LAW & Advertising

Current Legal Issues For Agencies, Advertisers And Attorneys.

[Dean K. Fueroghne]

THE COPY WORKSHOP
2144 N. HUDSON • CHICAGO, IL
(773) 871-1179 • FAX (773) 281-4643

First edition 1995. Second edition 2000.

This publication is designed to provide accurate and authoritative information with regard to the subject matter covered. It is sold with the understanding that neither the author nor the publisher is engaged in rendering legal, accounting, or other professional service. If legal advice or other expert assistance is required, the services of a competent professional person should be sought.

From a Declaration of Principles jointly adopted by a Committee of the American Bar Association and a Committee of Publishers.

LIBRARY OF CONGRESS
Library of Congress Cataloging-in-Publication Data

Fueroghne, Dean Keith.
Law & Advertising — Current Legal Issues for Agencies, Advertisers and Attorneys / Dean Keith Fueroghne.
p. cm.
Bibliography: p.
Includes index.
ISBN 1-887229-07-8
1. Advertising laws—United States—Popular works. I. Title.
1995

95-68129
CIP

Printed in the United States of America
1234567890

FOREWORD

Law & Advertising by Dean K. Fueroghne is an excellent compilation of the laws affecting advertising.

In one volume, Mr. Fueroghne has comprehensively brought together the major areas of legal concern in the review and preparation of advertising copy.

As an attorney who has specialized in the advertising field for 28 years, I can appreciate the effort and comprehensiveness of Mr. Fueroghne's publication.

I believe that *Law & Advertising* will act as an excellent reference tool for advertising practitioners regarding the legal framework in which they operate.

It is of course important that actual advertising copy and concerns be reviewed by an attorney experienced in these matters, as the law is constantly evolving and the interpretation of the applicable statutes, regulations, and policies will depend upon the specific advertisements involved.

Any attorney practicing in this area will be more effective in solving advertising problems and advising clients when the attorney is dealing with informed laymen.

Law & Advertising will greatly assist in informing the layman about legal concerns in order to prepare more effective advertising which complies with legal requirements, and to be more efficient and effective in dealing with their attorneys on such matters.

Congratulations on a job well done.

Stephen P. Durchslag
Attorney at Law
Winston & Strawn, Chicago

PREFACE

A number of years ago while studying law at U.C.L.A., I enrolled in an advertising law class. The class was attended mostly by lawyers and professionals in advertising. The professor began by announcing that there would not be a text for the course because none existed.

That experience combined with the naiveté about the implications of law that I've seen in the advertising business has led to the creation of this book. While advertising is a creative business, I have seen many agencies create more liability for themselves and their clients than awards for their ads. Most advertisers feel that advertising laws (the few that they are aware of) restrict the power of their message. Nonetheless, they need to understand these laws and their consequences.

The law has built a wall around itself with unfamiliar words and uncommon reasoning – a wall that most cannot break through. Until now there was simply no single source of ready access to information about the laws that impact the business of advertising. This book attempts to provide one source a person can use to learn about such areas of law as agency, contract, copyright, trademark, privacy and publicity rights, FTC regulations, the First Amendment, the Internet, and many others.

When I started writing this book, I decided that I wanted it to be useful for three audiences. This book is primarily addressed to all who produce, distribute, and prosper from advertising – the account executive, the art director, the copywriter, the creative director, the advertising manager – whether in the agency business or an in-house advertising department. This book also serves lawyers who need a compiled reference resource of advertising law. The book is also designed with the student in mind, whether in law school or in an advertising or communications law course.

I have tried to explain the legal principles as clearly as possible, believing that cases provide the best examples to illustrate each of the points. A project like this can't be all things to all people. I've had to select the information and material that I felt was the most relevant for all audiences. In some cases I've chosen examples and stories over in-depth legislative theory and history. To go past that is beyond the scope of these pages.

Because of the impact of legislation, court decisions, and consumerism on the advertising field, the law should be well understood by anyone who creates and implements advertising.

While I have tried to assure that the examples used in this updated 2000 edition of *Law & Advertising* are current, the case law, statutes, and regulations should not be used as authoritative unless the user researches them at the time of use to determine their validity or any changes or modifications since the date of publication. This book is intended to provide insight into the areas of law that affect advertising and to allow the advertiser to know when to seek specific legal advice. It is not intended to be construed as offering legal advice in any way. As with any legal problem, when in doubt, consult an attorney who specializes in that particular area.

I would like to thank Lee Lefton and Laurel Phillips for their help with the original manuscript. And thanks to Bruce and Lorelei Bendinger for their enthusiasm and help throughout this project.

To everyone I've worked with over the years in this business, who have provided the stories – sometimes humorous, sometimes sad – that have helped to illustrate the book, I extend my thanks. Many I have learned from; some I have walked away from shaking my head. But all have contributed to this book – some more than they would have liked.

Dean Keith Fueroghne

INTRODUCTION

The combined expenditure on advertising for the 10 largest companies in the United States is greater than the gross national product of most nations!

A major national television commercial will be viewed by more people than the total number of people who have seen *Gone with the Wind*. The average American is exposed to over 3,000 advertising messages each day. And that same person watches about 20,000 television commercials each year. A major manufacturer will spend a quarter of a million dollars to produce a 30-second television commercial that is designed to promote a 99-cent item.

What this trivia illustrates is that advertising is a very expensive, very pervasive, very specialized, and very institutionalized segment of our social and economic environment. But did you ever stop to ask yourself: How does advertising interact with the restrictions of society? This is one of the primary questions this book will explore.

It is generally accepted that advertising is a part of the business process. Advertising goes hand in hand with moving products and services from the rawest of materials to the ultimate consumer. Although it is difficult to precisely define advertising, in essence it is the catalyst that keeps a free enterprise market operating. Countries that don't have a free enterprise system don't have advertising in the commercial sense because they don't need it. A prime example of this situation is Red China. Before trade was opened up with the West, consumerism was controlled by the government. Afterwards, Western products were introduced into the Chinese culture along with something else new – "advertising."

Most textbooks teach that modern advertising began in the early 1900's. Greats like William Benton, George Batton, Albert Lasker, Chester Bowles, Bruce Barton, Ernest Elmo Calkins, Leo Burnett, David Ogilvy, and others whose names you may recognize, did not create the process of advertising. What we consider to be advertising in its purest sense was around for thousands, perhaps millions, of years before the time of these industry giants.

Because it is such a powerful marketing tool, advertising draws more than its share of criticism, despite an ever increasing awareness and emphasis on social responsibility.

The consumer's skeptical impression of advertising will continue to increase. Because of this, a major challenge for the advertising community is to restore the credibility of its product and to check public skepticism, lest it turn to cynicism.

The demands of advertising professionals require that they keep current on all aspects of their profession. Law is one of those areas that has a powerful effect on advertising. Therefore, the new policies dictated by regulatory agencies and the interpretations of court decisions must be well understood by advertising professionals.

As our economic system has grown over the years, it has become more complex by necessity. This complexity has forced the legal system to create an equally complex mechanism to maintain the delicate balance that exists between free enterprise and consumer protection.

On one side stand the advertiser and agency trying to display their product as favorably as possible. On the other side stands the consumer, guarded by a protective legal barrier which provides a sense of security in making purchasing decisions. The government has seen to that. Between these two constants lies a fine line. As you will see throughout the book, it is one beyond which neither side would be prudent to extend.

Throughout history, as promoters of products and advertising services have become more sophisticated and, indeed, cleverer, the legal system has had to keep pace. This book was written to discuss the relationship between advertiser and regulator, what brought it about, and its practical applications.

Many years ago, Calvin Coolidge said that "advertising ministers to the spiritual side of trade." While some consumers have expressed a fear of – and others have indicated a hope for – the demise of advertising, it is still integral to our market environment. Advertising provides a valuable service to the seller, the buyer, and the public and serves the spirit of trade only so long as it remains truthful and honest.

HOW TO USE THIS BOOK

As you read this book there are a few things I feel you should keep in mind. Advertising is affected by many areas of law, and each chapter of this book covers a separate area of law. The law tends to be compartmentalized. As a result, one area of law differs from another. And, therefore, the subject of each chapter differs. The regulation of each area of law varies; copyright has no effect on publicity rights, comparative advertising regulation has no effect on products liability.

You may see inconsistencies in logic from chapter to chapter. What you're actually noticing is the variations in the different areas of law. Always consider the subject of the chapter, and you'll see the law in the proper light. Also, read each chapter carefully and completely – do not skim. The subject matter is far too complex for that. I would strongly recommend reading the book straight through the first time. Many of the topics build on each other, and there is a reason that the chapters are in the order that they are. When questions arise about specific subjects, you can go back to the appropriate chapter for reference.

Another important point to consider is that, in the real world, you will find many examples of ads that were produced by others that violate the laws illustrated in this book. Citing such examples will not protect you if you are caught in similar violations. The fact that 20 people get away with robbery doesn't make it legal!

Finally, as you read, you will undoubtedly have questions

that will be brought up by the information in this book. That's the idea – and a clue that your question might best be answered by an attorney who specializes in that area. This book cannot answer every question that arises, although it should answer many. What it can do is teach you the basics and give you the wisdom to know when it's time to consult an attorney.

NOTES ON CITES

In this book you will notice that each case has a citation (cite) following the name of the case. For those who have a background in law, these cites are all too familiar. But for those who do not, they represent some unknown code. Here is how to decipher the code.

Citations indicate where the specific court opinions can be found, should you wish to read the entire court opinion. A typical cite may look like this: *Dawn Donut Co.* v. *Hart's Food Stores, Inc.*, 267 F.2d 358 (2d Cir. 1959).

The name of the case appears first: *Dawn Donut Co.* v. *Hart's Food Stores, Inc.* The first number following, indicates the volume of the reporter: 267. The next series indicates the name of the reporter: F.2d (in this instance: Federal Reporter, second series). The next set of numbers shows the page where the case begins: 358. In parentheses is the circuit court where the case was decided and the date it was decided.

The various sources are cited by abbreviations as we saw above. The following is a list of the most common published sources used in this book.

U.S.	United States Supreme Court Reports
F.	Federal Reporter (decisions by the Circuit Court of Appeals)
F.2d	Federal Reporter, second series
F. Supp.	Federal Supplement (decisions of the United States District Courts)

F.C.C.	Federal Communications Commission Reports
F.T.C.	Federal Trade Commission Reports
U.S.L.W.	United States Law Weekly
U.S.P.Q.	United States Patent Quarterly
A.	Atlantic Reporter
A.2d	Atlantic Reporter, second series
N.E.	North Eastern Reporter
N.E.2d	North Eastern Reporter, second series
N.W.	North Western Reporter
N.W.2d	North Western Reporter, second series
P.	Pacific Reporter
P.2d	Pacific Reporter, second series
S.E.	South Eastern Reporter
S.E.2d	South Eastern Reporter, second series
S.W.	South Western Reporter
S.W.2d	South Western Reporter, second series
S.	Southern Reporter
S.2d	Southern Reporter, second series

In addition, each state court system has its own reporters and digests where cases are recorded. While there are far too many to list here, I will give a few examples of the basic California sources. A complete list of abbreviations for all states can be found at any law library.

Cal.	California Reports (series one through three)
Cal.App.	California Appellate Reports (series one through three)
Cal.Dec.	California Decisions
Cal.Rptr.	California Reporter

Court decisions may be found in any law library. The Internet also allows you access to court opinions through LEXIS (www.lexis.com) and Find Law (www.findlaw.com). Federal Trade Commission cases may be found through www.ftc.gov.

ABOUT THE AUTHOR

Dean Keith Fueroghne has been an advertising professional for over 30 years as art director, advertising manager, creative director, and president of his own agency. He is currently a partner in Mousetrap Advertising & Marketing, Inc., located in Pasadena, California.

With degrees from the University of California and Edison State College, he has combined the study of law with daily involvement in advertising.

The author has also taught advertising law at the University of California at Los Angeles. He has consulted with law firms across the country on advertising law cases and has lectured and written articles on the subject.

Mr. Fueroghne has been inducted into *Who's Who in the World*, *Who's Who in America* and *Who's Who in Advertising*.

CONTENTS

CHAPTER 1

THE DEVELOPMENT OF CONTROL OVER ADVERTISING

There's a sucker born every minute.
— *P. T. Barnum*

W. C. Crosby was an astute businessman. He understood all too well the power of advertising. Crosby had a knack for practicing the subtle art of persuasion. He knew how to pique a person's interest by using the right words: how to light a fire in the prospect, how to promote, how to sell – abilities that any great ad man must possess. He lived during the early 1900's, when he eloquently described his profession as "a business, like all business," which "takes rise from the conditions of life about it and adapts itself as does social life. And...plays an invariable chord in the human make-up...according to the times and circumstances."

His was not a name that would go down in the history books as one of the great advertising giants. He would, however, be remembered as a craftsman of the art of persuasion. W. C. Crosby was a con man, and one of the best. He kept company at the turn of the century with such notables as Willie "The Sleepy Kid" Loftus, Jimmy McViccor, Charley (changed to Henry in the movie *The Sting*) Gondorf, "The Crying Kid," "Hungry Joe" Lewis, George Pole, and "Big Joe" Turley.

The con man's migration to America was a natural occurrence. One frontier opened itself up to another. Long before the Civil War, the con man could be found in the Gold Rush shanty towns of California, riding the paddle wheelers down the Mississippi to New Orleans, drifting through high society in the

East, and riding the first rails to the West.

W. C. Crosby and the others brought with them the skills of the great European harbinger, Richard Town, who had so incurred the wrath of his victims that on May 23, 1712, in London, he was hanged. His open-air execution was viewed by a cheering throng of spectators. "My friends, this is my birthday," Town stated coolly. "I see you have come to help me honor it...my compliments, and thank you for coming to my adventure."

THE POSTAL FRAUD LAWS – THE FIRST FORM OF ADVERTISING REGULATION

In 1872 stringent postal fraud laws were passed in order to wage a relentless war against the con man who was perpetrating his grandiose schemes through the mail. While these laws were needed, they did not do away with the con man overnight. Unfortunately, passage of these laws was only a small step toward stemming the tide of mail fraud. Even in the early 1900's, American con men still ran rampant among a gullible public – a public that responded to advertisements for mining rights, real estate, securities, inventions, cure-alls, and medicines of all types.

The bulk of advertising during that time was carried through the newspaper – the only media readily available to the masses. All that was required on the con man's part was the up-front capital to purchase relatively inexpensive newspaper space and postage stamps. Despite teeth-gritting indignation, the victims were virtually helpless against the guile of the con man. In fact, the Post Office estimated that in 1911 alone, con men netted $77 million from duped investors in mail-order schemes.

Peddlers placed advertisements offering nostrums and medicines guaranteed to cure anything. A man named Perkins sold through the mail two shiny rods he called "Metallic Tractors." These were to be passed over the ailing victim to redirect his "electrical" current and cure him of any disease. Perkins believed his own swindle so well that when he contracted yellow fever, he refused medical attention believing his "Metallic Tractors" would heal him. For three days the rods were passed over Perkins; then, as you might expect, he died.

The Essence Of Life

A newspaper ad appeared in the *Connecticut Courant* in October 1834:

MOORE'S ESSENCE OF LIFE
A safe and efficient remedy for whooping cough
Sold by appointment at the sign of
the Good Samaritan.

The Essence of Life was nothing more than colored water. Many bogus doctors and pharmacists offered products that would cure almost any ailment known to man. Turlington's Original Balsam, for example, promised to remedy 51 deadly diseases. In another instance, Dr. Spear offered his magic Balsam of Life through newspaper advertisements. It was claimed that the product would cure consumption (tuberculosis) overnight. The con man who offered Brandreth's Pills placed advertisements in newspapers for years which read:

Remember in all cases of disease
no matter whether
it be cold or cough, whether it be asthma or
consumption, whether it be rheumatism or pleurisy,
whether it be typhus fever and ague, or bilious fever,
cramp or whooping cough or measles, whether it be
scarlet fever or small pox, Brandreth's Pills will
surely do more than all the medicines of the drug stores
for your restoration to health.

A Portrait Of The President

When the mail-order fraud reached its peak, the perpetrators seemed to take a perverse pleasure not only in the fraud itself, but in pouring salt into their victims' wounds. They often exhibited the sort of "I dare you" attitude that challenged the victims to protest. The following classic nose-thumber appeared in over 200 newspapers in 1882 – the year after President Garfield's assassination caused immense national grief:

•••••••••••••

I HAVE SECURED
the authorized steel engravings of the late
President Garfield, executed by the United States Government,
approved by the President of the United States, by Congress,
and by every member of the President's family as the most
faithful of all the portraits of the President. It was
executed by the Government's most expert steel engravers,
and I will send a copy from the original plate, in full
colors approved by the Government,
postpaid, for one dollar each.

•••••••••••••••••••••

To each person sending in the required $1, the con man mailed the promised engraving of President Garfield – a 5-cent U.S. postage stamp.

Some 15 years later an offer appeared in newspapers promising a way to eliminate annoying moths:

•••••••••••••••••••••••••

DO THE MOTHS BOTHER YOU?
If so, send us fifty cents in stamps, and we will furnish
a recipe CERTAIN SURE to drive the pests from
furs or rugs or any other old things.

•••••••••••••••••••••••••

A few weeks later the consumer received the foolproof recipe, as advertised. The reply read as follows:

Dear Madam: Dampen the article in question in kerosene thoroughly (to soak it is even better) and add one lighted match.
If the moths do not disappear, your money will be cheerfully refunded.
Yours truly, The Buncomb Company

Indeed, it was the era of the con man – of getting wealthy off the gullibility of the consumer. Some got very wealthy. In 1927, (his last year of operation) a con man named Hugh B. Monjar brought in a cool $7,666,631 before being sent to a federal prison for mail fraud.

In the late 1800's and early 1900's, the exploits of the con man were the main form of deceptive advertising. This is without a doubt where consumers learned distrust for all advertising – a skepticism many consumers have to this day.

Times, however, have changed. No longer can the advertiser rampantly seek out the weaknesses in consumers and exploit them as did early con men. The consumer now has stiffer advertising controls on his side. These controls have brought heavy restrictions for today's advertiser, who has to deal with the problem of being heard in our over-communicated society. Yet the advertiser must be very careful about how he gets the consumer's attention. The myriad issues the advertiser must consider today are far more serious than they were in earlier days before regulation.

With the advent of the Federal Trade Commission (FTC) in 1914, a force of regulation against taking unfair advantage of the consumer began. Over the years since its inception, the consumer has gained substantial protection.

THE CREATION OF THE FEDERAL TRADE COMMISSION

The FTC was conceived by Congress in 1914 to enforce the country's faltering antitrust laws. Ironically, the first two cases it heard involved false advertising.[1] The only intent of the FTC at that time was to preserve fair competition between businesses by preventing restraint of trade – that is, such acts as creating a monopoly, which reduce or eliminate competition. Although this concerned only how businesses dealt with each other, in essence, the Federal Trade Commission Act protected consumers because it protected sellers against each other. This was an indirect consumer benefit at best.

Since its establishment, the scope of the FTC has been enlarged with the adoption of the Wheeler-Lea Amendments[2] in 1938. These brought direct protection for the consumer by modifying the authority of the FTC. The commission was originally authorized to regulate "unfair methods of competition in commerce." The Wheeler-Lea Amendments, however, added to this definition the phrase "...and unfair or deceptive acts or practices in commerce," thus expanding the act's coverage to consumers, as well as to competitors. The emphasis shifted to protecting the consumer against injury. This has been extended even further with the enactment of the FTC Improvement Act in 1975. We'll examine this act in more detail in Chapter 2 and 3.

In 1962 President John F. Kennedy gave a special message to the Congress on the importance of protecting the consumer interest.[3] He stated that every person, as a consumer, had four rights: To be informed; to be safe; to have a choice; and to be heard. And he promoted legislation to protect these rights.

This sparked the modern consumer movement. Since that time, major new legislation and amendments to prior regulation have been enacted. The FTC and the courts have dramatically increased their efforts to protect the consumer and to place him on equal ground with the advertiser.

The Long Arm Of The FTC

The FTC, as a federal organization, is assigned the task of policing advertising on a national level under Section 5 of the act. As a result, Section 5 only covers advertising that promotes products involving interstate commerce – transactions between one state and another. The advertiser must realize, however, that he is not safe from the FTC if his products are sold only in his own state. Courts are broadly interpreting the act to also bring intrastate activities within the authority of the FTC. This means that if any part or ingredient of the product was manufactured or purchased out of state, the courts consider interstate commerce to be involved; therefore, the product falls within the control of the federal act.

The FTC's influence reaches into state activities in another way. Most states have laws that carry the same implications as the federal act. These are known as "Little FTC Acts" and Uniform Deceptive Acts and Practices Acts (UDAP), and are discussed in Chapter 3. In fact, many of these state statutes direct the state courts to be guided by FTC decisions. California, for example, controls false and deceptive advertising under Section 17500 of the California Civil Code.

Disclosure Of Information

An obvious element in creating advertising is determining what to say in an ad. The advertiser must determine which of all the facts and points about a product should be featured in the limited space of an ad. Generally, regulation of advertising addresses the availability of information and how it is presented. Enough information should be made available to the consumer for him to make a valid purchasing decision – one in which he gets everything he bargained for, without surprise or deception.

In recent years, legislation has required that accurate information be disclosed in many areas of the marketplace, including the durability of light bulbs, octane ratings for gasoline, mileage-per-gallon statistics for new automobiles, care labeling of all textile wearing apparel, many telemarketing activities, and the Internet. The list continues to grow (see Chapters 3, 12, and 14 for specific information on many regulated products and industries).

The way in which the advertiser provides information and the relevance of that information are areas that must be carefully considered. Because of the competitive nature of the market system in the United States, every advertiser tries to show his product in the best possible light. As everyone in advertising knows, a good ad demonstrates the product's strengths while playing down its weaknesses. But when the strengths are distorted or when significant weaknesses are either played down or ignored altogether, a deception is created.

While it may be required, information disclosure creates certain problems simply by the nature of the marketplace. Well-established manufacturers may tend to avoid disclosing too much product information in their advertising for fear of opening opportunities for new competitors to enter or expand their market. An example of this situation is found in the history of the gasoline industry. Gasoline manufacturers attempted to avoid disclosing gasoline octane formulation because this would have highlighted the fact that ratings of high-priced brands were substantially the same as those of low-priced, unadvertised brands. Since the survival of the small independent manufacturers depended largely on their ability to maintain a cost advantage, they could not have easily undertaken expensive advertising campaigns to inform consumers about comparative octane ratings.

In other product areas, information disclosure may create an industrywide disadvantage for all sellers. Resistance in the past to an intensive advertising campaign promoting the smoking of low tar and nicotine cigarettes as a way to reduce health hazards would have obviously played up the fact that smoking any cigarette creates health problems. There was a reluctance to do this because total cigarette sales would suffer as a result.

Even after scientific evidence proved that smoking is harmful, advertisers of both low and high tar cigarettes played down negative comparison claims to avoid negative reactions toward other brands in their product lines. In fact, aggressive marketing of low tar, low nicotine brands has only recently occurred as a result of increased health issues and government pressure.

In December of 1970, cigarette manufacturers responded to threatened action by the government by voluntarily including the government test results for tar and nicotine contents in their advertisements. Soon after, television advertising of cigarettes ended. Cigarette advertising has come under intense pressure in recent years. We'll discuss cigarette, as well as alcohol, advertising and related issues in detail in Chapter 13.

Another problem in gathering and disclosing accurate product information is the extreme expense, especially in certain industries. For example, technical data such as chemical formulas for over-the-counter drugs probably have no meaning to the average consumer. Yet the cost of providing this information could, for many manufacturers, be prohibitive.

UNFAIRNESS VIOLATIONS

In contrast to straight deception, the FTC has developed a category of unfairness violations. Unfairness takes into account whether a practice, which is not considered unlawful, offends public policy as established by statute, common law, or otherwise. A practice is also considered unfair if it is immoral, unethical, oppressive, or unscrupulous, or causes substantial injury to consumers, competitors, or other business people. This gives the FTC room to maneuver. It allows the commission to pursue activities that it couldn't under the principle of straight deception.

As the FTC has expanded the unfairness concept in recent years, it has determined that there are certain types of advertisements that can be considered nondeceptive, yet still be unfair. These include claims made without prior substantiation, claims which exploit vulnerable groups like children and the elderly, and where the advertiser fails to provide consumers with certain information about competing products. We will discuss unfairness issues in more detail in Chapter 2.

CRIME AND PUNISHMENT – DECEPTIVE ADVERTISING

A major area of development since the advent of federal regulation of advertising involves sanctions for deceptive claims. Early on, the standard remedy for deceptive advertising was a cease-and-desist order. This consisted of an order to stop the action and not continue with the deceptive practice. Today, however, violation of the commission's cease-and-desist order can be quite expensive.

The original cease-and-desist order proved to be grossly inadequate. Advertisers, as well as their advertising agencies, routinely violated the law and went virtually unpunished, or more accurately, unnoticed. Advertisers were taking a calculated risk that the chance of being detected and ultimately prosecuted was extremely small, given the limited resources of the FTC and the tremendous amount of advertising that the commission was required to review.

However, in the years since, efforts by the FTC have focused on eliminating the gap in enforcement of sanctions for deceptive advertising violations. One development involves corrective advertising orders. These direct the guilty advertiser to spend a specific percentage of its future advertising budget to inform the public as to the false claim that was originally made. The reasoning behind corrective advertising was that it provided a way of dissipating the effects of a previously misleading advertisement since the original ad that misled could not be removed or discounted from the minds of the consumer. Yet, it could be counteracted (or at least neutralized) if the original deceiver was required to disclose information to "properly" inform the consumer. It was hoped that this corrective ad would offset the original inaccurate impression.

The price advertisers must pay under this sanction can be quite severe if they are found to have used misleading or deceptive advertising. For example, the manufacturer of Ocean Spray Cranberry Juice Cocktail was required to devote 25 percent of the company's advertising budget for one year to informing the public of a previous deception.[4] The makers of Profile bread were required to expend 25 percent of their advertising budget for one year toward advertisements stating: "Profile bread will not engender weight loss," contrary to the claims of its previous advertising.[5]

In 1975 the Commission proceeded against Warner-Lambert and the advertising of its product Listerine mouthwash.[6] Listerine's advertising had claimed that the product could prevent colds because it killed germs associated with colds. This was an unsubstantiated claim, which left an inaccurate message with the consumer. This case was the last time in which the Commission imposed the remedy of corrective advertising for the next 25 years.

This sanction lay unused since 1975, until recently. The FTC imposed this sanction on Novartis Corporation[7] for making the unsubstantiated claim that their Doan's analgesic product was superior to other over-the-counter (OTC) analgesics in treating back pain. Corrective advertising is intended to prevent the harm to consumers and competition that is caused when a false belief engendered by prior deceptive advertising lingers. Novartis made an implied superior efficacy claim for Doan's through short television advertisements that have not been disseminated since May 1996. The Commission concluded that these advertisements caused a false superior efficacy belief that has lingered and is likely to continue to linger until the corrective advertising provision terminates in July 2000 or beyond.

COMPARATIVE ADVERTISING

Other considerations for the advertiser lie in the area of comparative advertising. One form of this occurs when manufacturers go head-to-head to challenge each others' claims. Specific comparative advertising of products, if inaccurate, tends to open up the challenger to the possibility of a civil lawsuit or FTC intervention based on deceptive advertising practices.

Comparative advertising regulation stems basically from the Lanham Trademark Act of 1946,[8] Section 43(a). This Act allows a remedy for people or companies "likely to be damaged" by "false descriptions or representations" regarding comparisons of products or services. In other words, when Company X publishes an advertisement that compares its product to Company Y's product, and that ad proves to be untrue, Company X can be held liable.

Comparative advertising litigation concerns situations where a company implied a superiority of its own or an inferiority of the competitor's product. A good example of this can be found in *Smith* v. *Chanel, Inc.*[9] In this case, the perfume manufacturer Smith claimed in an advertisement that its version of Chanel perfume was "equal to the original." That claim was found by the court to be false, and under the Lanham Act, Smith was held liable.

In situations where the comparative ad claim does not fall under the federal Lanham Act, remedies are available under state law as well. False statements of this nature may well be actionable under laws against unfair competition or under tort remedies of disparagement or libel. We will discuss the Lanham Act and its relation to advertising claims more thoroughly in Chapter 8.

COUNTER-ADVERTISING TO CHANGE PUBLIC OPINION

In recent years, we have seen another form of advertising

take hold. It is a more useful and beneficial form, designed to offset public opinion about a specific product or industry. One example is Tampax's advertising campaign designed to counter the ill-effects it experienced because of the toxic shock syndrome scare. Another was Bristol Myers' advertising campaign attempting to offset fears about product safety after a series of tamperings and resultant poisonings had frightened consumers away from purchasing Tylenol.

INDUSTRY SELF-REGULATION

Consumer abuse or exploitation from false, misleading, or deceptive advertising doesn't necessarily have to be controlled by the government alone. Deceptive advertising may also be controlled by the advertising industry through self-regulation. We look at these issues in more depth in later chapters.

Self-regulation of advertising can be accomplished through a number of avenues. The various industry trade associations have established codes of conduct or ethics. Within the advertising industry such agencies as the American Association of Advertising Agencies (AAAA), the American Society of Magazine Photographers (ASMP), the American Advertising Federation (AAF), the Graphic Artists Guild (GAG), the Screen Actors Guild (SAG), and the American Federation of Television and Radio Artists (AFTRA) have specific conduct requirements for their members.

In addition, the National Advertising Division/National Advertising Review Board (NAD/NARB) inquires into complaints, evaluates them on their merits, and negotiates agreements. The board can also establish an arbitration panel to handle appeals. Lastly, the NAD/NARB can refer what it considers to be unlawful advertising to government agencies for action.

Media Regulation

The television networks also have rules about what they will and will not accept for commercials. Network clearance departments set standards that commercials must meet in order to be aired. These departments pass judgment on TV commercials, and will be discussed in more detail in Chapter 12.

In his well-known book on the ad agency business, *From Those Wonderful Folks Who Gave You Pearl Harbor* (Simon and Schuster, 1970), Jerry Della Femina says this about censorship (now referred to as "network clearance"): "One of the biggest problems that all agencies have is the headache of censorship. There is simply no reason for it. Censorship, any kind of censorship, is pure whim and fancy. It's one guy's idea of what is right for him. It's based on everything arbitrary. There are no rules, no standards, no laws."

In many instances, censorship can get out of control. An example is the time the Ted Bates agency produced a TV commercial for a toy company. The spot showed a little boy playing with the toy machine gun. The scene was shot on a mound of dirt with the kid blasting away at whomever it was we were blasting away at in the late 60's – Vietcong maybe.

"This commercial is not acceptable," said the network censor. The agency was sure that the rejection had something to do with the portrayal of war and violence with children. Not so. "Well, it's obvious that the mound of dirt is part of the game," said the censor. "The kid will obviously think that it's part of the game since it's on the screen for the entire commercial, and the kid spends his time on the top of the mound of dirt." The network, fearing that kids would expect to get a mound of dirt with the toy machine gun, would approve the spot only if it ran with a line of copy on the screen telling kids that the mound of dirt was not included. When the agency tried to explain that a child wouldn't actually believe that the dirt came with the gun, the censor replied, "It's not the five-year-olds we're worried about. It's the one- and two-year-olds who might be swayed." The irony was that the network censor wasn't concerned with the five-year-old who might be deceived, but rather about younger children who couldn't read anyway.

The smaller independent stations also tend to follow the lead of the networks. If the networks won't clear the spot, then the local stations probably won't run it either.

We in the U.S. are not the only ones who have to deal with media censorship. In the early 1970s the French agency Dupuy-Compton Advertising produced a television commercial for Levi-Strauss, to appear on French television. The commercial depicted a sad group of Boy Scouts all in grey uniforms, who were transformed into a bright new group dressed in Levi's. This happy group then undressed, scattering Levi's everywhere, and ran bare-bottoms-beaming down to a river to bathe in the cool sparkling water.

When the completed film was presented to RFP (Regie Francaise Publicitaire) for clearance, it was refused outright.

"No problem!" said Jed Falby, the agency's transplanted American director. "We have lots of other shots of Levi's on bushes and on the grass – we can cut around the nude bathing scenes."

The group at RFP looked at Falby as though he was mad.

"We aren't concerned about the nude bathing, Jed. Don't you realize you can't make fun of the Boy Scouts?!"

Falby had to reshoot the whole opening to change the Boy Scouts to college boys in school uniforms.

Print media has its codes as well. Some years ago, I produced an ad for vitamins. The ad was to run in a series of health and fitness magazines. One of these rejected the ad because they had limits as to the levels of each ingredient, e.g., if a multivitamin contained 500 mg. of vitamin C, the maximum that could be claimed was 300 mg., even if the product contained a higher level. We had to produce a special ad for that magazine showing lower levels of the vitamins.

While these self-regulation efforts don't have the force of law behind them, they have become an increasingly effective method of checks and balances. They do place additional burdens on advertisers, and they are gaining in power. It's only when these efforts get overly aggressive and arbitrary that they lose credibility. Yet these are issues with which the advertiser must deal.

DAVID VERSUS GOLIATH – CONSUMER ACTION

It is also possible for consumer interests to be protected directly by the consumers themselves. The consumer can sue an advertiser directly, although this rarely occurs. The rare consumer suit against an advertiser typifies a larger pattern in our legal system – one where consumers find themselves powerless to take advantage of their legitimate legal rights. Most people simply cannot afford the often prohibitive expense of a lawsuit, especially when battling the virtually unlimited resources of a major company.

In most cases, the deceptive practice involved a purchase of such small cost that it makes no practical sense to consider retaining an attorney to pursue the matter through the courts, other than for reasons of principle. Although fighting for a principle can be rewarding, it can also be very expensive.

The extent of consumer injury from a deceptive advertisement is difficult to prove, and the extent of the damage even more so. Unlike the FTC – who doesn't need to show that damage actually occurred (only a likelihood to deceive), the individual consumer has different burdens of proof in order to win an award. This adds to the complication and expense of a court battle.

As an alternative, class-action suits have become nearly impossible to pursue because federal court decisions do not allow individuals to combine separate claims in order to satisfy the minimum $10,000 damage amount required to file a lawsuit in federal court. While a few states have rejected the federal approach (notably California), opportunities for consumers to pursue class actions in state courts vary. What this all boils down to is that even when consumers are aware that their rights have been violated – and that retribution is available on their behalf – they are often frustrated by the obstacles that lie in their path.

Consumer protection organizations are a major force for advertisers to contend with in today's environment. As these organizations grow in strength, so does their power to effect change. The group Mothers Against Drunk Driving, for example, has had a tremendous impact on alcohol advertising practices in the United States.

ADVERTISING'S ROLE IN PRODUCTS LIABILITY

There is another area of real concern to advertisers. Consumers are recovering substantial damages in products liability litigation. These are actions to recover damages when a defective product causes injury. For example, a can of beans is intended to be edible. If a consumer buys the product and gets food poisoning, products liability is involved, and the consumer can sue for damages. Advertising has begun to play a large role in these lawsuits since product advertising can considerably influence liability. The problem occurs when the image created in advertising may not be substantiated by the product's actual performance. Courts assume that a product will perform as claimed. So does the consumer. When it doesn't and damage results, the advertising may be instrumental in showing the advertiser's failure to "live up to" the product's claim.

Products liability is an area where the FTC can become involved under false advertising violations, and the consumer can receive punitive damage awards in private lawsuits. The many areas of law that fall under "products liability" create an arsenal for the consumer who has been damaged from use of the product. As you can well imagine, cases of this nature can be a tremendous financial burden on an advertiser and its agency. Chapter 4 is devoted exclusively to the subject of products liability and advertising's impact on it.

OTHER AREAS OF LAW THAT AFFECT ADVERTISING

There are many different areas of law beyond those of misleading and deceptive advertising including First Amendment issues and free speech, copyright and trademark, the rights to privacy and publicity of individuals, and specific problems of advertising concerning warranties, guarantees, and contests. We explore these areas later in the book.

The client/agency relationship is another area of concern to the advertiser. A client/agency relationship is one where an individual or company makes use of the services of another to accomplish things that could not be accomplished alone. When such a relationship is created – whether intentionally or implied by the law – it involves a well-developed area of law. The law defines the rights and liabilities of the parties, their relation to each other, and their relation to third parties. Therefore, we have seen an increasing number of court actions in which the advertising agency is brought in with the miscreant advertiser and held jointly liable. In most cases, each party is liable for the actions of the other. This subject will be discussed in Chapter 11.

There are also areas that relate to specific products and services. Alcohol and tobacco regulation is an area of recent growth for example. Also, with the increase in telemarketing activities, regulation has attempted to keep pace. These are discussed in detail in Chapters 12 and 13.

And the newest area of regulation involves the Internet. Chapter 14 is devoted exclusively to this topic.

[1] *FTC* v. *Circle Cilk*, 1 F.T.C. 13 (1916) and *FTC* v. *Abbott*, 1 F.T.C. 16 (1916).
[2] 52 Stat. 11.
[3] 88th Cong., 1st Sess., pt. 1, at 465 (1963).
[4] *Ocean Spray Cranberry, Inc.*, 80 F.T.C. 975 (1971).
[5] *ITT Continental Baking Co.*, 79 F.T.C. 248 (1971).
[6] *Warner-Lambert Co.*, (1973-1976 Transfer Binder) Trade Reg. Rep. (CCH) & 21, 066 (F.T.C. 1975), appeal docketed, No. 76-1138 (D.C. Cir., filed Feb. 13,1976).
[7] *Novartis Corporation et al.*, Docket No. 9279 (1999)
[8] 15 USC, Section 1125a.
[9] *Smith* v. *Chanel, Inc.*, 402 F.2d 562 (9th Cir. 1968).

CHAPTER 2

AN OVERVIEW OF THE FEDERAL TRADE COMMISSION'S ROLE IN ADVERTISING REGULATION

Big brother is watching.
—*George Orwell*

In 1946 Frederic Wakeman wrote a novel about the exploits of an advertising agency and an arrogant client named Evan Evans. Since then, *The Hucksters* has become the public image of the advertising profession. In the movie adaptation, Clark Gable plays the part of the advertising account executive caught in a struggle of right and wrong with the ne'er-do-well soap king played by Sidney Greenstreet. As these two battle, symbols of good conscience and selfish motives dominate the screen. "Advertising," exclaimed the soap tycoon, "is nothing more than pompous ranting," which he relishes when accomplished with the poorest of taste.

George Washington Hill, the real-life Evan Evans and owner of the American Tobacco Company, was well-known for his exaggerated advertising claims. When "creating" his own preference test statistics, Hill said, "I know the great preference for Lucky Strike is a fact, but the public won't believe it. Anyway, two-to-one has a better ring to it."

The Hucksters was written in an era when the advertiser took many liberties in selling his merchandise. For almost fifty years, however, moviegoers have overlooked the fact that

Wakeman's book was a work of fiction. The book convinced the public that advertising flourished – with the consumer falling victim to the guile of the advertiser – in a sea of broken promises that were never intended to be kept. Unfortunately, this feeling has prevailed. Today, the type of blatant deception demonstrated in *The Hucksters* is rigidly policed, primarily through the efforts of the Federal Trade Commission, which has successfully raised the standard of conduct of the advertising industry.

THE FEDERAL TRADE COMMISSION

As most advertising people already know, the Federal Trade Commission (FTC) has the greatest control over advertising and the way it is used. Yet few understand the extent of the FTC's involvement. The formation of the FTC was an outgrowth of the Sherman Act, an antitrust law that prohibited conspiracies in restraint of trade and the formation of monopolies. The original mandate from Congress (under Section 5 of the Federal Trade Commission Act) was simple and straightforward: to prevent "unfair or deceptive acts or practices...[and]...unfair methods of competition."

In January 1914 President Wilson addressed Congress calling for the creation of a Federal Trade Commission saying:

> The business men of the country desire something more than that the menace of legal process in these matters be made explicit and intelligible. They desire advice, the definite guidance and information which can be supplied by an administrative body, an interstate trade commission.
>
> Constructive legislation, when successful, is always the embodiment of convincing experience, and of mature public opinion which finally springs out of that experience.... It is not recent or hasty opinion.
>
> The opinion of the country...would not wish to

> see it [the commission] empowered to make terms with monopoly or in any sort to assume control of business, as if the Government made itself responsible. It demands such a commission only as an indispensable instrument of information and publicity, as a clearing house of the facts by which both the public mind and the managers of great business undertakings should be guided, and as an instrumentality for doing justice to business where the processes of the courts are inadequate to adjust the remedy to wrong in a way that will meet all the equities and circumstances of the case.

In an early move, the Seventh Circuit of Appeals in 1919, stated its definition of the FTC's role in *Sears, Roebuck & Co.* v. *FTC*,[1] saying:

> The commissioners, representing the government as parens patriae, are to exercise their common sense, as informed by their knowledge of the general idea of unfair trade at common law, and stop all those trade practices that have a capacity or tendency to injure competitors directly or through deception of purchasers, quite irrespective of whether the specific practices in question have yet been denounced in common-law cases.

The commission, as part of its scope, has the task of preserving a variety of marketplace options for consumers. Its efforts against deception help ensure that consumers will not make choices on the basis of misleading information. The ban on unfair practices also broadens the FTC's scope by protecting consumers from practices that are "exploitative or inequitable...morally objectionable, [or] seriously detrimental to consumers or others."[2]

As we discussed earlier, Section 5 of the act, which was

once considered only a tool against unfair methods of competition between businesses, was expanded in 1938 with the Wheeler-Lea Amendments to cover unfair and deceptive acts against individuals as well. While the rationale to abolish unfair methods of competition grew from the need to protect competitors from each other, the reasoning against unfair and deceptive acts and practices evolved out of the desire to protect the consumer from the advertiser.

While the Wheeler-Lea Amendments specifically gave the FTC jurisdiction in the consumer protection area, the commission continued its fight against unfair trade practices and monopolistic power. At times these divergent roles were in conflict.

Reasoning Behind The FTC Act And The Wheeler-Lea Amendments

Here, we will examine the different stages that the FTC has gone through in its development and the reasoning behind these developments.

The FTC Act

First, look at this excerpt from the Senate Committee on Interstate Commerce Report, 1914, supporting the enactment of a trade commission bill.

> The committee gave careful consideration to the question as to whether it would attempt to define the many and variable unfair practices which prevail in commerce and to forbid their continuance or whether it would, by a general declaration condemning unfair practices, leave it to the Commission to determine what practices were unfair. It concluded that the latter course would be the better, for the reason, as stated by one of the representatives of the Illinois Manufacturers' Association, that there were too many unfair

practices to define, and after writing 20 of them into the law, it would be quite possible to invent others.

As we have seen, the original intent was to prohibit unfair trade practices as they existed between businesses.

The Wheeler-Lea Amendments

Now, look at this excerpt from Senator Burton Wheeler in debate on the Wheeler-Lea Amendments, 1938.[3]

> The Commission spent most of its time and most of its money allotted to it by the Congress, in running down the question of whether or not one man has lost some money by reason of unfair trade practices on the part of another. After all, Congress is not interested in whether John Smith lost some money as the result of the advertising complained of, but the question is whether or not the general public has been deceived or injured by reason of it. We are here to legislate with respect to that question.

This, then, also prohibited deceptive acts in commerce, thereby bringing consumer deception into the picture, and allowing the FTC to act on that as well.

The 1975 FTC Improvement Act

Essentially, the FTC Improvement Act of 1975,[4] modified section 5 of the FTC Act in one major way. It added the phrase "or affecting" to the existing phrase "in commerce." Now, as we'll see in the next section, the phrase reads "in *or affecting* commerce." This gives the FTC wider latitude in determining the existence of deception.

Key Sections Of The FTC Act

At this point, it may be valuable to look at the specifics of current key sections of the FTC Act.

Section 5. (a) (1) Unfair methods of competition in **or affecting** commerce, and unfair or deceptive acts or practices in **or affecting** commerce are hereby declared unlawful. (Underline added with Wheeler-Lea Amendments; bold added with 1975 FTC Improvement Act.)

Section 5. (b) Whenever the Commission shall have reason to believe that any such person, partnership, or corporation has been or is using any unfair method of competition or unfair or deceptive act or practice in **or affecting** commerce, and if it shall appear to the Commission that a proceeding by it in respect thereof *would be of interest to the public*, it shall issue and serve upon such person, partnership, or corporation a complaint stating its charges. (Italic shows concern for a public interest; bold added with 1975 FTC Improvement Act.)

Section 12. (a) It shall be unlawful for any person, partnership, or corporation to disseminate, or cause to be disseminated, any false advertisement.

(b) The dissemination or the causing to be disseminated of any false advertisement within the provisions of subsection (a) of this section shall be an unfair or deceptive act or practice in **or affecting** commerce within the meaning of section 5. (Section 12 added with Wheeler-Lea Amendments; bold added with 1975 FTC Improvement Act.)

Key Events In The History Of The FTC

The following list includes a history of events that have played an important role in the evolution of the Federal Trade Commission, many of which we will look at in this chapter.

1887 Interstate Commerce Commission created
1890 Sherman Antitrust Act passed
1903 Bureau of Corporations created
1914 Federal Trade Commission Act passed
Clayton Antitrust Act passed

1918 Webb-Pomerone Act passed
1919 *FTC* v. *Sears, Roebuck & Company*
1920 *FTC* v. *Gratz*
1921 Packers and Stockyard Act passed
1922 *FTC* v. *Winsted Hosiery*
1929 *FTC* v. *Klesner*
1931 *FTC* v. *Raladam*
1934 *FTC* v. *Keppel & Brothers, Inc.*
1935 *Humphrey's Executor* v. *United States*
1936 Robinson-Patman Act passed
1938 Wheeler-Lea Amendments passed, amending the 1914 FTC Act
1939 Wool Products Labeling Act passed
1949 Hoover Commission Report
1950 Celler-Kefauver Antimerger Act passed
Oleomargarine Act passed
1951 Fur Products Labeling Act passed
1952 McGuire Act passed
1953 Flammable Fabrics Act passed
1958 Textile and Fiber Products Act passed
1975 FTC Improvement Act passed
1984 *In the Matter of Cliffdale Associates*
1994 FTC Act Amendments on Unfairness passed

We see in this chapter how the FTC's activities have greatly expanded the definition of "unfair" and "deceptive." This chapter concentrates on the concepts that the commission and the courts have developed. In this chapter we also cover the guidelines that the FTC uses to determine if a violation exists. The next chapter will examine specific concerns and types of violations under the Federal Trade Commission Act.

THE FTC'S REGULATION OF ADVERTISING

Because the FTC's goal is to protect the consumer from false claims, deception, misrepresentation, and unfair acts and practices, the level of control it exerts over advertising has increased in recent years. The commission has gained increased authority and effectiveness for two reasons: first, through the cases it has heard and decided; and second, through the courts affirming the commission's decisions. In fact, courts have upheld the majority of the commission's decisions. For a specific discussion, see Chapter 3, Exhibit: 3-2.

An advertiser must understand how the FTC views an ad. Overall, what deceptive qualities does it look for? What qualifies as a deceptive ad? Or an unfair one? How does the advertiser know if the ad he creates will be acceptable in the eyes of the commission? This chapter addresses each of these questions in depth.

As mentioned, the FTC follows certain guidelines where advertising claims are alleged to be unfair or deceptive (see Chapter 3, Exhibit: 3-1). It first examines the advertisement to interpret all the information contained in it to determine if the ad is deceptive, or under current interpretation, if it is *likely* to deceive. The commission also looks at the net impression of the advertisement – the overall impression that the ad projects to the consumer. The commission views the materiality of all the representations in the advertisement and particularly the claims that are alleged to be false. The FTC also determines if the claims are simply sales exaggerations or puff.

The recent case, *In the Matter of Cliffdale Associates, Inc.*,[5] (which we will examine later in this chapter), establishes the commission's current stance on deception. Exhibit 2-1, includes a copy of a letter from then FTC Chairman James C. Miller, III to the Committee on Energy and Commerce. This letter, written in October 1983, attempts to explain the commission's position and interpretation of deception.

Now we'll examine each of the components of deception in more detail.

DECEPTIVENESS OF AN ADVERTISEMENT

From 1914 until 1984, "tendency or capacity" to deceive was the FTC's benchmark. One early case that dealt with this concept of "tendency or capacity" to deceive was *FTC* v. *Raladam Co.*[6] In that case the United States Supreme Court decided the issue of whether a cease-and-desist order by the commission (issued after a hearing in 1935) should stand. The case involved Raladam's product, Marmola. Marmola was a preparation for weight-reduction and was advertised as such. The company made claims in its advertisements that were misleading and deceptive. The statements concerned the product's qualities as a remedy for obesity.

Raladam did not argue whether the statements were deceptive (they had been caught before in 1929 as well). Its argument was that no proof was offered to show that injury occurred. However, the court held that no actual injury need be proven, only a tendency to deceive. The court felt that it was impossible to determine whether any injury occurred, or would occur in the future, because of Raladam's false claims. In fact, one of the principles of the act was "to prevent potential injury by stopping unfair methods of competition in their incipiency."

There's an interesting side note from the history of the con man's role in early advertising. A man named Edward Hayes, a con man extraordinaire, marketed a product for years called Man Medicine. Hayes claimed his product would bestow the purchaser "once more with gusto, the joyful satisfaction, the pulse and throb of physical pleasure, the keen sense of man sensation." Man Medicine was merely a laxative that Hayes used to bilk millions of dollars from a susceptible male market.

Hayes was caught and brought to trial by the Postmaster General for fraud. He was found guilty in April 1914, fined $5,000, and had to promise never to get involved with such wild schemes again. Only months later, Hayes was back out in the market advertising a new miracle product – a foolproof cure for obesity. The product was called Marmola, the same product which, with its new owner Raladam, was taken to court in 1929 and later in 1935.

Then in 1984, the case of *In the Matter of Cliffdale Associates, Inc.*, caused a change in the FTC's stance on deception. Today, the FTC uses a new standard to determine the existence of deception. "Tendency or capacity" to deceive has been replaced by "likely" to deceive. Since *Cliffdale*, the FTC takes a very close look at an advertisement to determine if a false representation or omission is "likely" to deceive a substantial number of consumers. As it was before 1984, actual deception is not necessary under the FTC act to constitute a violation.

In 1979 alone, Cliffdale Associates sold $692,998 in one of its products called the Ball-Matic Gas Saver Valve. The valve, what is commonly called an air-bleed device, was intended to be installed on an automobile engine to admit additional air into the engine to lean the air-fuel mixture, and thereby improve gas mileage. Ads promoted the sale of the Ball-Matic through mail order. Typical of these ads is the following:

GET UP TO 4 EXTRA MILES PER GALLON
– 100 EXTRA MILES BETWEEN FILL-UPS –
SAVE UP TO $200 A YEAR ON GAS.
GUARANTEED SAVINGS!
We firmly believe the Ball-Matic to be one of the best investments you can make to save money this year. The exact saving you will receive may vary significantly depending on the kind of car you drive, the condition of your engine, weather, your driving habits, and the amount of driving you do; however we guarantee that you MUST SAVE AT LEAST FIVE TIMES the amount you paid for your BALL-MATIC in the first year or you may return it for a full refund.
CONTROLLED TESTS CONFIRM BIG DOLLAR SAVING!
In the Spring of 1978, we arranged for a local Shell Service

Station to conduct a controlled, supervised test using seven different cars owned and driven by non-professional drivers. Each car was fitted with a locked gas cap and the keys kept in the possession of the testers.

After establishing base mileage consumption data for the various cars, the BALL-MATIC was installed and miles-per-gallon figures were re-checked. Every single car in the test showed meaningful improvement.

IMPROVEMENT RANGE...8% to 40%!

Yes, you can actually get up to 70...80...90...even 100 extra miles from every single tankful. No matter how old or rundown your car may be...no matter how many gallons of gasoline it now devours each week.

READ THE RESULTS FOR YOURSELF!

"The BALL-MATIC (gas saver) that I purchased has proven itself. I drive a 1970 Oldsmobile, now I get four miles more per gallon."

C.T. –Orange, California

"I want to express my thanks for the BALL-MATIC. Since it has been installed in my car, my gas mileage has not been under 18 miles per gallon. This is an increase of 5.5 miles per gallon."

Rev. R.N. –Claremont, California

••••••••••••••••••••••••

Ads like the one above were typical. Cliffdale's ads guaranteed an increase in gas mileage of 8 to 40 percent or more with the Ball-Matic. Part of the convincing nature of these ads were the claimed scientific tests and the consumer endorsement letters – all of which turned out to be false and clearly deceptive.

When this case went to court, it was proven that no valid scientific tests had been performed on the valve. The endorsements used in the ads were deceptive since all but one letter was written by someone connected with the company. In addition, the Ball-Matic was proven to not provide any measurable increase in gas mileage when tested by a series of credible university facilities.

The commission, stated that it:

> ...will find an act or practice deceptive if, first, there is a representation, omission, or practice that, second, is likely to mislead consumers acting reasonably under the circumstances, and third, the representation, omission, or practice is material. These elements articulate the factors actually used in most earlier Commission cases identifying whether or not an act or practice was deceptive, even though the language used in those cases was often couched in such terms as "a tendency and capacity to deceive." (Emphasis added.)
>
> The requirement that an act or practice be "likely to mislead," for example, reflects the long established principle that the Commission need not find actual deception to hold that a violation of Section 5 has occurred. (Emphasis added.)

The commission went on to expand on another new reference, a "reasonably acting consumer." They said that:

> The requirement that an act or practice be considered from the perspective of a 'consumer acting reasonably in the circumstances' is not new. Virtually all representations, even those that are true, can be misunderstood by some consumers. The Commission has long recognized that the law should not be applied in such a way as to find that honest representations are deceptive simply because they are misunderstood by a few.... [A]n advertisement would not be considered deceptive merely because it could be "unreasonably misunderstood by an insignificant and unrepresentative segment of the class of persons to whom the representation is addressed." (Emphasis

added.)

Now, the FTC has changed its requirement that a mere possibility of deception could occur, to a probability that deception will result from the claim. The new definition requires a higher degree of proof than the previous one. In essence, it provides less protection for the consumer than did the earlier "capacity or tendency" standard.

The change in the FTC's position on deception as a result of the *Cliffdale* case has been well articulated in the case's dissenting opinion of Commissioner Pertschuk.

> Under the guise of making the law more "clear and understandable," the [FTC] has actually raised the evidentiary threshold for deception cases. [We] have found it necessary to improve on language long understood by the courts and previous commissioners, by substituting the word "likely" for "tendency or capacity." "Likely to mislead," they insist, expresses more clearly the notion that actual deception need not be found!...the word "likely" suggests that some particular degree of likelihood of actual deception must be found. Therefore, it may create the impression, intentionally or not, that the burden of proof is higher than it has always been under the traditional "tendency or capacity" standard.

Commissioner Bailey also dissented in part to the *Cliffdale* decision, and stated:

> The [FTC's] first criterion for deception is that there be a claim, omission, or practice that is "likely to mislead" consumers. It is true that the courts have occasionally used this or similar phrasing, such as

> "the likelihood or propensity" of deception, interchangeable with tendency or capacity.
>
> Here, however, the majority makes unmistakable its intent to exchange the phrase tendency or capacity for the term likely, with only the brief explanation that it is meant to convey an understanding that "actual" deception need not be shown. As that was never in doubt, it does not explain the use of the term "likely" generally.
>
> A standard Webster's definition of likely, "having a high probability of occurring or being true," suggests, however, that the purposeful substitution of this term for tendency or capacity may well be intended to raise, or may be construed so as to raise, the burden of proof the Commission must meet in demonstrating that deception has occurred.

The commissioner concluded by saying: "Thus, use of the term 'likely' here may be fairly perceived to be at least a partial retreat from the Commission's traditional position that it may on the basis of its own expertise determine what representations a seller has made to the public."

THE MATERIALITY REQUIREMENT

To reach the conclusion that an ad is deceptive, the questionable representation (or omission) must also be a material one. A claim is material if it is likely to affect the consumer's choice of a product and his conduct in purchasing that product. In other words, it is material if it is important to the consumer in making his purchasing decision. Another way to understand this concept is in terms of injury to the consumer. Finding that a claim is material is finding that injury is likely, and injury exists if the consumer would have chosen differently had there been no deception. The consumer would be injured because he would be purchasing something other than what he thought he was purchasing. Thus, likelihood of injury and materiality are different sides of the same coin.

Let's utilize an example of this concept. In most of the cases throughout this chapter and the next, we will see deceptions that are material. The Rapid Shave case (which we will examine later in this chapter), where a television commercial demonstrates that the shave cream can shave sandpaper (when in reality it cannot), is a perfect example of a material deception. This ability is central to what the product is purchased for – its ability to shave sandpaper must mean that it is great for a beard. The consumer would probably be swayed to purchase the product after seeing this demonstration. Thus, the demonstration created a material deception. This case will be discussed in more detail later in this chapter.

Another example of a material deception occurred in 1990. Volvo ran into major legal trouble over a television commercial which it aired to dramatically demonstrate the structural strength of its automobile. A 13,000 pound "monster truck" called "Bear Foot" was shown rolling over a line-up of cars. All of the cars shown were crushed under the weight of the truck except the Volvo station wagon.

Later it was discovered that additional steel supports had been welded into the Volvo to reinforce it against the monster truck's weight. The other cars, on the other hand, were weakened by having their roof supports cut with a saw to aid them in collapsing.

As part of an out-of-court settlement, Volvo agreed to pull the commercial off the air and replace it with corrective ads. Volvo was also required to run newspaper ads apologizing to consumers for the deceptive advertising.

Scali, McCabe, Sloves in New York, Volvo's advertising agency for twenty-four years, and the creator of the commercial, resigned the $40 million account.

To look at the other side, when can a deception not be material? Some years ago I produced a television commercial for a resort community in Palm Springs, California. In the commercial a craftsman was shown carving a silver sign that was the logo of the community. This was done to develop a theme of pride and detail of the craftsmanship that went into the development of the community itself. In reality the craftsman was not carving the actual sign, but only chiseling silver wax from the sign. This was deceptive but not material. Why? Because the consumer would not purchase a home at this resort based on the carving of the sign. It had nothing to do with his decision to buy the product.

The commission feels that certain types of claims are unquestionably material in nature. Such claims include express claims; implied claims as intended by the advertiser; claims relating to health, safety, and other similar areas of concern to the consumer; claims that relate to the main characteristics of the product or service; claims establishing the purpose, efficiency, cost, durability, performance, warranty, or quality of a product; and statements regarding findings by a governmental agency concerning the product.

The *Cliffdale* case created much controversy in addition to new views on the three elements of deception; one of those being the materiality requirement. Commissioner Pertschuk, concurring in part and dissenting in part in the *Cliffdale* case, took exception with the new definition of materiality:

> The third element of deception is materiality. As the Supreme Court has explained, Section 5 prohibits the misrepresentation of "any fact which would constitute a material factor in a purchaser's decision whether to buy." Heretofore, any fact that is important to consumers has been considered material, regardless of whether consumer choices would actually turn on that fact. As the Commission has previously said, "[t]he fact that consumers were

> not harmed because they would have purchased the product anyway...is not relevant." The Commission has not required a showing of reliance or injury to establish deception.
>
> The majority opinion in this case [Cliffdale], however, suggests somewhat ambiguously that a misrepresentation is not material unless it is "likely to affect" consumers' conduct and "[c]onsumers thus are likely to suffer injury." Similarly, the October 14, 1983, Policy Statement on Deception states: "a finding of materiality is also a finding that injury is likely to exist.... Injury exists if consumers would have chosen differently but for the deception."
>
> If the majority commissioners intend to require proof of actual or likely reliance on the misrepresentations of respondents in future cases, they have changed the meaning of materiality and made it more difficult to establish violations of Section 5.

Commissioner Bailey also dissented in part to *Cliffdale* by saying:

> The Commission has long held that a challenged act or practice must be misleading in a material respect in order to be found deceptive. Just when all appears to be going well, however, the opinion...introduces a series of new concepts which appear to qualify standard principles of materiality in a restrictive fashion. At one point the opinion seems to equate materiality with the actual effects of claims or practices on consumer conduct, and the Policy Statement expressly states that "injury and materiality are different names for the same concept" and that deception will be found where an act or

practice "misleads...to the consumer's detriment." (Detriment is, of course, legally defined as injury.) The Policy Statement also notes that injury exists if consumers would have chosen differently "but for" the misleading act or practice, suggesting that reliance and causation are elements of materiality.

The commissioner went on to say:

Conclusions that injury and materiality are synonymous, that causation and reliance must be shown, or even that the likelihood of consumer detriment must be demonstrated in every case do not square with these accepted understandings of materiality.

I have no quarrel with the conclusions reached in this case, but analyzing it by applying these new elements is a wholly unnecessary exercise which demonstrates, I fear, the serious evidentiary difficulties and the exercise of even greater analytical gymnastics that will be necessary in future, more complicated Commission cases.

It appears that the *Cliffdale* case has stirred up much dust which will not soon settle.

THE EVOLUTION OF THE "REASONABLE MAN" STANDARD

Although the standard has gone through much change from the "reasonable man" to the "ignorant man" and back, the FTC has decided, for now, on the reasonable man standard. Yet, today the level has been raised to a stricter scale since the opinion in the *Cliffdale* case.

The reasonable man standard was first mentioned in 1837.[7] He is a man of average prudence and ordinary sense, who uses ordinary care and skill.

To understand why the FTC has changed its stance over the years regarding the reasonable man standard, it is helpful to look at the way the standard evolved. Soon after the Wheeler-Lea Amendments to the Federal Trade Commission Act were passed in 1938, the reasonable man standard began to be replaced with a new ideology: the ignorant man standard. This new standard was based largely on a case concerning an encyclopedia company that had used many false statements in a sales campaign. These were not simply innocent misrepresentations, but rather blatant untruths intended to deceive potential buyers.

However, some or all of these falsehoods could have been detected by consumers.

The case was *Federal Trade Commission* v. *Standard Education Society*.[8] In selling their *Standard Reference Work* and *New Standard Encyclopedia*, the company representative convinced the prospects that they had been selected because of their prestige and stature in the community from a small list of well connected, representative people in various areas. Allegedly, the company was presenting them with an "artcraft deluxe edition" of the encyclopedia free of charge. As the scheme developed the representative would state that "they [were] giving away a set of books...free as an advertising plan...that the prospect [had] been specially selected, and that the only return desired for the gift [was] permission to use the name of the prospect for advertising purposes."

The prospects were told that they would only have to pay for the loose-leaf extension service, which was $69.50. This, the prospects were told, was "a reduced price and that the regular price of the books and the extension service is $150, sometimes even as high as $200." These statements were false and were part of the scheme. In fact, the $69.50 price was the regular price for both the encyclopedia and the loose-leaf extension. Clearly, it was the practice of Standard Education Society to mislead customers into believing that they were being given a free encyclopedia, and that they only were to pay for the extension service. The record in this case is filled with testimony from people in 10 states that confirmed this.

What is interesting here is that the Circuit Court of Appeals for the Second Circuit (the lower court heard the case before the U.S. Supreme Court) had decided they could not seriously entertain the notion "that a man who is buying a set of books and a 10 year extension service, will be fatuous enough to be misled by the mere statement that the first are given away, and that he is paying only for the second."[9] Here the court felt that no reasonable man would believe the claim that he was getting one item for free if he paid for the other. The U.S. Supreme Court, however, felt – as did the FTC originally – that the lower court was wrong; an ignorant man could believe the claim.

To illustrate that point, Justice Black in the majority opinion authored by him in 1937 wrote:

> The fact that a false statement may be obviously false to those who are trained and experienced does not damage its character, nor take away its power to deceive others less experienced. There is no duty resting upon a citizen to suspect the honesty of those with whom he transacts business. Laws are made to protect the trusting as well as the suspicious. The best element of business has long since decided that honesty should govern competitive enterprises, and that the rule of caveat emptor should not be relied upon to reward fraud and deception.

This case could have been interpreted in several ways, and it was by the appeals court. However, it was interpreted by the U.S. Supreme Court as having abolished the reasonable man standard altogether. In fact, it firmly entrenched the ignorant man standard, which would continue for some time.

The Ignorant Man Standard

During the decade that followed, the ignorant man standard flourished, as was illustrated in *Gelb* v. *FTC*.[10] The case concerned an advertising claim that, among other things, a shampooing and coloring preparation known as Progressive Clairol and Instant Clairol permanently colored hair. One of the questions in this case dealt with the standard of perception of the consumer – specifically, whether an order should be upheld that would enjoin Clairol from "representing that the effect produced upon the color of the hair by the use of said preparation is permanent."

Looking at the advertisements for Clairol literally, it is obvious that the preparation permanently colors hair to which it is applied. But the commission found (and this would seem obvious) that the preparation has no effect on new hair as it grows in. Hence the commission concluded that the claim of the preparation "permanently" coloring hair was misleading. It seems absurd that any user of the preparation could be so simple-minded as to suppose that hair not yet grown out would be colored as well. (One witness was found who, after some prodding, finally testified "that you would think 'permanent' means you would never need to bother having it dyed again," although the witness knew better.) Yet the commission construed the advertisement as representing that it would do just that. Therefore, it ruled that the claim was false and deceptive.

The court, in this appeal from the earlier FTC ruling, validated the commission's earlier decision. Both the court and the commission reasoned that Section 5 of the act was designed for the protection of the trusting, as well as the suspicious. The result of this case was that evidence of deception, regardless of how unintended or unreasonable, was sufficient for a finding of deceptive advertising, even if only a single person were deceived, and even if that person was incompetent or a fool. The status quo at the time was that "people have a right to assume that fraudulent advertising traps will not be laid to ensnare them."[11] Yet it appears that the concept was taken to its extreme.

Back To The Reasonable Man Standard

Beginning in 1963 and modified in 1984, the FTC has moved back in the direction of a reasonable man standard of perception. The commission withdrew from the concept that deception of a single consumer, no matter how foolish or imperceptive, constitutes a deceptive practice.

True, the commission's responsibility is to prevent deception of the gullible and credulous, as well as the cautious and knowledgeable. This principle, however, loses its credibility if it is pushed to an absurd extreme as it was with the ignorant man standard. An advertiser cannot be held liable for every misconception, however outlandish. His representations cannot be subject to interpretation by the foolish or feeble-minded – the "ignorant man." Some people, because of ignorance or incomprehension, may be misled by even a scrupulously honest claim.

Perhaps a few misguided souls believe that all Danish pastry is made in Denmark. Is it deceptive to call a bakery item "Danish pastry" if it is made in California? Of course not! Under the reasonable man standard, an ad claim does not become false and deceptive merely because it will be misunderstood by an insignificant and nonrepresentative segment of people within the market the ad addresses.

In 1973 the commission presented its opinion, *In the Matter of Coca-Cola Company.*[12] In this case the commission dealt with an issue involving the Coca-Cola Company's marketing of a drink called Hi-C. It had been advertised as "the sensible drink ... made with fresh fruit...[and]...being high in Vitamin C,...[and that children]...can drink as much...as they like."

Television commercials and some package labels showed oranges and other fruits, from which the juices are used to make Hi-C. The complaint in this case stated that these advertisements compared Hi-C with natural citrus juices by implication. Therefore it was deceptive.

The commission maintained that Hi-C advertisements implicitly compared Hi-C with natural citrus juices and with orange juice in particular. It was alleged that consumers would likely take the advertisement to mean that Hi-C was made from fresh orange juice and was equal to, or better than, actual fresh orange juice in nutritional value.

Here the advertising representations were "not reasonably likely to have communicated" characteristics of Hi-C which were contrary to fact. It is possible to agree that the statements were "not reasonably likely" to deceive based purely on the facts. However, the statement of Commissioner Jones (dissenting) brings into play the standard of perception model:

> The commission's opinion ignores or perhaps reverses the standard model of the consumer as "the ignorant, the unthinking and the credulous" consumer which the commission has been commanded to use in determining whether a particular act is unfair or deceptive. Instead, without any evidence in the record to support it, the commission implicitly adopts a new consumer model as its standard for interpreting whether a claim is likely to deceive.
>
> This standard is actually one portraying the consumer as discriminating, sophisticated, and highly knowledgeable as well as skeptical and unbelieving. This consumer knows that fruit drinks are not the same as citrus juices despite what Hi-C ads said.

The commission has toughened its stance on the reasonable man standard as it exists today. The commission announced, through its 1984 *Cliffdale* decision, that only consumers "acting reasonably in the circumstances" were protected by the government. This new standard runs parallel with the "reasonableness" standard used in tort law negligence. Because of this, if the consumer is negligent in his behavior as a consumer, the FTC won't protect him.

It would appear then, that today the percentage of consumers affected would be required to be greater than with the earlier reasonable man standard. Perhaps we should call this the "prudent man standard." The main difference here is that in the past, the reasonable man standard was based on "a reasonable person in the situation," whereas now the issue involves "a consumer acting reasonably." (Emphasis added.)

In the *Cliffdale* case, much concern had been raised regarding the new direction that the commission had taken. Commissioner Pertschuk, concurring in part and dissenting in part to the *Cliffdale* decision, said that "[t]he new deception analysis has a more serious effect that is clearly not unintentional. That is, to withdraw the protection of Section 5 from consumers who do not act 'reasonably.'"

The Commissioner went on to say that:

> The sad fact is that a small segment of our society makes its livelihood preying upon consumers who are very trusting and unsophisticated. Others specialize in weakening the defenses of especially vulnerable, but normally cautious, consumers. Through skillful exploitation of such common desires as the wish to get rich quick or to provide some measure of security for one's old age, professional con men can prompt conduct that many of their victims will readily admit – in hindsight – is patently unreasonable.

> Of course, what strikes me as 'unreasonable' consumer behavior may not seem so to other commissioners. The very subjective nature of the 'reasonable consumer' standard is cause for concern. How can consumer conduct be measured for reasonableness? I know of no test for it, and I am fearful of the *ad hoc* determinations that will be made in the future.

Also concurring in part and dissenting in part to *Cliffdale* was Commissioner Bailey. She had trouble with the new distinction as well.

Commissioner Bailey said: "The second requirement is that an act or practice be likely to mislead consumers 'acting reasonably under the circumstances.' Of the three newly introduced elements, I believe this is on its face the most divorced from prior precedent and also the most likely to produce troubling results."

She went on to explain that:

> A claim or practice must deceive a "substantial number" of consumers in order to trigger a finding of deception.... Thus, while the Commission has indicated that it will not subject sellers to every interpretation made by an "insubstantial and unrepresentative segment" of the seller's audience, it has at the same time faithfully adhered to the enduring proposition that consumers are entitled to take commercial representations at face value and need not mistrust them. I believe the imposition of a "reasonable consumer" test as an element of the legal standard for deception may seriously jeopardize this guiding principle of deception law, which has permitted and encouraged the Commission to spread its protective mantle over the uninformed

> and credulous, those with understandable but often unreasonable hopes, those with limited reasoning abilities, such as children, and even "average" consumers whose guard may be down or who may behave somewhat carelessly in the face of deceptive conduct.

Clearly, this element of deception will, no doubt, see much activity and debate in the future.

SUSCEPTIBILITY OF THE AUDIENCE

In determining the consumer's interpretation, the guide is the susceptibility of the audience to which the advertisement is directed. The level of susceptibility is flexible and is adjusted to the norm of the intended audience. It is different for children than for adults. It is also different for the elderly or terminally ill than for the healthy young adult. This often falls into the area of "unfairness" claims, which we will discuss later in this chapter.

In the case *In the Matter of Doris Savitch*,[13] the commission measured the susceptibility of an audience to which the ad was directed. Personal Drug Co., owned by Doris Savitch and Leo Savitch, manufactured and advertised products under the names *Quick-Kaps* and *D-Lay Capsules*. Quick-Kaps were advertised as medication that would relieve a woman's overdue period.

• • • • • • • • • • • • • • •

PERIOD DELAYED?

(Overdue)

Don't Risk Disaster

Don't Worry

At last – it CAN BE SOLD, a new, extra effective, Doctor approved formula – "Quick-Kaps" capsules may relieve you of your biggest worry – when due to minor functional menstrual delay or borderline anemia. Scientifically prepared by registered

Pharmacists, "Quick-Kaps" capsules contain only medically recognized drugs, having no harmful after effects – Complete supply – packed in a confidential box only $5.00. Send no money and we will mail C.O.D. plus small postal and C.O.D. charges or send $5.00 cash and we will rush AIR MAIL.
"Just the thing to have on hand."

The implication here is strong: Relief from delayed menstruation due to pregnancy will be achieved by using *Quick-Kaps*. The advertisements also represented that its use would provide relief from delayed menstruation due to "minor functional disorders and borderline anemia." The first problem here is with the causes of delayed menstruation. The biggest cause is pregnancy. A more infrequent cause is iron deficiency anemia. Borderline anemia is not a cause of delayed menstruation other than in those rare cases when it is due to iron deficiency anemia.

Some of the phrases used in the advertisement are significant – for example, "Don't Worry" – "Don't Risk Disaster" – "May relieve you of your biggest worry" – "Medically recognized drugs having no harmful after effects" – "At last – it CAN BE SOLD, a new, extra effective, Doctor approved formula." The above-quoted phrase would seem to imply that, either because of a change in the law or recent medical discoveries, a new preparation was now being put on the market. This was not the case, and the ad was held to violate the FTC Act.

The commission felt that it was a commonly known fact that selling preparations or devices that would induce an abortion was prohibited by law. People looking for such a product would not expect to find it advertised as obviously and openly as products that were not prohibited. This advertisement seems to invite reading between the lines. It is reminiscent of bootlegging days when a knowing wink to a buyer implied that the "cold tea" being sold was in fact illegal liquor. Obviously, the implication about a product is as important as the literal truth of each sentence or picture. "The ultimate impression upon the mind of the reader (or viewer) arises not only from what is said, but also from what is reasonably implied."[14] We explore more on this area of interpretation of an ad later in this chapter.

The *Doris Savitch* case illustrates the susceptibility of an audience to which an advertisement is directed. It is reasonable to say that a woman would worry about delayed menstruation and could believe that this was caused by pregnancy. If she wanted to alleviate that situation, the advertisement for *Quick-Kaps* might be interpreted as promising that relief (an abortion). In any event, the commission stated in its conclusion to the case: "the mental condition of such a person is an element to be considered in arriving at which construction might reasonably be put upon the advertisement."

Ads Directed At A Specific Audience

Let's take another situation. Suppose that an advertisement appeared in a medical journal. The ad was not deceptive to a physician. Yet it fell into the hands of a layman who was actually deceived. Under these circumstances would the advertisement be deceptive even though a different person was actually deceived?

That was the situation in *Belmont Laboratories, Inc.* v. *FTC*.[15] Obviously false claims regarding the curing potential of Mazon, a soap and ointment, had been made. In medical pamphlets addressed to doctors and nurses, Mazon claimed to permanently eliminate specific ailments.

Mazon – an ethical preparation
compounded under the personal
supervision of its originator – is the original treatment of its
character for:

Eczema	Ring worm
Psoriasis	Athlete's foot
Head scalds	Barber's itch

Ivy poison Other skin disorders

The colloidal nature of the base of Mazon and its strong penetrating characteristics, together with its healing and soothing ingredients, afford quick and permanent elimination of Eczema and other skin disorders. No other treatment for permanent cure has ever been discovered. Some of the best-known skin specialists in the city are using it exclusively and praise it highly.

The claims found in the example were medically untrue. A major problem was with the claim that the product "permanently eliminated" certain diseases. The copy tends to convey that by an external application of an ointment, internal disorders can be cured. It fails to recognize the need to apply internal remedies to diseases caused by internal problems.

Many of the diseases listed (eczema, psoriasis, etc.) are caused by internal disturbances. The application of an external remedy can do little more than alleviate the exterior symptoms. The ad also creates an impression of newness. One may have a vision of thousands of doctors and druggists working diligently at hundreds of hospitals and laboratories to develop the new medical wonder – Mazon. This was certainly not the case.

These advertisements were found in pamphlets, which were circulated to the medical profession, and in a medical journal. Leaflets were also included inside the packages. The court said: "physicians and readers of professional journals are too smart to be deceived and that lay purchasers buy blind because the leaflet is inside the carton containing the ointment. We think that one position is untrue legally and the other factually."

In other words, the advertisements were blatantly untrue. Doctors and nurses would know that, but the consumer would not. The consumer would buy the product blindly because the leaflet was inside the package.

The benchmark of this concept is: who is deceived? If a person of low intellect is deceived by an advertisement for a Rolls

Royce, does this demonstrate a likelihood to deceive? The test for deception (or rather deceptiveness) is rooted in the market at which the advertisement is directed. However, if the advertisement reaches another market, the perception of that reader or viewer will be considered. Based on that reasoning, Belmont Laboratories lost.

THE ISSUE OF NET IMPRESSION

Whether an advertisement is deceptive must not be determined by viewing isolated parts of the advertisement (this has been alluded to earlier), but rather it should be based on the net impression of the entire ad. The net impression of the ad is the understanding that the reader walks away with after coming into contact with the advertisement. Keep in mind the reader will be determined by the current reasonable man standard, as we have discussed earlier.

Directly on this issue are statements by FTC Commissioner Mary L. Azcuenaga during a speech to the American Advertising Federation, National Government Affairs Conference, in Washington, D.C., on March 8, 1994. She addressed the relationship between claims made in a headline and claims or qualifications made in the text of the ad.

Azcuenaga pointed out that, "it would not be good policy to condone advertisements that make strong false or misleading claims in a headline, only to disclaim them in what is referred to as 'mouse print.'" She went on to say: "In evaluating the impact of the headline, the Commission will consider the 'net impression' created by the advertisement. The meaning of the advertisement should be construed in the context of the advertisement as a whole, not by individual elements of the ad taken out of context."

One very well-established case that demonstrated the principle of "net impression" is *Zenith Radio Corp.* v. *FTC*.[16] In this case, the commission alleged two primary issues in a series of advertisements for Zenith radios to determine if they were deceptive. The first involved Zenith's assertion regarding the capacity of its radio to receive foreign broadcasts. The second assertion involved the number of tubes contained in its radio sets.

These claims were found to be deceptive. A typical advertisement read as follows:

Europe is talking to you every night
in English. Are you listening?
With Zenith, the short wave radio that gives
you Europe direct, you can hear all the leaders,
all the daily news broadcasts.
You need not depend on re-broadcasts which bring
you only a small part.
Europe, South America, or the Orient every day
guaranteed or your money back on all short wave Zeniths.
1940 Zenith, the guaranteed short wave radio.

In truth, atmospheric conditions existed that made it impossible to receive satisfactory reception of foreign broadcasts. The Zenith radios were incapable of satisfactory reception of foreign broadcasts every day and under all conditions. The commission reasoned that the effect of the claims was to induce consumers to believe that radio reception problems would be completely overcome by using the Zenith radio. This is a good example of how deception was possible due to the consumers' lack of knowledge about the technical limitations of radio reception.

The second issue concerned the number of tubes contained in the radio. The ads listed different models available with the following tubes:

6-Tube Superheterodyne Table Model
8-Tube Superheterodyne with Wavemagnet Aerial

10-Tube Superheterodyne with Rotor Wavemagnet Aerial
11-Tube Superheterodyne with Rotor Wavemagnet Aerial

The commission defined "tubes" as devices that perform "the primary function of detecting, amplifying, or receiving radio signals." However, some of the tubes contained in the Zenith radio, and which were included in the advertised tube count, had nothing to do with receiving radio signals. They were, in fact, used for tuning and converting alternating current into direct current, and therefore the commission determined that they did not qualify under its definition. The commission, after concluding that a large portion of purchasers believed that a radio was better and more powerful because of the number of tubes it contained, ruled against Zenith.

The point in the Zenith case was that while the statements about the number of tubes contained in the sets were accurate, viewed as a whole the ad was deceptive. The consumer couldn't determine the relevance of the number of tubes, other than "the more tubes, the better the set." As for the first issue in the case, reception capability, the consumer would believe that reception problems would be overcome with the Zenith set. The net impression created by the ad was, therefore, a deceptive one.

DISTORTION OF FACTS

Let's take a look at another situation. In *Lorillard Co.* v. *FTC*,[17] isolated segments of an article taken from *Reader's Digest* were used in an advertisement for Old Gold cigarettes. Lorillard attempted to use the argument that the ads merely stated what had been stated in that article. By examining the advertisements however, the court determined that the meaning of the *Reader's Digest* article had been distorted. In essence, it amounted to the "use of the truth in such a way as to cause the reader to believe the exact opposite of what was intended by the writer of the article."

By comparing the advertisement with the article, we see

where the problem lies. The article, referring to results of independent laboratory tests of the leading brands of cigarettes, actually said:

The laboratory's general conclusion will be sad news for the advertising copywriters, but good news for the smoker, who need no longer worry as to which cigarette can most effectively nail down his coffin. For one nail is just about as good as another. The differences between brands are, practically speaking, small, and no single brand is so superior to its competitors as to justify its selection on the ground that it is less harmful. How small the variations are may be seen from the data tabulated on page 7.

That table showed the insignificance of the difference in the tar and nicotine content of the various brands. While the tests did show that Old Golds contained less nicotine, tars, and resins than the others, the difference was so small as to be entirely insignificant to the smoker. Yet the company advertised this difference as if it had been awarded a commendation for public health, rather than a slap in the face by *Reader's Digest*. Now that we know this, here's an example of one Old Gold advertisement:

OLD GOLDS FOUND
LOWEST IN NICOTINE
OLD GOLDS FOUND
LOWEST IN THROAT-IRRITATING
TARS AND RESINS

See Impartial Test by *Reader's Digest*
July Issue.
See How Your Brand Compares with Old Gold.
Reader's Digest assigned a scientific testing laboratory to find

out about cigarettes. They tested seven leading cigarettes
and *Reader's Digest* published the results.
The cigarette whose smoke was lowest in nicotine
was Old Gold. The cigarette with the least throat-irritating
tars and resins was Old Gold.
On both these major counts Old Gold was best among
all seven cigarettes tested.
Get July *Reader's Digest*. Turn to page 5.
See what this highly respected magazine reports.
You'll say, "From now on, my cigarette is Old Gold!"
Light one?
Note the mild, interesting flavor. Easier on the throat?
Sure. And more smoking pleasure? Yes. It's the new Old Gold
– finer yet, since "something new has been added."

Almost anyone reading the ad would get an entirely different impression from the actual facts. A person would think that Old Golds were less irritating and less harmful than the other leading brands, all because of the *Reader's Digest* research. Few, in fact, would have bothered to look up the article. As we have seen, the truth was exactly the opposite. In this case, the court concluded by saying:

> In determining whcthcr or not advertising is false or misleading...regard must be had, not to fine spun distinctions and arguments that may be made in excuse but to the effect which it might reasonably be expected to have upon the general public. The important criterion is the net impression which the advertisement is likely to make upon the general populace.

The Use Of Visual Distortion

In addition to the blatant deception we saw in the Volvo

case discussed earlier, the use of mock-ups (a model built to depict an actual situation) has also been an area of concern, particularly where television is employed.

A problem exists here since television, as well as other media, has certain limitations in the area of reproduction. As we'll see, the deception issue arises when these limitations are overcome in a way that portrays the product as something it isn't.

In television commercials aired in late 1959, Colgate-Palmolive Company promoted its product Rapid Shave in the following manner.

The spot opens showing a football being kicked and the ball zooming toward the camera. The scene then cuts to a football player whose face is hidden behind a mask of sandpaper.

Voice-over:

"Who is the man behind the sandpaper mask?"

The football player removes the mask revealing a heavy growth of beard. The player rubs his face.

Voice-over:

"It's triple-threat man, Frank Gifford – backfield sensation of the New York Giants...a man with a problem just like yours..."

Camera cuts to sandpaper mask and a hand brings a can of Rapid Shave into the frame in front of the sandpaper:

Voice-over:

"A beard as tough as sandpaper...a beard that needs . . . PALMOLIVE RAPID SHAVE...super-moisturized for the fastest, smoothest shaves possible."

Type is superimposed on screen, "Super Moisturized Fastest, Smoothest Shaves."

Hand presses the top of the Rapid Shave can to dispense a small amount of the lather into the other hand.

Voice-over:

"To prove RAPID SHAVE's super-moisturizing power, we put it right from the can..."

The lather is spread in one continuous motion onto the surface of the sandpaper. The first hand brings a razor into view and shaves a clean path through the lather and the gritty sandpaper.

Voice-over:

"...onto this tough, dry sandpaper. It was apply...soak . . . and off in a stroke."

The picture then cuts to Frank Gifford lathering his face.

Voice-over:

"And super-moisturizing PALMOLIVE RAPID SHAVE can do the same for you."

In a split-screen, on one side a hand applies Rapid Shave to sandpaper: On the other side a hand applies Rapid Shave to Frank Gifford's face. As Gifford makes a razor stroke down his face, a hand does the same to the sandpaper:

Voice-over:

"In this sandpaper test...or on your sandpaper beard, you just apply RAPID SHAVE...then...take your razor...and shave clean with a fast, smooth stroke."

Gifford then strokes his clean-shaven face with a look of satisfaction. Screen cuts to a picture of cans of Rapid Shave surrounded by the words Super-Moisturizing and Fastest, Smoothest Shaves.

Voice-over:

"Try RAPID SHAVE...or cooling, soothing RAPID SHAVE MENTHOL...both super-moisturized...for the fastest, smoothest shaves possible. They both outshave the tube...outshave the brush."

Musical tune ends spot with the lyrics: "RAPID SHAVE outshaves them all. Use RAPID SHAVE in the morning."

In an attempt to demonstrate the shaving power of its shave

cream, the Colgate-Palmolive Company showed the moistening and shaving of a piece of sandpaper, or so the viewer would think. The commercial purported to shave tough, dry sandpaper to demonstrate the moistening power of the cream, and it was blatantly demonstrated that way. However, the sandpaper turned out to be a sheet of plexiglass sprinkled with a layer of sand. The viewers were tricked into believing that they had actually seen the sandpaper test and they had been asked to make their purchasing decisions based on the test they had seen. In the case, *Federal Trade Commission* v. *Colgate-Palmolive Co.*,[18] the commission dealt directly with the issue of mock-ups in television. This case addressed a number of important sides to the mock-up issue. The court reasoned that "without this visible proof of Rapid Shave's claimed moisturizing ability, some viewers might not have been persuaded to buy the product."

Initially, it was determined that real sandpaper could be shaved if moistened for a sufficient length of time (in fact a very long time). However, it could not be shaved in the actual length of time used in the commercial, as the demonstration implied. They also found that, through the inadequacies of television, real sandpaper would appear to be only colored paper when photographed by the television camera. The advertiser attempted to use this as an excuse to justify the mock-up technique. It didn't work.

In a similar case, *In the Matter of Campbell Soup Co.*,[19] the commission looked at advertisements that showed a bowl of Campbell's soup. To all appearances, the soup had been prepared according to the directions on the can and was shown in a "ready to eat" situation. By viewing the ad the consumer apparently saw the abundance of "solid ingredients" that were present in a typical bowl of Campbell's soup.

The commission stated the reality of the advertisement:

> In truth and in fact, in many of the... advertisements, which purport to demonstrate or

> offer evidence of the quantity and abundance of solid ingredients in a can of Campbell soup, [the advertiser has] placed, or caused to be placed in the aforesaid bowl...a number of clear glass marbles which prevent the solid ingredients from sinking to the bottom, thereby giving the soup the appearance of containing more solid ingredients than it actually contains, which fact is not disclosed. The aforesaid demonstration exaggerates, misrepresents, and is not evidence of, the quantity or abundance of solid ingredients in a can of Campbell soup; therefore, the aforesaid advertisements are false, misleading, and deceptive.

Campbell Soup Co. had placed marbles in the bottom of a bowl of soup that was shown in an advertisement. This caused the solids in the soup to stay at the surface. Here again the respondent claimed that the limitations of the medium necessitated the use of this mock-up to portray the actual viscosity of the product. The commission didn't agree with that reasoning and ordered Campbell to stop using the ads. This case was settled by consent order; Campbell agreed to the commission's determination and consented to abide by it.

As seen in the above examples, the reality of an advertisement's net impression must be considered carefully.

UNFAIRNESS POLICY OF THE FTC

We touched on this earlier in Chapter 1. We should revisit the ever-expanding concept here. It is becoming more common that the FTC will attack a claim under the unfairness theory, so the advertiser must understand its implications. Until 1994 there were few notable cases to review. The ones worth noting include: *FTC* v. *Sperry & Hutchinson Co.*;[20] *In the Matter of Pfizer, Inc.*;[21] *In the Matter of I.T.T. Continental*;[22] and, *In the Matter of International*

Harvester Co.[23]

In 1980, the FTC issued a Policy Statement on Unfairness. The goal of the statement was to clarify the FTC's stance on unfairness violations. What follows is the bulk of that statement.

FTC Statement of Policy on the Scope of the Consumer Unfairness Jurisdiction

Section 5 of the FTC Act prohibits, in part, "unfair ... acts or practices in or affecting commerce." This is commonly referred to as the Commission's consumer unfairness jurisdiction.

The present understanding of the unfairness standard is the result of an evolutionary process. The statute was deliberately framed in general terms since Congress recognized the impossibility of drafting a complete list of unfair trade practices that would not quickly become outdated or leave loopholes for easy evasion. The task of identifying unfair trade practices was therefore assigned to the Commission, subject to judicial review, in the expectation that the underlying criteria would evolve and develop over time. As the Supreme Court observed as early as 1931, the ban on unfairness "belongs to that class of phrases which do not admit of precise definition, but the meaning and application of which must be arrived at by what this court elsewhere has called 'the gradual process of judicial inclusion and exclusion.'"

By 1964, enough cases had been decided to enable the Commission to identify three factors that it considered when applying the prohibition against consumer unfairness. These were: (1) whether the practice injures consumers; (2) whether it violates established public policy; (3) whether it is unethical or unscrupulous. These factors were later quoted with apparent approval by the Supreme Court in the 1972 case of *FTC* v. *Sperry & Hutchinson Co.*, 405 U.S. 233, 249 (1972), [referred to hereafter as *S&H*]. Since then the Commission has continued to refine the standard of unfairness in its cases and rules, and it has now reached a more detailed sense of both the definition and the limits of these criteria.

Consumer Injury

Unjustified consumer injury is the primary focus of the FTC Act, and the most important of the three *S&H* criteria. By itself it can be sufficient to warrant a finding of unfairness. The Commission's ability to rely on an independent criterion of consumer injury is consistent with the intent of the statute, which was to "[make] the consumer who may be injured by an unfair trade practice of equal concern before the law with the merchant injured by the unfair methods of a dishonest competitor."

The independent nature of the consumer injury criterion does not mean that every consumer injury is legally "unfair," however. To justify a finding of unfairness the injury must satisfy three tests. It must be substantial; it must not be outweighed by any countervailing benefits to consumers or competition that the practice produces; and it must be an injury that consumers themselves could not reasonably have avoided.

First of all, the injury must be substantial. The Commission is not concerned with trivial or merely speculative harms. In most cases a substantial injury involves monetary harm, as when sellers coerce consumers into purchasing unwanted goods or services or when consumers buy defective goods or services on credit but are unable to assert against the creditor claims or defenses arising from the transaction. Unwarranted health and safety risks may also support a finding of unfairness. Emotional impact and other more subjective types of harm, on the other hand, will not ordinarily make a practice unfair. Thus, for example, the Commission will not seek to ban an advertisement merely because it offends the tastes or social beliefs of some viewers, as has been suggested in some of the comments.

Second, the injury must not be outweighed by any offsetting consumer or competitive benefits that the sales practice also produces. Most business practices entail a mixture of economic and other costs and benefits for purchasers. A seller's failure to present complex technical data on his product may lessen a consumer's ability to choose, for example, but may also reduce the initial price he must pay for the article. The Commission is aware of these tradeoffs and will not find that a practice unfairly injures consumers unless it is injurious in its net effects. The Commission also takes account of the various costs that a remedy would entail. These include not only the costs to the parties directly before the agency, but also the burdens on society in general in the form of increased paperwork, increased regulatory burdens on the flow of information, reduced incentives to innovation and capital formation, and similar matters. Finally, the injury must be one which consumers could not reasonably have avoided. Normally we expect the marketplace to be self-correcting, and we rely on consumer choice – the ability of individual consumers to make their own private purchasing decisions without regulatory intervention – to govern the market. We anticipate that consumers will survey the available alternatives, choose those that are most desirable, and avoid those that are inadequate or unsatisfactory. However, it has long been recognized that certain types of sales techniques may prevent consumers from effectively making their own decisions and that corrective action may then become necessary. Most of the Commission's unfairness matters are brought under these circumstances. They are brought, not to second-guess the wisdom of particular consumer decisions, but rather to halt some form of seller behavior that unreasonably creates or takes advantage of an obstacle to the free exercise of consumer decision making.

Sellers may adopt a number of practices that unjustifiably hinder such free market decisions. Some may withhold or fail to generate critical price or performance data, for example, leaving buyers with insufficient information for informed comparisons. Some may engage in overt coercion, as by dismantling a home appliance for "inspection" and refusing to reassemble it until a service contract is signed. And some may exercise undue influence over highly susceptible classes of purchasers, as by promoting fraudulent "cures" to seriously ill cancer patients. Each of these practices undermines an essential precondition to a free and informed consumer transaction, and, in turn, to a well-functioning market. Each of them is therefore properly banned as an unfair practice under the FTC Act.

Violation of Public Policy

The second *S&H* standard asks whether the conduct violates public policy as it has been established by statute, common law, industry practice, or otherwise. This criterion may be applied in two different ways. It may be used to test the validity and strength of the evidence of consumer injury, or, less often, it may be cited for a dispositive legislative or judicial determination that such injury is present.

Although public policy was listed by the *S&H* Court as a separate consideration, it is used most frequently by the Commission as a means of providing additional evidence on the degree of consumer injury caused by specific practices. To be sure, most Commission actions are brought to redress relatively clear-cut injuries, and those determinations are based, in large part, on objective economic analysis. As we have indicated before, the Commission believes that considerable attention should be devoted to the analysis of whether substantial net harm has occurred, not only because that is part of the unfairness test, but also because the focus on injury is the best way to ensure that the Commission acts responsibly and uses its resources wisely. Nonetheless, the Commission wishes to emphasize the importance of examining outside statutory policies and established judicial principles for assistance in helping the agency ascertain whether a particular form of conduct does in fact tend to harm consumers. Thus the agency has referred to First Amendment decisions upholding consumers' rights to receive information, for example, to confirm that restrictions on advertising tend unfairly to hinder the informed exercise of consumer choice.

Conversely, statutes or other sources of public policy may affirmatively allow for a practice that the Commission tentatively views as unfair. The existence of such policies will then give the agency reason to reconsider its assessment of whether the practice is actually injurious in its net effects. In other situations there may be no clearly established public policies, or the policies may even be in conflict. While that does not necessarily preclude the Commission from taking action if there is strong evidence of net consumer injury, it does underscore the desirability of carefully examining public policies in all instances. In any event, whenever objective evidence of consumer injury is difficult to obtain, the need to identify and assess all relevant public policies assumes increased importance.

Sometimes public policy will independently support a Commission action. This occurs when the policy is so clear that it will entirely determine the question of consumer injury, so there is little need for separate analysis by the Commission. In these cases the legislature or court, in announcing the policy, has already determined that such injury does exist and thus it need not be expressly proved in each instance. An example of this approach arose in a case involving a mail-order firm. There the Commission was persuaded by an analogy to the due-process clause that it was unfair for the firm to bring collection suits in a forum that was unreasonably difficult for the defendants to reach. In a similar case the Commission applied the statutory policies of the Uniform Commercial Code to require that various automobile manufacturers and their distributors refund to their customers any surplus money that was realized after they repossessed and resold their customers' cars. The Commission acts on such a basis only where the public policy is suitable for administrative enforcement by this agency, however. Thus it turned down a petition for a rule to require fuller disclosure of aerosol propellants, reasoning that the subject of fluorocarbon safety was currently under study by other scientific and legislative bodies with more appropriate expertise or jurisdiction over the subject.

To the extent that the Commission relies heavily on public policy to support a finding of unfairness, the policy should be clear and well-established. In other words, the policy should be declared or embodied in formal sources such as statutes, judicial decisions, or the Constitution as interpreted by the courts, rather than being ascertained from the general sense of the national values. The policy should likewise be one that is widely shared, and not the isolated decision of a single state or a single court. If these two tests are not met, the policy cannot be considered as an "established" public policy for purposes of the *S&H* criterion. The Commission would then act only on the basis of convincing independent evidence that the practice was distorting the operation of the market and thereby causing unjustified consumer injury.

Unethical or Unscrupulous Conduct

Finally, the third *S&H* standard asks whether the conduct was immoral, unethical, oppressive, or unscrupulous. This test was presumably included in order to be sure of reaching all the purposes of the underlying statute, which forbids "unfair" acts or practices. It would therefore allow the Commission to reach conduct that violates generally recognized standards of business ethics. The test has proven, however, to be largely duplicative. Conduct that is truly unethical or unscrupulous will almost always injure consumers or violate public policy as well. The Commission has therefore never relied on the third element of *S&H* as an independent basis for a finding of unfairness, and it will act in the future only on the basis of the first two.

FTC Act Amendments Of 1994

On August 26, 1994, the FTC issued certain amendments of the FTC Act. Of the numerous changes made were two areas that impact advertising directly. The first was a change in the definition of an unfair act or practice. The second involved rulemaking based on unfairness. Let's take a closer look at those two amendments.

Definition of Unfair Act or Practice

Section 5 of the FTC Act was amended to provide that in order for the FTC to determine that an act is unfair, three new requirements must be met:

1. The act or practice causes, or is likely to cause, substantial injury to consumers;
2. The injury, or likelihood of injury, is not reasonably avoidable by consumers; and
3. The injury, or likelihood of injury, is not outweighed by a benefit to consumers or to competition.

In addition, the amendment allows the FTC to consider public policy evidence in determining whether a practice in unfair. However, public policy evidence may not be the primary basis in determining unfairness.

Rulemaking Based on Unfairness

Until 1994, the Commission was banned from issuing industry-wide rulemaking that related to unfair advertising practices. However, with these amendments, Section 18(b) of the FTC Act was modified to end this ban. The amendment provides that the FTC may "rulemake" under the unfairness definition when there is reason to believe that the conduct is "prevalent" in the industry. "Prevalance" is defined as either:

1. Where the FTC has previously issued cease and desist orders relating to the challenged act or practice; or
2. Any other information that indicates a widespread

pattern of unfair or deceptive acts or practices.

RESTRICTING NONDECEPTIVE, TRUTHFUL ADVERTISING

In contrast to deceptive advertising is the issue of FTC restrictions on advertising that is truthful and not deceptive. The courts have addressed that situation as well. Here's a case in point.

It's Like Pulling Teeth

In *California Dental Assn.* v. *FTC*,[24] the court held that the FTC's decision that the California Dental Association's (CDA) advertising rules unreasonably restrained trade and violated Section 5 of the FTC Act.

The California Dental Association's advertising policies stated:

> Any communication or advertisement which refers to the cost of dental services shall be exact, without omissions, and shall make each service clearly identifiable, without the use of such phrases as "as low as...and up," "lowest prices," or words or phrases of similar import.
>
> Any advertisement which refers to the cost of dental services and uses words of comparison or relativity – for example, "low fees" must be based on verifiable data substantiating the comparison or statement of relativity. The burden shall be on the dentist who advertises in such terms to establish the accuracy of the comparison or statement of relativity.
>
> Advertising claims as to the quality of services are not susceptible to measurement or verification; accordingly, such claims are likely to be false or misleading in any material respect.

The CDA's advertising rules about discount advertising required that advertisements disclose:

1. The dollar amount of the non-discounted fee for the service;
2. The dollar amount of the discount fee or the percentage of the discount for the specific service;
3. The length of time that the discount would be offered;
4. Verifiable fees; and
5. Specific groups who qualified for the discount or any other terms and conditions or restrictions for qualifying for the discount.

Essentially, the CDA's advertising policy prohibited its members from making truthful, nondeceptive statements in advertising that related to offering volume discounts as well as statements describing prices as "low" or "reasonable." The court noted, "restrictions on the ability to advertise prices normally make it more difficult for consumers to find a lower price and for dentists to compete on the basis of price."

Limiting advertisements about quality, safety, and other nonprice aspects of dental services prevented the dentists from fully describing the services they offered. The CDA contended that claims about quality were inherently unverifiable and as a result misleading. The court, in reply, determined that this did not justify banning all quality claims without regard to whether they were, in fact, false or misleading.

In this regard, the court said:

> Limiting advertisements about quality, safety, and other nonprice aspects of service prevents dentists from fully describing the package of services they offer, and thus limits their ability to compete. The restrictions may also affect output more directly, as quality and comfort advertising may induce some customers to obtain nonemergency care when they

might not otherwise do so. CDA contends that claims about quality are inherently unverifiable and therefore misleading. While this danger exists, it does not justify banning all quality claims without regard to whether they are, in fact, false or misleading. Under these circumstances, we think that the restriction is a sufficiently naked restraint on output to justify quick look analysis. We also note in this regard the Supreme Court's repeated holdings that the scope of inquiry under the rule of reason is intended to be flexible depending on the nature of the restraint and the circumstances in which it is used.

In upholding the FTC's ruling, the court further stated:

The Commission found that through its pattern of enforcement, the CDA went beyond the literal language of its rules to prohibit ads that were in fact true and nondeceptive.

The FTC correctly exercised its jurisdiction over the CDA. Substantial evidence supports the FTC's conclusion that the advertising rules of the CDA, as applied to truthful and non-deceptive advertisements, violate Section 1 of the Sherman Act and Section 5 of the FTC Act under an abbreviated rule of reason analysis.

On May 24, 1999, the U.S. Supreme Court unanimously upheld the FTC's jurisdiction over nonprofit professional associations but vacated and remanded to the court of appeals (*California Dental Association* v. *FTC*[25]).

THE ISSUE OF PUFFING

Puffing is an area of advertising where the law allows the advertiser to make certain exaggerated statements or opinions about his product. Ivan Preston, in his book *The Great American Blow-Up: Puffery in Advertising and Selling*, defined puffing as the use of advertising that praises with "subjective opinions, superlatives, or exaggerations, vaguely and generally, stating no specific facts." Such statements as "Coke is the real thing" and "Sleeping on a Sealy is like sleeping on a cloud" are perfect examples of puff. A certain degree of puffing has always been allowed in advertising. Yet, the tolerance for this practice is limited due to the inherent gray area in its use.

The use of puffing in advertising has generally been acceptable to both the FTC and courts, based on certain rationale. Courts have reasoned that consumers do not rely on expressions of opinion by advertisers about their products. Also, the FTC recognizes that certain statements of general praise are not likely to be relied on by consumers under its "capacity to deceive" standard. Lastly, certain forms of superlative praise are permissible simply because there is no way to establish that they are false.

LEGAL INTERPRETATION OF PUFFERY

If the puff takes the form of a pure statement of opinion, and if the law prohibits only false factual statements, then it may be impossible for courts to prove that a false representation was made. While exaggerations, superlatives, and unsupported opinions in advertising have been tolerated, it is also clear that the extent of puffing has been reduced over the years. This is because of the increased desire of the FTC and courts to recognize that false factual representations can arise by implication, as we have discussed. This occurs in the use of some forms of puffing.

The commission investigated a situation of puffing in the case of *In The Matter of Better Living, Inc.*[26] Better Living, Inc. was in the business of selling and distributing aluminum storm doors, storm windows, and aluminum awnings. They had published advertisements and sales literature that made many blatantly false statements. The company made two claims that illustrate puffing. The first was the statement, "WORLD'S LOWEST PRICES." The second was "Better Living, Inc., 'Beauty Prize' storm windows and doors. Acclaimed from Coast to Coast First Prize Winners for Beauty. Choice of Famous Home Stylists."

As to the claim that the products were offered at the world's lowest prices, the company's advertising agent claimed that "for several weeks prior to the publication of the advertisements, a check was made of local competitive prices and that the prices [thereafter] advertised were slightly lower than their competitors'." The advertising agent admitted that there was no real factual basis to support the claim and, in fact, stated that the claim was typical puffing.

At this point the commission expressed its definition of puffing saying:

> Puffing...is a term frequently used to denote exaggerations reasonable to be expected of a seller as to the degree of quality of his product, the truth or falsity of which cannot be precisely determined. In contrast,...the representation as to "the world's lowest price" is a statement of objective actuality, the truth or falsity of which is not variable and can be ascertained with factual precision. This representation cannot, therefore, properly be termed puffing. It is either true, or it is false; and, accordingly, such a determination must be made.

The other statement made by Better Living, Inc. related to the awards it had won in certain beauty contests. Despite the advertising claim, the advertising agent admitted that "these storm windows were never awarded a beauty prize of any kind." To this,

Better Living added that such a statement was mere subjective puffing, which is acceptable in advertising. The commission disagreed and held that such claims would mislead consumers. The statement was one of fact, which could be proven or – in this case – disproved.

The commission continued to develop this concept with the decision in *In The Matter of Dannon Milk Prods., Inc.*[27] Here, Dannon had made claims about its product, Dannon Yogurt. Specifically, Dannon claimed in advertisements, brochures, pamphlets, and radio broadcasts that "Dannon is known as nature's perfect food that science made better." Dannon argued that the perfect food claim was mere puffing. However, the commission reasoned that because of the present day emphasis on dieting, health, and nutrition, to make the claim that a food is perfect far exceeds puffing or exaggeration of qualities. It is a misrepresentation of a material fact.

The Federal Trade Commission is not authorized to foreclose expression of honest opinion. The same opinion, however, may not be utilized to mislead or deceive the public or to harm a competitor. Because the dividing line between permissible puffery and implied deception is vague and because false implications of fact can be easily found, there is an increasing risk of liability from using puffery in advertising. The continued rise in consumerism has affected when puffery will be regarded as appropriate. A claim considered as opinion and puffery years ago could now be considered a deception.

Therefore, advertisers must be very careful in using hyperbole in their advertisements. The test is whether the average consumer will recognize or perceive the hyperbole for what it is or be deceived by it. Advertiser be warned: the puffing rule is not a license to lie. Terms like "best," "perfect," "prime," "exceptional," "original," "comparable in quality," "wonderful," and so on have been dealt with by the commission and the courts and do not qualify as puff. It should be obvious that puffing can cross over into deception very easily.

EXHIBIT: 2-1

FEDERAL TRADE COMMISSION
WASHINGTON, D.C. 20580
October 14, 1983

The Honorable John D. Dingell
Chairman
Committee on Energy and Commerce
U.S. House of Representatives
Washington, D.C. 20515

Dear Mr. Chairman:

This letter responds to the Committee's inquiry regarding the Commission's enforcement policy against deceptive acts or practices. We also hope this letter will provide guidance to the public.

Section 5 of the FTC Act declares unfair or deceptive acts or practices unlawful. Section 12 specifically prohibits false ads likely to induce the purchase of food, drugs, devices, or cosmetics. Section 15 defines a false ad for purposes of Section 12 as one which is "misleading in a material respect." Numerous Commission and judicial decisions have defined and elaborated on the phrase "deceptive acts or practices" under both Sections 5 and 12. Nowhere, however, is there a single definitive statement of the Commission's view of its authority. The Commission believes that such a statement would be useful to the public, as well as the Committee in its continuing review of our jurisdiction.

We have therefore reviewed the decided cases to synthesize the most important principles of general applicability. We have attempted to provide a concrete indication of the manner in which the commission will enforce its deception mandate. In so doing, we intend to address the concerns that have been raised about the meaning of deception, and thereby attempt to provide a greater sense of certainty as to how the concept will be applied.

I. SUMMARY

Certain elements undergird all deception cases. First, there must be a representation, omission, or practice that is likely to mislead the consumer. Practices that have been found misleading or deceptive in specific cases include false oral or written representations, misleading price claims, sales of hazardous or systematically defective products or services without adequate disclosures, failure to disclose information regarding pyramid sales, use of bait and switch techniques, failure to perform promised services, and failure to meet warranty obligations.

Second, we examine the practice from the perspective of a consumer acting reasonably in the circumstances. If the representation or practice affects or is directed primarily to a particular group, the Commission examines reasonableness from the perspective of that group.

Third, the representation, omission, or practice must be a "material" one. The basic question is whether the act or practice is likely to affect the Consumer's conduct or decision with regard to a product or service. If so, the practice is material, and consumer injury is likely, because consumers are likely to have chosen differently but for the deception. In many instances, materiality, and hence injury, can be presumed from the nature of the practice. In other instances, evidence of materiality may be necessary.

Thus, the Commission will find deception if there is a representation, omission or practice that is likely to mislead the consumer acting reasonably in the circumstances, to the consumer's detriment. We discuss each of these elements below.

II. THERE MUST BE A REPRESENTATION, OMISSION, OR PRACTICE THAT IS LIKELY TO MISLEAD THE CONSUMER.

Most deception involves written or oral misrepresentations,

or omissions of material information. Deception may also occur in other forms of conduct associated with a sales transaction. The entire advertisement, transaction or course of dealing will be considered. The issue is whether the act or practice is likely to mislead, rather than whether it causes actual deception.

Of course, the Commission must find that a representation, omission, or practice occurred. In cases of express claims, the representation itself establishes the meaning. In cases of implied claims, the Commission will often be able to determine meaning through an examination of the representation itself, including an evaluation of such factors as the entire document, the juxtaposition of various phrases in the document, the nature of the claim, and the nature of the transaction. In other situations, the Commission will require extrinsic evidence that reasonable consumers reach the implied claims. In all instances, the Commission will carefully consider any extrinsic evidence that is introduced.

Some cases involve omission of material information, the disclosure of which is necessary to prevent the claim, practice, or sale from being misleading. Information may be omitted from written or oral representations or from the commercial transaction.

In some circumstances, the Commission can presume that consumers are likely to reach false beliefs about the product or service because of an omission. At other times, however, the Commission may require evidence on consumers' expectations.

Marketing and point-of-sales practices that are likely to mislead consumers are also deceptive. For instance, in bait and switch cases, a violation occurs when the offer to sell the product is not a bona fide offer. The Commission has also found deception where a sales representative misrepresented the purpose of the initial contact with customers. When a product is sold, there is an implied representation that the product is fit for the purposes for which it is sold. When it is not, deception occurs. There may be a concern about the way a product or service is marketed, such as where inaccurate or incomplete information is provided. A failure to perform services promised under a warranty or by contract can also be deceptive.

III. THE ACT OR PRACTICE MUST BE CONSIDERED FROM THE PERSPECTIVE OF THE REASONABLE CONSUMER

The Commission believes that to be deceptive the representation, omission or practice must be likely to mislead reasonable consumers under the circumstances. The test is whether the consumer's interpretation or reaction is reasonable. When representations or sales practices are targeted to a specific audience, the Commission determines the effect of the practice on a reasonable member of that group. In evaluating a particular practice, the Commission considers the totality of the practice in determining how reasonable consumers are likely to respond.

A company is not liable for every interpretation or action by a consumer. In an advertising context, this principle has been well-stated:

> An advertiser cannot be charged with liability with respect to every conceivable misconception, however outlandish, to which his representations might be subject among the foolish or feeble-minded. Some people, because of ignorance or incomprehension, may be misled by even a scrupulously honest claim. Perhaps a few misguided souls believe, for example, that all "Danish pastry" is made in Denmark. Is it therefore an actionable deception to advertise "Danish pastry" when it is made in this country? Of course not. A representation does not become "false and deceptive" merely because it will be unreasonably misunderstood by an insignificant and unrepresentative segment of the class of persons to whom the representation is addressed. *Heinz W.*

Kirchner.[28]

To be considered reasonable, the interpretation or reaction does not have to be the only one. When a seller's representation conveys more than one meaning to reasonable consumers, one of which is false, the seller is liable for the misleading interpretation. An interpretation will be presumed reasonable if it is the one the respondent intended to convey.

The Commission has used this standard in its past decisions. "The test applied by the Commission is whether the interpretation is reasonable in light of the claim." In the Listerine case, the Commission evaluated the claim from the perspective of the "average listener." In a case involving the sale of encyclopedias, the Commission observed "[i]n determining the meaning of an advertisement, a piece of promotional material or a sales presentation, the important criterion is the net impression that it is likely to make on the general populace." The decisions in *American Home Products*, *Bristol Myers*, and *Sterling Drug* are replete with references to reasonable consumer interpretations. In a land sales case, the Commission evaluated the oral statements and written representations "in light of the sophistication and understanding of the persons to whom they were directed." Omission cases are no different: the Commission examines the failure to disclose in light of expectations and understandings of the typical buyer regarding the claims made.

When representations or sales practices are targeted to a specific audience, such as children, the elderly, or the terminally ill, the Commission determines the effect of the practice on a reasonable member of that group. For instance, if a company markets a cure to the terminally ill, the practice will be evaluated from the perspective of how it affects the ordinary member of that group. Thus, terminally ill consumers might be particularly susceptible to exaggerated cure claims. By the same token, a practice or representation directed to a well-educated group, such as a prescription drug advertisement to doctors, would be judged in light of the knowledge and sophistication of that group.

As it has in the past, the Commission will evaluate the entire advertisement, transaction, or course of dealing in determining how reasonable consumers are likely to respond. Thus, in advertising the Commission will examine "the entire mosaic, rather than each title separately." As explained by a Court of Appeals in a recent case:

> The Commission's right to scrutinize the visual and aural imagery of advertisements follows from the principle that the Commission looks to the impression made by the advertisements as a whole. Without this mode of examination, the Commission would have limited recourse against crafty advertisers whose deceptive messages were conveyed by means other than, or in addition to, spoken words. *American Home Products*.[29]

Commission cases reveal specific guidelines. Depending on the circumstances, accurate information in the text may not remedy a false headline because reasonable consumers may glance only at the headline. Written disclosure or fine print may be insufficient to correct a misleading representation. Other practices of the company may direct consumers' attention away from the qualifying disclosures. Oral statements, label disclosures or point-of-sale material will not necessarily correct a deceptive representation or omission. Thus, when the first contact between a seller and a buyer occurs through a deceptive practice, the law may be violated even if the truth is subsequently made known to the purchaser. *Pro forma* statements or disclaimers may not cure otherwise deceptive messages or practices.

Qualifying disclosures must be legible and understandable. In evaluating such disclosures, the Commission recognizes that in many circumstances, reasonable consumers do not read the entirety of an ad or are directed away from the importance of the qualifying phrase by the acts or statements of the seller. Disclosures that conform to the Commission's Statement of Enforcement Policy regarding clear and conspicuous disclosures, which applies to television advertising, are generally adequate.[30] Less elaborate disclosures may also suffice.

Certain practices, however, are unlikely to deceive consumers acting reasonably. Thus, the Commission generally will not bring advertising cases based on subjective claims (taste, feel, appearance, smell) or on correctly stated opinion claims if consumers understand the source and limitations of the opinion. Claims phrased as opinions are actionable, however, if they are not honestly held, if they misrepresent the qualifications of the holder or the basis of his opinion or if the recipient reasonably interprets them as implied statements of fact.

The Commission generally will not pursue cases involving obviously exaggerated or puffing representations, i.e., those that the ordinary consumers do not take seriously. Some exaggerated claims, however, may be taken seriously by consumers and are actionable. For instance, in rejecting a respondent's argument that use of the words "electronic miracle" to describe a television antenna was puffery, the Commission stated:

> Although not insensitive to respondent's concern that the term miracle is commonly used in situations short of changing water into wine, we must conclude that the use of "electronic miracle" in the context of respondent's grossly exaggerated claims would lead consumers to give added credence to the overall suggestion that this device is superior to other types of antennae. *Jay Norris*.[31]

Finally, as a matter of policy, when consumers can easily evaluate the product or service, it is inexpensive, and it is frequently purchased, the Commission will examine the practice closely before issuing a complaint based on deception. There is little incentive for sellers to misrepresent (either by an explicit false statement or a deliberate false implied statement in these circumstances since they normally would seek to encourage repeat purchases. Where, as here, market incentives place strong constraints on the likelihood of deception, the Commission will examine a practice closely before proceeding.

In sum, the Commission will consider many factors in determining the reaction of the ordinary consumer to a claim or practice. As would any trier of fact, the Commission will evaluate the totality of the ad or the practice and ask questions such as: How clear is the representation? How conspicuous is any qualifying information? How important is the omitted information? Do other sources for the omitted information exist? How familiar is the public with the product or service?

IV. THE REPRESENTATION, OMISSION OR PRACTICE MUST BE MATERIAL

The third element of deception is materiality. That is, a representation, omission or practice must be a material one for deception to occur. A "material" misrepresentation or practice is one which is likely to affect a consumer's choice of or conduct regarding a product. In other words, it is information that is important to consumers. If inaccurate or omitted information is material, injury is likely.

The Commission considers certain categories of information presumptively material. First, the Commission presumes that express claims are material. As the Supreme Court stated recently, "[i]n the absence of factors that would distort the decision to advertise, we may assume that the willingness of a business to promote its products reflects a belief that consumers are interested in the advertising." Where the seller knew, or should have known, that an ordinary consumer would need omitted information to evaluate the product or service, or that the claim was false, materiality will be presumed because the manufacturer intended the information or omission to have an effect. Similarly, when evidence exists that a seller intended to make an implied claim, the Commission will infer materiality.

The Commission also considers claims or omissions material if they significantly involve health, safety, or other areas with which the reasonable consumer would be concerned. Depending on the facts, information pertaining to the central characteristics of the product or service will be presumed material. Information has been found material where it concerns the purpose, safety, efficacy, or cost of the product or service. Information is also likely to be material if it concerns durability, performance, warranties or quality. Information pertaining to a finding by another agency regarding the product may also be material.

Where the Commission cannot find materiality based on the above analysis, the Commission may require evidence that the claim or omission is likely to be considered important by consumers. This evidence can be the fact that the product or service with the feature represented costs more than an otherwise comparable product without the feature, a reliable survey of consumers, or credible testimony.

A finding of materiality is also a finding that injury is likely to exist because of the representation, omission, sales practice, or marketing technique. Injury to consumers can take many forms. Injury exists if consumers would have chosen differently but for the deception. If different choices are likely, the claim is material, and injury is likely as well. Thus, injury and materiality are different names for the same concept.

V. CONCLUSION

The Commission will find an act or practice deceptive if there is a misrepresentation, omission, or other practice that misleads the consumer acting reasonably in the circumstances, to the consumer's detriment. The Commission will not generally require extrinsic evidence concerning the representations understood by reasonable consumers or the materiality of a challenged claim, but in some instances extrinsic evidence will be necessary.

The Commission intends to enforce the FTC Act vigorously. We will investigate, and prosecute where appropriate, acts or practices that are deceptive. We hope this letter will help provide you and the public with a greater sense of certainty concerning how the Commission will exercise its jurisdiction over deception. Please do not hesitate to call if we can be of any further assistance.

By direction of the Commission, Commissioners Pertschuk and Bailey dissenting, with separate statements attached and with separate response to the Committee's request for a legal analysis to follow.

/s/James C. Miller III
Chairman

[1] *Sears, Roebuck & Co.* v. *FTC*, 258 F. 307 (7th Cir. 1919).
[2] 29 Fed. Reg. 8324, 8355 (July 2, 1964).
[3] (Harris and Milkis, 1989).
[4] P.L. 93-637, 88 Stat. 2183.
[5] *In the Matter of Cliffdale Associates, Inc.*, 103 F.T.C. 110 (1984).
[6] *FTC* v. *Raladam Co.*, 316 U.S. 149, 62 S.Ct. 966, 86 L.Ed. 1336 (1942).
[7] *Vaughan* v. *Menlowe*, 3 Bing. N.C. 468, 132 Eng. Rep. 490 (1837).
[8] *Federal Trade Commission* v. *Standard Education Society*, 302 U.S. 112, 58 S.Ct. 113, 82 L.Ed. 141 (1937).
[9] *Standard Education Society* v. *FTC*, 86 F.2d 692 (2d. Cir. 1936).
[10] *Gelb* v. *FTC*, 144 F.2d 580 (2d Cir. 1944).
[11] *Donaldson* v. *Read Magazine, Inc.*, 333 U.S. 178, 68 S.Ct. 591, 92 L.Ed. 628 (1948).
[12] *In the Matter of Coca-Cola Company*, F.T.C. Docket No. 8839.
[13] *In the Matter of Doris Savitch*, 50 F.T.C. 828 (1954), affirmed per curiam, 218 F.2d 817 (7th Cir. 1955).
[14] *Aronberg, trading as Positive Products Company* v. *FTC*, 132 F.2d 165 (7th Cir. 1943).
[15] *Belmont Laboratories, Inc.* v. *FTC*, 103 F. 2d 538, (3rd Cir. 1939).
[16] *Zenith Radio Corp.* v. *FTC*, 143 F.2d 29 (7th Cir. 1944).
[17] *Lorillard Co.* v. *FTC*, 186 F.2d 52 (4th Cir. 1950).
[18] *Federal Trade Commission* v. *Colgate-Palmolive Co.*, 380 U.S. 374, 85 S.Ct. 1035, 13 L.Ed. 2d 904 (1965).
[19] *In the Matter of Campbell Soup Co.*, 77 F.T.C. 664 (1970).
[20] *FTC* v. *Sperry & Hutchinson Co.*, 405 U.S. 233, 92 S.Ct. 898, 31 L.Ed. 2d 170 (1972).
[21] *In the Matter of Pfizer, Inc.*, 81 F.T.C. 23 (1972).
[22] *In the Matter of I.T.T. Continental*, 90 F.T.C. 181 (1977).
[23] *In the Matter of International Harvester Co.*, 104 F.T.C. 949 (1984).
[24] *California Dental Assn.* v. *FTC*, 128 F.3d 720 (9th Cir. 1997).
[25] *California Dental Association* v. *FTC*, U.S. Sup. Ct., No. 97-1625, cert. granted, 9/29/98.
[26] In *The Matter of Better Living, Inc.*, 54 F.T.C. 648 (1957), aff'd 259 F.2d 271 (1958).
[27] *In The Matter of Dannon Milk Prods., Inc.*, 61 F.T.C. 840 (1962).
[28] *Heinz W. Kirchner*, 63 F.T.C. 1282, 1290 (1963).
[29] *American Home Products*, 695 F.2d 681 (3d Cir. 1982).
[30] CCH Trade Regulation Reporter, ¶7569.09 (Oct. 21, 1970).
[31] *Jay Norris*, 91 F.T.C. 751, 847 n.20 (1978), affd. 598 F.2d 1244 (2d Cir.), cert. denied, 444 U.S. 980 (1979).

CHAPTER 3

SPECIFIC AREAS OF CONCERN UNDER THE FEDERAL TRADE COMMISSION ACT

Welcome back my friends to the show that never ends.
—*Keith Emerson*

In the previous chapter we discussed the scope of the jurisdiction of the Federal Trade Commission. The theory and reasoning the commission uses in its review of advertising was analyzed. In this chapter specific issue claims and language usage in advertising that can cause trouble are addressed.

We look at the types of advertising claims that the advertiser deals with almost every day, in almost every ad. We review examples of untruthful ads and explore problems with pricing, labeling, and endorsements. Also, we discuss the uses and pitfalls of using qualified language and ads containing claims that a product is unique or will perform in a certain way. Such other problem areas as deception by implication or inference, use of technical language, vagueness, and deceptive truth are also presented. Parallel state laws and FTC industry guidelines are additionally addressed. First, let's examine the most obvious type of deceptive ad, one that is strictly untrue.

UNTRUTH AND DECEPTION

This may seem to be contradictory, but an untrue claim is not, in and of itself, deceptive. The nature of the untruth must be explored to determine if it is deceptive. In simpler terms, there are claims that are factually untrue, but at the same time are certainly not deceptive.

Fantasy Claims

This type of claim is called fantasy advertising. While the claim "Coke adds life" is clearly untrue, it is not deceptive because an ordinary consumer would not believe such a blatant claim. As we have seen in Chapter 2, these types of claims are not considered deceptive if we look to the reasonable man standard, that is, the perception of any ordinary, reasonable consumer. While fantasy claims are very similar to puffery, they are more than subjective opinion. They are blatant absurdities.

Literally False Advertising

Literal untruths in any other form are almost always deceptive. Early examples of some of the more blatant in advertising run the gamut. For example, Alix Cohn, a junk dealer, was sued by the state of Connecticut for advertising his second-hand merchandise as being antique. The merchandise was certainly not "antique" in the true sense of the word.[1] In another case, a product designed to repair aluminum cookware, called So-Luminum, was advertised as being able to withstand a direct flame of 2,000 degrees. The company's claim was absolutely untrue.[2] Advertisements were created that gave the impression that goods were made of leather when they were not. Duraleather – a material used in cars, suitcases, and upholstery – contained no leather but was painted and embossed with a grain to look like leather.[3] In another example, a product called Sebrone claimed to permanently eliminate dandruff due to new discoveries of scientific research. In fact, the product only temporarily removed dandruff scales.[4]

In one case, Murry Space Shoes circulated reprints of a news article as an advertisement. The article claimed that the manufacturer's shoe would "cure many bodily ailments...corrects foot deformities (and cures)...corns, fallen arches, and bunions." Murry Space Shoes had no corrective or therapeutic value whatsoever and could not cure anything.[5]

To further illustrate untrue claims, let's take a more detailed look at two such cases where claims were considered to be plainly untrue. The first, *United States* v. *Hindman*,[6] involved the manufacturer of military uniforms. Seymour Hindman had been promoting his uniforms as custom-made and custom-tailored. In fact, the uniforms were all mass produced. Hindman argued that the term custom-tailored did not mean that the uniform was made individually to fit, but that it was given "particularly fine stitching or other tailoring finish." The court felt that the average consumer would not agree with such a definition, but rather would believe that the uniform was made to order. Therefore, it was untrue that Hindman's uniforms were custom-made.

The second case, *Prima Products* v. *Federal Trade Commission*,[7] involved the advertising of certain qualities of a masonry sealer called Aquella. The manufacturer, Prima Products, promoted to the public a waterproofing paint used mainly on brick walls. One of the claims that Aquella made was that it was "easy to apply...almost as simple as whitewashing." In fact, the application was somewhat more complex, including numerous washings and repeated applications. The court ruled that Aquella was not "easy to apply," as it was advertised.

More recently, under the FTC Act, the literal falsity of an advertisement is judged on the advertiser's reasonable basis, or lack thereof, for its claim. This is in comparison to a finding of falsity or a likelihood to deceive consumers that is required under the Lanham Act. Today, most of the FTC's actions here involve the existence and level of substantiation that supports the claim.

In 1983, the FTC developed *The FTC Policy Statement Regarding Advertising Substantiation* (CCH Trade Regulation Reports 139,060). Under this, advertisers must have a reasonable basis for advertising claims before the claims are made. With a claim like "tests show," "doctor recommended" or "studies prove," the advertiser must actually have literal, documented substantiation that supports these claims. The FTC looks to see that advertisers have a "reasonable basis" for their advertising claims even when no express or implied reference is made.

Consumer satisfaction also does not prevent an ad from being literally false. The court noted in *W.L.Gore & Assoc., Inc.* v. *Totes, Inc.*:[8] "[A] false claim is still a false claim, even if customers do not think the false claim is important enough to complain about it."

One area of heavy FTC activity in recent years involves health-related products. The manufacturers of self-help and health-related products have been rigorously investigated by the FTC for unsubstantiated claims. The FTC requires a high level of substantiation for any health- and safety-related claims. Generally, this would require reliable scientific evidence.

In a speech on February 29, 1996, Christine A. Varney, Commissioner of the Federal Trade Commission, outlined the FTC's stance on safety-related advertising. Here is an excerpt from that speech:

> Some...examples of recent Commission action include a host of cases against companies making deceptive health claims, including health claims for diet and weight loss products, dietary supplements, hearing aids, arthritis treatments, baldness cures, and acne treatments. In addition, we have brought cases against various medical centers and clinics deceptively touting varicose vein treatments, impotence treatments, stop-smoking hypnosis seminars, and dyslexia diagnosis and treatment. Again, our focus is on those claims that can cause the greatest consumer injury.
>
> We routinely cooperate with other federal

agencies, as well as state and local enforcement officials. This is particularly true in cases that involve health or safety claims, where we will rely on the expertise of such agencies as the CPSC, the EPA, and the FDA to help us analyze the validity of the underlying claim. Indeed, many of our cases are initiated by referrals from other agencies. For example, a case we settled last year with two marketers of home and office ozone generators was initiated in response to information submitted by the EPA. In that case, the companies marketed their products as the solution to "sick building syndrome," claiming their machines could clean the air of indoor pollutants, preventing allergies and relieving asthma. We alleged that these claims were unsubstantiated and, under the settlement, the companies are required to have competent and reliable scientific evidence to support such claims in the future.

A company's non-compliance with another agency's standards could, in some circumstances, also form the basis of a complaint. For example, under the Commission's unfairness jurisdiction, it might be possible to allege that a company that continues to market a product that was already the subject of, say, a CPSC recall is engaging in an unfair practice by selling an unsafe product. However, I expect that most of our cases will continue to focus only on the actual claims being made, and whether or not they are truthful and substantiated. And, as I just mentioned, we do try to coordinate our efforts with other agencies to avoid this sort of "double-whammy."

I would also like to mention briefly a few

matters that are currently under investigation, to give you a sense of areas of future interest. We are currently looking at a device that claims it can improve night vision and increase the safety of night driving. Experts from the FDA have indicated preliminarily that these claims are likely false and/or unsubstantiated.

We are also looking at athletic equipment that is being marketed as a safer alternative to traditional products; food storage and thawing products that allegedly can improve food safety and reduce contamination and food-borne illnesses; and claims for baby products that can reduce the chances of Sudden Infant Death.

A Thin Case

Trendmark had promoted its weight-loss program called "Thin-Thin," and two weight-loss products called Nuero-Thin and Lipo-Thin.

Trendmark's advertising made a number of claims, including: Neuro-Thin controls appetite; taking Neuro-Thin and Lipo-Thin together will cause long-term or permanent weight loss; Lipo-Thin lowers LDL cholesterol and boosts HDL cholesterol; Lipo-Thin promotes the healing of ulcers and lesions; Lipo-Thin helps prevent irritable bowel syndrome; Lipo-Thin helps improve cardiovascular health; and that testimonials from "consumers" appearing in the Thin-Thin Diet ads are typical of those who use Neuro-Thin and Lipo-Thin.

Typical of the ads included the following:

NEW ALL-NATURAL WEIGHT LOSS PRODUCT,
NOW ON THE MARKET!!!
If you've heard about the new "Phen/Fen" Diet,

and thought about trying it... DON'T!!!
With the ALL NATURAL "Thin-Thin Diet," you can achieve the same results, without the dangerous side-effect of Drugs! Eat the foods you want, and STILL lose 10-12 pounds per month!
Patent Pending Thin-Thin Diet works for you to lose weight and KEEP IT OFF.

The Thin-Thin Diet Program is a Nutritional Breakthrough Program with a NO DIET, NO WILL POWER, easy way to LOSE UP TO 20 POUNDS PER MONTH and KEEP IT OFF!!"
Read what a few of the THIN-THIN DIET users are saying:

"Because of the THIN-THIN Diet, I have reached my weight-loss goal and my diabetes is much less of a problem!"
–Toni H., Ohio
"After my husband died, I suffered from depression and gained 50 pounds. I tried several diets, but just couldn't lose any of the weight. I've lost 14 pounds already on the THIN-THIN DIET and feel great!"
–Kay M., Tennessee

NEURO-THIN turns your "hunger switch" off.
NEURO-THIN help[s] balance the levels of serotonin and dopamine in your brain. The result? Food cravings and hunger pangs are eliminated...and... you'll be on the way to achieving your goal!

LIPO-THIN Features:
*Absorbs and binds fat.
*Inhibits LDL cholesterol and boosts HDL cholesterol.
*Promotes healing of ulcers and lesions.
*Helps prevent irritable bowel syndrome.
*Reduces levels of uric acid in the blood.
*Correlates with improved cardiovascular health.

LIPO-THIN eliminates fat before your body can absorb it. Forbidden foods that you craved before beginning your THIN-THIN DIET can still be eaten in moderation because the fat they contain is blocked by the chitin fiber found in LIPO-THIN. This remarkable, naturally occurring ingredient acts like a "fat magnet" or a "fat sponge" in your digestive tract. It forms a non-digestible gel that binds with fat molecules and prevents their absorption into your body.

This program works. The THIN-THIN DIET is based on the latest scientific studies. It stops cravings and blocks fat absorption.

According to the complaint, the defendants did not have substantiation for their claims that consumers would lose significant amounts of weight and that following the program would lower their cholesterol, promote the healing of ulcers, and improve cardiovascular health, all without any change in diet.

The FTC determined that Trendmark did not possess any studies relating specifically to the Neuro-Thin or Lipo-Thin products. The "studies" submitted by Trendmark were test tube studies of rats. In addition, the consumer testimonials claimed in the ads were actually made by the company's distributors or their spouses.

In *TrendMark International, Inc.*,[9] the company agreed to settle FTC charges that their advertising claims about the efficacy of the program and the scientific tests that allegedly supported those claims were unsubstantiated. The settlement agreement prohibited Trendmark from misrepresenting the health benefits, performance, or efficacy of the program or any food, drug, or device without competent and reliable scientific substantiation. In addition, Trendmark would be prohibited from misrepresenting the results of any test, study, or research, and would be required to disclose clearly and prominently any material connection between a product endorser and Trendmark.

An Itchy Treatment

Three producers of over-the-counter head lice treatments agreed to change their advertising after they were found to have made false and unsubstantiated claims. The cases, *Care Technologies, Inc.*;[10] *Pfizer, Inc.*;[11] and *Del Pharmaceuticals, Inc.*,[12] all involved head lice shampoos that included a comb to remove lice eggs. All three companies made similar representations:

Their head lice products cured lice infestations with a single treatment;

The egg-removal comb was 100% effective;

Clinical studies proved the product cured lice infestations with a single treatment; and

Clinical studies proved that the egg-removal comb was 100% effective.

The FTC found the "single treatment" claim false since the pesticide used in the shampoo was not effective in a single treatment. Use of the shampoo required consumers to physically remove lice eggs and apply a second treatment in seven to ten days to kill any newly hatched lice. The study that the defendants relied on did not substantiate the claim because the study only used a single treatment.

As for the effectiveness of the egg removal comb, this could also not be substantiated. According to the FTC, lice eggs are difficult to see and remove. The effectiveness of the comb was largely dependent on the skill and tenacity of the user. As a result, the defendants could not make the blatant claim that the comb was 100% effective. Also, to substantiate the claim, the study relied on individuals trained in egg removal as opposed to an average consumer.

The cases were settled by consent order that required competent and reliable scientific substantiation for effectiveness claims in the future.

A Case To Clean The Air

Honeywell, a manufacturer of room air purifiers, settled a case with the FTC for false advertising in *Honeywell, Inc.*[13]

Honeywell claimed that its product removed nearly all or "99.97% of the impurities from the air that people breathe, including dust mite allergens, mold spores, bacteria, and viruses." Honeywell also claimed that its air cleaners provided noticeable allergy relief.

In court, it was revealed that the 99.97% figure referred to the filter's expected efficiency in removing particles that actually pass through the filter. While the filter's efficiency was a factor in determining its effectiveness, the FTC alleged that this figure overstated the actual effectiveness of the air purifier in removing pollutants from the air in a user's environment, as was stated by the advertising. The actual effectiveness of an air purifier depended on the amount of air that the purifier processes, the type of pollutant, and the rate at which the pollutant is being introduced into the environment.

According to the FTC, Honeywell's allergy relief claims were overstated because there was no proof that allergy sufferers would enjoy a noticeable reduction in symptoms by using the air purifier. This would depend on many variables, including the source and severity of their allergies, the rate at which the allergens are emitted into the environment, whether the allergens tend to remain airborne, and other environmental factors.

Somebody Stop Me

The FTC ordered Brake Guard Products, Inc., in *Brake Guard Products, Inc.*,[14] to stop advertising that its add-on braking system performed as effectively as factory installed antilock braking systems. The FTC also banned the company from using the term "ABS" in advertising. Because this case involved motor vehicle safety, the FTC took the case very seriously.

The FTC alleged that Brake Guard made false and unsubstantiated advertising claims by stating that its Brake Guard Safety System, also known as Advanced Braking System or Brake Guard ABS, was an antilock braking system as effective as manufacturer-installed ABS brakes; complied with a performance standard established by the Society for Automotive Engineers; would qualify a vehicle for automobile insurance discounts in a significant proportion of cases; complies with a performance standard pertaining to antilock braking systems as established by the National Highway Traffic Safety Administration; and reduces stopping distances by 20 to 30 percent.

USING QUALIFYING LANGUAGE TO OVERCOME DECEPTION

Another area of concern is the use of a deceptive statement made in an advertisement with the advertiser trying to offset the deception by clarifying it elsewhere with other language, the proverbial "small print." The practice of clarifying a deceptive – or possibly deceptive – claim with other language is sound policy for the advertiser. However, if the potentially deceptive statement is more noticeable than the qualification, either intentionally or unintentionally, then the statement will still be considered by the FTC to be false and deceptive.

The idea here is that the qualifying statement (often called a disclaimer) must relieve any misrepresentation made by the other statement. If this is effectively accomplished, deception has probably not occurred. But remember, this works only if the qualifying statement is made with the same weight and conspicuousness. But where the qualifying statement is made in an inconspicuous manner (compared to the qualified statement), then it has been held that deception probably exists.

Double Eagle Lubricants manufactured a motor oil that was re-refined from previously used oil. The oil was displayed in the standard one-quart can, the type found in any auto parts store. The trade name of the product was printed on the front of the can. On the side of the can was printed a statement that the oil was re-refined.

The cans were intended for display with the fronts showing, stacked side by side on the shelf. The front of the can faced the prospective customer to attract his attention. By placing the clarifying statements on the side of the can, the customer would conceivably pick up the can and purchase it based on the face label. For there to be a clear and conspicuous disclosure, the clarifying statement should have appeared on the front panel of the can.

The case, *Double Eagle Lubricants, Inc.* v. *FTC*,[15] discussed this situation and the court found that the labeling practice was deceptive. We will see more on labeling requirements later in this chapter. True, Double Eagle had made a disclosure about the product, but not with enough weight to avoid a misinformed purchase. What was interesting in this case was that Double Eagle brought in witnesses who testified that the labeling did not deceive them. Yet the court, in deciding against Double Eagle, said: "Evidence of [actual] deception is not necessary where the exhibits themselves sufficiently demonstrate their capacity to deceive." Remember, the test is now "likely" to deceive.

The court went on to say.

> If the commission can find deception without evidence that the public was deceived, we believe that it can make the same finding on the basis of its visual examination of exhibits even though numerous members of the public have testified that they were not deceived.

As we discussed in Chapter 2, actual deception is not required, only a likelihood of deception need be shown to satisfy the requirement of the FTC act.

Visibility Of A Qualifying Statement

In *Giant Food, Inc.* v. *FTC*,[16] the qualifying statement was not placed close to the statement that it was supposed to clarify. This case dealt with the small print in an ad. Giant Food, Inc., a large eastern retail chain, advertised its products through the newspapers, printing its sale price along with what it referred to as a regular price. The regular price was derived from a manufacturer's suggested price list and was not indicative of prices that the merchandise was ever actually sold at in the area.

A typical ad, which ran in three Washington, D.C., area newspapers, read as follows:

Procter Steam & Dry Iron #10010
Regular Price $15.95
Sale Price $8.47

Giant Food used the phrase "Regular Price" in a way that led the consumer to believe that it had sold the product at that price "in the recent, regular course of its business." That was untrue. Giant Food argued that its advertising was not deceptive because a disclaimer in small print ran at the bottom of the ad. The disclaimer was worded in a rather lengthy and confusing manner. The witnesses who testified at the trial said that they would not normally read the disclaimer, or that they would have been more confused if they had read it. The court said, "that the disclaimer might engender confusion appears to us...to be an understatement."

Giant Food also used the phrase "Manufacturer's List Price," which represented to the consumer the price at which the product was usually and customarily sold at retail. In fact, the manufacturer's list was substantially in excess of the usual and customary retail price. The way to look at this is if you state a "regular price" in an ad, the product must have actually been sold by you, at that price, generally within the previous 30 days. Specific pricing terms and their uses are discussed later in this chapter.

PRIOR KNOWLEDGE OF A FALSE STATEMENT

What happens when the consumer knows that an advertisement is false? Simply because the consumer knows that a claim is false does not relieve its being deceptive.

In *Heavenly Creations, Inc.* v. *FTC*,[17] knowledge of false statements was at issue. Although this case involved dealers, rather than consumers, the practice was still deceptive. Heavenly Creations sold a variety of products to distributors, jobbers, salesmen, and retailers. These products were then resold to consumers. The problem here was with the pricing of the manufacturer's product to the dealers.

Dealers knew that Heavenly Creations had a practice of preticketing goods at inflated prices. Heavenly, as a defense, tried to prove that there was a custom of fictitious pricing within the retail trade. However, the court maintained that "a practice does not cease to be...unfair because the falsity of the...representation has become so well-known to the trade that dealers...are no longer deceived."

CLAIMS OF UNIQUENESS

A claim of uniqueness about a product or service is another area of concern under Section 5 of the FTC Act. It is deceptive to state that a product has extraordinary features or is unique, if it is not. But what is considered to be a claim of uniqueness? Again, it's based on the average reasonable consumer of that type of product.

Fedders Corporation manufactured air conditioners and, in the mid-1970s, advertised them as being unique due to their having "reserve cooling power." This was a claim that could not be substantiated. In *Fedders Corp.* v. *FTC*,[18] they even admitted that the statement "reserve cooling power" was "intended to imply an unusual ability to produce cold air under extreme conditions of heat and humidity." The false claim that Fedders air conditioners possessed "reserve cooling power" implied to the consumer that some feature of the cooling, circulation, or dehumidifying systems in the air conditioner allowed them to outperform other brands in extreme temperature situations. In reality, Fedders air conditioners had no real technical advantage over its competitors' equipment.

The court ordered Fedders to cease and desist from making claims that its air conditioners were unique in any material respect, unless it was a fact which could be proven. In the commission's order, it prohibited Fedders from:

> Making, directly or indirectly, any statement or representation in any advertising or sales promotional material as to the air cooling, dehumidification, or circulation characteristics, capacity or capabilities of any air conditioner, unless at the time of such representation [they] have a reasonable basis for such statement or representation, which shall consist of competent scientific, engineering or other similar objective material or industry-wide standards based on such material.

PERFORMANCE CLAIMS

There are specific problems inherent in performance claims. These are claims that a product will do what the ad says it will do. The Fedders case we just looked at was a good example of this. In fact, uniqueness is a claim of performance.

Substantiation Of Performance Claims

In *Sears, Roebuck and Co. v. FTC,*[19] the claim that "our dishwasher cleans dishes so well that they do not have to be pre-rinsed" was an example of an absolute performance claim. If the claim were made that "our dishwasher cleans better than theirs," it would be considered as a relative or comparative performance claim. Sears, Roebuck & Co. is the largest retailer of general merchandise in the United States. In the early 1970's Sears devised a program to increase the sales of its "Lady Kenmore" dishwasher. Sears did not reengineer or redesign the product. Instead it attempted to change the image of – or reposition – the product. The objective was expressed by Sears advertising agency as seeking to "transform the consumer image [of the Lady Kenmore] from a price brand to a superior product at a reasonable price. Eventually, the brand should move from market leadership to market dominance as the market share increases."

Sears produced ads claiming that the Lady Kenmore "completely eliminated" the need for prescraping and prerinsing. Sears labeled the machine as the "Freedom Maker." In various media over a four-year period, and at a cost of over $8 million, Sears advertising for the Lady Kenmore claimed:

SEARS LADY KENMORE
THE DO-IT-ITSELF DISHWASHER
No scraping. No rinsing. Lady Kenmore has 6 powerful
hot water jets for the bottom rack,
surging hot water with enough force to
scrub every dish, pot and pan really clean.
Even baked-on food comes off.
And the dishes on top get as clean as those on the bottom.
With a Kenmore you'll never have to scrape or rinse again.
Even dishes crusty with leftover food.
Kenmore's 14 powerful hot water jets scour every dish clean

...with no scraping or rinsing.
It's great! You'll like the way it makes pre-rinsing
and soaking of heavily soiled dishes, pots and pans
a thing of the past.
Gets even the messiest baking dishes and roasting pans
spotlessly clean...without pre-rinsing!
Wouldn't the woman in your life love a Kenmore Dishwasher
for Mother's Day?
A Kenmore Dishwasher from Sears means no more dishpan hands,
she'll never have to touch dishwater again!
Egg, lipstick, peanut butter, jelly, even spaghetti sauce
come right off with no pre-rinsing.

• •

As a result of the Lady Kenmore campaign, unit sales rose more than 300 percent from 35,029 units in 1971 to 105,570 units in 1973. Sears total dishwasher sales rose from $73.47 million to $94.5 million during that period.

Now let's look at the reality of the case. Sears "no scraping, no pre-rinsing" claim was simply not true, and it had no reasonable basis upon which to make the claim. In fact, the instruction manual, which customers could only get after their purchase, contradicted the claim. The manual specifically instructed the owner to presoak or lightly scour certain dishes.

What the commission ordered Sears to do is worth noting. In addition to a cease-and-desist order, Sears was ordered to maintain written records "in connection with the advertising, offering for sale, sale, or distribution of dishwashers or other major home appliances." The records required included:

1. All materials that were relied upon in making any claim or representation in advertising...concerning the performance characteristics of any Sears...dishwashers or other major home appliances; and

2. All test reports, studies, surveys, or demonstrations...that contradict, qualify, or call into question any claim or

representation in advertising...on behalf of...Sears, Roebuck & Co.'s dishwashers or other major home appliances...for a period of three years.

Requirements Of Substantiation

The FTC has in recent years stepped up its activity regarding ad substantiation. Check the FTC's web site at www.ftc.gov for the *FTC Policy Statement Regarding Advertising Substantiation*.

We've seen that if you make a claim in an ad, you must be able to substantiate it. And note that substantiation must exist prior to making the statement. But what type of substantiation is acceptable? The courts have decided that the proof to support a claim must have a reasonable basis. In other words, the proof can't be contrived, out of context, or based on distorted facts or statistics. This was discussed in *FTC v. Pharmtech Research, Inc.*[20]

In July 1983, the following television commercial aired for a product manufactured by Pharmtech Research called Daily Greens:

•••••••••••••••••

The following message
concerns a revolutionary new concept in diet and nutrition.
According to this report, commissioned by the
National Cancer Institute, a combination of cruciferous and
carotene rich vegetables, has been proven to help our bodies build
certain important biological defenses.
Of course, to get the most benefit from any vegetable,
you should eat them raw. But that's difficult to do everyday.
So I'd like to introduce you to Daily Greens. Daily Greens
are not just another vitamin pill.
They're natural, fresh, cruciferous and carotene-rich vegetables,
dehydrated and compressed, to give you the important
nutritional supplements that could be so vital to your future

health. So, if you're not getting enough raw vegetables, everyday,
rely on Daily Greens – to help
your body defend itself.

Other advertisements ran in magazines, on the radio, and on television. While each ad varied somewhat, they all claimed that by taking Daily Greens the consumer would reduce the risk of certain cancers. The claim was also made that using Daily Greens would contribute to building certain biological defenses.

The advertisements didn't claim that the use of Daily Greens would prevent cancer. Yet the problem stemmed from the fact that Pharmtech relied solely on a report published by the National Academy of Sciences entitled *Diet, Nutrition, and Cancer.* The report itself states: "These recommendations apply only to foods as sources of nutrients – not to dietary supplements of individual nutrients." The report also warned "that the removal of water which occurs during dehydration may alter the protective effect of nutrients and other compounds."

Pharmtech's ads represented that the use of Daily Greens was connected to a reduction in the risk of cancer. The Daily Greens ads were deceptive for two reasons. First, they misstated the findings of the report – that the use of supplements reduces the risk of cancer or the building of biological defenses. Second, they fail to disclose some important material facts that the report's findings did not apply to processed supplements, but only whole foods. In other words, the report was taken and used out of context. The advertisement's substantiation did not have a reasonable basis.

DECEPTION BY IMPLICATION OR INFERENCE

In ads that contain deception by implication or inference, there is no specific untruth, yet for various reasons the advertisement's net impression is not one of truthfulness. In 1884

Mark Twain wrote *The Adventures of Huckleberry Finn.* In Chapter 1 Huck describes the way Twain had written about him earlier in *The Adventures of Tom Sawyer.* In Huck's honest opinion he said about Twain: "he told the truth, mainly. There was things which he stretched, but mainly he told the truth."

An ad can cause the same effect. Some mainly tell the truth while some are stretched quite a bit. But an ad is not a work of fiction. At least, it's not supposed to be. It's a commercial message that has to create an impression of truthfulness. And it has to live up to that impression. An important point is that an advertiser should not try to hide behind the excuse that there was no intention to deceive. A claim of an innocent deception is no defense. The ad speaks for itself.

Innuendo That Creates Deception

Obvious misrepresentations are one thing. But deception through innuendo is much more subtle. The makers of Hollywood brand bread created the impression that its product was a low calorie food. Specifically, the Hollywood bread advertisements claimed that its product was lower in calories than ordinary bread and, that by using Hollywood in a normal diet, the user would lose weight or prevent a weight gain.

The ads for Hollywood bread showed a picture of a beautiful movie star in a sleek full-length pose. The ads also showed a picture of the product. The copy read:

When a woman's Panther Slim,
she's vital as well as slender.
A good figure is more than luck when a lady
watches her weight the famous Hollywood Way.
Hollywood Bread is high in protein, vitamins
and minerals, yet has only 46 calories per 18 gram slice.
Choice of Golden Light or

Nut-like Dark Hollywood.

The court in *National Bakers Serv., Inc.* v. *FTC*,[21] found that the average consumer had no perception of the average caloric content or gram weight of a slice of bread. It also felt that the claim "only 46 calories per 18 gram slice" was intended to, and did, convey the impression that Hollywood bread had fewer calories than other breads. The claim also implied that by eating the same amount of Hollywood bread as other breads, the consumer could lose weight.

In reality, there is no significant difference in the caloric content of Hollywood bread and other commercial white breads. Both contain about 276 calories per 100 grams. However, other breads are sliced into twenty 23-gram slices while Hollywood is sliced into twenty-five 18-gram slices. The only reason that Hollywood bread contains fewer calories per slice is that it is sliced thinner.

The ad was technically true in that there were no incorrect facts. Yet, innuendo created an impression that was not altogether truthful. Hollywood bread had no fewer calories than other commercial breads, and, in fact, its only usefulness in a diet came from the fact that its thinner slices meant the consumer would consume smaller individual portions and therefore fewer calories.

Implication That Creates Deception

Another area of concern under Section 5 of the act is deception by inference or implication. Between 1967 and 1968, Firestone Tire Company ran ads which claimed:

THE SAFE TIRE. FIRESTONE.
When you buy a Firestone tire
– no matter how much or how little you pay –
you get a safe tire.

Firestone tires are custom-built one by one
by skilled craftsmen.
And they're personally inspected for an extra margin of safety.
If these tires don't pass all of the exacting
Firestone inspections, they don't get out.
Every new Firestone design goes through rugged tests
of safety and strength far exceeding any driving
condition you'll ever encounter.
We prove them in our test lab,
on our test track,
and in rigorous day-to-day driving conditions.
All Firestone tires meet or exceed the new
federal government testing requirements.
(They have for some time.)
Firestone. The Safe Tire.
At 60,000 Firestone Safe Tire Centers
At no more cost than ordinary tires.

Firestone, in *Firestone Tire & Rubber Co.* v. *FTC*,[22] admitted that it was technologically impossible to assure that a tire was free of defects. By implying an unqualified assertion of safety, they created a deceptive ad. While Firestone made no explicit claim about the safety of its tires under all driving and road conditions, it did imply a claim. The court said: "[Firestone's] advertisement asserts flatly that the Firestone tire is 'The Safe Tire' and describes the exacting, rugged tests...which the tires are put through to assure this safety. [Firestone's] advertisement gives no indication that there is any limit to the safety of this tire." As a result of this case Firestone was required to disclose clearly and conspicuously, in close proximity to any safety claim, that "the safety of any tire is affected by conditions of use, such as inflation pressure, vehicle weight, wear, and other operating conditions."

The Personal Computer Guarantee

Gateway 2000, a leading manufacturer of personal computers, settled with the FTC on charges that it made numerous false statements in advertisements for its refund policy and its on-site warranty service in *Gateway 2000, Inc.*[23]

Gateway advertising claimed that it would provide a "money-back guarantee" of a full refund. In reality, it deducted the cost of shipping the merchandise to consumers, about $62. The advertising also claimed that consumers would be provided free on-site service upon request. In reality, the on-site service was not provided unless the company diagnosed the problem over the telephone first.

The settlement prohibits Gateway from failing to make a full refund under any money-back guarantee unless it clearly disclosed in close proximity to the guarantee any deductions that would be made. It also prohibits Gateway from promising free on-site service unless its discloses any material limitations to that service.

THE USE OF TECHNICAL LANGUAGE AND VAGUENESS

Deception can be accomplished through the use of technical language that the consumer is not likely to understand, or by making vague or ambiguous statements. Technical language or complicated verbiage cannot be expected to be understood by the average consumer.

Use Of A Foreign Language

About 1840 Edouard Pinaud opened a business in Paris, France, to manufacture perfumes. His goods, as well as his name, became very well known. Monsieur Pinaud for many years built a reputation for the quality of his products. After Pinaud's death in 1868, the Koltz Company took over the Pinaud line.

From 1891 to 1895, a Mr. Hecht worked for Koltz. After leaving, Hecht began manufacturing, in the United States, his own line of toilet preparations. Hecht's bottles, contents, stoppers, and labels were all made in the United States. The labels, however, were printed in French. The labels contained the sentence:

Preparee par M. Hecht,
Dernierement avec Parfumerie Ed. Pinaud, Paris.

Roughly translated the line means "Prepared by Mr. Hecht, formerly with perfumer Ed. Pinaud, Paris." The court in *Koltz* v. *Hecht*,[24] stated that using foreign words, although literally true, can be considered deceptive. Hecht admitted at the trial that it was, in fact, his intent to mislead the public into believing that his domestic perfume was made in France, therefore trading on the reputation of French perfume and the name of Ed. Pinaud. While it was true that nowhere on the bottle was it stated that the product was foreign made, Hecht ingeniously conveyed that impression through his labeling, especially if the purchaser was not fluent in French.

Deception By Implying A Technical Term

Let's look at another example. The following ad ran in trade magazines (directed toward mattress manufacturers) by a manufacturer of mattress cloth:

STERITIZED FABRIC has a proven sales idea,
proven in shoes, proven in clothes, proven in hats.
The sales appeal of a STERITIZED FABRIC has been proven
in many other fields.
We are not guessing when we say that what has been done
in the shoe, the hat, and the dress industries
can also be done in the mattress industry.

In the Nation's Greatest Stores,
other merchandise has shown sales jumps by using the same
Germ-Repellent Method.
STERITIZED FABRIC – Repellent to Bacteria. Repellent to Water.
STERITIZED mattress ticking avoids
perspiration, stains, and odor.
STERITIZED FABRIC is absolutely noninjurious.
STERITIZED FABRIC Repels Germs,
Helps protect all the family against spread of infection,
is positively nonirritating, guards against odors.
STERITIZED Mattress Fabric...
Tested under standards stated in Circular 198,
U.S. Department of Agriculture,
made by Blumenthal Print Works, New Orleans, U.S.A.
Blumenthal Print Works, Converters of Cotton Cloth.

In *In the Matter of Blumenthal*,[25] the use of the word "Steritized" created a problem for the advertiser because the buyer perceived the word to say "sterilized." This was a natural assumption. Why was this a problem if the fabric lived up to the claims? Well, there's the rub. It didn't. The steritized fabric didn't do any of the things that the ad claimed it could. It was not sterile, sanitary, antiseptic, odorless, bacteriostatic, bacteria-, germ-, or water-repellent. It would not prevent perspiration odors, wear longer, or guard against the spread of infection. People would believe that, by some new sterilizing process, the Blumenthal fabric could have all of the claimed qualities. Blumenthal simply made up a name for its product, which bore an amazing resemblance to another word.

Deception Through Technical Language

In *Chrysler Corp.* v. *FTC*,[26] we see an example of confusing technical language. During the 1973-74 energy crisis, Chrysler ran ads for their Dodge Darts. A typical ad promoted the fuel efficiency of Chrysler cars and ran as follows:

• • • • • • • • • • • • •

THE SMALL CAR
VS.
THE SMALL CAR
You can buy a Chevrolet Nova OR
you can buy a small car that can beat
it on gas mileage*....

• • • • •

The answer is a small car at your
Chrysler-Plymouth and Dodge dealers....

• • • • •

See all the Darts at your
Dodge/Dodge Trucks dealer.
See the Dusters and Valiants at your
Chrysler-Plymouth dealer.

• • • • • • • • • • • • • • • • • •

The asterisk in the ad referred to a disclaimer which read: "Gas mileage figures based on October 1973 *Popular Science* magazine. Tests performed by *Popular Science* for its report were conducted on '73 vehicles with figures adjusted by *Popular Science* for 1974 model changes and the results of EPA tests."

That was one of a series of ads, all with the same message. The *Popular Science* tests referred to in the ad showed that the Plymouth Valiant and Dodge Dart equipped with 6-cylinder engines got better gas mileage than a Chevrolet Nova equipped with either a 6-cylinder or a V-8 engine. The same report also showed that Valiants and Darts equipped with V-8 engines got worse mileage results than Novas equipped with V-8s or 6-cylinder engines. In essence, the ads claimed that, based on the magazine report, all Chrysler small cars got better gas mileage than all Chevrolet Novas. In reality, however, the report covered only those cars equipped with 6-cylinder engines. But that was not stated clearly in the ad.

The Dream Vacation

In *Design Travel*,[27] the company used celebrities to promote luxury vacations in tropical settings. According to the FTC, consumers were promised "resort accommodations" and a "luxury cruise" with the payment of a small promotional fee. Those who took the trip found it was not the "world class" vacation they were led to believe. Others, faced with restrictions and extra costs, canceled their plans and lost their initial payment of up to $600.

Consumers were urged, at local fairs and trade shows, to "register" for a dream vacation. The names of those who registered were passed to telemarketers. The telemarketers called these consumers and led them to believe they had won a vacation. The telemarketers persuaded the consumers to provide credit card information and pay $598 for a luxury cruise to the Bahamas. After providing the information, the consumers learned that there were additional charges for "port reservation processing fees." Consumers who tried to cancel the vacation were told that there was a no-refund policy.

At the request of the FTC, the federal district court in Pittsburgh, Pennsylvania, froze the assets of the companies and temporarily halted the deceptive practices pending trial.

Jodie Bernstein, Director of the FTC Bureau of Consumer Protection, said: "These are major players in the vacation certificate industry, but their 'dream vacations' were a nightmare." According to Bernstein, complaints about travel plans rank among the top, and annual losses as a result of travel-related fraud are estimated to exceed $12 billion.

DECEPTIVE TRUTH

Up to this point, we have dealt with deceptive untruths.

But what about deceptive truth? There is a common element to all of the cases involving statements of deceptive, literal truth. That is, there is always some element missing, or a conclusion is inferable that is short of the truth.

In *Donaldson* v. *Read Magazine, Inc.*,[28] the U.S. Supreme Court discussed ads that, as a whole, may be misleading even though every sentence taken separately is literally true. This may occur when things are omitted or when ads are composed in such a way that they mislead.

Donaldson, who was the Postmaster General, sued *Read Magazine* based on its puzzle contests. Donaldson sued because he felt that *Read's* contest was "a scheme...for obtaining money through the mails by means of false and fraudulent pretenses, representations, and promises."[29]

In 1945 *Read Magazine* advertised its *Facts Magazine* Hall of Fame Puzzle Contest. Customers were led to believe that they would be eligible to win prizes by paying a $3 fee. In reality, they would have to pay up to $42. Customers were also led to believe that the contest was a puzzle contest. It was not. The puzzles were so easy to solve that most people would solve all of them. The prizes were awarded, if the truth be known, based on a tie-breaking letter-essay contest.

Read Magazine argued that it had explained all of these facts in its ads. The ads contained wording that specified that the first $3 puzzles might result in a tie. This would require a second and third series of $3 puzzles. Ultimately, if no winner appeared, one would be selected based on essays on "The Puzzle I Found Most Interesting and Educational in This Contest."

There were sentences in *Read's* advertisements which, taken alone, would have conveyed to a deliberate reader all of these details of the contest. But they were not sentences standing alone. They were small and inconspicuous bits of lengthy descriptions. *Read's* ads were very long, and its form letters to contestants were even more lengthy.

In bold one inch type their ads barked:

• •
$10,000 FIRST PRIZE PUZZLE CONTEST
• •

Pictures of sample puzzles covered the page. The ads left little doubt that the contest presented an opportunity to win large prizes (remember, this was 1947) by solving the puzzles. In the lower left corner of the ad appeared the "Official Rules of the Contest." There were 10 rules. Somewhere near the middle of the ninth rule appeared the only reference to the possible need for essay letters as a means of tie-breaking. While all of the information was in the ad, and no claims were made that were not factual, the ad was still deceptive. Granted there is a fine line here, but there is still a line.

This case is used to illustrate the principles of deceptive truth. Regulations that specifically control the advertising of contests and sweepstakes are explained in Chapter 9.

RULES FOR SPECIFIC PRODUCT AND SERVICE ADVERTISING

In addition to the general laws we've examined up to this point, there are also heavy regulations regarding some specific product and industry areas. These include types of products like real estate, jewelry, auto parts, and furniture, to mention a few. There are also areas which include pricing and credit advertising, which are important for advertisers to understand.

Specific information for the advertiser is available from the FTC, other government agencies, and industry trade associations. I would urge the advertiser or agency to familiarize yourself with the requirements of the particular area you're advertising, and you'll help avoid problems.

While most of these areas are covered by the FTC (under the auspices of policing deceptive and misleading advertising claims), other government agencies may be involved as well. Check with the appropriate group for information on the legalities of that specific trade or industry. The federal agencies are listed in the phone book under U.S. Government or through the Internet. In addition to the federal agencies listed, check with the applicable state government in the states where you advertise for specific local regulation information.

Here is a general reference list of the federal agencies that have an impact on advertising and marketing activities and the common products that each govern.

Federal Trade Commission

Light bulbs
Binoculars
Radios
Sewing machines
Amplifiers
Appliances
Consumer products
Foods
Drugs
Cosmetics
Medical devices
Wool, fur, and textile products
Cigarettes
Telemarketing
The Internet

Food and Drug Administration

Food
Drugs
Nonalcoholic beverages
Cosmetics
Medical devices

Biological products
Hearing aids
Radiation emitting devices (microwaves)

Department of Housing and Urban Development

Real estate
Land
Mobile homes
Apartments

Department of Transportation

Motor vehicles
Tires
Boats

Department of the Treasury

Imported goods
Alcoholic beverages
Tobacco products

Department of Agriculture

Meat products
Poultry products
Eggs and egg products
Fruits
Vegetables
Seeds

Department of Commerce

Seafood
Fire detection devices
Consumer products
Fruits
Vegetables

Consumer Product Safety Commission

Consumer products
Flammable fabrics
Poisons
Hazardous materials
Bicycles
Toys
Refrigerators

Department of Energy

Dishwashers
Refrigerators and freezers
Washers and dryers
Water heaters
Air conditioners
Heating devices
Televisions
Stereos
Furnaces
Ovens and ranges and microwaves

Environmental Protection Agency

Motor vehicles
Engines
Fuels and fuel additives
Noise emitting devices
Insecticides and pesticides
Poisons
Insect and rodent traps and repellents

INDUSTRY GUIDELINES

The Federal Trade Commission offers a series of guides, policy statements, and business education materials pertaining to the advertising, labeling and disclosure requirements of certain products and services. While these generally deal with misrepresentations and deceptions in advertising, they also provide information on other issues important to the advertiser. Recent FTC guides relate to subjects including telemarketing, the Internet, and advertising directed toward children. The reader should check with the FTC for up-to-date information on any current guides. Contact the FTC or check the FTC web site at www.ftc.gov.

Certain products and services also require that certain information be included in ads, such as the country of origin. As examples, the advertising regulations for jewelry, household furniture, appliances, televisions sets, audio equipment, fur products, wool products, and textiles are outlined below. These will give you an idea of the type of information that needs to be typically covered in these product messages

Other, more complex product and service areas are discussed in detail in later chapters of this book.

Jewelry

All forms of advertisement that mislead or deceive consumers about the type, quality, metallic content, size, weight, cut, and color of jewelry products are prohibited.

It is an unfair trade practice to misrepresent (or withhold) the place of origin, production, or manufacture of any jewelry item (or major components). It is also illegal to misrepresent gold, silver, precious, and semiprecious stones, as well as the use of quality designations such as "carat" and "sterling."

For example, it is illegal to use the word "gold" (or its abbreviation) to describe any product not composed throughout of fine (24-karat) gold.

Household Furniture

This covers advertising of articles of utility, convenience, or decoration which are suitable for use as furniture. It is illegal to misrepresent or fail to disclose any material facts that would likely mislead or deceive consumers and, therefore, influence their purchase decision. This includes situations where deception may result from the appearance alone, which in the absence of affirmative disclosures, could have the capacity and tendency or effect of misleading or deceiving. For example, using veneers or simulated materials without disclosure is an unfair trade practice in violation of the FTC Act.

If an advertiser makes representations regarding test results or performance characteristics of fabrics, they must be prepared to submit substantiating data that existed prior to making the claims. Because of this, it is wise to keep documentation for three years after a representation is made. The FTC can demand to review the proof within that three-year period.

If furniture is made in the United States, it should not be advertised by terms that suggest a foreign origin, such as "Danish" or "French." Unless, that is, the fact that the furniture was made in the U.S. is clearly and conspicuously disclosed in the ad. The ad should contain a disclaimer, such as "made in the U.S.A." or "manufactured by Acme Co., New York, NY, U.S.A."

It is also illegal to represent, either directly or implicitly, that the advertiser is also the manufacturer or owns or controls the factory where the products were made if this is not true.

Appliances And Electronic Goods

It is a violation of the FTC Act for an ad to represent the energy consumption of certain consumer appliances or the cost of energy consumed unless the product has been properly tested and the claim accurately portrays the results of the testing. This applies to refrigerators, refrigerator-freezers, dishwashers, water heaters, room air conditioners, clothes washers and dryers, and furnaces.

In order to comply, ads, brochures, and catalogs for appliances and electronic products must include the following information:

- The capacity of the model;
- Energy efficiency ratings for room air conditioners and furnaces;
- Estimated annual energy costs or energy efficiency ratings (as of the date of publication); and
- A clear and conspicuous statement that "Important energy information is available. Turn to page(s) 000." Or, "See your dealer for details."

Television Set

A major concern when advertising televisions sets involves the size of the viewable area of the picture tube. It is illegal to state the picture size of a television set unless it is the actual size of the viewable picture area as measured on a single plane basis.

If the stated size is other than the actual horizontal measurement of the set's picture area, the size designation must be accompanied by a clear and conspicuous clarification, in close connection and conjunction therewith. A footnote or other disclosure does not work. For example, making reference to a "19 inch diagonal picture tube" is acceptable, but "21 inch set" is not.

Home Entertainment Products

When stating the power output ratings for amplifiers used in radios, tape players, compact disc players, and component audio amplifiers, certain performance characteristics of the power amplification equipment must be made. If the ad doesn't include the required ratings, it is an unfair or deceptive ad. It is advisable to refer to the appropriate guide for details.

Textile Fiber Products

Textile fiber products are governed by the Textile Fiber Products Identification Act (the "Textile Identification Act").[30] This governs the advertising of textile fiber products when a reference to the fiber content is made or the ad includes a "fiber trademark" (identification of a particular fiber). The ad will be considered deceptive if it does not identify any constituent fiber content of the product. Let's look at an illustration. If a garment is made of 100 percent cotton, this can be stated. However, if it is only 60 percent cotton, the actual content of the other fibers must be listed: 60 percent cotton, 40 percent rayon.

Ads must include a clear and visible statement of the product's origin. A clarification that the product was made in the U.S.A., was imported, or both must be made in all advertising and labeling as well.

The requirements of the Textile Identification Act and its regulations do not apply to products regulated by the Wool Products Labeling Act of 1939.

Wool Products

The Wool Products Labeling Act of 1939,[31] (the "Wool Act") relates to the labeling of fabrics composed of wool.

When a wool product is advertised, a statement of origin must be made which makes a clear and conspicuous statement that the product was either made in the U.S.A., imported, or both. And, this statement must be consistent with the labeling on the actual product.

The Wool Act does not make any requirements for advertising other than those stated above. However, the FTC looks closely at advertising that violates the principles of the Wool Act and creates a deceptive or misleading claim.

Linings, paddings, stiffening, trimmings, facings (except where express or implied representations of fiber content are commonly made), or other products whose fiber content is customarily stated or whose fiber content is insignificant, do not fall under the Wool Act.

Fur Products

Advertising for furs and fur products must be in line with the Fur Products Labeling Act (the "Fur Act").[32] This act prohibits deceptive advertising, and specifically governs misrepresentation of pricing.

A statement of the country of origin is required in an ad for imported furs and fur products. If the ad shows a group of fur products made in more than one country, a statement such as: "Fur products labeled to show country of origin," is acceptable. This does not apply, however, to catalogue, mail-order, or other types of advertising where the purchaser cannot inspect the product and label before buying. In this case, a clear origin reference must be made.

ADVERTISING PRICE ISSUES

The Use Of The Word "Free"

Probably the single word that has caused the most anguish for advertisers is "free." Just plug the word "free" into an ad and you're asking for trouble. It is important for the advertiser to understand how the word "free" can be used and what bargain must be lived up to when it is. Indeed the guidelines in this area are quite clear-cut. The simplest form of free offer is a gift or sample truly given without any strings attached. The operative word here is <u>any</u>. The word "free" means the consumer pays nothing and is required to do nothing.

Often an advertisement offers a free sample that will be sent to the consumer for paying a small amount to cover mailing and handling. This is acceptable only if the amount requested is no more than the actual cost to the advertiser of the handling and mailing. But if the consumer must pay more than the actual cost, the offer is improper.

Mark Twain once said, "Few things are harder to put up

with than the annoyance of a good example." So here is one. It involves a major furniture retailer by whom I was once employed. The company found out what can happen when the word "free" is used too loosely.

These folks had been running advertisements for appliances. In these ads a simple, direct statement was made: "FREE DELIVERY." Things were going along fine, for many years in fact, until one day we got a call from a distraught older woman. She had not received satisfaction from our local store, so she called our general offices. She had purchased a new refrigerator at a competitor's store and wanted us to pick it up and deliver it to her home. After all, our ad did say "free delivery" and she wanted her refrigerator delivered – free.

The more we argued with her, the worse it got. We finally passed her off as a trouble-maker out to get a free ride, no pun intended. Sometime later we were contacted by the FTC, and they wanted some answers. Unfortunately the ones we gave them weren't the right ones. The statement had to be lived up to – literally – or be changed.

From that day on the ads read: "FREE DELIVERY INCLUDED." You had to buy our merchandise to get us to deliver it free of charge. Granted, the average consumer understands that we will only deliver our own merchandise. But the problem went beyond that because "free delivery" is a deceptive claim. The delivery is not actually free. The consumer has to do something – usually buy the merchandise. In basic contract law this action is called consideration. In this case delivery is not free; it is included in the price of the merchandise. You don't pay extra to receive it, but the point is, you do pay for it because it's built into the price.

A Free Offer Must Contain No Consideration

As we have just seen, consideration is the legal term for payment. But payment can be in forms other than the commonly used version, money. Consideration can be any action that induces someone into a contract. It can be a price, or an action, or a motive, or a forbearance (an agreement not to do something). *Black's Law Dictionary* defines consideration as: "Some right, interest, profit, or benefit accruing to one party, or some forbearance, detriment, loss, or responsibility, given, suffered, or undertaken by the other." In other words, an item is not free if it is given with some other consideration.

Along the same lines, *FTC* v. *The Book of the Month Club*,[33] dealt with the use of the word "free." In this case the Book-of-the-Month Club had published advertisements that read:

FREE
TO NEW MEMBERS OF THE
BOOK-OF-THE-MONTH CLUB

The "free" was another book. At the bottom of the ad was a coupon that the consumer filled out and sent in. This constituted a contract with the new member. The coupon stated that the consumer would receive the designated book free of charge, and that that person agreed to purchase at least four books a year from the club. However, in the court's opinion, there was no free book. If the member failed to buy the four other books within the year's time, the club would demand payment for the "free" book. The book was not a gift. It was not free.

In deciding this case the court looked at the definition developed by the FTC on January 14, 1948.[34] The definition read as follows:

> The use of the word 'free' or words of similar import, in advertising to designate or describe merchandise...that is not in truth and in fact a gift or gratuity or is not given to the recipient thereof without requiring the purchase of other merchandise or requiring the performance of some

other service...is considered by the commission to be a violation of the Federal Trade Commission Act.

"Free With Purchase" Offers

An offer of one item for "free" with the purchase of another item indicates to the consumer that they are paying nothing for the "free" item and not more than the regular price for the other item. The term "regular price" is taken to mean the price at which the advertiser has actively sold the same product, in the same market area. This must have occurred within a recent span of time and for a reasonably substantial period (usually thirty days).

The rationale is, a purchaser has a right to believe that the merchant will not directly and immediately recover, in whole or in part, the cost of the free merchandise or service by marking up the price of the article which must be purchased, by substituting inferior merchandise or services.

When creating a free offer, it is important to prevent the likelihood that the consumer might misunderstand the terms of the offer. To accomplish that, the FTC wants free offers to "set forth clearly and conspicuously at the outset of the offer" all limitations and conditions.

There are a few considerations for the timing and repetition of offers, as well. A "free" offer should not be advertised for more than six months in any twelve-month period. No more than three identical offers in the same area should be made in any twelve-month period, and at least 30 days should elapse before another such offer is promoted in the same area.

For another example of how not to use the word "free," let's look at *FTC v. Mary Carter Paint Co.*[35] Here, Mary Carter Paint had a practice of advertising that for every can of paint purchased the buyer would get a free can of equal quality. However, Mary Carter Paint Co. did not have a history of selling single cans of paint. In fact, it only sold two can sets. The company claimed in its advertising that the usual and customary retail price of each single can of paint was $6.98. This was actually the price needed to cover the cost of two cans of paint. What Mary Carter did, in essence, was double the retail price of its paint, sell the cans in twin sets, and then offer one of the cans as "free." Mary Carter's practice was deceptive and violated the FTC Act.

On February 8, 1968, an American Army officer firing on Ben Tre, Vietnam, said, "It became necessary to destroy the town in order to save it." It's not what you call it, it's what it is that counts.

Comparative Pricing And "Sale" Terminology

Advertisements that make price or value comparisons or that offer "sale" merchandise fall under the FTC's guides.

Pricing guides cover only "the most frequently employed forms of bargain advertising."[36] Yet "variations which appear from time to time...are...controlled by the same general principles." When advertising any bargain offer, the guides amplify the point that "advertisers should make certain that the bargain offer is genuine and truthful."

Advertising Price Reductions

A company may advertise that an item is being offered at a reduced price, if the former price "is the actual, bona fide price at which the article was offered to the public on a regular basis for a reasonably substantial period of time." But beware: the FTC has not defined a "reasonably substantial period of time."

One illegal tactic is to state an unusually high price to give a misleading impression of an actual saving and later reducing it to a "sale" price. To avoid this, it's important that the former price listed in the ad is not a fictitious one. Even if it's accompanied by terms like "regularly," "usually," or "formerly," make sure that the former price is not a false one.

The guides state that a "former price is not necessarily fictitious merely because no sales at the advertised price were made." Yet, be very careful that the former price is one that was "openly and actively offered, for a reasonably substantial period of time, in the recent, regular course of business, honestly and in good faith – and, of course, not for the purpose of establishing a fictitious higher price on which a deceptive comparison might be based." If substantial sales were not actually made at the former price, the advertiser "should scrupulously avoid any implication" that the former price is a "selling price" (for example, with language such as "Formerly sold at $000") as opposed to an "asking price."

What if the former price or the amount or percentage of the price reduction is not disclosed? When an ad simply states "sale," the amount of the reduction cannot be so insignificant as to be meaningless. The issue here is whether the price difference is large enough that the consumer, if he knew the difference, would believe that he was getting a genuine bargain or saving. That should be your guide.

Using Phrases Like "Formerly," "Originally," "Regularly," And "Usually"

Using phrases like "formerly," "originally," "regularly," and "usually" in relation to an advertised sale will project a certain impression to the consumer. Because of this, it is important that these terms are used properly, so as not to mislead the consumer.

"Originally," is defined as the advertiser's own original customary price offered in the recent, regular course of business. A price no higher than the first price used in the current selling season. If the original price is not the most recent price, it should be made clear along with any intermediate price reductions. One way to overcome this is to make a statement such as, "40 percent Off Original Prices (intermediate markdowns taken)," or, "Originally $299, Formerly $185, Now $149."

Terms like "formerly," "reduced," "Was $80, Now $60" or "$80 radio $60," convey to the consumer that this was the last, most recent previous price for the same article. As always, truth is the benchmark.

Using the term "regularly" means the last previous price. Using "regularly" also implies that the item will later return to that regular presale price. This needs to be the truth.

"Usually" is taken to mean the current or last previous price. This term may also mean the advertiser's own customary price for the same article or the usual customary price for the same article in the area. Therefore, it is wise for the ad to clearly disclose the basis used for the comparison.

Value Comparisons

It's a common practice for one company to advertise the same goods at prices lower than the competition in the area in which both companies do business. This is acceptable if the advertised higher price is based upon fact (not fictitious or misleading) and the advertiser is reasonably certain that the claimed competitor's price does not appreciably exceed the price at which substantial sales of the item are being made by typical sellers in the same area.

It is acceptable to show comparisons of prices charged by others in the same market for comparable goods, if such goods are of essentially similar quality and are obtainable in the area. It must be clear in the ad that a comparison is being made. However, as with comparisons of the same merchandise, the advertiser must be certain that the advertised price of comparable or competing goods does not exceed that at which it is being sold by other retail outlets in the area.

Advertising Manufacturer's Suggested Retail Or List Prices

Another common practice involves advertising price reductions based on a "manufacturer's list price" or "suggested retail price." This won't cause a problem if the listed price is the amount at which substantial (not isolated or insignificant) sales are made in the area in which the advertiser does business.

This general rule applies to national companies, regional manufacturers, mail-order and catalog distributors who deal directly with the public, or a local retailer. In other words, any company, any advertiser.

The key here is to determine whether the manufacturer's list price is actually the price regularly charged by other outlets in the area. This must be done before advertising the list price comparison. If the business operates on a large regional or national basis, they may advertise a suggested list price if the main retail outlets in a significant number of representative areas are selling the product at that price. To sum up, the retailer who engages in advertising a list price must act honestly and in good faith, and not with the intention of establishing a basis for a deceptive comparison in any trade area.

Bargain Offers Requiring The Purchase Of Other Merchandise

Ads that offer a bargain if another item is purchased by the consumer, must clearly state all of the terms and conditions of the offer. For example, by using language such as "Free," "2-For-l Sale," "Half Price Sale," or "Buy One-Get One Free." This must be done clearly in the ad and not in an attempt to mislead the consumer. Refer back to the *FTC* v. *Mary Carter Paint Co.* case that we discussed earlier in this chapter.

As stated in the *Mary Carter* case, a deception that violates the FTC Act would occur "[w]here the seller, in making such an offer, increases his regular price of the article required to be bought, or decreases the quantity and quality of that article, or otherwise attaches strings (other than the basic condition that the article be purchased)."

Introductory Sales

An introductory or "advance" sale may be promoted when the advertiser expects in good faith to increase the price at a later date. There is no requirement that the price in fact be raised later, but the intent must be made in good faith. It would be deceptive to advertise an introductory sale, while intending to keep the price at that level later.

"Cents-Off" And Other Savings Offers

Advertising that makes "cents-off" or other price representations may be required to comply with the Fair Packaging and Labeling Act and the FTC's regulations under the Fair Packaging Act,[37] or with regulations under the federal Food, Drug and Cosmetic Act.[38] The regulations under the two statutes require similar disclosures in advertisements and impose similar conditions. Let's take a closer look.

"Cents-Off" Promotions

A "cents-off representation" is any printed matter consisting of the words "cents-off" or similar words placed on any ad, label or packaging stating or implying that a consumer commodity is being sold at a price below the "customary retail sale price."

"Cents-off" representations are prohibited unless the labeled item has, recently and during regular business within the area, been sold at an ordinary and customary price and is currently sold at a reduction from the ordinary price in an amount at least equal to the "cents-off" amount that is shown on the package or label.

The "cents-off" claim must be marked as a savings from the retailer's regular price, such as, "Price Marked is 00¢ Off the Regular Price." The regular price must be clearly and conspicuously displayed on the package or label, or on a sign, placard or shelf-marker along with the display.

Within any twelve-month period, "cents-off" promotions for the same size item in the same trade area must not be initiated more than three times, extended more than six months, or exceed fifty-percent of the item's total sales volume. At least thirty days must have passed between each promotion. Invoices or other records should be maintained for at least one year following the twelve month period in which the promotion occurred.

A "cents-off" representation cannot be made where it is known or should be known that it will be used to deceive, e.g., where the retailer charges a price which does not fully pass on to the consumers the represented price reduction or fails to post the regular price, as required.

Introductory "Cents-Off" Offers

"Cents-off" representations made in connection with introductory offers are prohibited unless:

- The item is new, introduced into a new area for the first time, or has been substantially changed;
- The offer is clearly and conspicuously qualified as an "Introductory Offer;" and
- The offer does not continue within the area for more than six months.

At the time the introductory offer is made, the advertiser must intend in good faith to offer the item, alone, at the anticipated ordinary and customary price for a reasonably substantial period of time after the introductory promotion ends.

The term "economy size" or similar words should not be used unless the advertiser simultaneously offers the same brand of that commodity in at least one other size or form, and only if one size of the item is labeled "economy size." The item labeled "economy size" must be sold at a price-per-unit of weight or other measure which is substantially reduced, i.e., at least five percent.

THE FEDERAL FOOD, DRUG, AND COSMETIC ACT

The Federal Food, Drug, and Cosmetic Act also regulates "cents-off" and other savings claims used on labeling for food, drug, cosmetic products, or devices.

"Cents-off" representations may be made for an item if it has been openly and actively sold in the recent and regular course of business in the market area for at least thirty days, and if the selling price, "has been reduced by at least the savings differential represented on the package or labeling."

Sponsors of "cents-off" promotions, as well as persons involved at all other levels such as wholesalers and jobbers, must keep records of all promotions within any twelve-month period. These must be kept for at least twelve months after the end of the year in which the promotion occurs to document that the retailer has passed the represented savings on to the purchaser, should the FTC ask. And they just might.

Other savings offers, such as "two-for-one" or "one-cent" sales, which appear on the label or labeling of food, drug, or cosmetic items or devices "shall include all material facts relative to the offer and shall in no way be misleading."

BAIT-AND-SWITCH ADVERTISING

Bait-and-switch advertising is stringently prohibited. The FTC has defined bait-and-switch advertising as:

> An alluring but insincere offer to sell a product or service which the advertiser in truth does not intend or want to sell. Its purpose is to switch consumers from buying the advertised merchandise, in order to sell something else, usually at a higher price or on a basis more advantageous to the advertiser. The primary aim of a bait advertisement is to obtain leads as to persons interested in buying

merchandise of the type so advertised.

Remember, showing actual sales of the advertised items doesn't necessarily prove that a bait-and-switch scheme did not exist. The commission has determined that, on occasion, an actual sale is a "mere incidental by-product of the fundamental plan and is intended to provide an aura of legitimacy to the overall operation." Therefore, the FTC advises, "[n]o advertisement containing an offer to sell a product should be published when the offer is not a bona fide effort to sell the advertised product."

The ad must not create a false impression of the product or any of its characteristics, such as grade, make, color, availability, or otherwise misrepresent the product so that, "on disclosure of the true facts, the purchaser may be switched from the advertised product to another."

To determine whether the advertiser has created a bait-and-switch scheme, the FTC examines each of the following criteria:

- Refusal to demonstrate or sell the product as offered;
- Disparagement of the product as advertised, or features such as the guarantee or credit terms;
- Failure to meet reasonable demands for the advertised product unless the ad "clearly and adequately" discloses that "supply is limited" or item is "available only at designated outlets;"
- Refusal to accept orders for the advertised item, for delivery within a reasonable period;
- Showing an item that is "defective, unusable or impractical" for its advertised purpose; or
- Use of a sales program or compensation method that is designed to prevent, discourage, or penalize employees from selling the advertised product.

Attempts by a company to "unsell" merchandise or to sell other merchandise instead, is also prohibited. The FTC will consider that a sale was not made in good faith, but rather was a scam to sell other merchandise if it finds:

- Acceptance of a deposit for an advertised product and then switching the buyer to a more expensive item;
- Failure to deliver an advertised product within a reasonable time, or failing to offer a refund;
- Disparagement of the advertised product or any characteristic connected with it; or
- Delivery of the product in a condition that is defective, unusable, or impractical for its advertised purpose.

MAIL ORDER MERCHANDISE

The FTC's Mail Order Merchandise rule ("Mail Order Rule") controls advertising of all merchandise that is purchased by cash or credit through the mail. However, the Mail Order Rule doesn't cover orders made on a C.O.D. basis. This rule also excludes mail order items purchased by telephone and charged to a credit card.

The federal Mail Order Rule overrides any state law, municipal ordinance, or other local regulation that does not provide equal or greater rights to the buyer.

The Mail Order Rule states that it is "an unfair or deceptive act and practice" for a seller "[t]o solicit any order for the sale of merchandise to be ordered by the buyer through the mails unless, at the time of the solicitation, the seller has a reasonable basis to expect he will be able to ship [the] ordered merchandise to the buyer." The order must be shipped within the time specified in the ad or, if no date is specified, within thirty days after receipt of the order from the buyer.

What happens if the seller can't ship the ordered items before the thirty-day period or by the specified shipping date? Then the company must (without the consumer demanding) offer the buyer the option to either agree to a delay in shipping the item or cancel the order and receive a prompt refund.

The Not-So-Sweet Suite

Dell Computer Corporation, the country's largest seller of personal computers, agreed to pay a civil penalty of $800,000 to settle charges that it violated the FTC's Mail Order Rule in *Dell Computer Corp.*[39] The penalty was the largest ever paid (to date) by a single defendant for violating the Mail Order Rule.

The "Dell Software Suite" was advertised as being a part of the Dell Dimensions system. The FTC alleged that consumers who called to purchase a Dell Dimension system were not informed that the Dell Software Suite would not be included when their product was shipped. Instead, the company included a coupon for the software "when available." In reality, consumers did not receive the software for some time. Also, Dell did not offer purchasers the option of accepting the delay or canceling their orders and receiving a prompt refund, which was required by the rule.

CREDIT ADVERTISING

The federal Truth-in-Lending Act,[40] controls all advertising of consumer credit. That means credit offered to a consumer "primarily for personal, family, or household purposes." Anyone who advertises consumer credit in any form, must comply with the act's consumer credit regulation, also known as "Regulation Z."[41]

The FTC oversees and enforces Regulation Z as it applies to retailers, real estate developers, consumer finance companies, nonbank credit-card issuers, and all creditors not regulated by other agencies.

It would be advisable for anyone offering credit in an advertisement to get a copy of Regulation Z, and study its terms.

Definition Of Consumer Credit

The Truth-in-Lending Act defines two forms of consumer credit: "open-end" and "closed-end."

Open-end consumer credit generally includes credit cards and revolving charge accounts. It is extended in one of the following situations where:

- The creditor reasonably anticipates repeat transactions;
- The creditor may impose a finance charge from time-to-time on any outstanding balance; or
- The amount of credit that may be extended to the consumer during the term of the plan (up to the limit set by the creditor) is generally based upon how any outstanding balance has been repaid.

"Closed-end" credit, on the other hand, covers any other form of consumer credit.

Terms That Trigger Disclosure

The Truth-in-Lending Act includes a list of certain "triggering" terms. If any of these terms are used in an advertisement, the act requires certain additional disclosures to be made.

Triggering terms for open-end credit include any reference to one of the following:

- The circumstances when a finance charge will be imposed and an explanation of how it will be determined;
- A statement of when the finance charge begins to accrue, including any "free ride" period;
- The periodic rate used to calculate the finance charge, the range of balances to which it applies, and the annual percentage rate;
- The method used to determine the balance on which the finance charge is computed;
- The method used to determine the amount of the finance charge, including a description of how any finance charge (other than periodic rate) will be determined;
- Any amount, other than a finance charge, that may be imposed, or an explanation of how the charge is

determined. Examples include application fees charged to credit applicants, late and delinquent payment amounts, and annual or periodic charges;

- If the creditor has or will acquire any security interest in the property purchased under the plan, or in any other property; or
- A statement outlining the consumer's rights and the creditor's responsibilities.

If any triggering terms are used in an advertisement, it must also clearly and conspicuously explain each of the following points:

- Any minimum, fixed, transaction, activity, or similar charge that may be imposed;
- Any periodic rate that may be applied, shown as an annual percentage rate; and
- Any membership or participation fee that may be imposed.

Triggering terms for closed-end credit include any reference to one of the following:

- The amount or percentage of any down-payment;
- The number of payments or period of repayment;
- The amount of any payment; or
- The amount of any finance charge.

If any closed-end triggering terms are used in an advertisement, it must also clearly and conspicuously explain all of the following points:

- The amount or percentage of any down-payment;
- The terms of repayment; and
- The "annual percentage rate," using that term, and the details, if the rate may be increased.

In the case of a multi-page advertisement only one set of disclosures is required if a table or schedule fully explains each type of credit. If there is a triggering term anywhere in this type of promotional material, there must also be a reference to the page on which the table or schedule is located.

CONSUMER LEASING

In addition to the above, the Truth-in-Lending Act requires certain disclosures in ads promoting consumer lease transactions. The consumer leasing disclosure provisions of the Truth-in-Lending Act are implemented by "Regulation M."[42]

A "consumer lease" is "a contract in the form of a bailment or lease for the use of personal property by a natural person primarily for personal, family, or household purposes, for a period of time exceeding four months, for a total contractual obligation not exceeding $25,000, whether or not the lessee has the option to purchase or otherwise become the owner of the property at the expiration of the lease." Excluded from this section are leases that otherwise fall under the definition of a credit sale and therefore are controlled under Regulation Z.

As with consumer credit advertising under Regulation Z, certain triggering terms used in an ad for a consumer lease require that disclosures be made. In an ad for a consumer lease, triggering terms include any reference to the following:

- Statements as to the amount of any payment;
- The number of required payments; or
- Any or no down-payment, or other payment, is required upon entering into the lease.

Ads that include any triggering terms listed above must also clearly and conspicuously state all of the following:

- That the transaction advertised is a lease;
- The total amount of any required payment such as a security deposit or capitalized cost-reduction required at the execution of the lease, or that no such payments are required;
- The number, amounts, due dates, or periods of scheduled payments, and the total of such payments under the lease;
- If the lessee has the option to purchase the leased property and at what price and in what time. A statement of the method of determining such price is acceptable; and

- The amount (or method to determine it) of any liabilities the lease imposes upon the lessee at the end of the lease. Also required is a statement that the lessee shall be liable for the difference, if any, between the estimated value of the property and its actual value at the end of the lease.

As in the case of consumer credit examined earlier, a catalog, brochure, or multipage ad used to promote a consumer lease requires only one set of clear disclosures for the triggering terms. If a triggering term appears on other pages, a clear reference must be made to where the table or schedule begins.

In the case of point-of-sale tags (for items that include triggering terms) there must be a clear and conspicuous reference to where a table or schedule of the additional terms can be found.

USE OF ENDORSEMENTS AND TESTIMONIALS IN ADVERTISING

The FTC monitors testimonials and endorsements as part of its enforcement of the Federal Trade Commission Act. The FTC defines an endorsement as:

> Any advertising message (including verbal statements, demonstrations, or depiction's of the name, signature, likeness or other identifying personal characteristics of an individual or the name or seal of an organization) which message consumers are likely to believe reflects the opinions, beliefs, findings, or experience of a party other than the sponsoring advertiser.[43]

The FTC provides many examples of the type of representations it considers to be endorsements or testimonials. As an example, a film critic's excerpted statements regarding a specific film which were put into an ad would be considered an endorsement. This is because the consumer would readily believe that the statement is the critic's view rather than the view of the advertiser. Let's take another example: a television commercial for baseball bats showing a well-known professional ballplayer hitting balls would qualify as an endorsement, even if the professional makes no actual statement in the commercial.

On the other hand, an advertisement for a pain reliever using a long-standing spokesperson as the announcer would not be considered an endorsement by the spokesperson. The reasoning here is that the audience would recognize the announcer as a representative of the drug company and not a neutral and unbiased expert.

Note – An endorsement or testimonial can be created by any person; it does not need to be a celebrity. The FTC looks at any endorsement or testimonial regardless of who makes it. The fame (if any) of the person making the claim only affects how closely the FTC's magnifying glass is held to the issue.

FTC Principles

In order to be acceptable under the FTC's guidelines, testimonials and endorsements must accurately portray the honest beliefs and experiences of the endorser. Further, the endorser cannot make any representation that the advertiser could not directly make on its own. This means that the endorser cannot make any representation that would be deceptive or unsubstantiated even if it is his own belief.

We looked at the *Cliffdale* case in Chapter 2. We'll revisit it here. In *In the Matter of Cliffdale Assocs., Inc.*,[44] the FTC issued a complaint alleging Cliffdale, a mail-order company, with misrepresenting the value and performance qualities of an automobile engine part called the "Ball-Matic Gas Saver Valve." The advertisements stated that the Ball-Matic was "the most significant automotive breakthrough in the last 10 years," that "every car needs one," and that car owners could "save up to 20 percent and more" in gasoline costs.

Several of these advertisements included consumer "test

results" showing gasoline savings of 8 to 40 percent. Some ads included testimonials by consumers reporting gasoline savings of two to six miles per gallon. These claims were highlighted in a heavy-bordered box in the ad asking readers to "read the results for yourself."

It's of little surprise that the FTC ruled the Ball-Matic ads to be false and deceptive. After reviewing the substantiation provided by Cliffdale and the results of tests conducted by the FTC, they found that "even under conditions most likely to produce benefits from the Ball-Matic," the fuel savings did not even approach those claimed in the alleged consumer test or testimonials.

This points out that the advertiser is required to possess a reasonable basis for claims contained in testimonials, even if the testimonials reflect the honestly held views of the testifier. The commission rejected Cliffdale's argument that the testimonials, in and of themselves, validated the claims. The FTC stated that "consumer tests and testimonials...are not a recognized way of testing fuel economy." As the FTC stated, "irrespective of the veracity of the individual consumer testimonials, [the] use of the testimonials to make underlying claims that were false and deceptive was, itself, deceptive."

Cliffdale made substantial use of consumer endorsements to make performance claims about its product. About this, the commission said:

> The clear impression created was that the quotes came from actual, current users of the Ball-Matic. For example, several advertisements quote phrases such as 'Now I get four miles more per gallon,' and, 'Now that I have installed your unit...' Further,...the wording conveyed a sense that the testimonials were given voluntarily: 'It gives me great pleasure to express to you my satisfaction,' and 'Just a short note to inform you of the performance of your Ball-Matic.'

These claims were false, and the testimonials were not what they appeared to be.

In another case, *In re Cooga Mooga, Inc.*,[45] the FTC ordered the manufacturer of a topical acne medication to prohibit celebrity Pat Boone from representing (as it had in the ads) that all of his daughters used the medication with favorable results, unless those statements were true. The FTC reasoned that since not all of Boone's daughters used the acne medication, the statements were materially false and misleading.

If a person states in an ad that she uses a certain product, the advertiser may run the advertisement only if it knows that the endorser actually uses the product. In addition, an expert or celebrity can serve as an endorser only during the time when the endorser "continues to subscribe to the views presented."

CONSUMER ENDORSEMENTS

Requirement That Endorsements Must Be Typical

The FTC will examine an ad that represents a consumer's experience regarding a material attribute of the product. Further, the consumer claim must be representative of what an ordinary consumer will experience when using the product. Therefore, an advertiser should not employ endorsements in an ad unless it can adequately verify that the endorser's experience is representative of what will generally be achieved by others.

The *Cliffdale* case discussed above illustrates this requirement well. In this case, the advertiser stated that the claimed experiences were typical because the consumers (endorsers) represented a variety of locations, makes of cars, and occupations. In addition, the ads claimed "over 100,000 in use."

The commission, however, presumes that viewers will accept consumer testimonials as representative experiences, unless there is a clear disclaimer to the contrary. The scientific record in *Cliffdale* revealed the typical fuel economy improvement was, in the very best case, half that claimed in the consumer endorsements. The commission said: "We have already found that no competent scientific test supports respondents' performance claims." Therefore, the FTC ruled that the testimonials were deceptive since, "even if the individual experiences were accurate, they cannot be typical experiences...."

Use Of Disclaimers

The guides make it clear that, unless the endorser's experience is typical of what other consumers may generally expect to realize with the advertised product in actual use conditions, the advertiser must disclose the performance that would generally be found in similar circumstances or in the limited applicability of the endorser's experience. In other words, clarify the facts.

The FTC guides warn that "[t]he mere disclosure that 'not all consumers will get this result' is insufficient because it can imply that while all consumers cannot expect the advertised results, a substantial number can expect them." The FTC provides no general rule concerning how specific the disclaimer must be, so it would be wise to err on the safe side.

Advertisements for LaSalle Correspondence School (owned by Macmillan, Inc.) offered numerous testimonials of graduates reporting stunning careers and salary advances. Some ads did, in fact, imply that the testimonials were "exceptional cases" of "more successful graduates." However, the FTC found in *In re Macmillan, Inc.*[46] that the advertisements promoted an image that similar success could be readily expected by the reader. The commission, therefore, required all unrepresentative testimonials to be accompanied by the specific disclaimer: "This testimonial does not reflect the typical and ordinary experience of LaSalle students," in typeface that is as large as the testimonial itself.

Use Of Actual Consumers

Clearly, the advertiser should use actual consumers if it implies in an advertisement that the endorser is an actual consumer. To do otherwise would violate Section 5 of the FTC Act by creating a false and deceptive impression that is likely to mislead consumers.

Use Of Consumer Endorsements In Drug Ads

The manufacturer of a drug product should not use a lay person's endorsement in its ads unless: (a) the advertiser possesses comprehensive scientific substantiation to prove the validity of its claims, and (b) the claims do not violate any FDA regulation regarding the drug or device.

Going back to an earlier case *In re Cooga Mooga, Inc.*,[47] the FTC ordered the advertiser of acne medication to possess reliable information, tests, or studies that substantiated any results claimed in its consumer testimonials. Cooga Mooga, through the endorsement by Pat Boone, had falsely represented that its product penetrated the pores of the skin and cured acne. Nevertheless, the FTC permitted Cooga Mooga to rely solely on the personal experiences of the endorsers when the product or service was not related to health and safety and "where the evaluation of such products or services, for purposes of any endorsement, requires no professional expertise and such products or services can be reasonably evaluated through lay use."

In *American Home Prods. Corp.* v. *Johnson & Johnson*,[48] the court upheld American Home Product's (AHP) television advertisements in which an actor depicted as "a typical Anacin user" stated: "My headache's gone, and Anacin didn't upset my stomach."

The defendant had alleged that such statements falsely implied that "Anacin," an aspirin product, caused less stomach upset than ibuprofen or acetaminophen. The court rejected

McNeil's (manufacturer of Tylenol and a subsidiary of Johnson & Johnson) claims, stating that the only message the "Anacin" advertisement "literally communicates is that one user got pain relief without stomach upset."

The court further stated that while aspirin-based products are the most likely over-the-counter (OTC) analgesics to produce gastric discomfort, AHP's commercial made no implied claim that "Anacin" caused less stomach discomfort than non-aspirin pain relievers. The court reasoned that "Anacin's 'no stomach upset' advertising is within the acceptable and expectable limits of commercial puffery and is therefore unlikely to mislead consumers."

Endorsements By Experts

When using an expert to endorse a product or service, the expert must actually evaluate the product or service he or she is endorsing. It cannot be a blind claim where the endorser has not actually used and evaluated the product. Further, the evaluation must be "as extensive as someone with the same degree of expertise would normally need to conduct in order to support the conclusions presented in the endorsement."

Any endorsement made in the ad must be clearly supported by the endorser's actual evaluation. It also must be relevant to his area of expertise. This, however, does not prevent an expert from expressing a personal opinion about a product as long as it involves matters outside his area of expertise. But, as always, this situation (as an opinion) must be clear in the ad.

Another area where problems can arise involves comparisons of products. In cases where a endorsement is used, the expert endorser relying upon his expertise must have concluded that the endorsed product and the competitor's product are essentially equal. If the ad creates the impression that the endorsed product is superior to the competitor's product, it must be clear that it is the expert (not the advertiser) that concluded the product is superior to the competitor's product. An expert may not be used in an ad to falsely imply that he is endorsing a product.

When an endorsement is made by an organization that is claimed as an expert it must be based upon recognized experts within the organization, or by documented standards (that are suitable for evaluating the products) previously in existence within the organization. We'll look more into endorsements by organizations later in this chapter.

What Is Required To Be Considered An Expert

If an ad claims or implies that the person giving the endorsement is an expert, the endorser must actually possess qualifications as an expert in that area. Dan Mar Products manufactured and advertised a product called the G.R. Valve. This was an automotive retrofit device advertised as a product to improve fuel economy. NASA astronaut Leroy Gordon Cooper gave endorsements, as an expert, in ads for the G.R. Valve. In large part Cooper's credibility came from his fame as an astronaut and the implied scientific knowledge that went with that position.

In the case *In re Cooper*,[49] the FTC held that NASA astronaut Leroy Gordon Cooper was not qualified to represent himself as an expert with respect to fuel saving devices for automobiles. The commission held that "Gordon Cooper does not have the education, training, and knowledge to qualify him as an expert in the field of automotive engineering."

The commission reasoned that the ad falsely represented, either directly or by implication, that Gordon Cooper was a qualified expert in the field of automotive engineering. In fact, he was not.

Product Efficacy Claims

Dr. Bricklin, a professor of clinical psychology, had developed the basic "rotation" diet principles that were the basis for a weight reduction program marketed by Buckingham

Productions, Inc. He also served as director of the company. In addition, Dr. Bricklin personally participated in the promotion of the diet by appearing in print ads as an expert endorser.

The FTC initiated an action in June 1985 against Dr. Barry Bricklin, an expert endorser, as well as against Buckingham and others, claiming that ads for the so-called "rotation" diet plan made false and deceptive claims about typical weight losses achieved, ease of dieting, permanence of results, and the energizing, hunger-inhibiting, and fat-burning properties of the wafers and tablets used in the diet.

The FTC in *In re Bricklin*,[50] alleged that by virtue of his expert endorsements, Dr. Bricklin claimed he had a "reasonable basis" for his representations. Yet no such basis existed. A "reasonable basis" would consist of testing of the product and programs involved, which would support the conclusions presented in the endorsement. This is the standard required by the FTC in its guides.

The FTC prohibited Bricklin from representing in ads that consumers can lose weight without disclosing that weight loss depends on an overall reduction in caloric intake, and that a comparable weight loss can be obtained from any weight-control program. That is, unless these claims can be supported by a competent, reliable survey or other scientific evidence that substantiates the representation.

Implied Endorsements

"I want a pain reliever I can really trust," said the young lady. "When I sprained my ankle and went to the hospital, they gave me Tylenol. I learned that Tylenol is the pain reliever hospitals use most. Hospitals trust Tylenol. Last year, hospitals dispensed ten times as much Tylenol as the next four brands combined. If hospitals trust Tylenol, shouldn't your choice be Tylenol?" American Home Products (AHP), makers of Anacin, challenged the above ad for Tylenol.

The court in *American Home Prods. Corp.* v. *Johnson & Johnson*,[51] examined the assertion that the advertisement presented an implied expert endorsement. If you'll recall, we looked at another element of this case earlier.

AHP objected to the advertisement on the basis that it gave the false impression that hospitals use more Tylenol than other analgesics because Tylenol is a superior pain reliever. According to AHP, the real motivation in dispensing more Tylenol was that McNeil (a subsidiary of Johnson & Johnson) supplied Tylenol to them at extremely low prices.

The court reasoned that the Tylenol ad was not false or unfair, because hospitals would, in fact, not use Tylenol if it were ineffective or unsafe. The court said; "At worst, the statement is a half-truth, in that it omits to mention that hospitals choose Tylenol for the additional reason that it costs less than competitive analgesics."

In its counterclaim, McNeil complained of an AHP ad that used a similar marketing tactic. In response to McNeil's "hospitals trust" advertisements, AHP conducted a campaign in which it mailed free samples of Anacin-3 to 250,000 doctors with attached postage prepaid postcards, which when returned entitled doctors to additional free samples. AHP then surveyed a sample of the 108,000 doctors who returned the cards and computed a percentage from the sample of those who responded that they had recommended Anacin-3. AHP then multiplied the percentage by the 108,000 total responses to arrive at its advertising claim that 70,000 doctors recommended Anacin-3. McNeil complained that this advertisement falsely implied that most doctors recommend "Anacin-3" when 70,000 doctors represented only about ten percent of the doctors in the United States.

The court rejected McNeil's argument. Assuming that AHP's extrapolation was reliable, it held that AHP could say that "70,000 doctors recommend Anacin-3" whether or not most laymen understood the percentage of doctors that figure represented.

In addition, the court noted that the more problematic issue was that "the 70,000 doctors did not spontaneously recommend Anacin-3 [but v]ery likely, all that most of them did was to pass on to patients free samples which AHP had furnished them." It concluded that AHP had, in effect, carried "McNeil's scheme to its logical extreme" by reducing the price of Anacin-3 to zero. The court accordingly held that AHP's campaign was not false or "unacceptably misleading" since 70,000 doctors impliedly recommended Anacin-3.

OTHER CONSIDERATIONS CONCERNING ENDORSEMENTS AND TESTIMONIALS

Endorsements By Organizations

An organization's endorsement must fairly reflect the collective view of the group. This is because consumers view endorsements by organizations as a collective judgment, free from the sort of subjective influences inherent in an individual's judgment.

In the case *In re Biopractic Group, Inc.*,[52] the commission ordered the manufacturer of a treatment for arthritis and musculoskeletal ailments called "Ice Therapy" to stop representing that the treatment had been endorsed by various medical organizations and athletic groups. Biopractic's advertisement stated that "[d]octors, medical pain centers, physical therapists, health clinics, professional athletic teams, U.S. and Russian Olympic Track Teams Praise Ice Therapy." The commission alleged that no such medical or athletic organizations had given Biopractic the endorsements and found the ad to be false and misleading.

In another case, *In re Estee Corp.*,[53] the FTC ordered the maker of a fructose-sweetened food product to stop representing that its products had been recommended by the FDA or the American Diabetes Association when no such endorsements had been made. And in *In re Bristol-Myers Co.*,[54] the FTC ordered a drug manufacturer to stop representing in its ads that doctors recommended Bufferin more than any other pain reliever, without a reasonable basis for the claim.

In *In re Emergency Devices, Inc.*,[55] the commission ordered the manufacturer of a gas mask to stop ads containing an approval by any municipal, state, or federal agency when such an endorsement was not true. The ads had included statements such as "[t]ested and approved! In the U.S. and Canada, the mask has undergone vigorous testing by fire officials" and "[t]he filtering system was evaluated by an independent chemical testing lab, approved by OSHA and the California State Health Department." This was not true.

Disclosure Of Business Connection

Any connection between the endorser and the advertiser, which cannot reasonably be recognized by the audience, that might materially affect the credibility of the endorsement must be fully disclosed.

Consumers expect an advertiser to pay an expert or a well-known personality for an endorsement, but they do not expect such a payment for a noncelebrity endorsement. Therefore, if an advertiser is paying a noncelebrity for an endorsement, the compensation must be conspicuously disclosed in the advertisement.

The FTC reiterated its position concerning the disclosure of business connections in *In the Matter of Cliffdale Assocs., Inc.*,[56] a case which we looked at earlier. The FTC held that Cliffdale implied that the consumer endorsements in its advertising were "freely given by individuals who were unrelated to the marketers of the Ball-Matic" on the basis of specific language in the testimonials such as, "It gives me great pleasure to express to you my satisfaction" and "Just a short note to inform you of the performance of your Ball-Matic." In fact, many testimonials were solicited by Cliffdale employees from business associates.

As the commission states in their guidelines, when a connection exists between the endorser and the advertiser that might affect the weight and credibility of the endorsement, the connection must be disclosed. The FTC found the connection between the endorsers and Cliffdale to be material because potential purchasers would have difficulty evaluating the Ball-Matic on their own and would therefore be apt to rely heavily on endorsements of other users. The FTC also reasoned that the language used by the endorsers specifically implied that their testimonials had been unsolicited.

In another case we have looked at already, *In re Cooga Mooga, Inc.*, Pat Boone also had a financial interest in the advertised product, Acne-Statin. In fact, Boone had the majority control of the company. The commission maintained that "if a material connection exists between the endorser and the advertiser or its advertising agency, such connection must be disclosed in the advertisement(s) which contain the endorsement." The commission went on to further explain that: "A 'material connection' shall mean,...any financial interest in the sale of the product or service which is the subject of the endorsement or any familial connection between the endorser and the advertiser or its advertising agency."

However, the FTC guides do not require the disclosure that a testimonial is solicited.

LABELING

A number of labeling laws affect a wide variety of products. As an example, various provisions of the federal Food, Drug, and Cosmetic Act regulate labeling for those products. These regulations are administered by the Food and Drug Administration (FDA). Other examples include wool products (regulated by the Wool Products Labeling Act of 1939), textile products (regulated by the Textile Fiber Products Identification Act), and fur products (regulated by the Fur Products Labeling Act). These various acts outlaw mislabeling, which is often referred to as "misbranding" and are administered by the Federal Trade Commission.

THE RELATIONSHIP BETWEEN THE FDA AND THE FTC CONCERNING LABELING

As a general rule, the Food and Drug Administration (FDA) maintains jurisdiction for labeling of food, drug and cosmetic products, while the FTC has jurisdiction over the truth or falsity (and likelihood of deception) of any advertising used in relation to these products.

In the absence of an express agreement between the two agencies to the contrary, the FTC will exercise primary jurisdiction over all matters regulating the truth or falsity of advertising of food, drugs (with the exception of prescription drugs), devices, and cosmetics.

The Food And Drug Administration

The FDA controls labeling under the federal Food, Drug, and Cosmetic Act (FDC Act),[57] and the Fair Packaging and Labeling Act (FPL Act).[58] Both acts apply to foods and drugs for humans, as well as animals, cosmetics, and medical devices. In addition, many states have similar laws modeled after the FDC Act. Among other things, this act is designed to insure that labeling and packaging is truthful, nondeceptive, and informative. On the other hand, the FPL Act controls the location and contents of information on packages and labels.

Basically, the FDC Act forbids distribution within or importation into the United States of products that are adulterated or "misbranded." In this context, "misbranding" includes statements, designs, or pictures on labels that create a false or misleading impression. It also covers failure to display required information in labeling.

The FDC Act contains detailed definitions of "misbranding." For example, the FDC Act states that a product is "misbranded" if its label is false or misleading in any manner. As an example, use of testimonials constitute misbranding if the impression given is that the drug is effective for a particular condition when it isn't, or hasn't been proven effective for that condition.

The FDC Act defines "labeling" as all labels and other written, printed, or graphic matter accompanying the product. You should be aware that the FDA, and the courts, will interpret "accompanying" in very broad terms. Therefore, "labeling" may also include items that help identify the article, its uses, and give directions, even if it is not actually included with the product. Under this definition the FDA can proceed against a false or misleading food or drug ad. If the FDA believes a threat to the public health may exist in such an ad, they can attempt to link the ad with the product to give the agency the authority to act.

In 1981 then FDA Commissioner, Dr. Arthur Hull Hayes, Jr., stated in a speech to the American Advertising Federation Conference that:

> The line between advertising and labeling sometimes is very thin. In certain cases, advertising may become labeling when it accompanies a product. For example, tear sheets from newspapers or magazines, when they are placed on the counter next to the product, are labeling. Catalogues may be labeling, as may brochures used to promote a product. Courts have held that written, printed or graphic promotional material accompanying a product is labeling, regardless of the nature of the material, or the manner in which it became associated with or accompanies the article.

Dr. Hayes also provided three examples of situations where

the FDA might take action against an ad:

- A drug or medical device product is legally misbranded if its advertising contains conditions, purposes, or uses for which the labeling does not bear adequate directions for use;
- A drug or product may not be promoted, in either its labeling or advertising, with any representation or suggestion that approval by FDA is in effect; or
- A drug or medical device is illegally misbranded if its advertising is false or misleading in any way.

Labeling And Its Relationship To The Lanham Act

Recently, competitors have brought others into court in advertising cases. That trend is the result of Section 43(a) of the Lanham Trademark Act,[59] which we look at in detail in Chapter 8. While most of the cases to date have arisen as a result of problems with advertising, this statute applies to labeling. In fact, the statute specifically provides:

> Any person who shall affix, apply, or annex, or use in connection with any goods or services, or any container or containers for goods, a false designation of origin, or any false description or representation, including words or symbols tending falsely to describe or represent the same, and shall cause such goods or services to enter into commerce, and any person who shall with knowledge of the falsity of such designation of origin or description or representation cause or procure the same to be transported or used in commerce or deliver the same to any carrier to be transported or used, shall be liable to a civil action by any person doing business in the locality falsely indicated as that of origin or in the region in which said locality is situated, or by any person who believes that he is or

> is likely to be damaged by the use of any such false description or representation.

Keeping this in mind, what if you wanted to make reference to a competitor's trademark on your own product label? You can, if your label reference is truthful, according to a decision in *C. D. Searle & Co.* v. *Hudson Pharmaceutical Corp.*[60]

The case was brought under Section 43(a) of the Lanham Act and involved a vegetable laxative marketed and sold by two competitive pharmaceutical firms. Since 1934 Searle marketed a laxative product containing psyllium hydrophilic mucilloid using the registered trademark METAMUCIL. In 1964 Hudson Pharmaceutical Corp. marketed a laxative containing the same psyllium hydrophilic mucilloid, under the registered trademark name REGACILIUM.

Hudson had developed a comparative advertising campaign that ran for many years, not only in trade publications but also in point-of-purchase materials. Since 1972 Hudson had included in its comparative ads the claim that REGACILIUM is "Equivalent to METAMUCIL."

Until 1980 both of these companies' competitive products were packaged very differently. In that year, however, Hudson changed its product's packaging to resemble the METAMUCIL packaging. In addition to the ads, Hudson's new package label contained the statement Hudson had long used in trade catalogs and point-of-purchase advertising: "Equivalent to METAMUCIL."

The new packaging with its comparative statement brought on the lawsuit. Searle sued Hudson to halt any mention of METAMUCIL on the REGACILIUM container. The court held that Hudson could not make further reference to METAMUCIL on the REGACILIUM container, stating:

> Unless the defendant's container is changed such that "METAMUCI" appears in type no larger than the word "Equivalent" and in green letters on

> the white background. Defendant shall place an asterisk next to the METAMUCIL mark and shall state adjacent to said mark the statement "a product of G.D. Searle, not a Hudson product."

It was "proper for Hudson, on its REGACILIUM container, to truthfully characterize REGACILIUM as 'Equivalent to METAMUCIL.'" The court said: "Whether one is entitled to refer to a competitor's trademark depends not on where the reference appears, but on whether the reference is truthful."

STATE LAW PARALLELS TO THE FTC ACT

In addition to the federal regulations under Section 5 of the FTC Act just discussed, there are also state statutes and regulations. You should research and understand the unfair and deceptive acts and practices ("UDAP") statutes that exist in the states where you plan to advertise.

In the past twenty-five years, most states have developed some type of consumer protection law. Many of these statutes parallel the Federal Trade Commission Act and are appropriately called "Little FTC Acts" or "Mini FTC Acts." However, unlike the FTC Act many of these statutes afford consumers the right to bring a civil action for damages. There are four types of UDAP statutes which we will discuss in the following sections:

- Unfair trade practice and consumer protection laws;
- Uniform consumer sales practices acts;
- Uniform deceptive trade practices acts; and
- Consumer fraud acts.

Unfair Trade Practice And Consumer Protection Laws

This type of UDAP statute follows a form drafted by the Federal Trade Commission in association with the Committee on

Suggested State Legislation of the Council of State Governments. There are three versions of this model that are used in various states:

- Pure "Little FTC Acts" specifically outlawing unfair methods of competition and unfair or deceptive acts or practices. These have been adopted in states including: Connecticut, Florida, Hawaii, Illinois, Louisiana, Maine, Massachusetts, Montana, Nebraska, North Carolina, South Carolina, Vermont, Washington, and West Virginia;
- Acts prohibiting certain specific practices, in addition to any other practice that is essentially unfair or deceptive. These are found in states including: Alabama, Alaska, Georgia, Idaho, Maryland, Mississippi, New Hampshire, Pennsylvania, Rhode Island, and Tennessee; and
- Acts prohibiting false, misleading, or deceptive practices. These statutes are found in states including Kentucky and Texas.

Uniform Consumer Sales Practices Acts

Developed by the American Bar Association and the National Conference on Uniform State Laws, this act applies only to consumer transactions and makes deceptive and unconscionable practices illegal. This act has been adopted by states including Kansas, Ohio, and Utah.

Uniform Deceptive Trade Practices Acts

This type of act gives businesses the right to take action against a competitor that uses deceptive techniques to attract customers. In addition, the act has also been applied to consumer cases. This act in different forms is in effect in: Colorado, Delaware, Georgia, Hawaii, Illinois, Maine, Minnesota, Nebraska, New Mexico, Ohio, Oklahoma, and Oregon.

Consumer Fraud Acts

The Consumer Fraud Acts forbid misrepresentation, fraud, deception, and unfair or unconscionable acts. States that employ such acts include: Arizona, Arkansas, Delaware, Indiana, Iowa, Michigan, Missouri, Nevada, New Jersey, New York, North Dakota, South Dakota, Virginia, Wyoming, and the District of Columbia.

STATE LAW CASES

Failure To Disclose

We've seen recent cases that revolve around a failure to disclose facts. As a result, failure to disclose a fact may or may not be considered false advertising depending on the particular state's law. Take two cases that occurred in 1998, each involving AT&T's failure to disclose its practice of "rounding up" to the next full minute the cost of long distance telephone service. A New York court held that this was not false advertising under New York law, and a California court held that AT&T's omission was false advertising under California law.

The subject of a number of false advertising/deceptive practices actions in recent years, "rounding up" occurs when a long distance phone conversation lasts for one minute and ten seconds, and the customer is charged for two minutes of time. A typical defense against any request for monetary relief in such actions involves the filed rate doctrine. Telecommunications companies are required to file their rates with the Federal Communications Commission (FCC). As long as the company does not deviate from those rates, no civil action (based on rates) may be brought against the company. The theory here is that once the rates are filed, they become public record and therefore the public is presumed to be informed.

In *Marcus* v. *AT&T Corp.*,[61] AT&T's failure to disclose its rounding up practice in its advertising was not considered false advertising under New York law. AT&T did disclose its rounding-up practice when it filed with the FCC.

Under New York's false advertising statute,[62] a plaintiff must allege that the defendant made a material false misrepresentation, including how the advertising failed to reveal material facts.

The court stated:

> In order to establish a claim of false advertising under New York's General Business Law, appellants must demonstrate that AT&T's advertisements are "misleading in a material respect...[including] the extent to which the advertising fails to reveal [material] facts."
>
> Appellants claim that "[AT&T's] use of various forms of media to advertise, call attention to, or give publicity to the sale of long distance telephone service, which was falsely represented by [AT&T's] failure to disclose that residential consumers are billed for calls by the minute rounded up to the next higher full minute, constitutes false advertising."
>
> In Porr,[63] plaintiffs claimed that the advertisements of a local carrier were misleading in material respects because the advertisements failed to disclose the carrier's policy of rounding up phone charges to the next minute. The court concluded that, under the false advertisement statute, "[s]ince the defendants' tariffs were at all times a matter of public record and were in no way concealed, there is no underpinning for any cause of action for...false advertising." We agree with the Appellate Division's reasoning. In the instant case, AT&T's tariff is similarly a matter of public record, and is not concealed.
>
> We note, finally, that we do not hold that

> AT&T could avoid the imposition of injunctive relief if it affirmatively misrepresented to consumers as a whole what its rates are; we hold only that in cases such as this one, where AT&T has complied with federal laws regarding rates, filed those rates, and charged only those rates, its failure to more actively publicize those rates is not a basis of liability for breach of warranty, fraud and deceit, negligent misrepresentation, deceptive acts or practices, unjust enrichment, or false advertisement.

The court concluded that since AT&T's rates were at all times a matter of public record and were in no way concealed, there was no false advertising. The court stated:

> Plaintiffs who were able to prove their claims and recover damages would effectively receive a discounted rate for phone service over other AT&T customers. [I]f the plaintiff[s] were allowed to collect damages because of their purported reliance upon [the carrier's] non-disclosure, they would have won for themselves a reduced rate for their local telephone service. Nonparty subscribers to the same service would of necessity pay a higher rate. Such a "discriminatory" result cannot be squared with the filed rate doctrine's mandate of equal rates for equal service. Furthermore, the duty to file rates with the Commission and the obligation to charge only those rates have always been considered essential to preventing price discrimination and stabilizing rates.

In another case, *Day* v. *AT&T*,[64] consumers brought an action claiming that AT&T engaged in misleading and deceptive advertising in the sale of prepaid long distance phone cards. This occurred because AT&T failed to disclose in their advertising and packaging materials that calls made with the cards would be rounded up.

Under California law,[65] it was only necessary to show that consumers were likely to be deceived by the advertising. Proof of actual deception or confusion was not required.

The court said:

> [T]he statutes are meant to protect the public from a wide spectrum of improper conduct in advertising. They may be invoked where the advertising complained of is not actually false, but thought likely to mislead or deceive, or is in fact false. By their breadth, the statutes encompass not only those advertisements which have deceived or misled because they are untrue, but also those which may be accurate on some level, but will nonetheless tend to mislead or deceive.

The court in this case determined that since the phone cards were prepaid and the packaging of the cards did not reveal the practice of rounding up, AT&T's advertising was likely to mislead.

Specifically, the plaintiff argued that AT&T, who sells the prepaid phone cards, does not "reveal to the consumer, prior to purchase, that calls made with these cards are, in fact, rounded up to the next higher minutes." As an example, on the packaging of its "PrePaid Card" AT&T states the card is "worth 10 minutes of phone calls in the U.S." and that "1 minute of calling time requires 1 unit when calling within the U.S."

Based on the advertising, a consumer would not know that rounding up was done until the card was purchased.

The court reasoned:

> The State of California has no requirement that common carriers disclose their rates anywhere other

> than in the rate schedules filed with the PUC. Nonetheless, businesses are prohibited from engaging in advertising practices which are potentially misleading to the public, so that if they choose to promote their rates, they must do so with sufficient accuracy that they did not risk misleading or deceiving the consumer. We hold that under California's unfair business practices and deceptive advertising provisions, respondents are prohibited from disseminating misleading or deceptive packaging materials with their prepaid phone cards.

The court continued by stating:

> We hold that the policies which are furthered by the California statutes would be undermined by the filed rate doctrine's presumption of a consumer's omniscience of filed rates, and the resulting immunity to common carriers, regardless of any advertising deception used to lure the consumer.

Here, the court viewed *Marcus* differently because consumers were able to read their phone bills and see the rounding up practice.

The court specified:

> We decline to conclude on the facts alleged here that no reasonable consumer of prepaid phone cards would be likely to be misled or deceived by respondents' practices. The rationale of the holdings in...*Marcus* rested in part upon the consumers' ability to read the phone bills provided by the respondents there. With this document before them, they could see that only full minutes had been charged, but could not reasonably believe that each call they had made had been in increments of

precise minutes.

While in *Day*, the packaging of the phone cards did not discuss rounding up. Also, in *Day*, the court refused to consider the filed rate presumption of consumer knowledge.

In another case we see a contrast to the previous two cases. In *Tenore* v. *AT&T Wireless Services*,[66] the Washington Supreme Court held that AT&T Wireless could be liable for false advertising under Washington's consumer protection law for not disclosing its practice of rounding up.

The court stated:

> Respondent AT&T engaged in "deceptive, fraudulent, misleading and/or unfair conduct" by not disclosing its practice of "rounding" airtime in order to "induce cellular customers to use its cellular service, and/or in order to unfairly profit." "Rounding," "rounding up," or "full minute billing" is a common billing practice in the cellular and long distance telephone industry where fractions of a minute are rounded up to the next highest minute. For example, a call that lasts one minute and one second is charged as a two-minute call, but the subscriber is not informed of the actual duration of the call. Appellants claim this billing practice "results in millions of dollars of excess billing... all at the expense of the unwary customer." Appellants additionally claim this practice is "contrary to the 'Service Agreement'...which states that the customer is billed only for 'the time you press send until the time you press end.'"

The court added:

> Appellants claim cellular customers do not receive the full minutes they have contracted for at a

> fixed rate under their service plan because of rounding. For example, all subscribers are required to choose between plans that offer varying specified minutes of airtime, such as 30, 60, or 100 minutes, for a fixed monthly rate, beyond which calls are billed at a specified per-minute rate. But a 30-minute plan may not in fact provide 30 full minutes because of rounding. This is what Appellants claim AT&T should have disclosed.

The essential difference in *Tenore* was that AT&T Wireless Services was a cellular service provider. These providers are exempt from the FCC tariff filing requirements. *Marcus* and *Day* were long distance telephone service providers that were considered "common carriers" under the Federal Communication Act, which required the filing of tariffs. Since they weren't, AT&T Wireless could not use the filed rate doctrine as a defense. The court then looked at whether the doctrine of primary jurisdiction required the issues in the case to be decided by the FCC.

AT&T Wireless argued that finding false advertising under Washington's consumer protection statutes required a court to engage in rate regulation in determining a reasonable charge for partial minutes of airtime. Thus, the matter should have been referred to the FCC, which had special competence and expertise in rate regulation.

The court disagreed, relying primarily on the Supreme Court decision in *Nader* v. *Allegheny Airlines, Inc.*[67] In that case, a plaintiff brought actions against an airline for not disclosing its overbooking practices. The plaintiff had been "bumped" from a flight on which he had a confirmed reservation. The Supreme Court held that the doctrine of primary jurisdiction did not require the misrepresentation claim to be referred to the Civil Aeronautics Board.

The Court in *Nader* stated:

> The action brought by petitioner does not turn on a determination of the reasonableness of a challenged practice – a determination that could be facilitated by an informed evaluation of the economics or technology of the regulated industry. The standards to be applied in an action for fraudulent misrepresentation are within the conventional competence of the courts, and the judgment of a technically expert body is not likely to be helpful in the application of these standards to the facts of this case.

The plaintiffs were not challenging AT&T Wireless' practice of rounding up, but rather its failure to disclose the practice. The Washington Court reasoned that a court could award damages without it constituting rate-making.

A FEW FINAL WORDS ON THE SUBJECT

Having now studied the various problem areas involving the Federal Trade Commission Act and state parallels, the advertiser should be better equipped to avoid creating a deceptive ad. Advertisers and their agencies, with this knowledge in mind, must carefully and objectively evaluate their advertising to avoid trouble.

You should study the following document, reproduced in full in Exhibit 3-1, which was created in 1975 by the Federal Trade Commission. It contains a series of questions that the Commission uses to investigate advertising cases. In 1981, FTC Chairman, James C. Miller, III, stated that this protocol would be a key document during his tenure.

EXHIBIT 3-1:

Federal Trade Commission Policy Planning Protocol For Deceptive and Unsubstantiated Claims

These questions which follow are not cumulative. The answer to less than all of them may indicate the need for action. Moreover, answers to certain of these questions will frequently not be available at all, or may not be available except at considerable cost and delay. Answers to these questions therefore should not be required where obtaining the answers would be unduly burdensome or speculative, or where the answers to other of the questions indicate that the action proposed is a particularly good one, or, of course, where the answers could be obtained only by compulsory process and the action which the Commission is being asked to take is to authorize such process.

A. Consumer Interpretations of the Claim

1. List the main interpretations that consumers may place on the claim recommended for challenge, including those that might render the claim true/substantiated as well as those that might render the claim false/unsubstantiated.

2. Indicate which of these interpretations would be alleged to be implications of the claim for purposes of substantiation or litigation. For each interpretation so indicated, state the reasons, if any, for believing that the claim so interpreted would be false/unsubstantiated.

B. Scale of the Deception or Lack of Substantiation

3. What is known about the relative proportions of consumers adhering to each of the interpretations listed above in response to question 1?

4. What was the approximate advertising budget for the claim during the past year or during any other period of time that

would reflect the number of consumers actually exposed to the claim? Is there more direct information on the number of consumers exposed to the claim?

C. Materiality

5. If consumers do interpret the claim in the ways that would be alleged to be implications, what reasons are there for supposing that these interpretations would influence purchase decisions?

6. During the past year, approximately how many consumers purchased the product [refers to the particular brand] about which the claim was made?

7. Approximately what price did they pay?

8. Estimate, if possible, the proportion of consumers who would have purchased the product only at some price lower than they did pay, if at all, were they informed that the interpretations identified in response to question 2 were false.

9. Estimate, if possible, what the advertised product would be worth to the consumers identified by question 8 if they knew that the product did not have the positive (or unique) attributes suggested by the claim. If the claim can cause consumers to disregard some negative attribute, such as a risk to health and safety, to their possible physical or economic injury, so specify. If so, estimate, if possible, the annual number of such injuries attributable to the claim.

D. Adequacy of Corrective Market Forces

10. If the product to which the claim relates is a low ticket item, can consumers ordinarily determine prior to purchase whether the claim, as interpreted, is true or invest a small amount in purchase and then by experience with the product determine whether or not the claim is true? Does the claim relate to a credence quality, that is, a quality of the product that consumers ordinarily cannot evaluate during normal use of the product

without acquiring costly information from some source other than their own evaluative faculties?

11. Is the product to which the claim relates one that a consumer would typically purchase frequently? Have product sales increased or decreased substantially since the claim was made?

12. Are there sources of information about the subject matter of the claim in addition to the claim itself? If so, are they likely to be recalled by consumers when they purchase or use the product? Are they likely to be used by consumers who are not aggressive, effective shoppers? If not, why not?

E. Effect on the Flow of Truthful Information

13. Will the standard of truth/substantiation that would be applied to the claim under the recommendation to initiate proceedings make it extremely difficult as a practical matter to make the type of claim? Is this result reasonable?

14. What are the consequences to consumers of an erroneous determination by the Commission that the claim is false/unsubstantiated? What are the consequences to consumers of an erroneous determination by the Commission that the claim is true/substantiated?

F. Deterrence

15. Is there a possibility of getting significant relief with broad product or claim coverage? What relief is possible? Why would it be significant?

16. Do the facts of the matter recommended present an opportunity to elaborate a rule of law that would be applicable to claims or advertisers other than those that would be directly challenged by the recommended action? If so, describe this rule of law as you would wish the advertising community to understand it. If this rule of law would be a significant precedent, explain why.

17. Does the claim violate a Guide or is it inconsistent with relevant principles embodied in a Guide?

18. Is the fact of a violation so evident to other industry members that, if we do not act, our credibility and deterrence might be adversely affected?

19. Is there any aspect of the advertisement – e.g., the nature of the advertiser, the product, the theme, the volume of the advertising, the memorableness of the ad, the blatancy of the violation – which indicates that an enforcement action would have substantial impact on the advertising community?

20. What, if anything, do we know about the role advertising plays (as against other promotional techniques and other sources of information) in the decision to purchase the product?

21. What is the aggregate dollar volume spent on advertising by the advertiser to be joined in the recommended action?

22. What is the aggregate volume of sales of the advertised product and of products of the same type?

G. Law Enforcement Efficiency

23. Has another agency taken action or does another agency have expertise with respect to the claim or its subject matter? Are there reasons why the Commission should defer? What is the position of this other agency? If coordination is planned, what form would it take?

24. How difficult would it be to litigate a case challenging the claim? Would the theory of the proceeding recommended place the Commission in a position of resolving issues that are better left to other modes of resolution, for instance, debate among scientists? If so, explain? Is there a substantial possibility of whole or partial summary judgment?

25. Can the problem seen in the ad be handled by way of a rule? Are the violations widespread? Should they be handled by way of a rule?

H. Additional Considerations

26. What is the ratio of the advertiser's advertising expense to sales revenues? How, if at all, is this ratio relevant to the public interest in proceeding as recommended?

27. Does the claim specially affect a vulnerable group?

28. Does the advertising use deception or unfairness to offend important values or to exploit legitimate concerns of a substantial segment of the population, whether or not there is direct injury to person or pocketbook, e.g., minority hiring or environmental protection?

29. Are there additional considerations not elicited by previous questions that would affect the public interest in proceeding?

---

[1] *State* v. *Cohn*, 24 Conn. Supp. 188, 188 A.2d 878 (1962).
[2] *In the Matter of Perfect Mfg. Co.*, 43 F.T.C. 238 (1946).
[3] *Masland Duraleather Co.* v. *FTC*, 34 F.2d 733, 2 U.S.P.Q. 442 (3d Cir. 1929).
[4] *Sebrone Co.* v. *FTC*, 135 F.2d 676 (7th Cir. 1913).
[5] *Murry Space Shoe Corp.* v. *FTC*, 304 F.2d 270 (2d Cir. 1962).
[6] *United States* v. *Hindman*, 179 F.Supp. 926 (1960).
[7] *Prima Products* v. *Federal Trade Commission*, 209 F.2d 405 (1954).
[8] *W.L.Gore & Assoc., Inc.* v. *Totes, Inc.*, 788 F. Supp. 800, 808 (D. Del. 1992).
[9] *TrendMark International, Inc.*, CCH Trade Regulation Reports ¶ 24,448.
[10] *Care Technologies, Inc.*, CCH Trade Regulation Reports ¶ 24,502.
[11] *Pfizer Inc.*, CCH Trade Regulation Reports ¶ 124,503.
[12] *Del Pharmaceuticals, Inc.*, CCH Trade Regulation Reports ¶ 24,504.
[13] *Honeywell, Inc.*, CCH Trade Regulation Reports ¶ 24,358.
[14] *Brake Guard Products, Inc.*, CCH Trade Regulation Reports ¶ 24,380.
[15] *Double Eagle Lubricants, Inc.* v. *FTC*, 360 F.2d 268 (10th Cir. 1965).
[16] *Giant Food, Inc.* v. *FTC*, 322 F.2d 977 (D.C. Circuit 1963), *cert. dismissed*, 376 U.S. 976, 84 S.Ct. 1121, 12 L.Ed. 2d 82 (1964).
[17] *Heavenly Creations, Inc.* v. *FTC*, 339 F.2d 7 (2d Cir. 1964).
[18] *Fedders Corp.* v. *FTC*, 529 F.2d 1398 (2d Cir. 1976),
[19] *Sears, Roebuck and Co.* v. *FTC*, 676 F.2d 385 (9th Cir. 1982),
[20] *F.T.C.* v. *Pharmtech Research, Inc.*, 576 F. Supp. 294 (D.D.C. 1983).
[21] *National Bakers Serv., Inc.* v. *FTC*, 329 F.2d 365 (7th Cir. 1964).
[22] *Firestone Tire & Rubber Co.* v. *FTC*, 481 F.2d 246 (6th Cir. 1973).
[23] *Gateway 2000, Inc.*, CCH Trade Regulation Reports ¶ 24,467.
[24] *Koltz* v. *Hecht*, 73 F. 822 (2d Cir. 1896).
[25] *In the Matter of Blumenthal*, 43 F.T.C. 158 (1946).
[26] *Chrysler Corp.* v. *FTC*, 561 F.2d 357 (D.C. Cir. 1977).
[27] *Design Travel*, CCH Trade Regulation Reports ¶ 24,491.

28 *Donaldson* v. *Read Magazine, Inc.*, 333 U.S. 178, 68 S.Ct. 591, 92 L.Ed. 628 (1948).
29 39 U.S.C. 259, 732.
30 15 U.S.C. § 70.
31 15 U.S.C. § 68.
32 15 U.S.C. §§ 69-69j.
33 *FTC* v. *The Book of the Month Club*, 202 F.2d 486 (2nd Cir. 1953).
34 Federal Register, January 14, 1948, Administrative interpretations with reference to the use of the word *free* and words of similar import under certain conditions to describe merchandise.
35 *FTC* v. *Mary Carter Paint Co.*, 382 U.S. 46, 86 S.Ct. 219, 15 L.Ed. 2d 128 (1965).
36 16 C.F.R. § 233.5.
37 15 U.S.C. §§ 1451-1461 (1982); 16 C.F.R. §§ 502.100-.102 (1987).
38 16 C.F.R. § 1.35.
39 *Dell Computer Corp.*, CCH Trade Regulation Reports ¶ 24,411.
40 15 U.S.C. §§ 1601-1614,1661-1665a (1987).
41 12 C.F.R. pt. 226 (1987).
42 12 C.F.R. pt. 213. (1987).
43 16 C.F.R. § 255.0(a) (1987).
44 *In the Matter of Cliffdale Assocs., Inc.*, 103 F.T.C. 110 (1984).
45 *In re Cooga Mooga, Inc.*, 92 F.T.C. 310 (1978).
46 *In re Macmillan, Inc.*, 96 F.T.C. 208 (1980).
47 *In re Cooga Mooga, Inc.*, 92 F.T.C. 310 (1978).
48 *American Home Prods. Corp.* v. *Johnson & Johnson*, 654 F. Supp. 568 (S.D.N.Y. 1987).
49 *In re Cooper*, 94 F.T.C. 674 (1979).
50 *In re Bricklin*, 106 F.T.C. 115 (1985).
51 *American Home Prods. Corp.* v. *Johnson & Johnson*, 654 F. Supp. 568 (S.D.N.Y. 1987).
52 *In re Biopractic Group, Inc.*, 104 F.T.C. 845 (1984).
53 *In re Estee Corp.*, 102 F.T.C. 1804 (1983).
54 *In re Bristol-Myers Co.*, 102 F.T.C. 21 (1983), *aff'd*, 738 F.2d 554 (2d Cir. 1984), cert. denied, 469 U.S. 1189, 105 S.Ct. 960, 83 L.Ed. 2d. 966 (1985).
55 *In re Emergency Devices, Inc.*, 102 F.T.C. 1713 (1983).
56 *In the Matter of Cliffdale Assocs., Inc.*, 103 F.T.C. 110 (1984).
57 Food, Drug, and Cosmetic Act, 15 U.S.C. §§ 301-392.
58 Fair Packaging and Labeling Act, 15 U.S.C. §§1451-1461.
59 15 U.S.C. § 1125(a).
60 *C. D. Searle & Co.* v. *Hudson Pharmaceutical Corp.*, 715 F.2d 837 (3rd Cir. 1983).
61 *Marcus* v. *AT&T Corp.*, 136 F.3d 46 (2d Cir. 1998).
62 N.Y. Gen. Bus. L., §§ 349-350 (McKinney's 1988 & Supp. 1996).
63 660 N.Y.S.2d 440.
64 *Day* v. *AT&T*, 63 Cal. 4th 325, 74 Cal. Rptr. 2d 55 (1998).
65 Cal. Bus. & Prof. Code, §§ 17200 & 17500.
66 *Tenore* v. *AT&T Wireless Services*, No. 65609-6, 1998 Wash. LEXIS 593 (Wash S. Ct., September 10, 1998).
67 *Nader* v. *Allegheny Airlines, Inc.*, 426 U.S. 290 (1976).

CHAPTER 4

ADVERTISING'S PART IN PRODUCTS LIABILITY

It's such a perfectly imperfect human thing.
—*Charles Bragg*

"This is a stickup. Open the safe." Startled, John Klages turned toward the voice from the other side of the registration counter. Klages worked as a night clerk at Conley's Motel in Hampton Township, Pennsylvania. It was about 1:30 a.m. on an otherwise quiet March morning, and two armed men stood across the counter. Klages indicated that he didn't have the combination to the safe. In an instant, one of the robbers pointed a gun at him and fired.

The gun, fortunately, was only a starter pistol, and Klages suffered only minor injuries.

The day after the robbery attempt, Klages decided that he needed something to protect himself from future holdups. After reading some literature, a fellow employee, Bob McVay, suggested that they investigate mace as a weapon. McVay gathered four brochures from Markl Supply Company. The manufacturer of one of the mace weapons was General Ordnance Equipment Corporation. Klages selected the MKII model because it was easy to conceal yet, he felt assured, had the stopping power he needed.

The literature claimed that the product:

Rapidly vaporizes on face of assailant effecting instantaneous incapacitation...
It will instantly stop and subdue entire groups...
Instantly stops assailants in their tracks...

An attacker is subdued – instantly, for a period
of 15 to 20 minutes...
Time magazine stated the chemical mace is
"for police the first, if not the final,
answer to a nationwide need..."
A weapon that disables as effectively as a gun...
and yet does no permanent injury.
The effectiveness is the result of a unique
incapacitation formulation (patent pending)
projected in a shotgun-like pattern of heavy liquid droplets
that, upon contact with the face, cause extreme tearing,
and a stunned, winded condition, often accompanied
by dizziness and apathy.

•••••••••••••••••

McVay and Klages read the brochure and, after discussing it with their boss, purchased an MKII mace weapon from Markl Supply.

About 1:40 a.m. on the morning of September 22, 1968, two men entered the motel office where Klages was again on duty. The two men requested a room. Klages handed them a registration form and turned to reach for the room key. One of the men announced that it was a holdup, pulled out a gun, and demanded that Klages open the safe.

Klages moved behind the cash register where the mace was kept and, using the register as a shield, squirted the mace directly into the robber's face. Klages quickly ducked behind the counter. Unfortunately, the robber followed and shot him in the head – this time with a real gun, with real bullets. He survived the attack, but the bullet wound left Klages blind in his right eye.

Klages sued General Ordnance for damages. On March 4, 1974, a jury trial began in *Klages* v. *General Ordnance Equipment Corp.*[1] When it was over, the jury ruled in favor of Klages, awarding him $42,000.

This case is an example of products liability. Granted, the

advertising did not cause the injury. However, the advertising was the machinery that created the image in the mind of the consumer – an image that the product would perform in a certain way.

Here's how it works. The manufacturer made a product for a specific purpose. The consumer purchased the product for that purpose. When the product failed to live up to it, the manufacturer was liable for the injury that resulted.

A manufacturer, through its advertising, implies that its product is safe for – and will perform – its intended use. The manufacturer makes a promise or representation about his product. In the Klages case the manufacturer sold a product designed solely as a device to deter would-be assailants. Its sole use was to protect the purchasers from harm under extremely dangerous conditions. Klages bought the product with these specific purposes in mind. The product failed to live up to its promise, and the injury that resulted made the manufacturer liable.

PRODUCTS LIABILITY AND ITS EFFECT ON ADVERTISING

Products liability is an area of law that deals with a product's failure to perform whatever function for which it was sold. In this chapter we explore the connection between a company's advertising and products liability lawsuits.

The manufacturer's advertising or promotion may be a direct reason to bring suit or it may become evidence during a suit; evidence that can establish what the consumer expected from the product. The advertising may demonstrate the manufacturer's inability to live up to the representations made in the advertisement.

In the eyes of the law, a manufacturer is liable for any deficiency in its product. The point here is that in products liability lawsuits the plaintiff must prove that the advertising somehow lulled him into a false sense of security about the product's safety or capability enough to induce him into its purchase or use. This was the situation with Mr. Klages.

Theories Of Products Liability

To assess the role advertising plays in products liability litigation, we should understand that there are a number of legal theories under which a products liability lawsuit can be brought. Those theories are briefly described below with specific illustrative cases, which you'll find discussed later in the chapter.

Negligence exists when there is a failure to exercise reasonable care to protect others against high risks.
A manufacturer may be negligent for an act (such as poor quality control) or for a failure to act (such as not testing the product). See *Baxter* v. *Ford Motor Co.* on page 174.

Deceit occurs when there is intent to mislead regarding the existence or nonexistence of a material fact, the consumer relies on the misleading information and damages result. A good example is *Bahlman* v. *Hudson Motor Car Co.* on page 179.

Fraudulent concealment covers situations in which the manufacturer withholds information when he has a duty to speak. A case in point is *Hasson* v. *Ford Motor Co.* on page 187.

Negligent misrepresentation allows the consumer to bring suit when the manufacturer's statements become misrepresentations that he should have known were untrue or inaccurate. Again, this deals with the duty of reasonable care. See *Leichtamer* v. *American Motors Corp.* on page 184.

Strict liability holds the manufacturer liable for a consumer's physical injury resulting from a misrepresentation about the product. In these cases the consumer does not need to prove that the misrepresentation was made negligently or fraudulently. An example is *Procter & Gamble Mfg. Co.* v. *Superior Court.* on page 176.

Express warranty occurs when any specific warranty that becomes a part of the purchase. Any act, representation, affirmation of fact, or promise made by the manufacturer about the product becomes a part of the bargain.[2] This creates an express warranty that the product will live up to the act, representation, and so on. See *Greenman* v. *Yuba Power Prods., Inc.* on page 177.

Implied warranty exists by operation of law. Simply stated, it is implied in the sale of the product. One such warranty is for merchantability,[3] which means that the product is fit for the purpose for which it was sold. There is also a warranty of fitness for a particular purpose.[4] Two good examples are *Ford Motor Co.* v. *Lonon* on page 178 and *Filler* v. *Rayex Corp.* on page181.

Strict tort liability occurs when the product is defective and that defect causes injury or damage. It is not necessary to prove that the manufacturer or seller was negligent.[5] A good example is *Greenman* v. *Yuba Power Prods., Inc.* on page 177.

These theories form the basis for all of the cases in this chapter. In one form or another, all products liability litigation stems from these areas of law.

Placing Liability On Advertising Claims

In *Rogers* v. *Toni Home Permanent Co*,[6] Ms. Rogers purchased a Toni Home Permanent set marked "Very Gentle." She bought the product because of the manufacturer's claims in its advertising and on its packaging. After following the directions supplied with the kit, Rogers' hair became "cotton-like...and ...gummy." Her hair would not dry, and when the curlers supplied with the kit were removed, her hair fell out, leaving only one-half-inch of hair remaining.

This case is important because it was the first time the court made an effort to change how a manufacturer's liability was viewed. Originally, a consumer could sue only the seller of a product for breach of warranty. It was considered that a contract did not exist between the ultimate consumer and the manufacturer, and therefore no warranty existed. The only contract was between the consumer and the store where the item was purchased. The manufacturer could not be sued directly, except in cases of negligence.

Because of the *Rogers* case, the courts have taken the position that the consumer can sue the manufacturer directly for breach of warranty actions (otherwise known as products liability). The court said:

> Today, many manufacturers of merchandise, including the defendant herein, make extensive use of newspapers, periodicals, signboards, radio, and television to advertise their products. The worth, quality, and benefits of these products are described in glowing terms and in considerable detail, and the appeal is almost universally directed to the ultimate consumer. Many of these manufactured articles are shipped out in sealed containers by the manufacturer, and the retailers who dispense them to the ultimate consumers are but conduits or outlets through which the manufacturer distributes his goods. The consuming public ordinarily relies exclusively on the representations of the manufacturer in his advertisements. What sensible or sound reason then exists as to why, when the goods purchased by the ultimate consumer on the strength of the advertisements aimed squarely at him do not possess their described qualities and goodness and cause him harm, he should not be permitted to move against the manufacturer to recoup his loss. In our minds no good or valid reason exists for denying him that right. Surely under modern merchandising practices the manufacturer owes a very real obligation toward those who consume or use his products. The warranties made by the manufacturer in his advertisements and by the labels on his products are

> inducements to the ultimate consumers, and the manufacturer ought to be held to strict accountability to any consumer who buys the product in reliance on such representations and later suffers injury because the product proves to be defective.

Basically, products liability cases involve the performance that the consumer can reasonably expect from a product and also any resulting injury because of a consumer's reliance.

Products liability is not an area in which a manufacturer can be sued because of an advertising claim. However, products liability cases can be made using the advertising as proof of what the consumer expected from the product. Since advertising imparts an image, that image can become a large part of what the consumer expects when he or she purchases the product. If it fails, the advertising can be brought in to substantiate what the consumer expected. And, it can also confirm that the manufacturer is liable for any injury that resulted.

Now let's take a closer look at some cases that involve products liability issues and advertising.

THE SHATTERPROOF GLASS CASE

In one case, the literature about an automobile claimed that the windshield of the car was shatterproof. The case was *Baxter* v. *Ford Motor Co.*[7] During the month of May 1930, Mr. Baxter purchased a Model A Ford town sedan from St. John Motors, an authorized Ford dealer. Baxter had read and relied on statements made in Ford's promotional literature; statements that the windshield was made of glass that would not break or shatter. Baxter recovered damages because on October 12, 1930, while he was driving the car, a flying rock shattered the windshield of his car, causing small pieces of glass to destroy his left eye. The literature that Baxter read contained the following:

Triplex Shatterproof Glass Windshield

All of the new Ford cars have a Triplex shatterproof glass windshield – so made that it will not fly or shatter under the hardest impact. This is an important safety factor because it eliminates the dangers of flying glass – the cause of most of the injuries in automobile accidents. In these days of crowded, heavy traffic, the use of this Triplex glass is an absolute necessity. Its extra margin of safety is something that every motorist should look for in the purchase of a car – especially where there are women and children.

In essence, Ford should have known that the statements were true or it should not have made them. In other words, Ford was negligent. The court said:

> If a person states as true material facts...to one who relies and acts thereon to his injury, if the representations are false, it is immaterial that he did not know they were false or that he believed them to be true.

The automobile was represented as having a shatterproof windshield. By examining the car, the average consumer would not know if that representation was true. Statements of the manufacturer would have to be relied on.

Since the concept of caveat emptor (buyer beware) was first created, the complexity of doing business has undergone many changes. Advertising has become a major factor in creating the demand that causes goods to flow from manufacturer to ultimate consumer. As we discussed earlier, the manufacturer is bound to a form of strict liability to the buyer. Strict liability places absolute liability on the manufacturer for a consumer's physical injury resulting from a misrepresentation about the product. The manufacturer is liable to the buyer for representations that are proven to be false whether in advertisements, literature, or in a document that is passed along to the consumer by the dealer.

Let's look at a hypothetical situation. Acme Company manufactures hoists for cars. Acme distributes a manual that contains statements about the hoist's strength, lifting capacity, and so on. Mr. Jones goes into a local auto parts store and, after reading the literature, buys an Acme hoist. Jones uses the hoist to lift his car. The hoist does not have the lifting capacity that was stated in the literature, and as a result, the car crashes to the floor, injuring him. Acme is subject to strict liability to Jones.

Similar situations may occur in almost any situation; the form that the representation takes is not important. In fact, a representation may be in the form of an advertisement on the radio or television, in the newspaper, or in other literature (labels on the product, packaging material, etc.). It can be written or oral. For strict liability to exist, there must be an issue of fact in the advertising claim. In other words, the representation that the consumer relied on must be presented as a fact. This type of claim is more than just puffing, fantasy advertising, and the like. To illustrate this concept, let's go back to our earlier hypothetical example.

What if the hoist was advertised in the newspaper as "strong and safe for most uses," "the best available," "the best for the price," or even "the most desirable." Could these types of statements give rise to a legal action if the product fails? There is no definite answer, but the advertiser must be cautious. Even general statements can be considered to carry implications of fact. Such statements as a detergent being "kind to the hands" or a power tool being "rugged" have involved implications of fact, as we see in this chapter.

In *Procter & Gamble Mfg. Co.* v. *Superior Court*,[8] the claim of a detergent being kind to the hands was at issue. On February 3, 1953, Loretta and Robert Jones filed suit in the Marin County

Superior Court of California asking for $60,000 in damages. Loretta had been injured, as she alleged, while using Procter & Gamble's product, Cheer. Her injury was "a severe dermatitis and dermatosis, causing nervousness and illness and inability to perform her household duties for a six-month period, as well as permanent disfigurement of her hands, which prior to that time were beautiful and smooth." Proctor & Gamble lost the case.

Claims Of Quality Construction

In *Greenman v. Yuba Power Prods., Inc.*,[9] claims that a power tool was rugged were discussed. Mr. Greenman saw a demonstration of a product called a "Shopsmith." The Shopsmith was a combination power tool used as a drill, saw, and wood lathe. After studying a product brochure, Mr. Greenman decided that he wanted a Shopsmith. He told his wife this, and she purchased one for Christmas in 1955.

In 1957 Greenman purchased an attachment that would allow him to use the Shopsmith as a wood lathe. While working on a wood piece, it suddenly flew out of the lathe, striking Greenman in the head and causing serious injuries.

The jury returned an award for $65,000 in favor of Greenman after determining that Yuba Power Products had negligently constructed the Shopsmith. Expert witnesses testified that the set screws used to hold sections of the machine together were not adequate. Normal vibration would cause the screws to loosen, allowing the tailpiece of the lathe to move away from the spinning piece of wood, eventually allowing the wood to fly out of the lathe at high speed.

Here again, we see that the statements made in the manufacturer's product brochure were instrumental in determining the nature and extent of any express warranty that Yuba had made to the potential purchaser. As we saw earlier, an express warranty is created when any description, sample, model, fact, or promise is made by the seller to the buyer that relates to the goods and becomes part of the basis of the bargain. The express warranty is that the goods will live up to the promise. It does not matter that the advertiser knew or should have known that the express warranty was a misrepresentation.

The following information was contained in the Shopsmith brochure:

When Shopsmith is in Horizontal Position –
Rugged construction of frame provides rigid support from end to end.
Heavy, centerless-ground steel tubing ensures perfect alignment of components.
SHOPSMITH maintains its accuracy because every component has positive locks that hold adjustments through rough or precision work.

In this case, the court said: "A manufacturer is strictly liable ...when an article he places on the market, knowing that it is to be used without inspection for defects, proves to have a defect that causes injury to a human being." Simply because the Shopsmith was placed on the market, the consumer could assume that it was safe for the jobs for which it was built.

Those jobs were detailed in the product brochure on which the consumer who purchases the product would rely. It does not matter that the manufacturer did not intend to mislead or cause harm. The harm occurred, and the manufacturer was liable. This holds true as long as the injury results from a defect in the product that appears when the product is being used as intended.

Liability For Commercial Loss

In February of 1962, Mr. Lonon purchased a Fordson Major Diesel tractor from the Haywood Tractor Company. Lonon was a farmer and needed a large tractor capable of performing certain tasks. He had visited the Ford tractor dealers in the area and had read the sales literature. He also had seen the many advertisements Ford published in farm magazines and ran on television. The literature contained information about the live power take-off, the power steering lift, and other full specifications.

Over a period of time the tractor failed to perform the functions that were claimed it could perform. The tractor was taken in for repairs on many occasions with no effect. It was defective from the time that it was purchased. Lonon sued Ford after failing to receive any satisfaction. In *Ford Motor Co.* v. *Lonon*,[10] the jury award of $4,000 was upheld. Lonon received $4,000 plus court costs for a tractor that originally cost him $4,243.10.

What makes this case interesting is that, unlike other products liability cases, there was no injury to the plaintiff. Most of the decisions hold the manufacturer liable for physical injury that was a direct result of the manufacturer's breach of warranty. In this case, we see that the courts can apply the same principle to commercial losses (losses of time and work as opposed to physical injury) that result from a defectively manufactured product or product part.

THE SEAMLESS STEEL ROOF CASE – IMPLIED SAFETY CLAIMS

Mr. Bahlman, a traveling shoe salesman, bought a 1936 model Hudson Eight Sedan from the Hudson Motor Car Company, based in part on the claim that the car had a seamless steel roof. The manufacturer, in its promotional literature, had represented that the car had such a feature. In fact, the Hudson was touted as "A Rugged Fortress of Safety." However, in reality the roof was made of two separate parts. Typical of the advertising claims that Mr. Bahlman read were:

Beneath the bigness and beauty, the safest car on today's
highway, with the world's first safety engineering.
Safeness combined with the first bodies all of steel.
Bodies introduced last year by Hudson and now brought to new
heights of strength and beauty with an improved
seamless steel roof.

How, What, Why about the 1936 Hudsons and Terraplanes.
A steel top which is a smooth, solid unit with the body shell.
There are no seams or joints in the roof and body structure,
just a complete steel body made from a single sheet of steel.

In *Bahlman* v. *Hudson Motor Car Co.*,[11] the court held for the plaintiff. Bahlman had been injured by a jagged edge of the welded roof when his car overturned. Hudson had obviously conveyed an impression of a safety characteristic in its literature by claiming that the roof was one piece and therefore stronger than a welded roof. The construction of the roof of the car was represented as a specific safety feature, and specifically as protection against the type of injury that Bahlman suffered.

The fact that Bahlman's own negligent driving caused the accident was not significant because the safety feature existed to protect the people in the car from what actually took place – a crash. The safety features in a car are provided in the event of an accident regardless of who or what caused the accident.

THE ABSOLUTELY HARMLESS TOY CASE

On the packaging of the Ronson revolver, a toy pistol, was a picture of a small boy firing a Ronson revolver.

In looks and action
just like the real thing.

B-A-N-G! F-L-A-S-H! S-M-O-K-E!
Absolutely harmless.

Shortly before Christmas in 1926, William Crist was demonstrating a Ronson revolver in the Crist Department Store window in Circleville, Ohio. William, a child of less than 10, was dressed in a Santa Claus suit, complete with beard. When William fired one of the Ronson revolvers, the sparks from the toy ignited the soft cotton material of the Santa Claus suit. In seconds the boy was enveloped in flames and seriously injured. The court in *Crist v. Art Metal Works*,[12] described the boy's injury as "...serious, painful, and permanent injuries, both externally and internally, about his head, face and limbs,...and...serious permanent disability and shock to his nervous system."

The interesting aspect of this case was that no defect in the product was alleged or discussed. In fact quite the contrary, the toy revolver operated perfectly. It was the claim that the toy was "absolutely safe" for a child that gave rise to the lawsuit. The advertising convincingly relieved all fear of possible injury to a child user. Here was a key example of where advertising plays a strong role in establishing the expectations of a product's performance. The product did not fail, but it failed to live up to its claim of safety.

There are cases in which the advertising or literature only suggests a safety quality. Other times a reference to safety is specific and direct, as in the case we just discussed. What is important for the advertiser to know is that the courts tend not to differentiate between these when looking at liability.

THE BASEBALL SUNGLASSES CASE

Richard Beck, the baseball coach at Oak Hill High School in Marion, Indiana, would not allow his players to wear sunglasses because he thought they were too dangerous. Yet, before the 1966 season he read the following in *Sporting News*:

••••••••

PLAY BALL!
and Flip for Instant Eye Protection with
RAYEX
baseball
SUNGLASSES
Professional
FLIP-SPECS
Scientific lenses protect your eyes with a flip
from sun and glare anywhere...
baseball, beach, boat, driving, golfing, fishing,
just perfect for active and spectator sports
– world's finest sunglasses.

••••••••••••••••••

The product packaging stated: "Simply flip...for instant eye protection," and "Rayex lenses are guaranteed for life against breakage."

After reading the advertisement and packaging, coach Beck purchased Rayex flip-down sunglasses for his team. One of the teenage boys on the team, Michael Filler, wore the glasses while playing in a game. A batted ball struck the boy in the face, breaking the glasses. The shattered glasses splintered and damaged one of the boy's eyes so badly that it had to be removed. The court in *Filler* v. *Rayex Corp.*,[13] in awarding damages in excess of $101,000, said about the product:

> Since they lacked the safety features of plastic or shatterproof glass, the sunglasses were in truth not fit for baseball playing, the particular purpose for which they were sold.

There was no explicit advertising claim about the shatterproof quality of the glasses. The ad copy referred only to protection against sun and glare. But they were advertised in a sporting magazine, directed to athletes, and stated that they were safe for use in baseball. The obvious implication was that they were safe for use in that sport, even though the manufacturer had not made adequate tests to support that claim. This was a case of a safety claim being implied, but a safety claim nonetheless. Along with the sale, an implied warranty was created.

Regarding a point that we covered earlier, an implied warranty means that the warranty is implied with the sale of the product. As we have discussed, there are warranties of merchantability and fitness for a particular purpose. Merchantability refers to the fitness of the product for the ordinary purposes for which such goods are used. Fitness for a particular purpose implies a specific use by the buyer which is peculiar to the nature of his business.

THE OVERTURNED GOLF CART CASE

The Missouri Supreme Court upheld a $94,000 award in *Blevins v. Cushman Motors*[14] involving a man who was pinned under a golf cart that had overturned. Advertisements had appeared in golfing magazines promoting the Cushman golf cart. Typical of the ad's copy was:

Talk about a turned on ride. Smooooth.
With a beefier, low-slung 3-point rubber suspension.
New rubber suspensions between power frame and main frame
lets the GC tool through turns with super ease,
super safety, super stability.
Low ground-hugging center of gravity makes
for wide stance, razor-honed handling.
Fat, ground-gripping, turf-protecting 9.50 x 8 Terra Tires

are standard.
This baby floats the course.

On the afternoon of July 15, 1969, Albert Blevins and a friend met for a round of golf at the Stayton Meadows Golf Course. The two men began play using their Cushman Golf Cart. On the 13th hole the cart was being driven at about five miles per hour when it crossed a wet, shaded area. The cart skidded and turned over, throwing Blevins' friend clear of the cart. Blevins, however, fell on the ground and was pinned and injured by the overturned cart.

In order to win his case, Blevins needed to establish that the accident and damage resulted from a use of the product that was "reasonably anticipated." Blevins was required to show that the golf cart was used as that – a golf cart which could negotiate a golf course. Here the advertising clearly convinced the court that that use was not only anticipated but encouraged. The advertising showed a "justified use and reliance by the driver" of the cart. In fact, the advertising tended to draw the purchaser into a false sense of security as to the use of the cart and its safety.

PUNITIVE DAMAGES

Increasing indications show that advertising is being considered heavily as an influential factor in imposing punitive damages in certain lawsuits. Punitive damages are awarded to punish the wrongdoer. They are also a strong deterrent for others to consider.

In *Leichtamer* v. *American Motors Corp.*,[15] a four-wheel-drive vehicle overturned while going down an incline. On April 18, 1976, Paul Vance and his wife Cynthia invited Carl and Jeanne Leichtamer to go for a ride in the Vances' Jeep CJ-7. The Vances belonged to an off-road club located near Dundee, Ohio, which had been converted from an old strip mine.

While the Vances' Jeep was descending a double-terraced hill, the vehicle's rear end pitched over. The Jeep had cleared the first embankment; and after clearing the second, it landed on the front wheels. At that point, the rear end continued over the front end of the Jeep. The Jeep landed upside down pointing back up the hill. Paul and Cynthia Vance were killed. Carl Leichtamer sustained a skull fracture, and Jeanne Leichtamer became a paraplegic.

During the trial it was acknowledged that Paul Vance's negligence caused the accident. However, it was claimed that the Leichtamers' injuries were "substantially enhanced, intensified, aggravated, and prolonged" as a result of the failure of the factory-installed roll bar on the Jeep. The roll bar was offered as optional equipment on the Jeep CJ-7 and was promoted solely for protection in the event of a rollover. The roll bar was not structurally sound enough to withstand the pitchover that the Vances went through.

Jeep, then a division of American Motors Corporation, had produced a multimillion dollar television campaign that encouraged people to buy a Jeep:

Ever discover the rough,
exciting world of mountains,
forests, rugged terrain?
The original Jeep can get you there,
and Jeep guts will bring you back.

This case illustrates the role advertising can play in the imposition of liability. Certain expectations that the consumer develops about the safety of a product are formed largely through the product's advertising. The manner in which a product's use is advertised is relevant to the use that the product is intended for.

The Jeep commercials depicted its qualities and safety in an off-road situation and stressed the Jeep's ability to negotiate steep hills. One particular spot challenged a young man, accompanied by his girlfriend:

"You guys aren't yellow, are you?
Is it a steep hill?
Yeah, little lady, you could say it is a steep hill.
Let's try it.
The King of the Hill is about to discover the new Jeep CJ-7."

In fact, the advertising clearly depicted the Jeep going up and down steep and rugged terrain safely. Even the owner's manual claimed that the Jeep could "proceed in safety down a grade which could not safely be negotiated by a conventional 2-wheel drive vehicle."

The court felt that the advertising was a significant factor in supporting a finding for punitive damages since it showed the probable use of the vehicle while ignoring the danger that could likely result from that use saying: "The commercial advertising clearly contemplates off-road use of the vehicle."

The salesman's guide to the vehicle described the roll bar in the following terms: "Surround yourself and your passengers with the strength of a rugged, reinforced steel roll bar for added protection. A very practical item, and a must if you run competition with a 4WD club. Adds rugged good looks, too."

Given the foreseeability of roll-overs and pitch-overs, the failure of appellants to test to determine whether the roll bar "added protection" represents a flagrant indifference to the probability that a user might be exposed to an unreasonable risk of harm. For appellants to have encouraged off-the-road use while providing a roll bar that did little more than add "rugged good looks" was a sufficient basis for an award of punitive damages.

The Ohio Supreme Court granted a $2.2 million damage

award in the case. Over half of the damages were punitive.

The Extent Of Punitive Damages

In 1982, the California Supreme Court affirmed a $9.2 million award in *Hasson* v. *Ford Motor Co.*[16] About $4 million were in punitive damages. The case developed because of a catastrophic brain injury suffered by the driver of a 1965 Lincoln Continental when the brakes failed on a hill. The driver established that the manufacturer failed to warn dealers and owners of a known (to Ford) problem with the brakes, and how to correct it, because it was protecting the model's reputation among customers. The manufacturer deliberately failed to test for the problem with the brakes and subsequently failed to install a dual master cylinder, which would have overcome the defect.

Deceit and fraudulent concealment – which we discussed at the beginning of this chapter – occur when the advertiser intends to mislead the consumer regarding a material fact about the product and the consumer relies on that information to his detriment. If the advertiser expressly misstates a fact, it is deceit. If the advertiser withholds information when he should give it out, it is fraudulent concealment.

The issue here was Ford's knowing disregard for the safety of the vehicle, something that its advertising convinced otherwise. Ford management had a policy of advertising that the Lincoln Continental was free from the need for service for a large portion of its components.

CONCLUSION

Advertisers must be aware of all areas of product liability. The portrayal of the product in advertising or promotional literature can be a major factor in claims against the integrity of the product. The stakes are high today in products liability litigation. Now, proof of liability has become facilitated by recent legal activity in this area. Claims are higher. Awards are higher. Juries are more willing to award substantial punitive damages.

---

1 *Klages* v. *General Ordnance Equipment Corp.*, CCH Prods. Liab. Rep. Paragraph 7664 (Pa. Super. 1976).

2 Uniform Commercial Code, Section 2-313.

3 Uniform Commercial Code, Section 2-314.

4 Uniform Commercial Code, Section 2-315. Restatement of Torts (Second), Section 402A.

5 Restatement of Torts (Second), Section 402A.

6 *Rogers* v. *Toni Home Permanent Co.*, 167 Ohio St. 244, 147 N.E. 2d 612 (1958).

7 *Baxter* v. *Ford Motor Co.*, 12 F2d 409, aff'd on rehearing, 15 P.2d 1118 (Wash. Sup. Ct. 1932).

8 *Procter & Gamble Mfg. Co.* v. *Superior Court*, 268 P.2d 199 (Cal. App. 1954).

9 *Greenman* v. *Yuba Power Prods., Inc.*, 377 F.2d 897 (Cal. Sup. Ct. 1963).

10 *Ford Motor Co.* v. *Lonon*, 398 S.W.2d 240 (Tenn. 1966).

11 *Bahlman* v. *Hudson Motor Car Co.*, 288 N.W. 309 (Mich. 1939).

12 *Crist* v. *Art Metal Works*, 243 N.Y. Supp. 496 (1st Dep't. 1930).

13 *Filler* v. *Rayex Corp.*, 435 F.2d 336 (7th Cir. 1970).

14 *Blevins* v. *Cushman Motors*, 551 S.W. 2d 602 (Mo. 1977).

15 *Leichtamer* v. *American Motors Corp.*, 424 N.E. 2d 568 (Ohio 1981).

16 *Hasson* v. *Ford Motor Co.*, 19 Cal. 3d 530 (1977), CCH Prods. Liab. Rep. Paragraph 9398 (Sept. 16, 1982).

CHAPTER 5

THE RIGHTS OF PRIVACY AND PUBLICITY

Civilization is the progress toward a society of privacy.
—*Ayn Rand*

The year is 1913. The place is an empty horse barn recently converted into a "factory where pictures that move are made." It's daytime, but the inside of the big empty barn is dark. Only bright sunlight streams through a window at the end of the room. A few stagehands move camera equipment around in the distance. The air is dusty. The floor is covered with straw.

As the television commercial we're watching continues, a man's feet step into view. A megaphone sits on the floor in front of his feet. The name "Mr. DeMille" is stenciled on it. The legendary director rocks in place in his knee-high riding boots, tense in anticipation.

The camera moves around him while he clutches a pair of leather gloves behind his back. His hands squeeze the gloves with nervous excitement. DeMille takes in the activity happening within the room. We see, almost as if a ghost, the image of an early 1900's train approaching from the distance. Then we see the image of an early 1900's camera crew on the set.

We hear a recognizable voice: "In 1913 a young director prepared to step off the train in Flagstaff, Arizona. But it was raining. So he stayed on to the end of the line and shot his feature-length Western in a rented barn in a quiet farming town...called Hollywood."

The last of the crew members have moved away and the

director moves out of the picture. Through the stark light of the window emerges the figure of a man. He walks toward us and becomes recognizable as Gene Barry, the actor. "Now, at the barn where it all began, you can relive those early days when Hollywood first met the movies." He turns toward DeMille.

"Ready, Mr. DeMille." The actor finishes: "The Hollywood Studio Museum. Where the legend lives on."

What you've just read is a script from a television commercial that I produced a few years ago promoting the site of the first feature-length motion picture – a little yellow barn, located in Hollywood and preserved as a historical landmark. The place where, literally, "Hollywood" began.

I've used this example (and we'll return to it later) because the commercial involves the subject of this chapter – the right of publicity and the right of privacy. Both rights protect a person against the unauthorized use of his or her identity. As we see in this chapter, each area of law covers different injuries and promotes different values. Whenever an advertiser uses an image, likeness, or name of another person in an ad or for trade, certain rights must be considered. Here, we explore two of these rights: The right of privacy and the right of publicity.

THE RIGHT OF PRIVACY

We start with the oldest of the two rights, the right of privacy. The concept of a specific right of privacy began to take shape in the late 1800's to protect individuals who truly desired privacy, mainly private citizens.

Here's a little sociology lesson. Individuals, by becoming a part of a society, give up many rights and privileges that they would be free to exercise in nature. In exchange for this, they receive the benefits of being part of a society. But all rights are not given up. There are matters that are private that any intelligent member of society can recognize, and there is a right of privacy in those matters.

The intent of the right of privacy laws is to protect the essence of the individual person. To put it another way, privacy laws protect his or her persona from being taken and used without his or her knowledge or permission for the profit of another. The words Shakespeare wrote for Iago were straight to the point:

Good name in man or woman, dear my lord,
Is the immediate jewel of their souls;
Who steals my purse steals trash;
'tis something, nothing;
Twas mine, 'tis his, and has been slave to thousands;
But he that filches from me my good name
Robs me of that which not enriches him,
And makes me poor indeed.

Individuals have the right to live their lives in any way they see fit so long as it does not invade the rights of others or violate public laws or policies. People may make themselves visible to the public when they desire and may withdraw from the public when they wish.

In Roman law we see the beginnings of what would become the right of privacy. Anyone who brought public attention to another on a public road or on the other's own private grounds would be punished. Shouting until a crowd gathered or following an honest woman or child were banned under Roman law. In those days the law recognized a right "to be let alone." Even though, at the time, it was considered a property right, and property was an extremely valuable commodity.

In *Semayne's* case,[1] one of the oldest English cases to be reported, we find the first legal maxim applied that "the house of every one is to him as his castle and fortress, as well for his defense against injury and violence as for his repose." Today, we find Semayne's maxim recognizable in our phrase "every man's home is his castle."

The unreported case of *Manola* v. *Stevens*, heard before the

Supreme Court of New York in 1890, was the first case in this country where the right of privacy idea was used in an attempt to persuade the court that the lawful right existed. The complainant claimed that while the plaintiff performed on the Broadway stage in tights, she was photographed with the use of a flashlight. This was done without her knowledge or consent by the defendant sitting in a box seat. While the court permanently enjoined the display of the unauthorized photo, they steered clear of labeling this a right of privacy.

Right Of Privacy – The Early View

In 1902 the New York Court of Appeals rejected the existence of a common law right of privacy in *Roberson* v. *Rochester Folding Box Co.*[2] Abigail Roberson – at the time a child – sued for the unauthorized use of her photograph in posters (promoting a flour product) that were displayed in stores, warehouses, saloons, and so on. Even though the posters were complimentary – describing her as "The Flour of the Family" – the publication of the photo subjected her to "scoffs and jeers...causing her great distress and suffering both in body and mind."

In spite of this, the court refused to rule in favor of Roberson. They feared that this would open the flood gates once the principle of a privacy right was established. The court said:

> [T]he so-called right of privacy has not yet found an abiding place in our jurisprudence, and, as we view it, the doctrine cannot now be incorporated without doing violence to settled principles of law by which the profession and the public have long been guided.

However, the public reacted very strongly to what it considered to be an injustice and demanded that the legislature change the law. The New York legislature quickly enacted a statute prohibiting the use of a person's name, likeness, or picture, without prior written permission, for trade or advertising purposes.[3] This became the model law that other states have since followed.

The Right Of Privacy Becomes Law

The first court case to specifically recognize the right of privacy was *Pavesich* v. *New England Life Ins. Co.*[4] Paolo Pavesich's picture was published in a life insurance company's ad that had run in the *Atlanta Constitution* newspaper. His picture, that of a healthy and well-dressed man, appeared next to one of a sickly and badly dressed one. The caption above Pavesich read: "Do it now. The man who did." Above the sickly person ran the caption: "Do it while you can. The man who didn't." Below both pictures was the statement, "These two pictures tell their own story." Under Pavesich's picture was the following copy:

"In my healthy and productive
period of life
I bought insurance
in the New England Mutual Life Insurance Co.
of Boston, Mass.,
and today my family is protected
and I am drawing an annual
dividend on my paid-up policies."
– Thomas B. Lumpkin, General Agent.

The photo was used without Mr. Pavesich's knowledge or consent. The statement under his picture was also false; he never had a life insurance policy with the company. Pavesich asked for $25,000 in damages. He got it. In essence, the court allowed Pavesich to recover damages for injured feelings.

The Pavesich case established for the first time the precedent for future actions under a right of privacy, and the court, in an opinion over 30 pages long, addressed the issue in detail. In its conclusion to the case it said:

> So thoroughly satisfied are we that the law recognizes within proper limits, as a legal right, the right of privacy, and that the publication of one's picture without his consent by another as an advertisement, for the mere purpose of increasing the profits and gains of the advertiser, is an invasion of this right, that we venture to predict that the day will come when the American bar will marvel that a contrary view was ever entertained by judges of eminence and ability.

Since the time of the *Pavesich* decision and the passage of the New York statute, every state has developed (in one form or another) a right of privacy. The U.S. Supreme Court, in fact, established that the right of privacy stems from the specific guarantees in the Bill of Rights.[5]

All right of privacy laws protect against one of four forms of violations:

- The unauthorized use of another person's name or likeness for another's benefit;
- The invasion into an individual's seclusion;
- The public disclosure of embarrassing private facts; and
- The presentation of an individual in a false light in the public view. The common denominator between these four is the right to be left alone.

Waiver Of Privacy Rights

The right of privacy, like every other right of an individual, may be waived by voluntarily allowing one's image to be used in an ad. An advertiser must get written permission for such use in order to avoid a violation. A person may also imply that he or she waives privacy rights. A good example of this occurs when a private citizen runs for public office. Here, the person's rights are waived in order to allow the public to investigate how the candidate's private life is conducted. This is allowed to determine the person's qualifications for the office that the candidate wishes to hold. But the waiver of rights applies only to matters that affect competency for the office being sought. This type of implied waiver, however, is rarely involved in advertising situations.

THE RIGHT OF PUBLICITY

The right to privacy had its limitations. As years progressed, many people actually wanted publicity, not privacy. The right of publicity grew out of the need to aid people such as celebrities, entertainers, and athletes who wanted to protect the use of their marketable image.

Development Of The Right Of Publicity

Prior to the establishment of a right of publicity, it was not illegal for others to freely use entertainers' names or likenesses. Because entertainers sought publicity, they were making their lives public, and as such, waived their rights to privacy, it was felt.

In *O'Brien* v. *Pabst Sales Co.*,[6] a well-known football player claimed a violation of his right of privacy after Pabst used his picture on a calendar promoting its beer. While at Texas Christian University, David O'Brien was selected by Grantland Rice for his *Collier's* All American Football Team in 1938. O'Brien was probably the most publicized football player of the 1938-39 season. After graduating from TCU, he would play professionally for the Philadelphia Eagles.

Pabst Brewing Company published a calendar every year with the schedule of the entire football league included. Inland Lithographing Company printed 35,000 calendars for 1939 that used the picture of O'Brien in uniform. The headline read, "Pabst Blue Ribbon Football Calendar, 1939."

O'Brien claimed that he had not given his permission for the use of his picture. In fact, he did not even know that it had been used until quite some time after its release to stores. He claimed that he was greatly embarrassed by the publication of his picture in connection with the sale of beer, a product he personally was against using.

The court, however, stated that:

> [A]s a result of his activities and prowess in football, his chosen field, and the nationwide and deliberate publicizing with his consent and in his interest, he was no longer...a private but public person, and as to their additional publication he had no right of privacy.

The court decided that O'Brien had no case. He could not recover under a right of privacy claim because O'Brien was a famous National Football League figure and had purposefully publicized his name and photos. Because of this, he had waived his right of privacy. In fact the court said, "the publicity [he] got was only that which he had been constantly seeking."

Establishment Of The Right Of Publicity As Law

Essentially, celebrities had little chance of recovering damages for the appropriation of their names or likenesses for commercial use. However, this dim outlook was soon changed by the Court of Appeals for the Second Circuit. For the first time, a right of publicity was recognized in *Haelan Laboratories* v. *Topps Chewing Gum, Inc.*[7]

Haelan was a chewing gum company that had obtained the exclusive right to use a baseball player's photograph in connection with the sale of gum. The defendant Topps claimed that it had a contract for the use of the same ballplayer's photograph during that same time. Topps had, in fact, deceptively persuaded the ballplayer to enter into a contract with it while he was still bound by the contract with Haelan.

In this case, the court admitted that, in addition to rights of privacy, a person has a right of publicity. It protects a person's commercial interest in his or her identity, and that person has the right to authorize the publication of a picture of that identity. When this happens, it is an exclusive grant, and other advertisers are not allowed to use the picture. Haelan won its case because it owned the publicity rights to the ballplayer. Topps' contract was invalid.

Public Figures Do Not Waive Their Right Of Privacy

Public figures who do not market themselves commercially may suffer injury by being associated with commercial products. These people have not waived their rights of privacy simply by being public figures.

A good example of this occurred when the late Jacqueline Onassis won an action under a right of privacy claim in *Onassis* v. *Christian Dior, New York, Inc.*[8] What made the case unique was the way that Dior violated her right of privacy. Dior, through its ad agency, J. Walter Thompson, produced a campaign of 16 ads. Dior spent $2.5 million in publications including *Esquire, The New Yorker, Harper's Bazaar*, and the *New York Times*.

The ads featured a trio known as the Diors (one female and two men) who were to be the essence of the idle rich, decadent, and aggressively chic. The intent was to develop a group of characters that would become the most memorable personalities since Brooke Shields refused to let anything come between her and her Calvins. The copy for one of the ads read:

When the Diors
got away from it all,
they brought with them nothing except
The Decline of the West
and one toothbrush.

The ads led the reader through a progression of various situations that would include the marriage of two (but not the exclusion of the third), the birth of a baby, and their ascent to Heaven. One of the ads, the one for the wedding, ran:

Christian Dior:
Sportswear for Women and Clothing for Men.
The wedding of the Diors was everything
a wedding should be:
no tears, no rice, no in-laws, no smarmy toasts,
for once no Mendelssohn.
Just a legendary private affair.

The ad showed the trio along with their wedding party. Included in the group were movie critic Gene Shalit, model Shari Belafonte Harper, actress Ruth Gordon, and a secretary named Barbara Reynolds, who bears an amazing resemblance to Jacqueline Onassis. All were obviously delighted to be at the event.

Dior knew that there was no chance of Ms. Onassis consenting to being in the ad. She has never permitted the use of her name or picture to be used in connection with the promotion of any commercial products, but only for public service, art, educational, or civic projects. So, the agency and photographer Richard Avedon contacted Ron Smith Celebrity Look-Alikes to supply someone who resembled Onassis. That they did with Barbara Reynolds. The use of look-alikes requires the permission of the actual celebrity, nonetheless.

Even though Onassis' name was not used in the ad, and the image was not actually of Onassis, the public would naturally assume that it was Onassis. A visual pun was used to catch the reader's eye and draw attention to the ad. What they had was a recognizable likeness, which was not consistent with reality.

Dior also contended that having Onassis attend the

wedding of the Diors was "no more than a touch of humor" and therefore was protected as a form of free speech. However, simply claiming that a statement was intended to be funny does not make it permissible to make the statement. In this case, the humor was used only to promote Dior products, so absolutely no freedom of speech privilege existed to justify its use.

What is ironic about this case, as the court noted, was that Dior was attempting to "pass off the counterfeit as a legitimate marketing device," when it had in the past, so adamantly tried to prevent others from deceptively obtaining the "fruits of another's labor." For example, in a previous case, *Dior* v. *Milton,*[9] Dior complained bitterly of the misappropriation of its good name and reputation that had taken so long to develop. Now the shoe was on the other foot.

Although Onassis was a public figure, even a celebrity, she purposely avoided any connection with commercial products. Embarrassment and annoyance were her injury rather than loss of economic opportunity.

As a side note, we'll look at another aspect of using celebrity look-alikes in Chapter 8. There, comparative advertising has become another area of law that is involved in certain situations that use look-alikes.

When Freedom Of The Press Overcomes The Rights Of Privacy And Publicity

In 1978, the movie *Magic* was released and subsequently grossed over $13 million. One of the stars of the movie was Ann-Margret. For only the second time in her career she appeared in a scene nude. She made the decision to disrobe for artistic reasons, agreeing to do so only if there was a minimal crew at the filming and if no still photos were taken.

High Society magazine runs photographs of well-known women caught in revealing situations. In one particular issue, five pages were devoted exclusively to Ann-Margret. One of the photos was taken from the movie *Magic* and showed her nude from the waist up. After learning of this photo, suit was brought in *Ann-Margret v. High Society Magazine, Inc.*[10] for violation of her right of privacy and right of publicity.

There is no doubt that Ann-Margret is considered a celebrity, but simply because she is a celebrity she has not given up her right to privacy. However, she chose to appear in the motion picture, partially nude, knowing that the public would see her performance. The reproduction of scenes from that performance were faithful and accurate and not distorted, and therefore were not an invasion of her privacy.

The court said:

> Undoubtedly, the plaintiff is unhappy about the appearance of her picture in [the] magazine. And while the court can sympathize with her feelings, the fact that she does not like either the manner in which she is portrayed, or the medium in which her picture is reproduced...[does] not expand her rights or create any cause of action....

As far as her claim of violation of her right of publicity, the court felt that it also had no merit. There is only an action when the use is for "advertising purposes or for the purposes of trade." The fact that the magazine is sold for profit does not constitute such a use. The mere use of the photos in an editorial context is acceptable. The case was dismissed.

When The Right Of Publicity Exceeds Freedom Of The Press

"Ladies and gentlemen, children of all ages, I present the great Zacchini." Hugo Zacchini practiced a form of entertainment developed by his father and performed by his family for over 50 years. Zacchini was a human cannonball, and over the years he performed at many public fairs and events.

In August and September of 1972, Zacchini performed his act at the Geauga County Fair in Burton, Ohio. The performance took place in a fenced area surrounded by grandstands. He was shot from a cannon into a net 200 feet away, and the performance lasted 15 seconds.

A freelance reporter for Scripps-Howard Broadcasting, owner of the local television station, visited the fair on August 30, 1972, where Zacchini was performing. Zacchini spotted the reporter carrying a video camera and requested that he not tape the performance, but on the next day the reporter returned and videotaped the feat anyway. The event was broadcast on the 11 o'clock news along with a commentary, which was very complimentary.

When Zacchini learned of the unauthorized broadcast, he sued for damages for showing and commercializing his act without his consent. This was the first case involving the right of publicity to reach the United States Supreme Court: *Zacchini* v. *Scripps-Howard Broadcasting Co.*[11]

Scripps-Howard argued that its broadcast of the event was protected under the 1st and 14th Amendments – freedom of the press. The TV station had the right to broadcast items of legitimate public interest. However, the TV station broadcast the entire act, from start to finish, along with a description of the event. If the station had broadcast that Zacchini was performing at the fair, commented on the performance, and showed his picture on TV, this could have been a very different case.

But as the Court said, Zacchini:

> [H]ad a right of publicity that gave him personal control over commercial display and exploitation of his personality and the exercise of his talents. This right...was said to be such a valuable part of the benefit, which may be attained by his talents and efforts, that it was entitled to legal protection.

Zacchini did not sue to stop the broadcast of his performance; he simply wanted to be paid for it. The Court agreed that Zacchini's commercial interest in his act was protected under his right of publicity.

DESCENDIBILITY OF THE RIGHT OF PUBLICITY

The right of publicity is a property right, separate and distinct from the right of privacy. The right of privacy is a personal right and is nondescendible; it terminates at death. The right of publicity is a property right, on the other hand, and can be inherited by or assigned to someone.

While some courts disagree, the trend is clearly toward descendibility. Since it is a property right, it survives after the death of the owner. A valid reason exists for recognizing this survivability. It motivates celebrities' efforts and creativity in encouraging them to develop their image so that their heirs will also benefit. It's money in the bank, so to speak. It may take many years to develop a talent, ability and reputation that will create large economic returns. Along those lines, nonrelated persons should not be able to benefit from the efforts celebrities put into developing their own images.

In practice, the various state courts have adopted one of three views regarding descendibility (see Table 5-1). One view says that the commercial use of the person's name or likeness shifts to the public domain after death. In other words, the right of publicity is never descendible.

Another view recognizes descendibility only if the right of publicity has been sufficiently exploited before death. What constitutes sufficient exploitation? Generally, it must be exploited by the celebrity through the creation of a second business or through the use of his or her name or likeness in connection with a product or service promoted by the person.

Finally, some courts recognize the descendibility of the right of publicity without any other conditions. Let's take a closer look at the three views. It is important to remember that the theory that applies to each case is determined by the state law used to decide that case.

TABLE: 5-1

State Interpretation of the Descendibility of the Right of Publicity

State	Always Descendible To Heirs	Descendible: If Exploited During Life	Never Descendible: Public Domain
Alabama	√		
Alaska		√	
Arizona		√	
Arkansas			√
California	Δ		
Colorado		√	
Connecticut	Δ		
Delaware	√		
Florida		√	
Georgia	Δ		
Hawaii		√	
Idaho		√	
Illinois			√
Indiana			√
lowa			√
Kansas	√		
Kentucky			Δ
Louisiana	Δ		
Maine	√		
Maryland	√		
Massachusetts	√		

State	Always Descendible To Heirs	Descendible: If Exploited During Life	Never Descendible: Public Domain
Michigan			Δ
Minnesota			√
Mississippi	Δ		
Missouri			√
Montana		√	
Nebraska			√
Nevada		√	
New Hampshire	√		
New Jersey	√		
New York	Δ		
North Carolina	√		
North Dakota			√
Ohio			Δ
Oklahoma			√
Oregon		√	
Pennsylvania	√		
Rhode Island	√		
South Carolina	√		
South Dakota			√
Tennessee			Δ
Texas	Δ		
Utah		√	
Vermont	Δ		
Virginia	√		
Washington		√	
Washington, D.C.	√		
West Virginia	√		

Δ = States where the descendibility issue has been decided.
√ = States where no appellate decisions have been made

regarding descendibility.

These states should be checked for current accuracy since the position of these states may vary over time.

Nonsurvivable Theory – The Statue Of Elvis

The strict view of descendibility is illustrated in *Memphis Development Foundation* v. *Factors Etc. Inc.*,[12] an example of when the right of publicity is not descendible. Under Tennessee law the courts hold the opinion that the celebrity's right of publicity is not inheritable.

Elvis Presley died on August 16, 1977, in Memphis. In his honor, the Memphis Development Foundation, a nonprofit corporation, wanted to build a large bronze statue of Elvis in downtown Memphis. The foundation would collect the needed money from contributions. Contributors of $25 or more received an eight-inch pewter replica of the full-size statue.

The defendant, Factors Etc., was the assignee of Presley's right of publicity, and the company claimed that Memphis Development had taken away its right to market Presley's name and likeness. Memphis claimed that Factors' license did not allow for the distribution of the statuettes.

The court decided that, based on Tennessee law, Factors could not inherit Presley's right of publicity. It reasoned that "the basic motivations are the desire to achieve success or excellence in a chosen field, the desire to contribute to the happiness or improvement of one's fellows, and the desire to receive the psychic and financial rewards of achievement." Essentially, the court felt that this right should not be survivable to the heirs because the celebrity alone did not have complete control over developing the notoriety in the first place.

The court felt that the public was an integral element in the creation of an image. Therefore it had "serious reservations about making fame the permanent right of a few individuals to the exclusion of the general public." In conclusion, the court said: "Fame falls in the same category as reputation; it is an attribute from which others may benefit but may not own."

In other words, the right of publicity is not descendible, but rather becomes public domain after death. At least this is the case in Tennessee and other states that have adopted the same philosophy.

Descendibility If Exploited During Life

The second option is where there is no descendibility unless the right was sufficiently exploited during the person's life. To illustrate, let's look at a case involving Bela George Lugosi and his well-known character, Count Dracula, the legendary character created in 1897 by author Bram Stoker. In September of 1930, Lugosi entered into an agreement with Universal Pictures to star in the lead role in the film classic, *Dracula*.

The case was *Lugosi* v. *Universal Pictures*,[13] during which Justice Mosk rather sardonically stated, "not unlike the horror films that brought him fame, Bela Lugosi rises from the grave 20 years after death to haunt his former employer."

In this case, the heirs of Lugosi, his son and widow, claimed that Universal had taken property rights that the studio had not been given in the agreement for the production of *Dracula* in 1930. Between 1960 and 1966 Universal licensed many companies to manufacture items using the Count Dracula character. There was no doubt that the merchandising of the Count Dracula character was patterned after the likeness of Lugosi. It may well be true, also, that Lugosi is readily recognized as having been Count Dracula, even though Max Schreck, Christopher Lee, John Carradine, Lon Chaney, and others also have appeared in the role.

Yet, Lugosi never exploited the character of Dracula commercially during his lifetime. He also never exploited his own identity commercially. Let's assume, for the sake of argument, that

Lugosi had opened a company named Lugosi/Dracula Enterprises. This company made T-shirts and hats with a picture of the actor made up as Dracula. Under the picture was printed "Dracula Lives ...signed Bela Lugosi." This product created a large public awareness of the business. If the business existed and had not been sold before Lugosi's death in 1956, his heirs may have had a claim if the Dracula image was later misappropriated.

However, under California law at the time, the right to profit from one's name and likeness was personal and had to have been be exercised during lifetime in order for the right to survive after death. Since Lugosi hadn't used his name or likeness as Count Dracula in association with any business, service, or product (other than the part in the movie), he had no claim under the California interpretation of publicity rights. As a result, his heirs lost the case.

It is important to note that this case does not concern Lugosi's right of publicity for his likeness, but rather that of a character he played. Unless there is a contract to the contrary, merely playing a role creates no inheritable property rights – any more than George C. Scott has any rights to the character of General Patton, James Whitmore to that of Will Rogers, Gregory Peck of General MacArthur, or Charlton Heston of Moses.

The United States Court of Appeals for the Second Circuit agreed with the Lugosi decision when it decided a case involving three brothers Adolph, Julius, and Leo Marx. This case concerned the brothers' public image for which they were known as Harpo, Groucho, and Chico, respectively. The case was *Groucho Marx Productions, Inc.* v. *Day and Night Co., Inc.*[14]

At the New End Theatre in London, a play opened in January of 1979 called *A Day in Hollywood/A Night in the Ukraine*. In May of 1980, it came to Broadway. The second half of the play featured performers who simulated the Marx Brothers' unique style, appearance, and manner.

The Marx Brothers had assigned the rights to their names,

likenesses, and style prior to their deaths; and subsequently their heirs transferred that right to Groucho Marx Productions, the plaintiff. The Marx Brothers, it can be said, made a profession of capitalizing on the unique characters they had created. Their fame arose directly from their efforts to create their instantly recognizable characters. The Marx Brothers' characters bore little resemblance to their actual personalities. This was a key issue in the case.

The Marx Brothers had capitalized on the commercial value of the artificial personalities they created. Every appearance and advertisement they took part in demonstrated their awareness of the commercial value of their images as Chico, Harpo, and Groucho. In fact, the Marx Brothers had promoted many products during their lifetimes, including Plymouth cars and Smirnoff vodka.

The play created a duplication, as faithfully as possible, of the Marx Brothers' performances. Granted, it devised a new situation and used new lines. But the essential style of humor of the Marx Brothers was accurately reproduced. The court said:

> Although the [plaintiffs] may have intended to comment "about 1930s Hollywood, its techniques, its stars, and its excesses,"...the content of the relevant portion of the play attempts to accomplish that objective exactly as would the Marx Brothers themselves.

The court found that indeed the Marx Brothers had established a commercial use of their names, likenesses, and images during their lifetimes. This allowed their right of publicity to survive them; to be passed on to their heirs. They had won their case.

Always Descendible Theory

The third approach makes the right of publicity always

descendible. The case we see here was easier to determine than the Lugosi case because it featured actors playing themselves. Stanley Laurel and Oliver Hardy developed their own characters, which were theirs alone and certainly not fictional.

The heirs of Laurel and Hardy brought suit for $250,000 against Hal Roach Studios, which claimed that the studio had been given the exclusive rights to the Laurel and Hardy characters. Roach contended that the rights had been acquired through contracts between the studio and the comedy team in 1923. However, the specific rights acquired were those of copyright for the Laurel and Hardy films, not the unlimited usage of the Laurel and Hardy names and likenesses. We'll look more closely at copyright in Chapter 6.

Roach also claimed that the names and likenesses of the comedy team are in the public domain. The court, in *Price* v. *Hal Roach Studios, Inc.*,[15] disagreed. Its only question was whether the right of publicity terminated on the death of Laurel and Hardy or was it descendible.

The court felt that there was no reasonable basis to assume that the right was not assignable or that it should terminate with the death of the person. The court decided that the heirs of Laurel and Hardy were entitled to the commercial rights to the names and likenesses of the team. It also reasoned that the heirs were entitled to the actual damages sought in the lawsuit – for the appropriation of that right by Roach.

A further extension of the right of publicity for celebrities involved the late Dr. Martin Luther King, Jr., a public figure but not a celebrity. From 1955, Dr. King was the prime leader of the civil rights movement in the United States. For his efforts, he was awarded the Nobel Peace Prize in 1964. On April 4,1968, Dr. King was assassinated.

American Heritage Products manufactured plastic products. It developed the idea of marketing a bust of the late Dr. King. Although the company had asked permission for the endorsement of the product of the Martin Luther King, Jr. Center for Social Change (the nonprofit corporation that holds the rights to the King estate), the center refused to participate.

Despite the lack of endorsement, American Heritage hired an artist to produce a mold for the bust. It also hired an agent to promote the product. American bought two half-page ads in the November and December 1980 issues of *Ebony Magazine*. The ad offered:

An exclusive memorial.
An opportunity to support
the Martin Luther King, Jr. Center for Social Change.
A contribution from your order goes to
the King Center for Social Change.

American also printed 80,000 brochures that were inserted in newspapers across the country. Two hundred busts had been sold with orders for 23 more when the lawsuit was initiated in *Martin Luther King, Jr. Center for Social Change, Inc.* v. *American Heritage Products, Inc.*[16]

Generally, the right of publicity is the distillation of celebrities' exclusive rights to the use of their names and likenesses. These celebrities are most often actors, musicians, athletes, comedians, or other entertainers. Although Dr. King was none of these, he still had the right to control the use of his image for trade purposes and advertising.

Indeed a public figure, Dr. King avoided having his name exploited during his life, and he was protected from having it exploited after death. Under Georgia law, individuals do not have to commercially exploit their names or likenesses during their lifetimes in order to have the right of publicity extend beyond life to their heirs. The Center won its case against American Heritage.

PROBLEMS RELATING TO CONSENT

The most appropriate method of avoiding suits involving the right of privacy or publicity is to obtain the person's prior consent. Generally, this consent must be in writing, and it involves more than just the authorization to use a person's name, likeness, or image. Involved are questions of how the image is used, the media, the form, where and when it is used, and so on. The advertiser must make certain that these questions are answered by the consent release to avoid liability later.

Let's look at the different areas where consent problems are common.

Consent For A Specific Use

As a very successful fashion model, Christie Brinkley has appeared on the covers of many major magazines, including *Mademoiselle, Ladies Home Journal, Harper's Bazaar*, and *Sports Illustrated*. In September of 1979, John Casablancas, the president of Elite Model Management (Brinkley's agent), signed a licensing agreement with Galaxy Publishing. The agreement was to produce a series of posters of several models, including Brinkley.

Brinkley verbally agreed to the project and picked her own makeup artist, hair-stylist, and bathing suit for the photo session. Photographer Michael Reinhardt photographed Brinkley for the poster. Cable TV provider Home Box Office (HBO) filmed the photography session for use in a special entitled: "Beautiful, Baby, Beautiful," on the careers of this country's top models. Brinkley gave her written permission to appear in the broadcast in the same pose and suit that was to be used for the poster.

After the session, Brinkley reviewed the photos and requested some retouching be done on the specific shot she had intended for the poster. This was done. At that point, Galaxy proceeded to print the posters. The problem was that Brinkley never signed a model release authorizing the publication of her pictures in a poster. Brinkley stated that she "agreed to participate in a shooting from which a poster *may* have been the result, depending of course on my final judgment of the final product." She claimed that the printing and distribution of pinup posters was an unauthorized exploitation, for commercial purposes, of her name and image. The court agreed.

In *Brinkley* v. *Casablancas*,[17] Brinkley's consent for the use of her photo for a cable television show did not include consent for a poster of a different photo taken at the same session. There was no written permission given for that particular photo to be used as a poster.

Consent For A Specific Length Of Time

Another area where a problem can arise is the length of time allowed for the usage. In 1973 actor Charles Welch appeared in a television commercial for Mr. Christmas, a manufacturer of artificial Christmas trees. Welch was paid the sum of $1,000 for the commercial. According to the contract the $1,000 fee allowed the commercial to be run for no more than one year. However, the contract further provided for an additional year's option with the payment of an additional $1,000. Although Mr. Christmas had not paid Welch the additional fee to exercise the option for the second year, it allowed its distributors to air the commercial in 1974.

Welch found out about this and agreed to a financial settlement for the 1974 option. In March of 1975 Mr. Christmas was contacted by the Screen Actors Guild and cautioned that the spot could not be aired any longer without further negotiations. In spite of this warning, the commercial aired during 1975.

In the lawsuit that resulted, *Welch* v. *Mr. Christmas Inc.*,[18] the plaintiff was awarded compensatory damages of $1,000 and exemplary damages of $25,000. Here, the time limit was part of the original consent agreement. Using the commercial after the authorized period expired is the same as airing the commercial with no consent at all.

Mr. Christmas claimed as a defense that it did not use the commercial, claiming that its dealers were expected to purchase their own air time and that it did not know or have control over the spots used by them. However, Mr. Christmas encouraged its dealers to get the maximum use of the commercial, and made no attempt to notify the dealers that the usage period had ended. All of this made Mr. Christmas liable.

As we have seen before, not taking action when you have a responsibility to do so is also negligent. Since the agreement was with the actor and Mr. Christmas, those are the parties who are responsible to each other. If the dealers had aired the spot after they were notified in writing by Mr. Christmas not to do so, the situation may have been different.

We'll discuss such responsibilities in greater detail in Chapter 11, The Client/Agency Relationship.

Use In A Medium That Was Not Authorized

Frank Dzurenko is a model who participated in a photo session for Jordache jeans. At the end of the photo session, Dzurenko signed a model release inserting the phrase "magazine ad use only." His reason for adding the limitation was that in the photos he had posed with a female model who was wearing only a pair of jeans.

After the session one of those photos was blown up and produced as a poster, which was then distributed to retailers. This violated Dzurenko's right of publicity because the photo's use exceeded the limitations of the release. In *Dzurenko* v. *Jordache, Inc.*,[19] the court determined that a release can cover not only the use of a name, picture or likeness, but also the time, form, and media of its use. Dzurenko won the case.

Another interesting issue brought as a defense was that Dzurenko didn't sign the release with the limitation until after the photos had been taken. However, the court held that this didn't matter. Dzurenko had the absolute right to limit the usage of the photos in any way he desired, regardless of when the release was signed.

When Parental Consent Is Revocable

Another problem regarding consent can occur when a child's parent gives consent and then the child, on becoming an adult, attempts to withdraw it. This can pose a unique problem for advertisers. That was exactly what happened with Brooke Shields and Garry Gross.

In 1975 Brooke Shields was 10 years old. At the time she was registered with the Ford Model Agency, working as a child model (and a very famous one at that). One of the jobs she did was for Playboy Press that required her to pose nude in a bathtub. The intent was that the photos would be published in a publication called *Sugar and Spice*.

Before the photo session, Teri Shields, Brooke's mother, signed a consent for the photographer Garry Gross to "use, reuse and/or publish, and republish" the photos. Brooke's photos appeared in *Sugar and Spice,* as well as on posters and in other publications. Brooke even used the photos in a book about herself with the permission of the photographer. Gross, in fact, had shot Brooke on many occasions for *Penthouse* magazine, *New York Magazine*, and advertising for the Courtauldts and Avon Company.

In 1980 Brooke learned that the *Sugar and Spice* photos had appeared in the French magazine, *Photo*. At that point, she became disturbed by the publication of the photos and attempted to buy the negatives from Gross.

When that failed, she brought suit: *Shields* v. *Gross*.[20] The suit claimed, among other things, that her right of privacy had been violated and sought to cancel the consent given by her mother in 1975.

According to New York's Civil Rights Law, section 50, once the written consent is obtained, the photos can be published as agreed. If that person is a minor, his or her parents may give the consent.

Under common law, infants can disaffirm their own or their guardian's consent. However, where a specific statute permits a class of agreements to be made by a child, the discussion is ended, and the agreement is valid. Consent had been given, and it would stand under its original terms. Brooke lost her claim.

FORMS OF DEPICTION THAT CAN CAUSE LIABILITY

What type of depictions can cause trouble for advertisers? As we'll see, there are many. There is a difference between the right of privacy and the right of publicity regarding what depictions create a problem. The right of privacy is very specific, while the right of publicity is more broad.

Upholding Privacy Rights Requires Recognizability

The right of privacy generally requires that a visually recognizable likeness of the person is used even if the name is not. This right is narrower in scope than publicity rights because it protects citizens where there is a recognizability by others.

What constitutes a recognizable likeness? The New York Court of Appeals defined that in *Cohen v. Herbal Concepts, Inc.*[21] In 1977 on the July 4th weekend, a woman and her daughter were photographed while bathing in a stream in Woodstock, New York. The photo of Susan Cohen and her four-year-old daughter, Samantha, was photographed from behind while they bathed nude in the stream located on their friend's private property. Ira Cohen, the husband and father, saw the photographer taking pictures, became incensed, and chased him away. However, the photographer printed and sold the photos.

The photo showed the nude mother and daughter from behind and to the right in a full-length pose. The shot did not show their faces, but their backs and right sides are clearly visible, as was the mother's right breast. The photo later appeared in ads that ran in *House and Garden, House Beautiful,* and *Cosmopolitan* magazines.

The ad for Au Naturel, manufactured by Herbal Concepts, promoted a product intended to help eliminate body cellulite. As the ad said: "those fatty lumps and bumps that won't go away." While leafing through one of the magazines that contained the ad, Ira Cohen "recognized [his] wife and daughter immediately."

The issue here was whether a photograph of the nude mother and child constitutes a sufficiently identifiable likeness without showing their faces. The court established that it does. Features such as the mother's and child's hair, bone structure, body shape, stature, and posture all together could make the people in the photograph identifiable by someone familiar with them. The court ruled that the photo need not show the face. The plaintiff need only show that the photograph is reasonably recognizable. The photo was clear and sharp with no objects blocking the subjects. In New York, privacy claims are based on sections 50 and 51 of the Civil Rights Law. This statute, as with many other states, was designed to protect not only name, portrait, or picture, but a person's identity. The plaintiff must be "identifiable." The fact that Susan and Samantha were identified by Ira Cohen was acceptable.

THE MANY FORMS THAT CAN VIOLATE PUBLICITY RIGHTS

As for publicity rights, almost any form that can be devised can potentially cause trouble. Because of this, the advertiser must be very careful when using any form of celebrity or public figure in an ad. Name, image, likeness, voice imitations, commonly associated phrases, look-alikes, cartoons, and even identifiable situations are potential problem areas. Now, let us explore some of these areas in detail.

Use Of A Phrase

The use of a familiar phrase can be an infringement. In 1962 Johnny Carson began hosting *"The Tonight Show"* for NBC Television. Carson was introduced five nights a week with the phrase "Heeeeere's Johnny." Johnny Carson is a well-known entertainer, and a large segment of the television viewing public associated him with the particular phrase.

In 1967 Carson authorized the use of this phrase by another business. He allowed it to be used by a restaurant chain called "Here's Johnny Restaurants." In 1970 Carson formed a clothing manufacturer and used the phrase "Here's Johnny" on its clothing and in its advertising. And in 1977 Carson authorized Marcey Laboratories to use the phrase as a name for a line of toiletries.

However, in 1976 a Michigan corporation was formed to rent and sell a product it called "Here's Johnny" portable toilets. The owner developed a clever tag line for the product:

"Here's Johnny Portable Toilets. The World's Foremost Commodian." The owner claimed that this made "a good play on a phrase."

Not long after this, Carson brought suit for, among other things, infringement of his right of publicity in *Carson* v. *Here's Johnny Portable Toilets, Inc.*[22] This was a case of an appropriation of Carson's identity without the use of his name – the phrase is so recognizable that when the public heard it, no one else but Carson came to mind. The phrase "Here's Johnny" is a symbol of Carson's identity, just as is a name or picture. The president of the toilet company even admitted that he used the name because it identified Carson.

A celebrity's right of publicity is invaded when his identity is intentionally appropriated for commercial purposes. The fact that the defendant did not use Carson's last name did not lessen the offense. In fact, no violation would have occurred if his name had been used.

The court gave as examples of names that would not have violated Carson's right of publicity: "J. William Carson Portable Toilet," "John William Carson Portable Toilet," and "J. W. Carson Portable Toilet." The reason that these uses of his name would not have been violative of Carson's right is simple – there would have been no appropriation of Carson's identity as a celebrity. Even if his real name was used, the public would not have associated the two as the same person. Carson's full real name is not recognizable by the public anymore than Marion Michael Morrison would be for John Wayne's real name, or Creighton Chaney for Lon Chaney.

Use Of An Object

Here's another example of appropriation of an identity without the use of a name. This case involved an object commonly associated with a celebrity.

Lothar Motschenbacher was an internationally known race car driver. Part of his income came from product endorsements. Since 1966 all of Motschenbacher's cars were individualized to set them apart from other cars and to make them more recognizable as his. Each was red with a narrow white pinstripe, unlike any other car. The white background of his racing number 11 was always an oval, unlike the circular ones on other cars.

In 1970 R. J. Reynolds Tobacco Company and its agency William Esty produced a television commercial that used a stock photo showing several race cars on the track.

Motschenbacher's car was in the foreground. The driver could not be identified in the photo because of the helmet and driving suit.

The ad agency altered the photograph for the commercial. They changed the numbers on all of the cars; Motschenbacher's number 11 was changed to 17. A spoiler (wing) was attached to the car, displaying the name of the product, Winston. All other product names were removed from the other cars.

The agency then filmed the slide, adding a series of comic

book-type balloons with messages. Over Motschenbacher's car the balloon said: "Did you know that Winston tastes good, like a cigarette should?" The commercial was broadcast nationally.

Motschenbacher filed suit in *Motschenbacher* v. *R. J. Reynolds Tobacco Co.*[23] The court agreed that the plaintiff himself was not recognizable. However, the decoration of the car in the picture left little doubt that the car was Motschenbacher's, and implied that he was driving. Because of this, R. J. Reynolds lost the case.

Use Of A Performer's Style

Appropriation of a performer's style is another way that one's right of publicity can be violated. Guy Lombardo had invested 40 years in developing his image as "Mr. New Year's Eve." Add to this the combination of New Year's Eve, balloons, party hats, and "Auld Lang Syne" in the right context and you have an image that is unmistakable, and one that can be exploited commercially.

Doyle Dane Bernbach, the ad agency for Volkswagen at the time, entered into negotiations with Lombardo in late 1974 to obtain his appearance in a television commercial. The negotiations, however, fell through but the agency went on to produce the commercial featuring several products of the car manufacturer all set against the background of a New Year's Eve party.

Lombardo's name was never mentioned, but the actor used to portray the bandleader conducted the band using the same gestures and choice of music. Even the set resembled the one that Lombardo had become so closely associated with as "Mr. New Year's Eve." The case that resulted was *Lombardo* v. *Doyle Dane Bernbach, Inc.*[24] Lombardo won.

Use Of Three-Dimensional Objects

Eleanor Brown Young was, in 1941, a professional model of junior misses' clothes. She was employed by a department store and was asked to pose for the making of a mannequin. She allowed Greneker Studios to mold the mannequins in her image – her form, features, and likeness – for the exclusive use of her employer – the department store.

Later, it was learned that Greneker sold the mannequins to others. *Young* v. *Greneker Studios, Inc.*[25] was the case that followed. Young alleged that Greneker manufactured and sold mannequins in her likeness, without her permission, for the purposes of trade.

Under New York Civil Rights Law, section 51, an action may be brought by "any person whose name, portrait, or picture is used...for advertising purposes or for the purposes of trade without the written consent first obtained." Even though Young gave her permission for her employer to make and use the mannequins in her image, she had not given permission to the company who manufactured them to sell them to anyone else.

What this case points up is that the courts give broad latitude to what form constitutes a "portrait or picture" of a person. As we have seen a picture is not limited only to a photograph of the person, but to any representation of that person. The representation can be two-dimensional or, as in this case, three-dimensional. The words "picture" and "portrait" are general enough to encompass any form of an image, from a photograph to a painting to a sculpture.

Use Of Photo-Illustrations

Another form that can create a problem involves photo-realistic illustrations. On February 15, 1978, Leon Spinks defeated Muhammad Ali in a 15-round split decision. Until then, Ali had been the heavyweight boxing champion of the world. In the February 1978 issue of *Playgirl* magazine a picture ran with an article entitled "Mystery Man," showing a nude black man seated in a corner of a boxing ring. The illustration fell somewhere between cartoon and realistic art. The article was not editorial, but rather fictional writing, using, as the court determined, the picture of Ali solely "for the purposes of trade."

There was no question that the portrait was of Ali. In the court's words: "The cheekbones, broad nose, and wide-set brown eyes, together with the distinctive smile and close-cropped black hair are recognizable as the features of...one of the most widely known athletes of our time." In *Ali v. Playgirl, Inc.*,[26] the court agreed that Ali's right of publicity had been violated.

One important thing to note here is that not only was the magazine liable for the violation of the right of publicity, but the artist who drew the portrait was named as a defendant as well.

Use Of Modified Photos

When a photograph or picture is modified or altered slightly, but still identifiable as a specific person, a problem can result. A situation such as this happened quite some time ago in 1917 when Gladys Loftus, a 22-year-old Ziegfeld Girl, appeared in the rose garden scene in *Midnight Frolics* wearing a special costume known as "the rose costume," made by Lady Duff-Gordon.

Loftus had her picture taken wearing the rose costume by Alfred Johnson, a photographer employed to take pictures of some of the girls in the play, while in costume. Loftus became readily recognizable in her costume, and the public became very familiar with Johnson's photograph of her.

Sometime later The Greenwich Lithographing Company, a designer of theatrical and movie posters, was hired to produce a poster for the photoplay, *Shame*. The posters were distributed throughout the city of New York. The name *Shame* appeared very large on the poster along with copy that read:

••••••

Coming
Soon
to your
local

theatre
John W. Noble presents
the photoplay of the hour
SHAME
featuring
Zena Keefe
(A story of the world's unjust condemnation.)

On the poster was a picture of a man pointing his right hand in scorn at a woman who had her head slightly bowing. Greenwich admitted that it had copied the photograph of Loftus to use as the model of the woman in the poster.

The artist, Ira Cassidy, used the rose costume picture when he painted the poster art for *Shame*, making only slight variations:

- Changing the tilt of the head;
- Lowering the hair;
- Altering the outline of the nose, chin, and neck; and
- Removing the right arm from view.

All other aspects of the photo were duplicated in the final painting.

The court determined in *Loftus* v. *Greenwich Lithographing Co., Inc.*[27] that the poster was not a direct copy of the photo, but the image of Loftus was duplicated in such a way as to make it easily identifiable as being Loftus. Loftus won her case.

Use Of A Voice Impersonation

Here again, the advertiser must be careful. A very popular trend, especially in radio commercials, is to produce spots using voice impersonators. At the end of these spots an announcer states "celebrity voice impersonated." This is done to clarify that the voice is an imitation and to avoid a violation of the celebrity's right of publicity.

In 1985 Ford Motor Company, through it agency Young &

Rubicam, Inc., developed a campaign using the song "Do You Want To Dance?" After getting permission to the copyright of the song, they hired a backup singer to record the song. They wanted to get a singer that could match singer Bette Midler's voice and style as close as possible. They did. The fact that the rendition of the song sounded exactly like Midler allowed her to win in court. When a distinctive voice that is widely known and recognized is deliberately imitated to sell a product, that person's identity is pirated.

ISSUES IN RECENT RIGHT OF PUBLICITY CASES

Trading Places

In *Allison* v. *Vintage Sports Plaques*,[28] the plaintiffs were Elisa Allison, the widow of a well-known race car driver, Clifford Allison, and Orel Hershisher, the famous baseball pitcher. Clifford Allison had a licensing agreement with Maxx Race Cards ("MAXX") whereby Maxx would manufacture and market trading cards bearing his likeness for a royalty of 18 percent of sales, which is now paid to his estate. Orel Hershisher ("Hershisher") has a licensing agreement with the Major League Baseball Players Association ("MLBPA") that grants MLBPA the right to use and license his name and image for commercial purposes in exchange for a pro rata share of all revenues derived therefrom. MLBPA has licensed Hershisher's name and image to various trading card companies.

Vintage Sports purchased trading cards from manufacturers and (without modifying the cards at all) mounted them under acrylic on a wood board. Vintage then labeled each plaque with the celebrity's name. They market each plaque as a "Limited Edition" and an "Authentic Collectible." Vintage is not a party to any licensing agreement and has never paid a royalty or commission for the use of the celebrity's name or image. However, pursuant to their respective licensing agreements, royalties from the card manufacturers and distributors for the initial sale of the cards to Vintage were received.

Mrs. Allison, on behalf of her husband's estate, claimed that the resale of the cards violated her husband's right of publicity. The court held that while Alabama had never recognized a right of "publicity," the Alabama right of privacy contained an analogous right. The court found that the right of privacy included the appropriation of some element of the plaintiff's personality for commercial use. The court stated: "We read Alabama's commercial appropriation privacy right, however, to represent the same interests and address the same harms as does the right of publicity as customarily defined. Indeed, the elements of Alabama's commercial appropriation invasion of privacy tort, bases liability on commercial, rather than psychological, interests."

Having decided that Alabama law recognized publicity rights, the court then determined that the first-sale doctrine precluded Mrs. Allison's claim. The court explained:

> The first-sale doctrine provides that once the holder of an intellectual property right "consents to the sale of particular copies...of his work, he many not thereafter exercise the distribution right with respect to such copies...." Any other rule would extend the monopoly created by the intellectual property right so far as to permit control by the rightholder over the disposition of lawfully obtained tangible personal property.

The court went on to discuss the impact of ignoring the first-sale doctrine. They reasoned that:

> Accepting appellants' argument would have profoundly negative effects on numerous industries and would grant a monopoly to celebrities over their

> identities that would upset the delicate balance between the interests of the celebrity and those of the public.

Such a holding presumably also would prevent, for example, framing a magazine advertisement that bears the image of a celebrity and reselling it as a collector's item, reselling an empty cereal box that bears a celebrity's endorsement, or even reselling a used poster promoting a professional sports team. Refusing to apply the first-sale doctrine to the right of publicity also presumably would prevent a child from selling to his friend a baseball card that he had purchased, a consequence that undoubtedly would be contrary to the policies supporting that right.

The court rejected Mrs. Allison's argument that the first-sale doctrine should not apply. She argued that the right of publicity protected "identity," whereas the others protected "a particular photograph or product." The court found that accepting this argument would profoundly affect numerous industries, and would bestow a monopoly to celebrities over their identities that would upset the delicate "balance between the interests of the celebrity and those of the public." Not to apply the first-sale doctrine to the right of publicity would make the resale of sports trading cards and memorabilia actionable in court.

By applying the first-sale doctrine, however, the celebrity would continue to control the right to license his/her image initially and still have the ability to determine when, or if, that image could be distributed. The court reasoned:

> Because the application of the first sale doctrine to limit the right of publicity under Alabama law will maintain the appropriate balance between the rights of celebrities in their identities and the rights of the public to enjoy those identities, we conclude that the Alabama Supreme Court would apply the

> first-sale doctrine in this case and the district court properly so applied it.

Allison and Hershisher cannot win a commercial appropriation action if Vintage merely resells the trading cards that bear their likenesses, because the resale of licensed images falls under the protective scope of the first sale doctrine as we have seen.

So, the district court ruled correctly, and observed:

> Vintage would probably violate the right of publicity if [it] attached a trading card to a baseball glove and sold it as "an official Orel Hershisher glove" or if [it] affixed a Clifford Allison card onto a model car and sold it as "an official Clifford Allison car." Thus, this court must decide if the Vintage Clocks and plaques are more like reselling the trading cards or more like using Plaintiffs' names and likenesses to sell frames and clocks, similar to selling an Allison car or a Hershisher glove.

The district court concluded that Vintage was selling the trading cards after putting them in a more attractive display. Because the first-sale doctrine permits such resale, the court granted summary judgment on the right of publicity claim.

Dear Mortified

Jamie Messenger, a teenage fashion model from Florida, posed for photographs for the magazine *Young and Modern*. The photographs were used to illustrate a love and sexual advice column that was a monthly feature of the magazine. The column contained a letter from a teenager, signed as "Mortified," who sought advice because she had had sex with three boys and was then ostracized by her friends. The column, entitled "I got trashed and had sex with three guys," was illustrated by three provocative photographs of Messenger in various stages of undress.

The court rejected the publisher's argument that the photographs were "newsworthy" and, as a result, exempt under Sections 50 and 51 of the New York Civil Rights Law, in *Messenger v. Gruner & Jahr USA Publishing*.[29] Messenger claimed that the publisher created the false impression that she was the author of the letter, and therefore the use of the photographs violated the New York right of publicity law. In contrast, the publisher argued that its use of the photographs was not for trade or advertising purposes, but was used in connection with editorial: a matter of public interest.

The court reasoned that the use of a photograph to illustrate an article on a topic of public interest was not actionable unless the photograph had no relation to the article or unless the article was actually an advertisement. However, if the use of the photograph was false or misleading in connection with the article, this could be a violation of the person's right of publicity.

The court found that readers of the sex advice article could interpret the accompanying photographs to be of the writer of the "Mortified" letter. Thus, the publisher's "newsworthy" privilege could be lost.

The court stated:

> The fundamental issue is whether the publication created the impression that Messenger had had the experiences that were the subject of the column, a matter that turns on the interpretation that would be given to the column by readers. The problem is analogous to that presented in libel cases where the question is whether the accused publication is defamatory, and the mode of analysis is the same. The Court initially must determine as a matter of law whether readers reasonably could construe the article in the manner alleged by the plaintiff. If they could, the issue whether they

> actually did so is for the trier of fact. Although the defendants have pointed out several substantial indications that arguably would lead a reader to conclude that the photographs of Messenger were those of a model and not in fact of "Mortified," the purported author of the letter, the Court is not prepared on this record to say that this was the only reasonable conclusion.

Oh, Lay!

One Frito-Lay television commercial used the Muppet character "Miss Piggy" eating Baked Lays and singing "The Girl From Ipanema." The actual singer, Astrud Gilberto, who recorded the original version of "The Girl From Ipanema," filed a claim against Frito-Lay for its use of the recording in the television commercial. The case was *Oliveira* v. *Frito-Lay, Inc.*[30] This case is unique in that it deals with what elements or forms of a person's identity are covered under New York's right of publicity statute. This is a good example of how states vary on their views of this area of law.

The court here rejected Gilberto's "look-alike" theory under New York's right of publicity statute. While Gilberto claimed that Frito-Lay used a caricature of her in the commercial, the court held that Miss Piggy bared little resembelence to Gilberto or her likeness. They stated: "Although the question of recognizable likeness is ordinarily one for the jury, this is one of those rare instances in which a court can conclude as a matter of law that no reasonable jury could find that Miss Piggy resembles Gilberto."

At the trial level, the court dismissed the claim since sections 50 and 51 of the New York Civil Rights Law only covered a "name, portrait or picture." Yet, the law was revised in 1995 to include "name, portrait, picture or voice." As a result, that portion of the lower court's order, which held that section 51 does not provide protection to voice, was in error and was withdrawn. Oliveira was given the right to replead the case on this issue.

The Case Of The Run-Away Truck

"Bear Foot" was the name of a monster truck that competed in monster truck races across the country. Bear Foot, Inc., the owner of the truck, complained that while it participated in a monster truck show on November 28, 1987, in Houston, Texas, footage of Bear Foot's performance in a videotape was used by Robert Chandler and Bigfoot 4X4, Inc. (Bigfoot). "Bigfoot" was a competing monster truck.

There were two issues in this case. The first was a breach of contract claim, which was dismissed. The second was a right of publicity claim, which we'll discuss here.

Here is another example of state interpretation of right of publicity issues. In *Bear Foot, Inc.* v. *Chandler*,[31] the court held that corporations did not have a right of publicity. Under Missouri law, the right of publicity provided for a person to recover damages for pecuniary gain through misappropriation of the person's likeness. Essentially, the statute protected a person from losing the benefit of his or her work by developing a publicly recognizable person.

In contrast to the right of privacy, the right of publicity did not intend to protect the person's feelings, but rather provided remedy for the misappropriation of the person's valuable public persona or image. The court stated that "[w]hile some states have recognized a right of publicity in individuals or the deceased, we do not believe that a corporation has such a right. The right of publicity creates a cause of action only for misappropriation of a person's likeness."

On this issue, the court went further:

> Missouri courts have not addressed the "right of publicity" of a corporation. The right of publicity is frequently recognized as a cause of action distinct from the right of privacy. The right of publicity

> allows a person to recover damages for pecuniary gain from misappropriation of their likeness. It protects a person from losing the benefit of their work in creating a publicly recognizable persona. In contrast to the right of privacy, the right of publicity is not intended to protect the person's feelings, but provides a cause of action where a defendant has been unjustly enriched by misappropriation of the person's valuable public persona or image.

In holding against Bear Foot, the court ruled that: "Since there is no right of publicity in a corporation, Bear Foot failed to state a claim upon which relief could be granted."

Batter Up!

Donald Newcombe was a major league baseball all-star from 1949 until 1960. He pitched for the Brooklyn Dodgers and other teams during that time, and previously had played in the so-called Negro leagues. Newcombe was one of the first African-American players in the major leagues after Jackie Robinson broke the color barrier in 1947. Newcombe is the only player in major league history to have won the Most Valuable Player Award, the Cy Young Award, and the Rookie of the Year Award. He was a four-time member of the National League All Star Team, batted over .300 in four separate seasons, and had the most wins of any pitcher in the National League in 1950, 1951, 1955, and 1956.

Newcombe's baseball career was cut short due to a personal battle with alcohol. He is a recovering alcoholic, and he has devoted a substantial amount of time using his fame to advocate the dangers of alcohol, including serving as a spokesperson for the National Institute on Drug and Alcohol Abuse. At the time of trial in this case, Newcombe was the Director of Community Relations for the Los Angeles Dodgers, where he maintains an active role in battling alcohol abuse.

An advertisement in the February 1994 *Sports Illustrated* "swimsuit edition" for Killian's Irish Red Beer (manufactured by Coors) featured a drawing of an old-time baseball game. The drawing filled the left side of the full-page ad, while the right side was a picture of a glass of beer.

The court described the image in the ad:

> The baseball scene focused on a pitcher in the windup position and the background included a single infielder and an old-fashioned outfield fence. The players' uniforms did not depict an actual team, and the background did not depict an actual stadium.

However, Newcombe, along with family, friends and former teammates, immediately recognized the pitcher featured in the advertisement as Newcombe in his playing days.

While denying that the pitcher in the advertisement was a "likeness" of Newcombe, Coors admitted that the drawing was based on a newspaper photograph of Newcombe pitching in the 1949 World Series. In reality, the drawing and the newspaper photograph were virtually identical.

In *Newcombe* v. *Adolf Coors Co.*,[32] the court determined that there was an issue of fact regarding whether Newcombe was readily identifiable as the pitcher in the advertisement. Under both California statutory and common law, to prove a cause of action for commercial misappropriation, the plaintiff must prove that his or her likeness or identity had been used.

To accomplish this, the court looked to the statute's definition that a person is considered readily identifiable from a photograph "when one who views the photograph with the naked eye can reasonably determine that the person depicted in the photograph is the same person who is complaining of its unauthorized use."

In determining that Newcombe's image had been

appropriated, the court stated:

> Having viewed the advertisement, we hold that a triable issue of fact has been raised as to whether Newcombe is readily identifiable as the pitcher in the advertisement. Initially, we note that the drawing in the advertisement and the newspaper photograph of Newcombe upon which the drawing was based are virtually identical. The pitcher's stance, proportions and shape are identical to the newspaper photograph of Newcombe; even the styling of the uniform is identical, right down to the wrinkles in the pants. The defendants maintain that stance alone cannot suffice to render a person readily identifiable, and that even if it could, the drawing of the pitcher in the advertisement was essentially generic and could have been any one of thousands of people who have taken to the pitcher's mound to throw a baseball. We disagree.
>
> It may be the case that Newcombe's stance is essentially generic, but based on the record before us, Newcombe is the only one who has such a stance. The record contains pictures of other pitchers in the windup position but none of these pitchers has a stance similar to Newcombe's, thus giving us no basis to reach the conclusion proposed by the defendants that the pitcher in the advertisement is "generic." Furthermore, Matthew Reinhard, the Art Director at [Foote, Cone,] Belding, declared that a prior work of Cassidy's, which depicted former San Francisco Giant pitcher Juan Marichal in his unorthodox high-leg-kick windup, would not have been suitable for the advertisement at issue because Marichal's windup was too distinctive. Reinhard's admission that a pitcher's

windup could be so distinctive so as to make that player readily identifiable, regardless of the visibility of his face or the markings on the uniform, bolsters our determination that there is a genuine issue of material fact as to whether Newcombe's stance was so distinctive that the defendants used his likeness by using a picture of Newcombe's stance.

In addition to the identifiability of the pitcher in the advertisement as Newcombe based on the pitcher's stance, the pitcher's skin is moderately dark, which is quite similar to Newcombe's skin color. A jury could rationally find from this that Newcombe was readily identifiable, even though his facial features were not entirely visible.

Furthermore, while the drawing in the advertisement was slightly altered from the newspaper photograph, that does not alter our conclusion that there is a genuine issue of material fact as to whether the advertisement made use of Newcombe's likeness. For example, the uniform number in the advertisement ("39") is only slightly different than Newcombe's number ("36") – the first number is the same and the second number is simply inverted and the advertisement utilized the same block style numbers that were used on Newcombe's jersey – and it is arguable that the similarity in numbers could either consciously or subconsciously conjure up images of Newcombe. Also, we do not find persuasive the fact that the coloring of the bill of the hat in the advertisement is different, in light of the fact that the rest of the uniform is identical to the uniform in the newspaper photograph of Newcombe.

FEDERAL RIGHT OF PUBLICITY

The right of publicity is currently controlled under state law. Yet, the American Bar Association and the International Trademark Association (INTA) have recommended that the Lanham Act be amended to create a federal right of publicity.

INTA adopted a resolution in its Request For Action By The INTA Board Of Directory, Federal Right of Publicity, March 3, 1998, calling for the introduction of legislation, in the form of an amendment to the Lanham Act, for a federal right of publicity. INTA formed a subcommittee in 1994 to address the issue, and the committee presented its recommendations in a report on March 3, 1998. There is a variance in the right of publicity laws from state to state, and the subcommittee felt that there was a need to create a consistent standard on a national level.

The subcommittee created a working draft of the proposed statute. They feel that a federal right of publicity is needed to bring uniformity and predictability to this area. As of the date of the report, seven states had recognized the right exclusively by statute. Eleven states recognized the right by common law. Eight states recognized both a common law and a statutory right of publicity.

Whether the right of publicity survived the death of the holder was a point of sharp division among the various states, as we discussed earlier. Some states limit publicity rights to the lifetime of the person, in effect, making them non-descendible. Other states treated the right as descendible. Some states differed on the duration of descendible rights.

The subcommittee also proposed that the federal law be designed to accommodate First Amendment constitutional and fair use principles as well. It also considered using "aspects of a persona" as they relate to matters of public interest.

Ideally, the amendment to the Lanham Act should encompass the following standards:

1. Preempt all state law (statutory and common law).
2. Standardize the laws of various states in a way that

recognizes the principles underlying the right of publicity and fairly balances competing public interests.

3. Recognize the principles underlying the right of publicity by providing for a descendible and transferable right of publicity for a fixed term, without requiring that the right was exploited during a person's life.

4. Protect the public interest by "grandfathering" prior user rights that were acquired before enactment of federal right of publicity legislation.

5. Protect the public's interest by allowing uses of a persona that meet fair use or First Amendment standards such as news, biography, history, fiction, commentary, and parody.

While the above action clearly shows that a consistent right of publicity is desirable, no such change has occurred as of this printing.

THE HOLLYWOOD STUDIO MUSEUM COMMERCIAL

At the beginning of this chapter, I wrote about a television commercial that had been produced for The Hollywood Studio Museum. Now that you have read the chapter, I'm sure that you can see why I used the story to begin.

Let's analyze that commercial to see if and where a problem could arise. First, there is the image of the famous director C.B. DeMille. Do we have to be concerned with invasion of his privacy rights? What about his rights of publicity? Secondly, we must consider the rights of the actor who played DeMille in the commercial, Gene Barry. Think about these issues for a moment.

Let's start with DeMille. His privacy rights ended at the time of his death, so there is no problem. Regarding publicity rights, did we need the permission of the DeMille heirs to use his name and likeness? As we know, publicity rights are survivable under certain conditions. Under California law (that's where jurisdiction would have been), the publicity right is descendible, but only where it was exploited commercially during life. DeMille did, in fact, exploit his name and likeness during his life for commercial purposes. He was a very famous motion picture director, and his name alone sold many movies. Permission of the DeMille heirs was required and obtained.

As for Gene Barry, consent was required. Obviously, his appearance in the commercial was evidence of his consent to have his name and image used. However, there were questions of usage. Barry, through the Screen Actors Guild (SAG), authorized use for only one year. The consent was for television and radio (the voice portion) use only. Another required restriction imposed by Mr. Barry was that we clearly identify the spot as "a public service message." This was to clarify that he had donated his time and name and thereby not diminish his worth for commercials other than public service messages.

Noncompliance with any of these restrictions could give rise to a lawsuit for breach of his publicity rights and consent agreement.

As you can see, using a person's identity, and how it is used, brings with it many issues which must be considered.

[1] (5 Coke, 91), 1 Smith's Lead. Cas. 228.

[2] *Roberson* v. *Rochester Folding Box Co.*, 171 N.Y. 538, 64 N.E. 442 (1902).

[3] 1903 N.Y. Laws Ch. 132, sections 1-2 (codified as amended; N.Y. Civil Rights Law sections 50-51 (1976)).

[4] *Pavesich* v. *New England Life Ins. Co.*, 122 Ga. 190, 50 S.E. 68 (1905).

[5] See *Griswold* v. *Connecticut*, 381 U.S. 479, 85 S.Ct. 1678, 14 L.Ed. 2d 510 (1965).

[6] *O'Brien* v. *Pabst Sales Co.*, 124 F.2d 167 (5th Cir. 1941).

[7] *Haelan Laboratories* v. *Topps Chewing Gum, Inc.*, 202 F.2d 866 (2d Cir. 1953).

[8] *Onassis* v. *Christian Dior, New York, Inc.*, 122 Misc.2d 603, 472 N.Y.S.2d 254 (Sup. Ct. 1984).

[9] *Dior* v. *Milton*, 9 Misc.2d 425,155 N.Y.S.2d 443, aff'd. 2 A.D.2d 878, 156 N.Y.S.2d 996 (1956).

[10] *Ann-Margret* v. *High Society Magazine, Inc.*, 498 F.Supp. 401 (1980).

[11] *Zacchini* v. *Scripps-Howard Broadcasting Co.*, 433 U.S. 562, 97 S.Ct. 2849, 53 L.Ed 2d 965 (1977).

[12] *Memphis Development Foundation* v. *Factors Etc. Inc.*, 616 F.2d 956 (6th Cir. 1980).

[13] *Lugosi* v. *Universal Pictures*, 25 Cal.3d 813 (1979).

[14] *Groucho Marx Productions, Inc.* v. *Day and Night Co., Inc.*, 523 F. Supp. 485 (S.D.N.Y. 1981), rev'd, 689 F.2d 317 (2d Cir. 1982).

[15] *Price* v. *Hal Roach Studios, Inc.*, 400 F.Supp. 836 (S.D.N.Y. 1975).

[16] *Martin Luther King, Jr. Center for Social Change, Inc.* v. *American Heritage Products, Inc.*, 694 F.2d 674 (11th Cir. 1983).

[17] *Brinkley* v. *Casablancas*, 80 A.D.2d 428, 438 N.Y.S.2d 1004 (App. Div. 1981).

[18] *Welch* v. *Mr. Christmas Inc.*, 57 N.Y.2d 143, 440 N.E.2d 1317 (1982).

[19] *Dzurenko* v. *Jordache, Inc.*, 59 N.Y.2d 788, 451 N.E.2d 477 (1983).

[20] *Shields* v. *Gross*, 58 N.Y.2d 338 (1983).

[21] *Cohen* v. *Herbal Concepts, Inc.*, 63 N.Y.2d 379, 472 N.E.2d 307 (1984).

[22] *Carson* v. *Here's Johnny Portable Toilets, Inc.*, 698 F.2d 831 (6th Cir. 1983).

[23] *Motschenbacher* v. *R. J. Reynolds Tobacco Co.*, 498 F.2d 821 (9th Cir. 1974).

[24] *Lombardo* v. *Doyle Dane Bernbach, Inc.*, 58 A.D.2d 620, 396 N.Y.S.2d 661 (App. Div. 1977).

[25] *Young* v. *Greneker Studios, Inc.*, 176 Misc. 1027, 26 N.Y.S.2d 357 (Sup. Ct. 1941).

[26] *Ali* v. *Playgirl, Inc.*, 447 F. Supp. 723 (S.D.N.Y. 1978).

[27] *Loftus* v. *Greenwich Lithographing Co., Inc.*, 192 A.D. 251, 182 N.Y.S. 428 (App. Div. 1920).

[28] *Allison* v. *Vintage Sports Plaques*, 136 F.3d 1443 (11th Cir. 1998).

[29] *Messenger* v. *Gruner & Jahr USA Publishing*, 994 F. Supp. 525 (S.D.N.Y. 1998).

[30] *Oliveira* v. *Frito-Lay, Inc.*, No. 96 Civ. 9289 (LAP), 1998 U.S. Dist. LEXIS 4021 (S.D.N.Y., March 30, 1998); 46 U.S.P.Q.2d 1636.

[31] *Bear Foot, Inc.* v. *Chandler*, 965 S.W.2d 386 (Mo. Ct. App. 1998).

[32] *Newcombe* v. *Adolf Coors Co.*, No. 95-55688, U.S. App. LEXIS 23308 (9th Cir., September 22, 1998).

CHAPTER 6

COPYRIGHT REGULATION

Life is a copycat.
—*Heywood Broun*

Let's examine a situation involving an advertising agency. We'll call the agency Doofus-Wazoo Advertising. One of its clients, Acme Chemicals, made swimming pool chlorine and asked the agency to create a television commercial for its product. The creative team got together and devised a spot showing different shapes and styles of pools with the tag line: "No matter what the shape of your pool, Acme will keep it in shape."

The agency writer and creative director took the idea to Mr. Wazoo, the agency president (and Acme account executive), and explained that this could be a terrific spot with the right pools, scenes, and camera angles. Mr. Wazoo loved the idea. He wanted to produce an impressive commercial, but knew that the client didn't have much of a budget. Therefore, filming the commercial was out of the question.

So, Mr. Wazoo told the creative director to get a selection of the best pool shoots he could find from a stock photo house. The creative director ordered a group of 104 color slides. When the slides came in, Mr. Wazoo and the creative director looked them over and picked the best 14. But the fee for using the photos was $300 each. Mr. Wazoo ordered all 104 slides to be sent out and duplicated, instructing the creative director to use the 14 best in the commercial.

The creative director explained that the agency should not have duplicated all of the slides without prior permission from the stock photo house. He also explained that the agency could not use the photos in the commercial unless it had permission and paid the appropriate fee since the slides were copyrighted, and to do so would be illegal.

Mr. Wazoo claimed that the client did not have $4,200 to pay for all 14 slides, so here's what he did. He sent the slides back to the stock photo house, but told them that the agency only needed to use and pay for one slide in the commercial. The agency, however, used all 14. Mr. Wazoo boasted, "They'll never find out, and if they do, we'll just pay the fee."

The creative director, under protest, produced the commercial using the 14 slides, only one of which was paid for. The commercial aired, and Acme was thrilled with the results. Doofus-Wazoo beamed with pride at its creative work. Mr. Wazoo gloated at producing the commercial for next to nothing and for making the client happy. Everyone except the creative director – who saw the light from the oncoming train – was very pleased.

Not long after, a United States Marshall walked into the agency and handed Mr. Wazoo a summons. The agency, the photo lab that duplicated the photos, the editing company that made the commercial, the distributors who were listed on the commercial, and the client were all being sued for copyright violations. The stock photo house claimed over $5 million in damages. And then depression set in.

Could such a blatant violation of copyright really happen? Would an agency be naive enough to think it could get away with such a thing? Could this story be real? Absolutely. I know, because I was the creative director. Ultimately, the case was settled out of court.

This type of copyright abuse occurs quite often – in fact, too often. In many cases, the agency just doesn't understand what can and can't be done legally. Some know the rules and still ignore them and, as in the situation I just described, some learn the hard way. Since forewarned is forearmed, let's take a look at the areas of copyright law affecting advertisers. Keep in mind as you read this chapter, and the next on trademark, the differences between the two areas of law. Each is based on different principles and, therefore, must be thought of separately.

THE COPYRIGHT ACT OF 1976

The Copyright Act of 1976 protects the creators of artistic works as an incentive to pursue their creative talents. The United States Constitution – Article 1, Section 8, provides that Congress shall have the power: "To promote the Progress of Science and useful Arts, by securing for limited Times to Authors...the exclusive Right to their...Writings...." The original Copyright Act was passed by the first Congress in 1790, shortly after the signing of the Constitution. The act has been amended over the years in 1831, 1870, 1909, and most recently in 1976.

In 1976 Congress updated the Copyright Act, which went into effect on January 1, 1978. Any work produced after that date was covered by the new law. Works created prior to that date are covered by the Copyright Act of 1909. In this chapter we deal with the current act.

REQUIREMENTS TO QUALIFY FOR COPYRIGHT PROTECTION

It is important to understand what can qualify to be copyrighted. There are conditions that must be met in order to apply for protection under copyright law. To qualify, a work must be the product of the original author and meet the requirement of originality. It must also be considered a "writing" and be fixed in a tangible medium. Let us look at each of these requirements separately.

Definition Of A "Writing"

To be eligible for copyright protection an item must be put in a written form referred to as a "writing." The common definition of a writing is much different than the legal definition. Under the Copyright Act, the definition of a writing is quite broad, encompassing anything that is "fixed in any tangible medium of expression, now known or later developed, from which [the original] can be perceived, reproduced, or otherwise communicated, either directly or with the aid of a machine or device."[1]

At the time the Copyright Act was first written, about the only means of performance was the stage. There were, of course, books, maps, and so on, which were specifically listed in the original act. But other than those forms of creative expression, the stage was all that was left. In those years, the only medium to record the stage performance was the mind of the audience. Today, a performance can be recorded in many ways with incredible realism. Protection of the creative work, therefore, has had to expand with technology to keep pace with the times.

Between 1970 and 1971 Mr. Goldstein and his associates purchased copies of record albums or tape cassettes at local record stores, duplicated them on tape, and distributed them to retail stores for sale to the public. Goldstein never asked for permission from, and made no payments to, the artists, writers, performers, producers, or any other person involved with the original recordings. No payments were made for the use of the artists' names or the titles of the original albums.

Eventually the state of California, where this occurred, arrested and prosecuted Goldstein in *Goldstein* v. *California*[2] for record piracy: the unauthorized duplication of major artists' performances. In this case, the United States Supreme Court established that a writing covered "any physical rendering of the fruits of creative, intellectual, or aesthetic labor." Records and tape recordings certainly qualified under this heading.

Fixed In A Tangible Medium

As we saw earlier, in order for an original work to be

considered a writing, the work must exist in some tangible entity. A tangible entity can be paper, video tape, film, computer disk, record, recording tape, compact disc, or almost anything else capable of maintaining its form. Under the copyright statute, material is protected when it is created and fixed into a concrete medium so that it can be perceived by others.

David Brown wrote a term paper for Professor Hagendorf's law course in 1977. In the fall of 1978, Hagendorf adopted Brown's paper in an article he wrote for Commerce Clearing House, a legal publisher. Brown sued – and won – for copyright violation in *Hagendorf* v. *Brown*.[3] Even a term paper can be protected by copyright. It is a tangible form that can be perceived by others.

Definition Of Author

Only the original author of a work can receive copyright protection. This was first discussed in *Burrow-Giles Lithographic Co.* v. *Sarony*.[4] In this case, photographer Napoleon Sarony took a picture of Oscar Wilde in January of 1882. Sarony claimed that he was the author of the copyright to that picture entitled, "Oscar Wilde No. 18." Sarony printed a copyright notice on each copy of the photograph which read: "Copyright, 1882, by N. Sarony."

Burrow-Giles had printed reproductions of the Oscar Wilde picture without Sarony's permission. Burrow-Giles argued that a photographer cannot be considered an author and therefore cannot hold the copyright to the photo. However, the Court disagreed and awarded Sarony $600 in damages (remember, this was 1883). At the time of this case, photography was a rather new medium and did not exist at the time the original copyright act was created.

This case defined an author as the person "to whom anything owes its origin; originator; maker...." The Court in its opinion restated Lord Justice Cotton's earlier definition of an author: "In my opinion, author involves originating, making, producing, as the inventive or master-mind, the thing which is to be protected, whether it be a drawing, or a painting, or a photograph."

The author of a work protected under copyright has a variety of rights. These include the right to make and distribute copies of the work, to create adaptations, and to publicly display and perform the work.

Requirement Of Originality

Copyright protection is available only to original works. But what is the definition of original? An original work must be the result of an independent effort. Here's an example.

United Card Company and Roth Greeting Cards were both in the business of manufacturing greeting cards for sale through gift and card stores. United president, Mr. Koenig, and vice president, Mr. Letwenko, produced a series of seven cards that bore an amazing resemblance to seven cards already produced by Roth. When Roth found out about this, *Roth Greeting Cards* v. *United Card Co.*[5] resulted.

Roth's suit was for copyright infringement. While United claimed that the cards it produced were its own creations, it admitted to "visiting greeting card stores and gift shows in order to observe what was going on in the greeting card business." In addition, Roth had a complete staff of writers and artists, while United had none. In fact, most of United's work was done by Koenig and Letwenko themselves.

Although the United cards were not exact duplications of the Roth cards, they were "in total concept and feel the...same as the copyrighted cards of Roth," even to the casual observer. Since the Roth cards were the originals, they were protected by copyright. As a result, United lost the case.

THE SCOPE OF COPYRIGHT PROTECTION

Anyone who deals with advertising needs to understand copyright law and what it protects. Certain works can be copyrighted, others cannot. Now we take a closer look at what can and cannot be protected.

Under the current definition, almost any form of expression can be covered under the Copyright Act. For the advertiser, the most common forms of copyright works include:

- Photographs, television commercials, videos, computer files and images;
- Illustrations, renderings, cartoons, prints, charts, models, mock-ups, drawings;
- Sound recordings, radio commercials, music;
- Ads, billboards, brochures, displays; and
- Literary works.

Generally, items that are not eligible to be copyrighted include the following:

- Works that have not been fixed in a tangible form. For example, if a person creates a song in his mind, it must be put in writing or some other tangible form to be copyrighted. The thought is not tangible because others cannot perceive it;
- Titles, names, short phrases and slogans, symbols, or design elements. These items could be protected under trademark law in certain cases however. See Chapter 7;
- Ideas, procedures, methods, systems, processes, concepts, principles, discoveries, devices, and machines. These, would be protected under patent law, if the item qualified; and
- Works that are only common property information and have no original authorship. This includes items such as calendars, rulers, public lists, etc.

Copyright Protects Only A Specific Item

Copyright, as we have seen, protects the work from unauthorized duplication or copying. The work might be in any form, from a brochure to a photograph, a drawing, a sign, or a television commercial. However, copyright protects only the tangible medium used. As an example, if a photograph of a house is copyrighted, only the specific photograph is protected, not the house that is depicted in the photograph.

This situation actually occurred in *Modern Aids, Inc.* v. *R. H. Macy & Co.*[6] Modern Aids ran newspaper ads for its product, a massage machine. Macy duplicated the machine almost exactly, which was legal since there was no patent on the machine. However, Macy also copied Modern Aids' ad, which was illegal. The Modern Aids ad was copyrighted and therefore protected. Yet the machine shown in the ad was not protected by copyright.

Objects Of Use Are Not Copyrightable

Items that do not in and of themselves convey information are considered items of use. While a blank account book cannot be copyrighted, a specific one with entries in it can be.

Objects which are only objects of use may not be copyrighted. Things like time cards, account books, diaries, bank checks, score cards, address books, and order forms fall into this category.

Copyright Of Compilations, Derivative Works, And Collections

Derivative works such as compilations or collective works may be copyrighted in some cases. A derivative work may include a work based on one or a number of preexisting works: translations, abridgements, fictionalizations, a motion picture adapted from a novel, reproductions, or condensations. Collective works also include periodicals, anthologies, or encyclopedias, where a number of separate works are brought together into one entity.

A compilation is a collection or assemblage of preexisting works. According to the Copyright Act, a compilation is "data that are selected, coordinated, or arranged in such a way that the resulting work as a whole constitutes an original work of authorship."[7] It is important to keep in mind that in order for the derivative work or collection to be copyrighted, it must have enough originality in itself to merit protection. Also, it must not infringe any other existing copyrights. To avoid violations, permission must be obtained from the original authors.

A person who assembles these separate works into one unit would be considered the author of the collective work, and, if the work is copyrighted, that person would be the owner of that copyright. But the owner of the collection of works only owns the rights to the *collection*, not to the individual works composing the collection.

Rand McNally, in 1978 and again in 1982, produced the *Rand McNally Mileage Guides* for sale to the public. These guides listed mileage figures between various cities throughout the United States. Rand McNally gathered the distance figures for its guide from various city, county, and state maps in the public domain. It also examined road conditions, compensated for variations between map sources, and broke down the distances into smaller segments. Unavailable mileage figures between some cities were developed from scales between other cities. *Rand McNally Mileage Guides* were compilations and were copyrighted. As we saw earlier, individual facts cannot be copyrighted, yet certain compilations of facts can be protected under copyright.

A problem arose when Fleet Management System copied virtually all of the figures listed in the *Rand McNally Mileage Guides* to produce mileage guides of its own. This all came to light in *Rand McNally & Co.* v. *Fleet Management Sys. Inc.*,[8] where the court determined that Rand McNally held valid copyrights to the compilation and that Fleet Management had infringed on its copyright. Keep in mind that it was not the individual figures that were protected under the copyright but the collection of data that had been copied almost in total that constituted the violation.

PROTECTION OF COPYRIGHT

To be protected by copyright, the author must abide by certain rules.

Notice Of Copyright

When something is considered important enough to protect, it should be identified by a copyright notice. The notice must consist of three items: a "C" with a circle around it for visual works or a "P" with a circle around it for audio works (or the word "copyright" may be used), the year of first publication, and the copyright owner's name. Under the Copyright Statute, the following format should appear:

- Copyright 1987, John Doe & Company. All Rights Reserved; or
- ©1987 John Doe & Company. All Rights Reserved.

The phrase "all rights reserved," is not required in the United States, but is necessary for protection in foreign countries. Ideally, each copy of the material should bear this notice clearly and conspicuously. Proper notice shows the world that the owner claims the copyright to the work. Typically, copyright notice should be placed on:

- A photograph – printed on the back of the print;
- A slide or negative – attached to the sleeve;
- A TV commercial or video – legibly displayed on the screen at the beginning or end of the spot for at least two to three seconds;
- A magazine or newspaper ad – printed legibly in the corner of the ad;

- A radio commercial – printed on the box label and tape reel;
- Original artwork – printed on the back of the original; and
- A book, report, or other literary work – printed on the title page at the front of the work.

Publication Of Copyrightable Work

Publication is defined legally as "the distribution of copies ...of a work to the public by sale or other transfer of ownership, or by rental, lease or lending. The offering to distribute copies...to a group of persons for purposes of further distribution, public performance, or public display, constitutes publication."[9]

In other words, when someone gives a copy of an original work to another in connection with a proposal, the original is considered published, so it is important that the original and any copies clearly display the copyright notice. Unless this is done, an inadvertent publication by another may cause loss of protection.

Registering For Copyright

Ideally, a copyright should be registered as soon as the work is fixed in a concrete, tangible form, but in any case, must be registered with the Copyright Office within five years of the date of first publication. If notice was not placed on the work, the author must make a reasonable attempt to add the notice to all works distributed after discovery of the omission.

Although registering a work is not required to secure protection under copyright, there are valid reasons why the author should do so. Most importantly, registration of the copyright protects the author by providing evidence of ownership. This is a crucial point for legal support of an author's claim to copyright protection. If a work is infringed upon, prior registration is required before a lawsuit may be initiated.

To register a copyright, the appropriate form must be completed. This form, along with copies of the work and a fee must be sent to the Register of Copyrights, Copyright Office, Library of Congress, Washington, D.C. 20559.

That office can be contacted to obtain the required forms. Remember, there are different forms for different types of works, and it is important to use the proper one for registration. Here's a list of the current forms:

- **TX**: Nondramatic works, literary works;
- **SE**: Serials, successive items bearing numerical or chronological designations (newsletters, magazines, annuals, etc.);
- **PA**: Performing arts (musicals, dramatic works, motion pictures, audiovisual works, etc.);
- **VA**: Visual arts (pictorial, graphic works, sculpture, advertisements, etc.);
- **SR**: Sound recordings;
- **RE**: Renewal registration;
- **CA**: Corrections or amplifications; and
- **GR/CP**: Group contributions to periodicals.

Duration Of Copyright Protection

Copyright protection begins when the original work is fixed in some tangible form by the original author. Protection continues for the life of the author plus 50 years after his or her death. In works-for-hire situations, which we will discuss later in the chapter, the duration of protection is 75 years from the first publication date or 100 years from creation of the work, whichever is shorter.

TRANSFER OF COPYRIGHT TO OTHERS

The rights to a copyright are transferable, usually by assignment or licensing. The transfer of exclusive rights, i.e., where only the grantee (person to whom the rights are given) can use the rights, is valid only if made in writing and signed by the holder of the copyright, the grantor (person granting the rights). Transfer of nonexclusive rights need not be in writing. Remember though, whenever a copyright is transferred or licensed, it must be recorded with the Copyright Office.

Compulsory Licensing Of Copyright

Compulsory licensing covers certain works that others can use after the payment of a fee set by the Copyright Office, instead of the copyright owner agreeing to the use. This practice is common in the music industry. Here's how it works: If an agency wants to use a musical piece in a commercial, notice is served on the owner of the copyright, and monthly royalties are paid to the owner. Cable television can also obtain a compulsory license for the transmission of copyrighted works. Royalties are paid as a percentage of the gross receipts of the cable system to the Copyright Royalty Tribunal (a clearinghouse for accounting and disbursement of royalties) and later distributed to the owners.

Assignment Of Rights

Many authors assign their rights to organizations who, in turn, authorize usage by others for a fee. Organizations such as ASCAP (American Society for Composers, Artists and Publishers) hold copyrights for many musical works. Broadcasters and commercial users are required to pay a fee to ASCAP, which is then distributed to the owners for the use of material.

THE "WORKS-FOR-HIRE" RULE

When an employer, person or company has an employee or agent perform work, the employer is considered the author and the owner of the copyright of that work. Under copyright law this is called work "made-for-hire." In other words, when the work is made by an employee (work-for-hire), the actual person who created it does not own the copyright. The person who employed the worker does.

"Works-for-hire" include items produced by an employee within the scope of his employment. If an employee of the company is asked to photograph a product, the company is the owner of the copyright in the photograph and it is a work-for-hire. However, work created outside the scope of his employment is owned by the employee and not the employer. The concept or term also covers works specifically ordered or commissioned for a particular purpose, if there is an agreement in writing that the work was done for hire. However, a work-for-hire does not normally include routine professional services on behalf of a client, unless there is an agreement to the contrary.

Ownership problems can arise when an independent contractor is commissioned to create work. To illustrate, if a photographer is hired by a company to photograph a product made by that company, the photographer is the copyright owner. This is not considered a work-for-hire situation unless there is an agreement to the contrary.

The best way to avoid copyright ownership problems when dealing with independent contractors (including freelancers) is to have them sign a written document designating that all materials created by the freelancer are works "made for hire" and that the creator transfers and assigns all rights and interest to the company commissioning the work. This should be put into written form and given to the independent contractor to sign prior to beginning work. One document can be prepared that will cover any work performed after the effective date of the agreement. Remember, the independent contractor must transfer rights, establishing that the work is made for hire in writing, or ownership problems may arise.

COPYRIGHT AND PROTECTION OF IDEAS

One point about copyright must be made clear. Copyright does not protect an idea *per se*. It does, however, protect the *expression* of an idea. If the expression of the original idea is recognizable in another work, to the extent that an infringement is created, a lawsuit may result.

I'll clarify this point. If Widget Manufacturing Company designed and built a new widget refurbisher, the company cannot copyright the machine. We saw earlier that devices may not copyrighted. If anything, the machine would need to be protected under patent law. However, to produce a brochure for its new product, Widget Manufacturing had a photograph taken of the machine. That picture could be copyrighted as it is an expression of the idea. But the copyright only protects the photo, not the widget. Let's take a closer look at this concept.

Copyright Does Not Protect Ideas *Per Se*

As we saw in the previous section, copyright is limited in scope. It does not protect against the use of an idea. Copyright protection does not cover "any idea, procedure, system, method of operation, concept, principle, or discovery, regardless of the form in which it is described, explained, illustrated, or embodied in such work."[10]

Copyright Protects The Expression Of An Idea

Copyright might be used to stem an unauthorized expression of an idea. An expression of an idea can take almost any form. An advertisement, a movie, a book, and even a video game can all be expressions of ideas. Unlike a patent, copyright protects only the expression – the tangible fixed form used to allow others to perceive the idea – not the idea itself.

Atari and Midway own the exclusive copyrights for a video game called "PAC-MAN." Atari markets a home video version of the game. Shortly after PAC-MAN hit the market, another company, North American Philips Consumer Electronics, hired independent contractor Ed Averett to create a video game, which was named "K. C. Munchkin." Averett was very well qualified for the task since he had developed over 21 other such games. Mr. Staup, who was the head of North American's video game development department, and Averett got together and visited various sites to see and play PAC-MAN.

The two men discussed the PAC-MAN game, its strengths and weaknesses, and decided to develop a version of the game for North American's Odyssey line of home video games. Averett began work on the project and when it was completed, he showed it to North American, which examined the game and determined that it was totally different from PAC-MAN. However, its legal counsel told North American that the game should be changed even more to avoid any potential liability. Averett made a few changes to the game, which was then produced and marketed to the public.

Stores in various cities ran advertisements promoting the new game. Typical of these ads were those in the *Chicago SunTimes* and the *Tribune*, which described the K. C. Munchkin game as "a PAC-MAN type game." The ads also claimed that it was "as challenging as PAC-MAN." When Atari learned of the new game, it produced its own response: *Atari Inc.* v. *North American Philips Consumer Elecs.*[11]

Atari sued for copyright infringement because North American's game was so similar to PAC-MAN. Atari argued that an ordinary consumer would assume that K. C. Munchkin was taken directly from PAC-MAN. Atari needed to prove that K. C. Munchkin was "substantially similar" to PAC-MAN. And it did just that.

The problem in cases like this is that there is no concrete rule or test to determine if an idea or the expression of an idea has been taken. It is a very subjective decision, as was addressed in the Atari case. "Obviously, no principle can be stated as to when an imitator has gone beyond copying the 'idea,' and has borrowed its 'expression.'" The video board game "idea" cannot be protected. But the specific form, PAC-MAN, which is the expression of the game (idea), can be protected. It is the individual features of the game shapes, sizes, colors, sequences, arrangements, and sounds taken as a whole that form an expression. Exact duplication or almost exact duplication is not necessary. "[A]n infringement... includes also the various modes in which the matter...may be adopted, imitated, transferred, or reproduced, with more or less colorable alterations to disguise the piracy."[12]

The main consideration given by the courts in these situations is the overall similarities, not the minute differences between the works.

The features of K. C. Munchkin were very similar to PAC-MAN. Those of you who have played the game would instantly recognize it as a copy. The main "Gobbler" characters in both games are very similar in shape, mouth, and movement, as well as the sounds they make. The same applies to the other characters of the two games. The board field is also very similar, as is the method of play and the rules and object of the game. The K. C. Munchkin game uses the same role-reversal and regeneration characteristics of PAC-MAN, as well. There was no doubt in this case that there was copyright infringement. Atari won a permanent injunction and substantial damages.

THE FAIR USE DOCTRINE

All holders of copyright are susceptible to the "fair use doctrine," which permits certain copying of copyrighted material for purposes of criticism, news reporting, teaching, or research. Generally, however, copying for commercial use violates the rights of the copyright holder. The fair use doctrine will not protect advertisers who try to use copyrighted material for commercial purposes without paying for it.

Fair use was developed to balance authors' rights to protection of their copyrights and accompanying economic compensation against the public's desire for a free flow of ideas and information. Basically, the doctrine tries to achieve a safe area between copyright protection and freedom of speech.

Fair Use Protection Against Infringement

The main issue that the courts look to in determining if the use falls under the fair use doctrine is whether the usage substantially diminishes the value of the work.

One of the most notable examples of fair use was shown in the landmark case involving Universal City Studios and its suit against Sony. This case discussed a then new area of copyright – copying by home video recorders – that Congress could not have conceived would occur when it enacted the first Copyright Act. Sony manufactured millions of its Betamax video tape recorders and sold them through many retail outlets.

Universal owned the copyrights to many of the movies, television programs, and other programming it broadcast over television stations across the country. In *Sony Corp.* v. *Universal City Studios*,[13] Universal claimed that by Sony providing the means to copy or record these shows from television, people were violating copyright laws. Universal was claiming essentially contributory infringement in its suit because although Sony could not infringe on Universal's copyrights directly, Sony contributed to it through consumers who bought and used the video recorders to record movies. However, Universal's argument in court was not valid under the Copyright Act. Contributory infringement did not exist here anymore than it would for a camera manufacturer or a photocopy machine manufacturer.

Sony further argued that the video recorders allowed the consumer to time-record from television. This allowed the consumer to watch the show when it was more convenient, actually expanding the television viewing audience that would watch the program. Therefore, the copyright holder could not object to the home recording of copyrighted material. The key here was whether the home recording impaired the commercial value of the work now or in the future. In this case it was ruled that it did not.

The court determined, in a 22-page opinion, that noncommercial home recording of copyrighted material broadcast over public television was fair use and did not constitute copyright infringement. Noncommercial is the operative word here because there would be no reduction in the market for the original work.

Although every commercial use of copyrighted material without permission is a copyright infringement, noncommercial uses are a different matter. In order to uphold a claim of infringement through noncommercial uses, it must be shown that allowing the use could cause some harm or could damage the potential market for the work. If the copyrighted material is used for commercial use, that likelihood is presumed, but for noncommercial use it must be shown. Universal tried to argue that by allowing its shows to be recorded at home, "live television or movie audiences will decrease as more people watch Betamax tapes as an alternative." The court disagreed and Sony won.

Here's an example that relates to advertising directly. *The Miami Herald*, published by Knight-Ridder Newspapers, developed an ad campaign to promote the new format of its magazine-style television supplement to the newspaper. The Sunday supplement was introduced in the newspaper in November 1977. The campaign included print ads and television commercials.

The focus of the *Miami Herald's* campaign was to compare its television magazine to *TV Guide* magazine. The print ads showed the covers of both magazines in actual size, with the headline which read:

The *Herald's* new TV book.
It's a little bit bigger
and a little bit better.

The message in the ad was that the *Miami Herald's* book was bigger, had more listings, was easier to read, and was more up-to-date than *TV Guide* magazine. In the television commercials, the message was the same. A typical spot, based on the Goldilocks and the Three Bears theme, went like this:

Narrator:
"This is the story of Sidney Bear, Cindy Bear, and Junior Bear."
"They all loved to watch TV, but ...."

Older man:
"This TV book is too small."

Child:
"This TV book is too big."

Older woman:
"This TV section is just right."

Narrator:
"It was the *Sunday Herald's* new TV book at no extra cost. The three bears loved the new, just-right size with its up-to-date and more complete listings. "Til one day this little blonde kid—uh, but that's another story. Something for everybody. Everyday of the week."

When Triangle Publications, the owner of *TV Guide* magazine, heard about these ads, it brought suit. In *Triangle Publications* v. *Knight-Ridder*,[14] Triangle objected to the reproduction of a *TV Guide* cover in both print ads and television commercials. The issue was whether the use of the *TV Guide* cover in the Herald's ads was allowed under the fair use doctrine.

The court determined that the *Herald's* ads did not copy the essence of *TV Guide*; that is, the articles, schedules, and features contained inside. The *Herald* reproduced only the cover of the magazine. This, the court reasoned, was not enough to determine that the commercial value of *TV Guide's* copyright would be diminished. In fact, if the *Herald's* ads drew customers away from *TV Guide*, it would have been because of the validity of the message – the difference between the two publications rather than showing the *TV Guide* cover.

The court concluded by saying *TV Guide* "suffered no economic injury whatever from the alleged infringement of its copyright." The *Herald* won its claim of fair use. For a discussion of comparative advertising issues, which parallels this case, see Chapter 8.

The Final Insult

Paramount Pictures produced the movie *Naked Gun 33 1/3: The Final Insult.* Advertising to promote the movie included an image of Leslie Nielsen's smirking face superimposed on the body of a nude pregnant woman. Paramount superimposed Nielsen's face on a photograph that very closely resembled a photograph taken by Annie Leibovitz of actress Demi Moore that had run on the August 1991 cover of *Vanity Fair* magazine. The pregnant Moore, nude, was shown from the side, with her right hand and arm covering her breasts and her left hand supporting her stomach (ala Botticelli's Birth of Venus). Moore had a ring on her middle finger and was wearing a very serious expression.

In August 1993, Paramount hired the design firm, Dazu, Inc., to create and produce an advertising and promotional campaign for the upcoming movie. Dazu showed Paramount four ads with composite photographs of Nielsen's face in place of what had been the faces of Sharon Stone, Madonna, Jane Fonda, and Demi Moore. Each proposed ad included a slogan that related to the March release date of the film. The composite photograph depicting Nielsen as the pregnant Moore slyly announcing: "DUE THIS MARCH." Paramount approved the concept and selected the composite of Moore's body and Nielsen's face.

Instead of copying the original photograph, Paramount

hired another photographer to take the image of a nude pregnant woman, similarly posed. The photograph resembled, in great detail, Leibovitz's photo. Neilsen's face was then superimposed on the model's body.

Leibovitz v. *Paramount Pictures Corp.*[15] was the case that resulted. Paramount claimed that its advertising was a parody of Leibovitz's original photograph. And as such, was a fair use. According to the court, the fair use doctrine "permits the use of copyrighted material without the owner's consent in a reasonable manner for certain purposes." Leibovitz argued that because the advertising was used for commercial purposes, Paramount could not use the fair use defense.

As we have seen in other cases, whether a use is "fair" involves:

1. The purpose and character of the work;
2. The nature of the copyrighted work;
3. The amount and substantiality of the work used; and
4. The effect of the use on the market for the original.

Although "parody" is not specifically mentioned in the Copyright statute as permissible fair use, courts have long afforded such works some measure of protection. The court reasoned that the *Naked Gun* ad was commenting on, and essentially making fun of, the original Leibovitz photograph. The court said: "[B]ecause the smirking face of Nielsen contrasts so strikingly with the serious expression on the face of Moore, the ad may reasonably be perceived as commenting on the seriousness, even the pretentiousness, of the original."

The court cautioned, however, that simply being different from the original did not necessarily mean a work "commented" on the original. In this instance however, the Neilsen photograph could be perceived as commenting, through parody, on the original photograph.

The court analyzed its position on the parody by stating:

A. First factor. We inquire whether Paramount's advertisement "may reasonably be perceived," as a new work that "at least in part, comments on" Leibovitz's photograph. Plainly, the ad adds something new and qualifies as a "transformative" work. Whether it "comments" on the original is a somewhat closer question. Because the smirking face of Nielsen contrasts so strikingly with the serious expression on the face of Moore, the ad may reasonably be perceived as commenting on the seriousness, even the pretentiousness, of the original. The contrast achieves the effect of ridicule that the Court recognized in *Campbell* would serve as a sufficient "comment" to tip the first factor in a parodist's favor. ("It is this joinder of reference and ridicule that marks off the author's choice of parody from the other types of comment and criticism that traditionally have had a claim to fair use protection as transformative works.")

In saying this, however, we have some concern about the ease with which every purported parodist could win on the first factor simply by pointing out some feature that contrasts with the original. Being different from an original does not inevitably "comment" on the original. Nevertheless, the ad is not merely different; it differs in a way that may reasonably be perceived as commenting, through ridicule, on what a viewer might reasonably think is the undue self-importance conveyed by the subject of the Leibovitz photograph. A photographer posing a well known actress in a manner that calls to mind a well known painting must expect, or at least tolerate, a parodist's deflating ridicule.

Apart from ridiculing pretentiousness, the ad

might also be reasonably perceived as interpreting the Leibovitz photograph to extol the beauty of the pregnant female body, and, rather unchivalrously, to express disagreement with this message. The District Court thought such a comment was reasonably to be perceived from the contrast between "a serious portrayal of a beautiful woman taking great pride in the majesty of her pregnant body...[and] a ridiculous image of a smirking, foolish-looking pregnant man."

The fact that the ad makes a parodic comment on the original does not end the first-factor analysis, however, because the ad was created and displayed to promote a commercial product, the film. This advertising use lessens the "indulgence" to which the parodic ad is entitled. Paramount seeks to mitigate the negative force of the advertising purpose by arguing that the advertisement should be viewed as an extension of the film, rather than merely an advertisement for it. Paramount emphasizes the general jocular nature of the film, as well as the film's specific humorous treatment of pregnancy and parenthood.

Though the advertising purpose of a parodic copying should not be entirely discounted simply because the ad promotes a humorous work, there is some slight force to Paramount's argument. For those who see the movie, the parodic comment of the ad might reasonably be perceived as reenforced by the kidding comments of the movie concerning pregnancy and parenthood.

On balance, the strong parodic nature of the ad tips the first factor significantly toward fair use, even after making some discount for the fact that it promotes a commercial product. "[L]ess indulgence" does not mean no indulgence at all.

B. Second Factor. Though Paramount concedes the obvious point that Leibovitz's photograph exhibited significant creative expression, ...the creative nature of an original will normally not provide much help in determining whether a parody of the original is fair use. The second factor therefore favors Leibovitz, but the weight attributed to it in this case is slight.

C. Third Factor. In assessing the amount and substantiality of the portion used, we must focus only on the protected elements of the original. Leibovitz is entitled to no protection for the appearance in her photograph of the body of a nude, pregnant female. Only the photographer's particular expression of such a body is entitled to protection. Thus, to whatever extent Leibovitz is contending that the ad takes the "heart" of the original, she must limit her contention to the particular way the body of Moore is portrayed, rather than the fact that the ad copies the appearance of a nude, pregnant body. Moreover, in the context of parodies, "the heart is also what most readily conjures up the [original] for parody, and it is the heart at which parody takes aim." Thus, the third-factor inquiry in the parody context concerns "what else the parodist did besides go to the heart of the original."

Paramount went to great lengths to have its ad copy protectable aspects of the Leibovitz photograph. Even though the basic pose of a nude, pregnant body and the position of the hands, if ever protectable, were placed into the public domain by painters and sculptors long before Botticelli,

> Leibovitz is entitled to protection for such artistic elements as the particular lighting, the resulting skin tone of the subject, and the camera angle that she selected. ("Elements of originality in a photograph may include posing the subjects, lighting, angle, selection of film and camera, evoking the desired expression, and almost any other variant involved.")
>
> The copying of these elements, carried out to an extreme degree by the technique of digital computer enhancement, took more of the Leibovitz photograph than was minimally necessary to conjure it up, but *Campbell* instructs that a parodist's copying of more of an original than is necessary to conjure it up will not necessarily tip the third factor against fair use. On the contrary, "[o]nce enough has been taken to assure identification," as plainly occurred here, the reasonableness of taking additional aspects of the original depends on the extent to which the "overriding purpose and character" of the copy "is to parody the original," and "the likelihood that the parody may serve as a market substitute for the original." That approach leaves the third factor with little, if any, weight against fair use so long as the first and fourth factors favor the parodist. Since those factors favor fair use in this case, the third factor does not help Leibovitz, even though the degree of copying of protectable elements was extensive.

At the trial, it became apparent that the use of the parody did not weaken the market for the original photograph. While the court did determine that Paramount copied more of the original photo than necessary to conjure up the parody, the first and fourth factors allowed the use. The court held that the advertising was a parody.

When A Fair Use Argument Does Not Protect Against Infringement

The fair use doctrine has been used to allow certain forms of parody, i.e., when the "style of...[a] work is closely imitated for comic effect...."[16] But the advertiser must understand the limits of the doctrine. To determine whether the use made of a copyrighted work can be considered fair use, the following need to be considered:

- The purpose and character of the use, including whether such use is of a commercial nature or is for nonprofit educational purposes;
- The nature of the copyrighted work;
- The amount and substantiality of the portion used in relation to the copyrighted work as a whole; and
- The effect of the use upon the potential market for or value of the copyrighted work.[17]

On the other hand, in the advertising area, a parody can fall outside the fair use doctrine when another company's theme, tag line, or primary characteristic is taken. Sambo's restaurants found this out when Dr. Pepper sued it for copyright infringement.

Dr. Pepper developed its *"Be a Pepper"* campaign in 1978. Within four years the company had spent over $100 million on the campaign and had realized tremendous results. Dr. Pepper was so pleased with the results that it planned for the campaign to run another 10 years.

In many cases, success breeds imitation. Here, Dr. Pepper was the success, Sambo's was the imitation. While the Dr. Pepper campaign was in its fourth year, Sambo's ad agency, Bozell & Jacobs, developed a campaign called "Dancing Seniors."

Both commercials started with one person (the leader) dancing and singing the beginning of a jingle. In the Dr. Pepper commercial, the leader sang, "I drink Dr. Pepper and I'm proud. I'm part of an original crowd." In the Sambo's commercial: "I eat at Sambo's Restaurants every day. I get a special deal on my dinner meal." Both commercials used people dancing along with the leader to a chorus:

For Dr. Pepper: "Wouldn't you like to be a Pepper, too?"

For Sambo's: "Don't you want to be a senior, too?"

The Sambo's commercials first aired in late 1980, and when Dr. Pepper learned of this in January 1981, it sued in *Dr. Pepper Co.* v. *Sambo's Restaurants, Inc.*[18] Dr. Pepper held copyrights to its television commercials and to the "Be a Pepper" jingle. As a defense to the case, Sambo's claimed that it was entitled to parody the Dr. Pepper commercial under the Fair Use Doctrine.

However, any commercial use has a tendency to contradict the fair use doctrine. This is a very risky area for advertisers. Because of Sambo's use of the essence and substance of the Dr. Pepper commercial, it diminished that spot's value, uniqueness, and originality. This took the infringement out of the fair use arena. Sambo's impact on the useful life of the "Be a Pepper" campaign was an infringement and Sambo's lost.

What about fair use of copyrighted material that was not another commercial? Parody or satirization is a common and legal practice in all forms of entertainment and social commentary under the fair use doctrine. However, it is not allowed in advertising.

Miller Brewing Company, its advertising agency Backer & Spielvogel, and comedian (the performer in the commercial) Joe Piscopo were sued by a rap music group, the Fat Boys. The case, *Tin Pan Apple, Inc.* v. *Miller Brewing Co., Inc.*,[19] involved a television commercial that infringed the copyright of some of the Fat Boys' songs. Miller argued that the similarity between the Fat Boys composition was allowed under the Fair Use Doctrine because the commercial was simply a parody of rap music in general, and of the Fat Boys in particular. In Miller's argument, they discounted the fact that the music and action used in the commercial was "substantially similar," the test for copyright infringement, to the Fat Boys' songs and performances.

Miller tried to use a 1989 case where a federal court ruled that a song entitled "I Love Sodom," used in a skit on the television program *Saturday Night Live*, did not infringe the copyrighted song "I Love New York." This was clearly because the purpose of the skit was to satirize the way in which New York City had attempted to rectify its rather tarnished image through the use of a comprehensive advertising campaign. This form of parody was protected under the fair use rule because it was used for social satire, rather than commercial advertising.

Although the parody defense is viable in situations where parts of the copyrighted work are used for social comment or criticism, the defense did not apply in the *Miller* case because its use was solely for the purpose of promoting the sale of a commercial product; in this case, beer. Commercial advertising cannot use the doctrine of fair use to defend an illegal use of copyrighted material.

As we have just seen, the more unique the concept of the commercial, the greater the protection required against infringement. If the commercial is based on more general situations, greater latitude will be allowed. Any car commercial may use a showroom as its setting with a car salesman speaking to the audience. However, if the bulk of the commercial shows a salesman announcing claims about the car, which are obvious and blatant lies, and subtitles are shown (as in the past Isuzu commercials), the courts will be more inclined to consider this type of use an infringement.

The Big One

Columbia Picture's 1997 movie *Men in Black*, grossed over $250 million at the box office in the United States and over $337 million in its international theatrical run. Merchandise licensing included posters, toys, video games, T-shirts, hats, games, greeting cards, and books. Further, millions of copies of the single and musical soundtrack to *Men in Black* have been sold.

Michael Moore's documentary entitled *The Big One* (TBO) was advertised with posters that infringed the *Men in Black* (MIB) movie poster. *Columbia Pictures Industries, Inc.* v. *Miramax Films Corp.*[20] was the case.

The movie *The Big One* opened on April 10, 1998. It was a documentary about the consequences of corporate America's focus on achieving maximum profits while turning a blind eye to the consequences, including plant closings, employee layoffs, and employee benefit reductions.

The advertising and poster used to promote the MIB movie featured Will Smith and Tommy Lee Jones wearing black suits, white shirts, black ties, and sunglasses. They carried over-sized weapons and had serious expressions. The copy read: "Protecting the Earth from the scum of the Universe." On the other hand, the poster for *The Big One* featured Michael Moore wearing essentially the same cloths, standing in front of a skyline of New York City. Moore's hair was disheveled and he was also wearing a black baseball cap. He was carrying an over-sized microphone and was smirking. The copy read: "Protecting the Earth from the scum of Corporate America."

The court discussed the requirements to establish copyright infringement:

> Plaintiffs must prove: (1) that Plaintiffs owned the allegedly infringed work; and (2) that Defendants copied Plaintiffs' copyrighted work. "Copying" is composed of two parts: (1) circumstantial evidence of the defendant's access to the copyrighted work; and (2) substantial similarity between the copyrighted work and the defendant's work. "Substantial similarity" refers to similarity of expression, not merely similarity of ideas or concepts.

The court found that *The Big One* poster infringed the MIB poster. The court explained: "The TBO poster is substantially similar to the expressive ideas contained in the MIB poster in that both contain: (1) figures carrying a large object; (2) figures of a similar size with similar stances; (3) figures standing in front of a New York skyline at night; (4) a similar manner of expression; (5) similar color; and (6) an identical layout."

In addition to the poster infringement, the court also found that the TBO trailers infringed the MIB trailers. It said: "The MIB Trailers are substantially similar to the expressive ideas contained in the TBO Trailers. The trailers contain a virtually identical theme, format, pace, and sequence of events."

Miramax also attempted to use a fair use defense, claiming that its use of the copyrighted materials was a fair use. In support of their fair use argument, the defendants contend that the TBO Trailer pokes fun at the MIB image by suggesting that an unfit documentation may "assume the mantle of hero and do battle against the villains of corporate America, as the [*Men in Black*] do battle against aliens." The defendants argued that advertising for *The Big One* "does not merely use the original concept to promote itself or as a vehicle to satirize some other subject. Rather, [the] advertising directly targets [*Men in Black*] for comment."

The court explained:

> The fair use defense permits courts to avoid rigid application of the copyright statute when, on occasion, it would stifle the very creativity which that law is designed to foster.

The Copyright Act sets four factors for courts to consider in determining if a fair use defense exists in any given case: (1) the purpose and character of the accused use; (2) the nature of the copyrighted work; (3) the importance of the portion used in relation to the copyrighted work as a whole; and (4) the effect of the accused use on the potential market for or value of the copyrighted work.

Because of this, the court rejected the defendant's fair use defense. The poster and trailers were created for commercial purposes. The poster and trailers merely copied the bulk of the MIB poster and trailers and were clearly intended, according to the court, to get attention for *The Big One.*

The court stated:

> In this case, The TBO Poster and Trailer do not create a "transformative work." The TBO advertisements cannot reasonably be perceived as commenting on or criticizing the ads for "Men In Black." The TBO Poster merely incorporates several elements of the MIB Poster: figures with a particular stance carrying large weapons, standing in front of the New York skyline at night, with a similar layout. Similarly, the TBO Trailer appears to be little more than an effort to "get attention" for *The Big One* and "avoid the drudgery in working up something fresh."

The TBO poster and trailer were designed solely for the purpose of attracting viewers to see *The Big One.* As such, Miramax has merely used the copyrighted work as a vehicle to poke fun at another target – corporate America. It has not used its advertising to comment on or criticize the copyrighted work.

Carazy Copyright

Louis Psihoyos was a photographer who took the photo of Larry Fuente in front of his wildly decorated Cadillac called the Mad Cad. This was not your typical Cadillac. Fuente extended the tail fins of the car by several feet using a dazzling edifice of beads and rhinestones that look like flames rising into the air. The curly flames were really a mosaic of flamingoes, geese, ducks, and horses arranged one atop the other. The beads and rhinestones of many colors, including pink, gold, silver, and aqua, decorate these fins and the rest of the car.

The Examiner published a news magazine called *The National Examiner.* The Examiner claimed that it obtained a slide of Psihoyos' photograph from the publisher of the book: *Art Cars: Revolutionary Movement.* The Examiner maintained that it thought that the publisher had given authorization to reproduce the slide.

In its July 22, 1997, issue, the Examiner reproduced Psihoyos' photograph. The Examiner did not obtain permission from either Psihoyos or Fuente for the use the photograph. The photograph was used as part of a pictorial entitled "CARAZY: Take a ride on the wild side in kookie vehicles."

Along with the photo was the text:

> AMERICANS wheely love their cars, and some folks have even turned them into wacky works of movable art! They've let their imaginations run wild and used anything and everything to decorate their car-azy hot rods. So, next time you hit the road, see if you spot one of these awesome autos.

In *Psihoyos* v. *National Examiner*,[21] the Examiner contended that its use of the photograph was a fair use because it was being used for news reporting or commenting purposes. The court disagreed. The Examiner used the photo to create commercial interest in its magazine.

Moreover, the use adversely impacted the copyright owner's market for the original photograph. The court concluded that the Examiner's piece could compete with the original. According to the court: "Psihoyos states that the Examiner's piece adversely impacted the potential market for his work because he did not earn licensing fees from the Examiner and because the Examiner's piece can be used as a poster, reducing demands for the original.

The Court agrees."

The Examiner's fair use argument was rejected as well. The court stated:

> Fair use has been defined as "a privilege in others than the owner of the copyright to use the copyrighted material in a reasonable manner without his consent." Congress identified four factors, which are not intended to be exhaustive, to be used in evaluating a defense of fair use. These factors are: (1) the purpose and character of the use; (2) the nature of the copyrighted work; (3) the substantiality of the portion used in relation to the copyrighted work as a whole; and (4) the effect on the potential market for or value of the copyrighted work.

The court went on in detail:

> The central purpose of this investigation is to see...whether the new work merely 'supercede[s] the objects' of the original creation...or instead adds something new, with a further purpose or different character, altering the first with new expression, meaning, or message. Although such transformative use is not absolutely necessary for a finding of fair use,...the goal of copyright, to promote science and the arts, is generally furthered by the creation of transformative works. Such [transformative] works thus lie at the heart of the fair use doctrine's guarantee of breathing space within the confines of copyright...and the more transformative the new work, the less will be the significance of other factors like commercialism, that may weigh against a finding of fair use. The Examiner contends this factor weighs in favor of finding fair use because its

> use of Psihoyos' photo is transformative. Specifically, the Examiner states that as "a news magazine with wide distribution," it used the picture for news reporting or commenting purpose. The Court disagrees.

The Examiner's use is not transformative, because its piece uses the photo to show what it depicts. It is clear from examining the Examiner's article that its purpose was not to comment on the Psihoyos photo but to use it "for precisely a central purpose for which it was created" – to show how an art car looks. Thus, the Examiner's use is not transformative.

The fact that the Examiner used the photo for a commercial rather than a nonprofit educational purpose also weighs against a finding of fair use. The Supreme Court has stated that "the crux of the profit/nonprofit distinction is not whether the sole motive of the use is monetary gain but whether the user stands to profit from exploitation of copyrighted material without paying the customary price." Here, the commercial nature of the Examiner's use is undisputed. The Examiner has commercially exploited the Psihoyos photo to create news – a centerfold consisting of "car-azy hot rods."

The above facts demonstrated to the court that the Examiner's use does not constitute a fair use.

COPYRIGHT PROTECTION RELATING TO ADVERTISEMENTS

Copyright law can, as in the Dr. Pepper case, be used against an ad or commercial derived substantially from another piece. This goes back to the "expression of an idea" concept discussed earlier: that is, if the other commercial takes the same basic feeling or premise. Devising a concept for an advertisement is an idea. A specific ad is an expression of that idea and can be copyrighted.

When An Ad Takes The Expression Of Another Ad

To illustrate this point, let's take, for example, McDonald's campaign developed directly from the H. R. Pufnstuf cartoon characters. When McDonald's agency, Needham, Harper & Steers, developed the McDonaldland concept, it was patterned after the characters in the *H. R. Pufnstuf* TV show. The Pufnstuf television series, which began in 1969, featured a boy named Jimmy, who lived on "Living Island" – a fantasyland inhabited by mayors with large round heads and oversized mouths, Keystone-Cop-type assistants, crazy scientists, multiarmed evil creatures, animated trees having human faces, and talking books. The McDonaldland image used the same location, characters, and elements.

McDonald's even used the people who designed and constructed the sets and costumes for Pufnstuf, as well as some of the same voice people for the campaign. The set itself was the same Living Island concept used in Pufnstuf. In January 1971, the McDonaldland commercials began to air.

The Pufnstuf cartoon characters had previously been licensed for Kellogg's cereal, the *Ice Capades*, as well as other toys and games. In fact, the Ice Capades actually replaced the Pufnstuf characters with the McDonaldland characters after the McDonald's campaign began.

The creators of Pufnstuf sued McDonald's for copyright infringement in *Sid & Marty Krofft* v. *McDonald's*.[22] Even though the specifics of the McDonald's campaign were not identical, they were substantially similar enough to have captured the look and feel of the Pufnstuf characters. McDonald's lost, was required to stop using the ads, and had to pay $50,000 in damages. The credibility of the Pufnstuf characters had been eroded. Pufnstuf even showed loss of licensing (*Ice Capades*) as a direct result of the McDonaldland ad campaign.

The Department Store Wars

Sears ran an advertisement offering "10% off everything... even sale prices when you put it on your Sears card." The offer was good "Thursday, Friday & Saturday only" and claimed "you're in charge!" Menards, a home improvement retailer based in Eau Claire, Wisconsin (and competitor of Sears), ran an ad using the same words and meticulously recreating every detail and design element of the Sears ad. They copied the colors, product placement, offers, typeface, and layout style.

The uniqueness here is that this case deals with one company virtually duplicating the look of another company's ad. Not the usual copyright infringement case, but a situation that does occur. This is a prime example of when it does.

According to the complaint, Menards ran its ad on December 28, 1997, which was essentially "identical" to a Sears ad that had run on November 6, 1997.

Sears immediately contacted Menard demanding that they stop the ad, and Menard sent a letter to Sears stating that it would no longer use the advertisement. Yet, on March 1, 1998, Menard again ran an ad that was "strikingly similar" to Sears. After the second advertisement ran, Sears filed suit in U.S. District court in *Sears, Roebuck and Co.* v. *Menard, Inc.*[23] for copyright infringement. In addition to the copyright infringement, Sears claimed unfair competition.

Sears claimed that both ads had the same theme, included most of the same words, and copied the overall layout of the Sears ads. The shared layout elements included the typefaces, color, and relative size and placement of elements.

In court, Sears also complained that Menards "engaged in unfair competition by mimicking the timing and type of Sears sales" which created confusion in the marketplace.

The case was subsequently settled.

The Song Says It Best

Country singer Aaron Tippin recorded the song "You've Got to Stand for Something" in 1990. The song peaked in popularity in Feburary 1991, when it was the fifth-best-selling country music song in the United States. Although the initial copyright for the song listed Tippin and Buddy Brock as the only authors of the lyrics, in 1996 Acuff-Rose amended its copyright to list Brock's father, William Brock, as an additional author. According to Acuff-Rose (and William Brock), William Brock independently created the sentence "You've got to stand for something, or you'll fall for anything."

Acuff-Rose Music owned the copyright to the country song. In the song the lyrics repeat: "You've got to stand for something or you'll fall for anything."

Jostens was a manufacturer of custom rings. In December 1992 they launched a nationwide advertising campaign for its school class rings that used the theme: "If you don't stand for something, you'll fall for anything." The slogan was preceded by: "The song says it best."

In *Acuff-Rose Music, Inc.* v. *Jostens, Inc.*,[24] Jostens claimed that the line in the music could not be copyrighted, so there could be no infringement. The court said: "To qualify for copyright protection, a work must be original to the author. Originality does not signify novelty; a work may be original even though it closely resembles other works so long as the similarity is fortuitous, not the result of copying."

The court went on:

> The sine qua non of copyright is originality. To qualify for copyright protection, a work must be original to the author. Original, as the term is used in copyright, means only that the work was independently created by the author (as opposed to copied from other works), and that it possesses at least some minimal degree of creativity.

> Originality does not signify novelty; a work may be original even though it closely resembles other works so long as the similarity is fortuitous, not the result of copying.
>
> Referring to these prior uses of the saying, the district court decided that the phrase "enjoyed a robust existence in the public domain long before Tippin employed it for his song's title and in the key lyrics." It therefore concluded that the lines in Acuff-Rose's song lacked the requisite originality to warrant protection, in effect finding that, given the widespread popular usage of the phrase, William Brock most likely did not independently create the lyric lines of Acuff-Rose's song.

In its support, Jostens showed numerous instances when the line had been used that predated Acuff's song, including the Bible, Abraham Lincoln, Martin Luther King, Malcolm X, and Ginger Rogers. In 1985 popular singer/songwriter John Mellencamp included a song in his album entitled "You've Got to Stand for Somethin'," which included the lyrics, "You've got to stand for somethin'/Or you're gonna fall for anything."

The court held that the phrase had been in existence in the public domain long before the Acuff copyright. The court held that the line lacked the originality required to earn protection.

When There Is Not Enough Similarity Of Expression

Certain cases show a lack of similarity and therefore no infringement of copyright. The creators of the Pink Panther character tried at one time to sue Lincoln-Mercury for copyright infringement. When Lincoln-Mercury developed an animated cat character for use in its ads, the creators of the Pink Panther sued because of the similarities between the Lincoln-Mercury cat and the Pink Panther. It was claimed that both of the cats had human characteristics and mannerisms as well as elongated tails. But this was not enough to cause infringement.

Lincoln-Mercury had used a live cougar as its identity for many years prior to the alleged infringement. Also, the Lincoln-Mercury cat had a strong masculine personality as opposed to the glitzy Pink Panther personality. In fact, many companies have used animated cats, including Exxon, B. F. Goodrich's Tigerpaws tires, Kellogg's Tony the Tiger, Le Tigre shirts, and others.

LEGAL REMEDIES

Obviously, one should not take the copyrighted work of someone else and use it without permission. Congress, in creating the Copyright Act, felt that there were two good reasons for making this unauthorized use illegal. First, the author may have future plans to license the work. And infringement could severely interfere with these plans. We saw this in the Dr. Pepper case. Second, the author may consider that commercial exploitation of his work may demean his creative efforts and thereby erode its credibility. This is especially true in the case of literary works, although we saw the advertising version of this in the Pufnstuf case.

If actual damages cannot be shown, the statute provides for not less than $250 or more than $10,000 per infringement. This can be increased up to $50,000 for willful infringement. There is a wrinkle to the "per infringement" fine. If we go back to the Doofus-Wazoo story at the beginning of this chapter, you'll recall that the agency was slapped with a $5 million lawsuit. In that case the TV commercial used 14 copyrighted slides, and the use was willful; that's $50,000 multiplied by fourteen.

Also, each time the commercial airs another 14 infringements occur. It adds up fast!

Remedies for copyright violation include injunction, seizure, impounding and destruction of infringing items, damages and profits, and in many cases attorney's fees. Indeed, advertisers should be careful where copyright infringement is concerned. The penalties are very severe, as we have seen.

---

[1] 17 U.S.C. section 102(a)(1982).

[2] *Goldstein* v. *California*, 412 U.S. 546, 93 S.Ct. 2303, 37 L.Ed. 2d 163 (1973).

[3] *Hagendorf* v. *Brown*, 699 F.2d 478 (9th Cir. 1983).

[4] *Burrow-Giles Lithographic Co.* v. *Sarony,* 111 U.S. 53, 4 S.Ct. 279, 28 L.Ed. 349 (1884).

[5] *Roth Greeting Cards* v. *United Card Co.*, 429 F.2d 1106 (9th Cir. 1970).

[6] *Modern Aids, Inc.* v. *R. H. Macy & Co.*, 264 F.2d 93 (2d Cir. 1969).

[7] 17 U.S.C. section 101.

[8] *Rand McNally & Co.* v. *Fleet Management Sys. Inc.*, 600 F.Supp. 933 (N.D. Ill. 1984).

[9] 17 U.S.C. section 101.

[10] 17 U.S.C. section 102.

[11] *Atari Inc.* v. *North American Philips Consumer Elecs.*, 672 F.2d 607 (7th Cir. 1982).

[12] *Universal Pictures Co. Inc.* v. *Harold Lloyd Corp.*, 162 F.2d 354, 360 (9th Cir. 1947).

[13] *Sony Corp.* v. *Universal City Studios*, 52 U.S.L.W. 4090 (U.S. Jan 17,1984) rev'g 659 F.2d 963 (9th Cir. 1981).

[14] *Triangle Publications* v. *Knight-Ridder*, 626 F.2d 1171 (5th Cir. 1980).

[15] *Leibovitz* v. *Paramount Pictures Corp.*, 137 F.3d 109 (2d Cir. 1998).

[16] *Webster's New Collegiate Dictionary* (Springfield, Mass.: Merriam-Webster Inc., 1976).

[17] 17 U.S.C. section 107.

[18] *Dr. Pepper Co.* v. *Sambo's Restaurants, Inc.*, 517 F. Supp. 1202 (1981).

[19] *Tin Pan Apple, Inc.* v. *Miller Brewing Co., Inc.*, 737 F.Supp. 826 (S.D.N.Y. 1990).

[20] *Columbia Pictures Industries, Inc.* v. *Miramax Films Corp.*, No. CV98-2793 ABC (AIJx), 1998 U.S. Dist. LEXIS 11325 (C.D. Cal., June 2,1998).

[21] *Psihoyos* v. *National Examiner*, No. 97 Civ. 7624 USM), 1998 U.S. Dist. LEXIS 9192 (S.D.N.Y., June 22, 1998).

[22] *Sid & Marty Krofft* v. *McDonald's*, 562 F.2d 1157 (1977).

[23] *Sears, Roebuck and Co.* v. *Menard, Inc.*, Civil Action No. 98 C 1688, (3/19/98).

[24] *Acuff-Rose Music, Inc.* v. *Jostens, Inc.*, No. 987135, 1998 U.S. App. LEXIS 21599 (2d Cir., September 4,1998).

CHAPTER 7

TRADEMARK REGULATION

I hate the man who builds his name
On ruins of another's fame.
—*John Gay*

Within 20 years after the Civil War, a Columbus, Georgia, pharmacist named John S. Pemberton had invented, manufactured, and sold a variety of products. These ranged from Globe of Flower Cough Syrup and Indian Queen Hair Dye to Triplex Liver Pills, Gingerine, and Extract of Styllinger.

Pemberton later moved to Atlanta where he created a drink that combined an extract of kola nut, fruit syrup, and extract of coco leaf. In 1886 he took his syrup to Jacob's Drug Store in Atlanta where, on a trial basis, he was allowed to sell his drink at the soda fountain. The drink became modestly popular with the patrons of Jacob's Drug Store.

Eventually Pemberton became disillusioned with the drink and sold out to a man named Asa Chandler. Pemberton made $1,750. With his new product in hand, Chandler first advertised the drink as a "Wonderful Nerve and Brain Tonic and Remarkable Therapeutic Agent." By 1893 Chandler had sold 48,427 gallons of his tonic. A year later, soda water was added to the mixture, and it was bottled.

Chandler's tonic grew in popularity. In fact, the more a person drank, the more that person wanted. In part this was because of the caffeine and small amounts of cocaine that remained in the syrup after the brewing process. As sales of the drink grew, it became apparent to Chandler that he needed to market the product on a larger scale. So, in 1906 he hired the Massingale Agency in Atlanta to advertise his product. From that point on, Chandler's drink (which was named by the Jacob's Drug Store bookkeeper) soared into marketing history on the wings of a trademark the likes of which has not been seen since. The drink was Coca-Cola.

The strength and value of a trademark to identify goods and distinguish them from others cannot be overstressed. As Coca-Cola proved, a successful business gets that way by investing much of its efforts in building a favorable identity for itself and its products. This can be called *reputation*, and in many cases it is called *goodwill*. The public's knowledge of this image – what we in advertising work so hard to build and maintain – will draw first-time buyers and continue to bring back repeat buyers.

Once the buyer, let's say Ms. Jones, is satisfied with a product, she will seek it out to buy again. Ms. Jones seeks out the same product because of qualities she found in it before, and hopes to find again. Sociologists tell us that these qualities can range from actual product performance to ego gratification. Regardless, the consumer finds fulfillment in some form. This satisfaction in a brand also draws attention to new products introduced by the same manufacturer. It can create a built-in satisfaction with the product, even before it's purchased.

Take, for instance, the Chevrolet Corvette. Since the car's inception in 1953, its popularity has grown steadily. Even in the mid-1970's when oil prices were climbing, the 55 mph speed limit was invoked, and the V-8 engine was dying, demand for the Corvette continued to grow. Over the years, this demand has increased. Today, even before a new Corvette model is released, many people place orders for one. This demand exists, in large part, because of the reputation that the Corvette name has built over the years. I know from personal experience that this is true. I've owned nine of them.

Trademarks are an important part of indicating the origin of the product. They make the product recognizable and identifiable by the consumer. Often, the trademark can say more than any photo or amount of ad copy. The old adage claims that pictures speak louder than words. Well, a reputable trademark can speak louder than both. Take the Volkswagen ads in the early 1970's. One such ad ran the headline: "Here's What to Do to Get Your Volkswagen Ready for Winter." The rest of the page was blank – except for the Volkswagen logo. That shows how strong the Volkswagen trademark is.

When a consumer sees a product with a particular trademark on it, that person should be able to rely on the image that the name conjures up and to trust the quality of a product that carries a certain trademark. After all, trademark laws were created to support that trust. A trademark is intended to distinguish one manufacturer's goods from another's. That's why a company must protect its trademark, and also why a company must be careful not to infringe on another company's mark. These are concerns both the advertiser and its agency must heed.

While reading this chapter, the advertiser should be most concerned with how to protect its own mark while not infringing on another's mark. It is not my desire here to teach the reader how to search trademarks. That should be left to a competent trademark attorney.

QUALITIES OF A TRADEMARK

There are many aspects of trademark law that advertisers must understand. One of the first concerns the qualities need to exist in a trademark. The following section discusses this important issue.

The Difference Between A Trademark And A Trade Name

Under the Federal Trademark Act of 1946, trademarks may be registered, but trade names may not.

[A trademark is] word, name, symbol, or

device or any combination thereof adopted and used by a manufacturer or merchant to identify his goods and distinguish them from those manufactured by others. [Trade names are] "individual names and surnames, firm names and trade names used by manufacturers, industrialists, merchants, agriculturalists, and others to identify their businesses, vocations, or occupations.[1]

To distinguish the two terms, a trademark refers to products or services, and a trade name refers to the business entity itself. For example, Beatrice (the company) is a trade name while its product, Hunt's Ketchup, is a trademark; Kodak is a trademark while Eastman Kodak Company (the manufacturer) is a trade name.

Types Of Trademarks

The term "trademark" actually covers a number of marks of various uses. There are trademarks, service marks, certification marks, and collective marks. A trademark, as we have just discussed, is used in connection with a product.

A service mark may be used when referring to the sale of a service. Since services rarely have anything concrete to place a name or mark on, the service mark generally identifies the business itself. In this case, what would usually be considered a trade name would be registered as a service mark. As an example, if Acme Auto Repair Service, Inc., desired to protect its name, it would have to register it as a service mark. These services are identified with an "SM" symbol. The category of service marks also includes slogans, titles, characters, and symbols.

Another form of mark is called a "certification mark," which calls attention to the origin, material, nature, method of manufacture, accuracy, quality, or labor source of a product. Examples include the Good Housekeeping Seal of Approval, the mark used for the AFL-CIO, or the mark used by the cotton industry to designate 100 percent cotton composition of the item.

Collective marks, another form of trademark, are marks used to show membership in an organization or group. A collective mark has no relation to a specific product or service, but merely shows affiliation with the group. The marks used by the Elks' Lodge or the American Association of Advertising Agencies are prime examples.

STRONG MARKS AND WEAK MARKS

As far as trademarks are concerned, there are two strengths of marks: strong and weak. The law offers different protection for each type so it is important for the advertiser to be aware of the difference between the two types of marks.

Strong Marks

Strong marks can receive protection under trademark law simply because they are distinctive. Marks in this category can include those that are suggestive of the product. A strong mark is coined or fanciful, such as "Kodak," "Xerox," or "Exxon." "Sure" for deodorant, "Raid" for insect spray, and "Drano" for clogged drains are other examples of strong marks. Strong marks, while they are suggestive, are more than just descriptive of the product.

Weak Marks

Weak marks do not automatically qualify as trademarks and will be permitted protection only if the Trademark Office allows it. A weak mark would be composed of words that praise or describe a quality like "best" or "premium." However, a weak mark, as such, will be granted protection as a trademark only if it has acquired a secondary meaning. This implies that the consumer makes an automatic connection between the product or service that the mark refers to and its source. The consumer must associate the product and the mark with the manufacturer. If this connection can be shown, then protection can be afforded the mark. For example, when you hear the term "Big Mac," what do you think of? McDonald's of course. That's secondary meaning.

Another category of weak marks include the use of geographical names. Unless secondary meaning could be established, names using "Swiss" for watches, "Columbian" for coffee, "California" for oranges, and so on would not be protected under trademark law. These names only designate the geographic origin of the item, and a manufacturer cannot take such a designation for its own to the exclusion of others.

Weak marks also include surnames. Common names like Johnson, Smith, White, and Jones have probably already been trademarked at some time. If another company has already trademarked a surname, a manufacturer runs the risk of infringing on that mark. Even if the name is the person's legitimate one, it can still infringe on another's trademark.

Let's say that Smith's Oil begins manufacturing its product and trademarks the name. It runs a high risk that another trademark already exists under that name. If time goes by, and no claims are brought, consumers may become accustomed to associating Smith's Oil with the product. In this case, the name develops a secondary meaning. If another manufacturer begins selling an oil product under that same name, in the same marketing area, it would be infringing on Smith's trademark.

Marks that use descriptions of praise as trademarks also fall into the weak mark category. "Premium," "World's Finest," and others are very weak unless secondary meaning can be attributed to the trade name. However, this does occur, as we see later. Products such as Pabst Blue Ribbon beer, Gold Medal flour, and others have achieved this secondary meaning status through heavy and continued usage of the marks for many years within the market. As a result, they are protected under trademark.

REGISTRATION OF MARKS

Trademarks are registered with the U.S. Patent and Trademark Office in Washington, D.C. The importance of registering a mark is that doing so notifies others that the owner of the mark "claims" the exclusive rights to its use. But registering the mark alone is not enough to protect it. Notice of registration must be used along with the mark. Keep in mind that registering a mark does not create an unlimited legal right to ownership; rather it's a claim of ownership. To be protected, the mark must not infringe on another's mark. Until 1989 federal trademark law said that a company must actually use a trademark before it could be registered. However, in 1989, the statute was amended to allow trademark registration by showing an "intent to use" the mark, which may be inferred from marketing, advertising and distribution plans.

Length Of Registration

Once a trademark is registered, the claim is established for 10 years. After obtaining registration, the company has six months to begin using the trademark in commerce. Registration may thereafter be renewed for unlimited 10-year periods. An application must be filed within six months before the expiration of a trademark. As an alternative, a mark can be renewed up to three months after expiration if a penalty is paid.

Trademark Registers

Trademarks can be recorded in one of the two registers of the Trademark Office: the Principal Register or the Supplemental Register. All applications for registration go first to the Principal Register. If the mark does not meet the requirements of that register, it is passed on to the Supplemental Register for possible acceptance. This is an automatic process used by the Trademark Office.

It is important to note that, unlike copyright, registering a trademark does not provide any right of ownership. Any such right exists through common law as a property right. Because of this, many marks that are not registered are still afforded trademark status. We'll look at this later.

Also, some marks that are registered can have their trademark status revoked if challenged by a company that previously registered and used the same mark. The registers only provide a place where marks can be listed for public record. This doesn't mean that there are not good reasons to register a mark. Indeed there are, and we look into these reasons later.

The Principal Register accepts only marks that meet certain standards but keep in mind that the Trademark Office does not search for similar marks that have already been registered. The applicant must perform its own search or hire someone, such as a trademark attorney to do this. The Trademark Office only judges a mark against the standards of the office for acceptance, not against other marks already registered – that's the applicant's responsibility. Standards for acceptance include:

- The mark must be distinctive;
- The mark must not be immoral, deceptive, or scandalous;
- The mark must not consist of a flag, emblem, or insignia of the United States or other country;
- The mark must not consist of the picture or signature of an individual without prior consent;
- The mark must not resemble another mark;
- The mark must not be merely descriptive of the product;
- The mark must not be geographically descriptive of origin; and
- The mark must not be a surname.

The Supplemental Register is more lenient. All four of these requirements must be met for registration:

- The mark must be unqualified for registration on the

Principal Register;

- The mark must be able to distinguish the product;
- The mark must not fall into any category above for the Principal Register, except numbers 6, 7, or 8; and
- The mark must have been used in commerce for one year without opposition from another trademark owner.

NOTICE OF REGISTRATION

It is important to place a notice of registration along with a trademark. A notice of registration of a mark allows damages to be recovered if infringement of the mark occurs. Without that notice damages cannot be awarded; only the infringing usage of the mark may be stopped. Notice also lends credibility, which should help deter potential infringers. Registration notice also helps establish that the mark is a trademark rather than a generic term.

The Trademark Act states that "a registrant of a mark ...*may* give notice that his mark is registered by displaying with the mark as used...the letter 'R' enclosed within a circle."

The act goes on to say: "[I]n any suit for infringement under this chapter by such a registrant failing to give such notice of registration, no profits or damages shall be recovered...*unless the defendant had actual notice of registration....*" (emphasis added).[2] There are two alternate notice forms, which are acceptable, but seldomly used because of their sheer bulk: "Registered in U.S. Patent and Trademark Office" and "Reg. U.S. Pat. & Tm. Off."

Marks that are not yet registered, but for which application has been made, can be identified with a "TM." Be aware that it is legal to use a notice of actual registration "®" only after a certificate of registration has been issued.

The registration notice may be placed anywhere in relation to the mark and in any style. If a trademark is used more than once in an ad, it is not necessary for the notice to appear every time the mark appears, but it should appear with the mark that is used first or appears most prominent. Of course, the notice itself should be large enough to be readily recognizable and readable.

Another important consideration is that when using another company's trademark in your ad, always use the appropriate notice with the mark. Also, when you use someone else's trademark in an ad, capitalize the mark. For example, use "XEROX" or "Xerox," not "xerox." In other words, capitalizing lets the reader of the ad know that the mark is the trademark of another company. This may need to be clearly identified elsewhere in the ad if there is any chance of confusion, such as a credit line stating: "Acme is the registered trademark of Widget Manufacturing Company."

Using A Trademark Notice With A Mark That Has Not Been Registered

If a notice is placed with a trademark that is not registered, severe problems can result. Most importantly, the right to register the mark in the future can be lost. A trademark known as "Four Roses" is a good example. In 1925 Small Grain Distilling Company applied for and was granted the trademark "Four Roses" for its high-grade whiskey. "Four Roses" was a widely known brand name at the time.

Early in 1926 another company, Four Roses Products, began placing a notice of registration on its product of malt syrup used in making liquor. The name "Four Roses" was used on the product packaging along with the notice "Trade-Mark Reg. U.S. Pat. Off." When Small Grain learned of this, it brought the case to court in *Four Roses Products Co.* v. *Small Grain Distilling & Drug Co.*[3]

The fact was Four Roses Products had never received a registration of the trademark for "Four Roses:" It had applied for registration but had been denied. Four Roses Products used the registration notice even though it knew it had no registration. The court determined that Small Grain's trademark of Four Roses was legitimate and Four Roses Products' mark was not. Essentially, Four Roses Products tried, through the use of the registration notice, to imply that its product was authentic and that any other, including Small Grain's, was an infringement. This was not accurate.

Since Four Roses Products used the registration notice on an unregistered mark, it lost the case, had to pay damages for infringement, and lost any chance for future registration. As a side note, this must have been a heated case in court considering the time it occurred – not long after the 18th Amendment to the Constitution was adopted. The amendment repealed prohibition.

There is another reason not to use a registration notice if the mark has not been registered. The right to stop another company from using the same mark can be lost. Fox Photo learned about this in 1972. The company provided photo developing and finishing services to the public. The Fox Photo logo consisted of a red fox running with the name Fox Photo across it. Fox Photo also used, as part of its logo, a red "R" in a circle.

Sometime later, Harry Otaguro began publishing a photo magazine called *FOX*. Fox Photo decided that Otaguro's magazine infringed its trademark because of the similarity in the names and the fact that both products were in the same field – photography. *Fox-Stanley Photo Products, Inc.* v. *Otaguro*[4] resulted. Unfortunately Fox Photo had never registered the Fox Photo mark. That, however, did not deter it from placing a registration notice with the logo to imply registration of the mark.

Fox Photo lost its case at the outset simply because it did not own the trademark. Because it had used a registration notice on a mark that had not been registered, Fox also lost its right to be granted a trademark registration for its logo in the future.

ANOTHER FORM OF ERRONEOUS USE OF A TRADEMARK

Other than the situations described above, there is an additional form of trademark misuse that can cause problems. This involves using a mark with goods different from those for which it was registered. A trademark can be used only with the product or product line that it was registered for, i.e., registering a mark for use with a specific product does not automatically allow that mark to be used with other products. Here's an example. If Bonzo Company manufactures and owns a trademark for its line of cars, it cannot use that trademark for its new line of dishwashers.

In 1965 Cumberland Packing Company wanted to register the mark for "Sweet 'N Low." The low-calorie sugar substitute was to be marketed to the public in packet form. Cumberland had been assigned the rights from the inventor, May MacGregor.

Another company who sold only to the trade, Duffy-Mott Company, also owned a trademark to use the name "Sweet 'N Low." It, too, had been assigned rights to the name by MacGregor for use of her sugar-substitute formula in canned, frozen, and fresh fruits; vegetables; pudding; and cake mixes. Duffy-Mott opposed the registration of the mark for Cumberland's packet version of "Sweet 'N Low," claiming that it would infringe Duffy-Mott's use of the mark. *Duffy-Mott Co. v. Cumberland Packing Co.*,[5] was the case.

Duffy-Mott argued that by allowing registration of "Sweet 'N Low" for the sugar substitute sold in packets, its mark would be eroded. However, the court reasoned that the issuance of a registration for Cumberland would not infringe on the mark used by Duffy-Mott because Cumberland's mark would be directed to the public in raw form. On the other hand, Duffy-Mott's mark was directed to the trade to be included in a finished product. Since the product lines and markets were different for each company, the court allowed registration for Cumberland.

GENERICIDE: WHAT CAN HAPPEN WHEN A MARK IS MISUSED

Ultimately, when a mark is misused, it can be lost to the forgotten world of generic terms. The consumer may begin to consider a trademark as the name of the product line in general.

Then the trademark no longer identifies and distinguishes the product of a particular manufacturer. Instead of standing for one particular brand of the product, the mark stands for the type of product. This is called "genericide."

When a trademark is not handled properly, it can be weakened to the point that it is no longer protected as a trademark. Therefore, an advertiser must be very cautious. The manufacturer's own promotion, labeling, and advertising are at fault when this happens. Genericide has been the demise of many trademarks, which we now consider product lines, including "cellophane," "celluloid," "kerosene," "lanolin," "linoleum," "milk of magnesia," "dry ice," and (as we'll soon see) "aspirin," "thermos bottles," "escalators," and "PROMS." These trademarks were allowed to deteriorate to the point that they became synonymous with the product rather than the manufacturer.

The key to understanding this process is this: genericide happens in the mind of the consumer, not to the product. Yet, there is something that the advertiser can do to control how the consumer perceives the trademark. The easiest way to avoid genericide and to protect a trademark would be to use the word *brand* in connection with the name and product, i.e., "Xerox brand copiers" or "IBM brand computers," to forestall any assumption by consumers that the trademark is a generic term.

The Headache That Aspirin Caused

How many brands of aspirin can you think of? Bayer, Johnson & Johnson, Excedrin, Bufferin, and Anacin are some of the major ones. This is the problem that Bayer had to deal with in the early 1920's, because "aspirin" was originally a trademark.

"Aspirin" was the trademark for the drug acetyl salicylic acid, a powder that was patented by Bayer Company in 1898. In 1904 the name of the drug was changed to momoaceticacidester of salicylic acid. Bayer began allowing chemists, druggists, and physicians to make the powder into tablets for sale under names such as "Squibb Aspirin," "Smith, Klein & French Aspirin," or "United Drug Company Aspirin." United Drug, in particular, sold over 19 million tablets in its first two years. The consumer could not possibly have known the manufacturer of the drug, only the name on the bottle.

In 1915 Bayer changed its policy and discontinued selling to other manufacturers. From that time on Bayer prohibited others from manufacturing or selling the drug. It began selling aspirin itself in tablets to the general public. Tablets were sold in tin boxes with the legend:

The Trademark "Aspirin"
(Reg. U.S. Pat. Office)
is a guarantee that the momoaceticacidester of salicylic acid
in these tablets is of the reliable Bayer manufacture.

But it was too late; the harm had been done. Because of this change in policy, United Drug sued Bayer, claiming that the name *aspirin* had become a descriptive name, free for anyone to use. The case was *Bayer Co. v. United Drug Co.*[6] While the druggists knew that aspirin was a trademark, the general public did not. Its only knowledge of the product was through the over-the-counter brands that were available, especially since many manufacturers had used the name alone in labeling and advertising – all allowed by Bayer.

Bayer understood that the term "aspirin" had become generic. When it began to sell to the public in 1915, its labels read: "Bayer – Tablets of Aspirin." This meant that the tablets were Bayer's make of the drug known as "aspirin."

The public could not have known that "aspirin" was a trademark for momoaceticacidester of salicylic acid; it thought that *aspirin* was the name of the drug. By allowing this confusion to occur, Bayer failed to protect the trademark as such, and the

Trademark Office declared the trademark not valid as of 1918. The court in its decision agreed with both the Trademark Office and United Drug in determining that the name "aspirin" had become a generic term.

The Moving Stairway

Trademark registration number 34,724 was issued to Charles D. Seeberger in 1900. The trademark was for the term "escalator." Seeberger had invented the device and assigned the trademark to the Otis Elevator Company a number of years later, which manufactured not only elevators, but escalators as well.

A typical ad for Otis from a 1946 issue of *Architectural Forum* magazine contained the following:

Otis (logo)
THE MEANING OF THE OTIS TRADEMARK.
To the millions of daily passengers on the
Otis elevators and escalators, the Otis
trademark or name plate means
safe, convenient, energy-saving transportation.
To the thousands of building owners and managers,
the Otis trademark means the utmost in safe,
efficient, economical elevator and escalator operation.

Obviously, the Otis name was treated as the trademark, and the names "escalator" and "elevator" were merely descriptive of the product. This was plain from the ad copy. As a result, the Haughten Elevator Company attempted, in the late 1940's, to have the name "escalator" declared generic.

Haughten succeeded with its efforts in *Haughten Elevator Co.* v. *Seeberger*.[7] Here, the court determined that the term "escalator" was a generic term for a moving stairway. The court reasoned that the term "escalator" described any moving stairway made by any company. Otis, in large part, allowed this to occur through its literature and advertisements. The term "escalator" was not used by Otis to identify it as the originator and only source of an escalator. The word "escalator" became a generic term for any moving stairway. Trademark number 34,724, held by Otis, was cancelled.

Keeps Hot Things Hot And Cold Things Cold

A German company named Thermos-Gessellschaft M.B.H. manufactured vacuum-insulated containers that were adopted from Dewar's vacuum flask invention of 1893. In 1907 the German company sold out to a new American company, The American Thermos Bottle Company, which produced the now well-known thermos bottle. Initial sales were $114,987 in 1907, and by 1960 the company grossed $13,280,164 for the year.

As early as 1910, American Thermos was promoting the fact that "thermos" had become a household word synonymous with "vacuum-insulated;" thus Thermos bottle. The public adopted this term, and began referring to the thermos bottle as if it were a type of product.

A competitor, Aladdin Industries, also manufactured vacuum-bottles. When it started calling its product a "thermos bottle," American Thermos sued to stop this use in *American Thermos Products Co.* v. *Aladdin Industries, Inc.*[8] The court determined that "thermos" had become the generic term for the vacuum bottle. American Thermos used the combination of "Thermos bottle," not "Thermos brand bottle," or "Thermos vacuum-insulated bottle." American Thermos could still use the name, but so could anyone else.

The court stated that American Thermos, during the early 1900's, welcomed the public's conception that "Thermos" was synonymous with vacuum-bottle. American Thermos "recognized this as an 'enormous amount of free advertising' worth, at that time, between three and four million dollars...." On the other hand, it paid a high price for the free advertising; it lost its trademark protection forever.

The PROM That Never Was

Most losses of trademark protection to genericide occurred in the years when marketing and advertising techniques were young. As we have seen, many early trademarks were lost because of poor handling. But today's company is still at risk when it comes to trademark protection as clearly seen in a recent example involving the computer revolution and one of its components, the "PROM."

High-tech afficionados love to use initials for the names of components. For computer memories, RAM stands for Random Access Memory, SAM for Simultaneous Access Memory, CAM for Content-Addressable Memory, ROM for Read-Only Memory, and PROM for Programmable-Read-Only Memory.

The Harris Semiconductor Division of Radiation, Inc. developed the first field programmable-read-only memory. Harris adopted the acronym "PROM" for the product and put that name on its merchandise. Soon after, other companies developed similar programmable-read-only memories and also used the designation "PROM." Harris attempted to stop the other manufacturers from using the name, claiming that "PROM" was a trademark for its own products. Harris then attempted to register the term "PROM" as its trademark.

When this occurred, Intel (one of the other competitors) brought an action to stop Harris from acquiring the trademark. In *Intel Corp.* v. *Radiation, Inc.*,[9] the issue was whether the term "PROM" should be trademarked. Essentially, the court determined that "PROM" was merely the "descriptive letters [that] constitute the initials or abbreviations of the common name of the product."

In fact, the trade had already become well-acquainted with the term "PROM." The acronym had been used extensively by publications within the trade and in promotional materials of various manufacturers. It was common practice in the electronics industry to use abbreviations as an easy method for identifying the different components. It was also well known that these acronyms did not denote the manufacturer of the component. Indeed, "PROM" was only a descriptive name or acronym for the specific type of memory. Harris was not granted a trademark for the term "PROM" – it was a generic name.

HOW TO AVOID GENERICIDE

Al Ries and Jack Trout, in their inspiring book, *Positioning: The Battle for Your Mind*,[10] extol the virtues of positioning a product so that the brand name becomes generic with the product. It's the basis for positioning strategy, and anyone in advertising knows it. Let's take a short step back to our Bayer case. In their book Trout and Ries use it as an example to discuss the power in a name:

> The tablets in a bottle of aspirin are Bayer. Not aspirin manufactured by a company called Bayer.... The great strength of a generic brand name is this close identification with the product itself. In the consumer's mind, Bayer is aspirin, and every other aspirin brand becomes 'imitation' Bayer.[11]

The strength of positioning strategy cannot be questioned. But what is good for marketing may be terrible for protection of a trademark. The advertiser must be careful not to destroy a trademark in the process of building brand awareness.

The best method an advertiser can use to avoid genericide is to treat a trademark as a trademark. In other words, distinguish it from the type of product. How can you accomplish this? For copywriters, a trademark should always be an adjective that modifies the product name. It is not a noun; the noun names the type of product. Actually, the trademark is a proper adjective modifying a proper noun – allowing both words to be capitalized.

As an example, let's take a fictitious company called

Metropolis Manufacturing. It makes a car called the Metromobile. Now "Metromobile" is a trademark. In its advertising, to protect the trademark, Metropolis must not refer to its car merely as a Metromobile. It should refer to it as a Metromobile Automobile or Metromobile Car. (Also, note that a trademark is not a verb since you can't Metromobile to work.)

Here's the test to see if a trademark is treated as a trademark, therefore avoiding possible genericide. A typical advertisement headline to accomplish this might read: "Enjoy the Freedom of the Road in a Metromobile Car." If you eliminate the trademark, "Metromobile," does the remaining sentence make sense? Aside from the fact that it would be a horrible headline, it would read: "Enjoy the Freedom of the Road in a Car." The headline still makes sense grammatically. Compare this to an incorrect usage of the mark. If the type of product were left out, the headline would read, "Enjoy the Freedom of the Road in a Metromobile." Now remove the trademark from this version, and the headline would make no sense: "Enjoy the Freedom of the Road in a _____." The sentence must make grammatical sense if the trademark is removed.

But let's be realistic. Not all advertisers follow these rules. One reason is that some trademarks are so strong the consumer invariably knows exactly what product is being referred to. How is it that a consumer can drive a Ford, smoke a Salem, use a box of Tide, drink a Coke, or wear a pair of Nikes? It happens because some trademarks are very well understood by consumers. They know exactly what product is being referred to when the term is used. This is the secondary meaning we discussed earlier. The consumer places the generic name with the trademark automatically in his mind. We saw this earlier when we discussed positioning. Yet, all trademarks are not so fortunate as to have that status. Only in cases where the generic term is understood so thoroughly can the advertiser feel secure that the trademark can stand alone. For new products, or lesser-known ones, habitual use of the trademark without mention of the generic product should be avoided. When Bayer first heard people ask, "What brand of aspirin do you use?" it should have seen what was coming.

SLOGANS

In some cases slogans may be trademarked. But those situations are controlled by strict guidelines. Slogans, if they qualify for protection, fall into the category of service marks. A trademark may consist of any slogan, but it is allowed protection only if it distinguishes the product.

In 1932 American Enka adopted the mark of a black rectangle with a thread extending through it. Below the logo was the name American Enka; above the logo was the slogan, "The Fate of a Fabric Hangs on a Thread." By 1939 Enka had modified its mark. The slogan remained, but the logo became a tag with the words "Fashion Approved" in it. Underneath the tag were the words "Enka Rayon."

Then in 1947 Enka applied for registration of its mark with the slogan. The Commissioner of Patents and Trademarks, John Marzall, declined to register the slogan. Enka then filed suit in *American Enka Corp.* v. *Marzall*[12] to decide the matter.

The court determined that Enka could register its slogan with the logo. Enka was the only user of the slogan, and it had become widely known to identify its rayon yarn from any other. The slogan unquestionably indicated the origin of the mark.

Indeed, certain word combinations can operate as trademarks when they are so distinctive. The fact that the words comprise a slogan does not bar them from trademark status.

"We Smile More"

Marriott began using the slogan, "We Smile More," as an advertising and promotional line in 1964. In 1968 the hotel chain applied for registration of the slogan as a trademark after it learned that Ramada Inns had begun using the same line.

The case went to trial in *In re Marriott Corp.*,[13] where it was determined the slogan did qualify to be registered. A slogan does not have to be unique in verbiage to qualify. "[A] capability of identifying and distinguishing the source of goods or services is all that is required to support registration."

The court went on to say that "the function of a...mark is to indicate continuity of quality of services, i.e., that the quality of services rendered in connection with a particular mark is controlled by a single entity." Marriott showed that customers were aware of the slogan and recognized the mark as belonging to it. These consumers substantiated that they knew the slogan referred to Marriott, and only to Marriott. Indeed, the slogan indicated the source. The court allowed the registration of "We Smile More" as a trademark.

See the section on the Federal Trademark Dilution Act of 1995 that follows later in this chapter. The consideration of likelihood of consumer confusion (as was typical of the case here) is no longer a requirement for infringement.

The Slogan That's A Mouthful

Everyone in advertising will no doubt remember McDonald's campaign in the mid-1970's that used the slogan:

"TWOALLBEEFPATTIESSPECIALSAUCELETTUCECHEESE PICKLESONIONSONASESAMESEEDBUN."

McDonald's began using the slogan in its advertising in late 1974. It spent over $2 million in advertising, using the slogan as its theme through the end of 1975. The advertising campaign included almost every media available from TV, radio, newspaper, magazine, billboards, through point-of-purchase, contests, and premiums.

In essence, McDonald's saturated the market with "TWOALLBEEFPATTIESSPECIALSAUCELETTUCECHEESE-PICKLESONIONSONASESAMESEEDBUN."

McDonald's applied for registration of its slogan as a trademark in 1975, and *In re McDonald's Corp.*[14] resulted. At the hearing the argument was made in opposition to the application that the phrase was no more than a descriptive list of ingredients of a Big Mac sandwich. However, the phrase is a unique "and somewhat catchy arrangement and combination which in its entirety creates a commercial impression quite different from that of the individual words as they are ordinarily used."

Through its massive advertising campaign, McDonald's also met the second requirement for registration, that of knowledge of origin by the public. At the time, everyone who knew the name McDonald's knew the slogan. There was little doubt the public knew that the phrase meant only McDonald's.

"America's Freshest Ice Cream"

When a slogan is a mere statement, puff, or irrelevant phrase, it will not be allowed protection. A good example of this is evident in the case, *In re Carvel Corp.*,[15] involving Carvel Ice Cream. Carvel wanted to register its slogan, "America's Freshest Ice Cream," which it had been using since 1978, along with its logo. However, as the court put it, the mark "is not a mark capable of distinguishing [Carvel's] goods from like goods of others...."

Carvel attempted to argue its point that because it used the word *fresh* in relation to ice cream, it is a distinctive mark. It felt that the word *fresh* was not normally associated with ice cream, and therefore it was distinctive. The court was not convinced. This simple expression of praise was not capable of functioning as a trademark. A common expression, such as the one Carvel used, could not indicate anything other than a motive toward high quality. It certainly could not indicate the origin of the mark to the general public. Hypothetically though, if it could have been proven that the slogan was well understood by the public to mean Carvel, and only Carvel, the outcome may have been different.

Strictly speaking, the Trademark Act does not prohibit expressions of praise (even if they are self-inflicted) from being registered. But in order for one to be registered, there must be enough originality or uniqueness to set it apart from other marks in the consumer's mind. It must distinguish the origin or owner of the mark for the consumer. Clearly, Carvel's slogan failed to accomplish this and therefore was refused registration.

A Hog By Any Other Name

In 1969 Ronald Grottanelli opened a motorcycle repair shop and named it "The Hog Farm." Since then his shop was located at various sites in New York state. After 1981 Grottanelli began using the word "hog" in connection with events and merchandise for his shop. He also sponsored events known as "Hog Holidays" and "Hog Farm Holidays," and sold products such as "Hog Wash" engine degreaser and a "Hog Trivia" board game.

Beginning in the early 1970's, motorcyclists began using the term "hog" when referring to Harley-Davidson motorcycles. For several years the company tried to disassociate itself from the word "hog." The company wanted to distance itself from the connection between "hog" as applied to motorcycles and negative groups, such as Hell's Angels, who were among those associating the term to Harley-Davidson motorcycles.

However, in 1981, Harley-Davidson recognized that the term "hog" had significant financial value and began using the term in connection with its merchandise, accessories, advertising and promotions. In 1983 it formed the Harley Owners' Group, using the acronym "H.O.G." Four years later, in 1987, it registered the acronym in conjunction with various logos.

By 1979 Grottanelli started using his version of Harley-Davidson's bar-and-shield logo. In an ad he ran in 1979, he included a hand-drawn copy of the bar-and-shield logo, with the name "Harley-Davidson" displayed on the horizontal bar. When Harley-Davidson protested to this use, Grottanelli replaced the words "Harley-Davidson" on the horizontal bar of his logo with the words "American-Made." He also put a banner at the bottom of his logo with the words "UNAUTHORIZED DEALER." In 1986, Grottanelli began using his current logo, which adds an eagle's wings behind the shield. This addition, patterned after Harley-Davidson's bicentennial logo design mark, included an eagle above the shield. Grottanelli's 1986 version of his logo also features a drawing of a pig wearing sunglasses. Grottanelli acknowledged at trial that his version of the logo was "supposed to be similar, but confusing...[t]o a Harley-Davidson bar and shield."

Harley-Davidson, Inc. v. *Grottanelli*[16] was the case where this all came to a head. In court, Harley-Davidson argued that it is entitled to trademark protection for the term "HOG" as it is applied to motorcycles because a substantial segment of consumers used the term to refer to Harley-Davidson motorcycles.

The court reasoned on this point:

> Some decisions have invoked this principle to accord a company priority as to its subsequent trademark use of a term. See *National Cable Television Ass'n, Inc.* v. *American Cinema Editors, Inc.*,[17] (mark "ACE"); *Volkswagenwerk AG* v. *Hoffman*,[18] (mark "BUG"). Whether or not we would agree with these decisions, they present a significantly different situation. Neither "ACE" nor "BUG" was a generic term in the language as applied, respectively, to a category of film editors or a category of automobiles prior to the public's use of the terms to refer to the American Cinema Editors and Volkswagen cars. By contrast, "hog" was a generic term in the language as applied to large motorcycles before the public (or at least some segments of it) began using the word to refer to

> Harley-Davidson motorcycles. The public has no more right than a manufacturer to withdraw from the language a generic term, already applicable to the relevant category of products, and accord it trademark significance, at least as long as the term retains some generic meaning.

For all of these reasons, Harley-Davidson may not prohibit Grottanelli from using "hog" to identify his motorcycle products and services. Like any other manufacturer with a product identified by a word that is generic, Harley-Davidson will have to rely on all or a portion of its tradename (or other protectable marks) to identify its brand of motorcycles, e.g., "Harley Hogs."

Then the court turned to Grottanilli's use of the Harley-Davidson logo. Grottanelli claimed that his use of Harley-Davidson's logo was a parody, and therefore allowed.

The court reasoned that that argument:

> [I]s vulnerable not only because he uses it to market competing services but also because whatever protection is to be afforded a trademark parody must be informed by the Supreme Court's recent elucidation in the copyright context of parodies allegedly protected by the defense of fair use. See *Campbell* v. *Acuff-Rose Music, Inc.*,[19] "[T]he heart of any parodist's claim to quote from existing material is the use of some elements of a prior author's composition to create a new one that, at least in part, comments on that author's works." The comment must have some "critical bearing on the substance or style of the original composition." The Supreme Court's parody explication as to copyrights, set forth in the context of an expressive work, is relevant to trademarks, see Robert S. Shaughnessy, Note, Trademark Parody,[20] especially a trademark

> parody that endeavors to promote primarily non-expressive products such as a competing motorcycle repair service. Grottanelli's mark makes no comment on Harley's mark; it simply uses it somewhat humorously to promote his own products and services, which is not a permitted trademark parody use.

The court then looked at Grottanelli's use of his disclaimer as a defense. The court reasoned on this issue that:

> Grottanelli gains no protection by coyly adding to his version of the bar-and-shield logo the wording "UNAUTHORIZED DEALER." We have alluded to commentary questioning the capacity of brief negating words like "not" or "no" in disclaimers adequately to avoid confusion. Whatever the worth of such disclaimers in other contexts, the use of the prefix "UN" before "AUTHORIZED DEALER" provides Grottanelli with no defense when used on signage designed to attract speeding motorcyclists.

The court concluded that Grottanelli was properly enjoined from using his current bar-and-shield logo or any mark that resembles Harley-Davidson's trademark, but reversed the lower court's ruling that enjoined his use of the word "hog."

Typical Slogans That Have Been Refused Registration

The following list presents a few more examples of typical slogans that have been refused registration.

"Best and Biggest Cigar"	Lewis Cigar Company
"America's Finest Overall"	Levi Strauss
"Tender Fresh"	Nash-Finch Fresh Cut Chicken

"Sudsy"	Parsons Ammonia
"Champagne"	Demos Salad Dressing with Champagne
"The Professional Health Care People"	Career Employment Services
"More Gun for the Money"	Mossberg Firearms
"America's Most Luxurious Mattress"	Englander Mattress Company
"For a Day, a Week, a Month or More!"	Brock Residence Inns

CONSIDERATIONS IN CHOOSING A TRADEMARK

When a company develops a new product, it generally creates a new name for it – and possibly a trademark. In many cases the ad agency is involved in choosing the name, so it's important to know what to consider in selecting a trademark.

Marks That Infringe Existing Marks

The most important concern in developing a new mark is establishing that it does not infringe on an existing mark. The new mark must not be the same as another existing mark or confusingly similar to an existing mark.

Believe it or not, there is no single place where the applicant can look to find a list of all trademarks. Simply checking with the Trademark Office isn't enough. One reason for this is that some marks may be registered in a particular state (we look at this later in the chapter). Another reason is that a mark may have been used for many years without being registered. The original mark would be allowed protection in many cases under common law (refer to the section "Trademark Registers" for an explanation).

There are, however, professional trademark search services. These services are fairly thorough and use a number of sources to determine if the mark already exists as a trademark. But beware: They are not 100 percent conclusive.

It is important to check new trademarks before putting them into use, as Goodyear found out. Goodyear is the world's largest tire manufacturer; in 1974 its net sales reached over $5.25 billion. A minor competitor, Big O Tire Dealers, manufactured a private label tire of its own. In late 1973, Big O named its line of tires "Big Foot." The name appeared on the sidewall of each tire.

In July of 1974 Goodyear adopted the name "Big Foot" for its new Custom Polysteel Radial tire. The name also appeared on the side of the tire. The firm hired a trademark search firm to investigate any existing trademark conflicts. None were shown. Feeling secure, Goodyear developed an advertising campaign to promote its new tire, Big Foot. Within a year, Goodyear had spent over $9.6 million on the advertising of this single product. Typical headlines from Goodyear ads were:

Bigfoot, the new Polysteel Radial.
Bigfoot. The Polysteel Radial that keeps its feet even in the rain.
Only from Goodyear.

In August of 1974, Goodyear learned of the existing and previous trademark held by Big O Tires. Goodyear tried to buy the rights to use the name from Big O, but the offer was not accepted. When Big O refused the offer, it mentioned the possibility of a lawsuit if Goodyear did not stop using the trademark "Big Foot." As stated in court, Goodyear informed Big O president Norman Affleck, that if Big O did bring suit, "the case would be in litigation long enough that Goodyear might obtain all the benefits it desired from the term 'Big Foot.'"

In fact, Big O Tires did sue in *Big O Tire Dealers, Inc.* v. *Goodyear Tire & Rubber Co.*[21] The problem occurred because Goodyear, through their search firm, failed to verify an existing trademark for "Big Foot." Since there was such a trademark, Goodyear lost the case.

At trial it came to light that when Goodyear learned of the Big O trademark, not only did it not discontinue its ad campaign, which claimed exclusiveness, it continued to willfully infringe upon the existing mark. Goodyear basically thumbed its huge corporate nose at Big O. Because of Goodyear's action and its disregard for Big O's trademark, the court awarded $678,302 in compensatory damages and $4,069,812 in punitive damages.

The Case Of The Velvet Elvis

A Houston, Texas, nightclub called The Velvet Elvis, owned by Barry Capece, was designed to be a recreation of the eclectic bars of the 1960's. The decor included velvet paintings (including one of Elvis Presley), lava lamps, beaded curtains, and vinyl furniture. The club was a parody of the faddish sixties bars, and Capece claimed that the name The Velvet Elvis was symbolic, and had no specific connection to Elvis Presley.

However, the advertising for the club made direct references to Elvis and Graceland, and used phrases like "The King Lives," "Viva la Elvis," and "Hunka-Hunka Happy Hour." Also, in many of the advertisements the "Elvis" portion of the logo "The Velvet Elvis" was very large in relation to the word "Velvet." The bar served a wide variety of food and liquor with menu items ranging from appetizers to full entrees. The menu included "Love Me Blenders," a type of frozen drink; peanut butter and banana sandwiches, a favorite of Elvis's; and "Your Football Hound Dog," a hot dog. Live music was also regularly featured at the bar. Its decor included velvet paintings of celebrities and female nudes, including ones of Elvis and a bare-chested Mona Lisa. Other decorations included lava lamps, cheap ceramic sculptures, beaded curtains, and vinyl furniture. *Playboy* centerfolds covered the men's room walls. Magazine photographs of Elvis, a statuette of Elvis playing the guitar, and a bust of Elvis were also among the club's decorations.

The estate of Elvis Presley (EPE) sued the nightclub for trademark infringement and unfair competition in *Elvis Presley Enterprises, Inc.* v. *Capece*,[22] by claiming:

> [T]he inclusion of its "Elvis" trademark in the service mark "The Velvet Elvis" coupled with Defendants' use of the image and likeness of Elvis Presley in advertising, promoting, and rendering bar services creates confusion as to whether EPE licensed, approved, sponsored, endorsed or is otherwise affiliated with "The Velvet Elvis," constituting unfair competition and trademark infringement under the common law and Lanham Act.

In determining if there was any likelihood of consumer confusion, the lower court considered The Velvet Elvis service mark and the club's decor separately from the nightclub's advertising and promotional materials.

The lower court determined that the bar's decor was a parody and that there was no likelihood that consumers would believe that the nightclub was owned or authorized by Elvis Presley's estate. In contrast, the advertising did not convey the style of the club's decor but only the association with the name. Because of this, the lower court found that the ads were likely to deceive people into believing that the nightclub was associated with the estate of Elvis.

The appellate court, however, did not agree with the lower court's separating the service mark in the decor and its use in advertising.

The court noted:

> The use of a mark in advertising is highly probative of whether the mark creates a likelihood of confusion in relation to another mark. Evidence of the context in which a mark is used on labels, packages, or in advertising material directed to the goods is probative of the reaction of prospective purchasers to the mark. Courts consider marks in the context that a customer perceives them in the marketplace, which includes their presentation in advertisements. In the case of a service mark, advertising is of even greater relevance because the mark cannot be actually affixed to the service, as a trademark is to the goods. Many prospective purchasers first encounter the mark in advertising, rather than on the product; therefore, the service mark cannot be isolated from the advertising in which it appears.

The appellate court also disagreed with the district court's determination that the nightclub decor was a parody. According to the appellate court, parody (an element in determining trademark infringement) was not relevant to this case. Since the Fifth Circuit had not yet considered parody in a trademark case, the court looked to the Supreme Court's interpretation of parody in the copyright context. The Supreme Court noted:

> [T]he heart of any parodist's claim to quote from existing material, is the use of some elements of prior author's composition to create a new one that, at least in part, comments on that author's works. If, on the contrary, the commentary has no critical bearing on the substance or style of the original composition, which the alleged infringer merely uses to get attention or to avoid the drudgery

> in working up something fresh, the claim to fairness in borrowing from another's work diminishes accordingly (if it does not vanish), and other factors, like the extent of the commerciality loom larger. Parody needs to mimic an original to make its point, and so has some claim to sue the creation of its victim's (or victims') imagination, where as satire can stand on its own two feet and so requires justification for the vary act of borrowing.

In this case the nightclub owner claimed that the nightclub's decor was a parody of the sixties – the Las Vegas lounge scene, the velvet painting craze, and possibly the country's fascination with Elvis. In court, the owner stated that he was trying to make fun of clubs like Hard Rock Cafe and Planet Hollywood. The court found that "Without the necessity to use Elvis' name, parody does not weigh against a likelihood of confusion in relation to EPE's marks." In other words, parody is not a defense to trademark infringement, but rather another factor to be considered, which weighs against a finding of a likelihood of confusion.

To this point, the court said:

> This same need to conjure up the original exists when a parody targets a trademark or service mark. In the case of the standard likelihood-of-confusion analysis, a successful parody of the original mark weighs against a likelihood of confusion because, even though it portrays the original, it also sends the message that it is not the original and is a parody, thereby lessening any potential confusion.

The appellate court found that the nightclub's use of the name The Velvet Elvis, both in advertising and the interior decor infringed the trademarks owned by Elvis Presley's estate.

The appellate court agreed with the district court that advertising for The Velvet Elvis created the impression that the bars theme was to pay tribute to Elvis Presley. The advertising campaign alone could cause consumers to believe that the nightclub was sponsored by (or associated with) Elvis Presley's estate.

The court stated:

> Evidence of actual confusion is not necessary to a finding of a likelihood of confusion, but "it is nevertheless the best evidence of a likelihood of confusion." Actual confusion that is later dissipated by further inspection of the goods, services, or premises, as well as post-sale confusion, is relevant to a determination of a likelihood of confusion. Initial-interest confusion gives the junior user credibility during the early stages of a transaction and can possibly bar the senior user from consideration by the consumer once the confusion is dissipated.
>
> EPE presented witnesses who testified that they initially thought the Defendants' bar was a place that was associated with Elvis Presley and that it might have Elvis merchandise for sale. The witnesses all testified that, upon entering and looking around the bar, they had no doubt that EPE was not affiliated with it in any way. Despite the confusion being dissipated, this initial-interest confusion is beneficial to the Defendants because it brings patrons in the door; indeed, it brought at least one of EPE's witnesses into the bar. Once in the door, the confusion has succeeded because some patrons may stay, despite realizing that the bar has no relationship with EPE. This initial-interest confusion is even more significant because the Defendants' bar sometimes charges a cover charge for entry, which

> allows the Defendants to benefit from initial-interest confusion before it can be dissipated by entry into the bar. Additionally, the finding by the district court that the Defendants' advertising practices caused actual confusion shows that actual confusion occurred when consumers first observed the mark in commerce.

The court found that there was a likelihood that consumers would be confused by the nightclub's use of the mark The Velvet Elvis. The estate of Elvis Presley also owned a restaurant in Memphis. And, the court reasoned that the nightclub's use of The Velvet Elvis mark in advertising and in the bar showed an intent to build the market for the bar by trading on the name of Elvis. The appellate court overturned the lower court's ruling and held in favor of EPE.

A Fashionable Case

In May of 1997 the magazine *POLO*, which was devoted to the equestrian sport of polo and was aimed at "serious enthusiasts" of that sport, was purchased by Westchester Media. The new owners re-focused the magazine toward "adventure" and "elegance." The magazine regularly included advertising from companies such as Cartier and Neiman Marcus.

In *Westchester Media Co., L.P.* v. *PRL USA Holdings, Inc.*,[23] the court determined that Ralph Lauren's POLO marks were well known in fashion magazines and the general public. While Polo Ralph Lauren (PRL) did not publish a magazine, the court found that it was likely that consumers might believe that the *POLO* magazine was somehow connected with Ralph Lauren. Advertisers in *POLO* magazine were predominately "fashion oriented." The court also determined that Westchester attempted to capitalize on consumer familiarity with Ralph Lauren in the hope that consumers might believe that the magazine had some connection with Lauren.

The court said:

> [C]ourts must consider eight nonexclusive factors in determining the likelihood of confusion: (1) the type of mark allegedly infringed; (2) the similarity between the two marks; (3) the similarity of the products or services; (4) the identity of retail outlets and purchasers; (5) the identity of advertising media; (6) the defendant's intent; (7) any evidence of actual confusion; and (8) degree of care exercised by consumers.
>
> The list is neither exhaustive nor exclusive. In fact, "the absence or presence of any one factor ordinarily is not dispositive; indeed, a finding of likelihood of confusion need not be supported by even a majority of the [eight] factors." The court may find a likelihood of confusion even absent confusion as to source; liability can be established "if it appears that plaintiff may have sponsored or otherwise approved of defendant's use." The standard for a likelihood of confusion for trademark infringement and unfair competition is the same under federal law and Texas law and, therefore, those claims will be examined simultaneously.

The court concluded that:

> [F]rom the findings made on each of the eight factors set out above, that PRL has shown that there is a likelihood of confusion as to the source or affiliation of the *New Polo Magazine*.

The court granted limited relief by requiring that the magazine include a disclaimer on the front cover, in lettering at least as large as the *POLO* name, that the magazine was not affiliated with Ralph Lauren. While Westchester argued that the requirement of a disclaimer violated the First Amendment, the court reasoned that:

> In balancing Westchester's claim of harm with the expressed need for injunctive relief, the court finds that Westchester has an available outlet to publish, without any restrictions at all, a magazine devoted to the equestrian sport of polo, Polo Players Edition. The injunctive relief, as fashioned here, will not cause undue disruption to Westchester's operations. The threatened injury to PRL outweighs any damage that could be caused by the limited preliminary injunctive relief ordered.

The cases that Westchester has cited in support of its contention that a critical First Amendment issue is present are not pertinent to the relief granted here. In requiring Westchester to use a disclaimer in connection with the name POLO, as the name for its "lifestyles" magazine, there is no prior restraint in violation of the First Amendment.

Marks That Cannot Be Registered

There are a few areas that could disqualify a mark from registration. These were listed earlier in the section on the two registers and their requirements to qualify for registration. Now let's take a closer look.

Confusing or Deceptive Marks. Marks cannot be registered that are "likely...to cause confusion, or to cause mistake, or to deceive."[24] This could also occur through the use of a similar or exact duplication of another trademark.

Marks that Are Descriptive of a Place or Function. Marks cannot be registered as trademarks if they are only functionally or geographically descriptive, or if the mark is only a surname. In other words, the mark must be distinctive.

Use of Flags or Insignias. Marks cannot use flags, coats of arms, insignia of cities, states, the federal government, or foreign countries.

Use of Names or Personal Identities. Marks cannot use the name, image, or signature of a person, unless written permission is given.

Use of Immoral Marks. Marks cannot be "immoral" or "scandalous."[25] This includes names that are contemptuous or disparage a person, institution, established belief, or national symbol.

LIMITED PROTECTION FOR SPECIFIC USE

Keep in mind that a mark can only be registered for the specific category in which it is used. We saw this illustrated earlier in the *Sweet 'N Low* case. The Patent and Trademark Office maintains records for the classification of trademarks under the specific category of goods or services for which the mark is used.

The name Johnnie Walker has meant high-quality Scotch Whiskey since 1880, when the trademark was created. Since its inception, the name was heavily advertised and promoted. As a result, the name Johnnie Walker has gained an excellent and very recognizable reputation. I think I can safely say almost every adult knows the name "Johnnie Walker," and quickly associates it with whiskey.

In the early 1950's, Tampa Cigar Company began marketing one of its cigars under the name Johnnie Walker. This irritated John Walker & Sons (the whiskey company) enough to file a lawsuit: *Tampa Cigar Co.* v. *John Walker & Sons, Ltd.*[26] Clearly, the use of "Johnnie Walker" on cigars was an infringement. Tampa tried to take advantage of the fame and reputation built on the Johnnie Walker name. In effect, Tampa Cigar tried to create the impression that the makers of the whiskey were the makers of the cigars. This is called "palming off."

Tampa argued that because the products were different, it should be allowed to use the name. "That," the court said, "we decline to do." While the products, whiskey and cigars, are different, they are often sold to the public at the same time and in the same stores. Bars, liquor stores, restaurants, markets, convenience stores all sell these items. Johnnie Walker whiskey and cigars could literally be placed side by side and sold to the same person at the same time. Even though the products were different, the cigar's use of the mark was an infringement.

On the other hand, there are cases where no infringement exists. A good example of this can be seen in *Holiday Inns, Inc.* v. *Holiday Out In America*.[27]

Holiday Inns had developed a considerable reputation with the public for its chain of travel motels. Its reputation was one of consistent high quality. Keeping close watch over its marks of "Holiday Inn, Holiday Inns of America," and "The Nation's Innkeeper," Holiday Inns, Inc. guarded its service marks.

In 1966 another company opened a series of trailer parks under the name "Holiday Out" and "Holiday Out in America." Holiday Out registered its trademark on January 23, 1967, describing its business as "maintaining and operating campground facilities for campsite owners." When Holiday Inn learned of this, it filed suit in July of that year.

The court found that they were totally different markets, and no proof was shown to validate Holiday Inn's claim of infringement. The court felt that allowing both trademarks to be used "is not reasonably calculated to cause confusion or mistake or to deceive." Holiday Out was allowed to retain its trademark.

Hold The Presses

Sir Speedy, a California corporation, operates a nationwide chain of 705 print shops, including 41 in the greater Chicagoland area. A Sir Speedy franchise requires that the operator agree to run the business in accordance with Sir Speedy's guidelines and pay royalties to Sir Speedy. In exchange, the franchisee becomes licensed to use the Sir Speedy trademarks and reputation to build its business.

The owner of Express Printing Company had operated as a Sir Speedy franchise from 1979 until 1994. At that time he voluntarily terminated his franchise with Sir Speedy and immediately opened Express at the same location, using the same phone number. In 1996, Sir Speedy granted a franchise to another person, who opened up just three blocks down the road from Express. After Sir Speedy was told about Express' yellow pages advertisement, it sent a letter to Express demanding that it stop referencing Sir Speedy in its advertising.

In *Sir Speedy, Inc.* v. *Express Printing Center*,[28] the court viewed Express' yellow pages advertisement in context. The Express advertisement ran in the 1998-1999 Ameritech Yellow Pages, and was located on the same page, directly below a larger Sir Speedy advertisement. The phrase "formerly Sir Speedy" was in small type and placed below the much larger Express logo. "Indeed, it would take an extraordinary amount of oversight and a few Jordanesque leaps of logic to conclude that all Sir Speedy shops had become Express Printing Centers," the court reasoned.

In the case, the court stated:

> Sir Speedy requests injunctive relief because of Mr. Matye's and Express' damage to Sir Speedy's goodwill. However, aside from this naked allegation, Sir Speedy puts forth no supporting evidence. Furthermore, and much to its detriment, Sir Speedy admits that treble damages will suffice for damage "to Sir Speedy's goodwill, business, name, and mark resulting from Defendants' use of the name and mark since the time that defendants began his infringing use." Sir Speedy also requests Express' gross receipts during the infringement period, to be used to calculate the damage to Sir Speedy's

> goodwill. Therefore, a legal remedy will be adequate for Sir Speedy, and the fact that money will compensate the loss in itself suggests that the harm is not irreparable.

Sir Speedy also argued that by stating that Express was formerly a Sir Speedy franchise, the company was subtly claiming that it could provide the same service as a Sir Speedy. The court rejected Sir Speedy's argument that the phrase "formerly Sir Speedy" could be read to mean that "Express Printing Center provides the same quality of service as Sir Speedy."

Express was not claiming to be a Sir Speedy franchise. The phrase simply noted that, previously, Express had been a Sir Speedy franchise, but that it was no longer.

The court summed up the issue of balancing the harms that each party may experience:

> If this injunction is not issued, Sir Speedy claims that it will continue to suffer incompensable harm. It is imaginable that potential customers would be drawn away from the Sir Speedy of Deerfield and to Express Printing Center because of Mr. Matye's use of the phrase "formerly Sir Speedy." However, Sir Speedy's failure to present any evidence of this, as well as the fact that seven other print shops in the area have been using the same phrase in their advertisements for nearly a decade without Sir Speedy noticing, militates against such a finding. The potential harm to Sir Speedy, at worst, appears negligible.
>
> On the other hand, if this injunction is issued, specifically the portion which requires the changing of Express' telephone number, the harm to Mr. Matye would be disastrous. For over a decade, all of Mr. Matye's business has been acquired through the

> telephone, and correspondingly, the telephone number he has had for the last nineteen years. He has over one thousand customers who communicate with him only through that telephone number. If he is forced to change that number now, Express would likely be put out of business, and Mr. Matye, along with his six employees, would be unemployed.

Because Sir Speedy failed to sustain its initial burden, the court denied Sir Speedy's request for a preliminary injunction.

Playmate Of The Year

Terri Welles is a model and spokesperson who began her modeling career with *Playboy* magazine in 1980. In May of 1980 Ms. Welles appeared on the cover of *Playboy* magazine and in the December 1980 issue, was the "Playmate of the Month." Ms. Welles received the "Playmate of the Year" award in June of 1981. Since 1980 Ms. Welles has appeared in 13 issues of *Playboy* magazine and 18 special publications that were published by Playboy Enterprises, Inc. (PEI). Ms. Welles claims that since 1980 she has referred to herself as a "Playmate" or "Playmate of the Year," all with the full knowledge of PEI.

On June 29, 1997, Welles opened a web site (www.terriwelles.com) that included photographs of herself and others, a fan club posting board, an autobiography section, and so on. The heading for the web site was "Terri Welles-Playmate of the Year 1981" and the title of the link page was "Terri Welles-Playboy Playmate of the Year 1981." The web site included a disclaimer at the bottom of most pages which stated that: "This site is neither endorsed, nor sponsored by, nor affiliated with Playboy Enterprises, Inc. PLAYBOY, PLAYMATE OF THE YEAR and PLAYMATE OF THE MONTH are registered trademarks of Playboy Enterprises, Inc."

Playboy owned the trademarks Playboy, Playmate, Playmate

of the Month, and Playmate of the Year.

In *Playboy Enterprises, Inc.* v. *Welles*,[29] the court found that Welles' use of the term Playmate of the Year 1981 was a fair use of Playboy's trademarks.

The court noted:

> [T]he other trademarks such as Playmate are not only trademarks related to Playboy magazine, but they are titles bestowed upon particular models who appear in the magazine. From the papers submitted and oral arguments, it appears that the terms Playmate, Playmate of the Month, and Playmate of the Year are titles which Playboy magazine awards to certain Playboy models, who then use the title to describe themselves. Much like Academy Award winners, crowned Miss Americas, and Heisman Trophy winners, Playboy Playmates are given a title which becomes part of their identity and adds value to their name. Indisputably, these winners represent the awarding organization or sponsor, but the title becomes part of who they are to the public.

Moreover, it was learned that Playboy encouraged models to use the Playmate title for their own self-promotion as well as the promotion of Playboy's magazine. It was also determined that Welles was not contractually restricted from using the Playmate of the Year title in any way.

The court stated:

> This case is not a standard trademark case and does not lend itself to the systematic application of the eight factors. In the case at bar, defendant has used the terms Playmate of the Year and its abbreviation PMOY on her website. She has also used the terms Playboy and Playmate as meta tags

> for her site so that those using search engines on the Web can find her website if they were looking for a Playboy Playmate. The problem in this case is that the trademarks that defendant uses, and the manner in which she uses them, describe her and identify her. This raises a question of whether there is a "fair use" of these marks pursuant to 15 U.S.C. §§ 1115(b)(4) and 1125(c)(4). Terri Welles was and is the "Playmate of the Year for 1981." Plaintiff has conceded this fact and has not submitted any evidence for the court to conclude that PEI may prevent defendant from using that term to identify herself and her award, as noted above. PEI conceded that there are no contractual agreements between it and defendant which restrict her use of any of the marks. Thus, defendant has raised a "fair use" defense which must be overcome by the plaintiff before a potential infringement under Section 43(a) of the Lanham Act or trademark dilution under Section 43(c) of the Lanham Act may be found.

A fair use defense to trademark infringement arises when the trademark also describes a person, place, or an attribute of a product, the court found. The fair use defense prohibits the trademark owner from appropriating a descriptive term for its exclusive use and so prevents others from accurately describing themselves or a characteristic of their goods or services. Welles' use of disclaimers on her web pages confirmed that there was no attempt by Welles to confuse the public into thinking that her site was a Playboy-related site.

The court concluded:

> It is clear that defendant is selling Terri Welles and only Terri Welles on the website. There is no overt attempt to confuse the websurfer into

> believing that her site is a Playboy-related website. In this case, then, defendant's use of the term Playmate of the Year 1981 "is descriptive of and used fairly and in good faith only to describe [herself]."[30] As such, the use of the abbreviation PMOY '81 is also permissible since it makes reference to her title as "Playmate of the Year 1981." Since the court finds that "PMOY '81" is a fair description of Ms. Terri Welles, it is not necessary to rule on whether the abbreviation PMOY is a protected trademark.
>
> In addition, it is unclear that irreparable harm would ensue from the continued operation of Ms. Welles' website since plaintiff has not demonstrated that there is a likelihood of confusion. As such, the court, hereby, DENIES plaintiff's Motion for a Preliminary Injunction.

DECEPTIVE FORMS OF TRADEMARKS

In addition to the Trademark Office's regulations, the FTC can become involved if the trademark or trade name used is deceptive. The FTC's concern is any form of deception of the consumer, whether in an ad or a name. Having a trademark registered does not protect it against causing other violations of the law. In cases where the name does fall into the deceptive or false advertising arena, the FTC can force the company to stop using the name.

A rental car company using the trade name "Dollar-A-Day Car Rental" was brought into court by the FTC in *Resort Car Rental System, Inc.* v. *F.T.C.*[31] It was shown that the name created an obvious impression to the public. The court said: "The 'Dollar-A-Day' slogan carries strong psychological appeal. Its connotations are obvious." The consumer could expect to be charged $1 per day for a rental car. This was certainly not true, however.

This case turned on the issue of deceptive advertising. The point here is that trademark registration did not create a shield to protect what was essentially a deceptive claim in the guise of a trade name. Dollar-A-Day was required to change its name.

FOREIGN WORDS AS TRADEMARKS

Another area to consider is the use of foreign words in trademarks. Some companies try to register marks using foreign words in place of the English version that they could not ordinarily register in English. If the words are descriptive of the product in that foreign language, then the United States will also consider them not qualified to be protected under trademark law. The guide should be that if the mark would not qualify in English, for whatever reason, it wouldn't qualify using another language either.

On another point, if a company desires to market its product in other countries, it must consider the trademark laws of those governments. They all vary and may have a large impact on the choice of a trademark. A specialist should be consulted in this case, since the requirements of foreign countries far exceed the scope of this book.

THE FEDERAL TRADEMARK DILUTION ACT OF 1995

A recent development, the Federal Trademark Dilution Act of 1995 (Dilution Act) has significant impact on trademark law.

The Dilution Act[32] was signed by President Clinton on January 16, 1996, and became effective immediately. The act amended section 43 of the Trademark Act of 1946.[33] The new act creates a significant change in the law of trademarks. Until the act was passed, use of a mark was only actionable, under federal law, if it caused a likelihood of confusion as to the source. Now dilution of a famous mark is actionable under federal law. (Take note that some of the cases discussed in this chapter were viewed under the likelihood-of-confusion standard if they were decided prior to the 1995 Act.)

Owners of "famous" marks are now able to get injunctions, under federal trademark law, that will stop uses that weaken their marks or willfully trade on the reputation of the mark, even if that use does not cause consumer confusion. The idea of trademark dilution looks to the substantial investment an owner makes in the mark and the commercial value of the mark itself. Even in the absence of actual consumer confusion, the power of a mark may be weakened by another's use.

Twenty-five states have enacted dilution statutes. In general, the states have patterned their law after the Model State Trademark Bill,[34] which in part provides:

> Likelihood of injury to business reputation or of dilution of the distinctive quality of a mark registered under this Act, or a mark valid at common law or a trade name valid at common law, shall be a ground for injunctive relief notwithstanding the absence of competition between the parties or the absence of confusion as to the source of goods or services.

Three states, Michigan, New Jersey, and Ohio, also recognize dilution as a common law doctrine.

However, dilution protection is often viewed as inadequate, even in these twenty-eight states. According to Senator Orrin Hatch, "a federal dilution statute was needed because only twenty-five states currently prohibit dilution, making national protection a 'patch-work system.'" Until the act was passed, the form and extent of remedies for trademark dilution varied from state to state. Some courts required a showing of likelihood of confusion. Other courts maintained that only non-competitive, non-confusing uses were prohibited.

As originally introduced, the bill only applied to famous registered marks. However, Congresswoman Patricia Schroeder offered an amendment to the bill which would include all famous marks within the scope of the bill. The amendment also made registration one of the factors a court may consider in determining whether a mark is, in fact, famous.

Provisions Of The Dilution Act

The new Dilution Act contains certain provisions regarding trademarks. The owner of a famous mark is entitled to injunctive relief against another's use of the mark or trade name if the use causes dilution of the distinctive quality of the mark. In addition, if the violator trades on the owner's reputation or causes dilution intentionally, then the court may award the violator's profits, actual damages, treble damages, and costs of the suit as specified in sections 1117(a) and 1118 of the Lanham Act.[35]

The owners of famous marks may now obtain an injunction against use of their marks if such use begins after the mark has become famous, and if the use dilutes the distinctive quality of the mark. Under the Act, "fair use" of a mark in comparative advertising, noncommercial use of a mark, news reporting and commentary are not actionable.

When Is A Mark Famous And Distinctive?

One of the potential difficulties with the new act is determining when a mark is famous and distinctive. The act sets forth eight guidelines to be used in determining whether a mark is distinctive and famous (courts can also add their own, as well).

The eight factors include:

1. The degree of inherent or acquired distinctiveness of the mark;
2. The duration and extent of use of the mark in connection with the goods or services with

which the mark is used;

3. The duration and extent of advertising and publicity of the mark;
4. The geographical extent of the trading area in which the mark is used;
5. The channels of trade for the goods or services with which the mark is used;
6. The degree of recognition of the mark in the trading areas and channels of trade used by the mark's owner and the person against whom the injunction is sought;
7. The nature and extent of use of the same or similar marks by third parties; and
8. Whether the mark was registered under the Act of March 3, 1881, or the Act of February 20, 1905, or on the principal register.

Dilution Of The Distinctive Quality Of A Mark

Does the use cause dilution of the distinctive quality of the mark? To help determine this, Congress amended section 45 of the Trademark Act by inserting a definition of dilution. The act defines dilution as "the lessening of the capacity of a famous mark to identify and distinguish goods or services, regardless of the presence or absence of 'competition between the owner of the famous mark and other parties,' or likelihood of confusion."

A plaintiff, then, needs to prove both the capacity of a famous mark to be identified and distinguished and a lessening of that capacity. The phrase "lessening of the capacity" does not create a clear line. So, it is likely that courts will look to cases that have interpreted state dilution statutes.

Courts will probably look to cases that have interpreted state dilution statutes. The legislative history of the Dilution Act provides that dilution "is designed to encompass all of the forms of dilution recognized by the courts, including dilution by blurring, by tarnishment and disparagement, and by diminishment."[36]

The two most common forms of dilution are "blurring" and "tarnishment." Blurring involves the "whittling away of an established trademark's selling power and value through its unauthorized use by others upon dissimilar products."[37] Hypothetical examples were given in the New York Statute: DuPont shoes, Buick aspirin tablets, Schlitz varnish, Kodak pianos, and Bulova gowns.[38]

In addition, a trademark may be tarnished when it is linked to products of shoddy quality, or is portrayed in an unwholesome or unsavory context, with the result that the public will associate the lack of quality or lack of prestige in the defendant's goods with the plaintiff's unrelated goods. Some examples of tarnishment have been found when a mark's likeness is placed in the context of sexual activity, obscenity, or illegal activity.[39]

Carve-Outs

To deal with First Amendment concerns, the Dilution Act explicitly exempts certain trademark uses from liability. First Amendment groups had criticized the dilution legislation as endangering First Amendment rights. The criticism focused primarily on the fact that parody – traditionally regarded as a form of fair use under copyright law – is one type of potential trademark dilution. In response to this criticism, Congress carved out "fair use" of a mark in comparative advertising, "non-commercial" use of a mark, and news reporting and commentary from actionable uses. (Also, see the next chapter discussion on comparative advertising.)

Other Provisions

As mentioned earlier, the act encourages federal registration of marks. The bill was amended to include federal registration as one of the nonexclusive factors a court may consider in determining whether a mark is "famous and distinctive."

Essentially, the trademark office must determine a mark to be distinctive or to have acquired distinctiveness before it will be registered. It also reasons that federal registration is a valid step in establishing and protecting a famous mark.

Owning a federally registered trademark is a defense against an action brought under the common law or a state dilution statute. Therefore, federal registration of a trademark offers a new benefit – protection against later claims of dilution under common law or state laws. However, nothing in the new law prohibits an action under the Dilution Act against the owner of a federal or state registration.

In addition, the Dilution Act does not preempt existing state dilution statutes. State laws may continue to be applied in cases involving famous marks. For example, if a mark is not famous under the Dilution Act because its fame is limited to a particular state or region, an action may be available under state law. Stay tuned.

The Act is different than many state dilution laws since it applies to only famous marks, while many state statutes do not contain such a limitation. In general, though, court decisions interpreting state statutes only extend protection to well-known marks. However, the Act allows for a nationwide injunction, which state dilution law does not. The Act also confers federal jurisdiction for dilution regardless of whether there are other Lanham Act claims asserted.

The SPAM Case

Here's an example of a case decided under a state dilution statute. In *Hormel Foods Corp.* v. *Jim Henson Prods., Inc.*,[40] the Second Circuit held that the New York Anti-Dilution statute was not violated. Hormel brought an action against Jim Henson Productions for naming a puppet character "Spa'am." The plaintiff alleged infringement and dilution of its trademark, SPAM.

According to the court, no likelihood of dilution existed by blurring – the parody was not likely to weaken the association between SPAM and the food. Nor was the SPAM mark "tarnished" by the movie's use of a character named Spa'am. Evidence showed that the character was likable and would not generate any negative associations. In addition, the parody was not being used to sell another product that would compete with Hormel.

The Cat In The Hat Case

Several cases have been decided under the Dilution Act. For example, in *Dr. Seuss Enterprises, L.P.* v. *Penguin Books U.S.A., Inc.*,[41] the court held that the Dilution Act does not apply to parodies. Defendant, Alan Katz, wrote *The Cat Not in the Hat* – a parody based on the O.J. Simpson double-murder trial. The rhymes, illustrations, and book's packaging all imitated the unique style of the works created by Theodore S. Geisel (Dr. Seuss). As a result, Dr. Seuss brought this suit against the publisher and author seeking an injunction against publishing the book.

Penguin, the publisher of Katz's book, argued that the Act does not apply to its use of the mark because of the exception contained in § 1125(c)(4)(b), which permits "noncommercial use of a mark." Dr. Seuss argued, however, that Penguin's use cannot be accepted as noncommercial because the marks are used to make their books more entertaining, thereby selling more copies.

The court rejected Dr. Seuss' interpretation of the noncommercial exception by reasoning that an expressive use is not rendered commercial by the impact of the use on sales. The court quoted Senator Hatch who, in introducing the bill, defined the exception as including "parody, satire, editorial, and other forms of expression that are not part of a commercial transaction." According to the court, commercial speech is only that speech which is part of a commercial transaction. The court therefore held that the defendant's use is exempt from the reach of the Dilution Act.

The Candyland Case

In *Hasbro, Inc.* v. *Internet Entertainment Group, Ltd.*,[42] the court issued a preliminary injunction, holding that Hasbro demonstrated a likelihood of prevailing on its claims that the defendants violated the Dilution Act and the Washington state trademark anti-dilution statute. Hasbro, claimed that the defendant was diluting the value of Hasbro's CANDYLAND mark by using the name CANDYLAND to identify a sexually explicit Internet site.

The court held that there was a probability of proving that the defendants were diluting the value of Hasbro's CANDYLAND mark and, as a result, issued the preliminary injunction.

The Ringling Bros. Case

In contrast to the *Hasbro* case, the *Ringling Bros.-Barnum & Bailey Combined Shows, Inc.* v. *B.E. Windows Inc.*,[43] situation dealt with issues of dilution through blurring of the mark's strength rather than dilution through tarnishment of the mark.

Ringling Brothers went after an injunction claiming dilution of its trademark phrase THE GREATEST SHOW ON EARTH by defendant's use of the name "The Greatest Bar on Earth" for a bar at the top of the World Trade Center in New York. Ringling Brothers' claims were based on the Dilution Act and the New York Anti-Dilution statute. The court decided that although the two marks appear similar at first glance, differences in the words chosen for each phrase and the products represented prevented dilution by blurring. The court also found that despite the famousness of the Ringling Brothers' mark, the defendant's mark was little known and thus would not cause dilution.

It's not clear from this case what exactly is the role state statutes played in reaching the decision.

Another Ringling Bros. Case

Another Ringling Brother's case, *Ringling Bros.-Barnum & Bailey Combined Shows, Inc.* v. *Utah Division of Travel Development*[44] dealt with whether the anti-dilution provision operates only where the allegedly diluting mark is identical to the famous mark, or whether it is also triggered where the diluting mark is only similar to the famous mark.

In this case, Ringling Brothers sought relief for use of the slogan THE GREATEST SNOW ON EARTH in connection with license plates, advertisements, and other promotions for Utah's resorts. The defendant claimed that the Dilution Act applies only to situations where the mark used is identical to the famous mark. Specifically, the defendant argued that language in the Dilution Act stating that the owner of a famous mark is entitled to an injunction "against another person's commercial use in commerce of a mark or tradename" refers only to use of the famous mark.

However, the court disagreed, and stated that "Congress chose to use plain and unambiguous language to make clear that a famous mark may be diluted by the use of 'a mark,' not 'the [famous] mark.'" Applying the statute to protect against the use of same or similar marks is consistent with Congress' goal of creating uniformity among states and conforming to international provisions already enacted.

The WAWA Case

In *WAWA, Inc.* v. *Haaf*,[45] the court granted WAWA, Inc., a permanent injunction to prevent defendant's use of the name HAHA 24 HR. MARKET.

Both companies used the names in conjunction with convenience stores. The court reasoned that WAWA was a strong and famous mark that had become synonymous with the plaintiff's store and even though the HAHA mark was not as well known, the name was "inherently distinctive and not merely descriptive." On this basis, the court held that the Dilution Act was violated and granted plaintiff's request for a permanent injunction. Although the decision is based on dilution grounds, it is worth noting that at least part of the court's discussion looks to elements generally considered under a likelihood of confusion analysis. For example, the opinion includes a market comparison of the two stores and an analysis of the consumers' sophistication. Also, the decision is limited to "prohibiting Defendants from utilizing the phrase 'HAHA' directly or indirectly in regard to the operation of their 24-hour market." In a pure Dilution Act analysis, these issues would not need to be considered.

RESTRICTIONS IMPOSED BY STATE LAW

While the Trademark Act grants protection of trademarks on a federal level, the separate states can also grant trademark registration. For example, trademarks for professional services may be registered by the state. This applies only to businesses that the state categorizes as "professional" (doctors, attorneys, certified public accountants, etc.). These firms, which are prohibited from using fictitious names, may trademark their firm name even though they are using surnames. The regulations of the respective state should be considered in these situations.

Cities, counties and states also maintain registers of business names. While these are not federal trademark registers, a company should consult these sources for any conflicts of name, origin or identity, which could cause legal problems.

---

1 Trademark Act of 1946, section 45, 15 U.S.C., Section 1127 (1976).
2 15 U.S.C., section 1111.
3 *Four Roses Products Co.* v. *Small Grain Distilling & Drug Co.*, 29 F.2d 959 (D.C.Cir. 1928).
4 *Fox-Stanley Photo Products, Inc.* v. *Otaguro*, 339 F. Supp. 1293 (D. Mass 1972).
5 *Duffy-Mott Co.* v. *Cumberland Packing Co.*, 154 U.S.P.Q. 498 (TTAB 1967).
6 *Bayer Co.* v. *United Drug Co.*, 272 F. 605 (SDNY 1921).
7 *Haughten Elevator Co.* v. *Seeberger*, 85 U.S.P.Q. 80 (Comm'r 1950).
8 *American Thermos Products Co.* v. *Aladdin Industries, Inc.*, 169 U.S.P.Q. 85 (D. Conn. 1970).
9 *Intel Corp.* v. *Radiation, Inc.*, 184 U.S.P.Q. 54 (TTAB 1974).
10 Al Ries and Jack Trout, *Positioning: The Battle for Your Mind* (New York: McGraw-Hill).

11 *Positioning: The Battle for Your Mind*, Page 105.
12 *American Enka Corp.* v. *Marzall*, 92 U.S.P.Q. 111 (D.C.Cir. 1952).
13 *In re Marriott Corp.*, 517 F.2d 1364 (C.C.P.A. 1975).
14 *In re McDonald's Corp.*, 199 U.S.P.Q. 490 (TTAB 1978).
15 *In re Carvel Corp.*, 223 U.S.P.Q. 65 (TTAB 1984).
16 *Harley-Davidson, Inc.* v. *Grottanelli,* 164 F.3d 806 (2d Cir. 1999).
17 *National Cable Television Ass'n, Inc.* v. *American Cinema Editors, Inc.*, 937 F.2d 1572 (Fed. Cir. 1991).
18 *Volkswagenwerk AG* v. *Hoffman,* 489 F. Supp. 678 (D.S.C. 1980).
19 *Campbell* v. *Acuff-Rose Music, Inc.*, 510 U.S. 569 (1994).
20 Robert S. Shaughnessy, Note, Trademark Parody, 72 Va. L. Rev. 1079 (1986)..
21 *Big O Tire Dealers, Inc.* v. *Goodyear Tire & Rubber Co.*, 561 F.2d 1365 (1977).
22 *Elvis Presley Enterprises, Inc.* v. *Capece,* 141 F.3d 188 (5th Cir. 1998).
23 *Westchester Media Co., L.P.* v. *PRL USA Holdings, Inc.*, No. H-97-3278, 1998 U.S. Dist. LEXIS 11735 (S.D. Tex., July 2,1998).
24 15 U.S.C., § 1052(d).
25 15 U.S.C.,§ 1052(a).
26 *Tampa Cigar Co.* v. *John Walker & Sons, Ltd.*, 222 F.2d 460 (5th Cir. 1955), 110 U.S.P.Q. 249 (Com. Pat. 1956).
27 *Holiday Inns, Inc.* v. *Holiday Out In America*, 481 F.2d 445 (5th Cir. 1973).
28 *Sir Speedy, Inc.* v. *Express Printing Center*, No. 98C3762, 1998 U.S. Dist. LEXIS 11248 (N.D. Ill, July 17, 1998).
29 *Playboy Enterprises, Inc.* v. *Welles*, No. 98-CIV-0413-K (JFS), 1998 U.S. Dist. LEXIS 9180 (S.D. Cal., May 21, 1998), 47 U.S.P.Q.2d 1186.
30 15 U.S.C. § 1115(b)(4).
31 *Resort Car Rental System, Inc.* v. *FTC*, 518 F.2d 962 (9th Cir. 1975).
32 Pub. L. 104-98.
33 15 U.S.C. § 1125(c) (Supp. 1996).
34 Model State Trademark Bill, § 12 (USTA 1964).
35 15 U.S.C. § 1125(c)(2).
36 H.R. Rep. No. 374, 104th Cong., 1st Sess (1995), reprinted in 1996 U.S.C.C.A.N. 1029
37 *Mead Data Cent., Inc.* v. *Toyota Motor Sales, U.S.A.*, 875 F.2d 1026, 10 U.S.P.Q 2d 1961 (2nd Cir. 1989).
38 *Hormel Foods Corp.* v. *Jim Henson Prod., Inc.*, 73 F.3d 497, 37 U.S.P.Q. 2d 1516 (2nd Cir. 1996).
39 *Id.*
40 *Id.*
41 *Dr. Seuss Enters., L.P.* v. *Penguin Books U.S.A., Inc.*, 924 F. Supp. 1559 (S.D. Cal. 1996).
42 *Hasbro, Inc.* v. *Internet Entertainment Group, Ltd.*, No. C96-130WD, 1996 WL 84853 (W.D. Wash. Feb. 9, 1996).
43 *Ringling Bros.-Barnum & Bailey Combined Shows, Inc.* v. *B.E. Windows Inc.*, No. 96 Cov. 4758 (SAS), 1996 WL 391886)S.D.N.Y. July 11, 1996.
44 Civil Action No. 96-788-A (E.D. Va. Sept. 10, 1996).
45 *WAWA Inc.* v. *Haaf,* No. 96-4313, 1996 WL 460083 (E.D. Pa. Aug. 7, 1996).

CHAPTER 8

COMPARATIVE ADVERTISING

One man's ceiling is another man's floor.
—*Paul Simon*

The year was 1949, June to be exact. At 350 Madison Avenue in New York, Ned Doyle, Maxwell Dane, and William Bernbach, along with 13 employees, started an ad agency with a simple philosophy of Bernbach's: "Don't be slick. Tell the truth." Bernbach had a clear and deliberate approach to advertising. He felt that most advertising was dull and failed to motivate the consumer. "Business is spending money for advertising," he would say, "and is achieving boredom with typical American efficiency."

Doyle Dane Bernbach has produced its share of memorable ad campaigns over the years since its inception. In the beginning, the agency took on clients like Ohrbach's, Levy's Rye Bread, Polaroid, El Al Airlines and in 1959, Volkswagen. Doyle Dane Bernbach created the Volkswagen campaign that stands as one of the industry's best.

Then, in the fall of 1962, Avis moved its $1.5 million account from McCann-Erickson to Doyle Dane Bernbach. At that time Hertz was the car-rental leader and pulling way ahead of Avis. So, Doyle Dane Bernbach gathered art director Helmut Krone and copywriter Paula Green together. They came away with the first of a new series of Avis ads.

The first ad read:

Avis is only No. 2 in rent-a-cars.

So why go with us?

"We try harder. (When you're not the biggest, you have to.)
We can't afford dirty ashtrays. Or half-empty gas tanks.
Or worn wipers. Or unwashed cars. Or low tires.
Or anything less than seat-adjusters that adjust.
Heaters that heat. Defrosters that defrost.
Obviously, the thing we try hardest for is just to be nice.
To start you out right with a new car, like a lively
super-torque Ford, and a pleasant smile.
To let you know, say, where you can get a good, hot
pastrami sandwich in Duluth.
Why?
Because we can't afford to take you for granted.
Go with us the next time.
The line at our counter is shorter.

Before the client was shown the new ad, Bernbach commissioned a consumer survey to pretest the ad. It scored very poorly. Nonetheless, Bernbach sold the client on the ad. Two years later Avis had increased its market share by 28 percent.

While Avis never mentioned who it tried harder than, everyone knew. Hertz was the number one car rental company at the time. Because of this, the Avis ads have become acknowledged as the first major comparative advertising campaign.

While the Avis campaign might have been the first comparative ad campaign, many more have followed, and they have run the gamut. My personal favorite started life in the late 1970's. The commercial depicted a small, bulbous store owner standing in his electric light bulb store. On the phone he proclaims: "If those bulbs aren't here tomorrow morning, I am out of business!" In the next scene, Dingbat Air Freight pulls up in front of the store, two days late. The courier scurries around frantically looking at the front door. A sign across the front of the store reads: "OUT OF BUSINESS."

Federal Express took on the giants of air freight, Emery, United Parcel, and even the United States Postal Service. Its slogan, "Twice as good as the best in the business," became fighting words for Federal Express. The company started in 1971, and promptly fell $30 million into debt. But by 1983 Federal Express had broken the $1 billion mark in annual revenue. The Federal Express ads, created by Ally & Gargano Advertising, were classics of comparative advertising. They did the job and did it very well.

When a company compares its product to another, both are identified either by name, implication, or reputation. The use of another company's identity involves the use of its image trademark, or trade name. If this use is truthful, honest, and accurate the law allows products to compare themselves. On the other hand, if Bunko Company compares its product as being superior to Binko's product and a deception results, the image and therefore value of Binko's trademark can suffer. As we saw in Chapter 7, a company's trademark is of great value, and can be protected by its owner under the law.

Therefore, comparative advertising is based on trademark law. In fact, comparative advertising is controlled by a section of the Trademark Act, which will be discussed later. Under this law there is nothing illegal about comparing a product to that of a competitor unless a deception is created. When this happens, there are basically two avenues of court action for victims. One is under federal law: Section 43(a) of the Lanham Act.[1] The other is under state law: Antidilution statutes. We examine the advantages and disadvantages of both in this chapter.

THE DEVELOPMENT OF COMPARATIVE ADVERTISING

Today, comparative advertising bombards the consumer. But this hasn't always been the case. For the most part, comparative ads were not used prior to the 1970's. One main reason was that mentioning a competitor's name gave recognition to it and, in effect, free publicity. For this reason, major companies rarely had any interest in comparative ads. These companies felt that nothing was to be gained from mentioning competitors.

Many companies also felt that showing a competitor in a bad light would create consumer sympathy for the competitor, thereby causing consumers to buy its products. As a result, companies did not want to be pictured as a "big bully picking on the little kid."

Taking part in comparative advertising was also considered by many advertising agencies to be unethical, hitting below the belt so to speak. Many advertisers and their agencies also shied away from this practice for moral reasons. The main deterrent, however, was that the FTC and the television networks would not allow comparative ads.

There was a concern over the use of advertisements that compared products. Until 1972 two of the television networks and some major print publications banned comparative ads altogether. But in 1972 the FTC came out in favor of comparative ads, and the media changed its stance. The media finally accepted comparative advertisements. The FTC proclaimed that by having the ability to compare the features of various products, the consumer could make a more informed and intelligent purchasing decision, as long as the comparison was fair and accurate.

The FTC Policy Statement established the commission's position on comparative advertising. The commission has supported the use of brand comparisons where the bases of comparison are clearly identified. Comparative advertising, when truthful and nondeceptive, is a source of important information to consumers and assists them in making rational purchase decisions. Comparative advertising encourages product improvement and innovation, and can lead to lower prices in the marketplace.[2]

Suave Shampoo's comparative advertising is a good example of the FTC's position. The ads for Suave compared it to other leading brands and claimed that Suave performed as well, but at half the price. The consumer benefited because that person could purchase a product that would do the same job at a lower cost. Because of its campaign, Suave Shampoo increased its sales from $10 million to $50 million in just four years.

Comparative advertising also contributed to a 20 percent increase in sales in one month for Wendy's Restaurants. Wendy's superb "Where's the Beef?" campaign compared its single to McDonald's Big Mac and Burger King's Whopper.

Comparative advertising can have positive benefits for both the consumer and the advertiser, but it must be fair, truthful, and accurate. Otherwise it can be a dangerous instrument. This is why the FTC and the courts keep a very watchful eye on comparative ads.

The television networks, to help assure truthful comparative advertising, have established guidelines for advertisers to follow. The National Broadcasting Company's (NBC) guidelines are reproduced as an example in Exhibit 8-1 below.

EXHIBIT 8-1: NATIONAL BROADCASTING COMPANY DEPARTMENT OF BROADCAST STANDARDS

Comparative Advertising Guidelines

NBC will accept comparative advertising which identifies, directly or by implication, a competing product or service. As with all other advertising, each substantive claim, direct or implied, must be substantiated to NBC's satisfaction and the commercial must satisfy the following guidelines and standards for comparative advertising established by NBC:

1. Competitors shall be fairly and properly identified.

2. Advertisers shall refrain from disparaging or unfairly attacking competitors, competing products, services or other industries through the use of representation or claims, direct or

implied, that are false, deceptive, misleading or have the tendency to mislead.

3. The identification must be for comparison purposes and not simply to upgrade by association.

4. The advertising should compare related or similar properties or ingredients of the product, dimension to dimension, feature to feature, or wherever possible be a side-by-side demonstration.

5. The property being compared must be significant in terms of value or usefulness of the product or service to the consumer.

6. The difference in the properties being compared must be measurable and significant.

7. Pricing comparisons may raise special problems that could mislead, rather than enlighten, viewers. For certain classifications of products, retail prices may be extremely volatile, may be fixed by the retailer rather than the product advertiser, and may not only differ from outlet to outlet but from week to week within the same outlet. Where these circumstances might apply, NBC will accept commercials containing price comparisons only on a clear showing that the comparative claims accurately, fairly and substantially reflect the actual price differentials at retail outlets throughout the broadcast area, and that these price differentials are not likely to change during the period the commercial is broadcast.

8. When a commercial claim involves market relationships, other than price, which are also subject to fluctuation (such as but not limited to sales position or exclusivity), the substantiation for the claim will be considered valid only as long as the market conditions on which the claim is based continue to prevail.

9. As with all other advertising, whenever necessary, NBC may require substantiation to be updated from time to time, and may reexamine substantiation, where the need to do so is indicated as the result of a challenge or other developments.

Challenge Procedure

Where appropriate, NBC will implement the following procedures in the event a commercial is challenged by another advertiser.

1. If an advertiser elects to challenge the advertising of another advertiser, he shall present his challenge and supporting data to NBC in a form available for transmittal to the challenged advertiser.

2. The challenged advertiser will then have an opportunity to respond directly to the challenger. NBC will maintain the confidentiality of the advertiser's original supporting data which was submitted for substantiation of the claims made in the commercial. However, NBC will ask the challenged advertiser to provide it with a copy of its response to the challenger and, where the response is submitted directly to NBC, the challenged advertiser will be requested to forward a copy of its response to the challenger.

3. Where NBC personnel do not have the expertise to make a judgment on technical issues raised by a challenge, NBC will take appropriate measures in its discretion to assist the advertiser and challenger to resolve their differences, including encouraging them to obtain a determination from an acceptable third party.

4. NBC will not withdraw a challenged advertisement from the broadcast schedule unless:

a. it is directed to do so by the incumbent advertiser;

b. the incumbent advertiser refuses to submit the controversy for review by some appropriate agency when deemed necessary by NBC;

c. a decision is rendered by NBC against the incumbent advertiser;

d. the challenged advertiser, when requested, refuses to cooperate in some other substantive area; or

e. NBC, prior to final disposition of the challenge, determines that the substantiation for the advertising has been seriously brought into question that the advertising can no longer be considered substantiated to NBC's satisfaction.

5. NBC may take additional measures in its discretion to resolve questions raised by advertising claims.

(Excerpt courtesy of National Broadcasting Company, Inc. © National Broadcasting Company, Inc. All Rights Reserved.)

TYPES OF COMPARATIVE ADVERTISEMENTS

There are basically three types of comparative ads. The most obvious type includes ads that specifically name the competitor and the product. One form of this can be seen in Suave's advertising claim that it's as good as five other named shampoos at half the price. This includes ads that attack the other product. Here are some examples: Scope mouthwash ads claim that Listerine gives "medicine breath," and Minute Maid lemonade ads label Country Time as being the "no lemon lemonade."

The second type of comparative ad is more subtle. It does not name the competitor, but rather implies it. The Avis ad campaign discussed earlier falls into this area because Avis does not name the competitor, but the implication is understood by everyone; there's no doubt that it is Hertz.

The last type involves ads that do not identify the competitors. Comparisons between "our product" and "Brand X" are good examples. This type of comparative ad was very popular in years past, probably because it was safe.

THE LANHAM ACT

The federal government has developed a policing resource through private court action that can overcome the inherent drawbacks to an FTC suit for deception. Section 5 of the FTC Act allows the government to sue companies for deceptive advertising. But what about the company that was the victim of the deception?

The Lanham Act allows one company to sue another

company directly for damages due to deception and also serves as a way of avoiding the red tape, time, and expense of an FTC action. However, to qualify under the Lanham Act, the deceptive claim must involve a comparison of products. The Lanham Act provides for private litigation for "all actions...without regard to the amount in controversy or to...the citizenship of the parties."[3]

Congress passed Section 43(a) of the Lanham Act in 1946 providing:

> Any person who shall...use in connection with any goods...any false description or representation, including words or other symbols tending falsely to describe or represent the same, and shall cause such goods or services to enter into commerce...shall be liable to a civil action by...*any person who believes that he is or is likely to be damaged* by the use of any such false description or representation. (Emphasis added.)

The real power here is in the phrase, "believes that he is or is likely to be damaged." The important word is "likely." Unlike many other areas of law that we've seen, the Lanham Act does not require that proof of actual damage be shown, only that damage is likely. This is a very broad concept, which gives the act tremendous strength.

Another benefit to the Lanham Act is expressed in the phrase "any person." This means Section 43(a) actions are available not only to companies who are in competition, but individual consumers as well. For this reason, advertisers must be very aware of the Lanham Act and its provisions. The reasons a company may decide not to sue a competitor, even if it is the victim of a deceptive comparison, usually won't apply to the consumer. Deceived consumers, now, are a concern to advertisers.

The courts originally placed severe limitations on actions brought under Section 43(a) of the Lanham Act. As we have seen before, it takes time for courts to adjust to new legislation. Just as water seeks its own level, laws also need a period of adjustment to find their level in society. For example, the courts initially refused to act unless 30 or more cases were reported against an advertiser. However, all this changed in 1954 when the Lanham Act found its level as a result of the following case.

L'Aiglon Apparel manufactured and sold through an ad campaign a distinctively styled ladies dress for $17.95. In its advertisements, L'Aiglon pictured its dress along with the price. This combination of picture and price became very identifiable with the public at the time.

Lana Lobel, a retailer, sold a different dress of much lower quality. Lobel advertised its dress in a national magazine for the price of $6.95, available through mail order. The Lobel ad showed an actual photographic reproduction of the L'Aiglon dress. This fraudulently represented to the buying public that the L'Aiglon dress was being sold at $6.95 – a representation that was not true.

Lobel's ads provoked L'Aiglon to sue in *L'Aiglon Apparel, Inc.* v. *Lana Lobel Inc.*[4] L'Aiglon alleged that two forms of damage existed. First, Lobel's misrepresentation "caused some trade to be diverted" from L'Aiglon to Lobel. And, second, other trade was lost by L'Aiglon because of the inaccurate impression given to the public that L'Aiglon had been selling a dress worth only $6.95 for $17.95.

The resulting lawsuit was filed under Section 43(a) of the Lanham Act. And, the court gave a new and clear interpretation for future cases to follow. The court said:

> It seems to us that Congress has defined a statutory civil wrong of false representation of goods in commerce and has given a broad class of suitors injured or likely to be injured by such wrong the right to relief in the federal courts.

This case interpreted the Lanham Act to mean that a single

individual or company could bring suit. The earlier requirement that there be a minimum of 30 victims before a suit could be initiated was abolished. L'Aiglon won its case against Lobel and helped establish the Lanham Act as a versatile tool against deceptive comparative advertising.

THE TRADEMARK LAW REVISION ACT OF 1988

On October 19, 1988, Congress passed the Trademark Law Revision Act of 1988. Although the 1988 act deals primarily with trademark matters, it also changed comparative advertising law in several respects. Certain changes may prove significant, but whether they will actually have a material affect on advertising litigation remains an open issue.

Section 43(a) of the Lanham Act has been amended to read:

> (a) Any person who, on or in connection with any goods or services, or any container for goods, uses in commerce any word, term, name, symbol, or device, or any combination thereof, or any false designation of origin, false or misleading description of fact, or false or misleading representation of fact, which –
>
> (1) is likely to cause confusion, or to cause mistake, or to deceive as to the affiliation, connection, or association of such person with another person, or as to the origin, sponsorship, or approval of his or her goods, services, or commercial activities by another person, or
>
> (2) in commercial advertising or promotion, misrepresents the nature, characteristics, qualities, or geographic origin of his or her or another person's goods, services, or commercial activities, shall be liable in a civil action by any person who believes that he or she is or is likely to be damaged by such act.

As amended, section 43(a) will make illegal any advertising that disparages "another person's goods, services, or commercial activities." This change was intended to circumvent decisions in cases holding that section 43(a) extended only to false statements concerning the advertiser's own products and did not apply to claims that merely disparaged the products of another.

Disparagement (often referred to as trade libel or injurious falsehood) is a false and deliberate attack on the advertiser's product. This disparagement tends to diminish the respect, confidence or esteem in the product that is attacked. Disparagement exists where the quality of the advertiser's product is impugned, and violates the Lanham Act. While this a new element in section 43(a), it is one that the advertiser must be aware of.

Another change to section 43(a) was its application to false representations pertaining to, among other things, the "commercial activities" of the advertiser or of another person. Section 43(a) previously applied only to false representations pertaining to the "inherent quality or characteristics" of the defendant's "goods." After the 1988 amendment however, the section applies to false representations pertaining to any "commercial activities."

Failure To Disclose

In connection with the 1988 amendment of section 43(a) of the Lanham Act, Congress considered including a section that made actionable a failure to disclose. The section was eventually not included in Section 43(a) and the Senate report stated:

> To respond to concerns that it could be misread to require that all facts material to a consumer's decision to purchase a product or service be contained in each advertisement...the committee does not through the deletion indicate that it condones deceptive advertising, whether by

> affirmative misrepresentations or material omission, and leaves to the courts the task of further developing and applying this principle under section 43(a). *Gillette Co.* v. *Norelco Consumer Products Co.*[5]

For example, in *McNeilab, Inc.* v. *American Home Products Corp.*,[6] the court, in interpreting an alleged omission in an advertisement under the Lanham Act, stated "a failure to inform consumers of something, even something that they should know, is not per se a misrepresentation actionable under Section 43(a) of the Lanham Act."

Under state law, failure to disclose a fact may or may not be false advertising, depending on the particular state law. For example, in two cases that involved a claim by consumers that AT&T failed to disclose its practice of rounding up to the next full minute the cost of long distance telephone service, a New York court held that the failure to disclose was not actionable under New York law, while a California court held that AT&T's omission was false advertising under California law.

The Federal Trademark Dilution Act Of 1995

We discussed the Dilution Act in detail in Chapter 7 on trademark (please review). While trademark is where this act will have the most impact, it will nonetheless spill into the comparative advertising realm. In an effort to confront First Amendment concerns, the Dilution Act explicitly exempts certain trademark uses from liability. Congress carved out "fair use" of a mark in comparative advertising, "noncommercial" use of a mark, and news reporting and commentary from the universe of actionable uses.

While the following case was decided under a state dilution statute, it shows the reasoning of how the Dilution Act can impact comparative advertising directly. State dilution statutes are discussed specifically later in this chapter.

The Deere Case

Here's an example of a case decided under state dilution statute. In *Deere & Co.* v. *MTD Prod., Inc.*,[7] the court found that New York's Anti-Dilution statute applies to situations where a competitor's alteration of a company's well-known trademark does not necessarily result in the blurring or tarnishment of the mark.

Deere owns a trademark for a deer design ("Deere Logo"). MTD, the defendant, manufactures and sells lawn tractors that compete with products sold by Deere & Company. MTD ran an advertising campaign in which the Deere Logo was depicted in unflattering ways. In one of the commercials, the deer was running in fear, while being chased by a dog and an MTD tractor. Deere brought suit under the New York Anti-Dilution statute.

The district court ignored the federal trademark infringement claim that was part of the suit and ruled that the plaintiff had demonstrated a probability of prevailing on its state dilution count under "dilution by blurring." The district court issued a preliminary injunction limited strictly to activities within New York state.

The Second Circuit affirmed the district court's finding of a likelihood of dilution, but for different reasons. The Second Circuit did not believe that the defendant's use of the Deere Logo gave rise to a likelihood of dilution by blurring because such use posed a slight, if any, risk of impairing the identification of Deere's mark with its products. The court also did not think that such use constituted dilution by tarnishment since, according to the court, tarnishment is usually found where a mark is depicted in a context of sexual activity, obscenity, or illegal activity.

The Second Circuit found that the New York Anti-Dilution statute includes an undefined cause of action which protects trademark owners from attempts by others to increase sales of competing products by altering and satirizing the trademark.

According to the court, defendant's use of the Deere Logo fell within the proscribed range since it altered a well-known mark for the sole purpose of promoting a competing product rather than to make a social comment for its own sake.

The court did note that a seller of commercial products may, without violating the New York Anti-Dilution statute, use a competitor's mark to identify the competitor's product in a comparative advertisement. Provided "the mark is not altered, such use serves the beneficial purpose of imparting factual information about the relative merits of competing products and poses no risk of diluting the selling power of the competitor's mark." Additionally, a satirist may lawfully use another's mark in a parody to make a point of social commentary, so long as the satirist is only selling the publication that contains the parody and not another product. The case illustrates the growing strength of state dilution law. It also, however, illustrates the potential First Amendment concerns that arise under anti-dilution statutes.

GROUPS THAT CAN SUE UNDER THE LANHAM ACT

As mentioned earlier, under the Lanham Act any "person" may bring a civil suit "who believes that he is or is likely to be damaged by the use of any such false description or representation." This broad definition creates a huge group of people who are potential litigants. Under the Lanham Act the term "people" covers businesses, groups, or individuals. In the following sections we will examine consumer and business groups separately.

The Consumer's Standing To Sue

Although an individual consumer may bring suit under the Lanham Act, in practice, this is not very common, mainly because the cost of a court battle is so high.

Some, but not all, courts feel that individual consumers must show a "commercial interest" in order to bring suit. In the case that follows we see how the court dealt with both issues.

Arneson, an inventor, brought suit against the Raymond Lee Organization, a patent service. The suit claimed that Raymond Lee had lured clients through misleading advertisements. The case was *Arneson* v. *Raymond Lee Organization, Inc.*[8]

The court felt that the wording in the act should be taken literally, i.e., "any person" could bring an action under the Lanham Act. Arneson was "any person" and was allowed to sue Raymond Lee. That is what the act says, and that is what it means. After all, consumers can be injured by deceptive comparative advertising, as well as competitors. An ad can clearly compare two products, pointing out the flaws in one but if this is done through incorrect, misleading, or deceptive statements, the consumer will be damaged when the claim is relied on to make the purchase. As a result, the consumer will purchase the product based on incorrect information, and a commercial interest will become involved.

A Company's Standing To Sue

The most common Lanham Act issue involves direct competitors in business: companies having a commercial interest that is directly threatened by deceptive comparative advertising. Situations that are most likely to create court actions involve companies or products that compete directly for the same market. We see this in most of the cases illustrated throughout the rest of this chapter.

A company may, however, have a commercial interest even though it does not compete directly with the other company. As an example, two companies may be in totally different industries, selling to completely separate markets. Yet, one company may create a deception that affects the other company's name or image.

The best example I can recall to illustrate this point occurred in 1978. This is also one of the more unique cases we discuss in this book. In November of that year, Pussycat Cinemas began showing an X-rated movie called *Debbie Does Dallas*. The film was described by the court as "a gross and revolting sex film whose plot, to the extent that there is one, involves a cheerleader at a fictional high school, Debbie, who has been selected to become a Texas Cowgirl." (Courts sometimes make editorial opinions.) The movie ends with a scene showing Debbie in a cheerleader's uniform bearing a striking resemblance to the outfit worn by the Dallas Cowboys Cheerleaders. In fact, 12 minutes of the film shows Debbie engaging in various sexual acts while wearing all, or part, of the uniform.

The movie was promoted with a poster showing Debbie wearing the same outfit, i.e., a combination of white boots, white shorts, blue blouse, white star-studded vest and belt, all of the same style and cut as that used by the Dallas Cowboys Cheerleaders.

As soon as the Dallas Cowboys Football Club learned of the movie, the organization filed suit under the Lanham Act in *Dallas Cowboys Cheerleaders, Inc.* v. *Pussycat Cinema, Ltd.*[9] seeking an injunction to prohibit the distribution and showing of *Debbie Does Dallas* because of the movie's use of the Dallas Cowboy's image and trademark.

The actual Dallas Cowboys Football Club employs 36 women who perform as the Dallas Cowboys Cheerleaders. *The Dallas Cowboys Cheerleaders, Dallas Cowgirls*, and *Texas Cowgirls* are all registered trademarks. The group has gained worldwide exposure (excuse the pun) and has made many public appearances outside of football stadiums. As a result, the Dallas Cowboys organization has earned substantial revenue from its commercial ventures involving the Cheerleaders.

The Dallas Cowboys wanted the movie banned because it felt that the public was likely to be deceived by the representations in the movie and promotional poster. Pussycat claimed, as a defense, that the public would not be confused about the origin of the film. Such confusion is a requirement the courts look for in Section 43(a) actions. Yet, the court said about the existence of consumer confusion: "[T]he public's belief that the [trademark's] owner sponsored or otherwise approved the use of the trademark satisfies the confusion requirement."

Simply put, the issue here was the association between *Debbie Does Dallas* and the Dallas Cowboys Football Club – or, more accurately, the assumed association between the two. In fact, a commercial interest existed even though the two "products" did not directly compete. The movie did create a confusion in the consumer's mind and injured the Dallas Cowboys' business, name, and reputation. The Dallas Cowboys Cheerleaders won their case.

REQUIRED ELEMENTS THAT CREATE A LANHAM ACT VIOLATION

The concept of the Lanham Act is very simple. When an ad claims a superiority over another product, a comparison is used. This occurs many times in today's advertising – Mitsubishi compares itself against Toyota, Hebrew National against Oscar Mayer, and Chrysler against Ford.

However, if that comparison is disparaging, deceptive or misleading, a lawsuit may be brought by the victim. But certain specific conditions must exist in order to create a violation of the act. In fact, there are five elements that must exist:

- A false statement about the product must be made;
- The advertising must have actually deceived or have the tendency to deceive;
- The deception must be material;
- The advertised product must have entered interstate commerce; and
- There must be injury or a likelihood of injury.

One case where all of these requirements developed involved two power tool manufacturers, Skil and Rockwell. The two companies manufacture portable electric drills and jigsaws for sale to the consumer. In 1973 Rockwell began a major national advertising campaign using television, magazine, and newspaper. It was estimated that the campaign reached approximately 80 million people.

The Rockwell campaign revolved around a comparison of product testing, which had been done by an independent testing lab. Under "supposedly normal-use situations," Skil, Rockwell, and other manufacturers' tools were tested. The results of this independent testing was used in Rockwell's ad campaign. In the ads, Skil products were clearly shown and were identifiable by their labels.

The Lanham Act was violated because Rockwell's ads were not factually accurate regarding the performance of the Skil product line. Mainly, the test results used to compare product performance were biased. The testing was not conducted under normal-use conditions. The Skil products were put through much more demanding test conditions than would have been encountered in normal use, which was not disclosed in the advertising.

As a result, Rockwell used false, misleading, deceptive, and incomplete claims in its ads about Skil. When Skil realized the content of Rockwell's ads, it filed suit in *Skil Corp.* v. *Rockwell International Corp.*[10]

Skil not only sought an injunction against Rockwell, it also wanted damages for its loss of profits and damage to its name, which would affect future earning power. This one case developed the guidelines for the five elements required to bring a lawsuit under the Lanham Act. Now let's examine each requirement.

1. Making False Statements About A Product

The first requirement to bring suit under the Lanham Act is that the ad must create a deception in one form or another by making disparaging, false or partially correct claims, or failing to disclose material facts about its product.

Going back to our case, Rockwell made false statements about the performance qualities of Skil tools. The facts used in its ads were supposedly the result of testing the tools under normal-use conditions. This was not the case, however, so the results used in the ads were clearly false, misleading, and deceptive.

2. Requirement That Advertising Actually Deceived Or Has A Tendency To Deceive

The second element required is that the advertisement actually deceived consumers or had a tendency to deceive a substantial portion of the intended audience. This also refers to the confusion requirement we saw in the *Dallas* v. *Pussycat* case. Confusion is another way of saying "tendency to deceive."

Consumers who buy power tools base their decision on many factors: price, the features of the tool, performance, and durability. If a consumer buys a Rockwell power tool over a Skil tool, it would be for one or more of these reasons. If, as in this case, the consumer buys the Rockwell product based on the performance features it claims to have over Skil, the consumer has been clearly deceived. Since the Rockwell ads gave factually incorrect information in the comparison of Skil products, actual deception occurred.

3. The Deception Must Be Material

The third requirement necessary to bring suit is that any deception created must be a material one. That is, it must have been likely to have influenced the purchasing decision. We saw this in Chapters 2 and 3 in the discussion of deception and the FTC Act. The same reasoning applies here.

In the Rockwell case, its false and misleading claims involved the performance of Skil products. This is a primary criterion for purchasing a power tool, as discussed in the previous section. Statistics about the durability and performance of a power tool would weigh heavily in the consumer's decision to purchase or not to purchase a specific brand of product. Rockwell's deceptive statements were, without question, material.

4. The Advertised Product Must Have Entered Interstate Commerce

The fourth element required under the Lanham Act is that the goods advertised were involved in interstate commerce. Simply, the product must have been engaged in commerce between two or more states. At first glance this may seem to disqualify many products. However, the courts feel that if any portion of the product – during any stage of its manufacture – crossed state lines, or even if the product has an "effect" on interstate commerce, then the product is considered to have entered interstate commerce.

It is not just the final product that can meet the interstate requirement. If any part of the tool, say the power cord, is purchased out of state, then interstate commerce is involved. This means that many more products qualify under the interstate commerce requirement than would first appear.

In the case of Rockwell, both its and Skil's finished products were sold in every state and therefore were clearly involved in interstate commerce; there was no need to look into the manufacturing of either product to see if a more subtle form of interstate commerce was involved.

5. Injury Or Likelihood Of Injury Must Exist

The final requirement that must be present in order to sue under this act is that the advertisement has injured, or is likely to injure. Actual injury can result either from the diversion of sales or by the weakening of goodwill belonging to the product or service.

In the Rockwell case actual injury occurred in both forms. For Skil, the injury involved sales (lost profits) that were lost due to the deception. Skil also suffered potential future injury because, in the consumer's eye, Skil products were of a lesser quality as a result of Rockwell's deceptive advertising. In essence, the future selling power of Skil's long established name and reputation had been diminished. By the way, Skil won its case. It received an injunction and was awarded damages.

TYPES OF CLAIMS THAT VIOLATE THE LANHAM ACT

As the use of comparison advertisements grew, certain types of claims began to appear. Of those, a certain group has emerged that can violate the Lanham Act – claims that a product does something that others don't do. If the product claims are true, accurate and can be supported, this is legal.

However, claims that unjustifiably attack another product's qualities or performance or do so without support are another matter. There are a few different forms that this can take. The claim may be implied or it may be created, for example, through the use of a survey, disclaimer, or trademark.

Literally False Claims

A High-Pressure Case

Let's look at a literally false claim. K&M Plastics, Inc., was a manufacturer of fiberglass pressure tanks for use in the water treatment industry. K&M mailed advertising to customers stating that K&M was "the only manufacturer with NSF certification" and that it had a pending application for National Sanitation Foundation (NSF) certification for its pressure vessels. NSF certification indicated that it had been deemed suitable for holding drinking water. K&M's competitor, Park, claimed that the statements were false and misleading because it and other manufacturers in the industry were, in fact, NSF certified.

The court in *K&M Plastics, Inc.* v. *Park International, Inc.*[11] found that K&M's representations violated both the Illinois

Deceptive Trade Practices Act and the Lanham Act because they suggested that Park was not NSF certified when, in fact, it was.

K&M was enjoined from using advertising that implied that it was the only manufacturer of pressure tanks in the water treatment industry with certification by the NSF; that it had obtained certification for products when it had not; and that its competitor (Park International Corp.) did not have NSF certification for its products.

A Repelling Case

Avon's advertising claimed that its bath oil was an effective insect repellent. This was held not to be literally false under the Lanham Act. This case revolved around an advertiser's failure to inform the consumer that its product was not approved by a federal regulatory agency. The court in *Avon Products, Inc.* v. *S.C. Johnson, Inc.*,[12] came to the conclusion that as long as the advertiser did not falsely claim that it actually had Environmental Protection Agency (EPA) approval of its product, no approval would be assumed.

Laboratory testing showed that the bath oil did have some effect as a repellent. However, the bath oil did not meet EPA standards for insect repellents. The court stated that without specific claims by the manufacturer that the product was approved by the government, the law did not determine that the public would assume that it was approved. In addition, testing showed that the bath oil had some ability as a repellent. Avon had no duty to state in its advertising that the bath oil was not an insect repellent.

The court stated:

> In other words, the standard of falsity under the Lanham Act is distinct from federal licensing standards and, absent an explicit claim that a product has been approved by the relevant federal agency or that the product meets federal standards,

a Lanham Act plaintiff must prove that the defendant's efficacy claims are literally false, not simply that they fail to meet current federal licensing standards.

Implied Claims

Certain claims are literally true but create a misleading impression, as seen in the FTC's interpretation of deceptive advertising. This can also occur from a comparative advertising standpoint. A good example can be seen in a series of ads run by Hertz in early 1984 that contained the following copy:

Hertz
has more new cars
than Avis has cars.
If you'd like to drive some of the newest
cars on the road, rent from Hertz.
Because we have more
new 1984 cars than Avis
or anyone else has cars – new or old.
Hertz. The #1 way to rent a car.

The above ad was produced by Hertz's ad agency Scali, McCabe & Sloves. Obviously, the objective of the ad was to lure renters away from Avis and to Hertz. The lure was based on the claim that Hertz had more cars available for rental. Therefore, Hertz implied that it had an advantage over Avis, an advantage that consumers should exploit. The reality though was quite different. While the statements were literally accurate, they painted an inaccurate picture for the consumer.

Here's the problem. As of the time the ad ran, Hertz had a total of 97,000 (1984 model) cars. Avis, on the other hand, had a total of 95,224 (1984 model) cars. So, literally, the claim that Hertz had more 1984 model cars than Avis was true. However, of the 97,000 Hertz cars, only 91,000 were available for rental: The others were part of Hertz's licensee fleet. Although Hertz did own them, these cars were not part of the cars available to rent.

When an "apples-to-apples" comparison was made (that is, cars available for rental), Hertz had only 91,000 compared to Avis' 95,224. That is why the claim was misleading. The ad claimed that Hertz "has more new cars." But the impression on the potential car renter – to whom the ad was directed – was that Hertz "has more *rental* cars" than Avis. Because of this ad campaign, Avis sued Hertz for violation of the Lanham Act in *Avis Rent-A-Car* v. *Hertz Corp.*[13] Avis won.

Antibiotic Drugs

Eli Lilly claimed that its competitor, Roussel, was stating that cefaclor (a generic antibiotic drug) was an "alternative to brand name drugs." The implication according to Lilly was that the drug was approved by the Food and Drug Administration (FDA). While Roussel had originally received FDA approval for distribution of the drug in the United States, that approval was withdrawn by the FDA when it found misrepresentations in the application.

In *Eli Lilly and Co.* v. *Roussel Corp.*,[14] the court held that simply placing a drug on the market did not act as an implied representation that the FDA approved it. Such violations would need to be dealt with under the Federal Food, Drug, and Cosmetics Act (FFDCA). However, under the FFDCA, no private right of action existed, so Eli Lilly couldn't directly pursue action there. On the other hand, allowing Eli Lilly to proceed on a Section 43(a) basis (merely by placing its drug on the market) would permit Eli Lilly to enforce the Food, Drug, and Cosmetics Act, the court reasoned. Without any statement or representation in the competitor's advertising that declared that it had obtained "proper FDA approval," that portion of Eli Lilly's complaint was dismissed.

The Insulin Case

Novo Nordisk manufactured an insulin pen injection system for personal use by diabetics. Novo's system consisted of three parts: the actual pen, a disposable needle, and an insulin cartridge. The needle and the cartridge were replaceable. The system was designed as a convenient way for diabetics to administer insulin themselves.

The problem arose when Novo ran advertisements that stated that the pen injection system was to be used only with Novo disposable needles. And on the package for the pen system it also stated: "Use with Novolin PenFill cartridges and NovoFine disposable needles only."

Becton, a competitor, also sold disposable insulin needles, and charged that Novo's ads gave the impression that Becton's disposable needles were not compatible with the Novo's system. However, clinical tests showed that Becton's needles were compatible with the Novo system.

In *Novo Nordisk AIS* v. *Becton Dickinson and Co.*,[15] Novo claimed that these statements were merely sales statements and were not literally true or false.

However, the court reasoned that "Becton has submitted consumer survey evidence, as discussed below, that supplies 'the causative link between the advertising and [Becton's] potential lost sales.'"

Becton submitted three clinical tests that proved that its needles were, in fact, compatible with Novo's system.

Becton also submitted the results of a survey that included over 200 diabetics and 100 pharmacists. This consumer survey looked at Novo's statement that the pen system should only be used with Novo disposable needles. The results showed that 48 percent of the diabetics and 56 percent of the pharmacists said that the pen system could be used only with Novo needles. When asked directly if the pen system could be used with other needle brands, 90 percent of the diabetics and 96 percent of the pharmacists said no. The court found the survey reliable and held that Novo's "use only with" claim misled consumers to believe that other brand needles were incompatible with the Novo.

Initially, the court agreed with Novo that, considering that Novo's statement is a directive, it can't be deemed literally true or false. On its face, Novo's statement makes no factual claim. Taken literally, Novo's statements merely request diabetes patients to buy NovoFine needles. A sales recommendation, as long as it is non-deceptive, is proper and shows only that Novo is interested in promoting its product over others, the same as any other company.

The court said:

> The real issue before the Court is whether the "to be used only with" statement is deceptive, or implicitly false, such that it is likely to mislead and confuse consumers. Had Novo included the word "recommended" before its statements or deleted the word "only," the Court has little doubt that Novo's advertisements would be lawful. However, since Novo chose neither of these options, the Court is left to consider whether Novo's statements convey a misleading or confusing message.
>
> [T]he "to be used only with" language is understood in the diabetes treatment industry to mean that other needles are incompatible. Based on this evidence, Becton has demonstrated a likelihood that Novo's advertisements convey a message of incompatibility.

The court went on further to reveal:

> In addition...Becton points to litigation in Europe that resulted in Novo being enjoined from making analogous statements. There, a German court and the Commission of the European Communities found that Novo's advertisements

> were misleading because Becton's needles were compatible with Novo's pens. While this Court is not bound by the European findings, it does believe that these findings support Becton's current claim of compatibility.

The court granted Becton a preliminary injunction to keep Novo from making its claims.

The Unsafe, Safe Can Opener

Telebrands sold a patented hand-held can opener named "Safety Can." Its device opened cans by cutting through the rim of the lid so that no sharp edges were left either on the lid or on the rim of the opened can.

The Media Group, a competitor, also sold a can opener that it advertised as leaving the lid of the can smooth.

The Media Group's can opener was advertised on television, showing a woman opening a can with its can opener. The woman then rolled the lid of the can across her arm. The announcer claimed: "Sharp lids become a thing of the past...." What was not clear in the ad was that the can opener cut through the side of the can beneath the rim, leaving the rim of the can as sharp as a lid cut with a conventional top-cutting can opener.

This case is a good example of an implicitly false claim. The ad was challenged by Telebrands.

In *Telebrands Corp.* v. *The Media Group, Inc.*,[16] Telebrands claimed that the statement about sharp lids and the shots of the woman rolling the lid across her arm implied that a person using the Media Group's can opener would be handling cans that were left in a safe condition.

To make its point Telebrands conducted the following consumer survey:

The first question asked the respondents what the main message of the commercial was.

The second question asked: "[D]id the [commercial] say anything about the safety of the can opener, or was this not mentioned, or do you not recall what was said." If a respondent answered that the commercial did mention the safety of the can opener, that person was asked what the commercial said specifically.

The third question asked if the commercial mentioned anything about the availability of the can opener in different colors.

The fourth question asked: "[D]id the [commercial] say anything about the edge of the can after it has been opened, or was this not mentioned, or do you not recall what was said." If the respondent answered that the commercial did mention the edge of the can, that person was asked what the commercial said specifically.

Lastly, the fifth question asked: "[D]id the video say anything about the edge of the lid after the can has been opened, or was this not mentioned, or do you not recall what was said." If the respondent answered that the commercial mentioned the lid, that person was again asked what the commercial said.

In response to the first question, 20% of the respondents answered that the main message was "will not cut yourself/can't cut yourself."

The court determined that some consumers came away with the impression that use of the safety can opener would leave the lid and the rim of the can smooth. In other words, a user would not get cut. In reality, Media Group's can opener left the rim of the can as sharp as the lid of a can opened with a traditional top-cutting can opener. The court concluded:

> The context in which consumers are likely to view the commercial confirms the reliability of the survey's conclusion that some consumers are misled by defendant's advertising. In this country, prior to Safety Can's introduction to the market, hand-held

> can openers opened cans in a manner that almost universally left a lid with a sharp edge and a can with a smooth rim. Defendant's advertisement informs the public that its "amazing new" hand-held can opener leaves a safe lid, but does not warn the public that by doing so, the can rim, which is left smooth by an ordinary hand-held can opener's operation, is now sharp. No warning of this situation is given to the consumer viewing the advertisement. Accordingly, the consumer is misled into believing the sharp lid problem, associated with the use of traditional can openers, has been remedied while the smoothness of the rim remains unaffected. Therefore, the evidence that some respondents took away the message from the [commercial] that they "will not cut [themselves]/can't cut [themselves]" is not unsupportable.

Media Group contended that the order of some of the questions rendered the survey results unreliable. The court agreed that the order of the questions, especially four and five, could produce misleading results. Therefore, the court based its opinion that the advertisement was misleading on the responses to question one alone. As the court noted: "[E]ven recognizing the survey's limitations, the Court cannot conclude that it does not merit consideration."

As in this case, false advertising is not confined to literal falsehoods. It also encompasses claims that are literally true, but have a tendency to deceive when considered in the overall context of the message. In *American Home Products Corp.* v. *Johnson & Johnson*,[17] the court stated that the fact that:

> [S]ection 43(a) of the Lanham Act encompasses more than literal falsehoods cannot be questioned....

> Were it otherwise, clever use of innuendo, indirect intimations, and ambiguous suggestions could shield the advertisement from scrutiny precisely when protection against such sophisticated deception is most needed. It is equally well established that the truth or falsity of the advertisement should be tested by the reactions of the public.

First, the actual message or message conveyed by the advertisement is examined. Next, it must be determined whether the claim is likely to mislead a consumer. Typically, these determinations are made by looking at consumer surveys, market research, or clinical tests, although direct consumer testimony may also be used. As the court stated in *American Brands, Inc.* v. *R.J. Reynolds Tobacco Co.*,[18] under the Lanham Act: "The question in such cases is what does the person to whom the advertisement is addressed find to be the message?"

Using Consumer Surveys and Test Results Relating To Deception

One of the difficulties in succeeding in a Lanham Act case involves proving that a comparative ad is deceptive, or is likely to deceive. One method is by using market research or consumer surveys as evidence to prove that the consumer was deceived or is likely to be deceived. For this reason consumer surveys are widely used in Lanham Act cases.

A good case in point involved Coca-Cola. In early 1984 Tropicana Products began airing a television commercial for its orange juice product. Olympic athlete Bruce Jenner was shown squeezing an orange and claiming: "It's pure, pasteurized juice as it comes from the orange." In the next scene, Jenner poured the fresh-squeezed juice into a Tropicana carton while continuing: "It's the only leading brand not made with concentrate and water."

When the ad came to their attention, Coca-Cola the makers of Minute Maid orange juice filed suit in *The Coca-Cola Company* v. *Tropicana Products, Inc.*[19] In this case, Tropicana's claim was blatantly false. The ad claimed that Tropicana contained unprocessed, fresh-squeezed juice. In fact, it was pasteurized (heated to 200 degrees) and then frozen prior to being packaged. In the commercial, Jenner claims that Tropicana is "pasteurized juice as it comes from the orange." Well, pasteurized juice doesn't come from oranges. The representations in the commercial were clearly untrue.

Tropicana and Minute Maid, at the time, were the top selling ready-to-serve orange juices on the market. If Tropicana's advertising were allowed to mislead consumers into believing that its juice was better because it was fresh-squeezed and unprocessed, then Minute Maid would lose a significant share of the market.

Prior to the trial, Coca-Cola commissioned a consumer reaction test to be conducted by ASI Market Research, Inc. to measure consumer recall of the commercial. At trial, Coca-Cola produced this evidence showing that a "significant number of consumers would be likely to be misled" by the Tropicana ad. The court ruled in favor of Coca-Cola.

This does not mean that any survey can be used effectively in court. On the contrary, courts are very critical about the credibility and thoroughness of any survey brought into court as evidence. The intent of the court is to make certain that damage amounts are calculated accurately. Surveys are acceptable as evidence only if they accurately reflect the consumers' true impressions.

The Feminine Hygiene Case

Smithkline redesigned its feminine hygiene douche, Massengill, and began an advertising campaign to promote it. In the advertising, Smithkline claimed that its Massengill douche was

"Now Designed for Better Cleansing" (the claim was based on its improved design). C.B. Fleet, the manufacturer of a competing product, Summer's Eve, filed suit against Smithkline in *C.B. Fleet Co., Inc.* v. *Smithkline Beecham Consumer Healthcare, L.P.*[20] The issue here involved whether the claim was literally false.

After Smithkline began claiming an "improved design," it conducted several tests to study the new design against the old design. And also against the Summer's Eve product. Here's where it gets tricky: Regarding the "improved design" claim, the tests showed that the new Massengill design outperformed the Summer's Eve product, but that its old Massengill design outperformed its new Massengill design.

This case involved a comparative superiority claim. Smithkline claimed that its "improved design" claim wasn't false even though the tests showed that its previous design was better than its new design. Smithkline's experts described the new nozzle design and emphasized those features that improved its mechanical performance "overall" over the old model. The court agreed with Smithkline that its "improved design" claim referred to the entire new design and not just its cleansing capabilities. The court found that the claim was not literally false.

The court held that C.B. Fleet had to prove that the claim was literally false. The fact that no clinical tests had been done did not matter because the advertisement made no claim that the statement was based on any tests. There is a difference between advertising that implies a claim that is favorable and which is supported by tests, and an ad that makes no actual reference to tests but simply asserts a favorable fact (a "bald" claim). In these different situations, the burden of proof is different. When a "tests show" claim is challenged, the challenger must prove only that the referenced test did not validate the claim. When a "bald" claim is challenged, the challenger has the more difficult task of proving that the favorable fact asserted is itself false.

The court put it this way:

> As to the "improved-design" claim, SmithKline witnesses described the new nozzle design, emphasizing those features that improved its mechanical performance over that of the old model. Specifically, they noted that it has deeper side channels which improved outflow, a more rounded tip which made insertion easier, and improved flow dynamics which made the douching process more gentle and, possibly, safer. As to its actual cleansing properties, as measured by the blue-dye studies, they conceded that it did not perform better than did the earlier design (as they had hoped it would) though, per those studies, it did still outperform the Summer's Eve douche in this respect.

In this case the court stated: "[T]he relevant question for determining the required proof is whether the advertisement made an assertion of test-validation to the consumer public. If it was not asserted in the advertised claim, it was not made part of the claim being challenged as false. If it is later revealed, through discovery or otherwise, that the claim was test-based, the claimant obviously may challenge the test's reliability in attempting to prove false the advertised fact, but falsity of that fact remains the required object of proof."

Fleet argued that the superiority claim implied that it was based on clinical tests. The court disagreed because the advertising claim made no express claim of test validation and there was no language in the ad that implied testing. The court reasoned that "because the 'comparative superiority' claim was not a 'tests show' type, Fleet's burden was to prove affirmatively that the advertised claim of 'comparative superiority' was literally false."

After hearing testimony from experts on both sides, the court held that the tests conducted by Smithkline did support its superiority claim.

I Know What You Did Last Summer

Here's a recent case that examines implicitly false advertising in an advertising campaign for the horror movie *I Know What You Did Last Summer.* The ads claimed that the movie was by the same creator as the motion picture *Scream,* and was determined to be implicitly false in *Miramax Films Corp.* v. *Columbia Pictures Entertainment, Inc.*[21]

Miramax, the creator of the highly successful horror movie *Scream,* claimed that Columbia's advertising campaign for the movie *I Know What You Did Last Summer* (*Summer*) falsely created the impression that the two movies came from the same "creator," namely, Wes Craven, the director of *Scream.*

Columbia's advertising campaign used statements such as "From The Creator of *Scream*...Last Time He Made You Scream, This Time You Won't Have The Chance," and "From the Creator of *Scream* Comes A New Chapter in Terror."

In truth, the only connection between the two movies was the screenwriter Kevin Williamson. Williamson wrote the original screenplay for *Scream.* The screenplay for *Summer* was adapted from a novel. In the television and print ads, Williamson's name appears in small print but he's never named or otherwise identified as the "creator," as the advertisements referred.

Miramax submitted two consumer surveys to prove that consumers believed that the movie *Summer* was created by or somehow associated with Wes Craven. The first study surveyed consumers who saw *Summer* during its opening weekend. The second study surveyed consumers standing in line to view the movie *Summer*. Both surveys included 15-to-40-year-olds and were taken in the top 180 motion picture markets in the United States.

In the first study, 17 percent of the consumers responding to open-ended questions believed either that (1) *Summer* was a sequel to *Scream*; (2) the creator of *Summer* produced *Scream*; (3) the creator of *Summer* directed *Scream*; or (4) the creator of

Summer was Wes Craven. Only 2 percent of the consumers thought that the advertising for *Summer* communicated that *Summer* was by the writer of *Scream* or by Kevin Williamson. According to the second study, the results were 20 percent and 1 percent, respectively.

Based on this evidence, the court held that the *Summer* advertising was likely to mislead potential viewers into believing that *Summer* came from the same source as *Scream*. The consumer surveys proved that, based on the advertising, an appreciable number of consumers held the false belief that there was a significant connection between the two films. The advertisements failed to name Kevin Williamson, or the writer of the movie script, as the only link between the two films. Columbia allowed the advertisements to imply that the films were more closely related.

Using Consumer Surveys And Test Results As Comparison

Until now we've looked at surveys as a way of showing the existence of deception. However, surveys can also be used in an ad as a way of comparing products. Using consumer-survey information as part of a comparative advertisement may create a deception. This can occur if the results or methodology are misrepresented.

In the mid 1970's, two of the leading cigarette manufacturers in the United States were Phillip Morris and Lorillard (which was owned by Loew's Theatres). In 1972 Phillip Morris introduced Marlboro Lights, and in 1975 it introduced Merit. Merit was supported by an intensive ad campaign pushing a claim of good taste in a low-tar cigarette. In 1979 Lorillard began marketing its low-tar brand, Triumph.

In April of 1980 Lorillard hired SE Surveys to conduct "A National Taste Test: Triumph Menthol versus Winston Lights, Marlboro Lights, Vantage and Merit Non-Menthols." The results of that test were used in Triumph's advertising. Lorillard's ads for

Triumph claimed:

"Triumph. National Taste test Winner.
Triumph tastes as good or better than
Merit, or...Marlboro Lights.
In rating overall product preference,
more smokers independently
chose Triumph over Merit,
or...over Marlboro Lights."

As a result of these ads, Phillip Morris filed suit for an injunction. The case was *Phillip Morris, Inc.* v. *Loew's Theatres, Inc.*[22] At the time of the trial, Merit was the largest selling low-tar cigarette in the United States, generating over $350 million in revenue. About $80 million was spent on advertising that one brand alone.

The actual issue in this case revolved around the use of a taste test. Lorillard claimed that its brand Triumph was the "National Taste Test Winner." Yet, actual test results revealed that 36 percent preferred Triumph over Merit for taste; 24 percent considered the two brands to be equal; 40 percent preferred Merit.

Obviously, from the test results, Merit not Triumph was preferred for taste. The ad failed to inform the consumer that, based on the same criteria, 64 percent stated that Merit tastes as good or better than Triumph. In other words, Triumph stated a statistic, which was true, and implied that the figure made it the winner. In reality, the other brand scored higher, which the ad failed to report.

Obviously, the results of the taste test were not used accurately in the Triumph advertisements. Phillip Morris submitted evidence at trial that consumers believed credible tests had proven that Triumph tasted better than Merit. As a result, the court stated: "[T]here is convincing evidence that consumers are being deceived by Triumph's false claim of taste superiority."

The Roach Bait Case

A television commercial for Maxattrax, entitled "Side by Side," depicts a split-screen view of two roach bait products on two kitchen countertops. On the left is the Maxattrax box; on the right, a generic "Roach Bait" box that bears a vague similarity to the Combat brand sold by Clorox. The announcer asks: "Can you guess which bait kills roaches in 24 hours?" The camera moves past the boxes to reveal a clean, pristine kitchen, uninhabited by roaches, on the Maxattrax side. On the other side, the kitchen is in a chaotic state: cupboards and drawers are opening, items on the counter are turning over, paper towels are spinning off the dispenser, a spice rack is convulsing and losing its spices, apparently the result of a major roach attack. The message "Based on lab tests" is shown at the bottom of the screen. The two roach bait boxes then reappear on the split-screen, and several computer-animated roaches on the "Roach Bait" side appear to kick over the generic box and dance happily upon it. The final scene shows only the Maxattrax box, with the announcer concluding: "To kill roaches in 24 hours, it's hot-shot Maxattrax. Maxattrax, it's the no-wait roach bait."

In this case, *United Industries Corp.* v. *The Clorox Co.*,[23] we find another example of a claim that was not literally false.

Scientific testing by both companies showed that Maxattrax contained a fast-acting nerve toxin that actually killed roaches within 24 hours from the time they made contact with the product.

The court explained:

> The district court determined that the Maxattrax commercial conveyed an explicit message that the product killed roaches in 24 hours and found that this message was literally true. The court concluded that scientific testing performed both by United Industries and Clorox sufficiently demonstrated that Maxattrax, which contains the

> fast-acting nerve toxin known as chlorpyrifos or Dursban, will actually kill a roach within 24 hours of its coming into contact with the product. In response, Clorox argues that the district court erroneously "ignored the explicit visual statements in United's advertising that, as a matter of law, combine with its express audio statements to determine its literal meaning."
>
> Our review of the record satisfies us that the district court's determination that the commercial was literally true is not clearly erroneous. The court was clearly correct in its assessment that the audio and print components of the advertisement are literally true. The scientific evidence and expert testimony contained in the record satisfactorily established that Maxattrax roach bait "kills roaches in 24 hours." Clorox protests that this statement is literally true only in circumstances where a particular roach actually comes into contact with the product. This complaint rings hollow. The requirement that roaches must come into contact with the poison for it to be effective is the central premise of the roach bait line of products. We will not presume the average consumer to be incapable of comprehending the essential nature of a roach trap.

Combat argued that the commercial also projected three literally false messages: (1) that Maxattrax controlled roach infestations in consumers' homes within 24 hours; (2) that Combat, and others, were ineffective in consumers' homes within 24 hours; and (3) that Maxattrax provided superior performance in consumers' homes in comparison to Combat and other brands.

The court disagreed since the evidence, which included

clinical tests and expert testimony, established that the 24-hour claim was literally true and that the ad did not make any claims about complete infestation control.

The court reasoned:

> The depiction of a Maxattrax box in a pristine, roach-free kitchen, coupled with the depiction of a kitchen in disarray in which animated roaches happily dance about on a generic roach trap, is not sufficient, in our view, to constitute literal falsity in the manner in which it was presented. When the context is considered as a whole, moreover, the audio component of the advertisement, emphasizing only the 24-hour time frame and quick roach kill with no mention of complete infestation control, fosters ambiguity regarding the intended message and renders the commercial much more susceptible to differing, plausible interpretations. Thus, in our view, the district court's finding that the commercial did not explicitly convey a literally false message that Maxattrax will completely control a home roach infestation within 24 hours is not clearly erroneous.

Resource Versus Ensure

In *Abbott Laboratories* v. *Gerber Products Co.*,[24] an advertisement that claimed a liquid dietary supplement was "preferred" by consumers over a competitor's product became the point of contention. This case considered whether consumer test results were reliable. Gerber's advertising campaign for its nutritional supplement called Resource claimed: "America Prefers Resource over Ensure" and "National Preference Winner Resource Beats Ensure." The maker of Ensure (Abbott Laboratories) filed suit for false advertising, arguing that Gerber's tests did not substantiate its advertising claims.

The court stated:

> In the case at issue, Abbott argues that Gerber's claim that Resource is preferred over Ensure is literally false, and, therefore, Abbott need not show consumer confusion. This Court agrees that if Abbott can establish that Gerber's claim is literally false, that evidence of consumer confusion is not needed.
>
> Abbott asserts that Gerber's claim is false in two ways: (1) the tests Gerber relies upon to support its claim were conducted as taste tests and not as tests indicating overall preference, and (2) these tests do not show that Resource tastes better or is preferred over Ensure.

During the trial, the court found that Gerber's preference claim was in reality a taste claim. During the trial, experts established that the nutritional supplements of both brands were nutritionally the same. In fact, most consumers used the products for medical reasons and would chose the product that tasted better.

The "product preference test" conducted by Gerber included 4,000 consumers over the age of 55 who were users or potential users of a nutritional supplement. The test showed that consumers preferred Resource over Ensure in every category tested.

The court went on to state:

> This Court finds Gerber's use of test participants over the age of fifty-five, whether users or potential users, was appropriate. NSBs [nutritional supplement beverages] are in a dynamic market. Consumers are entering and leaving the market at a very high rate. Furthermore, consumers are in the market for a very short period of time,

> making it necessary for companies who market NSBs to reach potential users. If Gerber wanted to limit the test participants to users and potential users, the only way to limit the participants would be to have a requirement that test participants be over the age of fifty-five since a majority of the users of NSBs are over the age of fifty-five. Gerber limited its test participants to those most likely to have used or will use NSBs in the relatively near future. Furthermore, Gerber qualified its claim so that consumers would know that the test was limited to test participants over the age of fifty-five.

As we can see, the court rejected Abbott's contention that the test participants should have been restricted to consumers who actually used a nutritional supplement. The court determined that users as well as potential users of a product were acceptable participants in consumer tests.

The consumer tests conducted by the defendant were sufficiently reliable to substantiate the advertising claim.

Using Disclaimers In A Comparative Advertisement

There are situations in which an advertiser adds a disclaimer to an advertisement to offset what would otherwise be a deceptive claim. In 1984 the FDA authorized the sale of the drug ibuprofen in over-the-counter 200 mg tablet form. American Home Products marketed the aspirin substitute under the brand name "Advil." A competitor, Upjohn, marketed the drug under the brand name "Nuprin." Prior to the over-the-counter release of ibuprofen, Upjohn manufactured and sold ibuprofen only as a prescription under the trademark of "Motrin." Now, who's on first?

American Home Products produced an ad campaign for Advil through its ad agency, Young & Rubicam. The campaign included magazine ads and television commercials. In the ads, an

Advil tablet was shown. The tablet was orange in color and the same size and shape as the prescription drug Motrin. Copy in the ads exclaimed: "ADVIL contains ibuprofen, the same medicine as the prescription drug MOTRIN now in nonprescription strength."

When Upjohn learned of the ads, it contacted American Home Products requesting that it change them to avoid any confusion for the consumer. American Home Products changed the color of its Advil tablets to brown. It also changed the disclaimer used in its ads to read: "ADVIL contains a nonprescription strength of ibuprofen, the medicine found in the prescription brand, MOTRIN." American Home Products also added a visible line of copy to the television commercial that Advil is from Whitehall (a division of American Home Products) and that Motrin is manufactured by another company.

The revised print ads read:

ADVIL IS ADVANCED MEDICINE FOR PAIN

ADVIL isn't Tylenol and it isn't aspirin.
Advil contains ibuprofen—the medicine in the prescription brand Motrin, the product of another company.
Now ibuprofen is available in nonprescription strength in Advil. Ibuprofen has been proven so effective in relieving many types of pain that doctors have already prescribed it over 130 million times.

After American Home Products made these changes and added the disclaimers, Upjohn went to court requesting an injunction in *Upjohn Co.* v. *American Home Products Corp.*[25] Upjohn felt that the consuming public would still be misled and confused by American Home Product's ads for Advil. Upjohn wanted to stop any implication that Advil tablets were the same color as Motrin, that Advil was manufactured by Upjohn, that Advil was the equivalent of Motrin, or that the ingredient in Advil was Motrin.

The court examined these issues and determined that the new changes and disclaimers used in the Advil ads were sufficient. For the trial, consumer reaction surveys were instituted to determine the effect of the revised ads on the public. The surveys found that a higher percentage of consumers polled recalled the disclaimers as opposed to those who felt that Advil and Motrin were made by the same manufacturer. The court said: "[S]uch disclaimers are preferred to an absolute prohibition of the potentially misleading reference as a means of alleviating consumer confusion...."

The important point to remember is that consumer confusion can be alleviated through the use of disclaimers or qualifying language. However, if this is challenged in court by the competitor, consumer surveys will be relied on and the survey will be used to determine whether use of the disclaimer alleviates the majority of consumer confusion.

Fair Use Of Trademarks In Comparative Advertising

There is nothing illegal *per se* in referring to another company's trademark. But this is true only if the use is informational and not likely to cause confusion about the source of the product or its qualities. We see many instances where an ad will make reference to, or show another company's product. In most cases this is done fairly and to compare qualities or features that one product has making it distinctive from the other. These comparisons must be true and accurate. Comparisons must not be deceptive or mislead the consumer, and proof to support the claim must exist prior to making the claim.

Here is another example of deceptive comparisons. Johnson & Johnson Company is a major manufacturer of Johnson's Baby Oil, Johnson's Baby Powder, and Johnson's Baby Shampoo. Quality Pure also manufacturers skin oil, skin powder, and shampoo. Its products are packaged in containers that exhibit an amazing resemblance to the J & J products. In fact, at a quick glance, the competing product packages look the same. Such similarity can be an infringement of trademark. This close similarity, known as "palming off" involves the use of another company's trademark to cause a likely confusion as to the origin of the product.

As an example, let's look at the shampoo products. The Johnson & Johnson Baby Shampoo bottle is elongated and made of clear plastic. The clear, yellow shampoo can be seen through the container. The Quality Pure shampoo package was almost identical to J & J's, down to the style and color of label. The J & J label contained a tear drop with the slogan "No More Tears," while the Quality Pure label used three tear drops on the label with the words "Tear Free."

The packaging of all of the Johnson & Johnson products was distinctive and unique. Suffice it to say that Quality Pure was in competition with Johnson & Johnson. But the competitor is not allowed to package its product so as to ride on the coattails of the image, reputation, and goodwill built over many years by Johnson & Johnson.

Quality Pure produced and aired a 30-second commercial to promote its new line of products. In its commercial, an actress, Jane Paley, claimed that Quality Pure Shampoo "gave me the same lather" as Johnson & Johnson Baby Shampoo. The commercial also claimed that "both were extremely mild." The gist of the commercial was that while the products gave the same results and had the same qualities, Quality Pure was cheaper than Johnson & Johnson.

As a result Johnson & Johnson brought suit in *Johnson & Johnson v. Quality Pure Mfg., Inc.*[26] Two items were at issue in this case: the similarity of the packaging and the advertising claim of equal performance and lower price. The court expressed its opinion that competing on a price level is perfectly acceptable. Yet it is not acceptable to "sell a competing product on the basis of a lower price and at the same time use [packaging] designed and calculated to fool the customer into the belief that he is getting someone else's product." See Chapter 3 for more on labeling requirements.

Further, Quality Pure had no basis for the claims used in its commercial. Quality Pure conducted a "survey" by handing out samples of competing shampoos to shoppers at shopping centers. The competing shampoos were unidentified except for a mark on each bottle, either X or Y. Then Jane Paley was given the samples and, after using them, scored them as equal. This result is what appeared on the television commercial.

The problem rests on the credibility of the "survey." There was no way of determining which brand of shampoo was in which bottle, or even if the products were different. The test was rigged and without any substantiation, and in the court's eye "had far too much resemblance to three-card monte to be accepted...."

REMEDIES AVAILABLE UNDER THE LANHAM ACT

Originally, there were essentially three remedies available under the Lanham Act: an injunction against the deceptive ad, corrective advertising by the company that ran the deceptive ad, and monetary damages. In order to recover damages or require corrective advertising, however, it must be shown that the buying audience was actually deceived. If only a likelihood of deception can be shown, an injunction is the sole remedy allowed.

The 1988 act made the damage remedies set forth in section 35 of the Lanham Act applicable to actions under section 43(a).

Section 35(a) provides as follows:

> When a violation of any right of the registrant of a mark registered in the Patent and Trademark Office, or a violation under section 43(a), shall have been established in any civil action arising under this chapter, the plaintiff shall be entitled...subject to

> the principles of equity, to recover (1) defendant's profits, (2) any damages sustained by the plaintiff, and (3) the costs of the action. (Emphasis added.)

Prior to the amendment, most courts that had considered the question held that section 35(a) applied to actions under section 43(a), although most of those cases involved unregistered trademarks rather than advertising issues.

The 1988 act authorizes courts to apply the remedies provided in section 35, and provides damages and profits should continue to be "rarely assessed" in actions under section 43(a). The 1988 act also makes the remedies provided for in section 34 (injunction) and section 36 (destruction of infringing copies) applicable to actions under section 43(a). Injunctions, however, have always been available in false advertising cases.

Injunction As A Remedy

This is the most common (and quickest) remedy under the Lanham Act. Essentially, an injunction bans the ad from running. The most important function of an injunction is that it stops the publication of the deceptive ad.

Most people have the view that the legal system moves very slowly. It may be refreshing to learn that a preliminary injunction can be obtained within months or even weeks of filing a complaint. This can be a major consideration to the company who is the victim of an advertisement showing its product in an unfavorable, disparaging or misleading way.

Discussed earlier, one of the features of an injunction is that it stops further damage. The negative side, though, is that it does not remove the deception already created. Further, an injunction does not compensate the victim for injury either.

In order to be granted an injunction, the person or company requesting one must show the court that irreparable damage will be suffered if the injunction is not issued. Actual lost sales need not be proved, but it must establish that there is more than a belief of injury. If the advertising claim is explicitly false, no other proof is required. However, if the advertisement is less than explicit, some other evidence must be shown that establishes that the claim is likely to deceive the consumer.

The Toro Company and Jacobsen Manufacturing (a division of Textron) are manufacturers of various labor-saving machines for consumer use. A few years ago a controversy arose when Jacobsen produced an ad directed toward dealers. The ad showed a performance comparison between its Sno-Burst snow thrower and Toro's Snow Master. In the ad Jacobsen's Sno-Burst appeared to come out ahead in the categories rated.

When Toro learned of this, it filed suit seeking an injunction against the ad. Toro obviously felt the ad was deceptive. The court, in *Toro Co.* v. *Textron, Inc.*,[27] discussed whether the ad misled dealers about the features of both machines. The ad headline claimed: "The New Jacobsen. You Get More To Sell." The ad then proceeded to compare categories such as reserve power, engine size, starter priming, gas/oil ratio, wheel size, snow-throwing distance, fuel capacity, auger housing, handle adjustment, and warranty.

The basis for Jacobsen's comparison, however, proved to be insignificant and arbitrary. Here are some examples. Regarding the category under "starter," Jacobsen claimed that its machine didn't need to be primed to start, while the Toro did. The court found that, in fact, the Jacobsen required pulling the starter cord a number of times before the machine would start, just as with the Toro model. This, the court reasoned, constituted priming. The comparison was considered false.

Some of the other claims by Jacobsen were literally true, but they were insignificant as a valid comparison. Jacobsen claimed that its handle was adjustable and Toro's was not. A true statement. However, on closer examination, the Jacobsen handle was only adjustable one inch. The claim that the handle on the Jacobsen was adjustable was truly misleading.

As you can see, a number of the compared features between the two machines were found to be false or so insignificant that there was a likelihood of confusion of the buyer. While Toro could not show that purchasers were actually deceived (a requirement for damages), it could show that the ads had a tendency to deceive. In order to obtain an injunction, "[Toro] need only show that the misrepresentations of which it complains 'have a tendency to deceive'...[T]he three claims found to be false do have a tendency to mislead consumers into purchasing a Jacobsen rather than a Toro, and injunctive relief is, therefore, appropriate."

Toro was granted an injunction against Jacobsen for making the deceptive claims.

Corrective Advertising

This type of remedy is essentially an award of money. The company who created the deception is ordered by the court to use its own money to produce advertising that will offset the originally deceptive ads.

The intent of corrective advertising is for the new ads to correct the confusion created by the deceptive ad. The company must produce its own ads with a message that effectively counters the previous, deceptive message, much like a public apology.

Durbin Brass Works is a manufacturer of brass lamps, selling its lamps through, among other outlets, The Sharper Image stores and catalog. In the early 1980's, Richard Schuler also sold lamps of the same style and design as Durbin's. The Schuler lamps were sold through, among other outlets, the American Express Company catalog. Schuler's lamps were manufactured in Taiwan as opposed to Durbin's lamps, which were manufactured in the United States.

Durbin filed suit in *Durbin Brass Works, Inc.* v. *Schuler*[28] claiming that Schuler's lamps caused a decline in sales of its lamps because of consumer confusion between the two manufacturers. In other words, due to the identical appearance of the two brands of lamp, consumers were drawn to buy the cheaper version while believing that they were buying the original Durbin lamp.

Schuler sold over $60,000 worth of imitation lamps before Durbin brought suit. The court agreed with Durbin that these sales were a result of the public's confusion. Durbin testified at the trial that it would cost his company $10,000 in advertising to offset the deception created by the Schuler ads. The court concluded that Schuler's actions created actual consumer confusion, and therefore an award of corrective advertising was appropriate. Durbin was awarded $10,000 as damages plus court costs. It was ordered, by the court, that the $10,000 be spent by Schuler on corrective advertising to offset the deception that it had originally created.

Monetary Damages As A Remedy

Until the early 1980's no court had awarded monetary damages to a plaintiff under Section 43(a) of the Lanham Act. All prior awards were either injunctions or corrective advertising. This, however, was to change when a case came to court that was able to prove a direct loss of sales or potential sales. In seeking damages, two things must be shown: actual consumer deception and consumer reliance on the false claim.

Another section of the Lanham Act, Section 35, has been utilized in comparative advertising cases. This has given even more punch to an already strong law by expanding the damages allowed. Under Section 35, the lost profits, actual damages, and the cost of the lawsuit may be recovered. Treble (three times) damages and attorney's fees may also be recovered in certain extreme cases.

Ryder System was in the car and truck rental business. In the mid-1970's, James A. Ryder began to lose control of the company that he had begun. New internal management had largely ignored him for a few years.

Even though Ryder was over 60 years old, he decided to leave Ryder System and start a new company to compete with

Ryder. The new car and truck rental company was originally named "Jarpool," but was later renamed Jartran. Originally Jartran, with only mediocre results, leased large truck and trailer units to businesses. Seeing the potential in consumer rentals, Mr. Ryder wanted to expand into the self-move rental field. This would bring the new company directly into competition with the leader, U-Haul.

In order to put his plan into motion, Mr. Ryder went heavily into debt to acquire the vehicles that he needed. Once Jartran obtained its vehicles, it needed to get them on the road fast. And that meant competing head-to-head with U-Haul for customers. As anyone in advertising knows, it is extremely difficult to dislodge the number one company in any field. But Jartran was determined to do it.

So, Jartran, through its ad agency Sandra C. Tinsley Advertising, created an ad campaign to generate consumer rentals. The campaign was designed to compete on a price advantage over U-Haul. Did the campaign work? Jartran's gross revenues in 1979 (its first year) were $3 million. In 1980, however, gross revenue rose to $58 million, and in 1981 to $95 million. Yes, I'd say it worked. Within months Jartran had taken over more than 10 percent of the market.

The campaign worked so well that it won the Gold Effie award from the American Marketing Association for "its overall marketing effectiveness." In Mr. Ryder's opinion the campaign "knocked the competition (U-Haul) on their ass."

How did this affect U-Haul? In 1979 U-Haul had almost all of the self-move rental business in the United States. Others had entered the field over the years but with very little effect. U-Haul's largest competition came, coincidentally, from Ryder System in 1979. However, U-Haul's revenue began to decrease after Jartran's campaign broke. In 1981 U-Haul saw, for the first time, its revenue decrease with a loss of $49 million. To stem the tide, U-Haul tried to counteract Jartran's efforts with $13.6 million spent on advertising between 1981 and 1982.

Without its concentrated and comparative ad campaign directed at U-Haul, Jartran would not have gained the market share that it did. The ads were simple. The headlines claimed:

U-Haul It to Dallas for $0000.
...Jartran It to Dallas for $000.
Save big money...to almost any city.

The price stated for Jartran was always less than the stated U-Haul price. In the ads, a picture of each company's rental truck was shown. However, the size of the U-Haul truck used in the ad was smaller to make it look less attractive.

In June 1980 U-Haul filed suit to stop Jartran's campaign. *U-Haul International, Inc.* v. *Jartran, Inc.*[29] was the case. U-Haul claimed that Jartran's price comparison ads were false and that Jartran knew it. The court agreed.

The Jartran rental prices shown in the ads were "special promotion prices," although this very important point was never mentioned. The intent, which worked, was to convey that the advertised price was Jartran's regular price. Actually, the rates advertised were considerably lower than those stated on Jartran's one-way price sheet. Conversely, the price Jartran quoted for U-Haul rentals was its regular price plus a distribution fee. Again this was not disclosed in the ad. In fact, a distribution fee is charged in only certain unique rental cases.

The price claims that Jartran made were blatantly false and were intended to mislead the consumer into renting from Jartran instead of U-Haul. A series of consumer surveys were used as evidence to substantiate that: "The false and deceptive statements contained in the Jartran ads were material in influencing rental decisions of a substantial segment of the public interested in renting self-move equipment."

The claims in the Jartran ads were published deliberately.

They were known by Jartran to be false, and they were intended to damage U-Haul by taking business away through deception. Under the Lanham Act, "a court may award additional damages, up to three times the amount awarded for actual damages according to the circumstances of the case."

In this case, the court awarded actual damages of $20 million to U-Haul. In addition, the court felt that Jartran's advertising was "willful, malicious or in reckless disregard of the rights of [U-Haul]," and an additional $20 million was awarded – $40 million in all. U-Haul was also awarded court costs and attorney's fees.

DILUTION STATUTES: STATE ACTION AND COMPARATIVE ADVERTISING

What we've seen up to now is federal control over comparative advertising. But many states have also become involved by enacting what are termed "dilution statutes." In practice, through use of these statutes, each state controls deceptive comparative advertising within its borders. Since these are state laws, the necessity for interstate commerce is not a requirement.

Dilution is defined basically as any whittling away or general eroding of the trademark's selling power. In other words, any nonowner use of a trademark or trade name that diminishes the selling power of that mark violates the statute. As we saw with the Lanham Act, a comparative ad, if untrue, can diminish the selling power of the competitor's trademark.

Dilution actions can take place under three situations: generic usage, unrelated usage, and comparative advertising. The first is generic usage. This situation exists when a competitor uses another trademark to denote a class of product; in other words, using another's mark as if it were the generic type of product.

The second area, unrelated usage, covers use of a trademark on products that do not compete and have no connection. Here again this type of use erodes the value of the mark. We saw this earlier in *Dallas Cowboys Cheerleaders, Inc.* v. *Pussycat Cinema, Ltd.* Although that case was brought under the Lanham Act (federal law), the principle is the same.

The final area involves literal comparative advertising. As in federal cases, comparative advertising can injure a product's selling ability by re-directing the trademark's image to another company's product. This violates antidilution statutes because consumers no longer associate the reputation of the trademark exclusively. In other words, a dilution of the mark has occurred.

Twenty-five states have enacted dilution statutes. In general, the states have patterned their law after the Model State Trademark Bill,[30] which in part provides:

> Likelihood of injury to business reputation or of dilution of the distinctive quality of a mark registered under this Act, or a mark valid at common law or a trade name valid at common law, shall be a ground for injunctive relief notwithstanding the absence of competition between the parties or the absence of confusion as to the source of goods or services.

In addition, three states, Michigan, New Jersey, and Ohio, recognize dilution as a doctrine of common law.

CELEBRITY LOOK-ALIKES AND THE LANHAM ACT

In Chapter 5 look-alikes that can violate a celebrity's right of publicity or privacy were discussed. In 1985 the issue of look-alikes was taken one step further. It crossed over into the comparative advertising realm.

Early in 1984 a man named Phil Boroff appeared in an ad for National Video, a video rental service. Boroff was hired through his agency, Ron Smith's Celebrity Look-Alikes in Los Angeles,

California, because he bore a striking resemblance to Woody Allen.

In the National ads, Boroff appeared behind the counter where two of Woody Allen's films were displayed. The headlines for two of the ads claimed:

We'll Make You Feel Like A Star.
You Don't Need A Famous Face
To Be Treated To Some Famous Service.

These ads ran in national magazines including National Video's own publication and *Video Review* magazine. In the *Video Review* issues the ad carried the disclaimer: "Celebrity double provided by Ron Smith's Celebrity Look-Alikes, Los Angeles, Calif."

Allen was not amused by this. He filed suit in *Allen* v. *National Video, Inc.*[31] What made that case unique was that it was the first time that a suit of its type succeeded under the Lanham Act. Allen claimed a violation of Section 43(a). He argued that a likelihood of confusion existed between Boroff and himself.

Even if some consumers realized that the person in the ad was not Allen himself but a look-alike, these same people most probably will assume another possibility. That is, the public "may be led to believe by the intentional reference to [Allen] that he is somehow involved in, or approves of their product."

You might say that there was a disclaimer in the ad stating that the person was a double for Allen. Yet, a small disclaimer at the bottom of an ad was not sufficient to offset an overall deceptive advertisement.

The result of this case was that an injunction was issued, stopping the use of any of the ads with Boroff as Woody Allen. National Video paid Allen $425,000, and Boroff was barred from appearing as a look-alike for Allen in any advertising that "creates the likelihood that a reasonable person might believe that he was really [Allen] or that [Allen] had approved of the appearance."

However, Boroff could appear in advertising only if a "clear and bold" disclaimer or clarifying body copy was used.

While this case is relatively recent, not to mention revolutionary, it shows a trend. Other courts may follow; they may not. Only time will tell. Yet, the Lanham Act was effectively used to stop the use of a look-alike who in essence created a false impression by comparing Boroff to Allen. And after all, that's what the Lanham Act was created for. The moral of this story is that the deceptive comparison can be that of people as well as of products.

---

1 15 U.S.C., Section 1125(a).

2 S. Kanwit, *Regulatory Manual Series*, Federal Trade Commission, Section 22.17 n. 13 (1985).

3 Section 39 of the Lanham Act, 15 U.S.C. Section 1125(a).

4 *L'Aiglon Apparel, Inc.* v. *Lana Lobel Inc.*, 214 F.2d 649 (3rd Cir. 1954).

5 *Gillette Co.* v. *Norelco Consumer Products Co.*, 946 F. Supp. 115, 132 (D. Mass. 1996) (CCH 1996-2 Trade Cases 171,657).

6 *McNeilab, Inc.* v. *American Home Products Corp.*, 501 F. Supp. 517, 532 (S.D.N.Y. 1980).

7 Deere & Co. v. MTD Prod., Inc., 41 F.3d 39, 32 U.S.P.Q. 2d 1936 (2nd Cir. 1994).

8 *Arneson* v. *Raymond Lee Organization, Inc.*, 333 F. Supp. 116 (C.D. Cal. 1971).

9 *Dallas Cowboys Cheerleaders, Inc.* v. *Pussycat Cinema, Ltd.*, 604 F.2d 200 (1979).

10 *Skil Corp.* v. *Rockwell International Corp.*, 375 F. Supp 777 (N.D. Ill. 1974).

11 *K&M Plastics, Inc.* v. *Park International, Inc.*, No. 97C8018,1998 U.S. Dist. LEXIS 456 (N.D. Ill., January 7,1998).

12 *Avon Products, Inc.* v. *S.C. Johnson, Inc.*, 984 F. Supp. 768 (S.D.N.Y. 1997).

13 *Avis Rent-A-Car* v. *Hertz Corp.*, 782 F.2d 381 (2nd Cir. 1986).

14 *Eli Lilly and Co.* v. *Roussel Corp.*, No. 97-2009 (JAG), 1998 U.S. Dist. LEXIS 10063 (D.N.J., July 1, 1998).

15 *Novo Nordisk AIS* v. *Becton Dickinson and Co.*, 997 F. Supp. 470 (S.D.N.Y. 1998).

16 *Telebrands Corp.* v. *The Media Group, Inc.*, CCH 1998-1 Trade Cases 172,042.

17 *American Home Products Corp.* v. *Johnson & Johnson*, 577 F.2d 160 (2d Cir. 1978).

18 *American Brands, Inc.* v. *R.J. Reynolds Tobacco Co.*, 413 F. Supp. 1352 (S.D.N.Y. 1976).

[19] *The Coca-Cola Company* v. *Tropicana Products, Inc.*, 690 F.2d 312 (1982).
[20] *C.B. Fleet Co., Inc.* v. *Smithkline Beecham Consumer Healthcare, L.P.*, 131 F.3d 430 (4th Cir. 1997).
[21] *Miramax Films Corp.* v. *Columbia Pictures Entertainment, Inc.*, 996 F. Supp. 294 (S.D.N.Y. 1998).
[22] *Phillip Morris, Inc.* v. *Loew's Theatres, Inc.*, 511 F. Supp. 855 (S.D.N.Y. 1980).
[23] *United Industries Corp.* v. *The Clorox Co.*, 140 F.3d 1175 (8th Cir. 1998).
[24] *Abbott Laboratories* v. *Gerber Products Co.*, 979 F. Supp. 569 (W.D. Mich. 1997).
[25] *Upjohn Co.* v. *American Home Products Corp.*, 598 F. Supp. 550 (S.D.N.Y. 1984).
[26] *Johnson & Johnson* v. *Quality Pure Mfg., Inc.*, 484 F. Supp. 975 (D.N.J. 1979).
[27] *Toro Co.* v. *Textron, Inc.*, 499 F. Supp. 241 (D. Del. 1980).
[28] *Durbin Brass Works, Inc.* v. *Schuler*, 532 F. Supp. 41 (E.D. Mo. 1982).
[29] *U-Haul International. Inc.* v. *Jartran, Inc.*, 601 F. Supp. 1140 (D. Az. 1984).
[30]. Model State Trademark Bill, § 12 (USTA 1964).
[31] *Allen* v. *National Video, Inc.*, 610 F. Supp. 612 (S.D.N.Y. 1985).

CHAPTER 9

CONTESTS AND LOTTERIES

This is essentially a people's contest...
– to afford all an unfettered start, and a fair chance,
in the race of life.
—*Abraham Lincoln*

The summer of 1955 brought the era of the game show. All across America people tuned in to watch an immigrant welder win a fortune through his knowledge of art or a file clerk dazzle the audience with her grasp of opera trivia – the common citizen getting the chance to become richer than his or her wildest hopes. The things dreams are made of – to win a fortune on such shows as "Twenty-One" (portrayed in the movie *Quiz Show*), "The $64,000 Question," "Tic-Tac-Dough," "Name That Tune," "Dotto," and "The Big Surprise." That moment of glory. As Andy Warhol said, "...everyone will be world famous for fifteen minutes."

To assure honesty, the questions were guarded so that no one could discover them, or their answers. The audience was sure that contestants could not possibly have known what they would be asked. On many shows isolation booths were used so that the contestants could not get help from the audience. Some shows went so far as to use bank officials accompanied by armed guards to hand deliver the questions to the host. The questions had been locked in a bank vault until that time.

The tension would build with each question, and the audience would sigh with relief after each correct answer. The appeal of the game show was what appeared to be the unrehearsed spontaneity of the shows, and that the contestants were masters of certain areas of knowledge, memory, and intelligence. These game shows were a spectacle to behold. The audiences became engrossed in the show, and they were just that – all show.

In July 1958, the Federal Communications Commission (FCC) was drawn into the scene when a contestant of "Dotto" complained that the show was deceptive. Not much resulted from this investigation. The station denied any wrong-doing, and the case was dropped. But news had leaked out, and the game show scandal began to draw public attention. In late 1959, a subcommittee of the House Committee on Interstate and Foreign Commerce opened hearings on the matter.

Witnesses (previous contestants) who were called before the subcommittee testified that they were given the questions and in many cases the answers as well. Some were given scripts to memorize. Even the theatrics of their responses were coached. Despair, agony, exuberance, elation were all prerehearsed to create the desired effect for the audience.

Good-looking contestants were promoted to increase the television audience; unattractive ones were routinely eliminated (or so the producers would try). Dr. Joyce Brothers, the now well-known psychologist, was one such contestant. The producers of the game show tried to get her to lose the game, but her knowledge of boxing was so extensive that she answered every question they threw at her.

Quite obviously the game shows were fixed, and the advertising community was also involved. The advertisers and their agencies were the ones who were truly in control of the purse-strings. At that time it was common for a single advertiser to sponsor an entire show, therefore wielding a tremendous amount of control over the show and its content to the point where the advertiser actually directed the contestant briefing.

The television game show scandal caused the networks to re-think their priorities. As a result of the bad press, television began to move away from game shows, and in their place came the era of the Western. "Gunsmoke," "Wagon Train," "Have Gun, Will Travel," "Bonanza," "Wanted Dead or Alive," and many others saw the sun set on the era of the game show.

Since then, contests of every kind have drawn acute attention from the networks, the FTC, and courts, alike. That is why it is very important for advertisers and their agencies to understand the laws that apply to contests. Sometimes they are called games, sweepstakes, games-of-chance, or just contests. Regardless of the name, the intention is obvious. The advertiser expects that the consumer will enter the contest and be drawn to its product.

In other words, contests generate interest because they get the consumer involved. They appeal to a basic human trait – the desire to get something for nothing. The real intent, then, is to transfer this desire to the product and, with that, increase sales.

Somewhere, right now, people are filling out entry forms and dreaming of what they'll do with the money if they win. Winning a fortune in a contest is a dream of many Americans, an easy reward for very little effort. Yet, the odds of winning a contest are extremely low. For example, the odds to win first prize in the January 1969 *Reader's Digest* sweepstakes were about one in 480,000.[1]

But what does the advertiser need to be concerned with when creating and promoting a contest? Actually, the answer is very simple. There are guidelines that must be followed to run a contest and to prevent it from becoming a lottery. This chapter examines those guidelines. If the contest is structured according to the guidelines, these games are legal.

However, if the game falls outside the guidelines, it will be considered a lottery – which is gambling and illegal (unless state sponsored). To prevent an illegal lottery, there are specific and stringent laws that control contests. This heavy regulation evolved because contests closely resemble lotteries. In the states that permit this form of gambling, it is very heavily regulated. For the advertiser, a contest must not be allowed to cross over the line and become a lottery.

WHAT CONSTITUTES A LOTTERY

Recently, many of the states have sponsored lotteries to raise funds for various government institutions. In California, for example, the proceeds from the lottery were intended to benefit public education. In Colorado, lottery profits were intended to benefit state parks and recreation areas. With the growth and popularity of these lotteries, many companies have jumped on the contest bandwagon. Companies that had not been involved with contests in the past have begun promoting their products through contests and sweepstakes of every kind.

In order to remain within the boundaries of a legal contest, it is important to understand what situations will be considered an illegal lottery. The generally accepted definition of a lottery is "a chance or chances taken, for a consideration, in the hope or expectation that something would be obtained of greater value than that which was given up, but with the full knowledge that nothing at all might be obtained...."[2]

As mentioned earlier, contests are legal, but lotteries are not. The difference between a contest and a lottery is quite simple, and advertisers must understand the difference. Let's take a look at the three basic conditions that create a lottery:

- A prize must be offered;
- The entrant must give up something (consideration) in order to participate; and
- Winning must involve an element of chance rather than skill.

If one, or more, of these elements is missing, a lottery does not exist. All three are required for a lottery. Two elements occur in most all games of chance: a prize and chance. The tricky element, as you'll see, is consideration. We'll look into each of these areas in more detail.

In the late 1930's the government confiscated 83 cases of merchandise marked "Honest John," "Wonder Store," and "Diamond Store." Each of these boxes contained smaller boxes with a number on each. On the main display case were small pull-tabs, which a consumer would remove to reveal a number underneath.

The consumer purchased a chance to remove one pull-tab for 1, 2, or 5 cents. After the pull-tab was removed to reveal a number, the consumer got the prize in the small box that had the same number on it. Each box contained a small amount of inexpensive candy and some other trinket. The value of the items in the prize boxes was only a few cents, and each box contained a prize of equal value.

Now the question is, was that a legal contest or an illegal lottery? That question was answered by the court in *U.S. v. 83 Cases of Merchandise Labeled "Honest John."*[3] The court examined the three elements that needed to exist in order for this to be a lottery: a prize, consideration, and chance. In this case, "there is no single prize, no group of prizes, but a prize given for every chance that is taken."

In a lottery, the consumer takes a chance on winning a prize that is much greater than the price paid to participate. In this case there was no substantial difference between the amount of money that the participant paid and the value of what would be received. In essence there was no "prize" involved.

No chance was involved either, because all participants received an item for their participation in the game. This game, then, was a legal contest because it did not meet all three of the elements required of a lottery.

Prize As An Element

Most games of chance end with a winner, or a couple of winners, who receive a prize. A prize is a special item given to the winner. It is also what is used to induce the consumer to enter the game.

Prizes can range from cash, to cars, vacations, merchandise, to just about anything. A few years ago Zerex antifreeze, made by

DuPont Corporation, offered as first prize in its contest a radiator filled with Zerex antifreeze. What made this prize worth winning was the fact that the radiator was installed in a new Rolls-Royce.

If every entrant receives a gift of equal value, and in the same way, then no "prize" is awarded. We saw this in the case just discussed. If the gifts have different values, the game is considered a lottery (if the other two elements also exist).

In the early 1900's, a company in Georgia named Purvis Investments offered a plan to customers. The plan involved offering a loan on very favorable terms to the first few people who mailed in an investment of a specific amount. However, the investment return was not as good as other savings institutions at the time. The main feature of the scheme was the possibility of obtaining a loan at better than average rates. That was the incentive for entering the "contest" and paying the investment amount. The customer's payment of the investment constituted consideration.

When entries were received at the company, they were opened and numbered. But if a batch of entries were received in the same day's mail, it would be pure chance which envelope was opened first. So, we have the element of chance. When this scheme made its way to the courts in *United States* v. *Purvis*,[4] the court said, "it was of course a mere matter of chance as to which the...clerk...should take up first, as he opened and entered them."

The final element necessary for this to be a lottery was the existence of a prize. In this case the prize was an opportunity to obtain a loan on favorable terms. "It was the desire to obtain loans on the very attractive terms proposed...which made these contracts so much favored and which induced the purchase of these loan contracts." The investment return itself was not particularly attractive. Better returns could have been achieved at other savings institutions. But the chance to obtain one of the loans was a thing of value. It also made this qualify as the element of a prize. The scheme was held to be a lottery.

Consideration As An Element

The next element of a lottery is consideration. If the other two elements exist but there is no consideration, then there is no lottery. But what is the definition of consideration? Many acts can constitute consideration. Even a forbearance (a promise to not do something) can be consideration. Yet, the most obvious form of consideration is money. There are others, and we look at those here.

It is extremely important to understand that what we are discussing are general rules under federal law. Each state has specific laws concerning what it feels qualifies as consideration in relation to a lottery. We'll look at these later in this chapter. Without exception, the advertiser should check into the laws of any state in which it intends to promote a contest.

As just explained, the exact definition of consideration varies from state to state. But generally, consideration can be money or anything of value. It can also be an act such as exerting substantial time and effort in some way. In Wisconsin, which is unique in this respect, consideration is defined by statute as "anything which is a commercial or financial advantage to the promoter or a disadvantage to any participant."[5] What this means is that some states (including Wisconsin) feel that any burden put on the participant constitutes consideration. But, generally, the requirement that a consumer visit the store to obtain game pieces is not interpreted as consideration.

Around 1950 George Wagner was the Postmaster of Garden City, New York. Mr. Wagner wanted to ban the mailing of a card that he felt constituted a lottery. Here's how the game worked. The consumer who received the card in the mail would remove the coupon portion which contained a number. Then the consumer kept the coupon and mailed the other portion of the card to the Garden City Chamber of Commerce.

Later, the consumer visited the stores that participated in the game. If the consumer saw an article in the store window that had the same number as the person's coupon, the store would give the item as a prize. In essence, this was a treasure hunt.

The question is, does the act of visiting stores create a consideration which would make this a lottery? That question was answered in *Garden City Chamber of Commerce* v. *Wagner*.[6] The court agreed, on one point, with the Postmaster who brought the suit by stating: "consideration is present in the substantial amount of time and effort involved in examining the various prizes to ascertain whether one holds a winning ticket."

As seen earlier, consideration can take the form of a payment of money, purchase of a ticket, or the expenditure of substantial time or effort. The basis of the controversy in this case, however, is whether the act of visiting a store "actually involves an expenditure of substantial effort and time." The court ruled that it did not, saying: "[We] have found no case in which the element of consideration has resided in walking or driving to look in a window."

Generally, situations that are not classified as consideration include requiring participants to:

- Visit a store to enter;
- Return to store to learn of winners;
- Visit different stores;
- Witness a demonstration or take a demonstration ride; or
- Pay postage.

Once again, it is important to consult specific state statutes for exact current regulations.

Now let's look at typical situations involving consideration.

Use Of Consumer's Name Or Likeness

Requiring the authorization to use the name or likeness of a participant or winner could be held that consideration was given because there is consent to do something in the future. It is consideration notwithstanding the future performance aspects of the consent.

The Gift Enterprise

In many cases the consumer must purchase the advertiser's product to qualify for the contest. Then usually a proof of purchase in the form of a box top, wrapper, facsimile, or the like is sent in to register for the contest. This is known as a "gift enterprise."

Even though the price of the product remains the same, there is consideration because the consumer is required to do something. The consumer is required to make a purchase.

Therefore, a gift enterprise scheme involves the element of consideration. This explains the common "No purchase required" disclaimer used in many contests.

There is another situation that is very closely related to a pure gift enterprise. That involves games where a lottery is created when a customer must promise to buy a product to enter a game. A good example of this situation occurred in 1976, with a radio promotion called "Dial-a-Discount."

Don J. Plumridge Advertising in Washington, D.C., developed a radio campaign for one of its clients, Allyn's Pants Ranch. A typical commercial read:

Dial your own discount on a pair of pants.
This is our Pants Ranch Wheel of Fortune.
On it are various dollar amounts.
Two dollars, three dollars, four, five, and ten dollars.
After you purchase any pair of pants – and the Pants Ranch
has over 40,000 to choose from –
you get to dial your own discount.
What you spin on the wheel is what you save
on the purchase of your first pair of pants.
If the wheel stops on "freebie," lucky you!
Cause there's no charge.
The pants are on us!

The concept of the game was pretty straightforward. The customer took a pair of pants to the counter where the Wheel of Fortune was spun. Wherever the wheel stopped was the amount of the discount off the purchase price of the pants.

When the Federal Communications Commission found out about the game, a complaint was initiated: *In the Matter of Metromedia Inc.*[7] The commission discussed the following:

> Whether a 'Dial-a-Discount' participant's commitment to purchase a pair of pants alone [constituted] the requisite element of consideration, since if money has not yet changed hands, any participant may refuse to pay after spinning the discount wheel and return the pants to the shelf.

However, the game rules required this agreement to pay in order to participate, and therefore, consideration existed because there was an "agreement" to pay at least the regular price of a pair of pants in order to participate. This game was an illegal lottery because it required that the consumer purchase the pants without knowing, in advance, the amount of the discount. Metromedia lost the case and was required to pay a $16,000 fine for promoting an illegal lottery.

Free Airline Tickets

In *Consumer Protection Division* v. *Luskins, Inc.*,[8] the office of the Attorney General of Maryland proceeded against Luskin's for an appliance store advertisement that offered consumers two free airline tickets for any purchase of $200 or more. The state claimed that the offer violated Section 13-305 of Maryland's Consumer Protection Act that prohibits a person from notifying another person of eligibility to receive something of value if the purchase of goods or services is required.

The first print ad Luskin's ran included the following:

• • • • • • • • • • •

FREE* AIRFARE
FOR TWO...
TO FLORIDA, THE BAHAMAS OR HAWAII.

* Buy an Appliance, TV, Stereo, VCR, or any Purchase over $200 And You'll Get a Big Gift For Two (Round Trip Airfares).

Buy Selected Items for $200-$299.
Get Airfare for 2 To/From FLORIDA
Buy Selected Items for $300-$399.
Get Airfare for 2 To/From BAHAMAS.

Buy Selected Items over $400.
Get Airfare for 2 To/From HAWAII.

TICKETS MUST BE USED WITHIN ONE YEAR.
ASK FOR DETAILS.
* Vacations Premiums Offered Through Vacation Ventures, Inc. Which is not affiliated with Luskin's. Minimum Hotel Stay Required. See Store For Details....Applicable Taxes Apply. See Store For Details.

• • • • • • • • •

There were several versions of the television ad. All versions contained some form of disclaimer regarding the free airfare, typically, "minimum hotel stay required." The disclaimers, in fine print at the bottom of the screen, were shown only for brief periods. One advertisement stated, "Min. hotel stay req. Offered through Vacation Ventures, Inc. which is not affiliated [with] or guaranteed by Luskin's. Taxes apply. Details at store." Even the fastest speed reader could not have finished reading the statement before it disappeared from the screen.

The Luskin's ad stated that consumers would receive free airfare for two to Florida, the Bahamas, or Hawaii if the consumer purchased an appliance, TV, stereo, VCR, or any purchase over $200. The ads appeared in newspapers and on television.

Of the advertising, the court reasoned:

> Luskin's advertising campaign ran afoul of the definition set forth in section 13-301(1) by misleading consumers into thinking that they would receive free airfare when, in fact, they were given a travel certificate for a vacation program that would cost a minimum of "hundreds of dollars" to redeem. [E]ven if consumers had carefully read the advertisement, the disclaimer was ambiguous because "consumers reasonably could assume that they had to arrange for and pay for hotel accommodations themselves," which was not permitted under any of the travel packages. [T]he disclaimer did not dispel the impression that the "airfare primarily was conditioned upon the purchase of consumer goods at Luskin's and that any further condition or requirement would be secondary;" the cost of purchasing the consumer goods, however, became secondary, when compared with the cost of redeeming the travel certificate.

Sections 13-305 (a) and (b) of the Maryland statute reads as follows:

> (a) Exception. This section does not apply to:
>
> > 1) Trading stamps, as defined by § 13-101 of the Business Regulation Article;
> >
> > 2) State lottery tickets issued under the authority of Title 9, Subtitle 1 of the State Government Article;
> >
> > 3) Retail promotions, not involving the offer of gifts or prizes, which offer savings on consumer goods or

services including one-cent sales, two-for-the-price-of-one sales, or manufacturers cents-off coupons; or
4) Games of skill competition not involving sales promotion efforts.

(b) Prohibition. A person may not notify any other person by any means, as part of an advertising scheme or plan, that the other person has won a prize, received an award, or has been selected or is eligible to receive anything of value if the other person is required to purchase goods or services, pay any money to participate in, or submit to a sales promotion effort.

Luskin's argued that § 13-305(b) only applied in situations where individuals were notified by mail that they were specially selected to receive a prize. The court held, however, that § 13-305(b) applied since the statute clearly stated that a person may not notify any other person by any means that they had won a prize. The Luskin's promotion was illegal because it met each element of the statute:

1. Luskin's newspaper and television ads notified individuals;
2. The airline tickets qualified as something of value; and
3. Having to purchase a $200 item from Luskins qualified as a requirement to purchase goods.

Luskin's then argued that they were exempt under subsection (a)(3), which exempts offers of savings on consumer goods or services including one-cent sales, two-for-the-price-of-one sales, or manufacturers cents-off coupons. However, the court held that the Luskin's promotion did not offer any savings on consumer goods.

Presence At The Drawing

Here again there is a difference of opinion. But most courts feel that requiring participants to be present in order to win a drawing is consideration.

Obstacles In Obtaining Entry Blanks

If free entry blanks for a game are offered but the company has irregular office hours, a problem can result. Also, if the participant must, let's say, purchase a newspaper to obtain entry forms, an illegal lottery exists. The purchase of the newspaper is consideration. In other words, entry forms must be made readily available, and a purchase must not be required in order to obtain an entry form. Otherwise, consideration is given.

The following case provides a good example of obstacles for participants. Dreem Arts, Inc., published a newspaper in Chicago called *Nightmoves*. The paper cost $2 and contained a game called "Pick and Play." The idea of the game was for the reader to pick the winners of upcoming professional and college football games. All upcoming games were listed, along with the point spread. Participants mailed in their entry blank listing the teams they picked to win. If an entrant picked 10 winning teams, the prize was $1,000 in cash. Other prizes were available if a person picked at least four winning teams. The advertised contest rules were as follows:

> Free contest entry forms are available at office of publisher. Please send stamped self-addressed envelope and free entry form will be mailed to you; a reasonable hand-drawn facsimile can be used – in addition to stores and news stands, copies of Nightmoves are available at Chicago public libraries for your inspection (no limit to number of contest entries.)...No purchase necessary – tax liabilities for all prizes are the sole responsibility of winners.

Late in 1985 the Chicago Police Department confiscated newspapers from various locations, and *Dreem Arts, Inc.* v. *City of Chicago*[9] was the result. A detective investigated the case and found that the *Nightmoves* offices had no sign displayed. The office was closed, and no employees were present. He was unable to obtain the "free entry form." The detective also tried to obtain an entry blank by mail, but none was ever received. Another detective visited over 24 Chicago libraries, none of which had ever subscribed to the newspaper.

If the consumer is allowed to submit a reasonable facsimile for an entry, no consideration exists. There is a problem, though, when the consumer can't get a copy from which to make a facsimile without buying something. That was the case here.

Obviously the publisher devised the rules to "purposely [make] it more difficult to obtain free entry forms than to pay the $2 newsstand price of *Nightmoves*." The court found that the obstacles in obtaining free entry blanks made this option inordinately difficult. Because the only realistic way to enter the game was to pay the $2 price of the newspaper, this was consideration, and that made the game a lottery.

Scratch-And-Win

Treasured Arts, Inc. (TAI), sold the Treasured Arts Power Call Card for $2. The card allowed three minutes of long distance telephone time provided by United States Long Distance (USLD). The card was perforated so that it could be torn in half: one side was a "scratch-and-win" game piece, and the other side had instructions on how to receive the long distance time. With the "scratch-and-win" game, the purchaser could win prizes ranging from $1 to $50,000.

The Mississippi Gaming Commission (MGC) argued that the card constituted a lottery since the purchaser received nothing of value when purchasing the card. Therefore, the money paid for the card was actually consideration for an opportunity to play the game.

Here in *Mississippi Gaming Commission* v. *Treasured Arts, Inc.*,[10] we see an example of what was ultimately considered a legal promotion and not an illegal lottery under Mississippi law.

The relevant Mississippi Code[11] states that a lottery consists of: the offering of a prize; the awarding of a prize by chance; and the giving of consideration for the opportunity to win the prize. All three elements must exist to constitute an illegal lottery.

In analyzing the issues here, the court stated:

> The parties are in disagreement as to whether a purchaser of a Card actually pays any consideration for the opportunity to chance to win a prize such that there is a violation of subsection (a) of the statute. TAI asserts that the consideration paid for the Card is paid for the card itself and not for the game piece attached. If true, this would mean no consideration is paid for the opportunity to win a prize and the product does not constitute a lottery. However, the MGC claims the purchaser of a Card is paying more than the maximum retail value for per minute long distance time, which results in consideration for the opportunity to win the monetary prizes offered by TAI.

MGC presented evidence from another long distance carrier, LDDS WorldCom. The evidence indicated the price LDDS WorldCom charged per minute with its PhonePass prepaid phone card, and what it claimed was the maximum typical retail value of the per-minute phone time on these types of cards, was $0.45. MGC contended that since the price of the card exceeded the usual price per minute for long distance time, consumers were giving something of value for the chance to win a prize.

On the other hand, Treasured Arts presented testimony from USLD that the actual price charged by USLD per minute for long distance time was $0.66. The Treasured Arts card sold for $2 and provided three minutes of long distance time. Therefore, each minute cost a fraction over $0.66. It was determined that (essentially) no additional consideration was paid by the purchasers of the card for an opportunity to win a prize.

The court stated:

> In a capitalistic society competition is the axis on which a free market turns. The MGC's argument that a price charged by one long distance carrier which exceeds the price charged by another is necessarily consideration for an opportunity to win a prize is without merit. The lower court should have never considered the affidavit of [LDDS] as binding authority as to what "the maximum retail value" of long distance service should be. Granted it is authority as to what LDDS WorldCom charges for its long distance time. But there is not one scintilla of evidence that what one company charges for long distance time is binding on another as the maximum retail value.

In affirming the lower courts decision, this court went on:

> The lower court granted summary judgment based on evidence that the Card had some value. The court stated that it mattered not whether the Card was worth $.66 or $.14, it was apparent it was worth something. The court then narrowed its only issue to whether the consideration paid for the Card, which had some value, amounted to the giving of consideration for the game piece, which granted the chance to win a prize. The court then granted summary judgment based on its finding that the Card was an item that had value and consideration was paid for it and concluded no consideration was paid for the game piece. The lower court refused to get into a dispute as to whether the consideration paid for the Card was adequate or not, reasoning that this Court had never done so.
>
> We disagree that the amount of consideration is

> not at issue.... Nevertheless, the lower court reached the correct result based on the evidence in the record before this Court. The affidavit of Melley and the fact that the game pieces could be obtained free through the mail support TAI's Motion for Summary Judgment. The MGC provided no evidence in the record to constitute a genuine issue of material fact. Therefore, the Court holds that TAI was entitled to a judgment as a matter of law.

Chance As An Element

Chance is another element that must exist in order to qualify as a lottery. If chance dominates the game, rather than skill or judgment, it becomes a lottery. Chance is usually involved in games in which the participant must guess something to win – from guessing the number of beans in a jar to guessing the number of people that will attend a grand opening event. (There are other ways chance can create problems, and we look at those later.)

Chance is an interesting element. Pure chance is not the issue in most cases that have gone through the courts. Rather, the courts look to whether chance is the controlling factor in awarding prizes. For example, a dice game involves pure chance. On the other hand, a chess game involves pure skill. In the middle are card games, which are games of chance. They do not stop being games of chance simply because some element of skill is involved. Card games are still predominantly controlled by the luck of the draw.

One of my favorite examples of a game of chance involved a trade newspaper, the *United States Tobacco Journal*. The case occurred about 1900 and involved an advertisement for a game advertised in the newspaper. The ad read as follows:

The United States Tobacco Journal

SAVE OUR BANDS
Another free Distribution of
$142,500.00
Will be made in December, 1903
Based on the Month of November, 1903
TO SMOKERS OF
[Here follow the names of 30 brands of cigars.]
How many cigars (of all brands, no matter by whom manufactured) will the United States collect taxes on during the month of November, 1903?
(Cigars bearing $3.00 tax per thousand)
The persons who estimate nearest to the number of cigars on which $3.00 tax per thousand is paid during the month of November, 1903, as shown by the total sales of stamps made by the United States Internal Revenue Department during November, 1903, will be awarded as follows:
To the person estimating the closest...$5,000 in cash.

• •

The list continued for the number of people who guessed next closest in descending order. At the end of the list were people who won $5 or a box of free cigars. In theory, over 35,000 people could win something. Obviously, because of the newspaper's audience, the game was directed to retail sellers of cigars and other tobacco products. These retailers could make four estimates for every 100 cigar bands sent in.

The game was sponsored by a cigar manufacturer, the Florodora Company. As part of the rules, the company allowed each Florodora cigar band to count as two for the purpose of entering the game. Suffice it to say that the purpose of Florodora was to increase sales of its brand of cigar. There is nothing wrong or illegal in this.

Yet, the State of New York felt that the game was an illegal lottery, so they arrested the magazine publisher, Ismar Ellison. In many states, operating a lottery is a criminal offense; in this case it was a misdemeanor. The case was *People ex rel. Ellison* v. *Lavin.*[12]

According to the elements of a lottery, this game provided for awarding prizes. It also possessed the element of consideration by requiring the dealer to purchase cigars from which to get the bands required to enter the game. "Therefore," said the court, "the only question presented by the case is whether the distribution is made by chance or not."

This game was a lottery because the outcome was based primarily on chance. That is not to say that there is no skill or judgment involved, but it is slight compared to the chance involved. "A lottery," said the court, "does not cease to be such...because its result may be affected, to some slight extent, by the exercise of judgment." In this case, the controlling factor in receiving a prize was chance, rather than skill or judgment.

Earlier in this chapter we looked at a case that involved picking the winners of upcoming football games. Surely chance is involved in that game, you may think. Not so. Let's look at a situation to explain why that is.

Charles Rich and Frank Camarrata ran a game for which they were essentially bookmakers. The two men solicited bets or wagers on the outcome of sporting events from horse racing to baseball. They also took bets on elections. A complaint was filed against these two men charging that they were operating an illegal lottery in *United States* v. *Rich.*[13]

The participant wagered an amount by placing a bet. The requirement of consideration was met. The participant also stood to win a large return if the right team won. That meant that the requirement of a prize was also present. What was left to be determined was whether the game involved chance. That was the issue that the court was left to ponder.

The court said about "chance" that "...the word has reference to the attempt to attain certain ends, not by skill or any known or fixed rules, but by the happening of a subsequent event, incapable of ascertainment or accomplishment by means of human foresight or ingenuity." Obviously, a blindfolded man pulling a winning ticket from a jar involves pure chance. Here, though, it's a different story.

The government argued that choosing the winner of a horse race or baseball game offered extremely narrow odds. Because of the huge amount of uncertainty, the winner could attribute the win to nothing more than a guess.

The court, however, felt that "there is always something more than a mere guess" involved, and they said:

> The odds may often be long, and the chance of winning small so as to tempt the ignorant and the greedy to risk amounts small or large on the chance of getting a much larger return, and yet in every case there is a race or a game of skill or an election or something in which natural forces are involved and upon which knowledge, skill and judgment are brought into play.

In the case of a horse race, bets are placed on races that may be run quite some time in the future. Yet, the bets are placed based on information that can be obtained about the horses in advance. The stable that the horse comes from, the owner, the jockey, and the track are all considerations on which knowledge, skill, and judgment can be used to make a selection. There is no pure chance here as applied to lotteries. The government lost its case.

But chance in determining the winner is not the only way this element can be involved to turn a contest into a lottery. Chance is also created when the amount of the ultimate prize is unknown or undetermined. That is, when the amount of the prize is to be determined by some event yet to happen, like the dollar sales of a particular store on a certain day in the future. Another situation could exist when the prize depends on the number of people who ultimately enter the contest.

In 1963 Boris Zebelman was a car dealer in Gardner, Kansas. He developed a game to promote his dealership, which he advertised through the mail. He claimed that anyone who bought a car from him would become an "automobile owner representative." This rep would then submit names and addresses of others who would be potential buyers. For each person whose name was submitted and who purchased a car, also becoming a rep, the original rep would receive $100 in cash. Also, the original rep would receive $50 for each person whose name was submitted by the new participant, if that person bought a car and participated as a rep.

In other words, let's say Mr. Smith bought a car from Zebelman and became a rep. He would submit names of others including Ms. Jones. Now Ms. Jones buys a car and becomes a rep, and Mr. Smith receives $100. Then Ms. Jones submits the name of Mr. Adams, who buys a car and becomes a rep. In that case, Ms. Jones would receive $100, and Mr. Smith would receive $50. If this sounds like a pyramid scheme, it is.

Zebelman was caught and charged with 15 counts of running a lottery. The case was *Zebelman* v. *United States*.[14] The question here is tricky. Is chance involved? In the case of the original purchaser rep, the answer is no. In this phase of the game, chance is not the controlling factor. The person has control over this part of the game.

The chance element enters into the picture because "the original purchaser has no control over the payment or receipt of the $50 since it is the person whose name he submits that must locate another buyer." This situation requires, in large part, the element of chance, and this makes the scheme a lottery.

I Feel The Temperature Rising

Here's an interesting one. A group of car dealers (Classic Buick-GMC Truck, Inc., Bill Dodge Oldsmobile-Buick-Pontiac-GMC Truck, Inc., Westbrook Saturn, Inc., Infiniti of Falmouth,

Inc., and Bill Dodge Ford-Lincoln-Mercury, Inc.) ran a promotion that said that any person who leased a new vehicle at one of their participating dealerships during a certain four-week period would win twelve monthly lease payments (paid by the dealership) if the local temperature equaled or exceeded 96 degrees Fahrenheit at the Portland, Maine, airport on a specified date.

The dealers also offered that any person, without purchasing or leasing any vehicle, could submit their name for a drawing during the same four-week period. The winner of the drawing would be eligible to receive $5,000 cash if the temperature reached or exceeded 96 degrees.

In *Classic Oldsmobile-Cadillac-GMC Truck* v. *State of Maine*,[15] the court held the game to be an illegal game of chance under Maine law.

Under Maine law,[16] a game of chance is defined as:

A. A person stakes or risks something of value for the opportunity to win something of value;

B. The rules of operation or play require an event the result of which is determined by chance, outside the control of the contestant or participant; and

C. Chance enters as an element that influences the outcome in a manner that cannot be eliminated through the application of skill.

The dealership argued that the promotion was not an illegal lottery because it didn't require a purchase to participate. According to the second option, any person could submit his or her name and have the chance to win the $5,000 prize. However, the plan involved two promotions – one for those who entered into a lease agreement and one for those who did not. Under the plan, every lessee could win the lease payments if the specific temperature was reached, but the other entrants participated in a drawing in which only one person would win. The court found that these were two separate games. The promotion involving the vehicle lease constituted an unlawful game of chance.

The lease promotion involved an element of chance (the temperature on a future date at a particular location) that was outside the control of the entrants and one that could not be eliminated through the use of skill. The customer's lease and the twelve months of free lease payments constituted something of value. The only issue was if the entrant "staked or risked" any part of the lease consideration for the opportunity to win.

The dealership argued that purchasers of the lease agreements had not risked anything in the promotion because even if they did not win, they still had the car that they leased.

The court found:

> This present promotion is designed to increase the number of cars leased by offering lessees the chance to win twelve free monthly payments. Plaintiffs hope to derive profit from an increase in business, and customers hope to win the monthly payments. The mutual element of gain that characterizes a wager is therefore present. Turning to the element of risk, plaintiffs acknowledge their risk but argue that customers have nothing of value at stake and no risk of loss. They argue that even if the customers do not win, they have the car that they have leased.
>
> Plaintiffs ignore the obvious fact that if the prospect of winning induces anyone to enter into a lease, it follows inexorably that the lease consideration, in part, is provided for that chance. This is not a case in which the chance to win is gratuitously conferred after the parties make their bargain. By the express terms of the promotion, the chance to win is offered as part of the benefit of the bargain, even though the customer has the right to opt out. A customer responding to such an offer necessarily stakes some part of the consideration on

the chance to win.

This was not a case where the chance to win was gratuitously conferred after the parties made their bargain, it was part of the deal, the court found.

Use Of Skill

If skill or judgment is dominant, then the game is not a lottery. In games that ask for the "best letter," "best essay," or "best name," no chance is present. Also, as we saw in the *Rich* case involving sports games, skill or judgment is required because picking the winner is determined in part by the skill of the entrant.

As long as the winners are determined on the basis of a comparison of the skill of the entries, it is legal. In these games if a tie exists, both winners must receive prizes of equal value; otherwise chance enters into the picture again.

In 1912 the Armstrong-Byrd Music Company in Oklahoma City, Oklahoma, ran a promotion for a giveaway of one of its pianos. The company ran ads promoting the contest. The object of the game was to complete a puzzle by filling in spaces with numbers to make a total of fifteen. The puzzle was quite simple, but the challenge was to submit an entry that was the neatest or most unique design.

On May 10, 1912, a group of judges gathered together to pick the winner from the 6,500 entries. Most were simply filled in puzzles from the entry blank supplied in the newspaper ad. But a few were very original. One was actually made out of burnt wood, and another was embroidered on a pillow. The five most unique and original were awarded the promised prizes.

When the winners were notified of their prizes by mail, the Postmaster, H. G. Eastman, filed suit to stop what he considered an illegal lottery. The case was *Eastman v. Armstrong-Byrd Music Co.*[17] The court determined that the contest winners were picked based on a use of their skill and judgment. As the court said, "There was no element of chance in this scheme or plan." This contest was not a lottery and therefore legal.

Third Party Benefit: The Case Of The Disgruntled Consumer

This case arose out of an allegedly misleading promotion by Direct American Marketers (Direct American). A disgruntled consumer, Theodore Zekman, claimed that because AT&T provided (and profited from the telephone calls) the "900" telephone number used by consumers to respond to Direct American's promotion, it was liable. The case was *Zekman* v. *Direct American Marketers, Inc.*[18]

Mr. Zekman filed a lawsuit claiming that AT&T was secondarily liable for the allegedly fraudulent prize scheme promoted by Direct American. Under the promotion, consumers were sent a series of mailings that stated they had won either a large cash award or discount coupons. To collect the prize, consumers called a 900 number listed in the mailing. There were also instructions in the mailing on how to redeem the prizes by mail. Zekman made 11 phone calls in response to the various mailings and incurred a charge of about $8 to $10 dollars per call. The Illinois Supreme Court held that AT&T could not be liable under the Illinois Consumer Fraud and Deceptive Trade Practices Act for knowingly receiving the benefits of another's fraud.

The pertinent section of the statute reads:

> Unfair methods of competition and unfair or deceptive acts or practices, including but not limited to the use or employment of any deception, fraud, false pretense, false promise, misrepresentation or the concealment, suppression or omission of any material fact, with intent that others rely upon the concealment, suppression or omission of such material fact, or the use or employment of any

> practice described in Section 2 of the "Uniform Deceptive Trade Practices Act," approved August 5, 1965,[19] in the conduct of any trade or commerce are hereby declared unlawful whether any person has in fact been misled, deceived or damaged thereby.

The court stated: "[w]e agree with AT&T that the plain language of section 2 of the Act does not include anything that makes it unlawful to knowingly receive the benefits of another's fraud." The statute clearly contemplated that the entity perpetuating the misrepresentation was the entity liable under the statute. Using the canons of statutory interpretation, the court held that when a statute provided a list that was not exhaustive ("including but not limited to"), the class of unarticulated things must be interpreted as those things that are similar to the named things.

The court explained further:

> The common feature of the forms of conduct listed in section 2 of the Act is that they involve actions directly done by the perpetrator of the fraud. Knowingly receiving the benefits of another's fraud, however, more closely resembles a form of secondary liability. We believe that a claim for knowingly receiving the benefits of another's fraud is not so similar to the enumerated violations of section 2 of the Act that the legislature intended for it to be a cause of action under the statute. With no clear indication from the legislature that such conduct violates section 2 of the Act, we cannot extend liability to those who knowingly receive the benefits of another's fraud.

Zekman then tried for liability on AT&T under section 2P of the Consumer Fraud Act, which deals directly with disclosures of conditions on offers of free prizes and gifts.

The relevant section states:

> It is an unlawful practice for any person to promote or advertise any business, product, or interest in property, by means of offering free prizes, gifts or gratuities to any consumer, unless all material terms and conditions relating to the offer are clearly and conspicuously disclosed at the outset of the offer so as to leave no reasonable probability that the offering might be misunderstood.

Again, the Court stated: "[w]e believe that this provision clearly relates only to the person offering the free prizes, gifts or gratuities. The plain language of this statute does not pertain to those who knowingly receive the benefits of another's fraud."

Zekman also alleged that AT&T directly violated Section 2 of the Act by reviewing, revising, and approving Direct American's deceptive solicitations and recorded messages, and by billing Zekman for the 900-number calls in an allegedly misleading manner. In order to state a claim under Section 2, Zekman had to allege a deceptive act or practice by AT&T and that AT&T intended Zekman to rely on the deception. Illinois law also required that the fraud complained of be the proximate cause of the Zekman's injury.

The court maintained that AT&T did not cause Zekman's injury. In his deposition testimony, Zekman's acknowledged that when he received the mailings he did not know whether he had won a cash prize and that he made the 900-number calls in the hope of winning a prize. Zekman also understood that he would be charged for the calls and admitted that he heard the recorded message at the beginning of each call telling him that he could avoid any charges by immediately hanging up. As a result, clearly, there was no fraud on the part of AT&T.

You May Have Already Won: The American Family Publishers Case

American Family Publishers is widely known for its popular television commercials that feature Ed McMahon and Dick Clark. Thirty-two states and the District of Columbia joined in a $1.25 million settlement with American Family Publishers for violating state consumer protection laws by using deceptive advertising in connection with its sweepstakes.

Under the terms of the settlement, American Family agreed to revise its sweepstakes so that they would:

1. Only tell consumers that they were winners if they had in fact won;
2. Only tell consumers that they were among a select group that had a chance of winning a prize if the odds of winning were disclosed;
3. Tell consumers that no purchase was necessary to participate in the sweepstakes;
4. Clearly explain how to enter the sweepstakes without a purchase;
5. Make it clear to consumers who ordered magazines on an installment payment plan how much money was due each month; and
6. Not imply that consumers had a better chance of winning if they purchased magazines.

The states that joined in the settlement were: Alabama, Arizona, Arkansas, California, Hawaii, Idaho, Illinois, Kansas, Kentucky, Massachusetts, Michigan, Minnesota, Mississippi, Montana, Nebraska, New Hampshire, New Jersey, New Mexico, Nevada, North Carolina, Ohio, Oklahoma, Oregon, Pennsylvania, Rhode Island, South Dakota, Tennessee, Texas, Vermont, Virginia, Washington, Wisconsin, and Washington, D.C.

American Family Publishers still faces a number of actions involving its allegedly deceptive and unfair practices in connection with its sweepstakes and contests that have been consolidated to the federal district court in New Jersey.[20]

AGENCIES THAT HAVE REGULATION OVER CONTESTS

There are basically four federal agencies with control over contests and how they are promoted. The U.S. Postal Service has control over any contest that uses the mail in any way. The Federal Trade Commission has control over any activity which is deceptive or unfair, including contests. The Federal Communications Commission controls any contest advertised over radio or television. The Bureau of Alcohol, Tobacco and Firearms controls contests which affect those items. And, finally, each state has specific statutes that govern the use of contests, as do each of the television networks. We'll look at each of these in the remainder of this chapter.

U.S. Postal Service

The first form of regulation over gambling activities took place in 1868 in the form of postal regulations.[21] These laws were created in an attempt to curb the fraud and abuse in state-sponsored lotteries after the Civil War.

Under current law, it is a criminal offense to mail any advertisement of any lottery, gift enterprise, or similar scheme where prizes are awarded based on chance. Violation of this law carries a fine of $1,000 or two years in prison, or both.[22] In addition, the Postal Service is authorized to issue a cease-and-desist order and refuse processing any such advertisement in the U.S. mail.[23] Violation of a cease-and-desist order carries a civil fine of up to $10,000 per day.

Contests that use the mail in any way must be approved by the General Counsel, Mailability Division, U.S. Postal Service, Washington, D.C. 20006. When I say "contests that use the mail,"

I mean anything from mailing entry forms to mailing notification to winners after the contest.

We've seen cases earlier where the Postal Service brought suit because the mail was used in the scheme. *United States* v. *Purvis, Garden City Chamber of Commerce* v. *Wagner, Dreem Arts, Inc.* v. *City of Chicago, People ex rel. Ellison* v. *Lavin*, and *Eastman* v. *Armstrong-Byrd Music Co.* are good examples of cases where the Postal Service became involved.

Compliance with Postal Service rules, however, is going to be more difficult in the future. Effective January 2, 1985, the Postal Service no longer issues "no action letters" to advertisers who wish a ruling on whether or not their proposed contests are lotteries and as such would be challenged by the Postal Service under the postal lottery laws.[24] Its reason: Over the years the "number and complexity" of requests for such letters had increased dramatically.

Until recently, a game of chance enclosed in a product package violated the postal lottery law unless it was disclosed clearly in the advertising and on the package that a person could enter the contest by merely sending in a "facsimile" in the form of a 3 x 5″ card with the product's name or some other words or phrases written or printed by hand. However, in 1979 the Postal Service, by means of a "no action" letter, approved a promotion involving an in-pack game piece, if the package itself contained a notice of "no purchase necessary" and advised that a free game piece was available to persons who requested one by mail. In the view of the Postal Service this message offered potential entrants an accessible free entry alternative and that, therefore, persons who chose to enter by purchasing the package would be doing so voluntarily. In other words, the equivalent free entry offer eliminated the lottery element of consideration. Contrast this with the *Dreem Arts* case we looked at earlier, where it was much more difficult to obtain information with which to send in a facsimile entry.

Federal Trade Commission

The FTC, in 1925, began issuing cease-and-desist orders against lotteries. Since then the FTC has established rules that apply to contests. It requires the following:

- Disclosure of the exact number of prizes to be awarded;
- Disclosure of the odds of winning;
- Disclosure of the area within which the game will exist;
- Disclosure of the length of the contest;
- That all game pieces must be distributed to stores on a totally random basis; and
- That the game cannot end until all game pieces are handed out.

Also, any game that continues beyond 30 days must disclose the number of unredeemed prizes and revised odds on a weekly basis. Successive games must be separated by 30 days or the length of the previous game, whichever is shorter.

These rules do not apply to broadcast media; however, the same information must be made available to consumers. The company must disclose where the consumer can go, or write, to get complete contest information.

R. F. Keppel & Brothers operated a business which manufactured and placed in retail stores a candy game known as Break and Take. In the early 1930's, Keppel promoted its game in stores located near schools. It displayed the game in a way that would be attractive to children. The company earned about $234,000 a year from the game.

The game involved an assortment of wrapped candy. The participant would pay one cent and pick a piece of candy from the 120 pieces in the display. The candy would be opened to discover if it contained a penny as a prize, or a slip of paper with a purchase price of 1, 2, or 3 cents. In reality, only four pieces contained a penny. The other pieces of candy contained prices of 1 to 3 cents each. If the candy contained a ticket, that was the price that the participant had to pay. There was a possibility that the person could win back the initial penny investment and get the candy free. But the odds were very low.

Obviously, this game qualified as a lottery. All three essential elements were present: consideration, prize, and chance. Yet, the Federal Trade Commission brought suit in *Federal Trade Commission* v. *R. F. Keppel & Bros. Inc.*,[25] because of the game's effect on children. They were the audience at which the game was directed.

The Supreme Court, in upholding the FTC's decision, felt that "the method of competition adopted...induces children, too young to be capable of exercising an intelligent judgment of the transaction, to purchase an article less desirable in point of quality or quantity than that offered at a comparable price."

That is why the FTC became involved with the lottery. The method exploited children who were unable to protect themselves. The FTC, as we saw in Chapters 2 and 3, concerns itself with deception and unfairness. As the Court said, "It would seem a gross perversion...to hold that the method is not 'unfair.'" Keppel lost the case.

In many cases, the FTC may issue a cease-and-desist order for games that are not deemed to be literally illegal lotteries. Remember that the FTC has the authority to stop any activity that is unfair or deceptive, even if it does not violate specific lottery regulations.

A good example of this involved the *Reader's Digest* Sweepstakes. Entry forms were mailed to members of the public. The entry forms contained a number and a ticket with the same number printed on it. The participant was to return the ticket to *Reader's Digest* where it would be compared against preselected winning numbers. If the number on the ticket matched a winning number, that prize would be awarded.

The intent of the sweepstakes was to build sales in its products. To promote its sweepstakes, *Reader's Digest* made claims about the contest, including:

- Participants only needed to mail in their ticket to receive their prize if they were winners;
- Participants had a reasonable chance of winning;
- All advertised prizes had been purchased by *Reader's Digest* prior to the contest;
- Consumers who received entry forms were "selected," "chosen," or were "one of the few people to be invited;"
- Entry forms were mailed on a limited basis; and
- In January 1969 (a typical contest), 101,751 prizes were offered worth $999,000.

This well-known sweepstakes ran into trouble when the FTC stepped in and filed suit in *In the Matter of Reader's Digest Assn.*[26] The FTC took action, not because this was an illegal lottery, but because the sweepstakes was deceptive.

In reality, the claims that *Reader's Digest* made in its advertisements and promotion were not accurate. Participants were not "one of the few to be invited." In fact, millions of copies of the *Reader's Digest* Sweepstakes entry forms were mailed to consumers. In the January 1969 contest, there were not 101,751 prizes worth $999,000. In reality there were 40,517 prizes worth $441,789. Also, winners were required to do more than send in their ticket to receive a prize. They were required to do other undisclosed things – for example, submit to interviews by a private detective before being allowed to obtain their prize.

In addition, there was no "reasonable opportunity to win" in *Reader's Digest* Sweepstakes. As noted at the beginning of this chapter, the odds of winning first prize were about 1 in 480,000. The *Reader's Digest* Sweepstakes was simply not what it was promoted to be. Because of the deception, the FTC issued a cease-and-desist order.

Generally, there are specific situations regarding contests that the FTC does not allow. The following list represents a general outline of practices that are prohibited by the FTC as they apply to contests:

- Making false representations of the value of a prize;
- Promising cash and awarding merchandise instead;
- Failing to follow contest rules as established; and
- Offering a number of prizes that differ from those advertised.

In addition, the FTC does have a rule governing contests in the food retailing and gasoline industries. Issued in the wake of complaints that games were allegedly rigged, the commission adopted a rule, that is almost impossible to live with, requiring that the game pieces must be updated frequently.[27] This is difficult in a game that might be run by as many as 10,000 retail gas stations.

Federal Communications Commission

Congress first attempted to regulate the airwaves under the Radio Act of 1927.[28] However, lotteries were not regulated in broadcast until the Federal Communications Act of 1934.[29] Later these regulations were made a part of the Criminal Code as Section 1304.[30]

Under current law, Section 1304, it is a criminal offense to broadcast by radio or television any advertisement for a lottery, gift enterprise, or similar scheme. Specifically, the statute prohibits:

> Any advertisement of or information concerning any lottery, gift enterprise, or similar scheme, offering prizes dependent in whole or in part upon lot or chance, or any list of the prizes drawn or awarded by means of any such lottery, gift enterprise, or scheme, whether said list contains any part or all of such prizes....[31]

A good example of this occurred in 1973. The University of Florida radio station WRUF in Gainesville, Florida, broadcast a radio commercial for its client, Shaw and Keeter Fordtown. Any person who purchased an automobile from the dealership received a prize. Here's the radio copy:

Shaw and Keeter has an extra bonus for you...
A U.S. Savings Bond with every new car or truck delivered!
At least a $25 bond...it might be a $50 bond...
it could be a $500 bond!
After purchase, check the sealed envelope in the glove box
with the sealed envelope in the office.
It will be a $25 bond...
it might be a $50 bond...it could be a $500 bond!
Offer ends March 31st!
Hurry to Shaw and Keeter Fordtown,
downtown at 238 West University Avenue!

When the FCC learned of the commercial, it filed a complaint against the school. The FCC held that a violation of lottery restrictions was created with *In the Matter of University of Florida*.[32]

All three elements of a lottery existed in this case. A prize was offered in the form of a savings bond. While every purchaser received a bond, values varied of the bonds considerably. Consideration existed since the consumer was required to purchase a car or truck before being eligible to win a savings bond. Finally, chance was present as to which bond would be won. Since the University of Florida created, produced, and aired the spot, it was required to pay a fine of $2,000.

In any case where broadcast media is involved the advertisement should include information on the following:

- Who may participate;
- Type of entries required;
- Where, when, and how the entry is to be submitted;
- Number and nature of prizes;
- The existence of duplicate prizes in the case of ties;

- The closing date; and
- Where complete contest details can be obtained.

Bureau Of Alcohol, Tobacco And Firearms

The Bureau of Alcohol, Tobacco and Firearms (ATF) has jurisdiction over what's contained in, attached to, or printed on packages of certain tobacco products, such as cigarettes. The ATF view differs from the U.S. Postal Service's as to what constitutes a lottery. The ATF believes, for example, that the element of consideration exists even if no purchase of a tobacco product is required to take part in a contest. The statute in question is a section of the Internal Revenue Code of 1954[33] providing that no certificate or coupon representing a "ticket, chance, share or interest in or dependent, the event of a lottery" shall appear in or "on any package of tobacco products or cigarette papers or tubes."

The ATF also issues advisory letters involving the lottery aspects of proposed promotions. However, unlike the Postal Service, it has steadfastly refused to permit any kind of game promotion in which the game price is enclosed in the package with cigarettes or cigars.

RECENT FEDERAL LEGISLATION

Prompted by the $1.25 million settlement with American Family Publishers, Senator Ben Campbell (R-Colorado) introduced the "Honesty in Sweepstakes Act of 1998" (S. 2141) on June 5, 1998, which was referred to the Senate Committee on Governmental Affairs.

The legislation has two main provisions. The first provision requires that any solicitation or offer in connection with the sales promotion for a product or service that uses any game of chance in which a consumer has a chance of winning anything of value (including any sweepstakes) bear a conspicuous notice that states that the offer is not a game of chance (or sweepstakes, if applicable), or the statement "you have not already won," or some other words to that effect. The second provision requires any solicitation or offer that resembles a negotiable instrument to bear a conspicuous notice on the envelope that the instrument is not a check or has no negotiable value.

Specifically, the bill requires:

> An envelope containing a solicitation for a promotion would have to conspicuously disclose: "This is a game of chance (or sweepstakes). You have not automatically won."
>
> The following statement on the top of the first page of the material: "This is a game of chance (or sweepstakes). You may not have automatically won. Your chances of winning are (insert odds). No purchase is required either to win a prize or enhance your chances of winning a prize."
>
> These disclosures must be printed in a font which is: (1) 80% or more of the size of the largest font otherwise used in the solicitation; or (2) 16-point, whichever is larger.

In presenting the bill, Senator Campbell stated: "Every day millions of senior citizens and other innocent consumers receive sweepstakes announcements that boldly announce that they have just won millions of dollars or some other prize, perhaps a luxury cruise, when in fact they have not. Millions of Americans also receive cashier's check look-alikes, made out to their name, and written for thousands of dollars, as a ploy to get them to purchase some product or service. But upon close scrutiny, these cashier's check look-alikes are actually worthless."

A strength of the bill is that it does not preempt state law that regulates advertising or sales of goods and services associated with any game of chance. Senator Campbell stated that he consulted with the Attorneys General of his home state of

Colorado and of Florida and that they both expressed support for the bill.

An almost identical bill, H.R. 4340, was introduced in the House on July 28, 1998. Two additional bills introduced in Congress in September 1998, H. 4612 and S. 2460, would amend the U.S. Postal Code to require representations on sweepstakes solicitations. The requirements are similar to that set forth in the Honesty in Sweepstakes bill discussed above. The Senate bill includes limited subpoena power for investigations of sweepstakes fraud by the Postmaster General.

STATE REGULATION

Each of the states is in agreement as to what constitutes an illegal lottery, as we've discussed in the previous part of this chapter. They agree with the federal guidelines in most all cases. The difference shows up in how the states interpret the requirements. What constitutes "chance," "a prize," and especially "consideration" is where the states vary in some ways.

Each state has legislated specific requirements for contests. Current state statutes or amendments, regulation, or case law should be consulted before creating an advertisement involving a contest. It would also be wise to consult with an attorney in the applicable state. The following is a review of the law in many key states.

Alaska

Pyramid schemes occur where purchasers get consideration in the form of rebates or commission payments when they cause others to participate in the program. These are prohibited.[34]

Arizona

Pyramid schemes are programs where purchasers get consideration in the form of rebates or commission payments when they introduce other persons into participation in the program. These schemes are prohibited.[35]

Arkansas

Pyramid schemes are prohibited in Arkansas. These schemes occur where purchasers get consideration in the form of rebates or commissions when they bring others into the program. These schemes are prohibited.[36]

California

A leading case that extensively discusses the element of consideration when some participants receive a game chance with a purchase is *California Gasoline Retailers v. Regal Petroleum Corp*.[37]

California also requires that a form completed and filed with the State Department of Justice if telephone solicitation implies that a consumer may win a prize.[38]

California has antideception statutes that prohibit misrepresentations about the chances of winning a contest, the number of winners, and the value or availability of the prizes.[39]

In California there are disclosure requirements where a prize is offered as an inducement to either attend a sales presentation or visit a location.[40]

Pyramid schemes where purchasers get consideration in the form of rebates or commission payments when they introduce other persons into the program are illegal. These are prohibited.[41]

A bill in California, S. 1780, would prohibit solicitations containing contest entry materials from representing that an individual has won a prize unless that person has, in fact, won a prize. The bill passed the senate on May 21, 1998, and was sent to assembly committee.

Under the bill, the representation made on the envelope would be considered in the light of all the representations made. Contest materials would also be required to include contest rules and a prominent statement that no purchase is necessary to enter the contest.

Specifically, the bill:

1. States that solicitation materials containing sweepstakes entry materials shall not represent that a person is a winner or has already won a prize unless that person, has, in fact, won a prize. Factors reflecting the context of such a representation include print, size, color, location, and presentation of the representation.

2. States that if the representation is made on or is visible through the window of a mailing envelope, then the visible portion itself shall meet the above prohibition.

3. States that solicitation materials containing sweepstakes entry materials shall include a prominent "no purchase necessary" message, as specified by various provisions.

4. States that sweepstakes entries not including an order for product or services shall not be at any disadvantage in the selection process for the sweepstakes entered.

5. States that sweepstakes materials shall not represent that entries in the sweepstakes accompanied by an order for products or services will be eligible for additional prizes or will be more likely to win than entries from individuals not purchasing a product or service.

6. Defines "no purchase necessary message" and "official rules."

Under existing California law it is unlawful to notify a person that they have won a prize but that receiving the prize requires payment of money. It was felt that current law did not adequately protect against unfair or misleading advertising of sweepstakes. The intent of the bill was to provide for clearer rules and advertising restrictions on situations where a contest mailing falsely claims the recipient has won a prize.

Two other bills in the California legislature, S. 1069 and A. 953, would allow winegrowers and distilled spirits suppliers to sponsor sweepstakes and contests that offer the chance to win prizes. Existing law prohibits any alcoholic beverage licensee from giving any premium, gift, or free goods in connection with the sale or distribution of alcoholic beverage, except as provided for by rules adopted by the Department of Alcohol Beverage Control (ABC). The ABC is currently in the process of proposing new rules relating to consumer promotions that would restrict these types of promotions.

The Wine Institute and the Distilled Spirits Council of the United States sponsored the bills. The sponsors believed that sweepstakes advertise and promote a particular brand of alcohol and encourage those who choose to drink to select a particular brand. Similar sweepstakes are legal in nearly all other states and the marketing programs benefits both consumers and manufacturers.

The bill:

1. Authorizes winegrowers or brandy manufacturers to sponsor sweepstakes or contests that offer the chance to win prizes or other things of value. "Sweepstakes" is defined as an activity or event in which an entrant or entrants are furnished a prize or award based upon random selection. "Contest" is defined as an activity or event in which an entrant or entrants are furnished a prize or award based upon skill, knowledge, or ability.

2. Provides that no purchase may be required to enter any sweepstakes or contest and that a means of entry may be provided on neck hangers, corks, containers, etc., if both of the following

conditions are met: (a) an alternate means of entry is made available, and (b) no instant win based upon the material that comes with an alcoholic beverage purchase is permitted.

3. Provides that a retail licensee may not serve as the agent of a supplier to collect or forward entries or to award prizes to any sweepstakes winner. The matching of entries with numbers or pictures on point of sale is permitted so long as the entrants are offered the opportunity to utilize alternative means to determine prize-winning status.

4. Provides that entrants may be required to visit a retail premises to enter or compete in a contest. The bill further provides that no entry fee may be paid to a retail licensee.

5. Requires sweepstakes or contests to be available only to California adults and that the odds for winning any sweepstakes prize must be equal for all entrants. Alcoholic beverages may not be given as sweepstake or contest prizes, and prizes may not be awarded to any retail licensee or their employees. Additionally, no more than five percent of sweepstakes entrants may be awarded a prize costing in excess of five dollars.

6. Prohibits the use of point accumulation systems for contest and sweepstakes.

7. Prohibits any financial contribution by a wholesaler to any winegrower's or brandy manufacturer's sweepstakes or contest.

8. Authorizes winegrowers or brandy manufacturers to sponsor contests on their premises subject to specified conditions.

9. Authorizes winegrowers or brandy manufactures to provide a discount or rebate not

> exceeding three dollars (that may be adjusted every three years based on the Consumer Price Index) on any nonalcoholic merchandise or services in connection with the sale of wine and brandy. The monetary limit does not apply if there is no requirement to purchase wine or brandy and the person paying for the discount or rebate is not connected with the manufacturer. If there is a requirement to purchase wine or brandy, the monetary limit would not be required if the person paying for the discount or rebate on any nonalcoholic beverage merchandise or services is not connected with the manufacturer.

Another bill before the California legislature, S.B. 1476, would amend California's sweepstakes laws to prohibit a sweepstakes promoter from requiring winners to call an information access service, that is, a 900 or 976 number, to redeem their prize. The bill was prompted by the attorney general's office because of the numerous complaints the office was getting from consumers, particularly senior citizens, questioning why they had not received the prize they believed was promised through a mailer or telephone solicitation. Often the consumers had unwittingly telephoned a 900 number provided by the sweepstakes sponsor, at a cost of $4 to $6 per minute, only to be informed that they had not won the prize.

Current California law, like many other states, allows the use of 900 numbers in connection with sweepstakes as long as an alternative means of participating in the sweepstakes is provided is permitted. However, these solicitations often mislead consumers into believing they have already won a prize, and the consumer may not be aware that the use of a 900 number is very expensive. The California Commission on Aging, which supports the bill, believes that California's seniors are a particular target for such scams. The Commission said: "Misleading and deceptive sweepstakes promotions are victimizing our vulnerable elderly. The commission considers these types of practices to constitute financial abuse of the elderly. SB 1476 will provide a significant protection to this most vulnerable population."

The bill's approach would simply prohibit the use of information access services in any manner related to a sweepstakes.

Connecticut

This state has certain minor restrictions concerning the disclosure of prizes.[42]

Connecticut requires certain disclosures for contests relating to promotion of time-share plans.[43]

Pyramid schemes are illegal where purchasers get consideration in the form of rebates or commission payments when they induce other persons to participate in the program.[44]

In June 1998 the State of Connecticut broadened its Sweepstakes statute[45] to include in the definition of "advertising" solicitations that imply that someone has won a prize or that there is a strong likelihood that a person has won a prize. This language is consistent with the current trend of sweepstakes solicitations that deceptively imply that a person has won a prize. The law does not include any specific language defining a "strong likelihood that a person has won a prize," but the bill indicates that the Connecticut Commissioner of Consumer Protection may adopt regulations to that effect.

Currently under Connecticut law, advertising a sweepstakes that includes a condition or restriction on the receipt of the prize is permitted. In other words, the promoter may require the winner to make a local or 800-number call to redeem the prize, or even require the winner to visit a local retailer, as long as the winner is not required to attend a sales presentation.

Florida

In Florida the following are required for a game promotion:

- All rules and regulations must be filed with the Department of Legal Affairs thirty days in advance of game commencement;
- Rules and regulations must be posted in every retail outlet and published in all advertising copy;
- The promoter must establish a trust account or obtain a bond equivalent to the total value of all prizes offered;
- The promoter must provide the Department of Legal Affairs with a certified list of the names and addresses of all persons who have won a prize of more than $25 within sixty days after such winners have been determined;
- A list of winners must either be provided to persons who request it or published in a Florida newspaper of general circulation; and
- The promoter must hold all winning entries submitted for a period of ninety days after the close or completion of the game.[46]

This statute applies only to games in which the total value of the prizes exceeds $5,000, but applies to all game promotions, not only those offered by retailers. A nonrefundable filing fee of $100 must accompany the advance registration papers. Florida provides forms to aid game promoters in making the required filings.

Florida prohibits anyone connected with a game promotion from coercing a retail operator to participate in a promotion.[47]

Florida also has antideception statutes prohibiting misrepresentations about the chances of winning a contest, the number of winners, and the value or availability of the prizes.[48]

Florida prohibits the use of chance contests relating to promotion of time-share plans.[49]

Florida also prohibits promoters from notifying a person that he/she has won a prize or gift if the person must pay any money, do any act, or submit to a sales promotion effort.[50]

Georgia

Georgia has disclosure restrictions where a prize is offered as an inducement to either attend a sales presentation or visit a location.[51]

Georgia requires certain disclosures for contests relating to promotion of time-share plans.[52]

Hawaii

Hawaii prohibits telephone solicitors from offering prizes as a promotional device.[53]

Illinois

Illinois has conflicting precedents on the legality of grocery store promotions, but has not enforced any lottery restrictions against game promotions.

Louisiana

In Louisiana there are disclosure requirements when a prize is offered as an inducement to either attend a sales presentation or visit a location.[54]

Louisiana requires certain disclosures for contests relating to promotion of time-share plans.[55]

Maine

Maine forbids gas station games.[56] It is also illegal to award liquor as a prize in a contest.[57] This state also restricts the distribution of some live animals as prizes.[58]

Again, pyramid schemes are prohibited.[59] In these programs purchasers get consideration in the form of rebates or commission payments when they introduce others to the program.

Maryland

Maryland prohibits promoters from notifying a person that he/she has won a prize or gift if the person must pay any money, do any act, or submit to a sales promotion effort.[60]

This state specifically limits the ability of gas station operators from using games of chance as promotions.[61]

Maryland also requires certain disclosures for contests relating to promotion of time-share plans.[62]

Maryland has amended its business regulation law § 10-502 to allow refiners and other suppliers of motor fuel to sponsor, promote, advertise, or otherwise perform or participate in a game of chance offered to the public as long as the game of chance is not offered through a retail service station. Also, a supplier of motor fuel authorized to operate a retail service station may participate in a game of chance at the service station as long as the service station dealer is not required to pay for any costs related to the game of chance.

Massachusetts

Massachusetts forbids gas station games.[63] This state also restricts the distribution of some live animals as prizes.[64]

Michigan

Michigan requires disclosure of the prizes and information concerning the number of prizes to be awarded. Michigan prohibits anyone connected with a game promotion from coercing a retail operator to participate in a promotion.[65]

Minnesota

Minnesota specifically prohibits "in-package" promotional games unless participation is available free, without purchase of the package.[66]

Missouri

The Missouri electorate amended the state constitution to permit games of chance. The Supervisor of Liquor Control permits promotional games on the premises of licensees if consideration is not required for "participating in such games or contests or for receiving the award or prize therefrom."[67]

This language tracks part of the language of the constitutional amendment approved by the voters in November 1978. Section 39 (9) appears to outlaw games in which a purchase is required after the participant had been declared a winner.

However, the constitutional amendment also contains a definition of "lottery or gift enterprise," stating that these terms: "...shall mean only those games or contests whereby money or something of value is exchanged directly for the tickets or chance to participate in the game or contest."

The Division of Liquor Control will enforce regulations against food stores and others who have a license to sell 5 percent beer and, therefore, a retail game which requires a purchase "for receiving the award or prize" is unlawful for such licensees.

Missouri requires certain disclosures for contests relating to promotion of time-share plans.[68]

Montana

Pyramid schemes, programs where purchasers get consideration in the form of rebates or commission payments when they introduce other persons into participation in the program, are prohibited.[69]

Nevada

This state specifically limits gas station operators from using games of chance as promotions.[70]

Pyramid schemes are programs where purchasers get consideration in the form of rebates or commission payments when they introduce other persons into participation in the program. These schemes are prohibited.[71]

New Hampshire

Like Nevada, this state specifically limits gas station operators from using games of chance as promotions.[72]

New Jersey

Insofar as gasoline station promotions are concerned, it is immaterial in New Jersey whether consideration is or is not present because its Unfair Trade Practices (UTP) law[73] flatly prohibits "games of chance, in connection with the sale of motor fuels." The courts have ruled that the definition of a lottery contained in the state's antilottery law, which makes consideration an indispensable element of a lottery, does not control the interpretation or affect the application of its UTP law to gasoline retailers. See *United Stations of New Jersey* v. *Getty Oil Co.*[74]

New Jersey also prohibits promoters from notifying a person that she or she has won a prize or gift if the person must pay any money, do any act, or submit to a sales promotion effort.[75]

New Mexico

Pyramid schemes are programs where purchasers get consideration in the form of rebates or commission payments when they introduce other persons into participation in the program. These schemes are prohibited.[76]

New York

New York's General Business Law requires registration of promotional games with the Miscellaneous Records Section of the Department of State.[77] To register a game, you must complete an application form and enclose a $50 fee. The application form includes requests for the names of promoters, the odds of winning, and a copy of the rules. A trust account must be established or bond posted sufficient to cover the amount of the prize to be distributed in New York state. Winners must be disclosed to the New York Department of State within 90 days of the conclusion of the contest.

Contrary to many other states, New York does permit promoters to notify a person that has won a prize or gift when the person must pay some money, do an act, or submit to a sales promotion effort. But this is only allowed if the operator explicitly informs the person of these conditions to the receipt of the prize.[78]

New York prohibits anyone connected with a game promotion from coercing a retail operator to participate in a promotion.[79]

North Carolina

Pyramid schemes are illegal in North Carolina. These are programs where purchasers get consideration in the form of rebates or commission payments when they introduce others into participation in the program. These schemes are prohibited.[80]

A proposed North Carolina law, S.B. 253, would require registration with the state prior to promoting any telephone solicitation in connection with promotions and sweepstakes. The bill applies to any telephone communication designed to persuade a person to purchase goods or services or to enter a contest regardless of who initiated the offer. Under the statute, the seller is required to submit to the Secretary of State "the details of the promotion," including the complete rules, at least 10 days before commencement of any promotion offering any prize or gift with an actual or represented market value of $500 or more. The seller must post a bond, all prizes must be awarded, and all prizes must be forwarded within 30 days of the specified date of award. The statute also protects minors by requiring that all sellers inquire whether the prospective purchaser is 18 years old, and if the person is under 18, the seller must discontinue the call.

The bill also bans 900-number sweepstakes where a consumer is asked to call a pay-per-call number to find out what the consumer has won.

North Dakota

North Dakota addresses an ambiguity in the common law of lottery. The issue was: In a game promotion that requires only some contestants to give a consideration to enter, has one established a lottery against those who do not pay? In North Dakota if some patrons receive free chances to enter, their participation in the game may be prohibited if others have to pay.

Pyramid schemes are programs where purchasers get consideration in the form of rebates or commission payments when they introduce other persons into participation in the program. These schemes are prohibited.[81]

Ohio

Similar to New York, Ohio does permit promoters to notify a person that he/she has won a prize or gift when the person must pay some money, do an act, or submit to a sales promotion effort. But this is only allowed if the operator explicitly informs the person of the conditions to the receipt of the prize.[82]

Oregon

Oregon has antideception statutes prohibiting misrepresentations about the chances of winning a contest, the number of winners, and the value or availability of the prizes.[83]

Pyramid schemes are illegal here where purchasers get consideration in the form of rebates or commission payments when they induce others into participation in the program. These schemes are prohibited.[84]

Pennsylvania

Pennsylvania requires certain disclosures for contests relating to promotion of time-share plans.[85]

Rhode Island

Rhode Island has registration requirements similar to the laws of New York and Florida in that it only applies to games conducted by retail establishments. However, Rhode Island law applies to situations where the prize totals as little as $500.

Games by retail gasoline stations are not prohibited in this state. However, state law prohibits retail gasoline dealers from using games of chance or awarding any prizes which "permit any purchaser to obtain motor fuel from such retail dealer at a net price lower than the posted price applicable at the time of the sale."[86]

Pyramid schemes are programs where purchasers get consideration in the form of rebates or commission payments when they introduce other persons into participation in the program. These schemes are prohibited under *Roberts* v. *Communications Inv. Club*.[87]

Additionally, state law prohibits coercion of retail dealers to participate in a game of chance.[88]

Tennessee

Tennessee requires certain disclosures for contests relating to promotion of time-share plans.[89]

Pyramid schemes are programs where purchasers get consideration in the form of rebates or commission payments when they introduce other persons into participation in the program. These schemes are prohibited.[90]

Texas

Texas has antideception statutes prohibiting

misrepresentations about the chances of winning a contest, the number of winners, and the value or availability of the prizes.[91]

Texas requires certain disclosures for contests relating to promotion of time-share plans.[92]

Utah

Pyramid schemes are prohibited in Utah. These occur where purchasers get consideration in the form of rebates or commission payments when they introduce others into the program. These schemes are prohibited.[93]

Vermont

Vermont's antideception statutes prohibit misrepresentations about the chances of winning a contest, the number of winners, and the value or availability of the prizes.[94]

Pyramid schemes are programs where purchasers get consideration in the form of rebates or commission payments when they introduce other persons into participation in the program. These schemes are prohibited.[95]

Virginia

Virginia requires certain disclosures for contests relating to promotion of time-share plans.[96]

Washington

Article II, Section 24 of Washington's constitution was amended in 1972 to read in part: "lotteries shall be prohibited except as specifically authorized upon affirmative vote of 60% of the members of each house of the legislature...." The statute[97] defines the term "lottery" as meaning "a scheme for the distribution of money or property by chance, among persons who have paid or agreed to pay a valuable consideration for the chance."

Further, the statute states that the term "valuable consideration" does not include listening to or watching a television or radio show, filling out and returning a coupon or entry blank received through the mail or published in a newspaper or magazine, sending in an entry blank, visiting a business establishment to obtain a game piece, expending time, thought, attention, and energy in perusing game materials, or merely registering at a place of business or making or answering a telephone call.

The law provides that a "drawing" conducted by a retail outlet may not last more than seven consecutive days and only one such drawing can be conducted within a year. This does not prevent retailers from conducting other types of games, such as "instant winner" rub-off games and bingo games.

Pyramid schemes are programs where purchasers get consideration in the form of rebates or commission payments when they introduce other persons into participation in the program. These schemes are prohibited.[98]

West Virginia

Pyramid schemes are programs where purchasers get consideration in the form of rebates or commission payments when they introduce other persons into participation in the program. These schemes are prohibited.[99]

Wisconsin

Wisconsin is a state in flux regarding lotteries. In 1965 Wisconsin adopted a constitutional amendment. The state's attorney general then issued a decision that only skill contests were permissible. In 1982, however, Wisconsin courts upheld a bottle-top game in *Coca-Cola* v. *LaFollette*.[100] In 1983, another decision, *State* v. *Dahik*,[101] declared that chance must be the dominant element in a lottery. Yet, one remnant of the old view on lotteries is probably *Kayden* v. *Murphy*,[102] which offered that a game requiring a store visit would be void.

Pyramid schemes are programs where purchasers get consideration in the form of rebates or commission payments when they introduce other persons into participation in the program. These schemes are prohibited under *State* v. *Dahik*.

Wisconsin specifically prohibits "in-package" promotional games unless participation is available free, without purchase of the package.[103]

NETWORK STANDARDS

All major television networks have special rules to monitor ads that promote contests. Each has specific review procedures covering such advertising.

The advertiser of a proposed contest should present the storyboard and the game details, along with rules, entry prizes, game pieces, and any other elements to the network involved for approval.

CBS's Procedures

At CBS, the rules are outlined in "CBS Television Network Advertising Guidelines." A proposed ad will be reviewed initially and a questionnaire mailed out. Ad agencies are required to complete the form and enclose a copy of the official rules as they will actually be used, an entry blank and playing pieces, and a detailed breakdown of all prizes awarded during the contest. All related point-of-sale displays and print media ads must also to be enclosed.

CBS will review the following points:

- The final date by which one can enter the contest or claim a prize. This date must be clearly stated in the commercial;
- Where entry blanks and rules will be available and the manner in which they may be obtained without purchase;
- When the commercials will be aired and in what geographic area the contest will be promoted;

- What prizes are to be awarded and who will supply them (advertiser or prize company);
- Eligibility requirements must be clearly disclosed in the commercial. For example, whether one must be a licensed driver to enter;
- Any limitations on the number of times one can enter a contest;
- If a contest is limited to "participating dealers," will there be sufficient sources where contest materials will be available?;
- What print media will be running ads relating to the contest. (However, it does not need to know if another network will carry the ads.);
- Whether the commercials will be used in children's programming. If children are the target of a game, they must be informed very clearly what the odds of winning are. The commercial must show the prizes that will be awarded;
- Whether the contest is based on skill or chance. If the contest is based on chance, CBS wants to know whether the winners will be chosen by a random drawing. If so, where, when, and who will supervise the contest?;
- Will the winning contestant have to consent to use of his/her name to receive a prize?;
- If the contest is skilled in nature, the criteria for judging, the list of judges, and their qualifications must be disclosed;
- Will duplicate prizes will be awarded. If not, how will ties be broken?; and
- Will the public be able to obtain records of the contest, the list of correct answers, and the names of winners?

NBC's Procedures

The "NBC Broadcast Standards for Television" provide for

review of advertising of contests to assure that the proposed contest "is not a lottery, that the material terms are clearly stated, and that it is being conducted fairly, honestly and according to its rules." The following will need to be addressed:

- Submission of complete details of the program to the Broadcast Standards Department at least ten business days prior to the first public announcement of the contest (not the first NBC airing of the commercial);
- Submission of a complete copy of the contest rules, the entry blank, a complete questionnaire (similar to that outlined for CBS), all promotional material, and any print media ads and proposed broadcast copy;
- On-air contest disclosures are similar to CBS's. However, the criteria in which station call-in or call-out quizzes are handled must be explained;
- Game procedures must be free of tampering. NBC is very concerned with the security procedures used throughout the contest to maintain integrity and ensure that contest rules are followed fairly; and
- NBC also wants to know if any aspect of the contest could alarm the public over an imaginary danger; cause crowds, traffic violations or result in damage to public or private property or divert police officers from their normal duties; or result in significant numbers of telephone calls to government agencies or private lines.

ABC's Procedures

The "ABC Advertising Standards" allows advertising of contests as long as the contest offers a fair opportunity to all qualified contestants, it complies with all relevant laws and regulations, and it is not contrary to the public interest.

While ABC does not have a specific questionnaire procedure, the complete proposed ad and all details of the contest rules, prizes, and a copy of the entry blank must be approved by

ABC's department of Broadcast Standards and Practices. ABC reviews the following points:

- A free means of entering the contest must be provided if there is an element of chance involved;
- All contestants must have an equal chance of winning a chance-based contest;
- The network will refuse to broadcast any information concerning a private lottery;
- Methods of judging a contest must be disclosed; and
- Sweepstakes may be aimed at children if they have a fair chance of winning and the prizes are appropriate. The address to submit entries in children's sweepstakes must be both displayed visually and given in the audio portion of the commercial.

GUIDELINES IN CREATING CONTESTS

When developing contests there are certain items to consider. We've looked at these throughout this chapter. Here is a quick reference list of points to think about when developing contests and promoting them in ads. This is only a starting point. The specifics of the contest will determine what must be included.

Contest development should include the following:

- A description of the judging method;
- A statement that entries will not be returned;
- A statement that entries become the property of the company;
- A statement that winners will be notified by mail, if applicable;
- A statement regarding the limit on the number or frequency that a person may enter;
- A statement as to who may or may not enter the contest (e.g., children under 18, employees of the company);
- A list of places where the contest is void;

- A list of the prizes, including the retail value and cash substitute option if any;
- A clarification regarding whether certain prizes will only be given to parents or guardians, if a minor is the winner;
- A list of where entries may be sent, as well as where contest rules, a list of winners, and a list of prizes, may be obtained;
- A statement that the company reserves the right to use names and likenesses of entrants or winners for publicity purposes;
- A deadline (by final postmark date) for receipt of entries;
- Disclaimer of liability for any applicable taxes, licensing, or other fees on prizes;
- Disclaimer of liability for lost or stolen prizes;
- Disclaimer of liability for prizes supplied by others; and
- The termination date of the contest.

---

[1] *In the Matter of Reader's Digest Assn.*, 79 F.T.C. 696 (1971).

[2] *United States* v. *83 Cases of Merchandise Labeled "Honest John,"* 29 F. Supp. 912, at 915 (D.C. Md., 1939).

[3] *U.S.* v. *83 Cases of Merchandise Labeled "Honest John,"* 29 F. Supp. 912 (D.C. Md., 1939).

[4] *United States* v. *Purvis*, 195 F. 618 (N.D. Ga. 1912).

[5] Wisconsin Statutes Annotated, section 945.01(2)(b)(1)(1981).

[6] *Garden City Chamber of Commerce* v. *Wagner*, 100 F. Supp. 769 (E.D.N.Y. 1951).

[7] *In the Matter of Metromedia Inc.*, 60 F.C.C.2d 1075 (1976).

[8] *Consumer Protection Division* v. *Luskins, Inc.*, 706 A.2d 102 (1998).

[9] *Dreem Arts, Inc.* v. *City of Chicago*, 637 F. Supp. 53 (N.D. Ill. 1986).

[10] *Mississippi Gaming Commission* v. *Treasured Arts, Inc.*, 699 So.2d 936 (Miss. 1997).

[11] Miss. Code Ann. § 75-76-3.

[12] *People ex rel. Ellison* v. *Lavin*, 179 N.Y. 164 (1904).

[13] *United States* v. *Rich*, 90 F. Supp. 624 (E.D. Ill. 1950).

[14] *Zebelman* v. *United States*, 339 F.2d 484 (10th Cir. 1964).

[15] *Classic Oldsmobile-Cadillac-GMC Truck* v. *State of Maine*, 704 A.2d 333 (Me. 1997).

[16] 17 M.R.S.A. § 330(2) (Supp. 1996).

[17] *Eastman* v. *Armstrong-Byrd Music Co.*, 212 F. 662 (8th Cir. 1914).

[18] *Zekman* v. *Direct American Marketers, Inc.*, 695 N.E.2d 853 (Ill. 1998).

[19] 815 ILCS 510/2 (West 1992).

[20] *In re American Family Publishers Business Practices Litigation*, No. 1235, 1998 U.S. Dist. LEXIS 12514 (judicial Panel on Multistate Litigation, August 12, 1998).

[21] 15 Stat. 194 (1868).

[22] 18 U.S.C., section 1302 (1982).

[23] 39 U.S.C., section 3001, 3005 (1984 Supp.).

[24] 18 U.S.C. §1302; 39 U.S.C. §3005.

[25] *Federal Trade Commission* v. *R. F. Keppel & Bros. Inc.*, 291 U.S. 304, 54 S.Ct. 423, 78 L.Ed. 2d 814 (1934).

[26] *In the Matter of Reader's Digest Assn.*, 79 F.T.C. 696 (1971).

[27] 16 C.F.R. 419.

[28] 44 Stat. 1162 (1927).

[29] H. R. Rep. No. 72-2106, 72 Cong. 2d Sess. (1933).

[30] 18 U.S.C., section 312 (1982).

[31] 18 U.S.C., section 1304.

[32] *In the Matter of University of Florida*, 40 F.C.C.2d 188 (1973).

[33] 26 U.S.C. 5723(c).

[34] Alaska Stat. §45.50.471.

[35] Ariz. Rev. Stat. Ann. §44-1731.

[36] Ark. Stat. Ann. §41-3285.

[37] *California Gasoline Retailers* v. *Regal Petroleum Corp.*, 330 P.2d 778 (Cal. 1958).

[38] Cal. Bus. & Prof. Code §17511.3.

[39] Cal. Bus. & Prof. Code §17537.1.

[40] Cal. Bus. & Prof. Code. §17537.1.

[41] Cal. Penal Code. §327.

[42] Connecticut Statutes §53-290(a).

[43] Conn. Gen. Stat. Ann. §42-103-103bb.

[44] Conn. Gen. Stat. Ann. §42-145.

[45] Conn. Gen. Stat. § 42-295 (1997).

[46] Fla. Stat. Ann. §849.094.

[47] Fla. Stat. Ann. §849.091(7).

[48] Fla. Admin. Code Ann. 2-9.007.

[49] Fla. Stat. Ann. §721.111(2).

[50] Fla. Stat. Ann. §817.415.

[51] Ga. Code Ann. §16-12-36.

[52] Ga. Code Ann. §44-3-188.

[53] Haw. Rev. Stat. §468-4.

[54] La. Rev. Stat. Ann. §51:1721.

[55] La. Rev. Stat. Ann. §9:1131.12(g).

[56] Me. Rev. Stat. Ann. tit 17-2304.

[57] Me. Rev. Stat. Ann. tit 28, §305.

[58] Me. Rev. Stat. Ann. tit. 7, §3972.

[59] Me. Rev. Stat. Ann. tit. 17, §2305.

[60] Md. Com. Law Code Ann. §13-305.

[61] Md. Ann. Code Art. 56 §144A.

[62] Md. Real Prop. Code Ann. §11A-119.

[63] Massachusetts Statutes 271 §6c.
[64] Mass. Gen. Laws Ann. Ch. 272, §80F.
[65] Michigan Statutes §750.372a.
[66] Minn. Stat. Ann. §609.75.
[67] 11 CSR 70-2. 140.
[68] Mo. Ann. Stat. §407.610.
[69] Mont. Code Ann. §45-6-319.
[70] Nev. Rev. Stat. Ann. §1598.799.
[71] Nev. Rev. Stat. Ann. §598.100.
[72] N.H. Rev. Stat. Ann. §287-B:1.
[73] N.J. Stat. Ann., 56: 6-2 (f).
[74] *United Stations of New Jersey* v. *Getty Oil Co.*, 246 A.2d 150 (1968).
[75] N.J. Stat. Ann §56:8-2.3.
[76] N.M. Stat. Ann. §57-13-4.
[77] N.Y. Gen. Bus. Law §369(e).
[78] N.Y. Gen. Bus. Law §369(ee).
[79] N.Y. Gen. Bus. Law §369-e(7).
[80] N.C.. Gen. Stat. §14-291.2.
[81] N.D. Cent. Code. §51-16-01.
[82] Ohio Admin. Code §109:4-3-06.
[83] Or. Rev. Stat. §646.608(p).
[84] Or. Rev. Stat. §646.608.
[85] 63 Pa. Cons. Stat. Ann. §455.604(a)(18).
[86] R.I. Gen Laws §31-37-14.
[87] *Roberts* v. *Communications Inv. Club*, 431 A.2d 1206, 1212 (R.I. 1981).
[88] R.I. Gen Laws §11-50-7.
[89] Tenn. Code Ann. §66-32-133.
[90] Tenn. Code Ann. §39-6-625.
[91] Tex. Penal Code Ann. §32.42.
[92] Tex. Rev. Civ. Stat. Ann. art.6573c.
[93] Utah Code Ann. §76-6a-3.
[94] Vt. Admin. Proc. Comp. §109.01.
[95] Vt. Admin. Proc. Comp. §101.01.
[96] Va. Code Ann. §55-374.1.
[97] RCW 9.46.020.
[98] Wash. Rev. Code Ann. §19.102.010-020.
[99] W. Va. Code §47-15-2.
[100] *Coca-Cola* v. *LaFollette*, 316 N.W.2d 129 (Wisc. 1982).
[101] *State* v. *Dahik*, 330 N.W.2d 611 (Wisc. 1983).
[102] *Kayden* v. *Murphy*, 150 NW2d 447 (Wisc. 1967).
[103] Wis. Stat. Ann. §100.16.

CHAPTER 10

GUARANTEES AND WARRANTIES

Guarantees...are not worth the paper they are written on.
—*Johann Bernhard*

When someone mentions the word "guarantee," most people think of a piece of paper that comes with their new car, dishwasher, or compact disc player. In that case, the guarantee explains what the manufacturer will do if certain parts of the product fail within a certain time. This type of product guarantee is very common in today's market economy.

But there are other guarantees. Probably the most important and powerful one ever created was devised by a group of 55 men who met at a convention in Philadelphia. The first to show up for the meeting was a 36-year-old educator from Virginia named Jim Madison. The others who joined the meeting later were people from business, government, shipping, farming, education, and law. In fact, more than half of them were lawyers.

The group had the task of creating a guarantee for a new product. It was a different, rather revolutionary product, so they had to consider new situations that might arise and what would happen if they came about. This group continued their meeting for almost 17 weeks before they had ironed out the conditions of their guarantee. Finally, they were satisfied. And, then as with all good guarantees, they put it in writing so that anyone who needed to could rely on it, should a claim become necessary.

The guarantee that I have been discussing was written sometime ago – in 1791 to be exact. And it's still in effect today. It's called the Bill of Rights – the first ten amendments to the

Constitution of the United States. It's a guarantee for the people, a guarantee of personal freedom. It is probably the most powerful (the *Magna Carta* being the only other that comes close) and yet misunderstood guarantee ever written.

Although most people don't consider the Bill of Rights to be a guarantee, it surely is one. It guarantees the people of the United States certain "inalienable rights" that cannot be taken away or overlooked. Of all the cases that the U.S. Supreme Court hears involving constitutional liberties, most of them involve breaches of the Bill of Rights.

Since this chapter deals with guarantees, I thought it appropriate to start with the first ever written in this country. The Ninth and Tenth Amendments essentially say, "we mean what we said." Specifically, the Tenth specifies that powers not delegated are reserved. The Ninth guarantees "[T]he enumeration in the Constitution, of certain rights, shall not be construed to deny or disparage others retained by the people." For over 200 years this guarantee was ignored until the Supreme Court used it to announce that the privacy of the bedroom involved an "unenumerated" right. Specifically, the issue was contraception.

The Eighth Amendment disallows cruel and unusual punishment, as well as excessive bail and fines. The Seventh guarantees the right to a jury trial in civil cases "where the value in controversy exceeds twenty dollars." The Sixth begins, "The accused shall enjoy the right to a speedy and public trial...." That word "enjoy" still bothers me.

The Fifth Amendment declares two guarantees. The first specifies that no person "be subject for the same offense to be twice put in jeopardy of life and limb." Today we call this "double jeopardy." The other guarantee is that no person "shall be compelled in any criminal case to be a witness against himself." We call this "self-incrimination." This Amendment has caused the greatest amount of activity in the courts, from the "Communists-are-everywhere" era of Joe McCarthy and Richard Nixon to the "read-him-his-rights" era of the *Miranda*[1] rule in 1966.

The Fourth Amendment guarantees protection "...against unreasonable search and seizures." The Third touches on a person's right of privacy in his or her home. The Second Amendment specifies a guarantee that a "well regulated Militia being necessary to the security of a free State, the right of the people to keep and bear Arms shall not be infringed." This originally applied to the right of a militia to keep and bear arms, not the individual citizen.

The First Amendment, although it lay dormant for over 130 years, guarantees freedom of speech, freedom of the press, the right of people to peacefully assemble, and the right to practice one's religion. We will revisit the First Amendment and its impact on advertising more in Chapters 12 and 13.

So there you have it. The first guarantee written in this country. And yet it wasn't unanimously adopted by every state until 1939. Massachusetts, Georgia, and Connecticut were the holdouts.

All guarantees have the same purpose. They are intended as a protection. They give confidence to people who must rely on a claim. But the guarantees we are concerned with here are simpler. They are guarantees that involve the state of the marketplace, rather than the state of the Union.

In the fall of 1986, American Express started an ad campaign promoting its "Buyers Assurance Plan." American Express would automatically extend the manufacturer's warranty on any purchases made on its charge card. In some cases the manufacturer's warranty was extended for up to a year. The campaign was intended to run for only four months, but it was so successful that it was continued through 1987. The plan was instituted because American Express was used mostly for such business and travel purchases as air fare, hotels, and meals. But the company wanted to increase sales of retail merchandise with its charge card. As a result of the extended warranty, consumer use of the card increased considerably.

In the spring of 1987, Lufthansa German Airlines began a program for first class and business class passengers guaranteeing to pay $200 for any missed connecting flights or late baggage due to the airline's fault. Passenger ticket sales increased, as a consequence, with only minimal claims filed.

These examples show just how dominant the use of guarantees has become. Entire ad campaigns are built around them. Today, an increasing number of companies are turning to guarantees and warranties to increase sales. Companies recognize the value of customer satisfaction and tie that into their products with stronger guarantees. Airlines, appliances, banks, cars, computers, hotels, and many others are developing strong guarantees for products and services and advertising the fact heavily. Warranties and guarantees have become a part of comparative advertising and are major elements that one company can use to position itself against the competition.

Most of the car manufacturers now offer 6-year or 60,000 mile power-train warranties. A few years ago Ford offered a lifetime service guarantee covering major repairs for as long as the customer owns the car. Advertisements that exclaim "money-back guarantee," "quality assurance," "customer satisfaction," or "extended warranty" have become strong selling tools. Clearly, the advertiser must understand the legalities of promoting guarantees and warranties in its ads.

DIFFERENCE BETWEEN A GUARANTEE AND A WARRANTY

The terms "warranty" and "guarantee" are often used interchangeably. In reality there is very little difference between the two, but there is a distinction. To be technical, a warranty is an assumption by the seller of the quality, suitability, character, and performance of the product. On the other hand, a guarantee is the agreement that comes with the purchase of the merchandise that, if the product fails to live up to the claims, the seller will remedy the situation in some way.

A warranty is, simply put, a promise that becomes a contract between the manufacturer and the buyer. The contract goes into effect at the moment the consumer makes a purchase.

A guarantee is a promise that if something goes wrong with the product, the manufacturer will do certain things.

Let's say a roll of photographic film claims that it is "free from defects in workmanship and materials." That's a warranty. If the film turns out to be defective, the guarantee states that "if defective it will be replaced with a new roll of equivalent film free of charge." The warranty states what the manufacturer claims the product will do. The guarantee states what the manufacturer will do if the product fails to live up to the warranty.

THE SCOPE OF WARRANTIES AND GUARANTEES

As seen in Chapter 4 on the role of advertising in products liability actions, there are different forms of warranties. Warranties can be expressed, that is clearly stated, or they can be implied. I would recommend a review of that chapter to examine the ways in which warranties can have an impact on advertising.

Here, however, we will deal mainly with how guarantees should be advertised rather than discussing the legalities of developing guarantees. The balance of this chapter will be devoted to considerations about using guarantees in advertising.

REPRESENTATIONS MADE IN ADS ABOUT GUARANTEES

When advertisements discuss product guarantees the advertiser must be concerned with making certain representations. When claims are made in an ad about the quality, results, or effects of guaranteed merchandise, the advertiser must do certain things –

identify the guarantor and state the characteristics, performance, duration, conditions, and charges involved.

Identifying The Guarantor

In Maryland in the early 1960's, World Wide Television Corporation sold television sets and appliances to the public. As part of its promotion the company advertised in newspapers and on radio, focusing on a guarantee for its products.

The company had a unique way of selling its products. World Wide's giant screen Olympic console televisions were controlled by a coin meter, called the "Metermatic Plan." Instead of making monthly payments for the appliance, the purchaser would insert coins in a box to turn on the unit, similar to a coin-operated laundry. The purchaser couldn't use the appliance unless money was put in. A typical ad stated that the products were guaranteed. Here's what was claimed:

BRAND NEW GIANT SCREEN OLYMPIC CONSOLE TELEVISION

WITH ONE FULL-YEAR GUARANTEE including picture tube.
Service is fully guaranteed!
Service guarantee included!
The Metermatic Plan is better because service is guaranteed.

In truth, the Olympic televisions were guaranteed by Siegler Corporation, the makers of the television, and not World Wide. Yet this was not stated anywhere in the ads, but only in the instruction booklet included with the television set. The implication in the ad was that World Wide was guaranteeing the television sets. The consumer could not have known the true identity of the guarantor until after the television was delivered. This was deceptive.

There's another unique thing about World Wide's service

guarantee. Service was guaranteed because if the company didn't fix a broken set, it couldn't be used by the consumer – and the company wouldn't get paid. That's the only reason service was fully guaranteed. The FTC, learning of the situation, filed a complaint, *In the Matter of World Wide Television Corp.*[2]

In that case the commissioner stated:

> [World Wide's] products are not unconditionally guaranteed for one year. Said guarantee is subject to numerous requirements, limitations, and restrictions. The advertised guarantee fails to set forth the nature, conditions and extent of the guarantee, the manner in which the guarantor will perform...and the identity of the guarantor.

The commissioner ordered that World Wide could not claim its products were guaranteed unless the nature, extent, and duration were clearly stated. Further, World Wide had to clearly state the name and address of the guarantor.

Stating The Characteristics Or Attributes To Be Guaranteed

An advertiser can build whatever guarantee it wants into a product. In other words, an advertiser may create the limits of any guarantee on its products. However, it must state the characteristics, attributes, and limitations in its guarantee. But simply using the word "guaranteed" alone and without clarification must be avoided.

One of the earliest situations to establish this involved the Parker Pen Company. Parker manufactured fountain pens and sold them to the public. In 1946 Parker ran advertisements for its pens that contained a statement "Guaranteed for Life by Parker's." The specific terms of the guarantee were spelled out elsewhere in the ad: "Pens marked with a Blue Diamond are guaranteed for the life of the owner against everything except loss or intentional damage, subject only to a charge of 35 cents for postage, insurance and handling, provided complete pen is returned for service."

The Federal Trade Commission filed a complaint against Parker because it felt that by charging 35 cents a deception was created as to the "Lifetime Guarantee." The FTC claimed that the 35-cent charge limited the guarantee. The case was appealed to the Federal Circuit Court of Appeals in *Parker Pen Co.* v. *F.T.C.*[3]

There the court voiced its opinion. "Ordinarily the word, guarantee, is incomplete unless it is used in connection with other explanatory words." To say a pen or other object is guaranteed is meaningless. What is the guarantee? Is it a limited guarantee? Is it an unlimited guarantee? The answer to these questions gives meaning to the word "guaranteed." The same is true of the words "Guaranteed for Life" or "Life Guarantee."

In this case, Parker advertised its guarantee, claiming that it would make needed repairs during the life of the original buyer, if that person paid 35 cents per repair. There is nothing wrong with that. It clearly spelled out the terms of its guarantee. Parker won its case.

Specifying How The Guarantee Is To Be Performed

Another element of the claim that a product is guaranteed involves how the guarantee will be honored. In other words, what will be done if the product fails to perform as promised.

Capitol Manufacturing Company in New York offered watches represented as manufactured by Hamilton and Gruen Watch companies. In reality, Capitol did not sell Hamilton or Gruen watches, but rather cheap imitations. In its ads, Capitol made statements about its watches, including:

ELECTRA TWO-YEAR SERVICE GUARANTEE

We guarantee this watch for two years from date of purchase

against defects in material and workmanship.

This guarantee appears to name a company called Electra as the guarantor. It claims that any obligations that the company has under the guarantee will be performed fully, satisfactorily, and promptly. The ad also states that the watch will operate properly for at least two years.

Capitol's guarantee came to the attention of the Federal Trade Commission. Since the guarantee did not specify how the guarantor would fulfill the guarantee, the FTC filed a complaint, *In the Matter of Capitol Mfg. Corp.*,[4] charging that the guarantee was deceptive. The watches sold by Capitol were so cheaply made that "[f]ew, if any,...will operate for at least the two year period represented in the guarantee."

The problem with this guarantee was its failure to state what Capitol would do if the watch broke within the two-year period. Would it repair the watch? Would it replace the watch? Would it refund the purchase price? None of this was stated. In truth, it wasn't going to do anything. This is probably how the FTC learned about the situation in the first place.

When any guarantee is claimed, the "manner in which the guarantor will perform...[must be] clearly and conspicuously set forth in immediate connection therewith." Since Capitol failed to provide this information with its guarantee, the FTC issued a cease-and-desist order.

Duration Of The Guarantee

A guarantee should specify a limit as to the length of time it will be honored by the manufacturer. Advertisers can get into trouble with guarantees described as "for a season of use," or "for the year." The guarantee should specify when the time of the guarantee starts. For example, a statement such as, "guaranteed for one year from the date of retail purchase," leaves little to interpretation.

Another way to list the duration of a guarantee is to state its termination date. Let's go back to our example of photographic film, which is commonly guaranteed in this way. Film generally lists an expiration date for the "guaranteed" use of the product such as "not good after...."

A common way to start the clock running on a guarantee is through a mail-back registration card. Many products are guaranteed only after a registration card is filled out and returned to the manufacturer. Many home appliances, stereos, cameras, and watches are commonly guaranteed in this way.

In the late 1950's, a sewing machine manufacturer placed ads in national consumer magazines including *McCall's* magazine. The manufacturer, International Stitch-O-Matic in Chicago, promoted its guarantee in these ads. The guarantee stated that the product was backed by a "money-back" guarantee on the entire machine for 25 years. When it turned out that this was false, *In the Matter of International Stitch-O-Matic Corp.*[5] resulted. The guarantee claimed that the entire machine was covered for 25 years. In fact, only the motor was guaranteed, and for just one year. The Stitch-O-Matic guarantee had limitations, including time, which were blatantly misstated in its ads.

Stating Conditions Of The Guarantee

In the late 1960's Universe Chemicals, Incorporated, manufactured and sold a water-repellent paint by the name of "Kleer-Kote" and "Kolor-Kote." The sales demonstration of the product was quite impressive. Various items were shown to the prospective buyers, and they were told that the items were coated with Kleer-Kote or Kolor-Kote.

A piece of sheet metal, coated with Kolor-Kote, was shown, and the prospect was told that the paint would not crack, peel, or break even if the metal was bent. In another example, a treated brick showed the repellent quality of the coating when water was poured over it. The coating was heated with an infrared bulb to demonstrate its heat resistance. A sieve was coated with Kleer-Kote and was shown to hold water without leaking.

The product appeared to be truly amazing, and the demonstrations were convincing. Kleer-Kote and Kolor-Kote even came with a "10-year, unconditional guarantee." Unfortunately, the product failed to live up to its claims, and the guarantee turned out to be not much of a solution. The Federal Trade Commission became involved and filed *In the Matter of Universe Chemicals, Inc.*[6]

While the wording in the Kleer-Kote brochure stated that the product was "unconditionally guaranteed for 10 years," this was not the case. When a guarantee is claimed to be unconditional, it means just that: no conditions. If there are any conditions, the guarantee is not unconditional. In that case, it should be stated as a "limited guarantee" and then the limits must be specified.

Actually, in Universe Chemicals' case the company would only replace the product if defective. In certain cases the product was replaced, but in many cases the company refused. "The guarantee," said the commissioner, "was clearly not unconditional, and the conditions were not stated in the advertising."

Stating Charges Involved In A Guarantee

Western Radio Corporation manufactured pocket-sized radio transmitters and advertised them in such magazines as *Popular Science* in the mid 1960's. Its Radi-Vox transmitter was advertised with a "money-back guarantee." However, the company failed to inform the consumer that a service charge applied to the guarantee.

The case went to court in *Western Radio Corp. v. FTC.*[7] There, the court said the advertising had the capacity and tendency to mislead the public "by failure to disclose a service charge in connection with the advertised unconditional guarantee."

When a guarantee is advertised as a money-back guarantee, it means just that. Any guarantee must state "the terms and conditions of such guarantee...clearly and conspicuously... including the amount of any service or other charge which is imposed."

PROBLEMS WITH ADVERTISING GUARANTEES

The most obvious problem encountered in advertising a guarantee is whether the ad creates a deception about the actual guarantee. When there is a difference between the guarantee and the way it is advertised or where it is a blatant falsehood, the Federal Trade Commission can step in.

Variations Between An Advertised Guarantee And An Actual Guarantee

Montgomery Ward offered rebuilt car engines through its chain of retail department stores in the 1960's. In its advertisements the engines were promoted as having an unconditional guarantee. The customer would read the ad, go to the store, and purchase the engine only to learn later that the guarantee had quite a few restrictions.

The Montgomery Ward guarantee was not unconditional. It actually covered only a period of 90 days or 4,000 miles:

FOR A PERIOD OF NINETY DAYS
from the date installed or four thousand miles
(whichever comes first) we warrant this
rebuilt assembly for passenger car service
against defects in material and factory workmanship
provided our installation and
operating instructions are followed.

The guarantee also contained other restrictions. For instance, the guarantee only provided for the following:

- Replacement of parts, no labor;
- A claim for engines installed by Wards;
- A claim if required checkups are made;
- A claim if damage was not caused by misuse or accident; and
- A claim if a valid certificate was on file.

Eventually, the FTC learned of Montgomery Ward's guarantee and a complaint was filed: *Montgomery Ward & Co.* v. *FTC.*[8] Montgomery Ward argued that it had a policy of honoring claims for defective merchandise even though its guarantee stated many restrictions. In fact, the court acknowledged that there was no evidence "that any customer had any claim under any guarantee...or that [Ward] failed to satisfy any claim under its guarantees."

The point, however, was that Ward's actual guarantee placed many restrictions, which were not revealed in its advertising. Plain and simple, this is deceptive. If you'll recall from Chapters 2 and 3, the FTC does not require a showing that actual deception occurred, only that the ad has the likelihood to deceive.

"The capacity [or under current interpretation, likelihood] to deceive," said the court, "involved in Ward's advertisements lies in the inducement to buy created by the unlimited, advertised guarantee." It is clear from this case that an advertiser must specify the terms of its guarantee in an ad, unless it truly offers an "unconditional" guarantee. The advertising of a guarantee must clearly express the actual guarantee that the consumer will get with the purchase.

False Statements Regarding A Guarantee

Certain industries place specific restrictions and requirements on guarantees of quality, origin, and authenticity of merchandise. Industries such as alcohol, tobacco, medicines, textiles, and others have such regulations. An advertiser should consult the specific regulations of these industries.

M. Reiner & Sons was a fur dealer in New York. In 1969 the company advertised and sold furs with the guarantee that the furs were authentic and in compliance with specific laws governing the fur trade.[9] The company claimed that the proper guarantee, as required by the Fur Products Labeling Act, was on file with the Federal Trade Commission.

It was learned later that this was not the case; therefore, a complaint was filed by the FTC: *In the Matter of M. Reiner & Sons*.[10] The commission discovered that Reiner had no certificate of guarantee on file and therefore violated the law by creating a deception about its guarantee.

The commission stated that Reiner:

> [F]alsely represented in writing that [it] had a continuing [guarantee] on file with the Federal Trade Commission when [it] in furnishing such guarantees had reason to believe that the fur products so falsely guaranteed would be introduced, sold, transported, and distributed in commerce.

As a result, Reiner was ordered to cease-and-desist from such practices.

TYPES OF GUARANTEES

There are many different types of guarantees. Among the most common are money-back, satisfaction, lifetime, repair, limited, and refund or replacement guarantees. The type of guarantee offered is dependent on the manufacturer. Now let's take a look at each of these.

Money-Back Guarantees

This is one of the most common. A money-back guarantee

means just that. If the consumer is not satisfied, a full refund must be given. This type of guarantee must be honored in a timely manner. If a customer asks for a refund, he must not be made to make numerous attempts to collect the refund.

This guarantee can be offered in a number of situations, and should be clearly stated in any ads as well as on the packaging of the product. Typical money-back guarantees clarify what the manufacturer will do under the following situations:

- If the consumer is not satisfied with the product;
- If it can be purchased elsewhere for less;
- If it fails to perform a specific job; and
- If it does not do its job better than its competition.

Satisfaction Guaranteed

If an ad claims "satisfaction guaranteed," without any clarification, then the consumer is entitled to determine if the product satisfies or not.

In cases where the claim is "satisfactory-fit guaranteed" the consumer is still able to determine if satisfaction resulted from the purchase of the product. Satisfaction is a subjective judgment call, and the purchaser is allowed to use his or her judgment as to whether satisfaction exists.

Lifetime Guarantees

Lifetime guarantees are legal, but the terms of the guarantee should be clearly spelled out. The guarantee must be stated as "conditional" if charges are applied for service or replacement parts. A full disclosure of any conditions or service charges must accompany the guarantee. Terms such as "guaranteed forever" should not be used unless the manufacturer intends to live up to the claim, literally. The Sears Craftsman tool guarantee is a good example of a valid lifetime guarantee.

Claims that should not be made include the following:

- Guaranteed to last through the ages;

- Guaranteed to give a lifetime of service;
- Guarantee of a lifetime;
- Guaranteed for a lifetime; and
- Guaranteed forever.

Repair Guarantees

Certain guarantees involve service repairs. These guarantees, usually found with appliances or automobiles, should be carefully explained. The following elements should be included in any repair guarantee:

- Time restrictions;
- Service charges;
- Cost of repairs;
- Party responsible for repairs; and
- Types of defects that are covered.

Limited Guarantees

As seen earlier, any guarantee that is not unlimited is limited. If a guarantee is claimed in an ad and it is not unlimited, then it must be called a limited guarantee.

A good example of a limited guarantee can be found in our earlier example of film. Typically the manufacturer provides that if the film is defective the original roll of film will be replaced. But no other obligations exist; the company cannot be made to pay for loss of the photographic images or the costs to reshoot.

Refund Or Replacement Guarantees

Some guarantees may specify whether the manufacturer will refund the purchase price (sometimes pro-rated) or replace the item. The manufacturer may make this decision, but the term must be specified in the guarantee.

FTC GUIDELINES FOR ADVERTISING OF WARRANTIES AND GUARANTEES

The commission has guidelines to help advertisers avoid unfair or deceptive practices in the advertising of warranties and guarantees. These supplement the issues just discussed.

An advertiser generally is not required to state a warranty or guarantee offered on an advertised product, but is required only to disclose certain information if the warranty is mentioned. An advertiser should mention that a product is warranted or guaranteed only if the seller or manufacturer "promptly and fully performs its obligations under the warranty or guarantee."

Written Warranties On Consumer Products

If an advertisement for a consumer product costing more than $15 mentions a written warranty, the FTC states:

> The advertisement should disclose, with such clarity and prominence as will be noticed and understood by prospective purchasers, that prior to sale, at the place where the product is sold, prospective purchasers can see the written warranty or guarantee for complete details of the warranty coverage.
>
> If an advertisement in a catalog or other solicitation for mail order or telephone sales mentions a warranty, the advertisement must prominently and clearly, in close proximity to the description of the warranted product or in a clearly-referenced information section, set forth the full text of the warranty or disclose that prospective buyers can obtain complete details of the written warranty or guarantee free of charge upon specific written request from the seller or "from the catalogue or other solicitation."

Warranty Disclosure Requirements

Originally the FTC required disclosure of virtually all warranty terms in ads mentioning warranties. However, the FTC decided that to require disclosure of all warranty terms in ads might deter advertisers from mentioning warranty coverage at all. Since the Pre-Sale Availability Rule assures that warranty terms are available to consumers at the store, the FTC also concluded such detailed disclosures in ads are not needed. Instead, the revised position recommends disclosure in warranty ads promoting a product covered by the Pre-Sale Availability Rule 8, of the fact that the warranty document is available for examination before purchase of the product.

There is a similar approach for mail-order and catalog sales ads. One provision calls for mail-order or catalogue sales to disclose information sufficient to convey to consumers that they can obtain complete details on the written warranty free upon specific written request, or from the catalogue or solicitation (whichever is applicable).

The FTC also states (concerning disclosures) that text in the ad will clearly and prominently specify that warranties are available for inspection prior to sale.

Television ads will comply if the ads:

> Make the necessary disclosure simultaneously with or immediately following the warranty claim. The disclosure can be presented either in the audio portion or in the video portion as a printed disclosure, provided that a video disclosure appears on the screen for at least five seconds.

However, the FTC states:

> It may be necessary for multiple disclosures of the material limitations on a satisfaction guarantee to be disclosed in the audio portion of an advertisement, or to be disclosed for a longer period

of time than five seconds in order for the disclosures to be clear and prominent.

Satisfaction Guarantees

Satisfaction guarantees are very popular in advertising, particularly on television and in mail-order. The FTC states that "satisfaction guaranteed" claims should be used only if you plan to refund the full purchase price at the buyer's request. The guides also suggest that, if this type of representation is subject to material limitations or conditions (an express limitation of duration, or a limitation to products returned in their original packaging), the ad should disclose that limitation or condition.

"Lifetime" Representations

The FTC suggests that use of the term "lifetime" in describing the duration of a guarantee or warranty can mislead consumers unless clarified as to the definition of "life." They require clarification of the life to which the claim refers, i.e., whether or not it refers to the buyer's life.

Warranty Performance

The FTC warns "that a warrantor or guarantor should ensure performance on advertised warranties or guarantees."

SELF-REGULATORY BODIES

If you're planning to advertise a warranty, be aware of the various self-regulatory bodies. The most important industry self-regulatory mechanism is the Better Business Bureau's (BBB) National Advertising Division/National Advertising Review Board (NAD/NARB). The BBB's Code of Advertising contains basic advertising standards issued for the guidance of advertisers, ad agencies, and the advertising media. In particular, section 8 of that code (covering warranties and guarantees) provides:

a. When the term "warranty" (or "guarantee") is used in product advertising, the following disclosure should be made clearly and prominently: a statement that the complete details of the warranty can be seen at the advertiser's store prior to sale, or in the case of mail or telephone order sales, are available free on written request.

b. (1) "satisfaction guarantee," "money back guarantee," "free trial offer," or similar representations should be used in advertising only if the seller or manufacturer refunds the full purchase price of the advertised product at the purchaser's request.

b. (2) When "satisfaction guarantee" or similar representations are used in advertising, any material limitations or conditions that apply to the guarantee should be clearly and prominently disclosed.

c. When the term "lifetime," "life," or similar representations are used in advertising to describe the duration of the warranty or guarantee, the advertisement should clearly and prominently disclose the life to which the representation refers.

d. Sellers or manufacturers should advertise that a product is warranted or guaranteed only if the seller or manufacturer promptly and fully performs its obligations under the warranty or guarantee.

e. Advertisers should make certain that any advertising of warranties complies with the Consumer Products Warranty Act, effective July 4, 1975, relevant Federal Trade Commission requirements, and any applicable state and local laws.

NETWORK GUIDELINES RELATING TO THE ADVERTISING OF WARRANTIES

As with any network commercial, consult the network's clearance department before producing a television commercial. All networks have extensive guidelines pertaining to the advertising of warranties or guarantees. They will require clear and conspicuous disclosure in the commercial referring to a warranty or guarantee, whether the warranty is full or limited. In addition, both networks require additional disclosures in the audio or video portions of a commercial, or in both. ABC requires that the ad disclose: "specific duration, major limitations (e.g., parts excluded or costs or responsibilities the customer must undertake), and 'see dealer for details'" statements.

Under NBC's broadcast standards requirements, the ad must disclose: "the nature and extent of the guarantee; the identity of the guarantor; the manner in which the guarantor intends to perform; information concerning what a purchaser wishing to claim under the guarantee need do before the guarantor will perform pursuant to its obligations under the guarantee."

In addition, ABC has guidelines for "satisfaction or your money back" representations, "savings guarantees," "guarantees as a representative," "lifetime guarantees," and "prorated adjustment of guarantees."

THE MAGNUSON-MOSS WARRANTY ACT

When Congress enacted the Magnuson-Moss Warranty Act,[11] it gave the federal government a potentially dominant role in warranty law. While the act still hasn't lived up to initial expectations, it is, nonetheless, a major force to be reckoned with when offering a warranty or guarantee on a product or service. An initial determination should always be made whether the Magnuson-Moss Warranty Act applies. Magnuson-Moss is applicable to written warranties.

Essentially, there are two types of written warranties under the act: "full" and "limited." If you decide to offer your customers a "full" warranty, it means, among other things, that:

- You will fix or replace a defective product for free within a reasonable time;
- You won't require your customer to do anything unreasonable to get warranty service;
- Your warranty is good for anyone owning the product during the warranty period; and
- You will give your customer the choice of a new product or his or her money back if the product can't be fixed or hasn't been fixed after a reasonable number of attempts.

If you offer a "limited" warranty, it means you're offering less than what a full warranty provides. For example, a limited warranty may cover only parts and not labor, or cover only the first buyer, or charge for handling.

If a manufacturer or retailer offers a written warranty, the Magnuson-Moss act demands substantial analysis and compliance.

To get a copy of the Magnuson-Moss Act, implementing regulations, and explanatory pamphlets on the law, you should write to: the Federal Trade Commission, Washington, D.C. 20580, or check their web site at: www.ftc.gov.

---

[1] *Miranda* v. *Arizona*, 384 U.S. 436, 86 S.Ct. 1602, 16 L.Ed. 2d 694 (1966).
[2] *In the Matter of World Wide Television Corp.*, 66 F.T.C. 961 (1964).
[3] *Parker Pen Co.* v. *FTC*, 153 F.2d 509 (C.C.A. 1946).
[4] *In the Matter of Capitol Mfg. Corp.*, 73 F.T.C. 872 (1968).
[5] *In the Matter of International Stitch-O-Matic Corp.*, 54 F.T.C. 1308 (1959).
[6] *In the Matter of Universe Chemicals, Inc.*, 77 F.T.C. 598 (1970).
[7] *Western Radio Corp.* v. *FTC*, 339 F.2d 937 (7th Cir. 1964).
[8] *Montgomery Ward & Co.* v. *FTC*, 379 F.2d 666 (7th Cir. 1967).
[9] Fur Products Labeling Act, 15 U.S.C. § 69 et seq. (1988).
[10] *In the Matter of M. Reiner & Sons*, 77 F.T.C. 862 (1970).
[11] 15 U.S.C. § 45 (1988).

CHAPTER 11

THE CLIENT/AGENCY RELATIONSHIP

The client is, of course, god. And so it has been ever since the days of the first great ad man Jesus Christ.
—*Robert C. Pritikin*

If you'll allow me, I have a short story to tell you. A very long time ago, let's say somewhere around 10 million B.C., there lived a man we'll call Urr. He lived a simple life, mainly concerned with providing for his family. Back in those days, life could be pretty rigorous. Even cutting firewood could be a major ordeal. So, in order to make the job easier, Urr designed a crude but effective device, which he called for lack of a better name, a tree cutter. With it, the first tool was invented.

Everything went along fine until one day a fellow named Ogg happened by and saw Urr working with his tree cutter. Realizing that he could make excellent use of this device for his own daily chores, and being quite a bit larger in stature than Urr, Ogg used this advantage to negotiate for the cutter. As you'd expect, he took possession of it, thereby carrying out the first business transaction in history.

Thoroughly frustrated, Urr thought that there had to be a better way to do business. He soon realized that since he had built something that Ogg wanted, perhaps others would also want his invention. Urr reasoned that rather than letting others steal his device, he could make more and offer them in exchange for items other people possessed that he needed. Setting his plan into motion, he soon found to his pleasure that it worked.

Yet, it was only a matter of time before Urr became aware of a growing problem, competition. As expected, other people began making and selling their own brand of tree cutter. With salespeople cropping up (excuse the pun) everywhere, Urr knew that he had to do something. So he called on his cousin Aad.

Being a good salesman, Aad got the word out that Urr's tree cutters were better than any of the other cheap imitations on the market. Finding out that he had a real skill at this sort of thing, Aad decided to go into business promoting other products. He called his company The Aad Agency, and a new industry was born.

If you don't believe my version of how the first agency came about, here is another that can be better documented.

A common practice in Italy around 1250 was to sell wine by the flask. Many unscrupulous wine merchants filled the bottom of their bottles with wax, thereby reducing the amount of wine in the bottle and improving the profit margin substantially. When the public found out about this deception, wine sales dropped rapidly. So the legitimate wine merchants began sending agents out into the streets promoting wine with placards saying "Sine Cere," which means "without wax." From this phrase comes our word "sincere," and from this practice comes one of the earliest examples of an organized advertising agency.

THE ADVERTISING AGENCY

A professional agency is a business that acts on behalf of others. Attorneys, accountants, brokers, factors, auctioneers, and, yes, advertising agencies may fall into this category. Any profession – if it qualifies as an agent – is regulated by the same laws. As a result, some of the cases we examine in this chapter do not involve advertising agencies, but the principles are binding on any agency relationship.

First, there are a couple of terms that need to be clarified. An *agent* can be an individual alone, a group of people, a large corporation, or a full-time employee. A principal can be a client or an employer. But for purposes of clarity, we refer to a principal as the *client* throughout this chapter.

Advertising agencies that want the legal benefits of being an agency must abide by the duties that go along with the title. Simply calling a company an "advertising agency" does not mean that it is one legally. The legal relationship is what exists, not what is claimed. It must act like a true agency to be treated as one. We will examine this idea more closely in the balance of this chapter.

Now, you may ask why ad agencies are called "agencies" if they are not. It's more out of tradition than for any other reason. The title creates a trade name more than an establishment of legal status. It is actually a misnomer; a throwback from the early "space-broker" days when advertising agencies were merely brokers of media space.

The alternative to being an agency is being an independent contractor. Here's an example to illustrate. A person owns a Chevrolet dealership in Los Angeles. This dealer sells Chevrolet cars and trucks, and the business is referred to as a Chevrolet agency. However, this dealer is not an agent. The person simply sells Chevrolet products as an independent contractor, he or she does not work on behalf of others.

The distinguishing feature between an "agent" and "independent contractor" is the amount of control retained by the client over the physical conduct of the person performing the service. The independent contractor obligates herself or himself to produce a result and is free to pursue her or his own methods in the performance of the work.

For example, if Acme Company wants a new machine, it can use its own employees to build it. Or it can contract with Bosco Corporation to build the machine according to Acme's specifications and at an agreed-on price. If Acme hires Bosco to build the machine, Bosco is an independent contractor. Bosco has been hired to produce a result: a specific machine at a specific price. Acme has no physical control over how Bosco produces the machine.

However, in most cases advertising agencies are true agencies in the legal sense. They don't have the independent contractor's freedom of control. The ad agency is subject to direct control by the client. In the advertising business, most clients reserve the right to select, approve, confer, and be advised of the work of their advertising agencies during every stage of the process. Anyone who has ever worked in an agency can vouch for that. So most courts have maintained that agencies have, in fact, acted as agents for their clients.

DUTIES OF THE ADVERTISING AGENCY

An advertising agency is able to commit the client to contracts, and at the same time it owes a duty of confidence and trust (fiduciary) to the client. Duties that the agency owes to the client fall into one of two areas: specific duties that are spelled out in a written contract and duties that are imposed by law. Specific duties can be anything so long as they do not violate a law and that the client and agency want to make a part of the contract.

Even if no written contract exists between the client and agency, the agency's duties imposed by law still exist. These include the following:

- High level of skill required of agency;
- Full disclosure to client;
- Obligations regarding competitive accounts;
- Trustee of client and handling of funds;
- Accountability to client;
- Duty to cooperate with client;
- Obligation to preserve trade secrets; and
- No undisclosed interest in suppliers.

Now let's look at each of these duties in more detail.

High Level Of Skill Required Of Agency

An advertising agency represents itself as being an expert in its field. When an ad agency makes a presentation to a prospective client, it goes out of its way to impress upon the client that it possesses a tremendous degree of skill in both the area of advertising and that of the client's product. Once stated, the agency is then obligated to deliver. It must not merely show a general level of skill, but it must demonstrate the level of a highly skilled professional.

It is not enough that an advertising (or any other) agency apply the usual degree of care to the business entrusted it by its client. It must put forth its best efforts using its skill, experience, and knowledge to the best of its professional ability. When an agency fails to deliver on this, breach of contract may exist. The breach may be cause for the client to terminate the contract, or in some cases, bring suit for damages.

On the other hand, it is true that an agency is not required to guarantee the success of the advertising that it produces, only to put forth all of its best efforts toward the success of it. That means not doing anything that would diminish its chance for success.

Full Disclosure To Client

An agency owes its clients complete loyalty. This may seem simple to accomplish, but it can affect an agency in many ways. Part of this loyalty includes a responsibility to inform the client of any fact or occurrence that affects the client in any way. For instance, if the agency has been late in paying a supplier, who in turn threatens to cut off services, the agency is under a duty to inform its client. As unpleasant as this may be, the client is legally entitled to be informed quickly and thoroughly on all such matters.

Let me give you a good example. The disclosure required of an agent was discussed in *Crocker* v. *United States*.[1] Frank Crocker owned a company, which had a contract to furnish mail-carrier satchels to the U.S. Post Office. His company did so, but something happened to cause the Postmaster General to rescind the contract and refuse to pay for the satchels.

Two employees of Crocker, Mr. Lorenz and Mr. Crawford, made a secret agreement with Mr. Machen, who was superintendent of the division that needed the satchels. Machen arranged for the contract to go to Crocker's company in exchange for half of the profits. Crocker got the government contract, with Machen getting half the profits from the sales. The company furnished over 10,000 satchels before the Postmaster General learned of the collusion.

Lorenz and Crawford were agents of Crocker, and were acquiring the contract at the company's request. They were trying to secure the government contract by working out a fraudulent deal with Machen. By virtue of the agency relationship, Crocker in essence sanctioned what they did. Because the contract was obtained fraudulently, Crocker lost his claim for payment.

Obligations As To Competitive Clients

A problem arises when an agency tries to serve two clients who are in competition with each other. The agency can't serve both unless it has the consent of the two parties in advance. This became the issue in *Joyce Beverages of New York, Inc.* v. *Royal Crown Cola.*[2]

Joyce Beverages was a licensee, and as such an agent, of several soft drink manufacturers, including Royal Crown Cola, 7-Up, Diet 7-Up, A&W Root Beer, Sugar-Free A&W, Perrier, Nestea, Hawaiian Punch, and Nehi drinks. Royal Crown's licensing agreement with Joyce stated that Joyce must use its best efforts to build, maintain, and expand the sales of the Royal Crown drinks to Royal Crown's satisfaction.

The contract between the parties would not allow Joyce to distribute any soft drinks that were "substantially or reasonably similar" to Royal Crown products. The contract further provided that "any cola shall be deemed substantially or reasonably similar to any...cola [and] any diet cola to any...diet cola."

One of the ways Joyce could breach this agreement was to take on a competing drink. That's exactly what it did. In 1982 Joyce began marketing "LIKE," a decaffeinated cola drink manufactured by the 7-Up Company.

By handling another competitive cola in its market area, Joyce created "inevitable and corrosive divided loyalty and effort and made impossible a continued relationship...of confidence and cooperation." In essence, Joyce would be selling a new product to old customers, with advertising and promotion practices that it established for the old product. This breaches the duty of an agent not to handle competing clients without consent.

Joyce argued, in its defense, that Royal Crown would not be put in a position to "sink or swim" by itself. Joyce also claimed that Royal Crown wouldn't "go down the drain." This points out a common misconception, i.e., Joyce's duty to its client is to vigorously promote the product – to expand its market share, not simply to keep it alive. The court agreed and allowed Royal Crown to rescind the contract.

Sometimes it is not easy to determine whether two clients compete with each other. Clients compete, basically, when their products are similar or interchangeable or where one product may replace the need of the other. Such products that could replace the other might be toothpaste and dental cleaning powder, floor wax and a product that eliminates the need to wax, or bandages and a cut spray that replaces a bandage.

Another area of competition is situations in which products are advertised and sold in different geographic areas. In these cases there may be no direct competition of products, yet clients may not be pleased. Clients may claim that information obtained from one company is being used to benefit the other. While this may not violate any duty, the agency could have some very irritated clients on its hands. The best practice is to inform the agency's existing client and get its approval beforehand.

However, many agencies do represent different clients in competition for the same market. These agencies promote the fact that they specialize in a certain area: banking, real estate, or medical, for example. In many fields, this agency specialty is preferred by clients. In these cases, clients who know of this are considered to have consented to the agency's representing other competitors. If the client is told about representing other competitors in the same field before it becomes a client, it will have very little to complain about later. The point is that the client must be made aware of, and give its consent to, this multiple representation.

Trustee Of Client And Handling Of Funds

Handling Of Funds

The financial aspect of a client/agency relationship can be a major source of aggravation for both, especially in the area of commingling of funds, i.e., mixing the money that belongs to the agency with that which belongs to the client. The agency is the trustee of the funds taken in on behalf of the client and must treat that money accordingly.

Basic agency law requires that an agent must keep money belonging to its client separate from its own. The only time that this does not need to happen legally is when the client has knowledge and has consented in advance.

The common practice, however, is to the contrary for a number of reasons. When a client sends money to the agency, rarely does it identify what it should be applied to. It is very uncommon that a client will send a separate check for each type of payment. However, payments intended to cover the agency's fees and costs need not be kept separately. But, money that merely flows through the agency on the way to suppliers or media, less commissions, should not be mixed with the agency's money. To avoid problems later, this subject should be specifically addressed in the client/agency contract.

The best way to protect the agency is to have separate bank accounts: one as a trust account for the client's money, which can be drawn on as needed, and another for the agency's money, which is not subject to accountability to the client.

Trustee Of Rights And Materials

Everything that the agency creates for its client belongs to the client; the agency holds these items in trust for the client. This could include such materials as photographs, artwork, videotapes, or rights such as copyright, trademark rights, rights of publicity.

The agent does not own these items or rights, but it has a duty to guard them for its client. Here's an example which occurred between the Molle Company and its agency, Stack-Goble Advertising, in 1933.

Molle manufactured shaving cream and, through Stack-Goble, wanted to develop radio advertising. Stack-Goble hired Sedley Brown to produce and direct a program with Molle as the sponsor. We must remember that years ago it was common for advertisers to sponsor shows by themselves, and it was the job of the advertising agency to put the shows together. For example, "Amos 'n Andy" sold Pepsodent, "The Story of Mary Marlowe" sold Kleenex, "Fibber McGee and Molly" sold Johnson's Glo-Coat floor wax, "The Rhythm Boys" (featuring a youngster named Harry Lillis Crosby, later to be known as Bing) sold M. J. B. Coffee, and the list went on and on.

But back to Molle. As part of producing the show, Brown created a jingle out of Molle advertising slogans and set the words to the music of E. L. Gruber's "West Point Caisson Song."
The jingle went:

●●●●●●●●●●●

Mo-lle, Mo-lle,
The way to start your day,
As your razor goes sliding along,

Over cheek, over chin,
You don't have to rub it in,
As your razor goes sliding along.
Then it's sing, boys, sing,
Good-bye to pull and sting,
Your whisker troubles quickly fade away,
You can shave close and clean with this
brushless shaving cream,
So remember the name
Molle, Molle.

Brown produced the first radio show on September 25, 1933, and continued to do so until late December when he left the show. The show, along with the theme song, continued to air without any protest from Brown. In April 1934, Brown filed a copyright for the words to the song and gave notice to Molle of his claimed ownership in September of that year.

When Molle refused to acknowledge his claim, Brown brought suit for copyright infringement in *Brown v. Molle Co.*,[3] claiming ownership of the rights to the jingle. While it was true that the words were written by Brown, they belonged to Stack-Goble, who held them as trustee for Molle. Brown was employed by Stack-Goble to produce the program, including the theme song. Brown was an employee of Stack-Goble, and as such, anything he created as part of his duties became the property of Molle. When an agent creates work for, and at the direction of the client, it gives up, along with the work, any right to the work. Brown lost his case.

Accountability To Client

An agency is under a strict duty to account for all funds passing through the agency, or controlled by it, on behalf of its client. The client has the right to inspect books, records, papers, invoices, orders, receipts, and any other items that apply to its account with the agency. These must be made available to the client, at any time, for its inspection. Along these lines, the client can demand an accounting of all commissions or discounts, received from or credited by third parties (suppliers, media, etc.) to the agency on the client's account.

One major problem area regarding accountability involves hidden profits. This constitutes a serious breach of the agency's duty. Legally, this is called "fraudulent concealment." I have known of a few agencies that made a practice of stating in their contracts that they charged a 17.65 percent markup on third-party bills. Yet, the estimates and invoices given to clients actually included an undisclosed and considerable markup in excess of 30 percent.

If an agency makes a purchase for a client based on an estimate, and the actual billing comes in lower, the agency must pass this savings on to the client. It cannot legally keep the difference. At some agencies, the policy is to estimate a job and get the client to sign the estimate. Then the agency prebills the client for that amount before beginning the project, often receiving payment before the project is completed. Sometimes the final cost of the project comes out lower than the estimate. If the ultimate costs are lower than the estimate, and the difference is not returned to the client, the agency is breaching its duty.

If prebilling must be done, the best practice is to provide a recap of the project showing any amounts billed in excess of the estimate and credit them back to the client.

Purchase Orders

Another important duty is that the agency should document all purchases for its client with a written purchase order. The purchase order must establish what has been ordered and what will be paid. It should also establish that the order is being placed on behalf of the client. Exhibit 11-1 is a sample purchase order for reference.

Duty To Cooperate With The Client

Rarely do we hear mention of the duty of obedience when discussing the relationship between agency and client. This may be due to the fact that advertisers are usually inclined to bow to the expertise of the agency. Or it may be attributable to good business sense on the part of the agency. Whatever the reason, this is an area that needs to be discussed, nonetheless.

An advertising agency has a duty to do its best to cooperate with the client. Sometimes this can be difficult when an agency is determined to sell a campaign to its client. Let's say that the agency submits a campaign plan to its client. The client has the right to disapprove of the campaign plans – media, copy, art, or any other proposals of the agency – simply because it does not like them. An agency cannot force the client to produce advertising that it does not like or has not approved. The client cannot be deprived of the right to reject the agency's creative work in a campaign or in an individual ad.

Such a situation became the subject of *Medivox Productions, Inc. v. Hoffman-LaRoche, Inc.*[4] Hoffman-LaRoche, a well-known pharmaceutical manufacturer, entered into a contract with Medivox Productions as its agent in the production of a series of radio programs entitled "Milestones of Medicine." The contract called for 260 programs to be created and produced during one year at a total cost of $140,000. These programs were to be dramatic episodes depicting important medical events in history. Hoffman-LaRoche was to have a credit line in each episode. The intent was that of enhancing the public's image of those connected with medicine and health, while at the same time promoting the importance of drugs.

The contract stated that before being produced and broadcast, scripts would be submitted to Hoffman-LaRoche for their review and approval. Even without a contract this would be required. By the time Medivox had produced 135 of the programs (which the client had approved), Hoffman-LaRoche terminated the contract, having paid only $63,000. Medivox sued for breach of contract and sought to be allowed to complete the shows and receive the balance due on the contract. Hoffman-LaRoche claimed that they were entitled to terminate the contract because Medivox produced poor quality scripts.

Hoffman-LaRoche was dissatisfied with the scripts because they were inaccurate factually, and many of them discussed events that were not in keeping with the "Milestones of Medicine" theme. Medivox failed to satisfy its client, and as a result, Hoffman-LaRoche terminated the relationship. The court ruled that Medivox could not force the continuation of the relationship (legally this is called "specific performance") or collect the balance due on the contract. However, Hoffman-LaRoche could not recover the money that it had paid Medivox because it had accepted, used, and received the benefits of the 135 programs.

The client has the right, in an agency relationship, to approve or reject the work of its agency. Termination of the relationship, then, is based on the genuineness of its dissatisfaction, not necessarily on the reasonableness of it. Generally, the client makes this determination. Keep in mind, when the client expects satisfaction, the agency must allow the client to be the sole judge of its satisfaction.

The agency also has a duty to obey the instructions of its client in all but extreme situations. The agent has the right to refuse under certain extreme conditions without liability for damages. However, the client also has the right to terminate the contract if the agent does refuse to perform.

The four situations when the agent can legally refuse to obey its client are listed below.

1. The Instructions Are Unlawful

The agency has the right to refuse to produce advertising that is illegal – that is, advertising that violates any rights of others (including such things as publicity rights, copyrights, and trademarks), or when it would be engaging in unfair methods of competition or deception.

2. The Instructions Conflict With Other Duties Of The Agency

The agency may refuse to perform any instruction, such as the client's demand that the agency hold off paying certain media bills. Yet, this would be valid only if it would be a conflict of an agency duty. The agency may also refuse if the client demands that the agency take on a new product made by the existing client, which competes with another existing client of the agency.

3. The Instructions Defeat The Agency's Right To Protect Its Own Interests

A good example would be demanding the agency accept work on a speculative basis, with payment contingent on the client's sales or profits.

4. The Instructions Are Unreasonable

This fourth area may cause some problems, as we saw in the aforementioned *Medivox* case. What is considered unreasonable becomes the question. In many situations agencies feel that creating an ad it knows to be ineffective is unreasonable. An agency is hired for its expertise in a certain area and should be allowed to use its judgment. Logically, this may be true; legally, it may not.

Basic agency law states that, barring one of the above exceptions, an agent must obey the instructions of its client. Failure to abide by the instructions of the client could result in agency liability for damages. On the other hand, the agency may terminate the relationship at any time, with proper notice given, if it does not want to abide by the instructions.

The Obligation To Preserve Trade Secrets

Frequently it is necessary for a client to familiarize its agency with many matters it desires to keep secret. An advertising agency is under an obligation, both during and after its employment, to preserve those trade secrets, i.e., secrets that were disclosed or learned during the relationship.

Originally the issue was discussed in *E. I. Du Pont de Nemours Powder Co.* v. *Masland*.[5] A former employee, Mr. Masland (an agent), was sued to prevent him from disclosing or using secret trade processes learned while in the employ of Du Pont. Masland intended to open a company to manufacture artificial leather. He admitted that he intended to use processes related to those learned while employed with Du Pont. Masland's former employer did not want any of its secret trade processes divulged, and it had the right to enforce this. Masland had learned the facts about Du Pont's processes through a confidential relationship.

It is difficult to define what a trade secret is. However, some examples would be a specialized manufacturing process as we just saw, or special ingredients in a product such as Coca-Cola or Dr. Pepper. It seems that courts are more interested in the unfair use of the information than by the nature of the information itself.

The best story I can recall about trade secrets occurred a number of years ago. I was working for an agency that handled the Mitsubishi Electronics account. One day we got the news that two Mitsubishi executives had been arrested by the FBI. Evidently, Mitsubishi had paid $26,000 to undercover FBI agents who posed as grey-market electronics dealers. The money was paid in exchange for confidential trade secrets about IBM's newest computing products. This event was dubbed "Japanscam" by the press.

Note, any information that is easily accessible through other sources cannot be a trade secret. Lists of customers would be a good example. As a general rule these are not considered trade secrets because they are readily obtainable through such other public sources as trade publications.

There's another area to consider. Some years ago, Chiat/Day Advertising was in the running for the Godfather Pizza Parlor account. In order to prepare a speculative presentation to Godfather, the agency was given access to confidential information by the restaurant chain. A number of Chiat/Day employees were given this information, which contained many trade secrets.

Before the presentation was made to Godfather, Chiat/Day declined the account in favor of the Pizza Hut account. At that point, Godfather went to court to stop the use of the confidential information that Chiat/Day had obtained. The California Superior Court judge granted an injunction against Chiat/Day. The injunction stated that Chiat/Day could not use any of the confidential information it obtained from Godfather. In addition, the injunction banned the Chiat/Day employees involved in the Godfather presentation from being involved in any way with the Pizza Hut account. The point here is that, even at the presentation stage, the duty to preserve trade secrets is in force, and courts are backing this up by issuing injunctions.

Lastly, the agency has a continuing duty, even after termination, not to disclose or use trade secrets or other confidential information obtained during the course of its professional relationship.

No Undisclosed Interest In Suppliers

Another area of concern involves suppliers, vendors, or media that provide work for the agency's clients. The agency cannot have an undisclosed financial interest such as part ownership, kickback arrangement, etc., in these companies. Let's say that Acme Advertising produces brochures for its client, ABC Company. Bogus Photography Studio photographs ABC's products for the brochure. However, Acme Advertising owns 33 percent of Bogus Photography, and ABC doesn't know it. This would breach Acme's duty as an agency and make it impossible for the agency to make decisions in the client's best interests. The agent cannot perform as a true, impartial, and unbiased agent for its clients. Or at least it couldn't convince a court that it could.

Two other areas of this type of conflict of interest need to be discussed. First, the agency must not contract with suppliers who use them as their agency. To go back to our earlier example, if Bogus Photography uses Acme Advertising as its agency, Acme cannot let ABC Company's brochure be photographed by Bogus. Second, the agency must not perform work itself that it has been instructed to contract out. Again, let's say Acme is told by ABC Company to have Bogus photograph its brochure. Acme Advertising cannot photograph ABC's brochure itself, in-house.

Although these types of situations do exist, it is usually without the client's knowledge. If the agency has the client's consent, in writing, then it is not a breach of the agency's duty, since no trust has been violated.

DUTIES OWED BY CLIENTS TO THEIR AGENCIES

The most important duty the client has to its agency is to make the payments it owes to the agency. There are other duties, however, such as furnishing information to the agency and approving or disapproving programs or ads. The client must perform its duties within a reasonable time so as not to cause the agency additional delay and expense. It should make its decisions based on reason and good faith, not on a whim. Further, as seen earlier, the client does not have a right to demand the agency produce advertising that violates any laws. Finally, the client is bound by any contracts made by the agency on its behalf, again, provided the agency acted within the scope of its authority.

In 1869 the advertising agency was beginning to gain respect as a true agent of the client instead of a common space broker. In that year in Philadelphia, a man named Francis Wayland Ayer took $250 and opened an agency named after his father, N. W. Ayer & Son.

One of Ayer's clients, Devlen, manufactured Dent's Toothache Gum. In 1905 Devlen instructed Ayer to place an advertisement in daily newspapers. He also informed Ayer that he wanted "full position" (only editorial around the ad) for his small-space ad. Ayer informed its client that it was impossible to guarantee full position for a very small ad, and that in some papers such position was available only at an increased rate.

As the ad began to run, Devlen noticed that he was not getting full position in all newspapers. He complained to Ayer about this, but the ads continued to run for many months. Devlen also continued to make payments for the ads that ran.

In October 1907 Ayer terminated the contract with Devlen and in *Ayer* v. *Devlen*[6] asked the court for damages of $3,801.22 for the balance of the media charges. Devlen had wanted his ads to receive a certain position in newspapers, and although he had been told that this was not possible in most cases, he authorized the placement of the ads for some time while still demanding full position. The main issue here was whether Devlen had a contract for his ads to be placed in full position only. The court decided that Devlen did not, and he was ordered to pay the back media charges.

BREACH OF CONTRACT SITUATIONS

In the most simplistic terms, a contract is based on a promise or promises. When the promise is broken, a breach of contract can exist and a lawsuit can result. The client/agency contract can be breached when either party fails to perform in some area. For the agency, this can occur when it fails to comply with a duty, written in the contract or required by law. Placing an ad that the client had not approved or taking more than the amount of commission stated in the contract are examples. The client can also breach the contract if it fails to live up to its duties. Failure to pay the agency's bills is the most obvious example.

Generally, remedies for a breach of contract claim are

recision (canceling the contract), damages, specific performance (forcing the other to fulfill the contract), or termination. Specific performance does not apply to personal service situations; that is called slavery, and there are laws against that now. The two main remedies left are recision and damages. A party may find that recision is more realistic than seeking damages. And termination is always a remedy available to both parties.

In breach of contract cases the most common problem is not whether the contract has been breached, but rather determination of the amount of damages. Here's a good example of a breach of contract situation.

An ad agency, William B. Tanner Company, bought space from Action Transit Ads. Action sold space on buses and subways in New Jersey. Tanner, at the request of its client, Tanya Hawaiian Tanning Oil, entered into a contract for three years, 1969 through 1971. The contract provided for three things: the advertising was for Tanya, the agency would receive a 15 percent commission, and the contract could be canceled at the end of each year.

In mid-1971, another contract was entered into between Tanner and Action for Tanya for the years 1972 through 1974. As with the previous contract, Action was to be paid $22,500 per year. However, the difference here was that Tanner did not have the permission of its client to enter into this new contract. At the end of 1972, when Tanya refused to pay the bills, Tanner notified Action that it was terminating the contract. As a result, Action sued in *Action Ads, Inc.* v. *William B. Tanner Co.*[7]

William Tanner was authorized by Tanya to purchase the transit ads for the first three years, 1969 through 1971. However, it was not authorized by Tanya to make the second three-year contract. Because of that, Tanner was acting on its own in entering into the 1972 through 1974 contract. Tanner had breached its contract with its client and was itself liable for the $22,500 for the 1972 contract with Action.

DURATION OF CONTRACTS

In all written contracts the length of time that the agreement is to run must be stated. If it is indefinite, that should be stated as well. All contracts between advertising agencies and clients should be made in writing. Oral contracts are not a good idea for a variety of legal reasons, mainly because they can be found to be unenforceable in many situations.

TERMINATION OF CONTRACTS

Notice Of Termination

When a contract is terminated, the first thing to consider is the amount of time that must be given to the other party as notice. This "grace period" is built into client/agency contracts to allow the agency time to restructure for the change and for the client to settle its business with the agency. In other words, no undue hardship should be placed on either party.

The length of the notice period, according to industry trade custom, is usually 60 to 90 days, although it can be any period of time that both parties agree to. (A trade custom is law because of the length of time that the practice has been accepted and used.) To be on the safe side, the notice period should be stated in the contract. On this subject, Doyle Dane Bernbach tried to recover $126,729 for advertising from a former client, Avis Flowers, in *Doyle Dane Bernbach, Inc.* v. *Warren E. Avis*.[8]

Doyle Dane also handled the Avis Rent-A-Car account, which was started by the owner of Avis Flowers, Warren Avis, and later sold to a conglomerate. Avis Rent-A-Car put the agency on notice that it had to choose between the two clients due to the similarity in names and identity. Obviously, Doyle Dane opted to keep the Avis car account.

When Doyle Dane terminated the agreement with Avis Flowers in November 1977, it gave 90 days notice. During the notice period, Doyle Dane contacted the flower company to arrange for the transfer of the account to another agency. Even though it had given a notice of termination, Doyle Dane continued to handle the Avis Flowers account through the end of 1977, placing ads in *People* magazine that had been approved prior to when notice was given.

Avis Flowers claimed that Doyle Dane placed the ads after termination (breach of contract) and, therefore, was liable for any media charges incurred after the agency gave notice for those insertions. In fact, there was no written contract, so there was no stated notice period. However, the 90-day notice period is standard in the advertising industry and is accepted as a trade custom – one that Avis should have been well aware of. Doyle Dane gave Avis a sufficient amount of notice – the standard amount in the industry – and continued to perform through the notice period. As a result, Avis was required to pay the media fees incurred during the 90-day period.

Commissions Due After Termination

As just illustrated, certain postcontractual liabilities and duties are imposed on both parties. If the agency had entered into contracts with third parties on behalf of the advertiser before the relationship was terminated, the agency would be entitled to the commissions that it would have received.

In 1952 Hansman-Joslyn Advertising entered into a contract with Uddo & Tormina Company, makers of Progresso Italian foods. Hansman, as its agent, entered into a contract with WBOK radio. The one-year radio contract with Progresso was canceled after only a few months, causing the radio station to charge a "short rate" amount for the time because the full contract period was not used. The short rate policy is a trade custom in the advertising business.

In *Hansman v. Uddo and Tormina Co.*,[9] the court said:

> Contracts made with any kind of advertising

> media...providing therein a short rate cancellation, that is to say, the advertiser contracts to use the media for a stated length of time at a certain rate...if the advertiser sees fit to cancel the contract prematurely, then he is obligated to pay the rate which would be applicable had the contract...been for the number of advertisements actually used.

Uddo was ordered to pay the amount due the media.

Now, for the case of media contracts that were entered into by the previous agency. If the client takes its business to a new agency, the client is liable to the old agency for the media commissions, unless a contract agreement covers this occurrence.

To illustrate, let's go back to the hypothetical situation used earlier. Acme Advertising had placed media for an ad for its client, ABC Company, in *American Widget Monthly* magazine. A week later ABC notifies Acme that it is moving its account to a new agency, Dinkum Advertising, in 30 days. Even though Dinkum produces the ad and coordinates with the magazine, ABC must still pay Acme the amount of commission it would have received.

What if the client uses material from the former agency in preparation for another advertising campaign, after the termination of the relationship? If that material was never used or paid for, the client must compensate the original agency for its efforts. It cannot use the fruit of the agency's labor for future advertising without paying for it. In legal terms this principle is known as *quantum meruit*. In simpler terms, you don't get something for nothing.

When ABC Company transferred its account over to Dinkum Advertising, it also gave them campaign concepts and layouts that were developed by Acme Advertising. Acme had prepared the campaign on a speculative basis, but it was never approved by ABC. Since ABC never paid for the concepts and layouts, if it produces the campaign through Dinkum, it must compensate Acme for the work. On the other hand, if ABC had paid for the campaign to be created, the company would be free to produce it without further compensating Acme.

Soliciting New Accounts After Giving Notice Of Termination

When notice of termination has been given, can the agency service a competing account? It is certainly free to do so after termination. What is doubtful, though, is whether the agency is free to associate with prospective new clients who are in competition with the current client before termination becomes effective. The best advice would be that the agency should not jeopardize itself by creating a potential liability.

Limit To Use Of Information Gained

In the natural course of the advertising business an agency becomes familiar with the workings of its clients. It obtains a certain expertise in each client's line of business. There can be no doubt, however, that intimate knowledge of a client's trend of thought and method of doing business can become part of the agency's general knowledge and expertise.

Therefore, the postcontractual duty not to divulge or use details of the client must be restricted to actual trade secrets and the kind of confidential information that is separate from the general knowledge about a trade or business.

Here's a strong case in point. Murray Salit and other employees of Irving Serwer Advertising were sued by Serwer in *Irving Serwer, Inc. Advertising* v. *Salit*.[10] This occurred after the employees left the agency to open their own shop, Salit & Garlanda Advertising. Serwer claimed that Salit and the others had taken accounts over to the new agency by obtaining confidential information while in its employ and that they "entered into a course of conduct and conspiracy to destroy [Serwer's] business." However, the court held that simply gaining information about clients while working for an agency does not, in and of itself, constitute learning trade secrets or confidential information. As a result, Serwer lost his case.

While this situation involves employees of an agency, this reasoning applies to agencies who use knowledge gained from other clients. If the information does not constitute a trade secret and is not confidential (as discussed earlier), the agency cannot be stopped from making use of the knowledge.

LIABILITY TO MEDIA

Is a client liable for media commitments by the agency? There is a conflict here, but the general feeling is that the ultimate liability is on the advertiser. In essence, if the media knew who the client was and knew that the agency was acting in its behalf, any claims would be against the client. The agency would not be liable on the contract as long as it entered into the agreement with the client's knowledge and consent. One exception to this is a sole liability clause, which we'll discuss later in this chapter.

American Manufacturers Mutual Insurance contracted, through its agency Clinton E. Frank Advertising, to sponsor a news broadcast entitled "ABC Evening Report." At the end of one broadcast on November 9,1962, a promotional announcement was run that displeased American Manufacturers. The announcement promoted a show called "The Political Obituary of Richard M. Nixon." American Manufacturers terminated its sponsorship of the "ABC Evening Report" and refused to pay the media fees.

American Broadcasting Company filed suit for the amount due for media charges: *American Broadcasting-Paramount Theatres v. American Manufacturers Mutual.*[11] In this case, Clinton E. Frank Advertising was named as one of the defendants, but was held not to be liable for the media fees. Even though Clinton Frank was the agency and placed the order, it was not liable for any damages because ABC knew Frank was acting as the agency for American

Manufacturers. ABC also knew that the agency had entered into the contract on behalf of its client. ABC won the suit for breach of contract, and American was liable for the media.

The client/agency relationship may exist only with the knowledge and consent of both parties. The client who hires an agency voluntarily empowers it to bind the client to contracts with others. Simply put, when someone hires an agency it creates an implied acknowledgment that the client intends to be bound by any contract or transaction that the agent must enter into to fulfill his agency duties. Parties who deal with a known agent generally assume that the client intends to be bound by the agency's commitments.

In 1971 Lennon & Newell was the ad agency for Stokely-Van Camp foods company, as it had been for the previous 17 years. Lennon & Newell had purchased media space for Stokely on CBS. In 1967 the agency began to suffer substantial losses and by 1970 was in severe trouble. It had been paid by Stokely for media billings but had not, in turn, paid the media. By the end of 1971 Lennon owed CBS $714,000 out of total payables of $3 million and could not make its payments. About that time, Lennon & Newell filed for bankruptcy.

Because of the situation, CBS filed suit, *Columbia Broadcasting System, Inc.* v. *Stokely-Van Camp, Inc.*,[12] directly against the client. This was a case of liability when an agent goes bankrupt owing money to media. Does the media have a claim against the client? In this case, it did even though the client had paid the agency for the media.

In 1978 Sander Rodkin/Hechtman/Glantz Advertising purchased television time for its client Climate Control, an air conditioning distributor. At the time, Sander was having financial problems. When the agency received money from Climate Control for media, it did not pay the media. Climate Control, however, had paid its total bill and documented each payment. The final payment for $15,000 was designated as "final payment for WLS-

TV air time."

WLS-TV was the local ABC affiliate in Chicago. It sued Climate Control for the amount due in *American Broadcasting Companies, Inc.* v. *Climate Control Corporation.*[13] It was not until December 1979 that ABC contacted Climate Control and told them that it was liable for the unpaid balance. Right after that, this lawsuit was initiated.

In this case, Sander was the agency for Climate Control, and as such, bound Climate Control to any contracts it had made for the client. Climate Control was liable for the unpaid balance to ABC. Sander Rodkin went out of business.

For reference, I've included a sample media insertion order form (Exhibit 11-2). The format is typical of insertion order forms used in many agencies. This should serve as a general format for others to adapt and use as their needs dictate.

Sole Liability Clauses

The advertising agency is directly liable to the media under certain conditions. One is when the agency voluntarily agrees to be directly liable for media bills. The other is when the media contract contains a "sole liability" clause to which the agency has committed. In both cases the agency accepts full liability for media costs.

The sole liability clause, which is included in many media contracts, says that the agency is solely liable for the debts incurred on behalf of the client. As a consequence of the sole liability clause, the agency can impose on the client a duty to pay the media charges to the agency prior to the media's due dates. Failure to make these payments on time can easily lead to cancellation of the media space, as well as substantial damage claims by the agency against the client.

LIABILITY FOR ADVERTISING

As seen in other chapters, the agency can be liable along with the client for the advertising it produces. If the advertising makes deceptive or unfair claims, the agency as well as the client can be held liable for those claims. This has been proven many times in court. Claiming, as many agencies do, that they only did what the client told them to do does not relieve the agency's liability. The courts generally consider that an advertising agency should know what its clients are doing.

Other areas where the agency can be liable involve defamation (libel and slander), copyright and trademark infringement, violation of privacy and publicity rights, in addition to others. In general, advertising agencies must realize that the courts look on them as the professionals. This idea goes back to the "higher degree of skill" concept discussed earlier. More and more, agencies are being held liable for the joint actions stemming from the client/agency relationship. It is very important that agencies understand this idea.

The Invisible Window Case

A manufacturer of automobile windows set about to demonstrate how much clearer its windows were compared to those of its competition. The commercial exaggerated the demonstration by distorting the competition's windows with a coat of Vaseline. The clarity of the advertiser's windows was additionally enhanced by simply rolling down the window for the commercial.

When the FTC filed an action, the manufacturer's defense was that it had instructed its advertising agency to "present a fair commercial." The court reasoned, when it upheld the FTC's previous ruling in *Libbey-Owens-Ford Glass Co.* v. *FTC*,[14] that this statement did not allow the advertiser to escape liability by delegating the responsibility for the commercial to its agency.

ELEMENTS OF THE CLIENT/AGENCY CONTRACT

While it is not imperative that a written contract be created, it is the much wiser option. When the rights, duties, and intentions of both parties are fixed in writing, there is less interpretation and guesswork involved if a problem arises.

There are certain considerations that should be addressed when the contract provisions are made. The following list includes the most important ones:

- Appointment as the agency;
- Nature and extent of services to be provided;
- Compensation (commission, fees, etc.);
- How supplier contracts are to be handled;
- Rights upon termination of contract;
- Indemnity against claims;
- Handling of competitive clients; and
- Liability to media.

I have included a sample contract (Exhibit 11-3) and a project proposal (Exhibit 11-4) that are commonly used. The contract and project proposal work together and make reference to each other. The contract covers the general provisions of the relationship. The project proposal is used as an estimate for each specific project. While every agency should consult an attorney to have its specific contract drawn up, Exhibits 11-3 and 11-4 will serve as general formats to follow.

EMPLOYEE RELATIONS WITHIN THE AGENCY

One of the areas that agencies need to be aware of involves situations when an employee leaves and takes accounts. Account piracy is a growing internal problem for ad agencies. Many agencies are dealing with the problem by adopting restrictive covenants in employment contracts to prevent this.

Let's say that you own the Acme Advertising agency and your employees become increasingly dissatisfied with you and the way you run the agency. Some of the key people get together and decide that they will give you an ultimatum: sell them the agency and get out, or they will leave and take some of the accounts with them. Is this legal?

Let's take a look at just that type of situation to find the answer. The Duane Jones Company was an ad agency founded in 1942 by Duane Jones, who was the president and operating head of the agency until August 1951. At that time, the agency billed $9 million annually from about 25 accounts. But what happened in August 1951 threw a wrench into the machinery of the agency.

About that time the agency lost three accounts and $6.5 million with them. Along with that, three executives and numerous staff people resigned from the agency because, as the employees claimed, Duane Jones "had been guilty of certain behavioral lapses at his office, at business functions, and during interviews with actual and prospective customers. As a result... several of [Jones's] officers and directors expressed dissatisfaction with conditions – described as 'intolerable.'"

In June 1951 a private meeting had been held at a hotel in Manhattan between a number of the agency's officers, directors, and employees, led by one of the officers, Mr. Hayes. It was decided that these people would make an ultimatum to Jones: either sell them the agency or they would resign "en masse." Hayes told Jones of this plan and informed him that certain clients of the agency had been presold on the idea of leaving with the employees. Jones responded, "In other words, you are standing there with a Colt .45, holding it at my forehead, and there is not much I can do except to give up?" Hayes replied, "Well, you can call it anything you want, but that is what we are going to do."

At first, Jones decided to accept the buyout of the agency, but negotiations fell through in August 1951. That same month, six officers and directors resigned from the agency. A few days later the former employees of Jones opened a new agency, Scheideler, Beck & Werner, Inc. This agency employed 71 of the 132 Duane

Jones employees. Within a few weeks, the new agency had as accounts Manhattan Soap Co., Heublein, International Salt, Wesson Oil, C. F. Mueller Co., The Borden Co., Marlin Fire Arms, McIlhenny Corp., Haskins Bros., and Continental Briar Pipe – all former clients of Duane Jones.

When one acts as an agent or employee – the legal relationship is the same for either – a duty of loyalty, trust, and good faith is owed to the client or employer. We discussed this duty earlier. As a result, Duane Jones filed suit in *Duane Jones Co.* v. *Burke, et al.*[15]

The court awarded damages to Jones and said: "defendants ...while employees of [Jones], determined upon a course of conduct which, when subsequently carried out, resulted in benefit to themselves through destruction of [Jones's] business, in violation of the fiduciary duties of good faith and fair dealing imposed on defendants...."

There are situations in which taking accounts away from a former employer is acceptable, however. One example of such an occurrence is found in the case of *Nationwide Advertising Service, Inc.* v. *Kolar*.[16] Here, Nationwide sued a former employee, Martin Kolar, and his new employer, Bentley, Barnes & Lynn, for acquiring former accounts of Nationwide. Both agencies specialized in recruitment advertising. Not until after Kolar left Nationwide and became employed with Bentley did he solicit accounts of Nationwide. This was acceptable.

One of the issues in this case involved an implied covenant binding Kolar not to compete with his former employer. But this covenant covered only confidential information gained through his employment, and then used for his benefit, to the detriment of the employer. This was not the case here.

Granted, an agency's interest in its clients is proprietary by nature, but this is valid only when the client/agency relationship is near permanent. In the advertising business, this is a rare claim. In the recruitment advertising business, it is almost nonexistent.

Further, Nationwide's client list was not confidential, and no trade secrets were used to solicit the accounts. Kolar did not solicit any accounts until after leaving the employ of Nationwide. The court held that no breach of trust or confidence occurred; Nationwide lost the case.

Restrictive Covenants

Probably the best solution to account piracy involves the use of restrictive covenants in written employment contracts. This is the only way to legally enforce damages against former employees for account piracy.

Under an agreement containing a restrictive covenant, the employee agrees not to serve or contact any client of the former agency for a specific period of time. It is crucial that a specific period of time be stated in the agreement; otherwise it will be unenforceable. Also, the time must be reasonable, usually one to two years.

Restrictive covenants must be agreed to at the beginning of the employment. If an agency wishes to add restrictive covenants to existing employment situations, some additional consideration must be given. This can be any valuable offering: extension of employment, stock options, money, etc.

AGENCY LIABILITY

This is a very important subject for advertisers and their agencies. Almost every ad agency has dealt with children in the course of producing an ad, television commercial, billboard, or brochure. Any agency that works with children needs to understand the applicable restrictions and requirements. Few photographers and fewer art directors are aware of the current child labor laws governing employment of children.

The Problem

You're at the photo studio to photograph a client's project. Everything is going fine. The set looks good, the kids are great in their costumes, and the collie is behaving just fine. All of a sudden, the photo assistant kicks a light stand and the dog, startled, turns and bites one of the children. The child falls, knocking over a prop stand causing the entire set to crash down on top of another child. About then you wonder what else could go wrong.

Well, if the children were working without a valid work permit, you've only begun to hear your world come crashing down around you. If you, or your client, did not have the proper work permits, you could face criminal or civil prosecution, resulting in lawsuits, fines, and even jail. If the child is working without the proper permits, liability insurance could be useless. Insurance companies can deny coverage if a law was violated that led to the injury.

This was something John Landis learned the hard way. While filming the movie *Twilight Zone*, two child actors and actor Vic Morrow were killed when a helicopter crashed. The children were employed illegally for four reasons. First, they were working at 2:30 a.m. Second, they were in an extremely dangerous situation. Third, the children did not have work permits as required by California law. Fourth, no social worker was present. Had one been, the filming would probably not have been allowed. Had the laws been obeyed, the accident would not have killed the children or Morrow, since they would not have been on the set at that time.

Child Labor Laws

In the early 1900's child labor laws were created in response to an increase in serious injuries of children. Most of these injuries were the result of severe conditions in mills, sweatshops, and mines where children were used as cheap labor.

Child labor laws created restrictions on minimum wages, hours of employment, and working conditions. While some laws are federal, the most important are state statutes. The individual states have become more involved in this area and have adopted very stringent laws to protect children. New York and California are at the head of this list.

Note: anyone can be held liable – the photographer, the director, the ad agency, or the client. Each must protect itself by making sure that the proper permits are obtained and working conditions are met.

Guidelines For Working With Children

- **Check with the state agency** that oversees child labor laws to determine the state's requirements. For example, in California, it is the California Division of Labor Standards.
- **Obtain the proper permits** from the state where the photography takes place.
- **Abide by the hours of employment** allowed by law. For example, in California, children 6 to 18 years old can only work a maximum of four hours a day and not after 6:30 p.m. A one-hour lunch break must be provided no later than 1 p.m. For sessions out of the studio, lunch must be provided free to the child and teacher or welfare worker.
- **Provide the required supervision**. Again, in California, a studio teacher or welfare worker must be hired and present during any session.
- **Check insurance coverage**. Make sure that the photographer has valid workers' compensation and liability insurance.
- **Report any injury** that occurs to a child immediately to the insurance carrier and the state Workers' Compensation Board.
- **Provide medical attention**. Make sure that the child gets immediate medical attention.

- **Parents cannot waive liability**. Remember, a parent or guardian cannot give a release of liability by law. Even a written release will not protect you.

The Chilko River Incident

Over the years, Al Wolfe organized fishing and river rafting trips for many of his employees and clients. As Wolfe would later say of his trips: "If you could get away from the titles and pretense and really get to know each other, there would be a bond formed."

In 1987 Wolfe put together one such trip while he was the president of DDB Needham Worldwide's Chicago office. The plan was to take a group of eleven friends and business acquaintances for a weekend fishing and rafting trip on the Chilko river in British Columbia, Canada.

On a Saturday in August, the group set off down the Chilko, some of the roughest rapids in the world. Suddenly, after entering a stretch of river known as the "White Mile," the raft hit a rock and overturned. Five of the eleven perished in the river.

Those who never returned included Robert Goldstein, VP/advertising for Procter & Gamble; retired agency executive Richard O'Reilly; retired DDB Needham Senior VP James Fasules; Stuart Sharpe, Senior DDB Needham VP account manager; and, Gene Yovetich, Senior DDB Needham VP account manager.

The disaster, dramatized in the HBO movie *White Mile*, affected not only the participants but the agency as well. DDB Needham was sued by Mr. Fasules' family for his death due to the inadequate safety precautions and the negligence of Wolfe (in his capacity as president of DDB Needham). Fasules was not an employee of the agency at the time, and therefore the family could bring a negligence suit directly against DDB Needham. The agency employees, however, were limited to recover damages under workers' compensation actions. While the U.S. District Court determined that Fasules was 45 percent responsible for his own death, they also found that DDB Needham was 55 percent responsible. The court awarded Fasules's family $1.1 million in damages to be paid by DDB Needham.

The Chilko case illustrates how an action can bring liability to an agency, even if it did not actually involve work within the agency. Agencies (like any other company) can be held liable for the actions of their employees, at any time, when they are acting within the course and scope of their employment.

Avoiding Liability For Use Of Unsolicited Ideas Submitted By Outsiders

Occasionally, someone outside an agency or client may approach the company with an offer of a new idea for the company. While this is a common occurrence for advertising agencies, these situations present risks since subsequent use of the ideas can lead to an obligation to reasonably compensate the person who submitted the idea. This applies to creative ideas for ads, as well as marketing and product development ideas. A good example is Procter & Gamble, who received an idea from an outsider for putting a blue substance in a laundry powder. Later, when P&G marketed "Blue Cheer," liability was imposed by the court for using the submitted idea. The court in *Galanis* v. *Procter & Gamble Corp.*,[17] could have imposed liability on an express or implied contract theory, or on a misuse of trade secret theory, but they used a theory of unjust enrichment and ruled that Procter & Gamble was obligated to pay the outsider for the value of the idea it had received.

Although subsequent use by a company of information or ideas submitted to it is always somewhat risky, use of the information is not invariably illegal. Before liability is imposed, courts will insist that the outsider's idea be both novel and concrete; liability will not be imposed for use of vague and general ideas (unless, of course, there is a clear, express contract covering the matter). While the line between concrete and vague ideas is ambiguous, it's more prudent to err on the safe side to avoid the problems that can result from accepting unsolicited idea submissions. Formal records should be kept as to the date the idea was received and its specific content. Also, a written response should be made to the person submitting the idea explaining the company's position on not accepting unsolicited outside ideas.

If an outsider submission is accepted, it is wise to make a specific written agreement between the parties as to the use of, and compensation for, any ideas to be submitted. If an outside person submits an idea that had already been developed internally, there is no liability to compensate for the same suggestion. However, to guard against a possible argument that subsequent use of an internally developed idea actually came from an outsider, firms should keep accurate records as to the time and place of, and employees involved in, the discovery and development of new ideas and trade secrets.

CONCLUSION

As we have seen throughout this chapter, the ad agency has a lot to consider in the operation of its business. The agency business is a fascinating one indeed, but it also has many risks and pitfalls. An agency must deal with many areas of law in the operation of its business. While it has certain rights of its own, it also has duties to its clients and suppliers, as well as duties to the public and to its employees. And all of those parties have rights and duties of their own.

EXHIBIT 11-1
SAMPLE AGENCY PURCHASE ORDER

Purchase Order

ACME ADVERTISING

1234 Main Street
Hometown, CA 10000
(310) 555-1234

VENDOR:	PURCHASE ORDER NO: ______________	
	DATE:	
ATTENTION:	CLIENT:	
To Vendor: This order is placed by our agency as agents for our client as referenced on this order. All appropriate Sales Taxes must be billed on invoice. All invoices received after the 25th of the month are deemed to be the subsequent month's liability. Submit all invoices in triplicate. Job number and P.O. number must appear on invoice to receive payment.	JOB TITLE:	
	JOB NO:	
	TERMS:	

QUANTITY	DESCRIPTION	DUE DATE	PRICE QUOTED

SPECIAL INSTRUCTIONS:

DELIVERY INSTRUCTIONS:

ORDERED BY: ______________________________ DUE DATE: ________

EXHIBIT 11-2
SAMPLE MEDIA INSERTION ORDER

Purchase Order

ACME ADVERTISING

1234 Main Street
Hometown, CA 10000
(310) 555-1234

VENDOR:	PURCHASE ORDER NO: ______________	
	DATE:	
ATTENTION:	CLIENT:	
To Vendor: This order is placed by our agency as agents for our client as referenced on this order. All appropriate Sales Taxes must be billed on invoice. All invoices received after the 25th of the month are deemed to be the subsequent month's liability. Submit all invoices in triplicate. Job number and P.O. number must appear on invoice to receive payment.	JOB TITLE:	
	JOB NO:	
	TERMS:	

QUANTITY	DESCRIPTION	DUE DATE	PRICE QUOTED

SPECIAL INSTRUCTIONS:

DELIVERY INSTRUCTIONS:

ORDERED BY: ______________________________ DUE DATE: ________

EXHIBIT 11-3
SAMPLE AGENCY CONTRACT

THIS AGREEMENT, entered into this_____day of_______, 19__, by and between ACME ADVERTISING, a California corporation, ("Agency") and_________________________________ ____, ("Client").

ARTICLE I
ADVERTISING REPRESENTATION AND SERVICES

1.01 Term of Agreement. This Agreement shall become effective as of the execution date hereof and shall continue in effect until terminated as provided herein.

1.02 Appointment and Authorization of Agency. Client agrees to retain and appoint the Agency, as its agent, to represent it in carrying out its advertising program, subject to the terms and conditions of this Agreement. The Agency is authorized to enter into contracts with third parties to effectuate the purposes of this Agreement. In instances when a written project-proposal(s) shall be submitted for approval by Client, the terms and conditions of such project-proposals shall become a part of this Agreement

1.03 Agency Services. Agency agrees to act as the Client's advertising representative and to perform, upon authorization by Client, any and all of the following services to the extent necessary to meet the Client's needs.

(a) Study, research and analyze the Client's business and products or services and survey the market therefor.

(b) Develop and implement an advertising and marketing program designed to meet the Client's needs and budgetary limitations.

(c) Counsel the Client on his overall marketing and advertising program or make plans therefor.

(d) Determine and analyze the effect of the advertising used.

(e) Plan, create, write and prepare layouts and the actual copy and art to be used in advertisements of all types.

(f) Analyze all advertising media to determine those which are most suitable for use by the Client.

(g) Make contracts with the advertising media for space or time and with others to effectuate the advertising program and obtain the most favorable terms and rates available.

(h) Check and follow up on all contracts with the various media for proper performance in the best interests of the Client, including the appearance, accuracy, date, time, position, size, extent, site, workmanship and mechanical reproduction, as appropriate to the advertisements used.

(i) Negotiate, arrange and contract for any special talent and services required for all photography, cinematography, animation, models, special effects, layouts, and art work, and for all printing, including any required photography, separations, typography, film production, video and audio production, and any other necessary technical material for use in the advertising program.

(j) Make timely payment to all persons or firms supplying goods or services in connection with the advertising program.

(k) Advise and bill the Client for all amounts incurred by the Agency on behalf of the Client's account and maintain complete and accurate books and records in this regard.

1.04 <u>Prior Approval of Client</u>. Agency shall not incur any obligations or provide any services for the Client's account without first obtaining the approval from Client. The Agency shall submit a written project-proposal(s) to the Client, whenever possible, containing full descriptions of the proposed advertisements and estimates of the cost of obligations or services involved, including media costs, costs of preparation of the advertisement, costs of production, and any additional costs.

All estimates shall be submitted on the Agency's standard project-proposal forms with sufficient copies to meet the needs of the Client.

The Agency shall not be responsible for missed deadlines, closing dates or insertions caused by the delay of the Client in approving the advertisements to be used in connection therewith.

Production schedules shall be established and adhered to by Client and Agency, provided that neither shall incur any liability or penalty for delays caused by force majeure.

1.05 Property and Materials. All materials, sketches, copies, artwork, dummies, type, art, dies, photographs, illustrations, negatives, film stock, video tapes and other items supplied by Agency shall remain the exclusive property of Agency and no use shall be made, nor any ideas obtained therefrom may be used, except upon compensation to Agency to be determined by Agency. All such items shall remain the sole and exclusive property of Agency until compensation is made to Agency.

1.06 Delivery of Materials. Unless otherwise specified, any price quoted is for a single shipment without storage, F.O.B., local Client's place of business or F.O.B. printer's platform for out-of-town Clients. Proposals are based on continuous and uninterrupted delivery of complete order, unless specifications distinctly state otherwise. Charges related to delivery from Client to Agency or from Client's supplier to Agency are not included in any quotation unless specified.

ARTICLE II
COSTS AND PAYMENTS

2.01 Advertising Costs and Expenditures.

(a) Client shall reimburse Agency for all costs incurred and expenditures made on behalf of Client for approved advertising, for which client shall compensate the Agency as provided in Section 2.02.

(b) Client shall pay the Agency for its direct costs of mailing, packaging, shipping, taxes and duties, telegrams and telephones incurred by the Agency in connection with its performance under this Agreement.

(c) Client shall pay all of Agency's costs for any necessary travelling done on behalf of Client.

(d) In the event media or any other charges increase or decrease after the Agency has submitted an estimate, the Client shall pay for such increase or be given a credit for such reduction, as the case may be. In the event the Client, after having approved any planned advertising, cancels all or any part thereof, the Client shall pay for all costs incurred therefore to date of cancellation and any unavoidable costs incurred thereafter, including any noncancelable commitments for time or space. In addition, the Agency shall receive any commissions it would have earned had the proposal been fully performed.

2.02 <u>Agency's Compensation</u>.

(a) Agency shall receive a commission of fifteen percent (15%) of all gross media charges. The Agency shall charge an amount which, when added to the net cost of media allowing no commission or less than 15% commission, will yield 15% of the Agency's total media bill to the Client.

(b) The Agency shall receive a commission of fifteen percent (15%) of the charges made by third parties with whom the Agency has contracted for products or services which are to be used to implement the advertising approved by the Client.

2.03 <u>Billing and Payment</u>. The Agency shall bill the Client from time to time, and payment for which shall be made within thirty (30) days of the invoice date. Final billing to Client shall be adjusted based upon final invoices from vendors, plus Agency's commissions. Bills and project-proposals estimating the costs involved may be initially used, but final, detailed bills, supported by invoices of charges of third parties and showing all adjustments and credits, will be submitted to the Client as soon as available.

2.04 Internal Labor. All internal labor of Agency shall be charged at an hourly rate for: creative time, concept, design, art direction, copywriting, trademark, logo-type, mock-ups, research and development, market research, media research and planning, broadcast production, product development, analysis and public relations. Internal labor rates shall be as follows: [specify rates].

2.05 Speculative and Experimental Work. Speculative and experimental work performed by Agency for Client, at Client's request, such as sketches, research, drawings, composition, film and materials, including labor, will be charged Client at current rates and may not be utilized by Client without the prior written consent of Agency, and upon compensation to Agency.

ARTICLE III
TERMINATION OF AGREEMENT

3.01 Either Party may terminate this Agreement by giving the other Party written notice of at least ninety (90) days prior to the effective date of termination. Upon receipt of notice of termination, the Agency shall not commence work on any new projects or advertisements, but it shall complete and place all projects and advertisements previously approved by the Client. All the rights and duties of the Parties shall continue during the notice period, and the Client shall be responsible to the Agency for the payment of any contract obligations incurred by the Agency with third parties during this period.

3.02 In the event the Client of Agency desires to terminate all work in progress on all projects and advertisements commenced before receipt of notice of termination, it may be so agreed upon by the Parties' mutual consent and determination of the compensation to be received by the Agency for partially completed work.

3.03 Billing Upon Termination. Upon termination of the Agreement, the Agency shall bill the Client for all amounts not previously billed and due the Agency at that time under the terms of this Agreement.

Agency shall be entitled to payment for services and commissions for advertisements approved by Client prior to the effective date of termination.

ARTICLE IV
COMPLIANCE WITH LAW

4.01 Any controversy or claim arising out of or relating to this Agreement, or any project-proposal submitted pursuant to the terms of this Agreement, may be settled by arbitration in accordance with the rules of the American Arbitration Association, any judgment upon the award rendered by the arbitrator(s), may be entered in any court of competent jurisdiction. In the event of such claim, the prevailing party shall be awarded its reasonable attorney's fees and costs.

4.02 Neither Party may assign any rights or delegate any duties hereunder without the expressed prior written consent of the other.

4.03 This writing contains the entire Agreement of the Parties. No representations were made or relied upon by either Party, other than those expressly set forth herein. No agent, employee, or other representative of either Party has the power to alter any of the terms hereof, unless done in writing and signed by an authorized officer of the respective Parties hereto.

4.04 Validity, interpretation and performance of this Agreement shall be controlled by and construed under the laws of the State of California.

4.05 All notices pertaining to this Agreement shall be in writing and shall be transmitted either by personal hand-delivery or through the facilities of the United States Postal Service. The addresses contained herein for the respective Parties shall be the places where notices shall be sent, unless written notice of a change of address is given.

4.06 You represent and warrant that the information and materials provided Agency and which may be included in the work performed, will not at any time infringe upon or violate any copyright, artistic, personal, dramatic or any other rights, legal or equitable of any person. You agree to indemnify, defend and hold Agency harmless from any liability, claim or action arising out of or pertaining to the foregoing warranty. In the event of any such claim or action against Agency, you shall defend Agency with attorneys of your own choice, and at your own expense, and we agree to cooperate in all respects in connection with said defense.

IN WITNESS WHEREOF, the Parties have caused this Agreement to be executed on the date first hereinabove set forth.

____

"AGENCY"

BY:______________________________

____

"CLIENT"

BY:______________________________

EXHIBIT 11-4
SAMPLE AGENCY PROJECT PROPOSAL

Date:
To:

In accordance with your request, ACME ADVERTISING is pleased to submit the following project-proposal. Agency agrees to act as the Client's advertising representative and to perform any and all of the following services to the extent necessary to meet the Client's needs:

Our proposal is based upon estimates supplied by vendors. Final billing is subject to receipt of vendors' final invoices. This proposal does not include any applicable commissions, ACME ADVERTISING fees, expenses and costs, all of which will be contained in the final billing.

We shall furnish all elements and facilities necessary for the completion of the above-described work, except the following items which you shall provide:

This proposal shall remain valid for thirty (30) days from the date indicated, after which it may be withdrawn, or revised by ACME ADVERTISING. Any changes subsequent to approval of the proposal may affect the prices quoted and, therefore, must be approved by both parties. In the event of cancellation of the proposal by client after acceptance, ACME ADVERTISING shall be reimbursed for any expenses incurred and shall be paid any commissions it would have earned had the proposal been fully performed.

You represent and warrant that the information and materials provided ACME ADVERTISING and which may be included in the work performed, will not at any time infringe upon or violate any copyright, artistic, personal, dramatic or any other rights, legal or equitable of any person. You agree to indemnify, defend and hold ACME ADVERTISING harmless from any liability, claim or action arising out of or pertaining to the foregoing warranty. In the event of any such claim or action against ACME ADVERTISING, you shall defend ACME ADVERTISING with attorneys of your own choice, and at your own expense, and we agree to cooperate in all respects in connection with said defense.

Any disputes arising out of or pertaining to this agreement may be pursued in accordance with the rules of the American Arbitration Association, and any award made with respect to such arbitration shall be enforceable in any Court of competent jurisdiction. In the event of any such arbitration or any litigation arising out of or pertaining to this proposal, California law shall govern and the prevailing party shall be awarded its reasonable attorneys fees and costs.

All unpaid invoices in connection with the foregoing work shall bear interest at the rate of ten percent (10%) per annum until paid. All materials and/or other items produced and/or supplied by ACME ADVERTISING shall remain the exclusive property of ACME ADVERTISING and no other use or reproduction shall be made by client, without first obtaining the consent of ACME ADVERTISING, which consent shall include reasonable compensation to ACME ADVERTISING.

Very truly yours,
ACME ADVERTISING

BY:______________________

ACCEPTED AND AGREED TO BY CLIENT:

BY:_________ ______________DATED:__________

---

[1] *Crocker* v. *United States*, 240 U.S. 74, 36 S.Ct. 245, 60 L.Ed. 533 (1916).
[2] *Joyce Beverages of New York, Inc.* v. *Royal Crown Cola*, 555 F.Supp. 271 (1983).
[3] *Brown* v. *Molle Co.*, 20 F.Supp 135 (1937).
[4] *Medivox Productions, Inc.* v. *Hoffman-LaRoche, Inc.*, 107 N.J. Super. 47, 256 A.2d 803 (1969).
[5] *E. I. Du Pont de Nemours Powder Co.* v. *Masland*, 244 U.S. 100, 37 S.Ct. 575, 61 L.Ed. 1016 (1917).
[6] *Ayer* v. *Devlen*, 179 Mich. 81, 146 N.W. 257 (1914).
[7] *Action Ads, Inc.* v. *William B. Tanner Co.*, 592 S.W.2d 572 (1979).
[8] *Doyle Dane Bernbach, Inc.* v. *Warren E. Avis*, 526 F.Supp. 117 (1981).
[9] *Hansman* v. *Uddo and Tormina Co.*, 76 So.2d 753 (La. App. 1955).
[10] *Irving Serwer, Inc. Advertising* v. *Salit*, 17 A.D.2d 918 (1963).
[11] *American Broadcasting-Paramount Theatres* v. *American Manufacturers Mutual*, 42 Misc.2d 939, 249 N.Y.S.2d 481 (Sup.Ct. 1963), aff'd 251 N.Y.S.2d 906, aff'd 17 N.Y. 2d 849 (1966).
[12] *Columbia Broadcasting System, Inc.* v. *Stokely-Van Camp, Inc.*, 522 F.2d 369 (1975).
[13] *American Broadcasting Companies, Inc.* v. *Climate Control Corporation*, 524 F.Supp. 1014 (1981).
[14] *Libbey-Owens-Ford Glass Co.* v. *FTC*, 352 F.2d 415 (6th Cir. 1965).
[15] *Duane Jones Co.* v. *Burke, et al*, 281 N.Y.A.D. 622, (1953), aff'd 306 N.Y. 172 (1954).
[16] *Nationwide Advertising Service, Inc.* v. *Kolar*, 329 N.E.2d 300 (1975).
[17] *Galanis* v. *Procter & Gamble Corp.*, 153 F. Supp. 34 (S.D.N.Y. 1957).

CHAPTER 12

SPECIAL AREAS OF ADVERTISING CONCERN

You can tell the ideals of a nation by its advertisements.
—*Norman Douglas*

"The case is too hard for man," Maitland said, "so it is left to the judgment of God." That is how laws were tested for centuries. This is Occam's Razor in action. Actually it wasn't William of Occam, or Ockham, but Duns Scotus who created the Razor. Occam's Razor says that where there are several ways to account for a thing, the theory that involves the fewest hypotheses is to be preferred. And, around the 1300's, this was a handy way to dole out laws, indeed.

Laws were interpreted by God, the only one who could make such determinations as guilt and punishment. This was shown in the old concept of trial by ordeal which existed to let God determine such matters in his own way. The judges didn't presume to have the power or knowledge to do so on their own. And, after all, the judges answered only to the church.

Then, five hundred years later, the U.S. Constitution separated church and state. Man now has to decide all the intricate details of law. All the interpretations, the subtle nuances, the social ramifications. The drafters of the Bill of Rights could never have anticipated the consideration of issues like abortion, pornography, and commercial speech.

The First Amendment we are very aware of today. For 150 years, however, it was rarely noticed. Not because there was perfect freedom of speech and press, but because nobody thought there ought to be.

The First Amendment has been treated for about 150 years as a wicker basket that could not carry a heavy burden. In recent years, however, it has been treated more as a catch-all. Yet, recent events under the First Amendment dramatize the pendulum swings of history, and the dangers of doctrine, and tendency of doctrinaires to fight past wars.

Here, we are going to take a look at First Amendment issues regarding commercial speech: that is advertising. We'll look at the Commercial Speech Doctrine. We'll also look at other issues which have involved First Amendment issues such as attorney advertising and political advertising.

THE COMMERCIAL SPEECH DOCTRINE UNDER THE FIRST AMENDMENT TO THE U.S. CONSTITUTION

While it has not always been that way, the Supreme Court now recognizes that "commercial speech" (advertising falls into this category) is protected under the First Amendment to the U.S. Constitution. This means, among other things, that certain advertising of products and services cannot be banned by the government. Today, advertising and other forms of commercial speech are still not held in the same high regard as political or religious speech. Yet, the good news is that because of this change, fewer restrictions are being placed on advertisers. Those restrictions that are in place, or are considered, continue to cause debate on First Amendment issues.

The New And Improved Commercial Speech Doctrine

Until 1975 commercial speech was virtually unprotected by the First Amendment. However, in that year the Supreme Court overturned a criminal conviction for violation of a certain statute on the books in Virginia making it a misdemeanor to distribute any publication that encouraged or promoted an abortion in Virginia. The case arose when a newspaper published an ad for legal abortions in New York.

The argument was that the ad was unprotected because it was commercial. However, the court held that the message that legal abortions were available in New York "did more than simply propose a commercial transaction. It contained factual material of clear 'public interest.'" The court continued by saying that the ad related to abortions, a service with which, generally, the state couldn't interfere.

Because of the Supreme Court's 1973 decision in *Roe* v. *Wade,*[1] the Virginia court did not need to decide the "precise extent to which the First Amendment permits regulation of advertising that is related to activities the State may legitimately regulate or even prohibit." The goal of protecting commercial speech was to provide the consumer with the same access to information as his or her access to political and religious debate.

A year later the Supreme Court clearly settled the issue of whether there is an exception to First Amendment protection for commercial speech in a case involving a woman who was required to take prescription drugs on a daily basis. The Court ruled that commercial speech is protected under the First Amendment.

A Virginia law stated that a pharmacist licensed in Virginia would be guilty of unprofessional conduct if he "publishes, advertises or promotes, directly or indirectly, in any manner whatsoever, any amount, price, fee, premium, discount, rebate or credit terms...for any drugs which may be dispensed only by prescription."

The position was that prescription drug users would greatly benefit if advertising were allowed. The Virginia State Board of Pharmacy, however, argued that advertising prescription drug prices was not protected by the First Amendment because it involved commercial speech.

The Supreme Court, in *Virginia State Board of Pharmacy* v. *Virginia Citizens Consumer Council, Inc.*[2] decided that advertising is valuable in that it provides information about who is producing and selling what product, why, and at what price. "So long as we preserve a predominantly free enterprise economy, the allocation of our resources in large measure will be made through numerous private economic decisions." The Court maintained that it was in the public's interest to promote those decisions by being knowledgeable and well informed. "To this end, the free flow of commercial information is indispensable."

The Court went on to say "...that people will perceive their own best interests if only they are well enough informed, and that the best means to that end is to open the channels of communication rather than to close them." The end result was that Virginia could set whatever professional standards it wanted for its pharmacists; however, "it may not do so by keeping the public in ignorance of the entirely lawful terms that competing pharmacists are offering."

Limiting Commercial Speech: The Central Hudson Case

While First Amendment protection now extends to commercial speech, it still earns less protection than other forms of expression. The government can still limit First Amendment protection of some forms of commercial speech. In 1980 the Supreme Court created a four-part test used to determine if a certain restriction on commercial speech is allowed.

The New York Public Service Commission ordered electric utilities in the state to cease all advertising that "promot[ed] the use of electricity." This was put into place because New York did not have a sufficient fuel supply to meet the demands of the 1973-1974 winter.

Three years later the fuel shortage eased, and the commission proposed to continue the ban on promotional advertising. The Central Hudson Gas & Electric Corporation opposed the ban on First Amendment grounds.

The court in *Central Hudson Gas & Electric Corp.* v. *Public Service Commission*[3] recognized that commercial speech was entitled to First Amendment protection in some cases. However, the U.S. Constitution, the Court reasoned, affords less protection to commercial speech than to other constitutionally guaranteed forms of expression.

The First Amendment's protection of commercial speech is intended to allow and encourage the forms of advertising that provide consumer information. On the other hand, the Court ruled that there is no constitutional reason to support commercial messages that do not accurately inform the public about lawful activities. As a result, the government may ban communications that are more likely to deceive the public than to inform it. Governments may also ban commercial speech regarding an illegal activity.

The Central Hudson Test

The Court in the *Central Hudson* case established a four-part test for determining restrictions on commercial speech. This is known as the Central Hudson Test:

- Determine if the message qualifies for protection under the First Amendment. It must involve a legal activity and not be misleading;
- Determine whether the government's interest in restricting the commercial speech is substantial;
- If the first two points are met, the courts must then determine that regulation of the message directly supports the government's interest; and
- Lastly, the courts must determine whether regulating the message is more extensive than is necessary to further the government's interests.

The Court held that both the conservation of energy and

the state's desire to keep rates fair both represented valid governmental interests.

The Court also looked at whether the commission's complete suppression of speech, which would ordinarily be protected by the First Amendment, was too extensive and went further than necessary to justify the state's interest in energy conservation.

The commission's order covered all promotional advertising regardless of its impact on overall energy consumption. Yet, this rationale did not justify suppressing information about electric devices or services that would not increase total energy use. The commission could have limited the format and content of Central Hudson's advertising and required ads to include information about the relative efficiency and expense of the service. The Court reasoned that a complete ban on advertising violated the First Amendment.

The Puerto Rico Casino Case

With the Puerto Rico casino case, First Amendment protection for advertising took one step backward. This was the first time a court upheld a government's ban on truthful advertising of a legal product. The Games of Chance Act of 1948[4] was a law in Puerto Rico that legalized certain forms of casino gambling. The intent of the law was simply to promote tourism. In addition, the law prohibited casinos from advertising or promoting themselves to the public of Puerto Rico.

This law also banned casinos from using the word "casino" in matchbooks, interoffice and external correspondence, invoices, brochures, menus, elevator cards, lobby cards, flyers, telephone books, directories, lighters, envelopes, napkins, glasses, plates, banners, paper holders, pencils, bulletin boards, or any other hotel object that could be accessible to the public.

The Condado Holiday Inn Hotel and Sands Casino filed suit claiming that the law suppressed commercial speech by violating the First Amendment.

Using the *Central Hudson* test, the U.S. Supreme Court ruled in 1986 that the Puerto Rico law did not violate the First Amendment. The government of Puerto Rico had an important interest in restricting the ads because it would reduce the demand for casino gambling by the residents of Puerto Rico. This constituted a substantial governmental interest.

The Court also found that this view directly advanced the government's interest, saying, "In our view, the legislature's separate classification of casino gambling, for purposes of the advertising ban, satisfies the third step of the *Central Hudson* analysis."

The fourth step of the *Central Hudson* test was satisfied because the ban was no more extensive than necessary to further the government's interest.

But what about cases in which the Supreme Court had struck down a ban on any "advertisement or display" of contraceptives and the one we just looked at in which it reversed a criminal conviction based on the advertisement of an abortion clinic? There was a difference between those cases and the casino case. In the two cases involving contraceptives and abortion the promoted activities were constitutionally protected and could not have been prohibited by the government. However, in the casino case, "the Puerto Rico Legislature surely could have prohibited casino gambling by the residents of Puerto Rico altogether." Gambling is not protected as a constitutional right. So, in the Court's opinion, "the greater power to completely ban casino gambling necessarily includes the lesser power to ban advertising of casino gambling."

The casino case, *Posadas de Puerto Rico Associates* v. *Tourism Company of Puerto Rico*,[5] was heavily criticized, especially within the advertising community. This permitted virtually unlimited government regulation of commercial speech. This would all change in 1996, however.

The Liquormart Case

One of the most significant changes in connection with the *Central Hudson* test addressed in a recent case concerned interpretation of the third and fourth elements of the test. These elements cover the extent to which the government must show that its restriction of the speech directly advances its interests and that the restriction is not more extensive than necessary.

In 1996 the Supreme Court reversed the position it held in *Posadas*. In *44 Liquormart, Inc.* v. *Rhode Island*,[6] the Court found that *Posadas* "clearly erred in concluding that it was 'up to the legislature' to choose suppression over a less speech-restrictive policy. The *Posadas* majority's conclusion on that point cannot be reconciled with the unbroken line of prior cases striking down similarly broad regulations on truthful, nonmisleading advertising when non-speech-related alternatives were available."

The First Amendment makes it clear that the Constitution presumes that efforts to regulate speech are more dangerous than efforts to regulate conduct. That reasoning is consistent with the role that the free flow of information plays in a our society. The First Amendment, then, clarifies that the government may not suppress speech as easily as it may suppress conduct. Further, restrictions on speech cannot be treated as simply another way for the government to achieve its desires.

Complaints from competitors about an advertisement placed by 44 Liquormart in a Rhode Island newspaper in 1991 led to this litigation. The ad did not state the price of any alcoholic beverages. In fact, it stated that "state law prohibits advertising liquor prices." The ad did, however, state the low prices at which other items were being offered. It identified many brands of packaged liquor and included the word "WOW" in big letters next to pictures of bottles of vodka and rum. Based on this implied reference to bargain prices for liquor, the Rhode Island Liquor Control Administrator assessed a $400 fine. The case ultimately ended up at the Supreme Court.

In *44 Liquormart*, the Supreme Court overturned the Rhode Island statute that banned all advertising of liquor prices outside a beverage store's sales premises. In 1956 the Rhode Island Legislature had enacted two separate prohibitions against advertising the retail price of alcoholic beverages. The first prohibits vendors from "advertising in any manner whatsoever" the price of any alcoholic beverage offered for sale in the State (other than displayed with the merchandise within licensed premises and not visible from the street). The second statute applies to the Rhode Island news media. It does not allow the publication or broadcast of any advertisements – even those referring to sales in other States – that "make reference to the price of any alcoholic beverages."

The Court reasoned that the ban did not directly advance the state's interest in reducing alcohol consumption. The Court also reasoned that the state has the burden of justifying a complete ban on speech. A blanket ban on commercial speech is not valid unless the speech is deceptive or promotes an unlawful activity.

The Court went on to say:

> Advertising has been a part of our culture throughout our history. Even in colonial days, the public relied on "commercial speech" for vital information about the market. Early newspapers displayed advertisements for goods and services on their front pages, and town criers called out prices in public squares. Indeed, commercial messages played such a central role in public life prior to the Founding that Benjamin Franklin authored his early defense of a free press in support of his decision to print, of all things, an advertisement for voyages to Barbados.
>
> In accord with the role that commercial messages have long played, the law has developed to ensure that advertising provides consumers with

> accurate information about the availability of goods and services. In the early years, the common law, and later, statutes, served the consumers' interest in the receipt of accurate information in the commercial market by prohibiting fraudulent and misleading advertising. It was not until the 1970's, however, that this Court held that the First Amendment protected the dissemination of truthful and nonmisleading commercial messages about lawful products and services.

It's important to understand that the Court did not modify the *Central Hudson* test, yet it examined its interpretation of the third and fourth elements of the test. The Court required Rhode Island to show that the advertising ban significantly reduced alcohol consumption. It couldn't because truthful, nonmisleading speech does not relate to consumer protection. The Court also required that the restriction, although not perfect, must be reasonable and narrowly tailored to advance the government's interest. In this case, the ban only provides ineffective or remote support for the government's interest.

The Court said:

> In evaluating the ban's effectiveness in advancing the State's interest, we note that a commercial speech regulation "may not be sustained if it provides only ineffective or remote support for the government's purpose."
>
> For that reason, the State bears the burden of showing not merely that its regulation will advance its interest, but also that it will do so "to a material degree." The need for the State to make such a showing is particularly great given the drastic nature of its chosen means – the wholesale suppression of truthful, nonmisleading information. Accordingly,

> we must determine whether the State has shown that the price advertising ban will significantly reduce alcohol consumption.
>
> The Court went on:
>
> As is evident, any conclusion that elimination of the ban would significantly increase alcohol consumption would require us to engage in the sort of "speculation or conjecture" that is an unacceptable means of demonstrating that a restriction on commercial speech directly advances the State's asserted interest. Such speculation certainly does not suffice when the State takes aim at accurate commercial information for paternalistic ends.

In essence, the complete ban on liquor price advertising imposed by Rhode Island restricted speech under the First Amendment. Because Rhode Island failed to carry its heavy burden of justifying its complete ban on price advertising, it violated the First Amendment

The Greater New Orleans Gambling Case

Recently, two federal appeals courts each came to different conclusions regarding the *Central Hudson* test after the decision in *44 Liquormart*. Both of these cases involved a federal law that bans broadcast advertising for casino gambling, even in states where the practice of gambling is legal. In 1998 the Fifth Circuit in *Greater New Orleans Broadcasting Assn. v. United States*[7] held that the law (18 U.S.C. § 1304) was constitutional.

In the first case the Fifth Circuit in *Greater New Orleans* upheld the federal law banning radio and television advertising for casino gambling. The primary concern of the Fifth Circuit in *Greater New Orleans* was the test for determining whether the advertising restriction advanced the government's asserted interest. After *44 Liquormart*, determining what level of proof is required to demonstrate that banning a particular commercial speech directly advances a state's interest is unclear.

Concerning *Central Hudson's* forth element, the justices analyzed more carefully whether the state's ban of commercial speech serves the government's interests without unduly limiting free speech.

The court held that section 1304 passed both tests. Section 1304 prohibited broadcast advertising of "any advertisement of or information concerning any lottery, gift enterprise, or similar scheme, offering prizes depending in whole or in part upon lot or on chance...." There are exemptions to section 1304, including: fishing contests, wagers on sporting events, state lotteries, Indian gambling of all types, and charitable lotteries.

The court determined that while section 1304 allowed broadcast advertising of Indian casino gambling, the ban on advertising by private casinos directly advanced the government's interest in discouraging public participation in commercial gambling.

The court also found that the ban on broadcast advertising supported the policy of states, including Texas, that did not permit casino gambling.

The court reasoned that:

> The government may legitimately distinguish among certain kinds of gambling for advertising purposes, determining that the social impact of activities such as state-run lotteries, Indian and charitable gambling include social benefits as well as costs and that these other activities often have dramatically different geographic scope. That the broadcast advertising ban in [section] 1304 directly advances the government's policies must be evident from the casinos' vigorous pursuit of litigation to

overturn it.

On another related issue, the court also reasoned that the ban was not broader than necessary to control participation in casino gambling. The court said: "*44 Liquormart* does not disturb the series of decisions that has found a commonsense connection between promotional advertising and the stimulation of consumer demand for the products advertised."

Section 1304, please remember, was not a complete ban on advertising. Other media including newspapers, magazines, and outdoor billboards all remained as options. The court went on, "Section 1304 simply targets the powerful sensory appeal of gambling conveyed by television and radio, which are the most intrusive advertising media, and the most readily available to children." The court determined that a nationwide ban on radio and television advertising for casino gambling also served to protect those states that allow noncasino gambling. "*Central Hudson*, as applied after *44 Liquormart*, does not inhibit all legislative flexibility in confronting challenging social developments."

The Valley Broadcasting Case

Contrast to *Greater New Orleans*, in 1998 the Ninth Circuit held the federal law unconstitutional in *Valley Broadcasting Co. v. United States*.[8] Here, the court held an advertising ban was unconstitutional since it did not directly advance the government's interests. The court relied primarily on the exceptions in section 1304 that expressly allowed broadcast advertising for Indian-operated casino gambling, as well as other local charitable gambling. The court found these points inconsistent with the government's asserted interest.

In this case the government asserted two interests: first, an interest in reducing public participation in commercial lotteries; second, an interest in protecting those states that chose not to permit casino gambling. Certain states policies against casino gambling were of substantial interest. To support this, the government provided evidence that casino gambling attracted organized crime.

And, since broadcasts from states that permit casino gambling could be seen by people in other states that prohibited casino gambling, noncasino states would have no effective means to control the viewing of these advertisements by their residents.

The court, however, found that the restriction did not advance the government's interests. Section 1304 allowed broadcast advertising for such activities as Indian casino gambling, charitable gambling, state-run lotteries, and fishing contests. The court noted that the government had articulated its interest in reducing public participation in all commercial lotteries. The court reasoned that "because section 1304 permits the advertising of commercial lotteries by not-for-profit organizations, governmental organizations and Indian tribes, it is impossible for it materially to discourage public participation in commercial lotteries. To use the language from *Coors Brewing*,[9] '[t]here is little chance that [the challenged restriction] can directly and materially advance its aim, while other provisions of the same act directly undermine and counteract its effects.'"

DETERMINING COMMERCIAL OR NONCOMMERCIAL SPEECH UNDER THE FIRST AMENDMENT

Commercial and noncommercial forms of speech are granted different degrees of protection under the First Amendment. While the courts are becoming more liberal in their granting First Amendment protection of commercial speech (advertising), more latitude is still given to noncommercial speech. So, it is important to understand which speech falls into the commercial speech arena.

In *Bad Frog Brewery Inc.* v. *New York State Liquor Authority*,[10] the Second Circuit held that a beer manufacturer's bottle label that showed a frog, well, "giving the finger" was commercial speech and thereby protected under the First Amendment.

Bad Frog is a Michigan corporation that manufactures and markets several different types of beer products under the "Bad Frog" trademark. This case centers around labels used by the company for Bad Frog Beer, Bad Frog Lemon Lager, and Bad Frog Malt Liquor. The labels include an illustration of a frog making "the finger" gesture that is regarded as an offensive insult (the gesture of the extended middle finger is said to have been first used by Diogenes to insult Demosthenes), conveying a message that the company itself has characterized as "traditionally... negative and nasty." Versions of the label feature slogans including "He just don't care," "An amphibian with an attitude," "Turning bad into good," and "The beer so good...it's bad." Another slogan, originally used, but now abandoned, was "He's mean, green and obscene."

The New York State Liquor Authority (NYSLA) tried to ban the use of the offensive label in New York. The court held that the NYSLA failed to establish that the state's interest in protecting children from vulgar and profane advertising would be advanced by the ban.

Bad Frog contended that its beer label was noncommercial speech and, thus, afforded full First Amendment protection. Bad Frog argued that its labels did not purport to convey commercial information, but rather, communicated a "joke." Thus, the labels should enjoy full First Amendment protection, rather than the somewhat reduced protection accorded commercial speech.

Bad Frog contended that:

> Marketing gimmicks for beer such as the "Budweiser Frogs," "Spuds Mackenzie," the "Bud-Ice Penguins," and the "Red Dog" of Red Dog Beer [are] virtually indistinguishable from the Plaintiff's frog,

> promote intemperate behavior in the same way that the Defendants have alleged Plaintiff's label would... [and therefore the] regulation of the Plaintiff's label will have no tangible effect on underage drinking or intemperate behavior in general.

However, the New York State Liquor Authority argued that the labels conveyed no useful consumer information and should not be protected under the First Amendment.

After considering the Supreme Court's position with regard to commercial advertising, the Second Circuit ruled that Bad Frog's labels were, in fact, commercial speech. As a result, they were subject to the *Central Hudson* test. The court concluded that:

> The Supreme Court has not explicitly clarified whether commercial speech, such as a logo or a slogan that conveys no information, other than identifying the source of the product, but serves, to some degree, to "propose a commercial transaction" enjoys any First Amendment protection. The Court's opinion in *Posadas*, however, points in favor of protection.
>
> Bad Frog's label attempts to function, like a trademark, to identify the source of the product. The picture on a beer bottle of a frog behaving badly is reasonably to be understood as attempting to identify to consumers a product of the Bad Frog Brewery. In addition, the label serves to propose a commercial transaction. Though the label communicates no information beyond the source of the product, we think that minimal information, conveyed in the context of a proposal of a commercial transaction, suffices to invoke the protections for commercial speech articulated in *Central Hudson*.

Bad Frog then argued that its labels deserved full First Amendment protection because their "proposal of a commercial transaction" was combined with political or social commentary. The court agreed that there were forms of speech that combined both commercial and noncommercial elements. Whether a communication that combined those elements would be considered commercial speech depended on:

- Whether the message was an advertisement;
- Whether the message made reference to a specific product; and
- Whether the sender of the message had an economic motivation for the communication.

Clearly, these three elements existed in the beer label. Clearly, the labels were advertisements motivated by a desire to sell the product to which the labels were attached.

The court said:

> We are unpersuaded by Bad Frog's attempt to separate the purported social commentary in the labels from the hawking of beer. Bad Frog's labels meet the three criteria identified in Bolger: the labels are a form of advertising, identify a specific product, and serve the economic interest of the speaker. Moreover, the purported noncommercial message is not so "inextricably intertwined" with the commercial speech as to require a finding that the entire label must be treated as "pure" speech. Even viewed generously, Bad Frog's labels at most "link a product to a current debate," which is not enough to convert a proposal for a commercial transaction into "pure" noncommercial speech.
>
> We thus assess the prohibition of Bad Frog's labels under the commercial speech standards outlined in *Central Hudson*.

Well then, how does the *Central Hudson* test apply to *Bad Frog*? As we have already discussed, *Central Hudson* establishes the guidelines for determining the government's restrictions on commercial speech.

The court held that the Bad Frog labels involved legal activity and were not misleading. "The consumption of beer (at least by adults) is legal in New York, and the labels cannot be said to be deceptive, even if they are offensive." The interests asserted by the New York State Liquor Authority in protecting children from vulgar and profane advertising and promoting moderate and responsible use of alcohol among those above the legal drinking age and abstention among those below the drinking age were found to be substantial state interests.

The state failed, however, to show that a ban of the Bad Frog labels directly advanced its interests. "To meet the 'direct advancement' requirement, a state must demonstrate that the 'harms it recites are real and that its restriction will in fact alleviate them to a material degree.'" In fact, banning the Bad Frog labels would have made only a minute contribution to the state's interest in preventing exposure of children to vulgar advertising. The court stated:

> In the pending case, NYSLA endeavors to advance the state interest in preventing exposure of children to vulgar displays by taking only the limited step of barring such displays from the labels of alcoholic beverages. In view of the wide currency of vulgar displays throughout contemporary society, including comic books targeted directly at children, barring such displays from labels for alcoholic beverages cannot realistically be expected to reduce children's exposure to such displays to any significant degree.

A complete ban on the Bad Frog labels was also not

narrowly tailored to achieve the state's asserted interest. Bad Frog suggested several less intrusive alternatives such as "the restriction of advertising to point-of-sale locations; limitations on billboard advertising; restrictions on over-the-air-advertising; and segregation of the product in the store." The court agreed that a complete ban on the labels was overbroad and not reasonable with the goal of protecting minors. The court stated, "NYSLA's complete statewide ban on the use of Bad Frog's labels lacks a "reasonable fit" with the state's asserted interest in shielding minors from vulgarity, and NYSLA gave inadequate consideration to alternatives to this blanket suppression of commercial speech. [T]he government may not reduce the adult population...to reading only what is fit for children."

The court concluded that the NYSLA was prohibited from rejecting Bad Frog's label.

THE FIRST AMENDMENT, PUBLIC FORUM, AND PRIOR RESTRAINT ISSUES

Two other recent cases focused on the question of whether a government agency (in these cases, city public transportation authorities) had created a "public forum" for paid advertising on its city buses and stations. The cases further questioned whether restrictions on the content of those messages violated the First Amendment.

The Mayor Rudy Case

In New York, an advertisement ran on the sides of MTA buses that featured the *New York Magazine* logo along with the headline, "Possibly the only good thing in New York Rudy hasn't taken credit for."

In 1998, in *New York Magazine* v. *Metropolitan Transportation Authority*,[11] the court held that the New York Metropolitan Transportation Authority's (MTA) refusal to continue to display on its buses a *New York Magazine* advertisement that referred to Mayor Guiliani of New York City by his first name was an unlawful prior restraint.

New York Magazine had contracted with the MTA to place the ad on the side of MTA buses. Sometime later, the MTA removed the ad after receiving a complaint from the mayor's office, objecting to the use of the mayor's name to promote a commercial product, and claiming that the ad violated the mayor's rights under section 50 of the New York Civil Rights Law.[12] Section 50 prohibited the use, for advertising purposes, of the name, portrait, or picture of a living person without their consent. However, *New York Magazine* argued that the ad was protected under the First Amendment.

A federal district court granted *New York Magazine* a preliminary injunction prohibiting the MTA from removing the advertisements. The district court held that the ad was commercial speech and that the buses constituted a public forum. The district court also held that the government's interest in upholding section 50 was not directly advanced by removing the ad. The appellate court affirmed the preliminary injunction on the grounds that the MTA's standards in reviewing the advertisement for violation of section 50 constituted an unconstitutional prior restraint on speech.

The MTA was a public benefit corporation created by New York state law that owned and operated the majority of public buses in New York City. The MTA raised revenues for its operation, in part, by leasing advertising space on the buses.

The MTA had adopted standards that governed its acceptance of advertising on its buses. The standards prohibited the display of advertising that "violates New York Civil Rights Law section 50." Section 50 provides in part: "A person, firm or corporation that uses for advertising purposes, or for purposes of trade, the name, portrait, or picture of any living person without having first obtained the written consent of such person...is guilty of a misdemeanor."

One issue here is that of public forum. A designated public forum is one opened by the government for use by the public for expressive activity. The court held that since the MTA (operated by the government) allowed both political and commercial advertising on its buses, it was the MTA's intent to create a public forum. Regulations based on the content of the message in a designated public forum are allowed only if narrowly drawn to support a compelling governmental interest. The purpose behind the MTA's regulations, in this case, showed that the MTA was acting as a regulatory agency. The court stated:

> [T]he MTA's exclusion is based on a general interest in upholding the law, and a corollary interest in avoiding litigation. The MTA articulates its interest as "seeing to it that commercial advertising appearing on buses complies with section 50, the statutory codification of the rights of privacy and publicity." There is no commercial reason why MTA has any special interest in the policy behind section 50; MTA's interest is only the interest in upholding the law because it is the law.
>
> Given that MTA's standards allow both commercial and political speech, and given that the standard that MTA used to justify discontinuing the advertisement supports a legal characterization of MTA's action as regulatory, we conclude that the advertising space on the outside of MTA buses is a designated public forum.

Another issue in this case involves that of prior restraint. Having determined that the MTA intended to designate its advertising space as a public forum, the court reviewed MTA actions as an exercise of a prior restraint. The court held that the MTA's review of an advertisement for potential violation of section

50 was a prior restraint on speech that was more extensive than necessary to serve MTA's interest in avoiding litigation.

The court stated:

> In fact, the test that the Supreme Court regularly applies to commercial speech supports continuing to require procedural safeguards for prior restraints even where commercial speech is involved. That test requires us to consider "whether the regulation...is not more extensive than is necessary to serve [the asserted governmental] interest." If it is more extensive than necessary, the government's action fails. A prior prohibition of the Advertisement is certainly more extensive than is necessary to serve the governmental interest asserted here, particularly where this court found, when denying MTA's motion for a stay, that requiring MTA to display the Advertisement would not result in irreparable harm to MTA. In other words, we have already decided that applying section 50 before the Advertisement is displayed is more extensive than necessary. Because the advertising space is a designated public forum, MTA may not enforce section 50 through its advertising policy any more than a government agency, acting without procedural safeguards, could screen advertisements for violations of section 50 that private bus companies wished to display.

The result? Because the ad space is a designated public forum, the MTA may not enforce section 50 through its advertising policy. However, anyone (including Mayor Rudy) who feels his rights have been violated (under section 50) may bring an action privately under section 51.[13]

The Christ's Bride Case

The Southeastern Pennsylvania Transportation Authority (SEPTA), an agency of the Commonwealth of Pennsylvania, operated buses, subways, and regional rail lines in and around the city of Philadelphia. It sold advertising space in its stations and on its vehicles. In 1995 Christ's Bride Ministries (CBM) began a public service campaign to alert the public to what it believed to be the increased risk of breast cancer among women who had abortions. CBM's advertisements offered the headline: "Women Who Choose Abortion Suffer More and Deadlier Breast Cancer."

After the CBM posters were in place in stations and on buses, Dr. Philip Lee, Assistant Secretary of Health in the United States Department of Health and Human Services, claimed that the ads were misleading, unduly alarming, and did not accurately reflect the link between abortion and breast cancer. In a letter, Dr. Lee stated that the studies showing a link between breast cancer and abortion suffered from methodological weaknesses, that there was no consensus on the theorized relationship between breast cancer and abortion, and that Dr. Lee knew of no evidence supporting the claim that abortion causes "deadlier" breast cancer. Based on Dr. Lee's letter, SEPTA removed the posters.

When the case went to the appellate court, the Third Circuit ruled that SEPTA could not remove advertisements from its buses. In *Christ's Bride Ministries, Inc.* v. *Southeastern Pennsylvania Transportation Authority*,[14] the appellate court summarized its thinking as follows:

> SEPTA has accepted a broad range of advertisements for display. These include religious messages, such as "Follow this bus to FREEDOM, Christian Bible Fellowship Church;" an ad criticizing a political candidate; and explicitly worded advertisements such as "Safe Sex Isn't" and an advertisement reminding viewers that "Virginity-It's cool to keep" and "Don't give it up to shut 'em up."

Indeed, many ads address topics concerning sex, family planning, and related topics. Other examples include a controversial ad campaign on AIDS education and awareness, posters stating, "The Face of Adoption" "Consider Adoption" and "Every child deserves a family," and another ad reading "Pregnant? Scared? Confused? A.R.C. Can Help Call 1-800-884-4004 or (215-844-1082.)"

On the topic of abortion, SEPTA has accepted two ads. One read, "Choice Hotline, For Answers to Your Questions About: Birth Control * Pregnancy * Prenatal Care * Abortion * Adoption * HIV/AIDS * Sexually Transmitted Diseases (STDs), Call State Health Line 1-800-692-7254 For Free Booklet on Fetal Development." The other one addressed the health benefits of legalizing abortion: "When Abortion Was Illegal, Women Died. My Mother Was One of Them. Keep Abortion Legal and Safe. Support the Clara Bell Duvall Education Fund. 471-9110."

From the broad range of ads submitted, SEPTA has requested modification of only three. One was the large wrap-around bus ad for Haynes hosiery, which would have covered the entire bus with the picture of a "scantily clad" woman; it was too "risque." The same ad was accepted as a smaller "poster" ad on the sides of buses. SEPTA also asked for modification of an ad depicting a gun with a condom stretched over it. The text of the ad, "Safe Sex Isn't," ultimately ran without the graphics. SEPTA also requested that an advertisement for a personal injury law firm delete references to rail accidents.

We conclude then, based on SEPTA's written

> policies, which specifically provide for the exclusion of only a very narrow category of ads, based on SEPTA's goals of generating revenues through the sale of ad space, and based on SEPTA's practice of permitting virtually unlimited access to the forum, that SEPTA created a designated public forum. Moreover, it created a forum that is suitable for the speech in question, i.e., posters which presented messages concerning abortion and health issues. CBM paid for advertising space which had previously been used for ads on those topics.

> The court went on by saying:
>
> In light of the other advertisements, including those relating to abortion, which SEPTA had previously permitted to run on its property, and in light of SEPTA's own purposes in using and leasing the space, we have determined that SEPTA intended to create a designated public forum. We find that SEPTA's action in removing the posters does not survive the strict scrutiny applied to speech within the parameters of a designated public forum; nor does it pass the reasonableness test applied where property of a governmental agency has not been designated a public forum.

As it relates to the public forum issue (like the Guiliani case), the court first determined whether the advertising space on SEPTA's buses and in its stations constituted a public forum. That is, whether SEPTA clearly and deliberately opened its advertising space to the public. Clearly, the court concluded that it did.

The main goal of SEPTA's advertising space was to generate money. Other than tobacco and liquor advertising, SEPTA accepted many types of advertising, including religious messages, political advertising, advertisements concerning sex issues, family planning, and others. On the topic of abortion, SEPTA had accepted two advertisements in the past.

SEPTA argued that it asserted "tight control" over the forum. However, because the forum was limited in one way (refusing to run ads related to tobacco or alcohol) did not disqualify it as a public forum regarding other categories of speech, the court held.

In removing the advertisement without giving CBM a chance to prove the accuracy of the representation, SEPTA acted unreasonably. According to the court, SEPTA became a censor, thereby limiting speech it felt was misleading. SEPTA then argued that it could not investigate the accuracy of medical claims in ads submitted for placement on its buses. For that reason, it relied on Dr. Lee's letter. While SEPTA was under no obligation to "hire its own cadre of experts to evaluate medical claims made in ads," it was SEPTA that accepted the ad and then decided that it was misleading.

The court reasoned:

> Having decided to exclude the posters on this basis, SEPTA did not act reasonably when it failed to ask CBM to clarify the basis on which the claim was made. This is all the more true where SEPTA has failed to explain how its content-based distinctions are related to preserving the advertising space for its intended use, and where SEPTA has in place no policy, old or new, written or unwritten, governing the display of ads making contested claims.

THE FIRST AMENDMENT AND ADVANCING GOVERNMENT INTERESTS

In *Tillman* v. *Miller*,[15] Georgia's Workers' Compensation Truth in Advertising Act of 1995[16] was held to violate the First Amendment. This occurred because the Act did not advance the state's goal of deterring the filing of fraudulent workers' compensation claims and was too burdensome.

The Georgia statute provided:

> Any television advertisement, with broadcast originating in this state, which solicits persons to file workers' compensation claims or to engage or consult an attorney, medical care provider, or clinic for the purpose of giving consideration to a workers' compensation claim or to market workers' compensation insurance coverage shall contain a notice, which shall be in boldface Roman font 36 point type and appear in a dark background and remain on the screen for a minimum of five seconds as follows: NOTICE-Willfully making a false or misleading statement or representation to obtain or deny workers' compensation benefits is a crime carrying a penalty of imprisonment and/or fine of up to $10,000,000.

The state claimed that the motive was "to assure truthful and adequate disclosure of all material and relevant information in advertising" for workers' compensation claims. However, the court reasoned that the state had not proven that advertising of legal services caused fraudulent workers' compensation claims to be filed or that the inclusion of the notice in advertisements would likely reduce fraudulent claims. "In such circumstances, Georgia is not justified in placing, on a television advertiser, the burden of the cost of educating the public," said the court.

The Chiropractor's Case

In *Silverman* v. *Walkup*,[17] a Tennessee law that prohibited solicitation in person and by live telephone contact by chiropractors was also found to violate the First Amendment. Again, this was because the statutory restriction did not advance the state's asserted purpose of deterring "accident telemarketing."

The Tennessee law[18] prohibited the "solicitation, in person or by live telephone contact, by a licensee, or by an agent, servant, employee, or independent contractor of a licensee, of a patient with whom the licensee has no family or prior professional relationship." Silverman was a chiropractor who alleged that the law violated his First Amendment rights.

In contrast, the State argued that the law prohibited "solicitation," not advertising by chiropractors. It argued this on the grounds that the statute did not ban chiropractors from talking to prospective patients on the street or at health fairs or shopping malls. However, the court found the statute was clearly broader than merely prohibiting "telephone solicitation." In fact, the state's own regulations defined advertising as including "business solicitation."

Having determined that the statute regulated advertising by chiropractors, the court found that the restrictions were not narrowly tailored to the state's asserted interests. The state had a substantial interest in protecting the "tranquility, and privacy of the home" from the intrusion of telephone calls using personal information gleaned from accident reports. In addition, the protection of people from overreaching and pressure at a time when their judgment could be impaired and establishing standards for professional chiropractors that protected the reputation of the profession were at stake. The blanket ban of both in-person as well as telephone solicitation was too broad, according to the court. The court granted the plaintiff a preliminary injunction on enforcement of the statute until a full hearing on the merits.

U.S. CURRENCY RESTRICTIONS

One area of concern for advertisers is the use of certain elements in advertising. The use of U.S. currency in an ad has been a major issue for advertisers to deal with.

During the Civil War the first large issuance of paper

money in the United States was made. As a result, a law[19] was enacted to protect the uncontrolled counterfeiting that went with the wartime economy. At the time the law provided criminal liability for printing, photographing, or making any impression "in the likeness of any obligation or other security, or any part thereof ...." In other words, you could not photograph or copy any money or part of it.

However, in 1958 Congress enacted another law[20] that allowed the "printing, publishing...of illustrations of...any... obligation or other security of the United States...for philatelic, numismatic, educational, historical, or newsworthy purposes in articles, books, journals, newspapers, or albums...." Yet, this law limited how currency could be reproduced to avoid counterfeiting. The reproduction could only be in black and white, larger or smaller than actual size, and the negatives and plates had to be destroyed immediately after use.

The government, however, did not allow reproduction of currency for commercial advertising purposes to fall under this exception. In 1984 the U.S. Supreme Court made a decision in *Time, Inc.* v. *Donald T. Regan, Secretary of the Treasury, et al.*[21] that changed that. In that case, *Sports Illustrated* had used a color photograph of $100 bills pouring into a basketball hoop.

Time argued that Section 504 was unconstitutional in that it was a violation of free speech because the government could determine what was acceptable content or subject matter. The Court ruled in favor of Time in part.

In 1985 the Treasury Department formulated a policy statement regarding use of currency in ads.

The policy stated that the Department would:

> [P]ermit the use of photographic or other likenesses of U.S. and foreign currency for any purpose, provided that the items were reproduced in black and white and were less than 3/4 of, or greater than 1-1/2 times the size, in linear dimension, of each part of the original item.

> Furthermore, the negatives and plates used in making the likeness must be destroyed after their use. This decision will, for the first time, permit the use of currency reproduction in commercial advertisements, provided they conform to these size and color restrictions.

As a result, reproduction of currency is allowed in advertising under two conditions:

- It is not reproduced in full color; and
- It is reproduced less than 3/4 or more than 1-1/2 the size of the original.

Note: violating this law is a felony.

CONSIDERATIONS WHEN ADVERTISING PROFESSIONAL BUSINESSES

The first state to adopt an ethics code for attorneys was Alabama in the late nineteenth century. This specifically allowed newspaper ads to be used by members of the Alabama bar. However, in other states the practice was not allowed. In fact, a Denver, Colorado, attorney was suspended for six months by the state Supreme Court in *People ex rel. Maupin* v. *MacCabe*,[22] for running a newspaper ad which claimed: "Divorces legally obtained very quietly, good everywhere." The Court noted in that case, "The ethics of the legal profession forbid that an attorney should advertise his talents or his skills as a shopkeeper advertises his wares."

In 1908 The American Bar Association published its Canons of Professional Ethics, which discussed attorney advertising. Cannon 27 (1908) stated, in part, "...solicitation of business by circulars or advertisements, or by personal communications, or interviews, not warranted by personal relations, is unprofessional."

It was not until 1977 that a major change occurred

regarding attorney advertising. The landmark decision was the case of *Bates* v. *State Bar of Arizona.*[23] Here, the U.S. Supreme Court upheld the First Amendment right of attorneys to advertise their services. However, the *Bates* case did not grant carte blanche to attorneys to advertise in any manner they wanted. The Court stressed that attorney advertising must not be false, deceptive, or misleading. They noted: "As with other varieties of speech, it follows as well that there may be reasonable restrictions on the time, place and manner of advertising."

The state bar associations greeted *Bates* with little enthusiasm. In fact, they limited *Bates* to its facts, which essentially allowed price advertising of certain routine legal services.

Even though *Bates* dealt with advertising by attorneys, it led the way for advertising by all professionals. Accountants, attorneys, doctors, dentists, pharmacists, and other professionals have been using advertising to attract clientele ever since.

In 1978 *Ohralik* v. *Ohio State Bar Association*[24] decided the question of direct solicitation. The Court stated that truthful, restrained advertising of prices for routine legal services was not unprofessional conduct. However, the Court also indicated that states have a legitimate interest in protecting the public from attorney advertising involving fraud, undue influence, or intimidation.

The Court said:

> By discussing the origin and impact of the nonsolicitation rules, I do not mean to belittle those obviously substantial interests that the State has in regulating attorneys to protect the public from fraud, deceit, misrepresentation, overreaching, undue influence and invasions of privacy. But where honest, unpressed "commercial" solicitation is involved – a situation not presented in either of these cases – I believe it is open to doubt whether the State's interests are sufficiently compelling to

> warrant the restriction on the free flow of information which results from a sweeping nonsolicitation rule and against which the First Amendment ordinarily protects.

The Supreme Court went further in another landmark attorney advertising case, *In re R.M.J.*[25] The Missouri Supreme Court's Advisory Committee tried to disbar an attorney for violating attorney advertising regulations by using direct mail and advertising his expertise in his area of practice ("personal injury") using wording that varied from that allowed by the code. The Missouri Supreme Court upheld the constitutional validity of these rules and reprimanded the lawyer. The U.S. Supreme Court, however, reversed this decision by saying:

> Truthful advertising related to lawful activities is entitled to the protection of the First Amendment. But when the particular content or method of the advertising suggests that it is inherently misleading or when experience has proved that in fact such advertising is subject to abuse, the States may impose appropriate restrictions. Misleading advertising may be prohibited entirely. But the States may not place an absolute prohibition on certain types of potentially misleading information, e.g., a listing of areas of practice, if the information also may be presented in a way that is not deceptive. Thus, the Court in Bates suggested that the remedy in the first instance is not necessarily a prohibition but preferably a requirement of disclaimers or explanation.... Although the potential for deception and confusion is particularly strong in the context of advertising professional services, restrictions upon such advertising may be no broader than reasonably necessary to prevent the deception.

The Court went on:

> Even when a communication is not misleading, the State retains some authority to regulate. But the state must assert a substantial interest and the interference with speech must be in proportion to the interest served.... Restrictions must be narrowly drawn, and the State lawfully may regulate only to the extent regulation furthers the State's substantial interest.

In this case the Court clearly stated the broad parameters of an attorney's – and by inference any professional's – right to advertise.

The U.S. Supreme Court continued to show little patience for state restrictions on an attorney's right to advertise truthfully as demonstrated in it's decision in *Zauderer* v. *Office of Disciplinary Counsel of the Supreme Court of Ohio*.[26] Because of this ruling, attorneys may use accurate illustrations in their ads, as well as nondeceptive claims in ads that openly solicit specific types of clients. However, the decision requires some attorney ads to contain certain disclosures.

In 1981 Philip Zauderer, an attorney in Columbus, Ohio, began placing ads in Ohio newspapers. One ad included a line drawing of the Dalkon Shield, along with the following copy.

••••••••••••••••••

DID YOU USE THIS IUD?

The Dalkon Shield Intrauterine Device is alleged to have caused serious pelvic infections resulting in hospitalizations, tubal damage, infertility, and hysterectomies.

It is also alleged to have caused unplanned pregnancies ending in abortions, miscarriages, septic abortions, tubal or ectopic pregnancies and full term deliveries.

If you or a friend have had a similar experience
do not assume it is too late to take legal action
against the Shield's manufacturer.
Our law firm is presently representing
women on such cases.
The cases are handled on a
contingent fee basis of the amount recovered.
If there is no recovery, no legal fees
are owed by our clients.

• • • • • • • • • • • • • • • • •

The ad included Zauderer's firm name, address, and phone number for "free information."

Zauderer received over 200 inquiries from the ad and ultimately initiated lawsuits on behalf of 106 women.

Another ad noted Zauderer's availability to represent people charged for drunk driving. That ad contained the phrase: "full legal fee refunded if convicted of drunk driving."

The Ohio Supreme Court publicly reprimanded Zauderer after ruling that the ads violated several rules in the state's Code of Professional Conduct. On July 29, 1982, Ohio's Office of Disciplinary Counsel (ODC) charged Zauderer with several disciplinary violations because of these ads. The case claimed that the drunk-driving ad violated Ohio Disciplinary Rule 2-101 (A), saying that it was "false, fraudulent, misleading, and deceptive to the public." The rational for this was that it offered representation on a contingent-fee basis in a criminal case, a violation under another disciplinary rule.

The complaint also charged that the line drawing in the Dalkon Shield ad violated Disciplinary Rule 2-101(B), which forbid use of illustrations in attorney ads and limited the kind of information in such ads to an established list of 20 items. In addition, the ODC claimed that the ad violated another disciplinary rule forbidding a lawyer from "recommending employment, as a private practitioner, of himself, his partner, or associate to a non-lawyer who has not sought his advice regarding employment of a lawyer." Another rule stated that a "lawyer who has given unsolicited advice to a layman that he should obtain counsel or take legal action shall not accept employment resulting from that advice."

The case also dealt with another rule that required ads mentioning contingent-fee rates to "disclose whether percentages are computed before or after deduction of court costs and expenses." The failure to inform clients that they would be liable for costs (as opposed to legal fees) even if their claims were unsuccessful made the ad "deceptive."

It was never alleged that the Dalkon Shield ad was false or deceptive. In fact, the ODC stipulated that the information and advice in the ad relative to Dalkon Shield litigation was not false, fraudulent, misleading, or deceptive and that the line drawing accurately depicted the Dalkon Shield.

The Court said:

> Because all advertising is at least implicitly a plea for its audience's custom, a broad reading of the rules applied by the Ohio court (and particularly against self-recommendation) might suggest that they forbid all advertising by attorneys – a result obviously not in keeping with our decisions in *Bates* and *In re R.M.J.* Because appellant's statements regarding the Dalkon Shield were not false or deceptive, our decisions impose on the State the burden of establishing that prohibiting the use of such statements to solicit or obtain legal business directly advances a substantial governmental interest.

The Court concluded by saying the state did not meet that burden in this instance:

> An attorney may not be disciplined for

> soliciting legal business through printed advertising containing truthful and nondeceptive information and advice regarding the legal rights of potential clients.

Ohio's laws regarding the use of pictures or illustrations in an attorney's ad was invalid for similar reasons. The likely purpose behind the restrictions was to ensure that attorney ads are "dignified." However, the court said it was "unsure that the State's desire that attorneys maintain their dignity in their communications with the public is an interest substantial enough to justify the abridgment of their First Amendment rights."

Zauderer was unsuccessful with the disclosure issue. The problem here involved a failure to include in the Dalkon Shield ad "information that clients might be liable for significant litigation costs even if their lawsuits were unsuccessful." The Court noted that Ohio's disclosure requirements do not prevent lawyers from advertising. Rather, lawyers are required by these rules to "provide somewhat more information than they might otherwise be inclined to present."

Specifically, the Dalkon Shield ad said that "if there is no recovery, no legal fees are owed by our clients." The drunk-driving ad said "full legal fee...refunded...." However, the ads failed to mention the subtle distinction between "legal fees" and "costs." The problem with this technical point was that a layman might not be aware of the distinction between "fees" and "costs." Therefore, the U.S. Supreme Court affirmed the Ohio court's reprimand of Zauderer to the extent that it was based on the omission of material information concerning his contingent-fee arrangements in the Dalkon Shield ads and his terms of representation in the drunk-driving ads.

The FTC's Role In Attorney Advertising

It's not surprising that the Federal Trade Commission has actively encouraged truthful attorney advertising as well as truthful professional advertising in general. As we learned earlier in Chapters 2 and 3, the FTC is authorized to prevent unfair methods of competition and unfair or deceptive acts or practices in or affecting commerce. Under this mandate, the FTC encourages competition among professionals to a great extent. In recent years, the FTC has been looking into the competitive impact of restrictions on business arrangements that such state-licensed professionals as attorneys, doctors, and dentists can use. The commission's goal in that effort has been to urge the removal of those restrictions that restrain competition, raise prices, and hurt consumers without offering benefits.

In November 1984, for example, the FTC prepared a report, "Improving Consumer Access to Legal Services: The Case for Removing Restrictions on Truthful Advertising." Some 3,200 lawyers in 17 states were surveyed to find out if restricting attorney advertising affected the availability of legal services and the prices that consumers paid for these services. One of the main conclusions of the report was that "...restrictions on the manner, content, and form of lawyer advertising have limited the flow of information to consumers about lawyers and their services." The report also found "convincing support for the proposition that greater flexibility to engage in nondeceptive advertising will be associated with lower prices for consumers of legal services."

The FTC also plays a significant part in the area of professional advertising by offering recommendations to the state licensing authorities.

For example, in 1984 two Iowa attorneys televised three commercials that contained:

- More than a single nondramatic voice;
- Background sound;
- Visual displays other than words and numbers; and

- A list of four fields of practice which they would handle on either a percentage basis or a contingent fee basis.

While not alleging or demonstrating that these ads were false, misleading, or deceptive, the Iowa State Bar Association's Committee on Professional Ethics and Conduct obtained a temporary injunction and sought to permanently stop the attorneys from using these commercials to advertise their legal services.

It was charged that the three spots violated Iowa's Code of Professional Responsibility for Lawyers since they "contain more than a single non-dramatic voice, have background sound and visual displays of two or more people characterizing themselves as clients which make laudatory comment as to the defendants' services," and because they "list four areas of practice and contain no disclaimer."

As a result, the FTC urged the Iowa court not to restrict competition unnecessarily by limiting truthful, nondeceptive information. The commission listed three reasons why these ads were not deceptive:

- The ads did not make any misleading or deceptive statements or claims, nor was there any evidence on which the Iowa Supreme Court could base such a finding.
- A study submitted by the attorneys established that the public did not perceive the advertisements to be misleading or deceptive; and
- There was no evidence "in the record to support the premise generally that the technique of using dramatizations, background sounds or more than one nondramatic voice" in a television commercial is inherently misleading. The FTC noted that the plaintiff's witness "testified that in his professional opinion, the use of such format and techniques was not inherently misleading or deceptive."

The FTC also stated that the American Bar Association's

Commission on Advertising found no support that the use of graphic dramatizations and music in lawyer advertising is inherently misleading or potentially more misleading than advertisements which do not contain those elements.

Many state and local bar associations have used television commercials containing dramatizations, graphics, and music to advertise the availability of bar association-sponsored lawyer referral services. Therefore, the commission disagreed that a commercial featuring clients making laudatory comments about the attorney's services warranted an injunction. "All advertisements are, to some degree, self-laudatory," stated the commission.

As mentioned earlier, the FTC also offers advice to other professions. Generally, these comments also promote the FTC's strong opposition to restrictions on any truthful professional ad. For example, the New Jersey State Board of Dentistry proposed rules that would forbid "any statement offering gratuitous services or the substantial equivalent thereof." The FTC responded by stating that "a number of provisions in the proposed advertising rules would restrain truthful communication and thereby inhibit competition."

In fact, the FTC noted that this provision isn't needed to protect consumers: "To the contrary, truthful advertising of the availability of free services can be of great benefit to consumers and, in addition, such offers can be a valuable professional tool for new practitioners who are trying to establish themselves. While we are aware that there is a potential for deceptive schemes in the use of such advertising we believe that a total ban on the offering of free service is overly restrictive and unnecessary."

The ABA Code

Since the *Bates* decision, the American Bar Association (ABA) adopted its new Model Rules of Professional Conduct in 1983, which included rules dealing with attorney advertising. The FTC praised these new rules as promoting "a clearer and more objective standard for evaluating advertising content than appeared in previous ABA codes and in many state and local bar association codes. The proposed standard would allow truthful ads and prohibit only those that are false and deceptive."

Specifically, Rule 7.1 reads as follows:

> A lawyer shall not make any false or misleading communication about the lawyer or the lawyer's services. A communication is false or misleading if it:
>
> 1. Contains a material misrepresentation of fact or law, or omits a fact necessary to make the statement considered as a whole not materially misleading;
> 2. Is likely to create an unjustified expectation about results the lawyer can achieve, or states or implies that the lawyer can achieve results by means that violate the rules of professional conduct or other law; or
> 3. Compares the lawyer's service with other lawyers' services, unless the comparison can be factually substantiated.

Other areas of the Code cover the media in which an attorney can advertise and the use of trade names.

In fact, the FTC proposed its own "Model Code" (which follows) that would forbid "only false or deceptive advertising and false or deceptive trade names, and explicitly recognizes the legitimacy of using any media, including electronic broadcast or direct mail, to advertise legal services."

Model Code
COMMUNICATIONS CONCERNING A LAWYER'S SERVICES

A lawyer shall not make a false or deceptive communication about the lawyer or the lawyer's services.

Advertising

• A lawyer may advertise services through direct mail advertising or through public media, including but not limited to telephone directories, legal directories, newspapers or other periodicals, radio or television, provided the communication is not false or deceptive.

• A copy or recording of an advertisement or written communication shall be kept for (one year) after its dissemination along with a record of when and where it was used.

Direct Contact With Prospective Clients

A lawyer may initiate communications with a prospective client through personal contact, through individually directed written communication, or through telephonic communication for the purpose of obtaining professional employment, unless:

• The lawyer knows or reasonably should know that the physical, emotional or mental state of the person is such that the person could not exercise reasonable judgment in employing a lawyer;

• The person has made known to the lawyer a desire not to receive communications from the lawyer; or

• The lawyer knows or reasonably should know that the communication involves coercion, duress or harassment.

Communication Of Fields Of Practice

A lawyer may communicate the fact that the lawyer does or does not practice in particular fields of law. A lawyer shall not state or imply that the lawyer is an officially recognized or certified specialist except where the lawyer in fact has been certified in a particular field of practice.

Firm Names And Letterheads

A lawyer may use any firm name, letterhead or other professional designation provided it is not false or deceptive.

While the ABA code is clearly a key document, it is the various state bar associations – frequently acting in concert with state courts – that have direct authority over attorney conduct. So, it would be wise to check the specific state regulations for those states where ads will run.

It is important to understand that while *Bates*, *In re R.M. J.*, and *Ohralik* dealt with attorney advertising, the same principles are applicable to advertising by all professionals. Indeed, it was in the U.S. Supreme Court's ruling in *Virginia State Board of Pharmacy* v. *Virginia Citizens Consumer Council, Inc.*,[27] where the court overturned a Virginia statute forbidding licensed pharmacists from advertising prescription drug prices. And, for example, in December 1978, the U.S. District Court for the Eastern District of Louisiana held that truthful newspaper advertising concerning the availability or cost of routine dental services was commercial speech protected by the First Amendment, finding a statute unconstitutional to the extent it restricted such advertising.

ISSUES WITH POLITICAL ADVERTISING

Certainly, under the First Amendment to the U.S. Constitution no other form of speech enjoys more protection than does political advertising. Political advertising items such as posters, leaflets, and buttons have long been staples of our political system. Beginning with the campaign of John F. Kennedy, television advertising has come into its own as the dominant form of political advertising. Today political candidates spend tremendous sums of money on television ads. As a result, the use of television advertising brings up a variety of issues that must be understood by advertisers.

If you produce political advertising, you should be aware of an important federal statute – the Federal Election Campaign Act (FECA) of 1971.[28] Sections of this act, for example, discuss the disclosures a candidate should make in his or her ads, the time availability of the media, the contribution of services by an ad agency to a candidate, and many other relevant issues.

According to the FECA, ads involving a political candidate (or request for contributions to a campaign) must clearly name the candidate, authorized political committee, agent, or other person who paid for the ad. Campaign ads and other literature published by a political committee or person that are not authorized by a candidate to publish the material must also include notice that they are not authorized by the candidate.

The FECA requires broadcasters to allow reasonable access or allow candidates to buy reasonable amounts of time for federal elective office. On the other hand, newspapers and magazines aren't required to make space available to candidates.

The Federal Election Commission (FEC) was created by 1974 amendments to the FECA. The FEC regulations define "contribution" or "expenditure" as including any "direct or indirect payment distribution, loan, advance, deposit or gift of money, or any services...." This includes any materials or services that ad agencies offer to a candidate without requesting payment.

Ad agencies should also be aware of one important financial pitfall. If a candidate fails to pay an advertising agency, the agency must try to collect the debt or else the sum will be considered a political contribution.

The candidate, the candidate's ad agency, and the media should be aware of the American Association of Advertising Agencies' (4A's) guidelines for political advertising, which are reproduced below.

POLITICAL ADVERTISING – A SHARED RESPONSIBILITY

The Candidate

1. We regard the candidate as the advertiser. The candidate bears the same responsibility as any other advertiser for the content of any ad or commercial run in his behalf. This responsibility cannot be delegated to support groups.

2. We believe every candidate should sign and comply with the Code of Fair Campaign Practices administered by the Fair Campaign Practices Committee.

The Advertising Agency

1. We believe the advertising agency bears the same responsibility for the truth and accuracy of political advertising it prepares as it would for product advertising.

2. We believe the agency has a professional obligation to maintain standards of good taste and to avoid personal vilification and disparagement in the advertising it prepares for a candidate.

3. We see it as the agency's duty to use its communication skills to acquaint the electorate with the candidate, his character, programs, and stands on issues. Techniques of communication should be used to inform, not to distract from the real issues.

4. Should the agency find that it no longer exercises sufficient control over the content or execution of the messages, we think it is the duty of the agency to make a public statement to that effect and to cease activity on that campaign. The 4 A's will make its public relations resources available to any member or nonmember agency for such a statement.

The Media

1. We believe that all media should exercise the appropriate clearance standards and controls over the taste, content, truth, and accuracy of political advertising as it would for product advertising. Media have the professional responsibility to reject any political messages which do not meet their standards of fairness and good taste.

2. We suggest that in addition to selling conventional time segments for political messages, broadcasters offer segments of at least five minutes for political announcements.

(Reprinted by permission of the American Association of Advertising Agencies).

In addition, the American Association of Advertising Agencies' Board of Directors has reapproved the following "Code of Ethics for Political Campaign Advertising:"

CODE OF ETHICS FOR POLITICAL CAMPAIGN ADVERTISING

The advertising agency has become an increasingly important factor in the conduct of American political campaigns. Just as the political candidate must observe the highest standards of fairness and morality in his campaign, so must the advertising agency operate under a code that reflects the finest values of our political system rather than any unethical temptations that arise in the heat of the battle.

The advertising agency should not represent any candidate who has not signed or who does not observe the Code of Fair Campaign Practices of the Fair Campaign Practices Committee, endorsed by A.A.A.A.

The agency should not knowingly misrepresent the views or state record of any candidates nor quote them out of proper context.

The agency should not prepare any material which unfairly or prejudicially exploits the race, creed, or national origin of any candidate.

The agency should take care to avoid unsubstantiated charges and accusations, especially those deliberately made too late in the campaign for opposing candidates to answer.

The agency should stand as an independent judge of fair campaign practices, rather than automatically yield to the wishes of the candidate or his authorized representatives.

The agency should not indulge in any practices which might be deceptive or misleading in word, photograph, film, or sound.

(Reprinted by permission of the American Association of Advertising Agencies).

The 4A's Code of Fair Campaign Practices condemns the use of personal vilification, character defamation, whispering campaigns, libel, or misleading or falsified campaign material. Candidates that endorse the code agree to the following practices and constraints:

CODE OF FAIR CAMPAIGN PRACTICES

I SHALL CONDUCT my campaign in the best American tradition, discussing the issues as I see them, presenting my record and policies with sincerity and frankness, and criticizing without fear or favor the record and policies of my opponent and his party which merit such criticism.

I SHALL DEFEND AND UPHOLD the right of every qualified American voter to full and equal participation in the electoral process.

I SHALL CONDEMN the use of personal vilification, character defamation, whispering campaigns, libel, slander, or scurrilous attacks on any candidate or his personal or family life.

I SHALL CONDEMN the use of campaign material of any sort which misrepresents, distorts, or otherwise falsifies the facts regarding any candidate, as well as the use of malicious or unfounded accusations against any candidate which aim at creating or exploiting doubts without justification as to his loyalty and patriotism.

I SHALL CONDEMN any appeal to prejudice based on race, creed, or national origin.

I SHALL CONDEMN any dishonest or unethical practice which tends to corrupt or undermine our American system of free elections or which hampers or prevents the full and free expression of the will of the voters.

I SHALL IMMEDIATELY AND PUBLICLY REPUDIATE support deriving from any individual or group which resorts, on behalf of my candidacy or in opposition to that of my opponent, to the methods and tactics which I condemn.

(Reproduced by permission of the American Association of Advertising Agencies).

POLITICAL ADVERTISING AND THE FIRST AMENDMENT

Political advertising enjoys such an amazingly broad protection under the First Amendment that these ads are not reviewable by the Federal Trade Commission. For that matter, they are not reviewable by anyone else, either. Nevertheless, there are some limitations that can be placed on political advertising, specifically concerning where it is displayed. In 1984, for example, the United States Supreme Court ruled that a city's total ban on the posting of signs, including political signs, on public property did not violate the First Amendment. The case was *Members of City Council* v. *Taxpayers for Vincent*.[29]

In that case, Roland Vincent had run for the Los Angeles City Council. Some of his backers hired a political sign company to make and post signs with Vincent's name on them. The signs read: "Roland Vincent – City Council," and were attached to utility poles.

Acting under a town ordinance, city employees routinely removed all posters (including the political signs for Roland Vincent) attached to utility poles and similar objects.

On March 12, 1979, taxpayers and the political sign company filed suit in U.S. district court, seeking an injunction against enforcement of the ordinance as well as compensatory and punitive damages. However, the district court concluded that the ordinance was constitutional.

The U.S. Supreme Court agreed with the district court's decision saying that: "The problem addressed by this ordinance – the visual assault on the citizens of Los Angeles presented by an accumulation of signs posted on public property – constitutes a significant substantive evil within the City's power to prohibit."

The Court continued:

> As recognized in *Metromedia, Inc.* v. *San Diego*,[30] if the city has a sufficient basis for believing that billboards are traffic hazards and are unattractive, "then obviously the most direct and perhaps the only effective approach to solving the problems they create is to prohibit them".... As is true of billboards, the esthetic interests that are implicated by temporary signs are presumptively at work in all parts of the city, including those where appellees posted their signs, and there is no basis in the record in this case upon which to rebut that presumption. These interests are both psychological and economic. The character of the environment affects the quality of life and the value of property in both residential and commercial areas. We hold that on this record these interests are sufficiently substantial to justify this content neutral, impartially administered prohibition against the posting of appellees' temporary signs on public property and that such an application of the ordinance does not create an unacceptable threat to the profound national commitment to the principle that debate on public issues should be uninhibited, robust, and wide-open.

BROADCAST ADVERTISING

FCC's Role In Broadcast Advertising Regulation

Most restrictions that apply to advertising in print media apply to broadcast advertising as well. However, there's one major difference between advertising on television or radio and advertising on any other medium: Broadcasters operate under a license issued by the Federal Communications Commission. Congress created the FCC in 1934 with the institution of the Communications Act. This act was designed to regulate "interstate and foreign commerce in communication by wire and radio so as to make available, so far as possible, to all the people of the United States a rapid, efficient, nation-wide, and world-wide wire and radio communications service..." (The word "radio" also applies to television.) The Act authorizes the FCC to "make such regulations not inconsistent with law as it may deem necessary to prevent interference between stations and to carry out the provisions of [the] Act."

There are over 10,000 licensed radio and full-service television stations in the United States. More than 9,000 of these operate commercially and are supported by advertising revenues, the remainder are nonprofit, noncommercial stations.

The FCC's main authority lies in the fact that it has the power to grant applications to construct broadcast stations and license stations. The requirement that needs to be met, in the FCC's view, is whether these grants will serve the "public interest, convenience, and necessity."

Therefore, advertisers should be keenly aware of the following areas, as they directly affect advertising.

False Or Misleading Advertising

The Federal Trade Commission (FTC) has the main responsibility for protecting viewers and listeners from false, deceptive, or misleading advertising (see Chapters 2 and 3). Yet, the FCC expects licensed stations to be diligent in seeing that such ads are not aired. Because of this the FCC and the FTC have an agreement whereby they exchange information on matters of common interest.

Commercial Volume

The FCC has a policy statement which advises licensees

that objectionably loud commercials are contrary to the public interest. According to the FCC, licensees are responsible for making sure that objectionably loud commercials are not aired.

Subliminal Ads

The FCC strongly believes that the use of subliminal techniques in advertising is contrary to the public interest since, by their very existence, they're intended to be deceptive. This would also be a violation of the FTC Act.

Tobacco Ads

Federal law prohibits the advertising of cigarettes and little cigars on any medium that falls under the FCC's jurisdiction. However, broadcast advertising for other tobacco products such as pipes, smoking accessories, or cigarette-making machines is not forbidden.

Sponsor Identification Of Advertising

A station that broadcasts paid-for material must announce that it's paid for or sponsored, and by whom.

Despite its concerns with various aspects of broadcast advertising, the FCC is forbidden from censoring broadcast material including advertising. Accordingly, the FCC can't require its licensees to accept or reject ads for a particular product (unless Congress has passed a law forbidding its advertising, as in the case of cigarettes). In addition, the FCC cannot take actions against "offensive advertising," unless it's found to violate a specific law or regulation.

The End Of The NAB Code

On March 10, 1982, the National Association of Broadcasters (NAB) suspended enforcement of the advertising standards of its television and radio code. The NAB has never reinstated its code.

The NAB's action came in response to a decision on March 3, 1982, by a federal judge (*U.S.* v. *National Association of Broadcasters*[31]) finding that one of the code standards violated the Sherman Antitrust Act. Specifically, it was the NAB Television Code's multiple product standard forbidding the advertising of more than one product in a commercial lasting under sixty seconds.

The court found that:

> It is apparent from the fact of this standard that it has the effect of compelling some, perhaps many, advertisers to purchase more commercial time than their economic interest might dictate. In thus artificially increasing the demand for commercial time...the standard raises both the price of time and the revenues of the broadcasters, to the detriment of the users of the broadcast medium and the consumers of their products.

The NAB has argued that compliance with the Code is voluntary to each broadcaster and that it was not an agreement in restraint of trade. The court found that the Code "is not a mere set of advisory standards which subscribers may choose to ignore, but a contractual arrangement to which they are obligated to adhere." Essentially, the court reasoned that claiming that the code was voluntary was not a defense to a Sherman Act charge.

Following this case, the NAB agreed not to issue or enforce any rules that had been challenged by the government. After this decree was entered, NAB formally abandoned its Radio and Television Code Boards and halted all Code activities.

Network Standards

The demise of the NAB Code has placed even more importance on the network's own policing activities, and their advertising guidelines and standards. This is why every advertiser must have a good working knowledge of these guidelines and standards. Copies can be obtained from the following addresses:

- American Broadcasting Company, Department of Broadcast Standards & Practices, 1330 Avenue of the Americas, New York, NY 10019;
- CBS/Broadcast Group, CBS Inc., 51 West 52 Street, New York, NY 10019; and
- National Broadcasting Company, Inc., Broadcast Standards Department, 30 Rockefeller Plaza, New York, NY 10020.

It must be understood that each of the networks is separate and the standards adopted individually are unrelated to the other networks' standards. In fact, each network maintains individual practices specifically to avoid a Sherman Act violation. The result is that a commercial acceptable to one network may not be acceptable to another network.

Nevertheless, there are many areas of similarity among the networks' standards. This chapter discusses areas of concern to advertisers, and how each of the networks' standards deals with then.

Any questions regarding the networks' guidelines should be addressed to their clearance department for clarification.

Comparative Advertising Issues

All three networks accept comparative advertising.

CBS Guidelines

Comparative ads are acceptable, says CBS, if its claims are "truthful, fair and adequately substantiated."

NBC Guidelines

NBC will accept comparative ads if they meet the following guidelines:

- Competitors shall be fairly and properly identified.
- Advertisers shall refrain from disparaging or unfairly attacking competitors, competing products, services or

other industries through the use of representations or claims, direct or implied, that are false, deceptive, misleading or have the tendency to mislead.

- The identification must be for comparison purposes and not simply to upgrade by association.
- The advertising should compare related or similar properties or ingredients of the product, dimension to dimension, feature to feature, or wherever possible by a side-by-side demonstration.
- The property being compared must be significant in terms of value or usefulness of the product or service to the consumer.
- The difference in the properties being compared must be measurable and significant.
- Pricing comparisons may raise special problems that could mislead, rather than enlighten, viewers. For certain classifications of products, retail prices may be extremely volatile, may be fixed by the retailer rather than the product advertiser, and may not only differ from outlet to outlet but from week to week within the same outlet. Where these circumstances might apply, NBC will accept commercials containing price comparisons only on a clear showing that the comparative claims accurately, fairly and substantially reflect the actual price differentials at retail outlets throughout the broadcast area, and that these price differentials are not likely to change during the period the commercial is broadcast.
- When a commercial claim involves market relationships, other than price, which are also subject to fluctuation (such as but not limited to sales position or exclusivity), the substantiation for the claim will be considered valid only as long as the market conditions on which the claim is based continue to prevail.
- As with all other advertising, whenever necessary, NBC may require substantiation to be updated from time to

time, and may re-examine substantiation, where the need to do so is indicated as the result of a challenge or other developments.

ABC Guidelines

ABC's comparative advertising guidelines are more specific. Like CBS, ABC demands that such ads be "truthful and fair." In addition, many of ABC's standards are quite similar to NBC's:

- Competitive products or services must be accurately and clearly identified.
- False or misleading disparagement of competitive products or services shall not be used. Falsely claiming that a competitive product or service has little or no value (i.e., "ashcanning") is not permitted.
- Identification of a competitive product or service shall be for comparison purposes. Identification may not be used solely to upgrade the advertised product or service by associating it with a competitive product or service if such association creates a deceptive or misleading impression.
- Comparisons and demonstrations shall be based on specific differences between the products or services advertised, comparing similar or related properties or ingredients, dimension to dimension, feature to feature.
- When aspects of products or services are compared as to performance, they must be significant and meaningful to consumers.

ABC's standards provide specific guidance about commercials using superiority claims containing such words as "better" or "best." ABC also discusses subjective ("puffery") claims at length.

False, Misleading, Or Deceptive Ad Claims

The three major networks, of course, agree that all advertising broadcast on their networks must not violate the definitions of false, misleading, and unfair advertising as specified in Federal Trade Commission cases and decisions, as well as the definitions of unfair and deceptive under the Federal Trade Commission Act. According to CBS, "False, misleading or deceptive advertising claims are unacceptable." NBC will not accept in its ads "claims or representations, direct or implied, which are false or have the tendency to deceive, mislead or misrepresent." And ABC notes that all material broadcast on it facilities must comply with governmental laws and regulations. Clearly, a thorough knowledge of FTC law is important when working with the networks. See Chapters 2 and 3 for a discussion of FTC regulations.

Ads Directed At Children

Advertising to children poses sensitive compliance problems. Because of children's lower resistance to selling messages, it has long been recognized that more stringent safeguards are required for ads directed toward children.

Broadcasters also recognize their responsibility to protect children from certain kinds of child-directed advertising. Because of this, all three networks have fairly extensive guidelines for such advertising.

Before discussing these guidelines, however, it is first essential to define "child-directed ads."

NBC's Children's Advertising Guidelines, for example, apply to commercials:

- For products primarily used by children;
- Which are broadcast in or adjacent to children's programs; and
- Which are designed for or have the effect of primarily appealing to children.

ABC's guidelines apply to advertising that's "designed primarily for children 12 and under." CBS has a similar definition.

All three networks have similar concerns regarding ads

directed to children. For example, they all find the following to be unacceptable:

- "Extortive language;"
- "Exaggeration and distortion" of product attributes;
- "Frightening" commercials;
- Ads that use peer pressure to sell;
- Use of the words "only" or "just" in reference to price;
- Commercials for nonprescription medications and vitamins; and
- Commercials using celebrities or authority figures as endorsers.

However, there exist different approaches among the networks in some major areas. For instance, ABC flatly considers competitive and superiority claims in child-directed ads to be unacceptable. Both CBS and NBC, however, will consider such claims on a case-by-case basis.

In addition, all three networks have additional guidelines applicable to advertising for toys and food. Similar concerns guide all three broadcasters. For example, they all require that any view of a toy or how it works is one that a child must be "reasonably capable of reproducing" when using the toy.

Regarding food advertising directed to children, all three networks require such ads to "be in accord with the commonly accepted principles of good eating." In addition, all three networks have similar guidelines requiring at least one audio and one video showing a balanced meal in breakfast commercials. In addition, they all have guidelines for such foods that, essentially forbid suggestions of indiscriminate or immoderate use of such foods.

Both ABC and NBC have similar guidelines concerning children's premiums and offers:

- Forbid the use of fantasy, animation, stock footage, or real-life counterparts with such ads.
- Require the inclusion of such disclosures as price, offer dates, and separate purchase requirements in the audio

portion of the ad.
- Require simultaneous audio and video disclosure of conditions attached to "free" offers.

Ads For Professional Services

All three networks accept advertising for professional services.

CBS will accept "lawful advertising for accountants, chiropractors, dentists, lawyers, physicians, psychologists and other recognized and established professionals."

ABC permits such ads for "members of the medical and legal professions."

NBC does not accept ads "for professional services which do not comply with applicable law or ethical codes," which implies that those that do comply would be acceptable.

What standards do the networks apply? CBS won't accept ads containing "professional advice of the kind that, under sound practice, would be given only within the context of an established practitioner-client relationship."

ABC's Professional Advertising Guidelines are in two sections: Medical and Legal. These sections require that ads:
- Comply with federal, state, and local rules and ABC policy;
- Comply with stringent standards of taste and copy documentation;
- Not be aired when there's a substantial youthful audience;
- Avoid "hard-sell" techniques;
- Not play on viewers' fears or insecurities; and
- Must be approved by the network's New York Broadcast Standards and Practices department.

In addition, under the medical ad guidelines, words such as "safe" or "harmless" may not be used. And the legal ad guidelines list the elements of permissible content of the ad, including basic factual data such as name, address, and telephone number.

Contests/Sweepstakes Guidelines

All three networks allow the advertising of contests by advertisers, but forbid the advertising of lotteries (federal law forbids the broadcast of ads concerning lotteries) – except those conducted by the state. The FTC defines a lottery[32] as the combination of chance, consideration, and a prize. In addition, you should also be aware that the states have their own laws concerning sweepstakes and contests. See Chapter 9 for a detailed discussion of contests and lotteries.

However, before your proposed contest can air, you must submit detailed information to the network's Broadcast Standards and Practices Department for approval. CBS won't air such spots unless they've first been approved by their Commercial Clearance and Law Departments. It is highly recommended (and required by ABC) that you submit all such information before production of the commercial begins.

CBS has prepared a four-page "Contests/Sweepstakes Questionnaire" that seeks a wide variety of data about the proposed commercial, e.g., the final entry date, planned air dates for the spots, whether all prizes will be awarded, and any specific eligibility requirements. In addition to a completed contest questionnaire, CBS requires two copies of:

- Your contest's official rules;
- The actual entry blank and/or playing piece;
- A detailed statement of all prizes to be awarded; and
- Any applicable newspaper and magazine ads and point-of-sale displays.

A copy of the commercial itself must be submitted to CBS for review.

NBC also requires submission of a completed questionnaire, as well as a complete copy of the rules, an entry blank, promotional material and any published information about the contest, such as newspaper ads.

ABC needs to review all details of a proposed contest, an

entry blank or game card, complete rules, and list of prizes.

The benchmark for all three networks is complete disclosure of all pertinent information. Each network has devised its own method and guidelines to achieve that end. Please note, if your want to advertise a contest or sweepstakes on a network, it is critical that you contact the network's Broadcast Standards and Practices or Commercial Clearance Department as early in the planning stages as possible.

Alcoholic Beverage Advertising

The advertising of beer and wine is acceptable to all three networks, subject to federal and local laws. We look specifically at alcohol advertising in Chapter 13. Commercials for hard liquor (distilled spirits such as whiskey, vodka, and rum) are forbidden.

While wine and beer ads are acceptable, there are many network requirements advertisers must follow for such ads. For example, all three networks consider as unacceptable beer and wine commercials that:

- Encourage the use of such beverages by young people;
- Depict the use of such beverages in situations that may be hazardous or require a high level of alertness (e.g., driving); and
- Contain statements or implications concerning increased potency or alcoholic content (e.g., "extra strength").

Both NBC and ABC specifically forbid on-camera consumption of wine or beer. While CBS does not, apparently, specifically forbid such on-camera representations, it does forbid even implied references to excessive consumption and only accepts ads for beer and wine that are "presented tastefully." This means that ads featuring on-camera consumption will face a rigorous review by CBS's Clearance Department.

It should also be understood that alcoholic beverage advertising is undergoing much criticism. Groups such as Mothers Against Drunk Driving have launched a highly effective campaign against the problem of drunk driving. There have been proposals to forbid the use of celebrities and sports figures in wine and beer ads, and even suggestions to ban televised wine and beer ads altogether. Accordingly, standards that have prevailed for years may become obsolete overnight.

Multiple Product Commercials

Multiple product announcements contain advertising for two or more products. The now-defunct NAB Code, which was followed by the networks, forbid the advertisement of more than one product in a commercial lasting less than sixty seconds.

Current network guidelines allow multiple product announcements. CBS and NBC allow as many as two products to be advertised in a sixty-second commercial. Moreover, CBS will allow ads for more than one product in a thirty-second spot so long as the announcement is "integrated." That is, if "the products or services are related and interwoven within the framework of the announcement, and the voice(s), setting, background and continuity are used consistently throughout so as to appear to a viewer as a single message."

NBC will also allow multiple product announcements in commercials that are shorter than sixty seconds if the ad "presents the products or services of a primary and secondary advertiser."

ABC allows the integrated advertising of two or more products or services in thirty-second ads.

Unacceptable Products Or Services

There are certain products and services that the networks refuse to broadcast. NBC, for example, will not allow ads for the following products or services:

- Cigarettes;
- Hard liquor;
- Firearms, fireworks, ammunition, and other weapons;
- Presentations promoting a belief in the efficacy of

fortunetelling, astrology, phrenology, palm reading, numerology, mind reading, character reading, or other occult pursuits;
- Tip sheets and race track publications seeking to advertise for the purpose of giving odds or promoting betting;
- The sale of franchises;
- Matrimonial, escort, or dating services;
- Contraceptives;
- Adult or sex magazines;
- X-rated movies;
- Abortion services;
- Ethical drugs; and
- Anti-law enforcement devices.

ABC and CBS as well do not allow ads for cigarettes[33] or astrology, fortunetelling and similar services.

If you are aware that one network does not allow advertisements for your product, you should not assume that the other networks also follow suit. Pregnancy test kits are one example of this. CBS doesn't accept ads for such products. ABC does allow ads for these products if they are "restrained and inoffensive," avoid "graphic representations," and do not play on people's "fears and insecurities."

Substantiation

All three networks require prior substantiation of all material claims prior to airing:
- CBS requires that all claims must be "fully substantiated" before approval is granted;
- NBC requires "substantiation for all material claims and authentication of all demonstrations and testimonial statements;" and
- ABC requires that "when affirmative claims are made for a product or service, the advertiser must submit substantiation or documentation providing a reasonable basis for the claims." ABC's guidelines give many specifics

regarding the methodology of research done in substantiating claims.

It would be wise to contact the network's broadcast standards and practices or commercial clearance department before you conduct any claims research.

Other Areas Of Concern

There are many other areas covered in the various networks' guidelines. For instance, NBC has separate guidelines (in addition to those for advertising) that concern ads for children, health care products, personal products, alcohol products, products that control serum cholesterol, ads regarding weight reduction, gambling/lotteries, and games of chance. As we've discussed, it's wise to contact the network(s) while a commercial is still in the planning stage.

Challenge Procedure For Commercials Aired On The Networks

Any commercial aired on ABC, CBS, or NBC can be challenged. The challenges are handled by each network's Broadcast Standards and Practices Department. This is the same department that reviews all commercials before they are aired. ABC and NBC have written challenge procedures; CBS also has procedures, but they are not written.

Who May Challenge The Networks

Most challenges are made by competing advertisers. Because of this, the majority of commercials that are challenged involve comparative claims and are made by a competitor whose product is unfavorably compared in some manner to the advertiser's product. Additionally, challenges are filed by public officials and organizations, trade associations, consumer groups, disgruntled customers, and individual viewers.

Typically, challenges involve a comparative ad that distorts or exaggerates differences between competitive products or services, lacks adequate substantiation for the claims being made, or creates a false impression. Another issue arises if the ad implies a claim and, if so, whether that claim has been supported by the advertiser.

How To Use The Challenge Procedures

The networks require that a challenge be made in writing for review by the network's Broadcast Standards Department. ABC and CBS will send the complaint to the challenged advertiser for a response if they feel it has merit. NBC, on the other hand, will transmit the challenge under all circumstances. A challenge will not be pursued if it is considered to be without substance or involves advertising that has completed its schedule and will not be aired in the future. On the other hand, if a challenge is made to advertising that has not yet been approved, the substantive matters raised will generally be considered during the clearance process.

When a challenge is received, ABC generally requests a response within fourteen days. CBS requests a shorter response time. Yet, all three networks will accelerate the process if a matter is urgent or relatively simple, but will grant reasonable requests for extensions of time.

The networks maintain the confidentiality of the substantiation originally submitted by the challenged advertiser to support the claims made in the advertising. Advertisers, though, are encouraged by the networks to submit a response with supporting information.

The networks will generally permit a challenged commercial to continue to run until a response is received and the challenge is fully resolved. In extraordinary circumstances, approval may be withdrawn or airing may be suspended immediately after receipt of a challenge. And, in fact, some commercials are accepted "subject to challenge," which implies borderline approval. Under these circumstances either withdrawal of approval upon receipt of a responsible complaint or a short deadline for response to a challenge is in order. If approval is withdrawn or suspended, the advertiser may still proceed with the challenge and try to persuade the network to change its mind and reinstate the advertising.

Once the advertiser's response is received, the procedure used by each network is different. Later, after the challenge has been made each network may request a meeting with the challenger, advertiser, or both. The networks may encourage the parties to obtain a resolution from an acceptable third party mediator if they believe that they do not have the expertise necessary to make a judgment.

After receiving the initial challenge, ABC will review it, and will only pass it on to the challenger if rebuttal would be useful, such as if more information is needed or new arguments have been made.

NBC will direct the advertiser to respond straight to the challenger. The network will then make a decision after enough information has been gathered.

CBS's procedure is more formal. Each side generally is given a chance to respond to and rebut the other.

The Role Of The Network's Broadcast Standards Department

At the end of the process, the network's Broadcast Standards Department will make an independent decision as to how to resolve the challenge. The Broadcast Standards Department will generally allow a challenged commercial to run unless:

- It is voluntarily withdrawn by the challenged advertiser;
- The challenged advertiser refuses to cooperate with the challenge procedures; or
- A determination is made against the challenged advertiser by the network, by a third party to whom the matter has been referred, or by a government agency or an appropriate court.

Pros And Cons Of Network Challenge

In addition to filing a network challenge, the following actions are available:

- A complaint can be filed with the NAD or the FTC;
- Challenges can be made to individual stations or station groups that have aired a commercial;
- Suit can be filed against false comparative advertising under Section 43(a) of the Lanham Act; or
- Suit can be filed under state laws.

The following are some pros and cons of filing a network challenge:

- Network challenges are usually resolved more quickly than other types of complaints. They're less expensive to make and are more informal;
- A Lanham Act suit can produce the fastest result if the court is willing to grant a temporary restraining order or a preliminary injunction. However, there are difficult elements of proof. Discovery procedures are likely to be lengthy, time-consuming and expensive;
- Network challenges can be based on alleged violations of company policies, such as taste standards, as well as allegations of falsity or deceptiveness;
- The NAD will only consider complaints involving truth and accuracy;
- The National Advertising Review Board will consider complaints involving the taste, morality, or social responsibility of advertising in general;
- FTC will only consider alleged violations of the FTC Act; and
- Lanham Act suits must contain allegations that the plaintiff has been or is likely to be injured as a result of the false advertising.

Filing a challenge with the networks has its limitations. The networks do not have subpoena power or other discovery procedures; they must rely on the information voluntarily submitted by the parties. There is no hearing at which both sides appear and present arguments. Further, no monetary damages are allowed in such a challenge.

FOOD AND DRUG ADVERTISING

The FTC and FDA operate under a longstanding liaison agreement that divides the responsibilities between the two agencies. The FDA has primary responsibility for labeling, and the FTC has primary responsibility for advertising claims. Because of their shared jurisdiction, the two agencies work together.

Dietary Supplements

Nutritional Health Alliance, a nonprofit health association, brought a First Amendment challenge to FDA regulations that required FDA authorization in order to make health claims on labeling of dietary supplements. The regulations stated that the FDA would only allow health claims that were supported by scientific evidence. The regulations also set forth a timetable for submitting potential claims to the FDA for approval.

In *Nutritional Health Alliance* v. *Shalala*,[34] the court found that the First Amendment challenge was not appropriate because the plaintiff had not alleged any particular health claim that it wished to promote. Without a specific statement or claim to evaluate, the court could not determine if the proposed claim passed the first requirement of the *Central Hudson* test of truthful and nonmisleading speech.

The court stated:

> [W]ithout a specific proposed health claim to review, on evidence of record before the FDA, we cannot determine whether the "significant scientific agreement" requirement actually bars any truthful, non-misleading speech. In particular, we note that

> the parties have here argued at length over whether hypothetical health claims would, when combined with disclaimers of FDA acceptance, be misleading. That question seems to turn in part on whether the claims would confuse consumers with respect to possible side effects. And this issue is particularly difficult to resolve in the abstract and without a full record.

The court also determined that the FDA prior approval requirement for health claims in connection with dietary supplements was not an unconstitutional prior restraint of commercial speech. Because the prior restraint involved issues of health and safety, the court found that a 540-day prior restraint was acceptable. It granted a limited, but reasonable, time within which the FDA could evaluate the evidence of particular health claims. The waiting period also allowed for the development of a record on the matter so that a court could determine whether the regulated speech, was, in fact, truthful and nonmisleading.

FTC Guidelines

Due to the growth of the dietary supplement market, and to help ensure that advertising for dietary supplements is truthful and not misleading, the FTC released *A Guide for the Dietary Supplement Industry*. This guide describes the basic principles of the law and uses examples from the supplement industry to illustrate those principles. The guide should help resolve uncertainty about the connection between the FTC's advertising policy and the Food and Drug Administration's regulation of labeling under the Dietary Supplement and Health Education Act.

The guide explains how the FTC identifies advertising claims and how it evaluates the adequacy of the substantiation for those claims. It also covers consumer testimonials, expert endorsements, and adverting claims based on historical or traditional use of supplements.

Pending Legislation

On September 16, 1998, a bill (H.R. 4581) was introduced to provide that certain advertisements of dietary supplements not be considered unfair or deceptive. Under the bill, entitled "Dietary Supplement Fairness in Advertising Act," an advertisement for a dietary supplement that made claims about the usefulness or potential usefulness of a dietary supplement based on a study would not be considered to be an unfair method of competition or deceptive act or practice if the advertisement specifically identified the type of study conducted. For example, if the claims in the advertisement were based on an "in vitro" study, the ad would have to identify the study as an in vitro study and not a human study.

PAY-PER-CALL NUMBER RULE

The Federal Trade Commission's Pay-Per-Call Number Rule,[35] formerly known as the "900 Number Rule" enacted in 1993, took the guesswork out of these calls by requiring certain information in ads and preambles for pay-per-call number services. This is in addition to the protections under the Federal Communication Commission's own Pay-Per-Call Number Rule that governs telephone company practices.

Pay-Per-Call Number Ads

All print, radio, and television advertisements for pay-per-call number services must include:

1. The total cost of the call if there's a flat fee.

2. The per-minute rate if the call is charged by the minute, as well as any minimum charge. If the length of the program is known in advance, the ad also must state the total cost of the complete program.

3. The range of fees if there are different rates for different options. The ad also must state the initial cost of the call and any minimum charges.

4. The cost of any other pay-per-call number to which you may be transferred.

5. Any other fees the service might charge.

This information can't be hidden in small print: The cost of the call must be next to the pay-per-call number and printed in a size that's at least half the size of the pay-per-call number. In a television ad, an audio cost disclosure must also be made.

The Preamble

When a caller dials a pay-per-call number that costs more than $2, they should hear an introductory message or "preamble." They can't be charged for this message. It must briefly describe the service, the name of the company providing the service, and the cost of the call. It also must state that anyone under the age of 18 needs parental permission to complete the call. Once this information is provided, the caller must be given three seconds to hang up without incurring any charge.

Exceptions To The Rule

The Pay-Per-Call Number Rule does not apply if to a pre-existing contractual agreement with an information service.

The Rule also excludes calls charged to a credit card. However, the bills for such calls would be covered by the dispute resolution procedures of the Fair Credit Billing Act.

Children

The Rule essentially prohibits companies from promoting pay-per-call numbers to young children. Some companies have promoted pay-per-call numbers to children, encouraging them to pick up the phone to talk to a cartoon character. Under the FTC Pay-Per-Call Number Rule, companies are prohibited from advertising or offering pay-per-call services to children under age 12 unless the services are truly educational in nature.

Preambles for all pay-per-call number services must state that if the caller is under age 18, parental permission is required to make the call.

Recent Revisions

The Federal Trade Commission has announced a proposal to revise the Pay-Per-Call Rule, which was published in the Federal Register on October 30, 1998. The proposal is the result of developments since 1993 and is based in part on the Telecommunications Act of 1996, which granted the FTC authority to broaden the scope of the Pay-Per-Call Rule to include audiotext services that may be accessed through dialing patterns other than the 900 exchange.

Following is a breakdown of the proposed changes that relate to advertising disclosures:

The Rule, as amended, would continue to prescribe pay-per-call advertising disclosure standards. These disclosures are essential in order for consumers to understand the costs associated with the use of a pay-per-call number and any other pay-per-call service to which the caller might be transferred, and to prevent and prohibit certain unfair and deceptive practices in pay-per-call advertisements. Moreover, the disclosures are specifically required by the TDDRA.[36]

Proposed § 308.4(a)(1)(iii)(B) would require advertisements to disclose when the billing rate varies with time (i.e., variable time rate basis). This is consistent with the advertising disclosure[37] that is already required of the Rule when the billing rate varies with the particular options selected by the caller. The variable time rate disclosure, like the variable option rate disclosure, is necessary so that consumers can determine, before using an advertised pay-per-call service, how much the call will cost them.

The other new advertising disclosure requirement being proposed, a signal indicating the expiration of free time, is needed to ensure that consumers are left with no doubt as to when they must hang up to avoid being charged for a call. Sections 308.5(a) and (b) of the current Rule already require a signal or tone at the end of the free preamble or after any free time following the preamble. Similarly, § 308.6(b), as amended, would make clear that if any portion of a call is free, regardless when it occurs in the program, the vendor shall provide a clearly discernible signal or tone indicating the end of the free time.

TELEMARKETING SALES RULE

On August 16, 1994, President Clinton signed into law the Telemarketing and Consumer Fraud and Abuse Prevention Act (TCFAPA).[38] This law directs the FTC to develop rules that would prohibit deceptive and abusive telemarketing acts or practices.

The Telemarketing Sales Rule[39] grew out of the TCFAPA and relates directly to advertising and marketing practices.

Section 310.3 defines what consitiutes a deceptive telemarketing act or practice:

> (1) Before a customer pays for goods or services offered, failing to disclose, in a clear and conspicuous manner, the following material information:
>
> (i) The total costs to purchase, receive, or use, and the quantity of, any goods or services that are the subject of the sales offer;
>
> (ii) All material restrictions, limitations, or conditions to purchase, receive, or use the goods or services that are the subject of the sales offer;
>
> (iii) If the seller has a policy of not making refunds, cancellations, exchanges, or repurchases, a

statement informing the customer that this is the seller's policy; or, if the seller or telemarketer makes a representation about a refund, cancellation, exchange, or repurchase policy, a statement of all material terms and conditions of such policy;

(iv) In any prize promotion, the odds of being able to receive the prize, and if the odds are not calculable in advance, the factors used in calculating the odds; that no purchase or payment is required to win a prize or to participate in a prize promotion; and the no purchase/no payment method of participating in the prize promotion with either instructions on how to participate or an address or local or toll-free telephone number to which customers may write or call for information on how to participate; and

(v) All material costs or conditions to receive or redeem a prize that is the subject of the prize promotion;

(2) Misrepresenting, directly or by implication, any of the following material information:

(i) The total costs to purchase, receive, or use, and the quantity of, any goods or services that are the subject of a sales offer;

(ii) Any material restriction, limitation, or condition to purchase, receive, or use goods or services that are the subject of a sales offer;

(iii) Any material aspect of the performance, efficacy, nature, or central characteristics of goods or services that are the subject of a sales offer;

(iv) Any material aspect of the nature or terms of the seller's refund, cancellation, exchange, or repurchase policies;

(v) Any material aspect of a prize promotion

including, but not limited to, the odds of being able to receive a prize, the nature or value of a prize, or that a purchase or payment is required to win a prize or to participate in a prize promotion;

(vi) Any material aspect of an investment opportunity including, but not limited to, risk, liquidity, earnings potential, or profitability; or

(vii) A seller's or telemarketer's affiliation with, or endorsement by, any government or third-party organization;

(3) Obtaining or submitting for payment a check, draft, or other form of negotiable paper drawn on a person's checking, savings, share, or similar account, without that person's express verifiable authorization.

(4) Making a false or misleading statement to induce any person to pay for goods or services.

Section 310.6 discusses exemptions:

The following acts or practices are exempt from this Rule:

1. Telephone calls initiated by a customer in response to an advertisement through any media, other than direct mail solicitations; provided, however, that this exemption does not apply to calls initiated by a customer in response to an advertisement relating to investment opportunities, goods or services described in §§ 310.4(a)(2) or (3), or advertisements that guarantee or represent a high likelihood of success in obtaining or arranging for extensions of credit, if payment of a fee is required in advance of obtaining the extension of credit;

2. Telephone calls initiated by a customer in response to a direct mail solicitation that clearly,

conspicuously, and truthfully discloses all material information listed in § 310.3(a)(1) of this Rule for any item offered in the direct mail solicitation; provided, however, that this exemption does not apply to calls initiated by a customer in response to a direct mail solicitation relating to prize promotions, investment opportunities, goods or services described in §§ 310.4(a)(2) or (3), or direct mail solicitations that guarantee or represent a high likelihood of success in obtaining or arranging for extensions of credit, if payment of a fee is required in advance of obtaining the extension of credit.

---

[1] *Roe* v. *Wade,* 410 U.S. 113, 93 S.Ct. 705, 35 L.Ed. 2d 147 (1973).

[2] *Virginia State Board of Pharmacy* v. *Virginia Citizens Consumer Council, Inc.* 425 U.S. 748, 96 S.Ct. 1817, 48 L.Ed. 2d 346 (1976).

[3] *Central Hudson Gas & Electric Corp.* v. *Public Service Commission,* 447 U.S. 557, 100 S.Ct. 2343, 65 L.Ed. 2d 341 (1980).

[4] Games of Chance Act of 1948, Act No. 221, May 15, 1948, P.R. Laws Ann., Tit. 15, §71 (1972).

[5] *Posadas de Puerto Rico Associates* v. *Tourism Company of Puerto Rico,* 478 U.S. 328, 106 S.Ct. 2968, 92 L.Ed. 2d 266 (1986).

[6] *44 Liquormart, Inc.* v. *Rhode Island,* 517 U.S. 484, 116 S.Ct. 1495 (1996).

[7] *Greater New Orleans Broadcasting Assn.* v. *United States,* No. 94-30732, 1998 U.S. App. LEXIS 17608 (5th Cir., July 30, 1998).

[8] *Valley Broadcasting Co.* v. *United States,* 107 F.3d 1328 (9th Cir. 1997), cert. denied 140 L.Ed.2d 114, 118 S.Ct. 1050 (1998).

[9] *Rubin* v. *Coors Brewing Co.,* 115 S.Ct. 1585 (1995).

[10] *Bad Frog Brewery Inc.* v. *New York State Liquor Authority,* 134 F.3d 87 (2d Cir. 1998)

[11] *New York Magazine* v. *Metropolitan Transportation Authority,* 136 F.3d 123 (2d Cir. 1998).

[12] N.Y.Civ.Rights Law § 50 (McKinney 1997)

[13] N.Y.Civ.Rights Law § 51 (McKinney 1997)

[14] *Christ's Bride Ministries, Inc.* v. *Southeastern Pennsylvania Transportation Authority*, 148 F.3d 242 (3d Cir. 1998).

[15] *Tillman* v. *Miller*, 133 F.3d 1402 (1lth Cir. 1998).

[16] O.C.G.A. § 34-9-31.

[17] *Silverman* v. *Walkup*, No. 1:98-cv-208, 1998 U.S. Dist. LEXIS 15823 (E.D. Tenn., September 29, 1998).

[18] Tenn. Code Ann. § 63-4-114(5).

[19] 18 U.S.C. §474.

[20] 18 U.S.C. §504.

[21] *Time, Inc.* v. *Donald T. Regan, Secretary of the Treasury, et al*, 468 U.S. 641, 104 S.Ct. 3262, 82 L.Ed. 2d 487 (1981).

[22] *People ex rel. Maupin* v. *MacCabe*, 18 Colo. 186, 32 P. 280 (1893).

[23] *Bates* v. *State Bar of Arizona*, 433 U.S. 350, 97 S.Ct. 2691, 53 L.Ed. 2d 810 (1977).

[24] *Ohralik* v. *Ohio State Bar Association*, 436 U.S. 447, 98 S.Ct. 1912, 56 L.Ed. 2d 444 (1978).

[25] *In re R.M.J.*, 455 U.S. 191, 102 S.Ct. 929, 71 L.Ed. 2d 64 (1982).

[26] *Zauderer* v. *Office of Disciplinary Counsel of the Supreme Court of Ohio*, 471 U.S. 626, 105 S.Ct. 2265, 85 L.Ed. 2d 652 (1985).

[27] *Virginia State Board of Pharmacy* v. *Virginia Citizens Consumer Council, Inc.* 425 U.S. 748, 96 S.Ct. 1817, 48 L.Ed. 2d 346 (1976).

[28] Federal Election Campaign Act of 1971, 2 U.S.C. §431 (1982), P.L 92-225, 86 Stat. 3.

[29] *Members of City Council* v. *Taxpayers for Vincent*, 459 U.S. 1199, 105 S.Ct. 2265, 85 L.Ed. 2d 652 (1984).

[30] *Metromedia, Inc.* v. *San Diego*, 453 U.S. 490, 101 S.Ct. 2882, 69 L.Ed. 2d 800 (1981).

[31] *U.S.* v. *National Association of Broadcasters*, 395 U.S. 973, 89 S.Ct. 2126, 23 L.Ed. 2d 762 (1982).

[32] 16 C.F.R. 15.57.

[33] 15 U.S.C. 1335.

[34] *Nutritional Health Alliance* v. *Shalala*, 144 F.3d 220 (2d Cir. 1998).

[35] 16 CFR Part 308.

[36] § 201(a)(1), 15 U.S.C. § 5711(a)(1).

[37] § 308.4(a)(1)(iii).

[38] 15 U.S.C. 6101-6108.

[39] 16 CFR Part 310.

CHAPTER 13

ADVERTISING CONCERNS WITH ALCOHOL AND TOBACCO

> The most effective way of attacking vice is to expose it to public ridicule.
> —*Moliere*

A tall, powerful woman in a black dress marched into a saloon in Medicine Lodge, Kansas, one evening in 1890. For many days prior, she had stayed outside the saloon reading the Bible – intently praying for the close of the saloon. At the time, Kansas was a "dry" (no alcohol) state, but the law was not effectively enforced.

The woman had good reason for her vigil. Her drunkard husband had died shortly after their marriage, leaving her a lonely and angry widow.

When her prayers did not work, she turned to violence. The male patrons ran from the saloon, frantically stumbling, as she smashed the place to pieces with her axe. The well-placed blows struck by Carry A. Nation echoed far beyond the small town in Kansas. Around the beginning of the twentieth century there was increasing government regulation in many areas. Congress had begun to pass laws to protect the public from harmful foods and drugs and to conserve the nation's natural resources. The monopolies created by the Morgans and Rockefellers were beginning to be broken up. All this allowed the prohibition movement to catch fire as well.

It was not a new movement though. By the 1850's,

prohibition laws were in effect in thirteen states. The forces behind the movement had roots in religious fundamentalism and support from the Women's Christian Temperance Union, founded in Ohio in 1874. In many states, local counties had the ability to vote themselves dry. And many did in West Virginia, Maryland, Illinois, Georgia, Missouri, and Mississippi. But neighboring counties could still supply the product – and they did.

The temperance drive gained new momentum after 1900, however. Beer and whiskey sales had grown rapidly among the large numbers of Irish and German immigrants. And, as would be expected, this brought about an antiforeign ring to the cries for prohibition. And as women gained the vote for the first time, the temperance drive grew also.

The Committee of Fifty, formed in 1893 to study the "liquor problem," led the battle. The committee investigated the nation's poverty, crime, mental disease, and family decay and traced them all to alcohol use. They believed that national prohibition was the only answer because temperance – a supposed result of education and self-control – had not worked.

Congressmen and even president William McKinley had started to listen to the prohibitionists, and a nationwide law prohibiting alcohol sales went into effect. All this exasperated a man named Adolphus Busch, who personally took his argument to the president. Unfortunately, the president was a Methodist who as early as 1867 had been identified with "total abstinence."

If any single person energized the prohibition movement it was Adolphus Busch. He had the most visible profile, and his kingly demeanor and pro-German sentiments offended many Americans. Closely identified with his company, Anheuser-Busch Brewery, he became a prime target of the prohibitionists. Leading the industry as he did, he also had the most to lose; a long string of his descendants depended on beer for their livelihood. Adolphus had no intention of permitting the empire he had built for his children to be legislated out of existence. And it wasn't.

The stage was set when, nine days after his inauguration, president Roosevelt recommended that Congress officially sanction the return of beer. “I deem action at this time,” he said, “to be of the highest importance.” Congress – they were thirsty too – quickly approved a law authorizing the sale of beer with a 3.2 percent alcohol content. Moments after Roosevelt signed the beer bill, Busch sent a telegram praising him for his “wisdom and foresight” and for restoring to the “American people an old and time-honored industry.” Prohibition had survived for a little over thirteen years.

Prohibition ended on April 7, 1933, with a raucous, national street party. It was a coast-to-coast party unlike anything this country has ever seen. Not even the celebration that followed the armistice ending the Great War (now known as World War I) or Lindbergh's solo flight across the Atlantic compared. Beer was back, and Anheuser-Busch screamed the fact in full-page advertisements.

True to form, the company tried to hit upon a good advertising gimmick to celebrate beer's return. They picked a masterpiece. One that would become one of the most famous corporate symbols in the world – a team of high-stepping, solemnly majestic, champing at the bit, Clydesdale horses pulling a beautifully detailed red and yellow beer wagon assembled “for advertising purposes.”

The first truck out of the Busch plant had headed for the airport, carrying cases of the new Budweiser for president Roosevelt and the governor of New York. When the beer arrived in New York City and in Washington, D.C., it was loaded onto wagons drawn by teams of Clydesdales. In New York the horses caused a sensation as they clamored down Fifth Avenue and stopped at the Empire State building. In Washington, the team pulled up to a White House already deluged with similar shipments from other brewers.

Within 9 months, the required thirty-six states had ratified the twenty-first amendment, thereby repealing the eighteenth. But prohibition had taken a heavy toll on the nation's breweries. Of the 1,392 in operation in 1914, only 164 remained. For Anheuser-Busch the cost had been a staggering $34 million. But they had survived.

Today, however, efforts are being made to restrict, or even ban, the advertising of alcoholic beverages. These efforts are the result of a growing national concern over the serious problems of drunk driving and alcoholism. In this chapter we examine current restrictions on the advertising of both alcoholic beverages and tobacco products (another hot issue). We'll examine both state and federal levels, as well as voluntary controls, warning labels, the Surgeon General's efforts, and products liability issues.

THE ADVERTISING OF ALCOHOL

Significant Environmental Changes

There are three significant areas that have focused on alcohol abuse and its relation to advertising. State and federal governments may well look toward restrictions on the promotional practices used by alcoholic beverage marketers.

Alcohol Environment

There is America's new sobriety to consider, a reflection of the aging baby boomers' preoccupation with looking better and living longer. Baby boomers have stopped smoking. They exercise. They have begun to moderate or stop their use of alcohol.

We can see this trend in the annual increase in sales of seltzer and water products such as Perrier and Evian by 15 percent. There's an annual gain in sales of soft drinks, especially diet products and fruit juice by 5 percent.

These gains are being made at the expense of alcoholic beverage sales. Alcohol consumption has been declining steadily since 1982. In 1978, 71 percent of the American public was classified as drinkers. Today, that has dropped to 65 percent.

Marketing Environment

These societal changes in alcoholic beverage consumption have caused the development of new marketing strategies to cultivate the major market left to alcohol manufacturers – the twenty-one- to twenty-five-year-old market.

The creation of wine coolers and Peach Schnapps have been specifically targeted to the younger market. We have seen Bruce Willis of *Moonlighting* and *Die Hard* fame advertise Seagram's coolers. We have seen the Coors Light "Silver Bullet" campaign featuring animated characters. We have seen a repositioning of several brands that now cater to the youth market. A few years ago, Bud Light was introduced with the theme "bring out your best," and featured spokesdog Spuds MacKenzie. And Michelob produced a campaign that appealed to the youth market by using rock music and by showing rock stars including Eric Clapton, Phil Collins, and Steve Winwood.

The assault on the youth market runs in conflict with the consumer movement that advocates reduced alcohol use, and abuse, by youth.

Consumer Movement

The consumer anti-alcohol movement has been led by Mothers Against Drunk Driving and Students Against Drunk Driving, which have focused on better education about responsible drinking, training for servers in restaurants and bars, and stiffer penalties for drunk driving offenses.

Also, women's and medical groups are concerned that alcohol advertising may lead pregnant women to drink. Such drinking can lead to fetal alcohol syndrome in unborn children.

AREAS OF LAW CONCERNING ALCOHOL

Products Liability

Products liability lawsuits are coming to court in which alcohol is blamed for causing birth defects. The first such case, which was tried in a Seattle court in May 1980, involved Candace Thorp, a thirty-nine-year-old alcoholic, who sought $4 million in damages to support her four-year-old son. The child will require lifetime assistance for mental retardation and physical deformity, which were attributed to fetal alcohol syndrome. Thorp drank up to a half a fifth of Jim Beam bourbon a day while pregnant. She claimed in court that she would have quit if she had been warned about the risks that drinking posed for her baby.

Witnesses for Jim Beam Brands testified that Mrs. Thorp was repeatedly warned by relatives and friends about the dangers of drinking alcohol while pregnant, and that she and other alcoholics would not have heeded a label warning.

The jury reasoned that "there is overwhelming evidence that Candace Thorp would not have followed a label," even if there had been one on the bottle.

This case, of course, did not end the product's liability issue as it related to alcohol advertising.

Alcohol Warning Labels

Both public pressure and the fear of product's liability lawsuits caused the alcoholic beverage industry in 1988 to allow an alcohol warning label bill to pass Congress. Such warning labels have been required to appear in "a conspicuous and prominent place" on every container of beer, wine, and liquor sold in the United States since November l989. Congress prescribes the exact wording of the warning, which must read:

> GOVERNMENT WARNING: (1) According to the Surgeon General, women should not drink

alcoholic beverages during pregnancy because of the risk of birth defects, (2) Consumption of alcoholic beverages impairs your ability to drive a car or operate machinery, and may cause health problems.

The warnings may be placed on the back of the bottle, may be printed vertically, or may appear in any manner that the industry chooses.

Surgeon General's Workshop

When the 100th Congress asked U.S. Surgeon General C. Everett Koop to declare drunk driving a national crisis, he responded by organizing a workshop on drunk driving in December 1988. There were seven major advertising recommendations that emerged from the workshop's advertising and marketing panel. The panel's four major recommendations were directed to reducing the impact of alcohol beverage appeal to youth. These four recommendations are:

- Elimination of alcohol advertising and promotion on college campuses where a high proportion of the audience reached is under the legal drinking age;
- Elimination of alcohol advertising, promotion, and sponsorship of public events, such as musical concerts and athletic contests where the majority of the anticipated audience is under the legal drinking age;
- Elimination in alcohol advertising and promotion of the use of celebrities who have a strong appeal to youth; and
- Elimination of official sponsorship of athletic events, e.g., the Olympics, by the alcohol beverage industry.

Voluntary Efforts

In addition to organized action by government agencies and consumer groups, a number of individuals and organizations have taken steps to restrict alcoholic beverage advertising.

The Miller Brewing Company was forced to pull a March, 1989 ad entitled "Beachin' Times" that was a parody of spring break activities by college students. There were protests by students at several schools, including the University of Wisconsin and the University of Iowa. The University of Michigan's *Michigan Daily* and other college publications refused to run the ad. The University of Wisconsin at Madison passed a resolution calling for a boycott of Miller products unless the ad was withdrawn, and the company apologized. Student groups criticized the ad as depicting women in an insulting way (they were shown as scantily dressed "babes") and for including an account of a student vacationer's day: a twenty-four hour drinking marathon that included only two five-minute breaks for returning empties.

Even athletes have begun to speak out against the association between sports and alcohol beverage consumption. Houston Astros' first baseman Glenn Davis objected to the toast offered by local radio and television broadcasters for one of their sponsors after he, or one of his teammates, hit a home run: "Glenn Davis, this Bud's for you." Davis, who does not drink and is active in efforts to discourage youngsters from drinking, has objected to his implied endorsement of alcoholic beverages. As a result of his protest, Davis' name will no longer be used in the commercials.

Alcoholic beverage advertising is likely to be a point of controversy for many years. Not only will government officials and consumer advocates continue to press for restrictions, but private individuals and associations will seek changes as well.

FEDERAL REGULATION

As for the federal government, the Federal Communications Commission does not forbid the advertising of alcoholic beverages in broadcast media. On the other hand, the Federal Trade Commission and the Bureau of Alcohol, Tobacco and Firearms have joint authority over the advertising of alcoholic beverages.

FTC's Role In Alcohol Advertising

In September 1999, the FTC issued a Review of Industry Efforts to Avoid Promoting Alcohol to Underage Consumers. What follows is the complete text of that report.

EXECUTIVE SUMMARY

This report responds to a recent request from the Congressional Committees on Appropriations that the FTC examine the effectiveness of the alcohol industry's voluntary guidelines for advertising and marketing to underage audiences. The report provides company-specific information, supplied in response to orders by the Commission, only in an aggregate or anonymous fashion.

Underage alcohol use is a significant national concern. Last year, a third of twelfth graders reported binge drinking. Moreover, while underage alcohol use levels decreased from about 1980 to 1993, those decreases have stopped and some important markers of underage alcohol use appear to be on the rise. Finding ways to deter alcohol use by those under 21 is a constant challenge for the beverage alcohol industry – including beer, wine and distilled spirits producers – as well as for government agencies and consumer organizations.

One important industry initiative involves voluntary self-regulatory codes intended to prevent alcohol advertising and marketing that appeal to underage consumers. Self-regulation is a realistic, responsive and responsible approach to many of the issues raised by underage drinking. It can deal quickly and flexibly with a wide range of advertising issues and brings the accumulated experience and judgment of an industry to bear without the rigidity of government regulation. The Commission regards self-regulation as particularly suitable in this area, where government restriction – especially if it involves partial or total advertising bans – raises First Amendment issues.

The industry presently seeks to minimize the extent to

which underage consumers are exposed to and attracted by alcohol advertising by employing self-regulatory codes. Information supplied by trade associations and eight key industry members leads the Commission to conclude that for the most part, members of the industry comply with the current standards set by the voluntary advertising codes, which prohibit blatant appeals to young audiences and advertising in venues where most of the audience is under the legal drinking age. In addition, many individual companies follow their own internal standards that exceed code requirements when they are deciding what their ads should say and where they should be placed.

While the current codes provide important protections, improvements are needed both in code standards and implementation to ensure that the goals of the industry codes are met. The Commission recommends the following:

Third-Party Review: The industry should create independent external review boards with responsibility and authority to address complaints from the public or other industry members. This fundamental change would demonstrate to those in the industry – as well as to consumers – that code compliance is a high priority and that all members are held to reasonably consistent standards. Currently, none of the codes provides for an independent assessment of the merits of a complaint or follow-up procedures for complaint resolution.

Ad Placement: The industry should raise the current standard that permits advertising placement in media where just over 50 percent of the audience is 21 or older, and members should be able to demonstrate their compliance with that higher standard. Because the 50 percent standard permits alcohol advertising to reach large numbers of underage consumers, some companies already have raised their own internal placement standards, prohibiting ads where as little as 25 percent of the audience is underage.

Best Practices: Several industry members have put into

place practices that reduce the likelihood that their advertising and marketing will reach – and appeal to – underage consumers. All industry members should adopt and build upon these "best practices," as follows:

• For ad placement: Bar placement on TV series and in other media with the largest underage audiences, and conduct regular audits of previous placements.

• For ad content: Prohibit ads with substantial underage appeal, even if they also appeal to adults, or target ads to persons 25 and older.

• For product placement in movies and TV: Restrict the placement of alcohol products for which some form of payment is made to "R" and "NC-17" rated films (or, if unrated, to films with similarly mature themes) and apply the standards for placing traditional advertising to product placement on TV.

• For online advertising: Use available mechanisms to block underage access and avoid content that would attract underage consumers.

• For college marketing: Curb on-campus and spring break sponsorships and advertising.

The beverage alcohol industry has an opportunity to make its self-regulatory program more effective and credible. By strengthening enforcement mechanisms, raising th standard for the legal-age audience for ads beyond the 50 percent level, and adopting the best prevailing industry practices, the industry can improve compliance without sacrificing legitimate advertising and marketing activities.

I. Introduction

"The conferees are aware of concerns about the impact of alcohol advertising on underage drinking, and understand that the FTC is engaged in the ongoing monitoring of the advertising and marketing practices of manufacturers of beverage alcohol. The conferees expect the FTC to emphasize these activities, investigate when problematic practices are discovered, encourage the development of effective voluntary advertising codes, and report their findings back to the Committees on Appropriations."

This report, which responds to the Committees' request, is based on "special reports filed by eight key industry members whose budgets, taken together, account for a estimated 80 percent of the alcohol advertising in traditional media. It also is based on discussions with industry trade associations about their self-regulator efforts, a staff review of alcohol company web sites, and information provided by interested government and consumer groups. As the companies were advised at the onset, in order to address confidentiality concerns the information provided by the companies is presented only in an aggregate or anonymous fashion.

The report discusses the benefits of self-regulation in general, describes key provisions of the alcohol industry's voluntary advertising codes, considers those areas where self-regulation is successful and where it falls short, and recommends steps the industry could take to strengthen member compliance with the codes. The report evaluates the application of the industry codes to the placement and content of advertising, as well as product placement, online advertising, and college marketing.

II. Advertising Self-regulation

The Benefits of Self-Regulation

For decades, the FTC has recognized the important role that effective self-regulation can play and has worked with many industry groups to develop sound self-regulatory initiatives. These programs complement the Commission's law enforcement efforts to stop "unfair or deceptive acts or practices." The net effect is greater consumer protection in the marketplace.

Well-constructed industry self-regulatory efforts offer several advantages over government regulation or legislation. Self-regulation often can be more prompt, flexible, and effective than government regulation. It can permit application of the accumulated judgment and experience of an industry to issues that are sometimes difficult for the government to define with bright line rules. With respect to advertising practices, self-regulation is an appropriate mechanism because many forms of government intervention raise First Amendment concerns.

One especially effective model of self-regulation that has stood the test of time is the advertising industry's program. Operating since 1971, the National Advertising Division (NAD) of the Council of Better Business Bureaus expeditiously investigates complaints about the truthfulness of advertising made by consumers or competitors.

An advertiser that disagrees with the NAD's conclusion may appeal to the National Advertising Review Board (NARB), which includes members from inside and outside the industry.

Compliance with the NAD/NARB process is voluntary. Remarkably, NAD has handled over 3,500 cases since 1971, and in virtually all cases advertising found to be misleading has been discontinued or modified voluntarily. When an advertiser refuses to abide by a NAD decision, the matter often is referred to the FTC or another law enforcement agency. When appropriate, the FTC takes enforcement action.

Another aspect of this self-regulatory system is especially striking: NAD and NARB decisions are made public. This enhances the credibility of the program and provides valuable information to consumers and other industry members.

Self-Regulation in the Alcohol Industry

Each year the alcohol industry spends more than a billion dollars on television, radio, print, and outdoor advertising. Self-regulation plays an important role in the alcohol industry's overall efforts to address concerns that alcohol advertising not be directed to an underage audience. At the heart of this effort are three trade associations. The Beer Institute represents the interests of more than 200 brewers who produce more than 90 percent of the beer brewed in America as well as the importers of a majority of the imported beer consumed here. The Distilled Spirits Council of the United States (DISCUS) represents most of the major U.S. distilled spirits marketers; its members produce over 85 percent of the distilled spirits sold in America. The Wine Institute represents over 300 California vintners; its members market over 75 percent of the wine sold in America and most of the American wines sold abroad.

All three associations have voluntary advertising codes, with similar provisions about the placement and content of ads designed to prevent the marketing of alcohol to underage consumers. In addition, some beverage alcohol companies have their own self-regulatory guidelines. In most cases, the company guides parallel those of the trade associations, although some address specific issues such as marketing at college "spring break" locations. The codes are widely disseminated throughout the industry to promote awareness and compliance.

III. Alcohol Industry Codes

While many factors may influence an underage person's drinking decisions, including among other things parents, peers and the media, there is reason to believe that advertising also plays a role. Thus, the self-regulatory codes of the beverage alcohol industry provide that alcohol advertising and marketing efforts should not be directed to an audience that is primarily underage. Because substantial numbers of youngsters inevitably are exposed to alcohol advertising, the codes also provide that the content of the ads should not appeal primarily to an underage audience.

Advertising Placement

Although each code expresses the concept differently, industry members interpret code placement provisions to require that more than 50 percent of the audience for their advertising be over 21. The Beer Code prohibits placing ads in media where "most of the audience" is expected to be below the legal drinking age. The Spirits Code prohibits advertising from being placed in "any communication intended to appeal primarily" to individuals below the legal purchase age. The Wine Code specifies that wine advertising should not appear in programs or media "specifically oriented" to consumers below the legal drinking age.

To facilitate compliance, the Beer Code requires that members use audience composition data that reflect the percentage of viewers over the legal purchase age and that the data be updated and reviewed every six months. The Wine and Spirits Codes do not contain similar requirements. However, whether or not the codes expressly require it, audience composition data are the only effective measure of compliance with the code placement provisions. These data are readily available from independent monitoring services.

Advertising Content

The content provisions of the codes complement the placement restrictions, providing an important level of protection for consumers below the legal drinking age who may be exposed to alcohol advertising. For example, the Beer and Spirits Codes prohibit advertisers from using advertising content that is "intended to appeal primarily" to underage consumers. According to the Beer Code, "primary appeal" is defined as "special attractiveness to such persons above and beyond the general attractiveness it has for persons above the legal purchase age, including young adults above the legal purchase age." The Wine Code prohibits ads that have "particular appeal" to those under 21.

The special reports filed with the FTC indicate that members of the distilled spirits and wine industries interpret the content provisions of their codes the same way that members of the beer industry interpret the Beer Code. Additionally, they indicate that intent need not be proven to demonstrate a violation, despite the codes' references to intent.

The codes expressly prohibit the use of certain characters or people in alcohol ads: actors under 25; children; Santa Claus ; actors who appear to be under 21; actors who appear to be under 25; and sports celebrities or "current or traditional heroes of the young." At the same time, cartoon characters or similar images are allowed in ads as long as:

- Their use is not "intended to appeal primarily" to people below the legal drinking age;
- They are not "popular predominantly with children;" or
- They are not "specifically associated with or directed toward" those below the legal drinking age.

Product Placement

The practice of making alcohol products, logos, and signage available to producers so that a company's product will be featured in a television program, film, or music video is common across the alcohol industry. In 1997-98, the eight reporting companies made product placements in 233 motion pictures and in one or more episodes of 181 different TV series. Product placement can have significant promotional value for the alcohol company. Producers, in turn, rely on product placements to give their work a more authentic look. In some instances, they may receive some form of consideration for using the product, in the form of direct payment, goods, or assistance with promotion. Additionally, many industry members who participate in this practice retain agents or staff internal divisions specifically responsible for making product placements. While none of the codes specifically addresses product placement, the beverage alcohol associations indicate that the standard placement and content provisions of the codes apply to the placement of alcohol products in films and TV programs.

Online Advertising

Members of the beverage alcohol industry have created over 100 commercial web sites to promote their products. The content of these sites varies widely, from little more than basic brand information to chat rooms, "virtual bars," drink recipes, games, contests, and merchandise catalogues. A recent marketing report indicated that beer and wine companies spent approximately $1 million on Internet advertising in 1997. One major brand's web site was reported to be receiving 180,000 visitors per month, while another company report noted that its web site received over 21 million hits between 1995 and early 1997.

Although online advertising can be an effective and legal way to reach adults, many alcohol sites have been criticized because they are easily accessible by underage consumers and because some of their content likely is attractive to teens. The Wine Institute's code does not address online advertising, but the Beer Institute in 1997 and DISCUS in 1998 modified their codes to:

- Require advertisers to include on their web sites "reminders" that "brewer products are intended only for those of legal purchase age" or "a reminder of the legal purchase age;"
- Offer beverage alcohol web site addresses to operators of parental control software companies (the Spirits Code also promises to give web site information to parents who request it); and
- Clarify that the marketing provisions of the codes apply to web sites, including code provisions prohibiting advertising content that is "intended to appeal primarily" or is "particularly attractive" to kids.

College Marketing

An FTC staff investigation into the advertising and

marketing of alcoholic beverages on campuses 10 years ago revealed that some firms in the industry were directing advertising and promotions to an on-campus audience that may have been largely underage. In response to the inquiry, many members of the industry adopted voluntary guidelines that directly address alcohol promotions on campus and at "spring break" destinations.

DISCUS revised its code in 1995 to prohibit many of the college marketing practices that had been criticized – including advertising on campuses and in college newspapers – and to restrict other forms of campus marketing activities to licensed retail establishments. The Beer Institute revised its code in 1992 to continue to allow its members to advertise on college campuses and at college-sponsored events "only when permitted by appropriate college policy." The Wine Institute has not revised its code to address on-campus marketing practices, although according to the Institute, its code's placement provisions apply to marketing practices in all settings.

IV. Code Implementation And Best Practices

A strong and visible program of self-regulation is the most responsive and responsible approach to many of the concerns associated with alcohol beverage advertising and underage consumers. Meaningful industry self-regulatory programs can deal quickly and flexibly with a broad range of advertising issues. They can resolve difficult questions, such as whether the content of a certain ad may be unduly attractive to children, without raising the constitutional issues that less flexible government regulation might raise.

In the last 10 years, the beverage alcohol industry has responded voluntarily to FTC staff investigations with changes to its codes. In addition to the changes addressing college marketing described above, examples of voluntary industry responses to problematic practices include:

1. Withdrawing ads from television programs with majority

underage audiences: In the mid-1990's, FTC staff investigated the placement of beer ads on cable network programming that had majority underage audiences. The companies withdrew the ads from the programming at issue, and the Beer Institute adopted the requirement that demographic data be reviewed periodically to reduce the likelihood that the problem would recur.

2. Applying code protections to Internet ads: In 1997, FTC staff reviewed alcohol web sites, which some industry observers believed were potentially attractive to minors. At the time, it was unclear whether web sites were covered by the industry advertising codes. Responding to these concerns, the Beer Institute and DISCUS modified their codes to clarify that they applied to advertising online.

Although the current codes provide many important protections, some provisions could be strengthened to better ensure that alcohol advertising is not directed to underage consumers. Additionally, the special reports submitted to the FTC by the alcohol companies demonstrate that some industry members do not fully comply with the codes' provisions. Several companies, however, have adopted practices – "best practices" – that, if implemented industry-wide, would make the codes more effective and more credible. A discussion of the limitations in the code provisions and implementation and the companies' strategies to address them follows.

Advertising Placement

The special reports submitted to the FTC by the eight alcohol companies reflect mixed compliance with the codes' requirement that alcohol ads be placed only in media where more than 50 percent of the audience is of legal purchase age. Half of the companies were able to show that nearly all of their ads were shown to a majority legal-age audience. Two companies, however, entirely failed to obtain the age demographic data needed to evaluate their code compliance. Moreover, two other companies' data showed weeks when a large portion of ads (for one, 25 percent of its TV ads, for another, 11 percent of its radio ads) were shown to a majority underage audience.

Only 30 percent of the U.S. population is under the age of 21, and only ten percent is age 11 to 17. The 50 percent standard, therefore, permits placement of ads on programs where the underage audience far exceeds its representation in the population. Given this age composition of the population, large numbers of underage consumers can be exposed to alcohol ads even though a majority of the audience is of legal age. For example, the special reports indicate that alcohol ads have been placed on at least three of the 15 television shows reported to have the largest teen audiences. These shows may be among the best ways to reach teens, although they often have a majority legal-age audience.

Additionally, limitations in the available audience composition data can hinder companies' ability to determine how many underage persons are in the audience for an ad. For some media, the available demographic information does not measure the youngest portion of the audience. Radio audience demographics do not measure listeners under 12, who account for 17 percent of the population, and most magazine audience demographics do not measure those under 18, who account for 26 percent of the population. As a result, the underage audience may be larger than the demographics information reveals.

Best Practices: The special reports filed with the Commission indicate that some individual beverage alcohol companies have adopted ad placement policies that go beyond minimum code requirements in order to minimize underage exposure to their ads.

First, several companies have raised the standard for ad placement. Instead of adhering to the 50 percent requirement, these companies require a 60 to 70 percent legal-age audience for print media, a 55 to 60 percent legal-age audience for radio, and a 70 to 75 percent legal-age audience for television placements. This practice has two benefits: it provides a margin to compensate for limitations in audience composition data; and it minimizes the number of underage consumers reached by the alcohol advertising without unduly interfering with the advertiser's ability to reach a legal-age audience.

Second, some companies regularly review their past ad placements – as often as each quarter – and change their plans to avoid media that may not meet the 50 percent standard. Although these companies occasionally run ads in majority underage venues, their after-the-fact review procedures ensure quick discovery and correction. For example, periodic audits are useful in radio advertising, where changes in format and school season can result in sudden, substantial increases in underage audience composition.

Third, some alcohol advertisers maintain "no buy" lists of programs and magazines that are popular with underage audiences. Company lists vary but typically include animated, family, or teen-theme television programs and magazines – in short, vehicles that are likely to be effective ways to reach underage consumers.

Advertising Content

Since substantial underage exposure comes with any practical placement standard, compliance with the codes' content provisions is critical. The codes' content standards appear to require that companies contrast an ad's appeal to adults with its appeal to minors, and reject only those campaigns that are more appealing to those under the legal drinking age.

It is clear that industry makes a significant effort to comply with the codes' content standards. Alcohol companies rely on internal marketing and legal personnel, or ad agencies, to identify ad copy that might appeal primarily to children. The special reports document many instances where content was rejected or revised out of concern that it might have been especially attractive to children. The reports also show that most companies conduct consumer research, on persons 21 and over, to determine the effectiveness of proposed ad campaigns with the target audience. Companies often (but not always) will modify or reject a campaign if a research participant volunteers the opinion that an ad is "juvenile" or would attract those under 21.

The codes' standards permit advertising that has substantial appeal to teenagers, as long as it is equally appealing to audiences over 21. The special reports show that the reporting companies target 21 year olds for some brands – in fact, some companies' internal marketing documents discuss the importance of attracting new drinkers, noting that many consumers continue to drink, at least occasionally, the brands with which they started. Yet, the advertising campaigns targeted to 21 year olds also are likely to appeal to those under 21. Indeed, existing research and media reports have raised the question of whether several current or recent ad campaigns have high appeal to teens and even young children.

Although the codes prohibit marketing that promotes irresponsible drinking, documents provided with the company reports suggest that campaigns for a few of the brands targeted to 21 year olds may not comply with these provisions. Some marketing materials alert consumers to the usefulness of a brand for heavy drinking occasions – for example, promoting new or existing drinking rituals, or using ad language designed to communicate subtly the potency of the product. One company's market planning report noted that the top objective of 21 to 26-year-old drinkers was "to get wild, blitzed and be crazy."

Best Practices: Some companies have adopted strategies that reduce the likelihood that an ad will have substantial appeal to underage consumers. One company avoids ad content with substantial appeal to underage, by rejecting ad content – an idea, song or character – that would be effective to promote a child – or teen-targeted product.

Additionally, some companies limit the "spillover" appeal to a younger audience by setting the target audience for certain brands at age 25. They use campaign themes that are less likely to appeal to those under 21 by avoiding, for example, campaigns emphasizing a "wild" party theme. This practice also is consistent with code provisions that promote the responsible use of alcohol.

Product Placement

Companies state that they consider code standards when making product placements, and it is clear that they deny requests to place alcohol products in films and TV programs that show underage drinking. Still, alcohol product placement has occurred in "PG" and "PG-13" films with significant appeal to teens and children (including films with animal and "coming-of-age" themes); in films for which the advertiser knew that the primary target market included a sizeable underage market; and on eight of the 15 TV shows most popular with teens.

Best Practices: A few companies have taken steps to reduce the likelihood that a substantial underage audience will see their products promoted in movies and on television. They restrict product placements to movies that are "R" rated (or, if unrated, those with similarly mature themes) and prohibit placements in films and programs in which an underage person is a primary character. One company also prohibits promotional placements in movies and shows that deal strictly with college life.

Online Advertising

The Internet presents a special challenge for industry members in their efforts to prevent alcohol advertising and marketing to minors. Children under 18 represent a large and rapidly growing segment of the online community. One recent survey reported 18.5 million children online, including 9.5 million teens between 13 and 17.

Most industry members comply with the provisions of the

two codes (Beer and Spirits) that govern online alcohol advertising. A Commission staff review of 30 industry web sites revealed that most post the age reminders required by the codes. The Beer Institute and DISCUS also provide the web site addresses of their members to companies that produce parental control software, and many major Internet Service

Providers (ISP's) – AOL, ATT WorldNet, Bell Atlantic, Prodigy, and CompuServe – offer filtering programs to parents that can block access to commercial alcohol web sites. Currently, however, only one-third of parents use filtering software.

There are, of course, no foolproof measures to prevent underage access to inappropriate web sites. Companies therefore need to give special attention not only to restricting access, but to ensuring that web site content is not attractive to underage consumers.

Many alcohol web sites feature one or more promotional techniques – contests, games, cartoon and cartoon-like characters, chat rooms and bulletin boards – that underage visitors may find attractive and that alcohol companies generally do not use in other forms of advertising.

Best Practices: Some alcohol companies have taken extra steps in an attempt to address concerns about underage use of online alcohol sites. First, after the industry modified its codes, several companies eliminated or reduced web site content that underage consumers might have found attractive. For example, they dropped bulletin boards and/or chat rooms, often after inappropriate messages were posted.

Second, several companies make efforts to restrict underage access. Five of the 30 sites reviewed by the Commission staff seek to block younger consumers by requiring visitors to enter their age and denying access to those who enter an age under 21.

One company reported that nearly 10,000 visitors received a "virtual bounce" from its web site after entering an age under 21. Another company plans to ask for age information at various places on its web site and deny access to anyone who does not enter the same age each time.

Finally, a few sites supplement their beverage promotional efforts with messages discouraging underage and irresponsible drinking. These sites include many of the same materials that the industry members use in their responsibility campaigns, as well as links to other web sites that carry messages about responsible drinking.

College Marketing

Advertising on campuses remains a source of concern given the presence of a significant underage audience on most campuses and the high incidence of abusive college drinking. Company sponsorship of teams and athletic events – allowed under the Beer Code if permitted by the college – continues, producing substantial revenue for colleges and universities. Nonetheless, the number of campuses that restrict on-campus alcohol beverage advertising is growing. In a recent survey of 300 campuses, 72 percent said they prohibit on-campus alcohol advertising and 62 percent specifically prohibit industry sponsorship of athletic events. In the last year, the U.S. Congress, the U.S. Department of Health and Human Services, and others have called for an end to many or all of these arrangements.

Ads by local retail establishments are not subject to the codes or the direct control of the alcohol companies, but they can damage industry efforts to foster responsible drinking. One bar ad placed recently in a college paper invited customers to "Walk Over. Crawl Back." According to a 1997 survey, three-quarters of campus newspapers accept advertising from off-campus bars and other licensed retail establishments.

Best Practices: DISCUS and a growing number of colleges and universities prohibit marketing activities on campus, and most companies have stopped sponsoring special spring break activities (such as beach promotions and outdoor concerts) although the codes do not mandate it. These companies restrict their activities to bars and other licensed retail establishments where it is expected that most of the audience will be over the legal purchase age. In addition, some industry members are encouraging local licensed establishments to advertise responsibly and not promote excessive drinking.

V. Code Enforcement: The Need For Independent Review

The company special reports make clear that most industry members seek to comply with current code requirements. They instruct those that prepare and place the ads, design the web pages, and handle the product placements, that it is important to comply with the code provisions. Despite their efforts, however, compliance is not universal. Indeed, in the preparation of this report, a number of instances of code violations were uncovered.

Experience in other industries suggests that independent mechanisms for evaluating compliance, particularly in the face of complaints from the public or competitors, ensure that industry members are held to reasonably consistent standards. The beverage alcohol industry associations would do well to put external enforcement procedures into place not only to promote code compliance, but also to improve public confidence in the industry's efforts to police itself.

The Current Situation

The Beer and Wine Institutes refer complaints they receive about a member's advertising to that member for review and action. The referring body does not independently assess the merits of a complaint and no follow-up procedures exist to require the individual company to notify either the institute or the complaining party of the resolution.

DISCUS has a five-member Review Board that considers complaints received about member advertising and marketing.

Findings of the majority of the review board are communicated to the member and, when appropriate, to all members of the DISCUS Board of Directors. Occasionally, even absent an outside complaint, DISCUS has undertaken informal inquiries and urged members to discontinue practices that it believed had potential appeal to underage persons.

The beverage alcohol industry's enforcement mechanisms fall short of the advertising industry's model for effective self-regulation, the National Advertising Division of the Council of Better Business Bureaus, Inc., and its appeal board, the National Advertising Review Board. The system under the Beer and Wine Codes, where complaints are passed along to the member, does not provide for an impartial, objective consideration of the merits. The DISCUS procedure, where complaints are considered by a review board within the trade association, is superior to this model, but raises concerns that the responsibility of the association to represent its members in the best light might conflict with its responsibility under the code to criticize member behavior. No code provides for any "public" notice of a complaint or its resolution.

Finally, the current system does not ensure that code standards are applied consistently when complaints are considered. For example, one company routinely responds to consumer complaints about ad content by stating that it complies with placement standards and that there is no evidence that advertising significantly affects a child's drinking decisions. This type of response appears to fall short of objectively establishing the advertiser's compliance with the code's content provisions. Additionally, a trade association responded to a complaint charging that an ad appealed to underage consumers by stating that the icon depicted in the ad had been approved by the U.S. Trademark Office and the Bureau of Alcohol, Tobacco and Firearms (ATF), but did not address whether use of the icon violated code provisions. Neither the Trademark Office nor ATF has the authority to reject labels or icons due to potential youth appeal. Review by an expert, independent party presumably would avoid errors like these.

The industry trade associations have expressed concerns that third-party review and other self-regulatory improvements identified in this report would violate the antitrust statutes. In fact, while the antitrust laws prohibit collusive conduct that unreasonably restricts competition and harms consumers, they do not bar reasonable self-regulation designed to prevent alcohol advertising from being targeted to underage persons. (See Appendix H.)

VI. Recommendations

Through its self-regulatory codes, the industry seeks to minimize the extent to which underage persons are exposed to and attracted by alcohol advertising. While the current codes provide important protections, improvements are needed to ensure that the goals of the industry codes are met. The following are the Commission's recommendations:

1. Industry should provide for third-party review. The industry should create independent external review boards with responsibility and authority to address complaints from the public or other industry members.

2. Industry should raise standards for ad placement. The industry should raise the current standard that permits advertising placement in media where just over 50 percent of the audience is 21 or older. Because the 50 percent standard permits alcohol advertising to reach large numbers of underage consumers, some members of the industry already have raised their own placement standards, prohibiting ads where as few as 25 percent of the audience is underage. To ensure compliance with the higher placement standard, companies should measure their compliance against the most reliable up-to-date audience composition data available.

3. Trade associations and industry members should adopt and build upon the "best practices" of companies described in this report. These measures are demonstrated to be feasible and effective at reducing the risk that alcohol advertising will appeal to youth:

For ad placement: Maintain "no buy" lists barring placement on TV series and in other media with the largest underage audiences, and conduct regular after-the-fact audits of a sample of past placements to verify that past ad placements were in compliance.

For ad content: Raise the content standard by barring ads with substantial appeal to underage consumers, even if they also appeal to adults, or by targeting ads to persons 25 and older.

For product placement: Reduce the likelihood that alcohol product placement will occur in media with substantial underage appeal by restricting movie placements to films rated "R" or "NC-17" (or unrated films with similarly mature themes), prohibiting placements in films where an underage person is a primary character, and applying the standards for placing traditional ads to product placement on TV.

For online advertising: Use available mechanisms to prevent underage access to web sites, avoid content that would attract underage consumers, and post consumer education messages about underage and irresponsible drinking.

For college marketing: Further curb on-campus advertising and sponsorships and spring break marketing, and encourage licensed retail establishments to advertise responsibly.

The recommended changes would promote the goals underlying the codes as well as improve public confidence in industry's efforts to self-police. The Commission looks forward to the industry's implementation of these recommendations.

RECENT FTC CASES

The Case Of The Overboard Ad

An advertisement showed a sailing boat at sea. Almost all of the young adults on board were holding bottles of Beck's beer, with several of them sitting on the edge of the boat, where there was no railing. The complaint, *Beck's North America, Inc.*,[1] filed by the FTC charged that the advertisements constituted unfair acts or practices in violation of the FTC Act because they were likely to cause substantial injury to consumers. In addition, boating safety experts such as the U.S. Coast Guard stressed that boating accidents were greatly increased by the consumption of alcohol, the FTC said.

The case was settled and prohibited Beck's beer from producing television ads that depict a person having consumed or consuming alcohol on a boat while engaging in activities that pose a substantial risk of serious injury or that depict certain activities that would violate boating safety laws.

The Case Of The White Russian

Another case, *Allied Domecq Spirits & Wines Americas, Inc.*,[2] involved an advertisement claiming that Kahlua White Russian (a premixed cocktail) was a "low alcohol" beverage. According to the FTC, the beverage was not a low alcohol beverage because it contained 5.9 percent alcohol by volume, an amount equal to or greater than many other alcoholic beverages. A Kahlua White Russian had substantially more alcohol (ounce for ounce) than many beers, malt liquors, and wine coolers.

The U.S. Bureau of Alcohol, Tobacco and Firearms sets the limit that can be claimed to be low alcohol to 2.5 percent by volume. Again, this case was settled. And the consent order prohibits Kahlua from representing that any alcohol beverage containing 5.9 pecent by volume is a low alcohol beverage. The order does not prohibit the company from making truthful comparative claims about the alcohol level of its products, however.

CITY ORDINANCES

An ordinance in the City of Oakland, California, stated: "No person may place any advertising sign for alcoholic beverages or tobacco products in publicly visible locations." "Advertising sign" was defined as "any sign, poster, placard, device, graphic display, or any other form of advertising directing attention to, or otherwise pertaining to, a commodity, service, business, or profession which is not sold, produced, conducted, or offered by any activity on the same lot." The ordinance was challenged in court by Eller Media, an outdoor billboard company. The court in *Eller Media Co.* v. *City of Oakland,*[3] characterized the restriction as "off-site" advertising, as opposed to "on-site" advertising at liquor retail locations.

In addition, the ordinance did not apply to:

1. Alcoholic beverage advertising in commercial business districts;
2. Ads inside premises that lawfully sold alcoholic beverages;
3. Ads on commercial vehicles used for transporting products;
4. Ads in conjunction with temporary alcoholic beverage licenses;
5. Ads on taxicabs; and
6. Signs adjacent to and facing an interstate highway.

Prior to enacting the ordinance, the City of Oakland held public hearings during which it received testimony from school children, parents, teachers, nonprofit groups, and social scientists regarding the effect of alcoholic beverage advertising on underage drinking. The city also reviewed scientific literature that drew a direct correlation between a teenager's exposure to alcohol advertising and his or her propensities to "drink, drink heavily, and drink in hazardous situations such as in conjunction with driving." One report found that adolescents who suffered heightened exposure to alcohol advertising were more likely to associate drinking with attractiveness, athleticism, and success.

The court found that the purpose of the ordinance was to protect minors from the detrimental effects of alcohol consumption. The city tailored the ordinance to only include "off-site" billboards because of their ability to attract the attention of children. The court also found that the exceptions to the ordinance were crafted so as to leave other media available to advertisers, while limiting advertising in areas most likely to attract the attention of minors.

The federal district court upheld the ordinance passed by the City of Oakland that prohibited certain types of advertising for alcoholic beverages. The court ruled that the advertising restrictions in the ordinance advanced a substantial government interest and were narrowly tailored to serve that interest.

ATF'S ROLE: REGULATION ISSUES

The other important federal agency having jurisdiction over the advertising of alcoholic beverages is the Bureau of Alcohol, Tobacco and Firearms. The ATF groups alcoholic beverages into three major beverage groupings: malt beverages, wine, and distilled spirits and, treats each group differently.

1. Malt beverages –

Under the Federal Alcohol Administration Act, a malt beverage is:

> A beverage made by the alcoholic fermentation of an infusion or decoction, or combination of both, in potable brewing water, of malted barley with hops, or their parts, or their products, and with or without the addition of [certain additional ingredients].[4]

Malt beverages are low in alcohol content as a percentage of volume and occasionally escape regulations aimed at alcoholic beverages in general.

The ATF does not allow advertising the alcoholic content of malt beverages and does not allow any product containing less than one-half of one percent alcohol by volume to be called "beer," "lager beer," "lager," "ale," "porter," or "stout."

2. Wine –

Includes grape wine, sparkling grape wine, citrus wine, aperitif wine, raisin wine, and sake.

3. Distilled spirits –

Includes vodka, whisky, gin, brandy, rum, tequila, cordials and liqueurs, flavored spirits as well as imitations of any of these.

According to the ATF, the following rules must be followed:

- All ads must include the name and city of the manufacturer and the designation of the type of product involved;
- The ad may not make any false or misleading statements in any material respect or one that disparages a competitor's product;
- An ad may not make any statement that the manufacturer's beverage has intoxicating properties;
- Ads may not make any representation that the product has medicinal or therapeutic effects;
- Alcoholic beverage ads may not use any statement, design or representation regarding analysis, standards, or tests that may be considered misleading;
- An ad may not make a statement that's inconsistent with the product's label;
- An ad may not make any guarantee that is misleading; and
- An ad cannot use official flags, government insignia, or statements that can be construed as relating to the armed services.

In addition, there are other specific requirements regarding each type of alcoholic beverage.

BEER INSTITUTE ADVERTISING AND MARKETING CODE

The code that follows contains the voluntary advertising and marketing guidelines subscribed to by the members of the Beer Institute.

Introduction

Beer is a legal beverage meant to be consumed responsibly. Its origins are ancient, and it has held a respected position in nearly every culture and society since the dawn of recorded history. Advertising is a legitimate effort by brewers to make consumers aware of the particular types, brands, and prices of malt beverages that are available.

Three basic principles which have long been reflected in the policies of the brewing industry continue to underlie these guidelines. First, beer advertising should not suggest directly or indirectly that any of the laws applicable to the sale and consumption of beer should not be complied with. Second, brewers should adhere to standards of candor and good taste applicable to all commercial advertising. Third, brewers are responsible corporate citizens, sensitive to the problems of the society in which they exist, and their advertising should reflect that fact. Brewers strongly oppose abuse or inappropriate consumption of their products.

Guidelines

1. These guidelines apply to all brewer advertising and marketing materials, including Internet and other cyberspace media. These guidelines do not apply to educational materials or televised, printed or audio messages of a non-brand specific nature; nor to materials or messages designed specifically to

address issues of alcohol abuse or underage drinking.

2. Beer advertising and marketing materials should portray beer in a responsible manner.

a. Beer advertising and marketing materials should not portray, encourage or condone drunk driving.

b. Beer advertising and marketing materials should not depict situations where beer is being consumed excessively, in an irresponsible way, or in any way illegally.

c. Beer advertising and marketing materials should not portray persons in a state of intoxication or in any way suggest that intoxication is acceptable conduct.

d. Beer advertising and marketing materials should not portray or imply illegal activity of any kind.

e. Retail outlets or other places portrayed in advertising should be depicted as well kept and respectable establishments.

3. Brewers are committed to the policy and practice of responsible advertising and marketing directed to persons of legal purchase age. To facilitate this commitment, purchases by brewers, directly or indirectly, of Nielsen or other recognized TV viewer composition data shall reflect those viewers over the legal purchase age. Brewers shall review this Nielsen or other recognized TV viewer composition data on a regular basis (at least semi-annually) in order to ensure that advertisements are placed in compliance with this code.

4. Beer advertising and marketing materials are intended for adults of legal purchase age who choose to drink.

a. Beer advertising and marketing materials should not employ any symbol, language, music, gesture, or cartoon character that is intended to appeal primarily to persons below the legal purchase age. Advertising or marketing material has a "primary appeal" to persons under the legal purchase age if it has special attractiveness to such persons above and beyond the general attractiveness it has for persons above the legal purchase age, including young adults above the legal purchase age.

b. Beer advertising and marketing materials should not employ any entertainment figure or a group that is intended to appeal primarily to persons below the legal purchase age.

c. Beer advertising and marketing materials should not depict Santa Claus.

d. Beer advertising and marketing materials should not be placed in magazines, newspapers, television programs, radio programs, or other media where most of the audience is reasonably expected to be below the legal purchase age.

e. To help ensure that the people shown in beer advertising are and appear to be above the legal purchase age, models and actors employed should be a minimum of 25 years old, substantiated by proper identification, and should reasonably appear to be over 21 years of age.

f. Beer should not be advertised or marketed at any event where most of the audience is reasonably expected to be below the legal purchase age. This guideline does not prevent brewers from erecting advertising marketing at or near facilities that are used primarily for adult-oriented events, but which occasionally may be used for an event where most attendees are under age 21.

g. No beer identification, including logos, trademarks, or names should be used or licensed for use on clothing, toys, games or game equipment, or other materials intended for use primarily by persons below the legal purchase age.

h. Brewers recognize that parents play a significant role in educating their children about the legal and responsible use of alcohol and may wish to prevent their children from accessing Internet Web sites without parental supervision. To facilitate this exercise of parental responsibility, Beer Institute will provide to manufacturers of parental control software the names and Web site addresses of all member-company Web sites. Additionally, brewers will post reminders at appropriate locations in their Web site indicating that brewer products are indented only for those of legal purchase age. These locations include entrance into the Web site, purchase points within the Web site, and access into adult-oriented locations within the Web site, such as virtual bars.

5. Beer consumption is intended as a complement to leisure or social activity. Beer advertising and marketing activities should not associate or portray beer drinking before or during activities in situations which require a high degree of alertness or coordination.

6. Beer advertising and marketing materials should not make exaggerated product representations.

a. Beer advertising and marketing materials should not convey the impression that a beer has special or unique qualities if in fact it does not.

b. Beer advertising and marketing materials should make no scientifically unsubstantiated health claims.

c. Beer may be portrayed to be part of personal and social experiences and activities. Nevertheless, beer advertising and marketing materials should contain no claims or representations that individuals cannot obtain social, professional, educational, athletic or financial success or status without beer consumption; nor should they claim or represent that individuals cannot solve social, personal or physical problems without beer consumption.

7. Beer advertising and marketing materials reflect generally accepted contemporary standards of good taste.

a. Beer advertising and marketing materials should not contain any lewd or indecent language or images.

b. Beer advertising and marketing materials should not portray sexual passion, promiscuity or any other amorous activity as a result of consuming beer.

c. Beer advertising and marketing materials should not employ religion or religious themes.

8. Beer advertising and marketing materials should not disparage competing beers. In the event comparisons are drawn between competing beers, the claims made should be truthful and of value to consumers.

9. Beer advertising and marketing materials should never

suggest that competing beers contain objectionable additives or ingredients.

10. Beer advertising and marketing materials should not refer to any intoxicating effect that the product may produce.

11. Beer advertising and marketing materials should not depict the act of drinking.

12. Beer advertising and marketing materials should not show littering or otherwise improper disposal of beer containers, unless the scenes are used clearly to promote anti-littering and/or recycling campaigns.

13. Beer advertising and marketing activities on college and university campuses, or in college media, should not portray consumption of beer as being important to education, nor shall advertising directly or indirectly degrade studying. Beer may be advertised and marketed on college campuses or at college-sponsored events only when permitted by appropriate college policy.

Code Compliance and Dissemination

Each member of the Beer Institute is committed to the philosophy of the Code and is committed to compliance with the Code. When the Beer Institute receives complaints with regard to any member's advertising or marketing, it has long been its practice and it will continue to be its practice to promptly refer such complaints in writing to the member company for its review and action. To facilitate this end, the Beer Institute maintains an 800 number (1-800-379-2739). A copy of this code shall continue to be given to every brewery employee, wholesale distributor and outside agency whose responsibilities include advertising and marketing beer, as well as to any outside party who might request it.

THE WINE INSTITUTE

The ATF will not allow ad claims that tend to create the

impression that a wine contains distilled spirits, is comparable with a distilled spirit, or has intoxicating qualities. The use of vintage and bottling dates and of the word "old" is strictly controlled. So is the use of appellation of origin. Domestic products may not be described as imported.

The voluntary code originally created in 1978 governing wine producers is from the Wine Institute. Since all the members of the Wine Institute are located in California, the code only governs wines produced in that state. Check the Wine Institute's web site at: www.wineinstitute.org. They have a comprehensive list of reference materials on wine and related item advertising and marketing issues.

The Wine Institute's 1993 Code of Advertising Standards follows:

Code of Advertising Standards – Wine Institute

Preamble

Informal principles of good advertising practice for the winegrowing industry were first adopted in 1949. In recent years, California wine advertisers have desired more specific and significantly stronger standards to reflect the industry's concern with maximum social responsibility.

This code is designed to encourage continued high standards so that California wine advertising may increasingly be viewed as a positive contribution to society.

Guidelines

These guidelines shall apply only to voluntary subscribers of this Code of Advertising Standards.

1. Wine and wine cooler advertising should encourage the proper use of wine. Therefore subscribers to this code shall not depict or describe in their advertising:

a. The consumption of wine or wine coolers for the effects their alcohol content may produce.

b. Direct or indirect reference to alcohol content or extra strength, except as otherwise required by law or regulation.

c. Excessive drinking or persons who appear to have lost control or to be inappropriately uninhibited.

d. Any suggestion that excessive drinking or loss of control is amusing or a proper subject for amusement.

e. Any persons engaged in activities not normally associated with the moderate use of wine or wine coolers and a responsible life style. Association of wine use in conjunction with feats of daring or activities requiring unusual skill is specifically prohibited.

f. Wine or wine coolers in quantities inappropriate to the situation or inappropriate for moderate and responsible use.

g. The image of wine and wine coolers in advertising and promotion shall be adult-oriented and socially responsible. Comparative or competitor-derogatory advertising is inappropriate.

2. Advertising of wine has traditionally depicted wholesome persons enjoying their lives and illustrating the role of wine in a mature life style Any attempt to suggest that wine directly contributes to success or achievement is unacceptable. Therefore, the following restrictions shall apply to subscribers of this code:

a. Wine and wine coolers shall not be presented as being essential to personal performance, social attainment, achievement, success or wealth.

b. The use of wine and wine coolers shall not be directly associated with social, physical or personal problem solving.

c. Wine and wine coolers shall not be presented as vital to social acceptability and popularity.

d. It shall not be suggested that wine or wine coolers are crucial for successful entertaining.

3. Any advertisement which has particular appeal to persons below the legal drinking age is unacceptable. Therefore, wine and wine cooler advertising by code subscribers shall not:

a. Show models and personalities in advertisements who are under the legal drinking age. Models should appear to be 25 years of age or older.

b. Use music, language, gestures or cartoon characters specifically associated with or directed toward those below the legal drinking age.

c. Appear in children or juvenile magazines, newspapers, television programs, radio programs or other media specifically oriented to persons below the legal drinking age.

d. Be presented as being related to the attainment of adulthood or associated with "rites of passage" to adulthood.

e. Suggest that wine or a wine cooler product resembles or is similar to another type of beverage or product (milk, soda, candy) having particular appeal to persons below the legal drinking age.

f. Use current or traditional heroes of the young such as those engaged in pastimes and occupations having a particular appeal to persons below the legal drinking age.

g. Use amateur or professional sports celebrities, past or present.

4. Code subscribers shall not show motor vehicles in such a way as to suggest that they are to be operated in conjunction with wine or wine cooler use.

Advertising should in no way suggest that wine or wine coolers be used in connection with driving motorized vehicles such as automobiles, motorcycles, boats, snowmobiles, or airplanes.

5. Wine and wine cooler advertising shall not appear in or directly adjacent to television or radio programs or print media which dramatize or glamorize over-consumption or inappropriate use of alcoholic beverages.

6. Wine and wine cooler advertising by code subscribers shall make no reference to wine's medicinal or caloric values.

7. Wine and wine cooler advertising by code subscribers shall not degrade, demean, or objectify the human form, image or status of women, men, or of any ethnic, minority or other group, or feature provocative or enticing poses.

8. Wine and wine cooler advertising shall not be directed to underage drinkers or pregnant women. Wine and wine cooler advertising will not portray excessive drinking.

9. Wine and wine cooler advertising by code subscribers shall not exploit the human form, feature provocative or enticing poses, nor be demeaning to any individual. Wine and wine cooler advertising by code subscribers shall not reinforce nor trivialize the problem of violence in our society. Therefore, wine and wine cooler advertising shall not associate wine or wine coolers with abusive or violent relationships or situations.

10. A distinguishing and unique feature of wine is that it is traditionally served with meals or immediately before or following a meal.

Therefore, when subscribers to this code use wine advertising which visually depicts a scene or setting where wine is to be served, such advertising shall include foods and show that they are available and are being used or are intended to be used.

This guideline shall not apply to the depiction of a bottle of wine, vineyard, label, professional tasting etc. where emphasis is on the product.

All advertising – including, but not limited to direct mail, point-of-sale, outdoor, displays, radio, television and print media – should adhere to both the letter and the spirit of the above code.

DISTILLED SPIRITS

Under the ATF rules alcoholic content by proof must be stated for all distilled spirits. It may be stated in terms of percentage by volume for cordials and liqueurs, cocktails, highballs, bitters, and other specialties as approved by the ATF. The words "bond," "bonded," "bottled in bond," "aged in bond," or synonymous terms cannot be used unless they appear on the label pursuant to ATF regulations. "Pure" can only be used if part of the name of the permit holder or retailer for whom the distilled spirits is bonded. The words "double distilled" and "triple distilled" are strictly forbidden.

The Distilled Spirits Council of the United States (DISCUS), 1250 I St., N.W., Washington, D.C. 20005, is the voluntary authority that governs the advertising of distilled spirits. Check their web site at: www.discus.health.org.

The full text of the 1998 Code of Good Practice of the Distilled Spirits Council of the United States, Inc., follows:

Code of Good Practice for Distilled Spirits Advertising and Marketing

Preamble

The Distilled Spirits Council of the United States, Inc., (DISCUS) is the national trade association representing producers and marketers of distilled spirits sold in the United States. The members of DISCUS adopt this Code of Good Practice as guidelines concerning the placement and content of advertising and marketing materials. These guidelines have two overriding principles: (1) to ensure responsible, tasteful, and dignified advertising and marketing of distilled spirits to adult consumers who choose to drink and (2) to avoid targeting advertising and marketing of distilled spirits to individuals below the legal purchase age.

The consumption of beverage alcohol products has played an accepted and important role in the cultural and social traditions of both ancient and modern society. DISCUS members take special pride in their products and their commitment to promoting responsible consumption by those adults who choose to drink. Nevertheless, it is the obligation of each consumer who chooses to drink to enjoy beverage alcohol products in a responsible manner.

The distilled spirits industry acknowledges the problems inherent in abusive consumption of beverage alcohol, and DISCUS members remain commited to combatting alcohol abuse. To that end, the industry has joined with government and civic groups in efforts to encourage responsible use of beverage alcohol products. DISCUS also actively supports informational, educational, research, and treatment initiatives in an effort to better understand, prevent, and combat abuse of its products.

Scope

The producers and marketers of distilled spirits encourage responsible decision-making regarding drinking of beverage alcohol by adults, and discourage abusive consumption of their products. The distilled spirits industry urges that adults who choose to drink, do so responsibly. Towards this end, DISCUS members pledge voluntarily to conduct their advertising and marketing practices n the United States in accordance with the provisions of this Code. The provisions of the Code apply to every type of print and electronic media, including the Internet and any other on-line communications, used to advertise or market distilled spirits.

DISCUS members recognize that it is not possible to cover every eventuality and, therefore, agree to observe the spirit as well as the letter of this Code. Questions about the interpretation of the Code, member companies' compliance with the Code, and the application of its provisions are directed to the Code Review Board of DISCUS.

Responsible Placement

1. Distilled spirits should not be advertised or marketed in any manner directed or primarily intended to appeal to persons

below the legal purchase age.

2. Distilled spirits advertising and marketing should not be placed in any communication intended to appeal primarily to individuals below the legal purchase age.

3. Distilled spirits should not be advertised on college and university campuses or in college and university newspapers.

4. Marketing activities for distilled spirits should not be conducted on college and university campuses except in licensed retail establishments located on such campuses.

5. Distilled spirits advertising and marketing should not be specifically aimed at events where most of the audience is reasonably expected to be below the legal purchase age. Fixed distilled spirits advertising and marketing materials at facilities used primarily for adult-oriented events fall outside this guideline.

6. Distilled spirits advertising should not be placed on any outdoor stationary location within five hundred (500) feet of an established place of worship or an elementary school or secondary school except on a licensed premise.

Responsible Content – Underage Persons

1. Distilled spirits advertising and marketing materials are intended for adults of legal purchase age who choose to drink.

2. The content of distilled spirits advertising and marketing materials should not be intended to appeal primarily to individuals below the legal purchase age.

3. Distilled spirits advertising and marketing materials should not depict a child or portray objects, images, or cartoon figures that are popular predominantly with children.

4. Distilled spirits advertising and marketing materials should not contain the name of or depict Santa Claus or any religious figure.

5. Distilled spirits should not be advertised or marketed on the comic pages of newspapers, magazines, or other publications.

6. Distilled spirits should not be advertised or promoted by any person who is below the legal purchase age or who is made to appear, through clothing or otherwise, to be below the legal purchase age.

7. Distilled spirits web sites should contain a reminder of the legal purchase age on such web pages as the home page, access sites for the purchase of distilled spirits or brand-logoed consumer merchandise, and access sites depicting consumption of beverage alcohol, for example, a "virtual bar."

8. Distillers recognize the crucial role parents play in educating their children about the legal and responsible consumption of beverage alcohol. To enable parents who choose to prevent their children from accessing Internet web sites without their supervision, DISCUS will provide those parents and the manufacturers of parental control software upon request the web site address of each member company so that the parent or manufacturer can use this information.

Social Responsibility

9. Distilled spirits advertising and marketing materials should portray distilled spirits and drinkers in a responsible manner. These materials should not show a distilled spirits product being consumed abusively or irresponsibly.

10. On-premise promotions sponsored by distillers should encourage responsible consumption by those adults who choose to drink and discourage activities that reward excessive/abusive consumption.

11. Distilled spirits advertising and marketing materials should not promote the intoxicating effects of beverage alcohol consumption.

12. Distilled spirits advertising and marketing materials should not contain any curative or therapeutic claim except as permitted by law.

13. Distilled spirits advertising and marketing materials should contain no claims or representations that individuals ca obtain social, professional, educational, or athletic success or status as a result of beverage alcohol consumption.

14. Distilled spirits should not be advertised or marketed in any manner associated with abusive or violent relationships or situations.

15. Distilled spirits advertising and marketing materials should not imply illegal activity of any kind.

16. No distilled spirits advertising or marketing materials should portray distilled spirits being consumed by a person who is engaged in, or is immediately about to engage in, any activity that requires a high degree of alertness or physical coordination.

17. No distilled spirits advertising or marketing activity should be associated with anti-social or dangerous behavior.

18. Distilled spirits may be portrayed to be part of responsible personal and social experiences and activities, such as the depiction of persons in a social or romantic setting, persons who appear to be attractive or affluent, and persons who appear to be relaxing or in an enjoyable setting.

Drunk Driving

19. Driving while intoxicated is against the law. Distilled spirits advertising and marketing materials should not portray, encourage, or condone drunk driving.

Alcohol Content

20. Distilled spirits advertising and marketing materials should not refer to alcohol content except in a straightforward and factual manner.

Good Taste

21. No distilled spirits advertising or marketing materials should contain advertising copy or an illustration unless it is

dignified, modest, and in good taste.

22. No distilled spirits advertising or marketing materials should claim or depict sexual prowess as a result of beverage alcohol consumption.

23. Distilled spirits advertising and marketing materials should not degrade the image, form, or status of women, men, or of any ethnic, minority, sexually-oriented, religious, or other group.

24. Distilled spirits advertising and marketing materials should not employ religion or religious themes, nor should distilled spirits be advertised in publications devoted primarily to religious topics.

Code Review Board

There shall be established and maintained a Code Review Board, which shall meet when necessary to consider complaints lodged by DISCUS members or other interested parties.

The Code Review Board shall be compromised of no less than five (5) members in good standing of the Board of Directors of DISCUS. Each member shall be elected by a majority vote of the Board of Directors.

Findings of the majority of the members of the Code Review Board shall be communicated promptly to the responsible advertiser and in appropriate circumstances to all members of the Board of Directors of DISCUS.

NETWORK GUIDELINES

Wine and beer ads (but not those for distilled spirits) may appear on the three major television networks. NBC forbids the advertisement of alcoholic beverages as "necessary to maintain social status, obtain personal achievements, relieve stress or as a solution to personal problems."

On-camera consumption of alcohol is strictly forbidden. Ads for liquor outlets are acceptable to NBC if there is no reference to unacceptable wine or distilled spirits. Ads on NBC for airlines and restaurants may make incidental reference to cocktails, but advertising of mixed drinks is not acceptable, nor is the use of terms like "martini" or "Bloody Mary." Glassware associated with distilled spirits is not an acceptable prop to NBC, except in relation to the "incidental reference" mentioned above. NBC will review advertisements alerting the public to the dangers of alcohol abuse on a "case-by-case" basis.

ABC has a very similar set of guidelines; one minor difference is that ABC prohibits even the incidental display of cocktail props.

CBS has a policy against direct or implied references to excessive consumption of beer and wine.

RECENT STEPS BY THE BUREAU OF ALCOHOL, TOBACCO AND FIREARMS

In 1984 the ATF published regulations controlling the advertising and labeling of alcoholic beverages. The agency delayed decision, however, on such controversial issues as the use of the terms "natural" and "light."

A significant part of the regulations deals with comparative advertising of alcoholic beverages, requiring that comparative ads shall "not be disparaging of a competitive product." The regulations also require advertisers to follow "any scientifically accepted procedure" in so-called taste tests. Advertisers must also include the name and address of the testing administrator in taste-test ads. Both broadcast and print ads must comply with these rules.

The regulations state unequivocally that "subliminal or similar techniques are prohibited." Subliminal messages are defined as the "use of any device or technique that is used to convey or attempts to convey a message to a person by means of images or sounds of a very brief nature that cannot be perceived at a normal level of awareness."

The ATF is undecided about the issue of athlete endorsement of alcoholic beverages. Ads by currently active athletes have long been precluded:

> References to the illustrations of prominent athletes consuming or preparing to consume the advertised malt beverages are considered likely to mislead the public and therefore are subject to provisions (concerning misleading alcohol advertising).[5]

Likewise, the use of illustrations of athletic activities in connection with distilled spirits is forbidden.[6]

STATE CONTROLS

The most extensive control over advertising of alcohol comes from the individual states. They have restricted advertising on billboards, in circulars, and on radio and television. Displays on retail premises, newspaper and magazine advertising, retailer novelties, consumer novelties, premium offers, cents-off offers, samples, contests, and refunds are also considered state issues. It is important for any advertiser to investigate the specific regulations in any state in which he advertises. The detailed regulations of each state are too overwhelming for discussion in this chapter.

The Twenty-first Amendment to the Constitution gives the states some special powers. In *Capital Cities Cable, Inc.* v. *Crisp*,[7] the U.S. Supreme Court ruled against Oklahoma's advertising ban requiring cable television operators to screen out alcoholic beverage advertising that was part of the out-of-state signals they retransmitted by cable to their subscribers. The main reasoning behind the Court's ruling was that since cable television operates under FCC regulations, Oklahoma must follow federal law. In addition, Oklahoma's ban ran against established FCC regulations and their goal of making the benefits of cable television available nationally.

Two other important cases have upheld state control of liquor ads. In *Queensgate Inv. Co.* v. *Liquor Control Comm'n*,[8] the United States Supreme Court dismissed an appeal from an Ohio state court's ruling upholding an Ohio regulation prohibiting retail liquor permittees from advertising the price of alcoholic beverages off their premises. The Fifth Federal Circuit then followed that precedent and upheld Mississippi statutes and regulations banning liquor ads on billboards, in print, and over the air within the state in *Dunagin* v. *City of Oxford, Mississippi*.[9]

CIGARETTE ADVERTISING

Each year, heroin and cocaine together cause the death of approximately 5,000 Americans. Yet, this tragedy is dwarfed by the Surgeon General's conclusion that cigarette smoking is responsible for over 390,000 unnecessary deaths each year in this country alone. According to these numbers, almost 1 out of 6 deaths in the United States can be traced back to cigarette smoking. Although smoking among adults dropped from 40 percent in 1965 to 29 percent in 1987, approximately 55 million Americans still smoke.

The Controversy Over Cigarette Marketing And Advertising

The controversy over cigarette advertising continues to grow. Critics condemn all types of advertising and promotion used to market cigarettes. On the other hand, many industry voices claim advertising is highly overrated as a factor in causing people to smoke. They cite peer pressure and parental role-modeling as more relevant causes.

Here we'll take a look at some of the concerns about cigarette marketing and advertising in more depth. First, there is the concern over the scope of cigarette advertising. In 1988 the tobacco industry spent close to $2.5 billion (that's about $6.5

million a day) for advertising and promotion.

The vast majority of new smokers are teenagers or younger. By one estimate, 60 percent are under the age of fourteen. This statistic is a cause for particular concern over the effects of cigarette advertising on children and teenagers.

In addition, there has been a dramatic shift in the allocation of overall marketing budgets. The result of this is that promotional expenditures today account for over 60 percent of marketing expenditures, compared to only 25 percent in 1975. Increasingly, cigarette companies are promoting their brands through sponsorship of sporting events and concerts, which reach a youthful segment of the market.

The industry also uses logos on nontobacco products having special appeal to teenagers and pays to have cigarettes displayed in youth-oriented movies, including a recent James Bond film (for which Philip Morris paid $350,000), *Superman II*, and *Supergirl* (Luken 1989), to mention a few.

The tobacco industry, on the other hand, has argued that advertising informs consumers about brand differences and leads to brand switching rather than to smoking initiation. Critics emphasize advertising's role in the glamorization of smoking, attracting new smokers, and impeding the efforts of smokers to quit. There simply is no way to determine which view is provable.

Since most smokers merely switch among the brands of Philip Morris and R.J. Reynolds, who control approximately two-thirds of the U.S. cigarette market, this seems to validate the critics' charges that the goals of advertising and promotion are somewhat broader than would be guessed.

Restrictions On Cigarette Sales

The suggestion of an outright ban on the sale of cigarettes often invokes the response that Prohibition didn't work and further, that making the sale of cigarettes illegal and thereby branding many millions of people criminals is not in the public interest. Sentiment over freedom of choice runs very deep, especially on matters that appear to involve personal consequences rather than broad societal concerns. However, several types of lesser restrictions are receiving consideration, though the regulatory setting is a stumbling block to action.

As an example, under the Federal Food, Drug, and Cosmetic Act,[10] a drug is misbranded and can be removed from sale if it is falsely labeled. One might argue that failing to reveal the fact that the product contains nicotine (an addictive drug), the fact that forty-three known carcinogenic agents are contained in tobacco smoke, and the types of additives employed to make low tar cigarettes each constitute mislabeling.[11] The Food and Drug Administration has, however, taken the position that it does not have authority over tobacco products.

Further, Congress has apparently exempted tobacco from regulation under the Consumer Products Safety Act,[12] the Toxic Substances Control Act,[13] the Fair Packaging and Labeling Act,[14] the Controlled Substances Act,[15] and the Federal Hazardous Substances Labeling Act.[16] Thus, new legislation seems necessary for any restrictions on the sale of mislabeled cigarettes.

ISSUES WITH TOBACCO AND CIGARETTE ADVERTISING

In recent years there has been much activity in the courts regarding the advertising of tobacco and cigarettes. The most visible of which may have been the Joe Camel Case. There has also been a great deal of activity in other government bodies, including individual states.

The Joe Camel Case

As most people know, R. J. Reynolds' recent Camel cigarettes advertising campaign centered around a cartoon character named Joe Camel.

In May 1997 the FTC alleged that R. J. Reynolds, through its Joe Camel advertising campaign, unlawfully caused or was likely to cause substantial and ongoing injury to the health and safety of children and adolescents under the age of 18. The agency sought an order: (1) prohibiting Reynolds from advertising to children Camel cigarettes through the use of themes or images relating to "Joe Camel;" (2) requiring that Reynolds disseminate public education messages discouraging persons under 18 from smoking; and (3) requiring the company to collect and make available data concerning the sales of each brand of its cigarettes to persons under 18 and each brand's share of smokers under 18.

On January 27, 1999, the Federal Trade Commission announced that it dismissed the case against R. J. Reynolds Tobacco Company for its Joe Camel advertising campaign. The Commission decided that the result it sought was accomplished by the recent multistate tobacco settlement and revisions of the U.S. Department of Health and Human Services' data collection methods.

The November 23, 1998, Master Settlement Agreement with 46 attorneys general and five major cigarette companies covered the first and second issues.

That agreement, the Commission said:

> Specifically bans the use of all cartoon characters, including Joe Camel, in the advertising, promotion, packaging, and labeling of any tobacco product...[and] the settlement requires the tobacco companies to help finance a national public education fund designed to carry out on a nationwide basis sustained advertising and education programs to counter underage usage of tobacco products and to educate consumers about the causes of prevention of diseases associated with the use of tobacco products.

As it relates to the third issue, the FTC said that the "Substance Abuse and Mental Health Services Administration of the U.S. Department of Health and Human Services is revising the protocol for its annual national household survey on drug abuse to add specific questions to elicit brand share of smokers under 18."

The Food And Drug Administration

A number of tobacco companies, convenience store retailers, and advertisers recently challenged FDA rules that restricted the sale, distribution, and advertising of tobacco products. As a result, the Fourth Circuit has determined that the Food and Drug Administration does not have jurisdiction to regulate tobacco products in *Brown & Williamson Tobacco Corp.* v. *FDA.*[17] The court reasoned that Congress (by its creation of the Food, Drug and Cosmetics Act) had not intended to allow the FDA the right to regulate tobacco products.

The FDA asserted jurisdiction over tobacco products under the "drugs" and "device" definitions in the Act. The Act defines "drugs" as "articles (other than food) intended to affect the structure or any function of the body of man or animals." "Device" is defined as an article which is intended to affect the structure or any function of the body of man or other animals, and which does not achieve its primary intended purposes through chemical action within or on the body of man or other animals and which is not dependent upon being metabolized for the achievement of its primary intended purposes.[18]

According to the FDA, tobacco products fit under the Act's definitions because they were "intended to affect the structure or any function of the body." The FDA claimed that tobacco products were "combination products consisting of nicotine, a drug that causes addiction and other significant pharmacological effects on the human body, and device components that deliver nicotine to the body."

The court, however, reasoned that it was not Congress'

intent to grant the FDA the authority to regulate tobacco products. The provisions of the Food, Drug, and Cosmetics Act did not support bestowing that authority, the court found. During its rulemaking process regarding tobacco products, the FDA found that tobacco products were "dangerous," "unsafe," and the cause of "great pain and suffering from illness such as cancer, respiratory illnesses, and heart disease." In addition, the FDA determined that over 400,000 people die each year from tobacco use.

However, the court stated:

> The FDA has proposed to regulate tobacco products under a statutory provision that requires conditions on sale and distribution which provide a reasonable assurance of safety. According to the FDA, a determination of safety under the Act requires consideration of the risks of a product compared to the "countervailing effects of use of that product, including the consequences of not permitting the product to be marketed." Thus, the FDA concluded that withdrawal of tobacco from the market poses significant health risks to addicted adults which outweighs the risks of leaving tobacco products on the market. But that test is contrary to the statute: A statutory provision,[19] provides that safety and effectiveness are to be determined by "weighing any probable benefit to health from the use of the device against any probable risk of injury or illness from such use."

Analyzing the statute shows that the FDA must strike a balance between the risks and benefits of the use of a certain product, not weigh the risks of leaving a product on the market against the risks of taking it off the market. The FDA was unable to state any real health benefit derived from leaving tobacco products on the market. "[B]ased on the FDA's characterization of tobacco products as unsafe, it is impossible to create regulations which will provide a reasonable assurance of safety. Thus, the FDA cannot comply with the terms of the very statutory provision it has chosen as its basis for regulation," the court concluded.

Preemption Issues

The Chicago Tobacco Ordinance

In *Federation of Advertising Industry Representatives* v. *City of Chicago*,[20] a Chicago ordinance that restricted advertising of both cigarettes and alcohol in any "publicly visible location" was preempted by the Federal Cigarette Labeling and Advertising Act.[21]

The Federal Cigarette Labeling and Advertising Act established a comprehensive set of restrictions on cigarette advertising and labeling as they related to the health effects of smoking. The Act was designed to ensure that consumers received adequate, clear, uniform information about the dangers of smoking. In the interest of such uniformity, the Act contained an express preemption clause which stated: "No requirement or prohibition based on smoking and health shall be imposed under State law with respect to the advertising or promotion of any cigarettes the packages of which are labeled in conformity with the provisions of this chapter."

The Chicago ordinance stated:

> (a) No person may place any sign, poster, placard or graphic display that advertises cigarettes or alcoholic beverages in a publicly visible location. In this section, "publicly visible location" includes outdoor billboards, sides of buildings, and freestanding signboards.

The ordinance also had 10 exceptions that permitted advertising within retail premises, on city buses, at the major sports stadiums, and on interstate highways.

The court decided that it did not need to look beyond the express language of the preemption statute to find that the Chicago ordinance was preempted under the federal law. The ordinance clearly contained a "prohibition" and it was "with respect to the advertising and promotion of cigarettes." The contested issue was whether the ordinance's prohibition was "based on smoking and health."

The city argued that the purpose of the ordinance was to reduce sales of cigarettes to minors and, thus, the ordinance's prohibition was not "based on smoking and health."

The city argued:

> The Ordinance explicitly states that its purpose is to reduce illegal transactions, i.e., cigarette sales to or purchased by minors. Furthermore, the preamble is focused on illegal transactions, not health, and on the connection between outdoor advertising and illegal activities. Indeed, the very first section of the Ordinance recites that it is unlawful for any individual under the age of 18 to purchase or be sold cigarettes. All of the recitals, or "whereas" clauses, deal with the illegality of cigarette sales to or purchases by minors, the degree of cigarette consumption by minors, the extent of outdoor advertising of cigarettes, the unique nature of cigarette billboards, the relationship between advertising of cigarettes and consumption of cigarettes, and the need for the Ordinance. Nothing in the recitals indicates that the purpose of the Ordinance, vis-à-vis cigarettes, is anything other than preventing illegal transactions.

The court rejected the city's arguments, finding that the real reason the ordinance was passed was the link between smoking and health. The reason it was illegal to sell cigarettes to minors in Illinois in the first place was because the legislature's desire to protect minors from the health risks associated with smoking. The court rejected the city's attempt to narrowly define the purpose behind the ordinance.

Because the ordinance prohibited cigarette advertising that was based on smoking and health, the court found that the ordinance was preempted by federal law.

The Vermont Ordinance

In Vermont, a city ordinance that restricted retail tobacco advertising was preempted by federal law. Similar to the City of Chicago ordinance, the court in *Rockwood* v. *City of Burlington*[22] found that the Vermont ordinance was a "requirement or prohibition" "based on smoking and health...with respect to the advertising or promotion of any cigarettes." The court rejected the city's argument that the ordinance was enacted for the purpose of reducing the illegal sale of tobacco to minors.

The relevant part the ordinance prohibited:

> (a) Point-of-sale advertising of tobacco products by any means other than a maximum of two black and white, text only, 12 by 14 inch signs ("Tombstone Signs") in or on any retail establishment where tobacco products are offered for sale. The text could not exceed one inch in height, and could include only the brand name, description of the product, tar and nicotine content, price, and any warnings required by law. The Ordinance made it unlawful for city retailers to use any promotional items inside or outside their stores, such as clocks, grocery dividers, display racks, ashtrays, trash cans, catalogues, uniforms, T-shirts, or other clothing;
>
> (b) Any tobacco advertising within one

thousand feet of a school;

(c) The distribution of free samples of tobacco products or coupons redeemable for tobacco products;

(d) Any manufacturer, distributor, or retailer from sponsoring any athletic, musical, artistic, or other social event using a tobacco product brand name, logo, motto, or image; and

(e) Self-service displays of cigarettes or tobacco products.

The stated purpose of the ordinance was to decrease the illegal use of tobacco by minors. However, after reviewing the records of city council meetings and other public hearings held in connection with the ordinance, it became clear that health concerns were an important component of the city's concerns. The court stated: "It strains credulity to adopt the rationale that the City's Ordinance is unrelated to smoking and health, merely because the City has stressed its purpose of reducing illegal activity by minors. Clearly the dominant reason that lawmakers in Vermont as elsewhere seek to restrict the use of tobacco products by minors is the grave concern that addiction to nicotine in their youth will have long-term health consequences for them."

The court also rejected the city's argument that the ordinance did not regulate cigarette advertising within the meaning of the preemption statute. This, it claimed, was because it regulated the location and format of the advertising, but not its content, and did not limit the ability of cigarette manufacturers and vendors from advertising in the mass media. The court found, however, that one section of the ordinance specifically prescribed the content of tobacco product advertising signs as well as limiting their location. The text of the signs could only include the brand name, description of the product, tar and nicotine content, price, and any warnings required by federal law. On the other hand, the preemption statute made no distinction between prohibitions on advertising language and advertising locations.

This case also involved commercial speech issues. The court found that the city ordinance could not withstand First Amendment scrutiny since it restricted advertising of a lawful activity that was not misleading. There was no evidence that the tobacco companies targeted their advertising specifically to minors. And the court reasoned that the state had a valid state interest in reducing illegal (underage) smoking and that restricting tobacco advertising could possibly advance that interest.

The ordinance failed the *Central Hudson*[23] test because it was not narrowly tailored to serve the city's asserted interest. The ordinance completely banned publicly visible tobacco advertising within one thousand feet of a school. It restricted point-of-sale advertising to two black-and-white signs in a retail establishment, and limited what could be displayed on the signs. Further, the ordinance banned sponsorship advertising and the distribution of free samples. None of these provisions were narrowly tailored to affect advertising targeted at minors, the court determined. The court found that there was not a "reasonable fit" between the ordinance and the city's interest in reducing underage smoking.

State Attorneys General Actions

In June 1997 five tobacco companies and 40 state attorneys general reached a settlement that involved the advertising and marketing of tobacco products. Among the provisions of the settlement were bans on billboard and Internet advertising, tougher labeling requirements, and an extensive counter-advertising campaign. Also, the use of characters such as Joe Camel would be prohibited. To take effect, the settlement required federal legislation which has yet to pass.

In 1998 nine state attorneys generals (California, Colorado, Massachusetts, New York, North Carolina, North Dakota, Oklahoma, Pennsylvania, and Washington) negotiated with tobacco companies on advertising restrictions that would not require Congress' involvement. On November 16, 1998, a proposed $206 billion agreement was announced. According to the agreement, Brown & Williamson, Lorillard, Philip Morris, and R. J. Reynolds agreed to fund a $1.5 billion antismoking campaign.

The settlement requires that the companies pay $25 million per year, for ten years, to a foundation that will study programs to reduce teen smoking and substance abuse as well as study the prevention of diseases associated with tobacco. Another element provides that the foundation will carry out a nationwide, sustained advertising and education program designed to reduce youth smoking and educate consumers. The foundation will also commission studies, fund research, and publish reports on youth smoking and substance abuse.

As it related to tobacco advertising:

- The settlement bans use of cartoons in the advertising, promotion, packaging, or labeling of tobacco products.
- The settlement prohibits targeting of youths in advertising, promotions, or marketing.
- The settlement bans industry actions aimed at initiating, maintaining, or increasing youth smoking.
- The settlement requires companies to: (1) develop and regularly communicate corporate principles that commit to complying with the Master Settlement Agreement and reducing youth smoking; (2) designate an executive level manager to identify ways to reduce youth access and consumption of tobacco; and (3) encourage employees to identify additional methods to reduce youth access and consumption.
- The settlement bans all outdoor advertising, including billboards, signs and placards in arenas, stadiums, shopping malls, and video game arcades, and limits advertising outside retail establishments to 14 square feet.

- The settlement bans transit advertising of tobacco products and allows states to substitute, for the duration of billboard lease periods, alternative advertising which discourages youth smoking.
- Beginning on July 1, 1999, the settlement bans distribution and sale of apparel and merchandise with brand name logos, including caps, T-shirts, backpacks, and the like.
- The settlement bans payments to promote tobacco products in movies, television shows, theater productions or live performances, live or recorded music performances, videos, and video games.
- The settlement prohibits brand-name sponsorship of events with significant youth audience or team sports, such as football, basketball, baseball, hockey, and soccer and prohibits sponsorship of events where paid participants or contestants are underage. Bans tobacco brand names from stadiums and arenas.
- The settlement limits tobacco companies to one brand-name sponsorship per year after current contracts expire or after three years, whichever comes first.
- The settlement limits distribution of free samples to facilities or enclosed areas where the operator ensures no underage person is present.

On September 17, 1998, tobacco companies agreed to pay $1.7 billion to the state of Florida and accept additional advertising restrictions as part of that state's antismoking lawsuit. New advertising restrictions in Florida cover merchandise promotions such as Marlboro T-shirts and an agreement to not pay to have tobacco brands shown in movies.

In its antitrust case against tobacco companies, the State of Washington settled with two of the defendants on October 2, 1998. The settlements involved Smokeless Tobacco Council, Inc., and U.S. Tobacco Co. Here, U.S. Tobacco agreed to stop all billboard and transit advertising of tobacco products.

The company also agreed not to oppose legislation banning tobacco vending machines except in adult-only facilities, and legislation that would strengthen penalties for selling tobacco to minors. The company also agreed pay the state $2 million for reimbursement of legal costs.

PRODUCTS LIABILITY LAWSUITS

A final economic disincentive is the threat of product liability suits. We looked at this subject in detail in Chapter 4. A recent jury verdict went against tobacco interests in *Cipollone* v. *Liggett Group, Inc.*,[24] producing three major results:

- The monetary award of $400,000;
- The release of extensive and previously confidential strategy and research documents from company and Tobacco Institute files, paving the way for future cases; and
- The willingness of a jury to determine that cigarette advertising has made express warranties about health aspects of cigarettes and that these contributed to the person's smoking and death.

In several cases, including *Cipollone*, courts did not allow the introduction of evidence of company failure to warn and negligence after 1966 (when the Cigarette Labeling and Advertising Act took effect). Both the likelihood and magnitude of awards in the future will depend on judicial clarification of:

- Underlying liability theories (risk-utility concepts, implied warranties); and
- Admissibility and weight given to the conduct of both the smoker and the cigarette company after 1966.

A number of jurists and legislators have subsequently expressed the conviction that Congress, by mandating a particular warning, could not possibly have intended to shield tobacco companies from all responsibility to warn consumers or to give companies license to fail intentionally to disclose important health information by mandating a particular warning.

> The ultimate irony is: the cigarette companies can now escape liability for their deceptive ads because the federal courts have misinterpreted a law which was intended to impede the use of this death-dealing product by giving consumers more, not less, information.[25]

However, until Congress acts or the Supreme Court overturns lower court decisions, consumers' injuries resulting primarily from smoking in the period after 1966 may be immune from recovery under products liability theories.

Increased Regulatory Control

We have already discussed the regulatory problems associated with a lack of oversight by any agency specifically charged with protecting the health and safety of the public. There is substantial interest in possible congressional action to declare tobacco products an addictive drug (to be regulated by the Food and Drug Administration). Thus, there is at least the potential for the Food and Drug Administration to acquire broad power to examine tobacco additives and constituents, require appropriate disclosures of potential harm, require reductions or deletion of certain additives, and ensure that the information provided in advertising is not in conflict with these determinations.

[1] *Beck's North America, Inc.*, CCH Trade Regulation Reports ¶ 24,481.

[2] *Allied Domecq Spirits & Wines Americas, Inc.*, Trade Regulation Reports ¶ 24,482.

[3] *Eller Media Co.* v. *City of Oakland,* No. C98-2237 FMS, 1998 U.S. Dist. LEXIS 13319 (N.D. Cal., August 28, 1998).

[4] Federal Alcohol Administration Act, 27 CFR 7.20.

[5] Rev. Rul. 54-513.

[6] Rev. Rul. 54-326.

[7] *Capital Cities Cable, Inc.* v. *Crisp*, 467 U.S. 691, 104 S.Ct. 2694, 81 L.Ed. 2d 580 (1984), reversing *Oklahoma Telecasters* v. *Crisp*, 699 F.2d. 490 (10th Cir. 1983).

[8] *Queensgate Inv. Co.* v. *Liquor Control Comm'n*, 459 U.S. 807, 103 S. Ct. 31, 74 L.Ed. 2d 45 dismissing appeal from 69 Ohio St. 2d 361, 433 N.E. 2d. 138 (1982) (per curiam).

[9] *Dunagin* v. *City of Oxford, Mississippi*, 718 F.2d. 738 (5th Cir. 1983).

[10] Federal Food, Drug, and Cosmetic Act, 21 U.S.C. §301.

[11] Report of the Surgeon General 1989, 79-94.

[12] Consumer Products Safety Act, 15 U.S.C. §1193 (1988).

[13] Toxic Substances Control Act, 15 U.S.C. §2601 (1988).

[14] Fair Packaging and Labeling Act, 15 U.S.C. §1451 (1988).

[15] Controlled Substances Act, 21 U.S.C. §801 (1988).

[16] Federal Hazardous Substances Act, 15 U.S.C. §1261 (1988).

[17] *Brown & Williamson Tobacco Corp.* v. *FDA*, No. 97-1604, 1998 U.S. App. LEXIS 18821 (4th Cir., August 14, 1998).

[18] 21 U.S.C. § 321(h)(3).

[19] 21 U.S.C. § 360(a)(2)(C).

[20] *Federation of Advertising Industry Representatives* v. *City of Chicago,* No. 97C7619, 1998 U.S. Dist. LEXIS 11777 (N.D. Ill., July 29, 1998).

[21] 15 U.S.C. §§ 1131-1341.

[22] *Rockwood* v. *City of Burlington*, No. 2:98-CV-223, 1998 U.S. Dist. LEXIS 15021 (D. Vt., September 21, 1998).

[23] *Central Hudson Gas & Electric Corp.* v. *Public Service Commission of New York,* 447 U.S. 557 (1980).

[24] *Cipollone* v. *Liggett Group, Inc.*, 789 F.2d 181 (3d Cir. 1986), cert. denied, 479 U.S. 1043, 107 S.Ct. 907, 93 L.Ed. 2d 857 (1987).

[25] Excerpt from a letter from Representatives Whittaker and Luken urging co-sponsorship of the Cigarette Testing and Liability Act, May 11, 1988.

CHAPTER 14

The Internet

The hurrier I go, the behinder I get.
—*My Mom*

It was the 1960's. The era of the Beatles, Flower-Power, the Hippies, and the Zodiac Killer. Toyota sold its first car in the U.S., and the Eagle landed at Tranquility Base. It was also the time of the cold war between the Soviet Union and the U.S. Both countries built more and more atomic weapons, and both had the power to wipe out the whole planet.

So America's premier Cold War thinking machine, the Rand Corporation, approached a strategic problem. If one computer in a network was destroyed, communication was also. And if there was a central hub, it would surely be the first target for an atomic attack. So how could the US authorities successfully communicate after a nuclear attack? RAND invented a new kind of network in 1964 that would have no center – all the nodes would be equal in status, each could send and receive messages. That means that if one node was destroyed, the rest of the nodes would still be able to communicate.

The first test network built on these principles was installed in National Research Laboratory in Great Britain in 1968. Soon after, the Pentagon's Advanced Research Projects Agency (ARPA) installed a more advanced network based on the same principles in the USA. The network consisted of four high speed computers. In 1969, the first node was installed in UCLA.

In 1972, Ray Tomlinson of BBN invented the first e-mail program. But why is this that important? Over the years, an odd fact became clear. Instead of using the net for long distance computing, the scientists used it to communicate with each other – for sharing results of their experiments – but mainly for gossiping!

In 1992, the WWW was invented at CERN, an institute for particle physics situated in Switzerland. Originally, WWW was developed only for high energy physics (for world-wide communication). The number of hosts reached 1 million – an unexpected side effect of particle physics.

One year later, the first browser, Mosaic, was released. The growth rate of the Internet reached an incredible 341 percent and it stills grows at an alarming rate.

What can you say about the future of the Internet? One can only guess what it will look like in ten years.

Since the 1995 edition of *Law & Advertising*, the Internet has provided the largest amount of new activity in the area of advertising law. In fact, the Internet was not included in the earlier edition of this book, since advertising on the internet only began in 1994 when the first banner ads were sold. As television was 40 years ago, the Internet is the "new media" du jour.

As one court so well put it:

> The Internet has no territorial boundaries. To paraphrase Gertrude Stein, as far as the Internet is concerned, not only is there perhaps "no there there," the "there" is everywhere where there is Internet access. When business is transacted over a computer network via a Web-site accessed by a computer in Massachusetts, it takes place as much in Massachusetts, literally or figuratively, as it does anywhere.[1]

THE FTC

As with other forms of advertising, the same regulations apply to Internet marketing. A claim may be considered misleading if relevant information is left out or if the claim implies something that is untrue.

To help understand the Internet, the FTC has developed a guide that covers advertising and marketing on the Internet, entitled *Advertising and Marketing on the Internet: The Rules of the Road* (April 1998).

Disclaimers On Internet Advertising

In May 1998, the FTC asked for feedback from the marketing industry regarding interpretation of its current rules and guides as they applied to the Internet.[2] As mentioned, advertising a product or service on the Internet will be subject to the same standards as advertising in other media. However, the FTC maintains that there were some issues that are unique to the Internet and that require special rules or guidance.

The FTC is investigating the use of disclaimers in advertisements that appear on the Internet. In print advertisements, for example, disclaimers usually appear in smaller print than the rest of the ad copy. In television commercials, a disclaimer might be made through the voice-over. The question presented by the FTC is where and in what form should a disclaimer be for an Internet web site so that it is clear and conspicuous to the reader. As with other forms of advertising, the FTC views the disclaimer in the context of all of the other elements of the ad to determine whether it is effectively communicated. "Ordinarily, a disclosure [disclaimer] is clear and conspicuous, and therefore is effectively communicated, when it is displayed in a manner that is readily noticeable, readable and/or audible (depending on the medium), and understandable to the audience to whom it is disseminated."[3]

However, applying this standard to Internet ads involves several issues that are unique to Internet advertising.

The FTC stated the issues as follows:

> Many Internet advertisements, for example,

> include scroll bars to maneuver down pages that usually exceed one screen in length. They also often include hyperlinks, both to other pages on a web site as well as directly to other web sites. On the Internet and in other electronic media, new graphics technologies create messages that scroll, blink, spin, pop-up, relocate, etc. These unique features may require the Commission to give special consideration to certain factors in determining whether a disclosure is effectively communicated on electronic media. As is true for any medium, the specific elements necessary to effectively communicate a disclosure may vary depending on the nature of the advertisement and the nature of the claim.[4]

The FTC recommends that disclaimers in Internet ads should be very apparent to "reasonable" consumers. Consumers should not have to take any special action to see the disclaimer, such as scrolling down a page, clicking on a link to other pages, activating a "pop-up," or entering a search term. The Commission also feels that the disclaimer should be accessible at all times. In other words, a consumer who hyperlinks to another page should not be prevented from going back to the page containing the disclaimer. The disclaimer should also be close to the representation it clarifies.

The FTC also suggests that if the representation is made visually, the disclaimer should be made visually also. The same standard applies for audio representations.

Electronic Mail

The FTC is exploring a concern. That is, should the definition of "direct mail" be interpreted to include electronic mail. The Telemarketing Sales Rule, for example, applies to telephone calls initiated by consumers in response to "direct mail solicitations."[5] The FTC is proposing that the term "direct mail" refer to private communications. In other words, the term will encompass traditional mail as well as electronic communications that are individually addressed and capable of being received privately. "This interpretation would clarify that direct mail includes those communications that are directed to particular individuals, such as facsimiles or email, but not directed to the public at large, as are internet bulletin boards."[6]

E-mail requires the sender to address the message to an individual e-mail address. Therefore, telemarketers or sellers who send individually addressed e-mail that provides a telephone number for consumers to call may be subject to the Telemarketing Sales Rule. The Commission is investigating whether its interpretation of "direct mail" accurately reflects the term and encompasses this electronic version of "direct mail."[7]

Pyramid Schemes

The FTC has brought several cases to stop alleged pyramid schemes that find victims through the Internet. In the Commission's largest Internet pyramid case to date, *FTC* v. *Fortuna Alliance*,[8] Fortuna allegedly promised consumers that, for $250, they would receive profits of over $5,000 per month. The court determined that 95 percent of the consumers who joined the program could never make more than they paid. The Commission obtained a temporary restraining order halting the unlawful practices and freezing the assets of the individuals who developed and operated the Fortuna program. The court order also required the defendants to repatriate the assets they had deposited overseas. In February 1997, the defendants stipulated to a permanent injunction that prohibited their scheme and provided for redress to consumers who requested refunds. The defendants subsequently balked at paying many consumers, and the Commission filed two separate contempt motions. On June 5,

1998, the court issued a contempt order against the defendants, prohibiting them from promoting any marketing or investment program until they had paid $2 million, plus interest, owed to consumers.

Another Internet pyramid case was *FTC* v. *Nia Cano d/b/a Credit Development Int'l & Drivers Seat Network*.[9] The scheme included false promises that those who joined CDI would receive an unsecured Visa or MasterCard credit card with a $5,000 limit and a low interest rate, as well as the opportunity to receive monthly income of $18,000 or more. The court granted a temporary restraining order, appointed a receiver to oversee the corporate defendants, and froze both the corporate and individual defendants' assets. After a hearing on November 20, 1997, the court issued a preliminary injunction against the defendants. The FTC estimates that over 30,000 consumers may have lost $3 million to $4 million in this scam.

Credit Repair Programs

This is an area that has seen a fair amount of activity on the Internet, and the FTC has pursued the issues. Here we'll look at two cases.

The $99 Case

In its first case targeting advertising on the "information superhighway," the Federal Trade Commission charged a Sacramento, California, man with making false claims in the course of promoting his credit-repair program online. In *FTC* v. *Corzine*,[10] the FTC charged Brian Corzine, doing business as Chase Consulting, for promoting his scheme on America Online. The program advised consumers to take steps to repair their credit records, while representing that it is "100% legal."

According to FTC Chairman Janet D. Steiger: "As these computer networks continue to grow, we will not tolerate the use of deceptive practices here any more than we have tolerated them on other recently-emerged technologies for marketing products and services to consumers."

Consumers were instructed to contact Chase Consulting through the computer service. Corzine allegedly enticed consumers through statements such as:

"FOR JUST $99.00 WE WILL SHOW YOU
HOW TO CREATE A BRAND NEW CREDIT FILE
AT ALL 3 OF THE MAJOR CREDIT BUREAUS:
100% LEGAL AND 200% GUARANTEED."

Consumers who contacted Chase Consulting by computer were instructed to obtain a "taxpayer identification number" from the Internal Revenue Service and then to use this number in place of their Social Security number on credit applications. The complete "file segregation" program included a booklet which instructed consumers to obtain two new addresses: one for use on their driver's licenses and one for use on credit applications. Corzine allegedly represented that the program is legal. However, consumers who falsify statements on certain loan and credit applications or falsify their Social Security number would violate one or more federal criminal statutes.

The $125 Case

The Federal Trade Commission settled a case in 1996 regarding a deceptive advertisement for credit repair services that was posted on about 3,000 Internet news groups. The settlement in *FTC* v. *Consumer Credit Advocates, P.C.*,[11] prevents engaging in fraudulent credit repair practices and requires the defendant to provide a warning to its customers that consumers have no legal right to have accurate information removed from their credit reports. The order also requires the defendants to pay $17,500 in consumer redress.

The defendants in this case charged fees ranging from $125 to $750 for each derogatory item challenged. According to the FTC complaint, Consumer Credit and Legal Services offered credit improvement and other services since about May 1993. In May 1994, they created Consumer Credit Advocates and, in February 1995, that firm hired a consultant which posted the challenged ad on the Internet.

The ad stated, in part:

> Our LAW FIRM offers direct guaranteed effective credit restoration services by experienced attorneys.... We have successfully facilitated the removal of Late Payments, Charge-offs, Foreclosures, Repossessions, Collection Accounts, Loan Defaults, Tax Liens, Judgments and Bankruptcies from our clients' credit reports.
> WE GUARANTEE THAT YOUR CREDIT CAN BE RESTORED! ! !

In fact, the FTC charged, the defendants cannot remove derogatory information such as bankruptcies, late payments, and defaulted loans from a credit report when the information is accurate and not obsolete. The defendants have not substantially improved thousands of clients' credit reports as they had represented.

The consent decree prohibits the defendants, among other things, from misrepresenting their success rate for improving consumers' credit reports and from misrepresenting that they can remove derogatory information from credit reports regardless of the accuracy or the age of the information.

The Audiotex Case

While most of the cases pursued by the FTC involved deceptive claims, one dealt with a unique scheme. Consumers who visited this web site were prompted to download a "viewer program" where they could see computer images for free. Once downloaded, the consumers' computer was "hijacked." The viewer program was turned off and an international number was then dialed and connected with the computer. The international call cost over $2 per minute, and charges continued until the computer was turned off. In come cases, consumers were charged thousands of dollars. The FTC, along with AT&T and the Secret Service, located the group. The case was *FTC* v. *Audiotex Connection, Inc.*[12]

Since December 1996, Audiotex operated and promoted one or more World Wide Web sites offering "adult" images. Web sites included "www.sexygirls.com," "www.beavisbutthead.com," and "www.1adult.com." Through these web sites, Audiotex represented that consumers could view "adult" images for free at sites on the Internet.

At one or more of the Audiotex web sites, they offer images for viewing at "FREE ADULT SITES." In addition, at one or more of the Audiotex web sites, they claim:

NO MEMBERSHIP FEES!
NO CREDIT CARDS NEEDED!
NO 900# CHARGES!

MORE SEX for FREE
ALL NUDE ALL FREE PICTURES.

The Audiotex web sites instruct consumers that to view the "adult" images, the consumer must first "download a special image viewer." This "image viewer" is a software program, which is identified as "david.exe," or "david7.exe," or other similar names.

Contrary to the clear implication of the term "image viewer," the "david.exe" (or similarly named software) is not a means for reading computer data and converting such data into visual images.

According to the complaint in this case:

> If downloaded, installed, and activated, ["david.exe"] will, without any explanations or adequate disclosures: (a) automatically terminate the consumer's computer modem connection to the consumer's local Internet service provider while maintaining the appearance that the computer modem remains connected to such local Internet service provider; (b) automatically direct the consumer's computer modem to dial an international telephone number to re-connect to the Internet; (c) maintain the international long distance telephone connection thus established unless and until the consumer turns off the power switch to his computer or modem, or takes other unusual action to terminate the telephone connection; and (d) cause the consumer to incur international long distance telephone charges on his telephone bill at rates in excess of $2.00 per minute for as long as the international long distance telephone connection is maintained. One of the techniques that this software employs to maintain the appearance that the computer modem remains connected to the consumer's local Internet service provider is to automatically turn off the speaker on the consumer's modem before dialing, thus preventing the consumer from hearing the sound of the international number being automatically dialed.

Spam: Unsolicited Electronic Mail

The FTC has a "long history of promoting competition and protecting consumers in new marketing media." Door-to-door sales, television and print adverting, direct mail marketing, pay-per-call number sales, and telemarketing were all marked by early struggles between legitimate merchants and fraud artists battling for potential profits of the new marketplace.

The FTC monitors deceptive, unsolicited electronic mail, commonly called "spam." FTC Commissioner Shelia F. Anthony told the Senate Commerce, Science and Transportation Committee on June 17, 1998, that the Commission views the problem of deception as a significant issue in the debate over unsolicited e-mail and other Internet schemes. The Commission closely monitors e-mail for deception and fraud. Consumers can forward fraudulent e-mail to an FTC e-mail address: uce@ftc.gov.

FTC Chairman Robert Pitofsky stated: "The actions taken between the FTC and its partners have been very effective thus far in fighting consumer fraud. But with increased activity on the Internet, scam artists are coming up with inexpensive and efficient ways to reach vast numbers of consumers. The FTC and its law enforcement partners, using technology for enforcement, detection, deterrence, and education, will continue our full-fledged campaign."

Other Common Internet Schemes

The FTC has produced a list of the 12 most common scams found in unsolicited e-mail.[13]

The most common include:

Making Money By Sending Bulk E-Mail:

These companies offer to sell a list of e-mail addresses or software to allow the consumer to send bulk e-mail. However, sending bulk e-mail violates the terms of service of most Internet service providers. Virtually no legitimate business engages in bulk e-mailings. Several states have laws regulating the sending of bulk e-mail as well.

Chain Letters:

These are simply electronic versions of the old-fashioned chain letter. They usually make claims that the consumer will make a large amount of money in a short amount of time.

Work-At-Home Schemes:

E-mail messages offer the chance to earn money in the comfort of your own home. They usually involve envelope stuffing or assembly type operations.

Health And Diet Scams:

These offers attempt to sell products claiming the product is a "scientific breakthrough," "miracle cure," or "secret formula." Some come with testimonials from "cured" consumers or endorsements from "experts."

Easy Money:

These offers make claims such as "Learn how to make $4,000 in one day" or "Make unlimited profits exchanging money on currency markets."

Get Something Free:

These solicitations offer valuable free items like computers or long distance phone cards to get consumers to pay membership fees to sign up with the scams. Consumers later learn that they don't qualify for the "free" gift until they recruit other members.

Investment Opportunities:

These scams offer outrageously high rates of return with no risk. Promoters suggest they have high level financial connections or are privy to inside information.

Cable Descrambler Kits:

For a small initial investment you can buy a cable

descrambler kit so you can receive cable without paying the subscription fee. These kits don't work and pirating cable signals is illegal.

Guaranteed Loans or Credit on Easy Terms:

Some offer home equity loans even if you don't have any equity in your home. Others offer guaranteed, unsecured credit, regardless of credit history.

Credit Repair Scams:

These scams target consumers with poor credit, claiming that for an up-front fee they can clear up bad credit. They may also offer to give the consumer a completely clean credit slate by showing the consumer how to get an Employer Identification Number.

Vacation Prize Promotions:

Like their mail counterparts, these e-mail promotions inform the person that they have been selected to receive a "luxury" vacation at a bargain-basement price.

Business Opportunity Scams:

These scams promise great income for a small initial investment in time and money.

FTC Enforcement

In the first law enforcement action targeting fraudulent, unsolicited commercial e-mail, the FTC charged a company using unsolicited, false, and misleading commercial e-mail, or "spam," to induce consumers to advertise on its Internet newspaper sites. According to the charges, the company claimed that investors in the Internet "billboards" could sublease advertising space and earn a guaranteed return on their investment. The company claimed that purchasers could reasonably expect to sublease 25 percent of their billboard, realizing earnings up to $800 per month. In fact, the FTC alleged, few purchasers achieved the levels of earnings claimed and the company did not provide a refund as promised. In addition, the business ventures sold by the company were franchises, and the company failed to make complete and accurate disclosures as required by the FTC's franchise rule.

Jodie Bernstein, Director of the FTC Bureau of Consumer Protection, stated: "The rules for advertising by e-mail are the same as the rules for advertising through the regular mail: don't mislead or lie to consumers, or the FTC will come after you."[14]

STATE INVOLVEMENT

Typical of the actions taken by state attorneys general are the following two cases.

Jackie Don Lewis was indicted in May 1998 by the Missouri Attorney General for fraudulently selling computer equipment over the Internet. He'd receive money from consumers who responded to his Internet ad but failed to deliver the computer equipment and would not return phone calls or e-mails. According to the Attorney General, "Consumers should exercise a certain amount of caution and direction when they intend to make large purchases over the Internet from businesses or individuals they have not dealt with before." Because Lewis had prior felony convictions, he was sentenced to three years in prison.[15]

In New York, John Chen and Carl Schwartz sold pepper spray through bulk e-mail offers. Although pepper spray sales are legal in New York, only authorized firearms dealers, pharmacists, and other vendors approved by the Superintendent of State Police are permitted to sell the product. Neither Chen nor Schwartz were authorized to sell pepper spray. New York Attorney General Dennis Vacco fined the two men and took away their computers.[16]

PRIVATE LAWSUITS

EarthLink Goes To Court

In *Earthlink Network, Inc.* v. *Cyber Promotions, Inc.*,[17] junk e-mail was the focus. EarthLink had charged Cyber Promotions with falsely labeling messages with EarthLink's addresses and clogging members' mailboxes with thousands of unwanted e-mails. Cyber Promotions settled the $2 million case, with the following provisions. In addition to writing a formal letter of apology to EarthLink and its members for the inconvenience it may have caused, Cyber Promotions was prohibited from:

> 1. Causing, authorizing, participating in, or intentionally or recklessly assisting or enabling others in the sending of any commercial or promotional messages or solicitations through e-mails to any EarthLink e-mail address without the express permission of the EarthLink subscriber. "Express permission" shall mean (1) written permission sent by some means other than e-mail; and/or (2) e-mail permission, if, and only if, prior to the transmission of the commercial or promotional message, the user allegedly granting permission affirmatively responds to a separate request for confirmation of the permission (i.e., the validity of the user's request is confirmed via a "three-way handshake").
>
> 2. Intentionally or recklessly assisting or enabling others in the use of any false or misleading reference to EarthLink, an EarthLink e-mail address, EarthLink equipment, or EarthLink's computer system or resources in the header of, or in connection with in any way, any electronic message or newsgroup posting.

3. Causing, authorizing, participating in, or intentionally or recklessly assisting or enabling others in the modification, disguise, elimination, or erasure of the identification of the originating address and/or header of or for any e-mail sent to an EarthLink subscriber.

4. The sale, offer or other distribution of any e-mail address of any EarthLink subscriber and/or any list of e-mail addresses that contains the address of any Earthlink subscriber.

Cyber Promotions would also be liable for up to $1 million if it violates the settlement agreement.

The Hotmail Case

Hotmail is an Internet Service Provider (ISP) that provided free e-mail to over 10 million subscribers. Every e-mail sent by a Hotmail subscriber automatically displayed a header depicting Hotmail's domain name, "hotmail.com," and a footer depicting Hotmail's "signature" at the bottom of the e-mail, which read: "Get Your Private, Free E-mail at http://www.hotmail.com." To become a Hotmail subscriber, the consumer agreed to abide by a service agreement that specifically prohibited subscribers from using Hotmail's services to send unsolicited commercial bulk e-mail, or "spam," or to send obscene or pornographic messages.

Hotmail found out that several individuals were sending spam e-mails which contained Hotmail's return address to thousands of Internet users. The spam messages advertised pornography, bulk e-mailing software, and "get rich quick" schemes. Hotmail also discovered that a number of Hotmail accounts were created to collect responses to these e-mails and "bounced back" messages to a "drop box" whose contents were never opened, read, or responded to. These Hotmail accounts were used as return addresses instead of actual return addresses.

As a result, Hotmail was inundated with hundreds of

thousands of misdirected responses, including complaints from Hotmail subscribers. The overwhelming number of e-mails took up a substantial amount of Hotmail's computer space, threatened to delay Hotmail's subscribers in sending and receiving e-mail, and resulted in significant costs to Hotmail in dealing with the problem. It also damaged Hotmail's reputation and goodwill.

Typical of the spamming that went on were the following that were stated in the complaint:

> Hotmail discovered a spam e-mail message advertising pornographic material that was sent by ALS. While this spam originated from ALS and was transmitted through an e-mail provider other than Hotmail, ALS falsely designated a real Hotmail e-mail address as the point of origin. The e-mail address chosen for this purpose was "geri748@hotmail.com."
>
> Hotmail also discovered a number of spam e-mail messages advertising pornographic material that were sent by LCGM. While these spam e-mails originated from LCGM and were transmitted through an e-mail provider other than Hotmail, LCGM falsely designated a number of real Hotmail e-mail address as the points of origin. The e-mail address chosen for this purpose was "becky167@hotmail.com" [etc.].
>
> Hotmail also discovered a spam e-mail message advertising pornographic material that was sent by Moss. While this spam originated from Moss and was transmitted through an e-mail provider other than Hotmail, Moss falsely designated a real Hotmail e-mail address as the point of origin. The e-mail address chosen for this purpose was "rebecca_h19@hotmail.com."
>
> Hotmail also discovered a spam e-mail message

> advertising a cable descrambler kit that was sent by Palmer. While this spam originated from Palmer and was transmitted through an e-mail provider other than Hotmail, Palmer falsely designated two real Hotmail e-mail addresses as the points of origin. The e-mail addresses chosen for this purpose were "kelCA@hotmail.com" and "angiCA@hotmail.com."
>
> Hotmail also discovered a spam e-mail message advertising a service that matches people seeking cash grants that was sent by Financial. While this spam originated from Financial and was transmitted through an e-mail provider other than Hotmail, Financial falsely designated a real Hotmail e-mail address as the point of origin. The e-mail address chosen for this purpose was "order_desk66@hotmail.com."
>
> Hotmail also discovered a number of spam e-mail messages advertising pornography that were sent by Snow. While this spam originated from Snow and was transmitted through an e-mail provider other than Hotmail, Snow falsely designated several real Hotmail e-mail address as the point of origin. The e-mail addresses chosen for this purpose were "bettyharris123@hotmail.com," "annharris123@hotmail. com," "cindyharris123@hotmail.com," "wilmasimpson@hotmail.com," "rw3570@hotmail.com;" "rw3560@hotmail.com," and "jw2244@hotmail.com."

The court in *Hotmail Corp.* v. *Van Money Pie, Inc.*[18] granted Hotmail a preliminary injunction for unfair competition under the Lanham Act and for violation of the Computer Fraud and Abuse Act.[19] The court found that the defendants' use of Hotmail's domain name and return address was likely to cause consumers to believe that the defendants were somehow associated with or sponsored by Hotmail.

Under the federal dilution statute, ownership of a famous mark and dilution of the distinctive quality of that mark, regardless of whether consumers are confused about the parties' goods, is actionable.[20] And, under the California dilution statute, actual injury or likelihood of confusion need not be shown; plaintiff need only show its business reputation is likely to be injured or the distinctive value of its mark is likely to be diluted.[21]

Here, the court stated:

> [T]he evidence supports a finding that plaintiff will likely prevail on its federal and state dilution claims and that there are at least serious questions going to the merits of these claims. First, there is sufficient evidence to lead to a finding that plaintiff's trademark is "famous" within the meaning of 15 U.S.C. § 1125(c)(1) and also that it is entitled to state dilution protection. Plaintiff's mark is distinctive, has been advertised and used extensively both nationally and internationally in connection with plaintiff's services, and has established considerable consumer recognition. Moreover, the use of identical marks by defendants who are sending e-mails to thousands of e-mail users across the country and the world through identical trade channels threatens to dilute the distinctiveness of plaintiff's trademark and threatens to harm plaintiff's business reputation.

The Computer Fraud and Abuse Act prohibits any person from knowingly causing the transmission of information which intentionally causes damage, without authorization, to a protected computer.

In supporting its computer fraud claim, the court stated:

> The evidence supports a finding that plaintiff will likely prevail on its Computer Fraud and Abuse Act claim and that there are at least serious questions going to the merits of this claim in that plaintiff has presented evidence of the following: that defendants knowingly falsified return e-mail addresses so that they included, in place of the actual sender's return address, a number of Hotmail addresses; that such addresses were tied to Hotmail accounts set up by defendants with the intention of collecting never-to-be-read consumer complaints and "bounced back" e-mails; that defendants knowingly caused this false information to be transmitted to thousands of e-mail recipients; that defendants took this action knowing such recipients would use the "reply to" feature to transmit numerous responses to the fraudulently created Hotmail accounts, knowing thousands of messages would be "bounced back" to Hotmail instead of to defendants, and knowing that numerous recipients of defendants' spam would e-mail complaints to Hotmail; that defendants took such actions knowing the risks caused thereby to Hotmail's computer system and online services, which include risks that Hotmail would be forced to withhold or delay the use of computer services to its legitimate subscribers; that defendants' actions caused damage to Hotmail; and that such actions were done by defendants without Hotmail's authorization.

LEGISLATION

Federal Level

A bill entitled Anti-Slamming Amendments Act[22] passed the Senate on May 12, 1998. Under the bill, commercial electronic mail that contains an advertisement for the sale of a product or service or that contains a solicitation for the use of a telephone number that connects the user to a person or service that advertises goods or services, must include:

1. The name, physical address, electronic mail address, and telephone number of the person initiating the transmission.
2. The name, physical address, electronic mail address, and telephone number of the person who created the content of the message if different from the transmitter.
3. A statement that further transmissions of unsolicited commercial e-mail to the recipient may be stopped at no cost to the recipient by sending a reply to the originating e-mail address with the word "remove" in the subject line. All Internet routing information contained in the message must be accurate and valid.

The bill gives the FTC the authority to investigate these situations and impose penalties of up to $15,000. The states may also take action on behalf of their citizens under the law with prior notice to the FTC. Internet service providers are not covered by the law unless they send unsolicited e-mail to noncustomers.

Three anti-spamming bills have been introduced in the House. Two of the bills[23] amend the Communications Act of 1934, and ban the transmission of unsolicited ads by e-mail where there is no preexisting business or personal relationship. They also require the sender to supply identifying information, including a return e-mail address.

The third bill, entitled "E-mail User Protection Act of 1998,"[24] asks Congress to make the following findings:

1. The Internet has become a critical mode of global communication and now presents unprecedented opportunities for the development and growth of global commerce and an integrated worldwide economy.

2. The receipt of unsolicited commercial e-mail may result in undue monetary costs to recipients who cannot refuse to accept such mail and who incur costs for the storage of such mail, or for the time spent accessing, reviewing, and discarding such mail, or for both.

3. An increasing number of senders of unsolicited commercial e-mail purposefully disguise the source of such mail so as to prevent recipients from responding to such mail quickly and easily.

4. Because recipients of unsolicited commercial e-mail that does not provide a return address are unable to avoid the receipt of such mail through reasonable means, such mail may threaten the privacy of recipients.

5. By providing remedies similar to those provided with respect to unsolicited facsimile transmissions and automated dialing equipment in the Telephone Consumer Protection Act of 1991, the Congress can provide privacy protections without infringing important Constitutional rights or imperiling the commercial development of the Internet.

Under the bill, it would be unlawful for anyone to intentionally send an unsolicited commercial e-mail from an unregistered or fictitious Internet domain for the purpose of preventing replies to the message. The bill would also prohibit an individual from failing to comply with the e-mail recipient's request to cease sending e-mail in the future.

State Laws

According to the National Conference of State Legislatures, 17 states have proposed legislation to restrict unsolicited e-mail containing advertisements. To date, only Washington and Nevada have enacted laws regarding unsolicited e-mail.

Washington

Under the Washington law, it is illegal to transmit a commercial e-mail message from a computer located in Washington or to an e-mail address that the sender "knows, or has reason to know, is held by a Washington resident" that uses a third party's Internet domain name or otherwise misrepresents the source of the message or contains false or misleading information on the subject line.

Interactive computer services, which are defined as an "information service, system or access software provider that provides or enables computer access by multiple users to a computer server, including specifically a service or system that provides access to the Internet," may also block the receipt or transmission through its service of any commercial electronic mail that it reasonably believes is, or will be, sent in violation of the law.

In addition, violating the spam law also violates the Washington consumer protection act.

In enacting the law the legislature stated:

> The legislature finds that the volume of commercial electronic mail is growing, and the consumer protection division of the attorney general's office reports an increasing number of consumer complaints about commercial electronic mail. Interactive computer service providers indicate that their systems sometimes cannot handle the volume of commercial electronic mail being sent and that filtering systems fail to screen out unsolicited commercial electronic mail messages when senders use a third party's Internet domain name without the third party's permission, or otherwise misrepresent the message's point of origin. The legislature seeks to provide some immediate

> relief to interactive computer service providers by prohibiting the sending of commercial electronic mail messages that use a third party's Internet domain name without the third party's permission, misrepresent the message's point of origin, or contain untrue or misleading information on the subject line.

On October 22, 1998, the Attorney General of Washington State filed the first lawsuit under the new law. The suit, filed in King County Superior Court, alleges that Natural Instincts and its owner, Jason Heckel, sent unsolicited e-mail to millions of Internet users to sell his online book entitled, *How to Profit from the Internet*. Many of the people who received the spam were residents of Washington state.

Heckel used a misleading subject line, which read, "Did I get the right email address?" The goal was to entice recipients to download and read his entire message. The "message" was actually a sales pitch for Heckel's book. Heckel also used an invalid return e-mail address, which violated the new Washington law.

Commenting on the case, Attorney General Christine Gregoire said: "Washington Internet users were bombarded by this spammer with e-mail advertisements for a get-rich-quick scheme. Consumers didn't know where the message was coming from and weren't told in the subject line of the message what it was about. His spam clearly crossed the boundary from being annoying to being illegal."[25]

Nevada

Nevada law makes it unlawful to e-mail an advertisement unless it is readily identifiable as a promotion and clearly provides the "legal name, complete street address and e-mail address of the person sending the e-mail, along with a statement that the recipient may decline to receive additionals and the procedures for declining such e-mail."[26]

Proposed Anti-Spamming Legislation

California

Several bills have been introduced in California. One Assembly Bill[27] would expand California law that prohibits persons from faxing unsolicited advertising to also include unsolicited e-mail.

The proposed bill:

1. Expands the existing prohibition against unsolicited faxed advertisements by amending it to include the transmission of unsolicited advertising by e-mail.

2. Requires the sender of unsolicited e-mail advertisement to provide either a toll-free telephone number or valid sender operated return e-mail address that the recipient of the advertisement may call or e-mail to notify the sender not to e-mail further unsolicited documents ("opt-out" provision).

3.Requires the unsolicited e-mail advertisements to contain a statement of specified size type, disclosing the toll-free number or e-mail address which the recipient may notify to stop further unsolicited e-mail advertisements.

4. Prohibits sending unsolicited e-mail ads to any recipient who has notified the sender to stop further unsolicited e-mails.

5. Specifies that, in the case of e-mail, the bill shall apply when the unsolicited e-mailed documents are delivered to a California resident via an electronic mail service provider's service or equipment located in the state.

6. Requires any unsolicited e-mail advertisements for the sale, lease, rental, gift offer, or other disposition of property or services, or for the extension of credit, to include the acronym label "ADY" in the first four characters of the e-mail's subject line, and to include the acronym label "ADV:ADLT" in the first eight characters of an e-mail's subject line when the goods or services

may only be viewed or purchased by someone 18 years of age or older.

7. Becomes inoperative if federal law on this subject is enacted.

The bill also provides the right to opt out of spam distribution lists. It would also penalize spammers who do not provide consumers with a means to opt out or who fail to comply with a request to stop sending the unsolicited e-mail.

Another California bill[28] is more powerful and would prevent spamming and domain-name fraud. This bill would allow Internet service providers to sue spammers for any damage they cause to the provider's network. It would also make use of an unauthorized domain name a criminal offense. Service providers could recover damages of $50 for each unsolicited e-mail, up to a maximum of $25,000 per day.

New York

A bill in New York[29] deals with the fact that unsolicited e-mail is not covered under current law like unsolicited facsimiles are. This bill would protect consumers from unwanted and unsolicited e-mail while respecting those consumers who do want to receive the advertisements. The bill would also protect the privacy interests of consumers who have their e-mail address and other personal identifying information "harvested."

The bill would:

1. Make it unlawful to send an unsolicited e-mail advertisement unless the sender clearly and conspicuously indicates that the mail is an advertisement and provides the sender's identity, postal address, telephone number, and the means to prevent further unsolicited e-mail from the sender.

2. Make it unlawful to sell, lease, or exchange any consumer's e-mail address or any other personal identifying information that was obtained online without the consumer's knowledge or consent.

3. Provide for private action for damages.

New Jersey

The New Jersey bill[30] would prohibit sending unsolicited advertisements to an e-mail address unless the person has a business or personal relationship with the person receiving the advertisement or unless the individual has expressly requested the e-mail. The sender would be required to provide the identity of the business or other entity sending the message and include the return e-mail address. This bill allows a private action with the possibility of recovering actual damages or $200 per violation, whichever is greater.

North Carolina

A North Carolina bill[31] would impose civil liability for sending e-mail that includes an advertisement, unless:

1. The person transmitting the item has a preexisting business or personal relationship with the recipient.

2. The recipient has expressly consented to receive the item.

3. The ad is readily identifiable as promotional (or states that it is an advertisement) and clearly provides the name and address of the transmitting person, a notice that the recipient may decline to receive additional advertisements, and the procedures for declining such electronic mail. Remedies would include actual damages or damages of $10 per item of electronic mail received, attorneys' fees and costs, and injunctive relief.

INTERNET SERVICE PROVIDERS

FTC Enforcement

In March 1998 the FTC settled a case against America Online, Inc., Prodigy Services Corp., and Compuserve, Inc., for their "free trial" offers that actually resulted in charges to consumers. The FTC claimed that the three Internet service providers had not made it clear that consumers had an affirmative obligation to cancel before the trial period ended. So, as a result, consumers that did not cancel were automatically enrolled as members and were charged monthly service charges. The provisions of the consent order stop the companies from misrepresenting the terms or conditions of any trial offer. They must also not represent that the service is free without disclosing clearly any obligation to cancel or state action that must be taken to avoid charges. The case was *America Online, Inc.*[32]

State Enforcement

The Illinois Attorney General (and attorneys general for the states of Alabama, Arizona, Arkansas, California, Connecticut, Florida, Georgia, Idaho, Illinois, Indiana, Kansas, Kentucky, Louisiana, Maine, Maryland, Massachusetts, Michigan, Mississippi, Missouri, Nebraska, Nevada, New Jersey, New Mexico, New York, North Carolina, North Dakota, Ohio, Oklahoma, Oregon, Pennsylvania, Rhode Island, South Carolina, Tennessee, Texas, Utah, Vermont, Virginia, Washington, West Virginia, and Wisconsin) settled with American Online (AOL) in *In The Matter of America Online, Inc.*[33] This settlement provides new protections when prices or services are altered.

The settlement provides the following:

Disclosures for Free Offers:

Under the terms of AOL's "Free Trial Offer," the company must make new disclosures, including that the 50-hour free trial must be used within a month, that the consumer must cancel the trial to avoid billing, and that consumers should be careful to determine if AOL maintains a local access number in their area to avoid long-distance charges. If

> consumers cancel their AOL service, procedures must be explained clearly in AOL under "Keyword: Cancel" and "Terms of Service." The company also must mail a notice of cancellation.
>
> Disclosures Concerning Pricing:
>
> If AOL increases its monthly fees or otherwise modifies its contract, it must provide clear notice of the change at least 30 days in advance. The notice must describe the change, state its effective date, and direct the subscriber to an area where the change is described in greater detail. If such notice is not delivered, a subscriber is entitled to a refund on any price increase.
>
> Disclosures Concerning Premium Areas:
>
> AOL has agreed to notify all consumers, via pop-up screen, when they enter a game or other premium service area where charges are incurred beyond the monthly fee. The pop-up box will state the rate per minute of the extra charges.
>
> Disclosure Regarding Advertising to Minors:
>
> In advertisements for AOL service directed towards persons under the age of 18 or which are placed in a medium directed or disseminated primarily to persons under the age of 18, AOL shall: (1) use language generally understandable to the youngest age group to which the advertisement is directed; (2) present disclosure information in such a manner to attract the attention of the youngest age group; and (3) explain that a person must be 18 years or older to subscribe to AOL, if that is AOL's policy.

AOL agreed to two earlier settlements in 1996 and 1997 with numerous states regarding the company's $19.95-a-month unlimited service promotion.

"We are demystifying the relationship between consumers and online services," said Illinois Attorney General Ryan. "Under this settlement AOL must notify consumers in advance whenever there is a price increase or substantial service change. The notification must be clear and direct. The goal is to make sure that consumers know all the facts so they can make informed choices."[34]

Communications Decency Act of 1996

In February of 1996, Congress chose to "promote the continued development of the Internet and other interactive computer services and other interactive media" and "to preserve the vibrant and competitive free market" for such services, largely "unfettered by Federal or State regulation...."[35] It effectively immunized providers of interactive computer services from civil liability in tort with respect to material disseminated by them that was actually created by others. By recognizing the speed of information and the near impossibility of controlling information content, Congress decided not to treat providers of interactive computer services like newspapers, magazines, and television and radio stations. All of these may be held liable for publishing or distributing obscene or defamatory material written or prepared by others. While Congress could have made a different policy choice, but because of the uniquenesses of the Internet it choose not to hold interactive computer services liable for their failure to edit, withhold, or restrict access to offensive material disseminated through this medium.

Section 230(c) of the Communications Decency Act of 1996 provides: "No provider or user of an interactive computer service shall be treated as the publisher or speaker of any information provided by another information content provider."

In another case, the court, in *Zeran* v. *America Online, Inc.*,[36] stated:

> The purpose of this statutory immunity is not difficult to discern. Congress recognized the threat that tort-based lawsuits pose to freedom of speech in the new and burgeoning Internet medium. The imposition of tort liability on service providers for the communications of others represented, for Congress, simply another form of intrusive government regulation of speech. Section 230 was enacted, in part, to maintain the robust nature of Internet communication and, accordingly, to keep government interference in the medium to a minimum.
>
> None of this means, of course, that the original culpable party who posts defamatory messages would escape accountability. While Congress acted to keep government regulation of the Internet to a minimum, it also found it to be the policy of the United States "to ensure vigorous enforcement of Federal criminal laws to deter and punish trafficking in obscenity, stalking, and harassment by means of computer" Id. § 230(b)(5). Congress made a policy choice, however, not to deter harmful online speech through the separate route of imposing tort liability on companies that serve as intermediaries for other parties' potentially injurious messages.

The Drudge Report

In *Blumenthal* v. *Drudge*,[37] the court ruled that America Online (AOL) was immune from defamation claims that arose out of a defamatory statement made in a gossip column published by AOL. The Communications Decency Act of 1996 granted Internet service providers immunity from civil tort liability for material disseminated by them that was created by others.

The defamation suit by two White House employees

against Matt Drudge (author of an Internet gossip column called the "Drudge Report") was about an allegedly defamatory statement about Mr. Sidney Blumenthal and Jacqueline Jordan Blumenthal. The Drudge Report (www.drudgereport.com) was published by AOL and was written exclusively by Matt Drudge. AOL did not edit or verify any of the information in the report. Blumenthal included AOL as a defendant because AOL had a contract with Matt Drudge to publish the gossip column to AOL subscribers.

On August 10, 1997, the following article was available on the Internet:

> The DRUDGE REPORT has learned that top GOP operatives who feel there is a double-standard of only reporting republican shame believe they are holding an ace card: New White House recruit Sidney Blumenthal has a spousal abuse past that has been effectively covered up.
>
> The accusations are explosive.
>
> There are court records of Blumenthal's violence against his wife, one influential republican, who demanded anonymity, tells the DRUDGE REPORT.
>
> If they begin to use [Don] Sipple and his problems against us, against the Republican Party... to show hypocrisy, Blumenthal would become fair game. Wasn't it Clinton who signed the Violence Against Women Act?
>
> There goes the budget deal honeymoon.
>
> One White House source, also requesting anonymity, says the Blumenthal wife-beating allegation is a pure fiction that has been created by Clinton enemies. [The First Lady] would not have brought him in if he had this in his background, assures the well-placed staffer. This story about Blumenthal has been in circulation for years.

> Last month President Clinton named Sidney Blumenthal an Assistant to the President as part of the Communications Team. He's brought in to work on communications strategy, special projects theming – a newly created position.
>
> Every attempt to reach Blumenthal proved unsuccessful.

AOL argued that it be dismissed from the case since it was immune from the defamation suit based on the Communications Decency Act.

Section 230(c) of the Act provides:

> No provider or user of an interactive computer service shall be treated as the publisher or speaker of any information provided by another information content provider.

The Communications Decency Act was enacted to deal with the new challenges the Internet provided in connection with the publishing of information. In the Act, Congress chose to "promote the continued development of the Internet and other interactive media" and "to preserve the vibrant and competitive free market" for such services "unfettered by Federal or State regulation...."[38]

The court interpreted § 230 as follows:

> By its plain language, § 230 creates a federal immunity to any cause of action that would make service providers liable for information originating with a third-party user of the service. Specifically, § 230 precludes courts from entertaining claims that would place a computer service provider in a publisher's role. Thus, lawsuits seeking to hold a service provider liable for its exercise of a publisher's traditional editorial functions – such as deciding

whether to publish, withdraw, postpone or alter content – are barred.

The court stated: "AOL was nothing more than a provider of an interactive computer service on which the Drudge Report was carried, and Congress has said quite clearly that such a provider shall not be treated as a "publisher or speaker" and therefore may not be held liable in tort."[39]

COPYRIGHT ISSUES AND THE INTERNET

In *Playboy Enterprise, Inc.* v. *Frena*,[40] Playboy sued an online service provider because a subscriber of the service downloaded digital copies of copyrighted Playboy photographs.

The Court held the online service provider directly liable for the distribution of unauthorized copies on the service as well as the display of unauthorized copies to subscribers even though the provider did not have knowledge that the subscriber had downloaded the photographs.

The Court further stated that "[i]t does not matter that [the online service provider] may have been unaware of the copyright infringement.... Intent or knowledge is not an element of infringement, and thus even an innocent infringer is liable...."

This decision seems to impose a next-to-impossible burden on an online service provider to screen all uploaded information and material. The problem is that an online service provider has no way of knowing whether the information or material is subject to copyright protection. The courts have justified imposing this heavy burden by relying on the fact that the Copyright Act gives courts the discretion to consider the innocent intent of the infringer in determining the amount of damages to be awarded.

Protection Against Infringement

An online service provider may protect itself by having a

written, signed contract with its subscribers. The contract should state that:

1. The subscriber acknowledges that the Internet service provider does not regulate the content of its online service.

2. The subscriber acknowledges that the information it is downloading will be considered in the public domain.

3. The subscriber warrants that it has all rights necessary to submit such information it is downloading.

4. The Internet service provider will not take any responsibility to determine what information is protected nor will it be responsible for the use of the information by other subscribers.

In addition, the contract should include an indemnity clause which requires the subscriber to indemnify the online service provider against actions brought by a third party alleging improper use, publication, distribution or display of the protected material. This is not absolute protection, but it should help the online service provider if a legal action is ever brought for posting copyrighted materials.

Another option is including a disclaimer on the front screen every time a subscriber logs on. This should also be used by online service providers who already have written contracts with their subscribers. The disclaimer should simply incorporate the elements listed above. However, this type of disclaimer offers much less protection than a written contract.

The Digital Millennium Copyright Act

In October of 1998 Congress passed the Digital Millennium Copyright Act,[41] which was signed into law by President Clinton on October 28, 1998. The Act establishes limitations on the liability of Internet and online service providers for copyright violations by their subscribers, provided that certain conditions are satisfied. The Act immunizes an Internet or online service provider from claims for its storage of infringing materials on its system at the direction of the user of those materials. Providers are also shielded from claims based on their referring or linking users to a site containing infringing materials. These limitations on liability do not apply, however, if the provider knew or had reason to know that the materials were infringing, derived a financial benefit from the infringing activity, or failed to remove the infringing materials expeditiously upon notice.

Section 512 of the Act states:

> Limitations on liability relating to material online include:
>
> (a) TRANSITORY DIGITAL NETWORK COMMUNICATIONS – A service provider shall not be liable for monetary relief, or, except as provided in subsection (j), for injunctive or other equitable relief, for infringement of copyright by reason of the provider's transmitting, routing, or providing connections for, material through a system or network controlled or operated by or for the service provider, or by reason of the intermediate and transient storage of that material in the course of such transmitting, routing, or providing connections, if
>
> (1) the transmission of the material was initiated by or at the direction of a person other than the service provider;
>
> (2) the transmission, routing, provision of connections, or storage is carried out through an automatic technical process without selection of the material by the service provider;
>
> (3) the service provider does not select the recipients of the material except as an automatic response to the request of another person;
>
> (4) no copy of the material made by the service

provider in the course of such intermediate or transient storage is maintained on the system or network in a manner ordinarily accessible to anyone other than anticipated recipients, and no such copy is maintained on the system or network in a manner ordinarily accessible to such anticipated recipients for a longer period than is reasonably necessary for the transmission, routing, or provision of connections; and

(5) the material is transmitted through the system or network without modification of its content.

(b) SYSTEM CACHING –

(1) LIMITATION ON LIABILITY – A service provider shall not be liable for monetary relief, or, except as provided in subsection (j), for injunctive or other equitable relief, for infringement of copyright by reason of the intermediate and temporary storage of material on a system or network controlled or operated by or for the service provider in a case in which –

(A) the material is made available online by a person other than the service provider;

(B) the material is transmitted from the person described in subparagraph (A) through the system or network to a person other than the person described in subparagraph (A) at the direction of that other person; and

(C) the storage is carried out through an automatic technical process for the purpose of making the material available to users of the system or network who, after the material is transmitted as described in subparagraph (B), request access to the material from the person described in subparagraph

(A), if the conditions set forth in paragraph (2) are met.

(2) CONDITIONS – The conditions referred to in paragraph (1) are that –

(A) the material described in paragraph (1) is transmitted to the subsequent users described in paragraph (1)(C) without modification to its content from the manner in which the material was transmitted from the person described in paragraph (1)(A);

(B) the service provider described in paragraph (1) complies with rules concerning the refreshing, reloading, or other updating of the material when specified by the person making the material available online in accordance with a generally accepted industry standard data communications protocol for the system or network through which that person makes the material available, except that this subparagraph applies only if those rules are not used by the person described in paragraph (1)(A) to prevent or unreasonably impair the intermediate storage to which this subsection applies.

PRIVACY ISSUES

One of the major concerns of the Internet involves the amount of privacy protection consumers have when using the Internet. Especially when it involves children.

FTC Chairman Robert Pitofsky, before a House subcommittee on July 21, 1998, pointed out: "The Commission believes that, unless industry can demonstrate that it has developed and implemented broad-based and effective self-regulatory programs by the end of this year, additional governmental authority in this area would be appropriate and necessary."

In the area of children's online privacy, the FTC recommends legislation that would place parents in control of the online collection and use of personal identifying information from their children.

FTC Enforcement

GeoCities settled FTC charges that it misrepresented why it collected personal identifying information from children and adults. This was the first FTC case involving Internet privacy. Under the terms of a proposed consent order, GeoCities would be required to post on its site a clear and prominent privacy notice. Consumers would need to be notified of the information that was being collected and the purpose, whom it will be disclosed to, and how to access and remove the information. GeoCities also would have to obtain parental consent before collecting information from children 12 and under.

Jodie Bernstein, Director of the FTC Bureau of Consumer Protection, stated: "GeoCities misled its customers, both children and adults, by not telling the truth about how it was using their personal information."

Through an online registration process, GeoCities created a database that included e-mail and postal addresses, member interest areas, and demographics including income, education, gender, marital status, and occupation. GeoCities told consumers that its membership application form was used only to provide members the specific advertising offers and products or services they requested and that "optional" information (education level, income, marital status, occupation, and interests) would not be released without the member's permission. However, this personal identifying information of children and adults was released to third-party marketers. The FTC complaint also charges that GeoCities engaged in deceptive practices relating to its collection of information from children.[42]

Federal Legislation

Several bills were introduced in Congress regarding online consumer privacy.

The Consumer Internet Privacy Protection Act of 1997[43] would prohibit disclosure to a third party any personally identifiable information provided by a subscriber without the subscriber's prior written consent. The bill also provides that subscribers be permitted to revoke such consent at any time. In addition, at the subscriber's request, the service would be required to (1) provide the subscriber with his or her personally identifiable information maintained by the service; (2) permit the subscriber to verify the information; (3) permit the subscriber to correct any errors in the information; and (4) provide the subscriber with the identity of any third-party recipients of the subscriber's personal information.

The Federal Internet Privacy Protection Act of 1997[44] would prohibit federal agencies from revealing (through the Internet) an individual's education, financial, medical, or employment history records and to provide for remedies in cases in which such records are released.

Another bill[45] would require the FTC to commence proceedings to determine whether consumers are able to learn if information about them is being collected, whether the information is being used without their authority, and whether consumers can exercise control over the information.

Children's Online Privacy Protection Act

Bill S. 2326 was introduced on July 17, 1998, and was adopted as part of the Omnibus Spending Bill that was approved by Congress. Moving quickly, the Children's Online Privacy Protection Act (COPPA) was signed by the President in October 1998. The Act will take effect on April 21, 2000. The Act requires operators of web sites (or online services) directed at children under 13 to provide notice on the web site of what personal information is collected, how the information will be used, and the disclosure practices for the information. The Act also requires that verifiable parental consent be obtained before collecting information (known as the "opt-in" requirement) from children under 13.

Personal information means individual information such as first and last name, home address, e-mail address, and social security number. A clearly labeled link to the notice of the site's children's information practices policy must be clearly and prominently placed (a) on the home page and (b) on every page where personal information is sought or collected from a child. If the web site is a general audience site with a separate children's area, the site must post the link on the home page of the children's area.

The notice of children's information practices must contain specified information. The contact information for all of the web site operators collecting or maintaining personal information must be included in the notice. The type of personal information that will be collected, the manner in which it will be collected, and how such information will be used must also be disclosed. The notice must state whether and for what purposes the personal information will be disclosed to third parties. In addition, it must be disclosed that parents are able to review the personal information collected from their children and prohibit further use or collection of such by the site and/or third parties. The notice must also state the procedures to follow. Finally, the notice must expressly inform parents that operators cannot condition a child's participation in an activity on the provision of more personal information than is reasonably necessary for the activity.

According to the Act, "verifiable parental consent" means any reasonable effort to ensure that a parent gets notice of the collection, use, and disclosure practices, and authorizes that collection, use, and disclosure. This must be done before any personal information is collected. The Act has not defined "reasonable effort," however. Yet, the FTC suggests some methods of satisfying this requirement. For example, the site could require a parent to print out a consent form and return it to the sponsor, or a toll-free number may be provided for the parent to call and confirm authorization.

There are several exemptions to the prior consent issue. It is not required where online contact information is used only one time in responding to a child, or where a child's or parent's online contact information is requested only for the purpose of obtaining parental consent or notice under the Act, and it is not maintained. Prior consent is also not required where online contact information is gathered more than once from a child in response to the child and is not used beyond that purpose so long as after the initial response to the child, the service uses reasonable efforts to provide notice to the parents that the information is being collected, how it is being used, and provide an opportunity for the parent to stop its use.

If a web site operator collects information from a child who is under 13 (without prior verifiable parental consent), in order to respond to a specific request from the child more than once, the operator must make reasonable efforts to ensure that the parent receives notice immediately after the first response. The notice must include all the information required in the web site's information collection practices notice. In addition, the service must state that information has been collected from the child, that the service has contacted the child once, and that it needs to contact the child again to respond to the child's request. The notice must also provide the parent with the opportunity to request that the operator cease using the information and delete it. The information collected in this manner cannot be used for any purpose other than to send the parental notice and to respond to the child's request. Until verifiable consent is obtained, the web site cannot respond to any more requests from the child. However, if the parent fails to respond to the notice, the information may be used for the purpose stated in the notice.

The act also requires that a service provide to a parent whose child has given personal information a description of the specific types of personal information gathered from the child and a reasonable means for the parent to obtain that information. Under the "opt-out" rule, any parent may, at any time, refuse to permit further use of the information or future collection of information.

For more information, the FTC produced a guide entitled *How to Comply With The Children's Online Privacy Protection Rule* (November 1999).

---

1 *Digital Equipment Corp.* v. *Altavista Technology, Inc.*, 960 F. Supp 456, 462 (D. Mass. 1997.

2 63 Federal Register 24996, May 6, 1998.

3 63 Federal Register 25002, May 6, 1998.

4 63 Federal Register 25002, May 6, 1998.

5 16 CFR § 310.6(e); (CCH Trade Regulation Reports ¶ 38,050).

6 63 Federal Register 25001, May 6, 1998.

7 63 Federal Register 25001, May 6, 1998.

8 *FTC* v. *Fortuna Alliance*, (15. Civ. No. C96-799M (W.D. Wash., filed May 23, 1996).

9 *FTC* v. *Nia Cano d/b/a Credit Development Int'l & Drivers Seat Network*, No. 97-7947 IH (AJWx) (C.D. Cal. filed Oct. 29, 1997).

10 *FTC* v. *Corzine*, (FTC File No. 9423295, 1995).

11 *FTC* v. *Consumer Credit Advocates, P.C.*, (FTC File No. 952 3236, 1996).

12 *FTC* v. *Audiotex Connection, Inc.*, CV-97 0726 (DRH) (filed Feb. 13, 1997; final order and permanent injunction entered Nov. 13, 1997) (E.D.N.Y.).

13 Dirty Dozen Spam Scams, FTC Press Release, July 14, 1998.

14 *Maher*, CCH Trade Regulation Reports ¶ 24,397.

15 Missouri Attorney General Press Release, 7/31/98.

16 NAAG Press Release, 9/22/98.

17 *Earthlink Network, Inc.* v. *Cyber Promotions, Inc.*, BC 167502, Cal. Sup. Ct., March 30,1998.

18 *Hotmail Corp.* v. *Van Money Pie, Inc.*, No. C98-20064 JW, 1998 U.S. Dist. LEXIS 10729, 47 U.S.P.Q.2D (BNA) 1020 (N.D. Cal., April 30,1998).

19 18 U.S.C. § 1030.
20 15 U.S.C. § 1125(c)(1).
21 Cal. Bus. & Prof. Code § 14330.
22 S. 1618.
23 H. 1748 and 4176.
24 H. 4124.
25 Washington Attorney General Press Release, 10/22/98.
26 Nev. Rev. Stat. Ann. § 41.730 (1997).
27 Assembly Bill No. 1676.
28 Bill No. 1629.
29 A06805.
30 A. 513.
31 H. 1744.
32 *America Online, Inc.*, CCH Trade Regulation Reports ¶ 24,260.
33 *In The Matter of America Online, Inc.*, 98-2-131837SEA, Assurance of Voluntary Reliance, King County Wash. Sup. Ct., May 28,1998.
34 Ryan Leads 44-State Settlement with America Online That Provides New Protections For Consumers, Illinois Attorney General Press Release, May 28, 1998.
35 47 U.S.C. § 230(b)(1) and (2).
36 *Zeran* v. *America Online, Inc.*, 129 F.3d 327 (4th Cir. 1997).
37 *Blumenthal* v. *Drudge*, 992 F. Supp. 44 (D.D.C. 1998).
38 47 U.S.C. § 230(l) and (2).
39 47 U.S.C. § 230(c)(1).
40 *Playboy Enterprise, Inc.* v. *Frena*, 839 F. Supp. 1552 (M.D. Fla. 1993).
41 HR 2281, 17 USC 1.
42 *GeoCities*, CCH Trade Regulation Reports ¶ 24,485.
43 H.R. 98.
44 H.R. 1367.
45 H.R. 1964.

APPENDIX A

NBC BROADCAST STANDARDS FOR TELEVISION

The product, service, and research guidelines published herein are for the purpose of assisting network advertisers and their agencies in the development and production of advertising in the most favorable light while avoiding techniques, presentations, approaches, and claims that are likely to mislead or offend viewers or competing advertisers.

While it is our intention to apply the guidelines fairly and consistently, none are immutable and the Advertising Standards Department will consider reasonable variances, where appropriate.

These guidelines were developed primarily for application by network advertising standards editors. Local advertisers should consult NBC owned station broadcast standards personnel for guidance on policies applicable in the particular community of license.

NBC ADVERTISING STANDARDS, PROCEDURES AND POLICIES

Clearance Procedures

The ultimate responsibility for advertising rests with the advertiser. Advertising agencies preparing commercial messages intended for broadcast on NBC Network facilities should consult the Advertising Standards Department in advance of production. Such advance discussion enables the Department to assist agencies in the preparation of advertising that will be consistent with their clients' responsibilities to the consumer.

For each commercial, advertising agencies are asked to submit a shooting script or storyboard, a new product sample and label/package insert, substantiation for all material claims, authentication of all demonstrations and testimonial statements. When the pre-production discussions have concluded and the agency has produced the commercial, the finished version must be submitted for screening and final clearance.

Inasmuch as the following policies and guidelines are neither all-inclusive nor exhaustive and are subject to modification, it is suggested that agencies and/or their clients maintain contact with the Advertising Standards Department throughout the pre-production process.

For commercials intended for local broadcast on any NBC Owned Television Station, advertising agencies should consult the local Broadcast Standards. representative in advance of production. Policies specific to the NBC Television Network are identified as such in subject headings or in text. In all other instances NBC Network and NBC Television Station Division policies are identical or similar.

Acupuncture

Advertising for reputable clinical acupuncture services will be considered on a case-by-case basis.

Advisories

The use of advisories, e.g., "The following ... contains adult subject matter, parental discretion advised," as well as content editing techniques, e.g. , "bleeps, soundtrack drop-outs, and the like are reserved for use by NBC and may not be utilized in advertising.

American Flag

The American Flag may be depicted in advertising provided its use is dignified and incidental to the primary selling objectives of the announcement.

Animals

The use of animals in commercials shall be in conformity with accepted standards of humane treatment.

Billboards

Billboards may be used as stipulated by NBC Network Sales, provided they include 'no more than the identity of the program and the sponsor's name, product or service, and a brief factual description of the general nature thereof. Only products, services, or companies being advertised in the program may be billboarded. Any claims allowed must be supported. Billboards may not mention contests, offers, promotional teasers, or cross-references to other programs.

Basic Unit Of Sale

The basic unit of sale on the NBC Television Network is the 30 second advertisement. Except for spots placed in "newscapsules" and the like, no sponsorship opportunities will be made available in units of less than 15 seconds in length.

Cast And Talent Commercials

It is the general policy of the NBC Television Network to discourage inclusion of "traditional" cast commercials within programs identified with the featured talent, i.e., commercials which utilize talent in costume and on set.

If approved, the placement of Network cast commercials (other than the foregoing), is administered by NBC Sales Services in accordance with applicable policies of the Entertainment Division, News, Sports, Advertising Standards and the Broadcast Standards and Practices departments. Any such approvals and/or placements are solely within the discretion of NBC.

All questions concerning the use of cast commercials should be directed to NBC Sales Services.

Charitable Appeals

An advertiser may surrender NBC Network commercial time to schedule an approved public service announcement or theme. Solicitation of funds is not acceptable. Clear sponsorship identification is required.

Children

1. Commercial messages placed within children's programs or in station breaks between consecutive programs designed specifically for children, advertising of products designed primarily for children, and advertising or other messages designed primarily for children are subject to all applicable provisions of NBC's Children's Advertising Guidelines. Those guidelines specifically cover child-directed commercials for toys, premiums and offers, food, feature film "trailers," sweepstakes, contests, and adult-oriented children's product commercials.

2. Within programs designed primarily for children 12 years of age or under, appropriate separator devices shall be used to clearly delineate the program material from commercial material.

3. Advertising concerning health and related matters which are more appropriately the responsibility of physicians and other adults shall not be primarily directed to children.

4. Commercial messages shall not be presented by a children's program personality, host or character, whether live or animated, within or adjacent to the programs in which such personality, host or character regularly appears.

5. Taking into account the age of the actors appearing within a commercial as well as the composition of the audience it is likely to reach, advertising approaches and techniques shall not disregard accepted safety precautions.

Comparative Advertising Guidelines – NBC Television Network

NBC will accept comparative advertising which identifies, directly or by implication, a competing product or service. As with all other advertising, each substantive claim, direct or implied, must be substantiated. The following are NBC's guidelines and standards for comparative advertising:

1. Competitors shall be fairly and properly identified.

2. Advertisers shall refrain from unfairly attacking competitors, competing products, services or other industries through the use of representations or claims, direct or implied, that are false, deceptive, misleading or have the tendency to mislead.

3. The identification must be for comparison purposes and not simply to upgrade by association.

4. The advertising should compare related or similar properties or ingredients of the product, dimension to dimension, feature to feature, or wherever possible, by a side-by-side demonstration.

5. The property being compared must be significant in terms of value or usefulness of the product or service to the consumer.

6. The difference in the properties being compared must be measurable and significant.

7. Pricing comparisons may raise special problems that could mislead, rather than enlighten, viewers. For certain classifications of products, retail prices may be extremely volatile, may be fixed by the retailer rather than the product advertiser, and may not only differ from outlet to outlet but from week to week within the same outlet. Where these circumstances might apply, NBC will accept commercials containing price comparisons only upon certification from the advertiser that the comparative claims accurately, fairly and substantially reflect the actual price differentials at retail outlets throughout the broadcast area, and

that these price differentials are not likely to change during the period the commercial is broadcast.

8. When a commercial claim involves market relationships, other than price, which are also subject to fluctuation (such as, but not limited to, sales position or exclusivity), the substantiation for the claim will be considered valid only as long as the advertiser continues to certify that the market conditions on which the claim is based continue to prevail.

9. As with all other advertising, whenever necessary, NBC may require substantiation to be updated from time to time, and may re-examine substantiation, where the need to do so is indicated as the result of a challenge or other developments.

Challenge Procedures

Where appropriate in its sole discretion, NBC will implement the following procedures in the event a commercial is challenged by another advertiser:

1. (a) If an advertiser or agency seeks to challenge the advertising on NBC of another advertiser using the NBC challenge procedures, it must agree that by submitting to the NBC challenge procedures, it will release and dis charge any claims it has, had, or may have in the future against NBC, or its agents and employees in connection with the challenged ad and/or challenge procedures, and will not commence any legal action against NBC in connection with the challenged ad and/or the challenge procedures.

(b) If upon receipt of a challenge, the incumbent advertiser does not want NBC to withdraw the challenged advertisement from the broadcast schedule, it must agree to participate in the challenge procedures and agree further that by submitting to the NBC challenge procedures, it will release and discharge any claims it has, had, or may have in the future against NBC, its agents and employees in connection with the challenged ad and/or the challenge procedures.

2. If an advertiser elects to challenge the advertising of, another advertiser and is willing to accept the agreements and undertakings specified in Paragraph 1 (a) above, it shall present its challenge and supporting data to NBC in a form available for transmittal to the challenged advertiser.

3. NBC will take all reasonable efforts to maintain the confidentiality of the advertiser's original supporting data which was submitted for substantiation of the claims made in the commercial. Either party to a challenge may request that specific material, data, surveys, etc., provided to NBC during the course of a challenge be considered confidential and not be shared with the other party on the basis that it is a trade secret or is otherwise privileged or confidential. If, in NBC's judgment, such request for confidentiality is unreasonable and the material for which confidentiality is claimed is not subsequently made available f or rebuttal by the opposing party, such material will be deemed to have no probative value in the challenge.

4. Where NBC personnel do not have the expertise to make a judgment on technical issues raised by a challenge, NBC will take appropriate measures in its discretion to assist the advertiser and challenger to resolve their differences, including encouraging them to obtain a determination from an acceptable third party.

5. NBC will not withdraw a challenged advertisement from the broadcast schedule unless:

a. The incumbent advertiser fails to agree to the requirements of the challenge procedure as provided in paragraph 1(b) above;

b. It is directed to do so by the incumbent advertiser;

c. The incumbent advertiser refuses to submit the controversy for review by some appropriate agency when deemed necessary by NBC;

d. A decision is rendered by NBC against the incumbent advertiser;

e. The challenged advertiser, when requested, refuses to

cooperate in some other substantive area; or,

f. NBC, prior to final disposition of the challenge, determines that the substantiation for the advertising has been so seriously brought into question that the advertising can no longer be considered substantiated.

6. NBC may take additional measures within its discretion to resolve questions raised by advertising claims.

Contests

Any advertiser-supplied contest furnished to NBC for proposed broadcast must be initially reviewed to insure that it is not a lottery, that the material terms are clearly stated, and that it is being conducted fairly, honestly and according to its rules.

1. Contest information is further reviewed to make certain that:

a. The security arrangements are adequate to prevent $frigging";

b. The terms, conditions, and requirements under which contestants compete for prizes are clearly stated in the "Rules" so that there is no reasonable opportunity f or any misunderstanding;

c. The value, nature and extent of the prizes is clear;

d. The public interest will not be adversely affected;

e. The contest meets with federal, state, and local laws.

2. Complete details and continuity must be submitted to the Advertising Standards Department at least ten business days prior to the first public announcement of the contest.

3. All broadcast copy regarding contests must contain clear and complete information regarding:

a. Complete contest rules or when and how they may be obtained by the public;

b. The availability of entry forms and how to enter, including alternate means of entry where appropriate;

c. The termination date of the contest;

d. Any restrictions or eligibility requirements;

e. The prize suppliers, when applicable;

f. For chance contests, the necessary language:

No Purchase Necessary
Void Where Prohibited

g. For skill contests, judging criteria must be stated.

4. A complete copy of the rules, the entry blank, promotional material and/or any published information e.g., newspaper advertisements, about the contest should be included with the broadcast copy submitted to the Department.

5. All contest rules must be complete and contain:

a. Eligibility requirements;,

b. Restrictions as to the number of entries made by an individual;

c. The nature, extent and value of the prizes;

d. Where, when and how entries are 'Submitted;

e. The basis on which prizes will be awarded;

f. The termination date of the contest;

g. When and how winners will be selected, including tie breaking procedures when necessary, and procedures to be followed in the event winner is ineligible or disqualified;

h. How winners will be notified;

i. Time limits to claim or use prizes, if any;

j. Restrictions as to the number of times an individual can win;

k. Reference to "participating dealers" if not all outlets are involved.

Controversial Issue Advertising

As a general rule and subject to the exceptions stated below, time will not be sold on NBC Network facilities for the presentation of views on controversial issues and advertisers may not use their commercial positions for addressing such issues. This policy does not apply during campaign periods to announcements on behalf of candidates for public office and to issues to be voted on by the electorate. In non-campaign periods, the NBC Television Network will, on a case-by-case basis, consider requests for time on behalf of significant political parties or their spokespersons.

NBC Owned stations may accept controversial issue advertising subject to the discretion and approval of the General Manager.

Cross Reference And Promotion Of Other Media

References by NBC Network advertisers within their commercial time to another program they are sponsoring are permitted provided that the references do not identify a competing facility, the day, date, or hour of the program. Statements urging the viewer to check television listings for such information are permissible.

Advertisers may not refer to other programs scheduled at a later hour on the same day on a competing facility.

Advertising by cable systems, syndicators, cable program services, pay-per-view, direct broadcast satellite and similar services will be considered on a case-by-case basis. In no event may such advertising be day, date, or time specific. Mention of a program to be aired "tomorrow" is not acceptable while references to "next week" or "next month" may be considered. As a general matter, references to time, day and facility should be made in the following form: "Consult your local paper listings for time and station."

Demonstrations

Commercials which include demonstrations, tests, experiments or other technical, mechanical, electronic or chemical exhibitions, must be accompanied by an affidavit signed by the producer of the commercial or another responsible supervisory individual who personally observed the production.

The affidavit must truthfully attest to the accuracy of the demonstration, etc., and must honestly represent that the demonstration was performed with samples of the product available to consumers or prototypes that perform no differently than actual product and that no mock-up, modification or alteration was employed.

In appropriate circumstances, alterations or modifications of products or demonstrations may be utilized provided that such alteration or modification is disclosed to the viewer and, provided further, that viewers are not in any manner misled with respect to the performance of a material product feature or characteristic.

Distribution And Availability Of Products And Services

In the event that distribution to 50% of the advertising market has not been achieved, the following will be required:

1. If distribution is imminent but has not yet commenced, the advertising must disclose this fact, e.g., "Coming Soon;"

2. If distribution has commenced but is less than 50% of the advertised market, the advertising must disclose this fact, e.g., "not available in all areas."

Unless total availability is documented, advertising for franchise or chain retail outlets must indicate that the product or service is available at "participating stores."

Door-To-Door Sales Representatives And In-Home Selling

All such advertising must be in accordance with applicable federal, state, and local laws and shall be reviewed with special care. The reputation and reliability of the sponsor and the supervision exercised by the advertiser over its sales representatives are important considerations. Each proposed commercial will be evaluated on a case-by-case basis to insure its acceptability.

In general, advertising recruiting door-to-door representatives primarily for the sale of medical products and services having direct health considerations is not acceptable.

Dramatizations And Reenactments

Dramatizations or reenactments of actual events must be clearly disclosed as such. Fictional dramatizations which are readily apparent to the viewer ("slice of life") require no such disclosure.

Endorsements And Testimonials

All endorsements and testimonials must comply with the Federal Trade Commission Final Guides concerning Endorsements and Testimonials in Advertising which are enumerated in 16 C.F.R. 255. The following is a brief summary of FTC policy relating to endorsements and testimonials included in advertising of products, services and organizations:

1. Endorsements and testimonials used, in whole or in part, must honestly reflect in spirit and content the sentiments of the individuals represented;

2. All claims and statements in endorsements and testimonials, including subjective evaluations of testifiers, must be supportable by facts and free of misleading implication. They shall contain no statement that cannot be supported if presented in the advertiser's own words;

3. Advertisers are required to disclose any connection between the advertiser and the endorser that might materially affect the weight or credibility of the endorsement;

4. In the event a consumer endorsement does not fairly reflect what a substantial proportion of other consumers are likely to experience, the advertising must clearly disclose this fact;

5. Expert endorsements are permitted only as long as the endorser continues to hold those views.

Financial Advertising

Advertising for banks, funds, stocks, bonds, commodities, insurance, real estate, and other investments which conform to applicable law is acceptable provided that the advertiser supplies assurances that the investment is not highly speculative and that material restrictions and risks are disclosed. "Tips" on specific stocks, bonds, commodities and other ventures are not acceptable. Other mentions of specific securities will be considered on a case-by-case basis.

Franchised Business Advertising

The network advertising of franchise businesses to prospective entrepreneurs is acceptable subject to the following:

1. A franchisor must demonstrate its financial integrity and satisfactory past performance. No advertising will be accepted from any franchisor who has operated for less than one year;

2. All claims must be documented and each franchisor/advertiser should submit a copy of its standard Franchise Agreement for review by the Advertising Standards Department; and,

3. Testimonials, endorsements, or other specific claims relating to potential or actual profits must fairly reflect what a substantial proportion of other franchisees have experienced.

Guarantee And Warranty Offers

Whenever the terms "guarantee," "warranty" or similar words that constitute a promise or representation in the nature of a guarantee or warranty appear in a television advertisement, NBC may require certain additional information concerning the material terms and conditions of such guarantee or warranty offer to be disclosed to the viewer pursuant to 16 C.F.R. 239.

Health Related Product Advertising

All advertisements for health related products shall comply with the NBC Advertising Guidelines for Pharmaceutical Products.

1. Prescription Drugs

Subject to the aforementioned guidelines the NBC Television Network will consider advertising from prescription drug manufacturers limited to corporate, institutional and "reminder" advertising. Prescription drug advertising which requires a "brief summary" or which carries a "boxed warning," is not acceptable.

2. Nonprescription Drugs

The advertising of nonprescription medications presents important considerations to the health of consumers. The following principles govern the acceptability of such advertising on the NBC Television Network:

a. The advertiser must give assurance that the advertising for the product complies with all applicable governmental rules and regulations;

b. Advertising for nonprescription products is accepted only after relevant data, including adequate substantiation regarding product efficacy, safety and any particular claims asserted, have been submitted to Advertising Standards for examination and appraisal;

c. No claims may be made or implied that the product is a panacea or alone will effect a cure;

d. Words such as "safe," "without risk," "harmless," or terms of similar meaning may not be used without adequate qualification or documentation;

e. Advertising appeals may not be made to children for such products.

Statements From the Medical Profession

Physicians, dentists or nurses, or actors representing them, may not be employed directly or by implication in any commercial for products involving health considerations. Advertisements of an institutional nature which are not intended to sell specific products or services to the consumer, public service announcements by non-profit organizations, as well as presentations for professional services, may be presented by physicians, dentists, nurses, or other professionals subject to prior approval by Advertising Standards.

Hypnotism

Advertising for reputable clinical hypnosis services will be considered for broadcast on a case-by-case basis. Notwithstanding the foregoing, imitable demonstration of hypnosis is unacceptable.

Lean-ins, Lead-outs

Subject to approval, NBC Network commercial messages may be introduced by lead-in language when required for transition from live program material to a recorded commercial. Such lead-ins shall not exceed 5 seconds and may not contain a direct selling message, nor can there be visual identification of products, product logo or backdrop identifying the product or client. The product or client name, if used, must be the last word(s) in the lead-in. Lead-outs are not permitted. Notwithstanding the foregoing, talent on the "Today" and "Tonight" shows may display and briefly describe the product.

Legalized Lotteries And Gambling

The lawful advertising of government and private organizations that conduct legalized lotteries and/or the lawful advertising for legalized betting on sporting contests are subject to the provisions of the NBC Guidelines on Gambling, Betting, Lotteries and Games of Chance.

Mail Order (Direct Response)

I. All commercials must conform to applicable FTC Guidelines (16 C.F.R. 435).

2. Advertisers are required to submit a sample of the offered product and any other material to be sent to the customer.

3. Each commercial must include the name, street address, city, state and zip code of the sponsor, and/or the order address.

4. When applicable, any charges beyond the advertised purchase price must also be disclosed e.g., postage, handling, etc..

5. If time for delivery will exceed 30 days, commercials must indicate actual anticipated time for such delivery.

6. The sponsor must provide consumers with a cash refund for returned items.

Motion Picture Advertising

1. All advertising for domestic theatrical films must include an MPAA rating aurally and visually. NBC may accept advertising for films pending a rating subject to review of both the film and its proposed advertisement, and provided that the advertisement discloses that the film "has not yet been rated."

2. While the content of the film advertisement and its accurate reflection of the underlying film is the primary Advertising Standards concern, the department also considers the substance of the advertised feature.

3. Placement of advertising will be determined on the basis of audience composition and program compatibility.

4. "XXX rated and similar "adult" film fare is unacceptable.

5. All proposed commercials for films carrying the MPAA NC-17 rating (no children under 17 admitted) will be reviewed on a case-by-case basis, taking into account both the content of the commercial as well as the content of the underlying theatrical film.

If judged acceptable for a network television audience, such commercials must contain an audio disclosure that the film is "Rated NC-17, No Children Under 17 Admitted," and an appropriate MPAA video disclosure.

In no event may such commercials be scheduled to air earlier than 9:55 P.M. Central and Mountain time zones and 10:55 P.M., Eastern and Pacific. In certain circumstances, later scheduling may be deemed appropriate.

"New" Use In Advertising

Advertisers may only use the term "new" for a period of six months from the time a product has achieved general distribution in its market.

News And Newsroom Simulations

Advertising may not contain aural or visual approaches or formats which could confuse viewers as to the origin of the material being telecast. Unacceptable techniques include the phrase “We interrupt this program (commercial) to bring you ... 11, “bulletin”, “flash”, “This just in ... 11, newsroom settings, lower third horizontal crawls, and teletype sound effects.

Placement And Scheduling

NBC reserves the right to determine the scheduling, format and length of commercial breaks during and adjacent to programs carried over its facilities and the acceptability, number and placement of commercials, promotions and other announcements within such breaks, including those involving cast or celebrities.

In-program advertisements must be placed within the framework of the sponsored program. The program must be announced and clearly identified before the first commercial placement and terminated after the last commercial placement.

Premiums And Offers

1. Full details and continuity including “build-up copy”, and a sample of the premium offer, must be submitted to Advertising Standards well in advance of commitment.

2. The termination date of any offer should be announced as far in advance as possible. Such announcement will include the statement that responses postmarked not later than midnight of the business day following withdrawal of the offer shall be honored.

3. All audience responses to premiums, offers or contests made by advertisers must be sent to a stated Post Office Box or to an outside address arranged for by the advertiser.

4. As to the premium merchandise offered:

a. The advertiser must warrant that the premium or offer will not be harmful to person or property;

b. Premiums and offers scheduled within children’s

programs will be subject to all applicable Premium and Toy advertising requirements of the NBC Children's Advertising Guidelines;

c. Descriptions or visual representations of premiums or offers may not enlarge their value or otherwise be misleading;

d. The advertiser must provide NBC with written assurance that it will honor any request for return of money based on dissatisfaction with premiums or offers, and that a sufficient supply of the premium or offer is readily available so as to avoid audience ill will caused by delivery delay or impossibility of delivery.

5. The premium or offer may not appeal to superstition on the basis of "luck-bearing" powers or otherwise.

6. Mail order offers should indicate any additional postage/ handling charges, as well as expected delivery time.

Religious Advertising

1. NBC will, within it's discretion, accept commercial announcements for the sale of products which have a religious theme e.g., books, recordings, artifacts, etc.

2. NBC will also accept, within its discretion, commercial announcements of a general moral or ethical nature on behalf of religious organizations, and for the announcement of meetings, religious services, or for the promotion of approved public service and charitable.activities.

3. All advertising copy will be subject to NBC commercial clearance policies and must not depict, proselytize, promote, or discuss sectarian doctrine or dogma.

4. No solicitation of funds will be permitted.

5. Advertising copy which denigrates, attacks or negatively stereotypes any group or individual is unacceptable.

6. The discussion of controversial issues of public importance is not acceptable.

7. NBC may, within its discretion, review any books,

periodicals or other products advertised to insure that they do not attack any group or individual or otherwise violate NBC's advertising policies.

8. Each announcement must disclose that it has been "paid for" or "sponsored by" the appropriate advertiser unless such fact is otherwise obvious to the audience.

Safety

It is the advertiser's responsibility to assure compliance with normal safety precautions such as the use of seatbelts in vehicles and adult supervision of children who demonstrate or who are in proximity to potentially hazardous products.

Solicitation Of Funds

As a general matter the NBC Television Network does not sell time for the solicitation of funds.

Sound Level

The sound level of commercials should not appear to exceed that of the surrounding program.

Sponsor Identification

Identification of sponsorship shall be made in all commercials in accordance with the requirements of the Communications Act and the rules and policies of the Federal Communications commission.

Stereotyping

Special sensitivity is necessary in presenting commercial material relating to sex, sexual orientation, age, race, color, creed, religion, or national or ethnic derivation to avoid contributing to damaging or demeaning stereotypes. Similarly, special precautions must be taken to avoid demeaning or ridiculing members of the audience who suffer from physical or mental afflictions or deformities.

Unacceptable Commercial Presentations, Approaches And Techniques

NBC does not knowingly accept in advertising:

1. Claims or representations, direct or implied, which are false or have the tendency to deceive, mislead or misrepresent;

2. Unqualified references to the safety of a product, if package, label or insert contains a caution, or the normal use of the product presents a possible hazard;

3. "Bait and Switch" tactics which feature goods or services not intended for sale but designed to lure the public into purchasing higher priced substitutes;

4. The use of "subliminal perception" or other techniques attempting to convey information to viewers by transmitting messages below the threshold of normal awareness;

5. Unacceptable products or services promoted through advertising devoted to an acceptable product;

6. The misuse of distress signals;

7. Disrespectful use of the flag, national emblems, anthems and monuments;

8. Direct or implied use of the off ice of the President of the United States or any governmental body without official approval;

9. Sensational headline announcements in advertising of publications prior to the identification of sponsor;

10. Scare approaches and presentations with the capacity to induce fear;

11. Unsupported or exaggerated promises of employment or earnings; and,

12. Presentations for professional services which do not comply with applicable law or ethical codes.

Unacceptable Commercial Classifications

1. Cigarettes, chewing tobacco, snuff, tobacco and small cigars.

2. Hard liquor and references to distilled spirits.

3. Firearms, fireworks, ammunition and other weapons.

4. Presentations promoting a belief in the efficacy of fortune telling, astrology, phrenology, palm reading, numerology, mind reading, character reading or other occult pursuits. (Such presentations for the purpose of entertainment will be considered on a case-by-case basis).

5. Tip sheets and race track publications seeking to advertise for the purpose of promoting illegal betting (See Lotteries)

6. Contraceptives.

7. "Adult" or Sex Magazines.

8. X-Rated Movies.

9. Abortion Services.

10. Anti-Law Enforcement Devices.

11. Products, services or publications relating to illegal drugs.

12. Massage parlors.

13.Matrimonial, escort or dating services.

Visual Supers & Horizontal Crawls

When superimposed copy is essential to qualify advertising claims, it must be presented so it can be read easily against a plain, contrasting background and must be located within the safe title area of the television screen.

For purposes of reference, an ideal display of copy would have letter height of 4.5% of the vertical dimensions of the scanned area (approximately 22 video scan lines) and each line of copy would be viewed for 3 seconds. Supers not meeting this reference standard will be reviewed on a case-by-case basis.

The use of horizontal crawls in commercials is unacceptable.

GLOSSARY

Advertising Terms

Body copy: The text copy in an advertisement other that the headline.

Comparative advertising: An advertisement or campaign that compares the advertiser's product or service to that of a competitor either by name, implication, or reputation.

Comprehensive layout: A rough depiction of an advertisement to show basic placement of elements. Used to represent what the final advertisement will look before it is produced.

Deceptive advertising: Advertising that, in any way, creates a false, misleading, or deceptive message within the mind of the average consumer to which the ad was directed.

Endorsement: A claim, either implied or express, by a person or entity of significant standing, image or reputation in support of an advertiser, his product or service.

Freelancer: An independent contractor. A person who is not an employee of either the principal or agency, but sells his work or services to various parties on a project basis.

Genericide: The term used to describe a situation where a trademark is allowed to be used improperly so that the mark looses its status as an mark (which is owned) and therefore becomes a generic item.

Good will: The value of a business in patronage and reputation above and beyond its tangible assets.

Look-alikes: One person who bears a strong resemblance to another. Usually used in the context of a person who looks very much like a specific celebrity. The look-alike is used (as if he were the actual celebrity) in advertising to enhance the advertiser's image and promote a product or service.

Marks: A trade mark or service mark. The physical combination of symbols and words which make up the trademark.

Palming-off: The practice of creating the false impression that the advertiser's product is actually made by a manufacturer of greater reputation, thereby trading on another's image and status.

Puffery: Exaggerated sales talk or boasting by an advertiser about the quality of his product or service. Puffery claims have no material way of being proven or disproven.

Qualifying language: Language used in an advertisement to clarify or offset another claim in the same ad which would otherwise be deceptive if taken on its own merit. Qualifying language must have the same weight and visibility as the otherwise deceptive statement.

Royalties: The share of the proceeds from his work, usually a specified percentage, paid to an author or artist.

Service marks: A trademark used in connection with a business that sells a service, as opposed to a product to which a trademark can be affixed. See also: trademark.

Small print: Also called a disclaimer: Small type used to clarify a previously mentioned point within an advertisement.

Storyboard: A depiction, in drawn form, of what a final television commercial will look like. Usually drawn scene-by-scene to depict the sequence of the final commercial.

Testimonial: A statement testifying to a person's or company's qualifications, abilities, and character or to the value of some product or service.

Trade secret: A proprietary fact, process or item of knowledge gained through a working relationship with a company that would not be commonly know to the public.

Trademark: A mark used in connection with a product or service to which value attaches, and which is owned by the company as a property right.

Voice-Over: The narrated voice portion of a television or radio commercial.

Legal Terms

Actual damages: Compensation for actual injury or loss suffered by the plaintiff.

Bailment: A delivery of goods or personal property for the execution of a contract, usually for the benefit of both the bailor (one who delivers) and the bailee (one who receives). Example: Bailor parks her car in a parking garage. Bailee provides parking space.

Basis of bargain: That on which any affirmation of fact or promise relating to goods sold is based, creating an express warranty.

Breach of contract: Failure without legal excuse to perform a promise which forms the whole of part of a contract.

Breach of warranty: Failure without legal excuse to meet the obligations created by the representations or promises made contemporaneously with a sale.

Cease and desist order: An order of an administrative agency or court prohibiting a course of conduct from continuing.

Class actions: A legal action by or on behalf of a large group of persons who are similarly interested in the matter. Available in federal and most state courts. Usually, the number of plaintiffs must be so numerous that it would not be practical or possible to bring separate suits. Also called "representative action."

Common law: The body of law that comes from the decrees of courts and hence the customs of the people, as opposed to laws created by state legislatures or the Congress in the form of a statute.

Compensatory damages: An award in an amount sufficient to compensate for the injury sustained and no more.

Consent: Voluntary agreement by a person with sufficient mental and legal capacity who is not acting on the basis of fraud or under duress.

Consideration: A giving over of a sum, right, interest, or benefit in return for the promise of another in creating a contract. Consideration may also be a promise or forbearance, detriment, or loss again given up as part of the contractual agreement.

Contract: An agreement by which the parties promise to do or not to do that which is the basis of the contract.
Lit. I promise to do this if you promise to do that.

Damages: Financial compensation which may be recovered through the courts by a plaintiff who has suffered loss, detriment or injury as a result of the unlawful act, omission, or negligence of the defendant.

Foreseeability: Reasonable anticipation that an act or failure to act may result in injury or harm.

Fraudulent concealment: The deliberate failure to reveal a material fact with the intent to defraud.

Injunction: A court order issued at the request of one party to an action against another party in that action to refrain from an act. May be temporary pending the outcome of the action, or may be made permanent as a part of the decision of the court.

Jurisdiction: The legal right by which courts exercise their authority over parties and subject matter. May also literally refer to the physical location or boundaries where the courts or law enforcement agencies may exercise their authority.

Liability: Legal responsibility for the consequences of an action or inaction which may give rise to the award of damages to an injured party.

Merchantability (fitness for a particular purpose): In sales context that the article sold is fit for the purpose it is sold when used in the ordinary way normally to be expected.

Monetary damages: Also can be called pecuniary damages. Those damages that can be calculated and compensated by an award of the court in the form of the payment of money.

Prior restraint: The concept that under the First Amendment to the United States Constitution a publication cannot be prohibited unless extreme circumstances require. The corollary concept is that if anyone is harmed or defamed by the publication, that party is free to pursue damages in a libel action after the fact.

Products liability: The concept that manufacturers are responsible for the goods they produce when defects in those products cause injury to the purchaser or user.

Public domain: The status of publications, products or processes that are not protected under patent or copyright and hence belong to the public rather than the creator, writer, inventor, or developer.

Punitive damages: Also called exemplary damages. An amount awarded by the court over and above the damages required to make an injured party whole where the injury was caused by particular malice, fraud, or deliberate conduct on the part of the party at fault. These damages are intended to punish the party at fault, comfort the injured party, and set an example to society as a whole in an effort to deter future similar acts.

Quantum meruit: The concept that no one should benefit unjustly from the labor of others under which a court will award a reasonable amount under an implied contract.

Reasonable man: An imaginary individual used by the court to determine if an injured party's conduct or expectations were that of the average person in similar circumstances. The standard one must have in mind to avoid liability for negligence.

Recision: In contract law the right to cancel a contract when a certain kind of default by the other party occurs. Note: Not every default creates a right to rescind the contract.

Regulation: A set of rules set out by an agency of either a state or the federal government, i.e. a department, at the direction of the legislative body in the form of a statute.

Remedies: The recourse available an injured party either by contract or by order of a court to rectify a wrong or injury whether by an award of money or an order to do or not to do something.

Restrictive covenants: Agreements to refrain from doing something specified in the agreement. May be used in deeds, but for purposes of this book refers to employment contracts where an employee promises not to compete with the employer, in the event the employment is terminated, for a certain period of time within a certain geographic area. A restrictive covenant will only be enforced by the courts if it is reasonable.

Sole liability clauses: In a principal/agency relationship, a provision in a contract with a third party where the agent assumes full liability for any breach of the contract. Specifically, in advertising, sole liability clauses are commonly found in media contracts entered into between the media and the agent whereby the agent agrees to be fully liable for the debts incurred on behalf of the principal.

Specific performance: A provision in a contract or an order by a court that money damages will not suffice to compensate an individual for losses incurred as a result of the breach of a contract. In these cases, the breaching party must actually perform the promise made in the contract.

Standing: The concept that a party has sufficient stake in a matter to take it to court. Lit. Standing to sue.

Statutes: An act of a state legislature or the federal Congress that creates a law requiring or prohibiting certain actions by citizens.

Strict liability in tort: The concept that everyone involved in the manufacture and sale of a product is liable for any injury received by a consumer as a result of a defective product that is expected to and does reach the user without substantial change after manufacture or assembly.

Warranty: A statement or representation made by a seller of goods, contemporaneously with and as a part of the contract of sale having reference to the character, quality, or title of goods and by which the seller promises to insure that certain facts are or shall be as they are represented.

BIBLIOGRAPHY

Cone, Fairfax M. *With All Its Faults*. Boston: Little, Brown & Company, 1969.

Cooke, Alistair. *America.* New York: Alfred A. Knopf, 1973.

Della Femina, Jerry. *From Those Wonderful Folks Who Gave You Pearl Harbor.* New York: Simon & Schuster, 1970.

Fox, Stephen. *The Mirror Makers*. New York: Vintage Books, Random House, 1984.

Hernon, Peter, and Terry Ganey. *Under The Influence*. New York: Avon Books, 1991.

Kotler, Philip. *Principles of Marketing*. Englewood Cliffs, N.J.: Prentice-Hall, 1980.

Nash, Jay Robert. *Hustlers and Con Men*. New York: M. Evans & Co., 1976.

Nayak, P Ranganath, and John Ketteringham. *Breakthroughs!* New York: Rawson Associates, 1986.

Preston, Ivan L. *The Great American Blow-Up: Puffery in Advertising and Selling*. University of Wisconsin Press, 1975.

Pritikin, Robert C. *Christ Was an Adman*. San Francisco: Harbor Publishing, 1980.

Rembar, Charles. *The Law of the Land*. New York: Touchstone, 1980.

Ries, Al, and Jack Trout. *Positioning: The Battle for Your Mind.* New York: McGraw-Hill, 1986.

Rosden, George, and Peter Rosden. *The Law of Advertising.* New York: Mathew Bender, 1978.

Wakeman, Frederic. *The Hucksters*. New York: Buccaneer Books, 1993.

INDEX OF CASES

C

D

G

H

I

J

K

L

M

N

O

P

Q

R

S

T

U

V

W

Y

Z

INDEX

A

D

G

M

N

O

Q

R

S

T

U

V

W

X